W9-CQY-844

IRISH AND SCOTCH-IRISH

ANCESTRAL RESEARCH

*A Guide to the Genealogical Records,
Methods and Sources in Ireland*

VOLUME I
REPOSITORIES AND RECORDS

BY

MARGARET DICKSON FALLEY, B.S.
Fellow of the American Society of Genealogists

Originally published: Strasburg, Virginia, 1962
Reprinted: Genealogical Publishing Co., Inc.
1001 N. Calvert St., Baltimore, Md. 21202
First printing: 1981
Second printing: 1984
Third printing: 1988
Fourth printing: 1998

Library of Congress Catalogue Card Number 80-83867
International Standard Book Number: Volume I: 0-8063-0918-0
Set ISBN Number: 0-8063-0916-4
Made in the United States of America

PREFACE

There are now more than 30,000,000 descendants of the Irish and Scotch-Irish who emigrated from Ireland to the American Colonies, the United States or Canada. This is a conservative estimate, computed from the emigration figures in various published sources noted in these two volumes; allowing an average of thirty years from the birth of one generation to another, after the arrival in America, and only doubling the descendants of an emigrant in each of the succeeding generations.

It is a matter of common knowledge in America that the people of Irish and Scotch-Irish ancestry take pride in their heritage. They freely demonstrate that they have preserved a warm tradition of affection and loyalty toward Ireland in general, and particularly for the province and county wherein their respective family roots grew deep.

Americans have previously had little hope of discovering the historical and genealogical records of their forbears, due to the lack of any comprehensive and detailed guide to the methods of work and the collections of genealogical source materials of all classes, scattered among the many repositories of records in Ireland.

These two volumes, offering the first complete guide to Irish and Scotch-Irish genealogical research ever published in America or abroad, are the result of three extended periods of work in the principal repositories of records throughout Ireland in 1951, 1952 and 1955; consultation and correspondence with the directors of repositories; the accumulation of a private library of historical and genealogical source materials of over two thousand volumes (including microfilms of some seven hundred MSS. volumes of indexes, other MSS. materials, and a few rare printed works) ; and eleven years devoted to concentrated study while compiling this work.

The two volumes are arranged to meet the requirements in the way of guidance, in the following manner:

(1) The genealogist must first locate the geographical area of his earliest known branch of the family, and also the geographical origin of the earliest known ancestor, whether he lived and died in Ireland or emigrated. Hence, the first two chapters of this Volume I, and the bibliography in Part Five of Volume II, are presented for Americans who might not understand the value and necessity of thorough preliminary research in the United States to establish, if possible, the geographical origin of an emigrant before attempting work with the historical and genealogical records of Ireland. It goes without saying that descendants of Irish and Scotch-Irish emigrants who settled in any other country have the same need for preliminary research, and the pattern for their work is similar to that in America.

(2) Every genealogist who contemplates work with the records of Ireland must first become familiar with the existing classes of materials in each of the principal repositories of historical and genealogical records in Ireland, and must know about the important published works, manuscript collections, and microfilmed materials thereof. If a genealogist cannot go to Ireland to accomplish his own research, he can employ the services of a record searcher or another genealogist, to work under his direction at a reasonable charge. The six chapters of Part Two of this Volume I furnish an outline of the available collections in the most important repositories. Upon reading these chapters, it becomes evident that the various collections of any one class (census records, deeds, leases, marriage records, wills, vital records, etc.), are widely scattered among the various public and private repositories.

(3) Therefore, the family historian or genealogist, who would work efficiently, must know the extent and location of each collection of the class of records he chooses to investigate. For this reason, Part Three of this Volume I contains a chapter regarding each class of records, with lists of the classified collections and their places of deposit.

(4) The local or family historian, the genealogist, and the record searcher, all require a bibliography of printed works, MSS. materials, and microfilms thereof, containing family his-

tory and records of the members, genealogical notes, pedigrees, personal documents, etc. The accompanying Volume
II answers this need. It contains five parts, each a separate
bibliography.

(5) Quick reference to all classes and collections of materials may be made by using the General Index and the Family
Name Index in this Volume I, and the Subject Index in Volume II. A Family Name Index for Volume II was contemplated but, as the family records in numerous classified collections are listed according to surname, alphabetically, the
work of compiling one general Family Name Index appeared
to be a duplication of effort, and the extra hundred or more
pages would materially increase the cost of the volume.

Grateful acknowledgement is offered the following people
for their inspiration and aid, without which this work could
not have been accomplished:

Mr. Meredith B. Colket, Jr., F.A.S.G., past Director of the
General Reference Section, National Archives, Washington,
D. C. (since 1957, Director of the Western Reserve Historical
Society, Cleveland, Ohio). He served, 1950-1961, as Director
of the Institute of Genealogical Research of the American
University and The National Archives, in co-operation with
the Maryland Hall of Records, and sponsored by the American
Society of Genealogists. He first interested this compiler in
Irish records at the Institute in June 1951, with an assignment
to survey the original Irish passenger lists in The National
Archives, particularly those contained in the Ships Manifests
of Captains sailing from Irish ports or from Liverpool, and
landing at American ports. He called the attention of Mr.
Wayne C. Grover, Archivist of the United States, to this compiler's report on her survey. He also contributed an outline
of the collections of Passenger Lists deposited in The National
Archives (see pp. 22-26, herein).

Mr. Wayne C. Grover, Archivist of the United States, on
July 20, 1951, wrote letters of introduction for this compiler
to Dr. Richard J. Hayes, Director of the National Library of
Ireland, Dublin; to Mr. Diarmid Coffey, Assistant Deputy

Keeper of the Public Records in Ireland, Public Record Office of Ireland, Dublin; and to Mr. E. Heatly, Deputy Keeper of the Public Records of Northern Ireland, Public Record Office of Northern Ireland, Belfast. These letters of introduction provided a reception for this compiler soon afterward in Ireland, which resulted in further introductions to the Directors of other repositories.

Perhaps the most crucial period in this compiler's experience in Ireland occurred in Belfast in July 1951, with her first genealogical contacts in the country. Thanks to the kindly interest of people there who knew the records, this compiler's budding curiosity developed immediately into a deep determination to become well acquainted with all classes and collections of genealogical source materials, both MSS. and printed, throughout Ireland. The compiler is greatly indebted to the following individuals in Belfast for their information, patience, and continuous co-operation over the years in providing printed books, lists of collections of genealogical materials, photostats and certified copies of single documents and extensive MSS. collections.

The Rev. Dr. David Stewart, retired Director of the Presbyterian Historical Society, Belfast, in 1951 at the age of eighty, became this compiler's friend and mentor as he opened the door to the field of genealogical research in Northern Ireland. In the library of the Presbyterian Historical Society and in his own extensive private library, he called attention to published and MSS. works which are necessary tools of the genealogist. He prepared the way for an understanding and appreciation of the records in the Public Record Office of Northern Ireland, the Linen Hall Library, and in the repositories of Dublin and elsewhere.

Miss Jeannie L. M. Stewart, Assistant Secretary of the Presbyterian Historical Society, generously supplemented the help of the Rev. Dr. Stewart. She furnished this compiler with the lists of the Presbyterian Church Registers deposited in the vaults of the Society and in local custody. She typed and sent certified copies of the extensive MSS. 1740 Householder's List; the 1766 Religious Returns; the 1775 (some earlier and later)

Petitions of Dissenters. She also sent the printed *Fasti of the Presbyterian Church,* and other publications of the Society.

Mr. E. Heatly, Deputy Keeper of the Public Records of Northern Ireland, 1948 to July 1955, gave this compiler courteous attention in 1951 and 1952, while members of the staff explained the collections of printed and MSS. records and opened them for inspection.

Mr. Kenneth Darwin, Assistant Deputy Keeper of the Public Records of Northern Ireland in 1951 and 1952, and Deputy Keeper of the Records from 1955 onward, has given this compiler help of major importance regarding the records of Northern Ireland. He has furnished much information noted within this text, and has sent photostats or certified copies of many single documents and MSS. collections of family records. His Assistant, Miss Margaret Johnston, has kindly offered attention and given assistance in 1955 and thereafter.

Mr. John M. Douglas, Headmaster of Friends School, Lisburn, 1929-1952, and Keeper of the Archives in Friends House, Lisburn, gave permission for this compiler to spend a day examining the 17th and 18th century records in the vault. Mr. C. Ivan Gray, Headmaster of Friends School, Lisburn, from 1952 onward, arranged for the permission to see the records; conducted this compiler to the vault in Friends House, and brought lunch on a bitterly cold day in November 1955, to allow an uninterrupted period of work.

Mr. T. MacCallum Walker who was Librarian of Magee University College Library, Londonderry, in 1955 (and presently Deputy Librarian of the University Library of Glasgow, Scotland), received this compiler in Londonderry and provided information about the MSS. collections of Presbyterian Church records, old newspapers, printed books, etc. Also with the permission of the Rev. L. R. Lawrenson, Dean of St. Columb's Cathedral, Londonderry, Mr. Walker conducted the compiler to the vault of the Cathedral to inspect the Parish Registers, 1642-1703, and 1703-onward.

Dr. Richard J. Hayes, Director of the National Library of Ireland, Dublin, has provided this compiler with information of major importance during interviews in 1951, 1952, and

1955, and by correspondence from time to time over the years, regarding collections of MSS. materials, printed works and microfilmed records in the National Library, in other repositories throughout Ireland and Great Britain, all of which have been noted within this text. He called attention to some of the most important published source materials for an Irish genealogical library. In 1952, he made it possible for this compiler to acquire microfilm copies of the Names and Land Indexes of the records in the Registry of Deeds, 1708-1860. In 1955, he provided microfilm copies of the Registers of the Society of Friends, Dublin; a microfilm of the list of Roman Catholic Parish Registers (as far as they were filmed in 1955), with the inclusive dates of the records, in some fourteen dioceses in the Republic of Ireland; also some other series of records mentioned within the text. On January 30, 1961, Dr. Hayes wrote regarding this two-volume work which was nearing completion, "No praise can be too great for the arduous and most useful task you have undertaken and I have never thought it more worth-while assisting any scholar than in giving some small help to you. Your work will be known and quoted for many generations."

Directors and members of the staff of other repositories in Dublin, who have given particular assistance in explaining their records and in showing important collections of original documents, transcripts, abstracts, etc., in 1951, 1952, and 1955, and in sending from time to time requested photostats of the records or certified copies thereof, are Mr. Gerard Slevin, Chief Herald, Genealogical Office (Office of Arms), Dublin Castle; Mr. Diarmid Coffey, Assistant Deputy Keeper of the Public Records in Ireland, and Mr. MacGiolla Choille, Keeper of the State Papers in the Public Record Office of Ireland, Dublin; Mr. J. W. Dobbs, Assistant Registrar, Registry of Deeds, in 1951 and 1952, also Mr. J. P. Kenny, Senior Assistant Registrar and Mr. P. F. McKeown, Junior Assistant Registrar in 1955, and Mr. Henry M. Havelin who gave special attention in 1951 and thereafter; Miss Helen D. Jones, Secretary of the Society of Friends, who allowed the 17th Century registers to be examined in November 1955, and Miss Olive C. Goodbody, Keeper of the Manuscripts in Friends House Library; also members of the staff of Trinity College Library who assisted with examination of certain records at the request of Dr. Richard J. Hayes.

The following persons in the city of Cork gave some information regarding county families or permission to work with library collections: Mr. John T. Collins and Mr. J. Lankford, genealogists; Mr. P. J. Madden, Librarian of the County Cork Library, and Mr. W. Cahill, Librarian of the University Library, Cork.

In January 1962, this compiler had the pleasure of meeting in Chicago, Mr. Alfred MacLochlainn, Assistant Keeper of the Manuscripts in the National Library of Ireland, and Dr. R. Dudley Edwards, Professor of Modern Irish History in University College, Dublin, who furnished some needed information. Dr. Edwards was engaged in revising the chapter on Irish sources in the 1959 edition of the *Bibliography of British History*. He has been joint editor with Dr. T. W. Moody, of *Irish Historical Studies*, 1938-1955; a member of the Irish Committee of Historical Sciences, from 1939 onward; member of the Irish Manuscripts Commission, whereon he is a colleague of Dr. Richard J. Hayes, Dr. Edward MacLysaght, Dr. James Hogan, Dr. T. W. Moody, Mr. Kenneth Darwin and others. Dr. Edwards spent parts of two days examining this compiler's nearly finished two-volume work; visited her private Irish library; read her Irish chapter in *Genealogical Research; Methods and Sources*, published by the American Society of Genealogists, 1960 (2nd printing, 1962), and offered various important suggestions.

This compiler is indebted to Sir Anthony Wagner, formerly Richmond Herald in the College of Arms, London. He was knighted on July 7, 1961; made a Knight Commander of the Victorian Order, invested as Garter Principal King of Arms, and as Genealogist of the Order of the Bath. At a later date he was made Inspector of Regimental Colors, and Genealogist of the Order of St. John of Jerusalem. He is the author of several works concerning English Heraldry and of *English Genealogy*, Oxford Press, 1959, and *English Ancestry*, Oxford Press, 1961. He was elected a Fellow of the American Society of Genealogists, some ten years ago. In 1955, he conducted this compiler on an inspection tour of the records in the College of Arms (including Irish source materials and other rare manuscripts and age old documents) and later gave an evening to a conference on Irish records.

During the past eleven years a steady flow of influence, encouragement and practical assistance has come to this compiler from her American colleagues who are all Fellows of the American Society of Genealogists. Those who have particularly contributed are:

Dr. Arthur Adams, deceased, President of the American Society of Genealogists for many years until 1959; Librarian of the New England Historic Genealogical Society and Editor of its *Register*. He closely followed this compiler's Irish work with encouragement and suggestions.

Mr. Meredith B. Colket, Jr., mentioned above, invited this compiler to lecture on "Irish Genealogical Source Materials," at four annual sessions of the Institute of Genealogical Research, in The National Archives, Washington, D. C.

Mr. Walter Goodwin Davis, President of the American Society of Genealogists, 1959-1961, sent Church records of early settlers in the District of Maine, showing Irish origins. He closely checked this compiler's progress.

Mr. Gilbert H. Doane, for many years Librarian of the University of Wisconsin and presently Editor of the *New England Historical and Genealogical Register;* author of *Searching for Your Ancestors*, Minneapolis, 1948, 1960. He assisted with compiling the announcements for this two-volume work.

Mrs. Winifred Lovering Holman (married in January 1962, to Rear Admiral Frank Riley Dodge, U.S.N., retired), Vice-President of the American Society of Genealogists, 1958-1959; author of numerous published genealogical works. She was responsible for the beginning of this Irish work, in that she urged the compiler to attend the Institute of Genealogical Research at The National Archives in June 1951. She has offered important suggestions and assisted with announcements.

Mr. Donald Lines Jacobus, Editor of the *American Gene-*

alogist, published this compiler's early and incomplete survey of Irish records in the July and October 1952 issues, which furnished encouragement to pursue the work.

Mr. George H. S. King, Treasurer of the American Society of Genealogists for many years until 1959. He sent references for numerous Virginia land records of colonists, showing Irish origins.

Mr. Milton Rubincam, President of the American Society of Genealogists, 1961-1962; past President of the National Genealogical Society, and for some years to date Editor of its *Quarterly;* Editor (with Dr. Jean Stephenson) of *Genealogical Research; Methods and Sources,* published by the American Society of Genealogists, 1960, 1962. It contains this compiler's chapter on Irish research, requested by Mr. Rubincam. He also assisted with announcements concerning this two-volume work.

Mr. Walter Lee Sheppard, Secretary of the American Society of Genealogists, 1958-1961. He has repeatedly sent this compiler notes on Irish records and has assisted with announcements concerning this two-volume work.

Dr. Jean Stephenson, Secretary of the American Society of Genealogists, 1961-1962; Director with Mr. Frank Bridgers of The National Archives, of the Institute of Genealogical Research of the American University and The National Archives, in co-operation with the Maryland Hall of Records. Dr. Stephenson, who has had considerable experience in publishing various works, offered to guide this compiler through the maze of technical publication details. She has advised, edited the material, served as technical authority for the compiler with the printer and binder. Dr. Stephenson's professional assistant, Miss Thekla G. Stephan of Washington, D. C., has prepared the manuscript for these two volumes for the printer. Both Dr. Stephenson and Miss Stephan have repeatedly read and corrected the proof sheets. Dr. Stephenson has compiled the General or Subject Indexes for both volumes, while Miss Stephan compiled the Names Index for Volume One. Without the selfless generosity, loyal interest and great skill of these two gifted women, the material for these two volumes might have been laid away unpublished.

Recognition and appreciation are also due countless persons of the present and the past, whose works of recording, compiling and preserving historical and genealogical source materials are mentioned within this text. They are the ones who have served as antiquaries, archivists, clergymen, ministers, priests, genealogists, government officials and agents, historians, librarians, record searchers, and solicitors, all of whom have contributed to making genealogical research a rewarding activity.

The esteemed Irish historians of national or local affairs have served, perforce, as careful genealogists, schooled in the use and value of genealogical source materials which amplify and personalize their work. The genealogists of high repute have ever qualified as students of Irish history, recognizing it as a guide to the meaning and continuity of the various collections of public and private records which constitute genealogical source materials.

March 17, 1962   Margaret Dickson Falley

FOREWORD

The term "Irish" in the title of this work is broadly construed to include the Gaelic-Irish and the descendants of the Anglo-Norman or English settlers in Ireland who intermarried with the Gaelic-Irish.

The appellation "Scotch-Irish" is peculiarly American and never has been recognized in Scotland or Ireland as a distinctive race-name, nor does it denote a mixture of Scottish and Gaelic-Irish blood. It might be regarded as a misnomer by some who adhere to the term "Ulster-Scot" as applicable to the descendants of early Scotch Presbyterians who emigrated from Scotland to settle in the Province of Ulster in Northern Ireland during the 17th century, and were unmixed with other races when many of them moved on to the American colonies.

The term "Scotch-Irish" was coined in America in about 1750, to distinguish the Ulster emigrants of Scottish blood from the other Irish settlers in the colonies. It came into general use, instead of the term "Ulster-Scot", following the American Revolution. However, the colonial records prior to 1750 show that the Ulster-Scots or Scotch-Irish who settled in America in the latter part of the 17th century and the first decades of the 18th century were universally called "Irish" by their English colonial neighbors.

This misrepresentation of their race as "Irish" on the strength of having lived in Northern Ireland was deeply resented on their part, as shown by the Rev. James MacGregor who brought a body of Scotch Presbyterians, mostly from County Londonderry, Ireland, to settle and name Londonderry, New Hampshire. A letter of the Rev. James MacGregor to Governor Shute stated: "We are surprised to hear ourselves termed Irish people, when we so frequently ventured our all for the British Crown and liberties against the Irish Papists and gave all tests of our loyalty which the government of Ireland required, and are always ready to do the same when required." (*History of Londonderry, New Hampshire,* by Edward L. Parker, Boston, 1851, p. 68.)

Edmund Burke wrote in 1757: "The number of white people in Virginia is between sixty and seventy thousand; and they are growing every day more numerous, by the migration of the Irish, who, not succeeding so well in Pennsylvania as the more frugal and industrious Germans, sell their lands in that province to the latter, and take up new ground in the remote countries in Virginia, Maryland and North Carolina. These are chiefly Presbyterians from the Northern part of Ireland, who in America are generally called Scotch-Irish." (*European Settlements in America.* Vol. II, p. 216.)

In 1763-1764, the term "Scotch-Irish" was used in the Legislature of the Province of Pennsylvania, to denote the Scotch Presbyterian settlers from Ireland, particularly those in the Paxtang settlement. (See the *History of Dauphin County, Pennsylvania,* by William H. Egle, p. 60.)

March 17, 1962   Margaret Dickson Falley

Contents of Volume I

PART ONE

PRELIMINARY RESEARCH

CHAPTER I

PRELIMINARY RESEARCH IN THE UNITED STATES

The most usual and immediate problem of an American who wishes to begin Irish or Scotch-Irish ancestral research is that he does not know the parentage of his forbear who emigrated from Ireland to America. He may also lack information sufficient to establish with certainty the place of the emigrant's birth or his residence at the time he left Ireland. In all cases, it is of the utmost importance that the genealogist, for purposes of identification, shall locate the geographical origin of the emigrant.

Much time and expense can be saved during the Irish research, and the probability of ultimate success will be greatly increased, if the work is begun with an effort to learn everything possible about the immigrant and his family from their American records.

Too many people are under the impression that only their own private family records could hold information regarding the parentage and the geographical origin of an ancestor who came from Ireland. Not enough realize how successfully some identifying facts or clues may be found among the publications and manuscripts in American genealogical and historical libraries; in the town, church, and county court records of the localities wherein the immigrant and his children settled; also among state archives and the government records deposited in The National Archives, Washington, D. C.

It is hoped that preliminary research in America will reveal such facts as the parentage of the immigrant, his exact place of birth, or residence at the time of emigration, his certain or approximate age upon departure from his Irish home, the time of his marriage which would indicate whether he was a householder in Ireland and therefore held property by lease or deed shortly before or at the time of his emigration, the names of his wife and her parents which, if Irish, might provide a clue to his origin, the given names of brothers and sisters in Ireland or America, the given names of his children, in order of their birth, a record of the first property owned in America, the names and origins of any Irish who settled in the same community, and finally the time and place of his death.

The given names of the immigrant, his brothers, sisters and children, in order of their birth, are important identifying factors, especially if any unusual given names are included. They may serve to direct serious attention to the records of a family of his surname, in the general area of his geographical origin, if it is found that duplicate given names in significant order were used in the Irish family. An immigrant, more often than not, named his eldest son in honor of his father and another son for his grandfather, while the two elder daughters were frequently given the names of their grandmothers. Clues of this nature must be sought and used as a guide to further search if the immigrant came to America unmarried, too young to have held property by lease or deed in Ireland, and when only the name of the county of his origin is known. These clues will help in the selection of the records to be searched, such as wills, parish records, and miscellaneous land records of any possible father, on the chance that the immigrant was named in some identifying way.

The date of an adult householder's emigration directs attention to the indexes of the Registry of Deeds, Dublin, for a number of reasons. As marriage settlements were fairly common, even in families of modest circumstances, he might have been named in a settlement between his father and the father of his bride or, in a settlement made for a brother or sister, his portion may have been mentioned. A deed, lease or partition frequently names sons or daughters who are to inherit, in order of their birth and sex, in the event of the death of the elder heir without issue. Such records have named children of all ages, and sometimes mention a son, "gone to America." Some wills have named a son who is to inherit if he returns from America to receive his portion. The indexes of the Registry of Deeds, covering a fairly brief period before and after an adult householder's emigration, should be examined in a search for any lease or deed or assignment by which he disposed of property or assigned his rights.   As the leases deposited in the Registry of Deeds concern only those of three or more years' duration, the estate records of any large landowner in the area of the emigrant's origin would also be searched for any record of a lease or tenant by which he could be identified.   Such a lease might include the names of his father and/or brothers.   Irish property owned or held on a long term lease, which an adult immigrant failed to dispose of or inherited after immigration, may have been mentioned in his will if it was in his possession at death.   In such cases, relatives in Ireland are usually named as beneficiaries.   These brief suggestions indicate some of the reasons for learning everything possible about the first and second generation Irish and Scotch-Irish in America.

Several directors of important repositories of genealogical records in Ireland have expressed the hope that some mention of the value of preliminary research in America will be contained in this GUIDE.   In numerous interviews throughout Ireland during the past ten years, this compiler has been impressed with the kindly interest and wish of these men and their assistants to help all Americans who write for the records of their Irish or Scotch-Irish forbears.   These archivists, historians and scholars say that they are too often disappointed over letters of Americans requesting genealogical assistance, because of the lack of some identifying information of the above nature regarding the immigrant ancestor.   They term such letters "vague inquiries."   They believe that they indicate either insufficient preliminary research in America, or failure to offer all known information about the immigrant and his family which could provide an Irish record searcher with facts and clues necessary for beginning the research.   They regret that even a small accompanying fee has been wasted, and can only hope that further research in America will eventually be accomplished and all known facts will then be presented to prepare the way for an efficient selection and search of Irish records.

The hope of this compiler is that anyone in possession of the identifying facts, gleaned from American genealogical sources, can then direct his own Irish research from his home or in Ireland with the help of information contained in this GUIDE.

An exhaustive search should cover all of the primary and secondary source materials which could relate to the first American settler and his children. Their Bible records, notes, old letters, diaries, memoirs, newspaper obituaries, and manuscripts containing family history are all original sources to be sought among relatives. Public records, as primary sources which might also reveal information concerning the immigrant's origin or family, include probate and marriage records, deeds, mortgages, chancery and other court records, pension documents, passenger lists, naturalization papers and records of indenture. Church and cemetery records, tombstone inscriptions, and vital records of the town, county or state are also reliable primary sources. Secondary sources which require checking include manuscript materials contained in family collections in genealogical or historical society libraries, published family histories, biographical material in local and regional histories, and collected genealogies.

Before proceeding with preliminary research in America it is well to become aware of the various types of evidence which may be found, relating to the immigrant's Irish family and origin. Records in his handwriting or his oral statements recorded by children or grandchildren may be quoted or copied with alterations caused by misinterpretation, due to incorrect conclusions recorded as fact, as well as by careless or forgetful omissions. Tradition, subject to all of these errors, also reflects the personality and imagination of any who quote it. Thus, in establishing the geographical or family origin of the immigrant, it must be recognized that there are certain possibilities of error in the records or statements of fact which should be kept in mind.

A written statement of the immigrant or quotation of his oral wording, that he emigrated from a certain city or came from there, must not be construed to mean that he lived there or was born in that place if it is a seaport city from which he could have sailed. Such a record is suspect if it concerns any one of the following cities: Belfast, Coleraine, Cork, Dublin, Galway, Larne, Londonderry, Waterford, Wexford, Wicklow, Youghal, etc. Too often the words "came from" and "emigrated from" are transcribed or misquoted as "lived in" or "born in."

Descendants may have strengthened their conclusions incorrectly because of an added statement of the immigrant that he worked in the named city or was in business there before emigrating. It may then be repeated with certainty that he lived there with his family, was married there and his children were born there, if he came to America with a wife and children. Two such mistakes occurred in this compiler's own family records, causing some delay and fruitless research before proof to the contrary was established.

In weighing evidence of this nature, the early conditions of emigration must be kept in mind. There were no exact sailing schedules, even as late as 1850. The emigrant who had reserved and paid for his passage, wherever he lived, was notified of the approximate date of sailing. He, and any other members of the family going with him, packed a few possessions and traveled to the seaport city to await the ship. Frequently, because of bad weather or for other reasons, the ship was delayed. In such cases, men and women, who wished to preserve their funds for later establishment in America, at once sought work in the city to support themselves until the day of departure.

Tradition may be even more confusing when it relates that the immigrant ancestor was Irish, his family having resided in a certain city, town, or county in Ireland, but that he emigrated from Liverpool, where he was engaged in business. This person might have been one of the many thousands who annually embarked from an Irish port on a small vessel and were taken to Liverpool, there to board a larger ship for the long trip to America. In Liverpool, also, there were delays. Perhaps the emigrant sought employment in order to save his funds. Or, as in so many cases from about 1650 on, he may have been an indentured servant, his land confiscated by the English government with consequent impoverishment in Ireland after one of the repeated Catholic uprisings, who chose voluntary servitude for a period of years in the new world, in order to rebuild his fortunes. Many, also, were sold and exiled to the southern colonial plantations after being convicted of treason for political reasons or for disloyalty to the English Government. Irish history, documented by government records, describes this custom in all of its aspects. The land records of Virginia and Maryland list the arrivals by name, in large shipments of Irish indentured servants. As late as 1851, the *Census of Ireland,* Volume I, Part 5, p. 227, states, "The total colonial and foreign emigration from Ireland between 1831 and 1841 equalled 403,459, or an average of 40,346 per annum. Of these, 214,047 embarked from Irish ports, 152,738 from Liverpool, and 10% was added for imperfect returns." An American genealogist, unfamiliar with the Irish customs of transportation, employment, and indentured servitude, might be inclined to accept a specific Liverpool tradition and conclude that the emigrant's family may have only briefly resided in Ireland. Being unable to relate the seemingly conflicting facts, he might even disbelieve the family tradition of an Irish or Scotch-Irish ancestry, particularly if the surname is of early English, Welsh, or Scottish origin.

Conflicting records in more than one branch of the family, regarding the geographical origin of the immigrant, may occur because the place-name of his origin is a strange or lengthy one and difficult to spell. An oral statement of the name by the immigrant may have been written by a descendant as it sounded with the Irish pronunciation. If the immigrant also said he came from or sailed from a certain city, this gives rise to conflicting records in different branches of the family. One branch may retain the strange name as the place of origin, in spite of the fact that it cannot be found on a modern map of Ireland. Another branch, from preference or in the cause of accuracy, might drop the strange name while retaining the familiar one and, in the course of time, adopt it as the place of origin. In all probability, the strange name is that of a very small village, townland (acreage), or parish, unrecorded on a modern map, or it may be that of a larger town but badly misspelled. When such a conflict in records is discovered, preference must be given to the strange or unfamiliar name. Sources listed in the next chapter will help to identify it.

If the place-name is that of both a county and a city or town within the county, without a distinguishing prefix to identify it, then one should keep an open mind as to whether the immigrant came from the city or town, or from some other place out in the county. Place-names which require a distinguishing prefix of "County," "City of," or "Town of," before them, are as follows: Antrim, Armagh, Carlow, Cavan, Clare, Cork, Donegal, Dublin, Galway, Kildare, Kilkenny, Leitrim, Limerick, Londonderry, Longford, Louth, Mayo, Monaghan, Roscommon, Sligo, Tipperary, Waterford, Wexford, Wicklow. As the Irish were, and are today, careful to prefix such place-names, it is probable that if the distinguishing term is lacking in connection with one of these given as the place of the immigrant's origin, then undoubtedly it was dropped in a later generation. Further trouble develops when a descendant notes the omission of a prefix and jumps to the conclusion most desired, that the ancestor came from the city or town of the name. Good examples of the care with which these place-names were prefixed by the people who had lived in Ireland, or knew the importance of the distinction, are shown in many tombstone inscriptions giving the place of nativity or origin of the deceased Irish and Scotch-Irish, published in *Some Early Epitaphs in Georgia*, compiled by Mrs. Peter W. Meldrim and published by the Georgia Society of the Colonial Dames of America, Durham, N. C., 1924; also in *The History of Western Maryland*, volume 2, by J. Thomas Scharf, Philadelphia, 1882. Thus, if the later family records state that an ancestor came from Londonderry, or the city of Londonderry, while his tombstone gives the place as the county of Londonderry, it is best to believe the tombstone inscription.

This problem of confusion was mentioned to this compiler during an interview in Magee University College Library, in the city of Londonderry. Some concern was expressed over the number of Americans who write requesting that old newspapers published in the city of Londonderry and other records be examined for information about their ancestors, stating positively that the emigrant came from there or that he lived there or was born there, but supplying insufficient evidence to support the fact.

If the only place-name found in the family ancestral records of the immigrant is that of Ulster, which was a Province embracing nine counties before 1920, then certainly more identifying information is needed before attempting Irish work.

With these objectives and precautions regarding the preliminary research well in mind, the beginner should first investigate the private family records. He must never be certain that his own branch of the family kept the most accurate or complete information. All known and elderly relatives, who are descendants of the ancestor in question, should be consulted and enlisted in the search. Through them, distant and unknown cousins can be contacted. An early family Bible may in this way be located. Brief family histories, jotted down on scraps of paper, have been found in Bibles and among old letters. The least intellectual branch of the family may have preserved early original documents and genealogy.

As Bibles and other ancestral records are jealously guarded, a request to borrow them might alienate the owner. However, the accuracy of a copy made by a relative cannot be trusted. Handwriting which is a century old may be hard to decipher and place-names might be misread or statements misinterpreted. Thus, it is wise to offer to pay for photostats of any old records. A promise to share any information discovered in the future, in return for present co-operation, usually produces results.

More often that not, the searcher will find that records which come from various branches of the family will differ as to length, detail, and spelling. An Irish place-name, offering a clue in one record, may be added to information retained in some other report. The stated facts can be pieced together as the sections of a puzzle, often with amazing results.

For the purpose of aiding preliminary research among American records, a bibliography of important published source material has been compiled and is presented in the accompanying VOLUME II, PART FIVE. It is arranged in three sections. The first section provides a list of authoritative guides to American research. This is to facilitate the work of beginners who may wish to check such sources for guidance. The second section presents a list of general reference and source materials, selected particularly as containing information about individual Irish or Scotch-Irish settlers in various American localities. The third section contains a list of published source materials pertaining to, and arranged under the names of the states in which, as colonies or states, the first generation Irish and Scotch-Irish in America are known to have settled during the seventeenth, eighteenth, and early nineteenth centuries. Fortunately, many of the listed sources will also serve for a study of later arrivals who settled in these early states.

Space does not permit the list to include the hundreds of important county and local histories which contain a wealth of biographical and genealogical information about the early residents and those of a later date, who contributed to the affairs of their communities. These histories may be found in the many large genealogical libraries throughout the country.

An evaluation of the genealogical data in county, town, and regional histories must, of course, be made. Any family history of three generations may be accepted as within the knowledge of the person who contributed his family records. Earlier genealogical material should be checked with primary sources. Tradition, as quoted, is too often inaccurate. However, it may contain some seeds of truth which will provide clues worth checking and evaluating. The indexes of these histories, in many cases, omit the names included in the lists of first settlers, tax lists, tombstone records, early marriages, abstracts of wills, church records, etc. The reader who will painstakingly leaf through a volume may be well rewarded.

Lists of first settlers and those of an early date in the community are important. Previous to the Revolution, and often at a later date, emigrants were prone to move in groups, with a leader. In many cases, he was a minister, or an enterprising man in his Irish community who also became important in the place of settlement in America. His records would help to identify the origin of any who came with him.

Before 1763, the records show no mention of the term, "Scotch-Irish." Previously, all people who came from Ireland were referred to as "Irish." In 1763, in the Legislature of the Province of Pennsylvania, the Ulster people of Scottish origin who settled in America were spoken of as "Scotch-Irish." The descriptive term became a popular one, and has since been commonly used in America to denote the origin of a Scottish family which resided in Ireland for some generations before coming to America.

County probate, land, and other records may reveal an immigrant's origin in surprising detail. A good illustration was sent to this compiler by Mr. George H. S. King, F.A.S.G., of Fredericksburg, Va., as follows: Copy made in the Virginia State Library, Westmoreland County, Va. W&D Book, No. 9, p. 231. "20 June 1742. James Mercer of Stafford County, Gentleman, one of the sons of John Mercer, late of the City of Dublin, Ireland, merchant, deceased, by Grace his wife, conveys to John Mercer of Marlborough in the County of Stafford, Colony of Virginia, eldest son and heir of the said John Mercer by Grace his wife . . . reciting that whereas by a decree in the Chancery Court of Ireland in a suit then depending wherein the aforesaid Grace Mercer, widow and the said John Mercer and James Mercer, parties to these presents, Joseph Mercer, Mary Mercer, Elizabeth Mercer and Jemima Mercer the other children of the said John Mercer, deceased, by Grace, his wife, were plaintiffs and William Alcock and Richard Leigh, surviving executors of William Alcock, deceased, and others were defendants, it was on the 7th day of June 1738 decreed by the Chancery Court . . ." (Here follows a long detail of the holdings of John Mercer in Dublin.) The conclusion of this deed is that James Mercer deeds to his brother, John Mercer, of "Marlborough," all his interest in and to the property involved in this chancery cause which was formerly the property of John Mercer, merchant, deceased, their father.

Two deeds discovered in Washington County, Pa., are as follows: Deed Book 2 C, p. 324. "Indenture made on 24 April 1818 between William Dickson of the townland of Mullaghbane in the County of Tyrone in the Kingdom of Ireland, and Hannah his wife (she the said Hannah being one of the sisters and heirs at law of James McFarland, late of Washington County in the Commonwealth of Pennsylvania, deceased) of the one part, and John Dickson now in America and Francis Dickson of Mullaghbane, in the Kingdom of Ireland, both sons of the said Hannah . . . James McFarland died intestate without issue, leaving four brothers and three sisters to wit: Andrew, David, Francis and Hugh, and Mary, Sarah, and Hannah . . . William Dickson and Hannah his wife . . . unto the said John and Francis Dickson." At the bottom of this deed was the record that, on 15 October 1818, a deed of partition was signed by William and Hannah Dickson, before William Murray, Esq., Chief Magistrate and Provost of the Town of Dungannon, County of Tyrone, Kingdom of Ireland. It was witnessed by Christopher Ross, James Brown and Mathew Dickson. On that day, Hannah Dickson was examined, separately from her husband. Deed Book 2 D, p. 404, Washington County, Pa., continues the record, whereby, on 7 September 1819, John Dickson and Francis Dickson, both of Washington County, Pennsylvania, sold their one-seventh interest in the property of their uncle, James McFarland, to Robert McFarland, for $800.00.

The value of church records is illustrated by a number of items taken from the records of the First (Presbyterian) Church of Wells, Maine, sent to this compiler by Mr. Walter Goodwin Davis, F. A. S. G., of Portland, Maine. Each item shows the recommendation of a person from a church in Ireland to the church in Wells, Maine, giving the date, name of the church location in Ireland, name of the minister or Presbytery, and date received at Wells, Maine. One item read: "May 6: 1722. John Ross of the Kingdom of Ireland, received to Communion, upon his letter of Recommendation from Mr: Samll: Henry, Pastor at Sligo in Ireland: of June 9: 1719." Other people were listed as having come from Mogwater. Three were named from Donathkeady, recommended by the minister, Mr. Thomas Wensley. The *History of Con-*

gregations of the Presbyterian Church in Ireland, by the Rev. W. D. Killen, Belfast, 1886, identifies all of the places and ministers. Under the town of Sligo, p. 252, "The Rev. Samuel Henry was the first minister of this congregation of whom there is any record. He was ordained to the joint-charge of Sligo and Moywater (Killala) by the Presbytery of Convoy in May, 1695. In July, 1698, Moywater was separated from Sligo, which latter was still under Mr. Henry's care. In 1727 Mr. Henry resigned the pastorate of Sligo and settled at Abbeyfoile." Thus, "Mog-Water," as it was written by the minister of Wells, Maine, was actually Moywater. "Donathkeady," as it was spelled in Wells, Maine, was the congregation of Donagheady, under which heading on p. 113, is the following: "The next (2nd) minister was Mr. Thomas Winsley, who had been licensed by the Presbytery of Edinburgh, and had come to Ireland in 1698. He was ordained here (Donagheady) by the Presbytery of Lagan on the 18th of January, 1699; he died October 28th, 1736. He was succeeded by Mr. William Armstrong . . . " This also shows that the name Winsley was misspelled in Wells, Maine, as "Wensley." With the aid of sources listed in the next chapter, the full description of the geographical origin of these people was ascertained.

The Revolutionary War pension and bounty land records of the Veterans Administration Archives, in The National Archives, Washington, D. C., include the papers of a very large number of men and their widows who were of Irish or Scotch-Irish origin.

Because of the great genealogical value of the entire collection of documents, the National Genealogical Society, in March, 1943, began the continued publication of a "Supplement" in its *Quarterly,* containing the "Index of Revolutionary War Pension Applications." This index had, in March, 1961, reached the name "Vance." It shows for each man, the state from which his service was rendered, the file number of his papers, and before the number a letter "S" for survivor, "W" for widow in which case the widow's given name follows that of her husband, or "R" for rejected claim. The original papers of each file are in linen-lined envelopes, deposited in The National Archives, where they may be examined in the Central Search Room. Bounty Land Warrants are also listed in the index after the soldier's name, with a number preceded by "B L Wt." together with the number of acres and the date granted. This published index makes it possible for anyone to send a written request for photostats of the original papers in any file. A price schedule and estimate of the expense will be furnished upon inquiry.

Each person who applied for a pension was required to make application at the court house of the county wherein he resided at that time. In every case, his affidavit or sworn statement was taken by a county officer. In support of this evidence, the affidavits of other veterans who had served with the applicant or could attest to his war record were taken. Statements under oath regarding his financial condition, often with the names of those who were dependent upon him at the time of the claim, were also submitted. All papers were sent to the War Department, Washington, D. C., for approval.

Facts required in all of the applicant's affidavits were the dates and places of enlistment (frequently more than one for a person), names of his commanding officers, designation of the company (one or more) in which he served, and particulars of service during each and every enlistment; also a statement of financial condition, including the names of dependents. Data regarding personal history varied. If an immigrant, he was required to give the year of birth and the country of nativity. In many cases, full information was recorded, including the exact date and place of birth, parentage, record of marriage, time of arrival in America, and all places of residence in the United States.

The widow of a veteran, who made application for a pension, frequently submitted one or more pages of the family Bible as supporting evidence of the date of her marriage and the names and birth dates of their children. These Bible records sometimes revealed the parentage of the husband and wife, and even further notes regarding ancestry. Other files contain transcripts of Bible records and attested statements of relatives and friends, in support of claims.

Pensions were established by the Congress of the United

States, and their issue was controlled by Acts of the Congress of various dates, setting forth various conditions under which a veteran or his widow could qualify for a pension. The first pensions were voted by the Continental Congress during the Revolution, to take effect at the end of the war, and to be issued to officers who had served for the duration. These granted half pay for seven years. An Act of 1792 provided for pensions to officers and soldiers who were permanently disabled during the war. A few of these records have been found, abstracted, and published in the National Genealogical Society *Quarterly* of March and June, 1958. These only afford information regarding military rank of the applicant, his residence at time of application, particulars of accident and disability, and proportion of pension to which the veteran is entitled. Not many pension records of dates prior to 1818 are in existence. All those which have survived two fires in the War Department offices before this date pertain to disability cases of officers and soldiers.

The dates and provisions of the Pension Acts of the Congress, beginning in 1818, will be listed here as a guide to the possibility of an ancestor having qualified and applied before his or her death date: On March 18, 1818, Army and Navy officers and enlisted men were granted pensions, if proof could be given of "reduced circumstances," nine months of service, or active service at the end of the Revolution. By December 22, 1819, it was estimated that over 16,000 pensions were granted. This led to the "Alarm Act" of May 1, 1820, requiring a schedule of property of all pensioners to be filed, which resulted in many cancelled pensions. The Act of May 15, 1828, provided pensions for all who were in service at the end of the war. The Act of June 7, 1832, allowed volunteers and militia officers and men to apply. By the Act of July 4, 1836, widows who had been married to officers and soldiers before or during service were qualified to apply for a pension. The Act of July 7, 1838, added all widows who were married to veterans by January 1, 1794. This date was advanced to January 1, 1800, by the Acts of March 3, 1843, February 2, 1848, and July 29, 1848.   The Act of February 3, 1853, included widows married after January 1, 1800, and also provided that the children of a widow who failed to receive the pension from July 29, 1848, could collect the amount due from that date to her death.   Finally, by the Act of March 9, 1878, all widows of veterans of the Revolution could apply.

Often it is found that a Revolutionary War pension file, marked "R" for rejected claim, will offer more personal data than a more easily proven claim.

Many men of Irish and Scotch-Irish origin also took part in the War of 1812.   Pensions for veterans were first provided by Act of Congress in 1871, and applicants were required to submit affidavits setting forth their qualifications and proof of service.   These frequently contain full statements of the time and place of birth, marriage, and sometimes even parentage.   The application papers are filed in linen-lined envelopes in The National Archives, and may be examined in the Central Search Room.   The index to these records may be consulted there.   It has not been published.

The first 1812 Pension Act was the Act of February 14, 1871, which provided pensions for soldiers and sailors who had been enlisted for sixty days during the war, and their widows who could prove marriage prior to February 17, 1815.   On March 9, 1878, the required time of service was shortened to fourteen days and included all widows of veterans.

The immigration records identifying new arrivals in America are an important source for those who have been unable to determine the geographical origin of the first generation settler, his full name, age at time of landing in America, occupation in Ireland, and the names and ages of any members of his family who came with him, including a wife and children.   Adult relatives and members of their families who came with him may also be identified in the same way.

The available sources in The National Archives, Washington, D. C., are the passenger lists of the ships which landed at the Atlantic and Gulf Coast ports, 1798-1919 (records before 1820 are few and those dated after 1919 are not open to the public) ; lists of aliens, 1798-1800; the abstracts of lists of aliens arriving at Boston, 1848-1891; and various printed passenger lists. The sources in The National Archives will be described in the above order, followed by miscellaneous printed lists in the United States and Ireland.

The passenger lists are contained in the Ships Manifests, each compiled at the end of the voyage by the captain of the ship, who presented it under oath at his port of entry, upon arrival. A Ships Manifest contains the name and tonnage of the vessel, the name of the captain, the port of embarkation, the date and port of arrival, a record of the cargo, and a complete list of all passengers, including a record of any deaths which occurred at sea.

The passenger list contains the full name of each passenger, his or her age, sex, occupation if adult, the name of the country to which he owes allegiance, and the country in which he intends to settle. Many lists of Irish passengers give particulars of the town, city, or county of past residence and the city or state in America which they intend to inhabit. In some cases, a description of the passenger was given as "light," "dark," or "fair."

The passenger lists provide further information, by the grouping of names of those in a family party. They are usually listed in the following order: The adult male head of the family; the adult woman, as head of the family or wife; their children in age order; other adult or young relatives in the party. Adult brothers and sisters without families were listed together.

In 1951, this compiler had the opportunity to make a survey of original passenger lists in The National Archives, under the direction of Mr. Meredith B. Colket, Jr., F.A.S.G., who was then director of the General Reference Section, and is now director of the Western Reserve Historical Society, Cleveland, Ohio. The Ships Manifests, numbering 386, for the port of New York, 1822-1837, with their passenger lists, were selected from the files of this port, dated 1820-1919.

When examining the Ships Manifests in search of Irish arrival lists, it was found that care must be taken to inspect the manifests with passenger lists of those who sailed from any large West Coast port of England or Scotland, especially

Liverpool, as well as for Irish ports of embarkation. Liverpool was a port of departure to which the Irish were commonly sent by small ships to transfer to the larger vessels for the long trip across the Atlantic. To illustrate: In June, 1835, the ship, *Victoria*, 601-79/95 tons, James Campbell, Captain, arrived in the port of New York from Liverpool, carrying 115 passengers, all but one from Ireland. They were listed respectively by name as coming from the following places: Armagh, Belfast, Cavan, Cork, Donegal, Dublin, Kerry, Kildare, Kilkenny, Londonderry, Longford, Monaghan, Tipperary, Tyrone, and Wexford. One passenger declared intention of settling in Albany, six in Boston, three in Maryland, four in Massachusetts, seventy-three in New York, four in Pennsylvania, ten in Philadelphia, and thirteen in Ohio. On May 11, 1837, the brig, *John Cumming*, from Liverpool, landed 281 passengers at the port of New York, who came from the following Irish counties: Antrim, Cavan, Cork, Donegal, Dublin, Kerry, Kilkenny, Londonderry, Longford, Louth, Meath, Monaghan, Tipperary, Waterford, West Meath, and Wexford.

To illustrate the value of passenger lists, a copy of a Ships Manifest will be given below. This is for the brig, *Harriet*, from Londonderry, which landed at the port of New York on July 14, 1837. It appears that the captain listed the counties of Ireland from which the passengers emigrated under "Country to which they severally belong." He spelled Donegal variously as Donagel, Donnegil, Donegil, and Donegal. Londonderry was first listed as "L Derry" and afterwards as "Derry," a usual contraction. This ship, of 285-58/95 tons, carried 114 passengers, while the ship *Victoria* from Liverpool to New York, June, 1835, was listed at 601-79/95 tons and carried 115 passengers.

BRIG HARRIET

PORT OF LONDONDERRY FOR NEW YORK

14th July, 1837

I William Collins do solomnly, sincerely and truly swear that the following list of passengers subscribed with my name and now delivered by me to the Collector of Customs for the District of New York contains to the best of my knowledge and belief a just and true account of all the passengers received on board the brig *Harriet* whereof I am Master from Londonderry.

July, 14, 1837   So help me God,
                                                William Collins.

Report of the list of the Passengers taken on board the brig *Harriet* of Providence, Rhode Island.

Whereof William Collins is Master.   Burthen 285 tons and 58/95 of a ton bound from the port of Londonderry for New York.

Names	Age	Sex	Occupation or Profession	Country to which they severally belong	Country in which they intend to become inhabitants
John Gallagher	25	Male	Farmer	Donagel	New York
Nancy O'Neil	18	Fem.		Tyrone	"
John McNabb	6	Male		"	"
Robert Robb	18	"		"	Philadelphia
Robert Burnett	20	"		"	"
Lum Danley	22	"		"	"
Mary Sheryveen	20	Fem.		Donnegil	New York
Catherine Aitt	23	"		"	"
Mrs. McLaughlen	48	"		L Derry	"
John McLaughlen	21	Male	Carpenter	"	"
Charles McLaughlen	19	"		"	"
James McLaughlen	15	"		"	"
William McLaughlen	18	"		"	"
Daniel McLaughlen	11	"		"	"
Anna McLaughlen	13	Fem.		"	"
Mary Miller	50	"		"	"
James Miller	11	Male		"	"
Lume Miller	22	"	Farmer	Donegil	"
John Miller	22	"		"	"
Sarah Ann Kennedy	18	Fem.		"	"
Margt McElwie	20	"		"	"
Sarah McElwie	17	"		"	"
Isabella Ralston	20	"		"	"
Patrick Sweeny	25	Male		"	Penn.
Patrick Melby	23	"		"	Ohio
Mary Melby	23	Fem.		"	"
James Melby	1	Male		"	"
Hugh Melby	60	"		"	"
Peggy Melby	20	Fem.		"	"
Nancy Hamleton	18	"		"	New York
Margaret Hamleton	16	"		"	"
Eliza Hamleton	56	"		"	"
Sally Hamleton	20	"		Derry	"
Edward McCrew	26	Male	Carpenter	"	"
Barney Keenan	30	"	Farmer	Donegil	"
Mary Stewart	50	Fem.		"	Hartford
John Stewart	18	Male		"	"

Names	Age	Sex	Occupation or Profession	Country to which they severally belong	Country in which they intend to become inhabitants
Edward McKeown	25	Male	Weaver	Donegil	Hartford
Mary McKeown	25	Fem.		"	"
John McKeown	1½	Male		"	"
John Bradley	40	"	Weaver	"	"
George Robertson	19	"	Farmer	Tyrone	L (Prob. L Derry)
Mrs. Rea	69	Fem.		Donegil	Philadelphia
Rebecca Hunter	15	"		Tyrone	New York
Andrew Sprowle	18	Male	Farmer	"	Hartford
Margaret Mooney	20	Fem.		Donegil	New York
Margaret McClane	18	"		"	"
Mary Carland	20	"		"	"
Francis Quigley	14	Male		Derry	"
Nancy McWilliams	28	Fem.		"	"
Eleanor McGowen	15	"		Donegil	"
Mary Sweeny	17	Fem.		"	"
Maria Rogers	35	"		Tyrone	"
Moses Rogers	55	Male	Weaver	"	Indiana
Aaron Rogers	25	"	"	"	"
Catherine Rogers	60	Fem.		"	"
Margaret Rogers	23	"		"	"
Catherine Rogers	16	"		"	"
Robert Rea	50	Male	Carpenter	Donegal	New York
Elsie Rea	49	Fem.		"	"
Maria Rea	24	"		"	"
Eliza Rea	21	"		"	"
Samuel Rea	18	Male		"	"
John Rea	15	"		"	"
Michell McGillium	21	"	Weaver	Derry	"
Jane Otherty	24	Fem.		"	"
Patrick Duffey	29	Male	Farmer	Donegil	"
Biddy Conahun	18	Fem.		"	"
Michael Shutes	19	Male	Farmer	"	"
Patrick Kelly	20	"	Mason	Derry	"
Arthur Gormly	20	"		Tyrone	Rochester
Margaret Murnurn	20	Fem.		Donegal	New York
John Beatty	24	Male	Carpenter	"	"
Mary Meenan	15	Fem.		"	"
James Harayhy	20	Male	Farmer	Donegel	Philadelphia
James Harayhy	21	"	"	"	"
Dennis Connor	28	"	"	"	Ohio
Thos McNeilens	25	"	Weaver	Tyrone	"
Jane McNeilens	20	Fem.		"	"
Mary McNeilens	17	"		"	"
Hanna Stewart	21	"		"	"
Andy Cuthburton	20	Male	Carpenter	"	"
Mary Clark	30	Fem.		"	Philadelphia
Mary Sharkey	20	"		Donegil	New York
Seth McGonagle	16	Male		"	"
Patrick Hughes	21	"	Farmer	"	"
Catherine Hughes	19	Fem.		"	"
William Stewart	50	Male	Weaver	Tyrone	"
Jane Stewart	48	Fem.		"	"
June Stewart	23	"		"	"
Nancy Stewart	23	"		"	"

Names	Age	Sex	Occupation or Profession	Country to which they severally belong	Country in which they intend to become inhabitants
William Clowford	18	Male		Derry	New York
Mary Clowford	20	Fem.		"	"
John Donelly	40	Male	Farmer	"	Pittsburgh
Briget Donelly	30	Fem.		"	"
Chas McColegan	46	Male	Taylor	Tyrone	Philadelphia
Lucy McColegan	40	Fem.		"	"
Henry McColegan	17	Male		"	"
Margaret McColegan	16	Fem.		"	"
Lucy McColegan	14	Fem.		"	"
Eliza McColegan	12	"		"	"
Charles McColegan	8	Male		"	"
William McColegan	6½	"		"	"
James Wallace	5	"		"	"
Alex McCafferty	22	"	Farmer	Derry	Baltimore
Marg McCullough	24	Fem.		"	New York
Marg Fresh	18	"		Donegil	Philadelphia
Mary Gallagher	19	"		"	New York
John Scott	22	Male	Carpenter	Tyrone	"
Margaret Johnson	20	Fem.		"	Philadelphia
Thos Johnson	2	Male		"	"
Catherine McCowen	20	Fem.		Donegal	
Frank Gallagher	26	Male	Farmer	"	New York
Joseph Smith	28	Male	Blacksmith	"	New Haven

This compiler is indebted to Mr. Meredith B. Colket, Jr., previously mentioned, for the following information concerning the arrangement, classification, and extent of the passenger arrival records of people from all countries, including Ireland, now deposited in The National Archives. These records are dated 1798-1945. The files dated before 1820 are incomplete and those of dates after 1919 are not open to the public. The original documents have been withdrawn from the public, due to their fragile condition. However, these are being microfilmed and, by 1960, most of the records for the ports of New York and New Orleans had been filmed.

The passenger arrival records are preserved in three forms: Original records; transcripts of records, including card indexes which contain information amounting to abstracts; and microfilm copies of the records. The original records, transcripts, and card indexes are in the Bureau of Customs records deposited in The National Archives (Record Group 36). (The microfilm copies of the records are in R G 85.) There is also a list of immigrants entering all ports from 1819-1820, among the General Records of the United States Government (R G 11).

The names of the immigrants on this list have been printed in SENATE DOCUMENT 118, *16th Congress, 2nd session*. All transcripts, consolidated card indexes, and microfilms listed below may be consulted at The National Archives.

Passenger arrival records include the following: Lists of aliens, 1798-1800; passenger lists (described above) 1819-1945; abstracts of lists of aliens arriving at Boston, 1848-1891. Baggage lists, 1799-1819, which also contain some lists of names of arrivals, are not noted here as they are not sufficiently informative.

I. *Lists of Aliens, 1798-1800.* The records give the name of the vessel, port of embarkation, port and date of arrival, list of passengers giving for each, his name, age, place of birth, country from which he came, country to which he owes allegiance, his occupation, and his personal description. The records are for the following ports:

1. Alexandria, Virginia, 1798-1800.

2. Beverly and Salem, Massachusetts, 1798-1800. These lists are abstracted in the *New England Historical and Genealogical Register*, 106: 203-09 (July 1952).

3. Philadelphia, Pennsylvania, 1798-1800. The lists are card indexed, with the above information, and form a part of a consolidated card index of passenger lists which will be described below.

II. *Passenger Lists* (appearing on Ships Manifests) created under Customs legislation, 1819-1919. The records have been described above. The original records are for the following ports:

1. Baltimore, 1820-1919 (gaps, 1822-35; 1856-59). Records are card indexed, 1820-1899. Each card is coded; surnames of like sound being grouped together. Entries are located by reference to a key to the code. The index also covers entries in a bound volume for 1820, cited below under *Transcripts of the Passenger Lists.* (NOTE: The Department of Legislative Reference, City Hall, Baltimore 2, Md., answers requests for information from its alphabetically arranged card file on alien arrivals, 1833-1875, giving information noted above under *Lists of Aliens, 1798-1800.*)

2. Boston, 1883-1899 (lack of earlier records has been attributed to a fire in 1894).

3. Mobile, Alabama, 1820-1862. The lists are fragmentary for some years and completely missing for others.

4. New Bedford, Massachusetts, 1823-1899. Indexes, 1875-1896.

5. New Orleans, La., 1820-1899. Indexes, 1813, 1815, 1820-1867. The National Archives Library has a typescript, "Passenger Lists Taken from Manifests of the Customs Service Port of New Orleans," consisting of five separately indexed volumes as follows: 1813, 1815, 1821-33; 1834-38; 1839-49; 1850-61; 1864-67. Entries show the name of the vessel, place of embarkation, destination, name of the passenger and date of arrival. This is a Work Projects Administration product and omits the records of a number of passenger lists (original records) existing, as well as a large number of names on listed records. Also discrepancies appear in the spelling of many names, when compared with the original records.

6. New York, N. Y., 1820-1919.

7. Philadelphia, Pa., 1820-1899. Indexes, 1798-1819; 1820-1899. Lists before 1835 are interfiled with Customs manifests. The card index includes entries referring to the earlier lists of aliens and baggage lists.

III. *Transcripts of Passenger Lists,* created under Customs legislation, 1819-1875. This collection includes the transcripts of passenger lists of many smaller ports, the original records of which have been lost or destroyed. Transcripts are arranged under three headings:

1. Transcripts (unbound) arranged by name of the port, 1820-1874. Under each port, the transcripts are arranged chronologically. For each of the following ports there are 25 or more transcripts, dated within the years indicated: Alexandria, Va., 1820-52, 1865; Baltimore, Md., 1820-1869; Boston, Mass., 1820-69; Bristol (and Warren), R. I., 1820-71; Charleston, S. C., 1820-29, 1858; Edgartown, Mass., 1820-33; Fall River, Mass., 1833-65; Galveston, Texas, 1846-71; Key West, Fla., 1837-68; Mobile, Ala., 1832, 1848-52; New Bedford, Mass., 1826-69; New Berne, N. C., 1820-44, 1865; Newburyport, Mass., 1821-39; New Haven, Conn., 1820-45, 1865-73; New London, Conn., 1820-48; Newport, R. I., 1820-57; New Orleans, La., 1820-73; New York, N. Y., 1820-74; Norfolk (and Portsmouth), Va., 1820-50, 1857; Passamaquoddy, Me., 1820-59; Philadelphia, Pa., 1820-73; Portland (and Falmouth), Me., 1820-73; Portsmouth, N. H., 1820-61; Providence, R. I., 1820-67; Savannah, Ga., 1820-68; Wilmington, Del., 1820-49. A consolidated master card index for all Atlantic and Gulf Coast ports, except New York, is compiled on 3" x 5" cards. These have abstracts of the information in the transcripts. A separate card index is compiled for the tran-

scripts of the New York records but includes chiefly entries dated 1820-40, with a few as late as 1846.

2. Transcripts arranged by quarter year of arrivals by name of port, 1819-1832. Records were entered in nine volumes. Volume two is missing (dates between Sept. 30, 1820 and Sept. 30, 1821). All entries were presumably copied in the Office of the Secretary of State from the unbound transcripts of passenger lists sent to Washington by Customs officials. They are not complete. Fragmentary entries dated 1819 are only for the ports of Deighton, Mass., Petersburg, Va., and Wiscasset, Maine. Entries after 1826 do not include records of the ports of Boston and New York. All entries in volume one (Dec. 31, 1819-Sept. 30, 1820) and some entries from the missing volume two, were printed in U. S. Department of State *Letters from the Secretary of State, with a Transcript of the List of Passengers who Arrived in the United States from the 1st October, 1819 to the 30th September, 1820* (Washington, Gales and Seaton, 1821. *16th Congress, 2nd session*, S. DOCT. 118; serial 45). The National Archives has a transcript index to this volume.

3. Bound Transcripts of Baltimore Passenger Lists, 1820: One volume. The index to entries in this volume is consolidated with the index to the Customs passenger lists.

4. Bound Transcripts of New Orleans Passenger Lists, 1845-1875: Twenty-three volumes. Details such as full given names of passengers are sometimes lacking.

IV. *Abstracts of Lists of Aliens Arriving at Boston, 1848-1891.* The records of aliens who entered the port of Boston during this period were listed in the passenger arrival records, under terms of Massachusetts legislation of May 10, 1848 (*Massachusetts Acts and Resolves*, 1848, chap. 313, sec. 4) ; the records now being in the custody of the Archives Division, Office of the Secretary of the Commonwealth, 438 State House, Boston 33, Massachusetts. As this period covers the time of the greatest immigration of the Irish into the United States, and Boston became the port of entry for an enormous number of Irish arriving in this country, these records are extremely important to Irish genealogy. Abstracts of the records were taken from the passenger arrival lists on 4" x 6" cards which were prepared by the Work Projects Administration. This collection comprises an alphabetized card index arranged under dates of arrival. Each card shows the name of the passenger, his age, sex, date of arrival, the name of the vessel on which he came, his occupation if adult, his birth-place, the place of his last residence if he was in the United States previously, and his destination. Thus, these abstracts of the orig-

inal passenger arrival records are fully as valuable as the
original records, for genealogical purposes. In 1956, The
National Archives borrowed the cards for the purpose of
microfilming them.

V. *Microfilms of Passenger Lists.*

1. A microfilm of Irish Passenger Lists, Ireland to Ports
in the U. S. A., 1803-1806. The original passenger lists are
contained in the Ships Manifests drawn up by the captains of
the vessels which sailed from various Irish ports, and declared
under oath at ports of entry in the United States, 1803-1806.
The entire collection comprises 267 Ships Manifests, which are
now deposited in the British Museum, London, where they are
beautifully bound in one red leather volume of 399 pages
(catalogued, British Museum Additional Manuscript, No.
35932). In 1952, this compiler personally examined the
volume and had the contents microfilmed for The National
Archives, Washington, D. C. The manifests contain the complete passenger lists with information as to the name, age,
occupation if adult, Irish county, etc., of origin, and destination of each passenger. The collection contains the records
of over 3,000 arrivals. The ships sailed, for the most part,
from Belfast, Ballyshannon, Cork, Dublin, Londonderry,
Newry, Sligo, and Warrenspoint. The port of entry was, in
over half the cases, New York. Other ports of entry were
Baltimore, Boston, Charleston, New Bedford, Newcastle, and
Philadelphia. The emigrants were mostly from the counties
of Antrim, Armagh, Down, Fermanagh, Londonderry, and
Tyrone, with a smaller proportion coming from Southern Ireland. A copy of the records made by Fothergill is printed in
the *New England Historical and Genealogical Register,* vols.
60, 61, 62, 66. This is contained in some forty pages and does
not appear to be complete.

2. Microfilms of the Original Passenger Lists in The
National Archives: Passenger lists are in the process of being
microfilmed and, by 1960, most of the passenger arrival lists
for the ports of New York and New Orleans had been filmed.
These may be consulted and copies of the films may be purchased.

* * * * *

BIBLIOGRAPHY OF PUBLISHED IRISH PASSENGER LISTS:

This concerns Irish passenger lists, and references to the
records:

American-Irish Historical Society Journal, New York, volume
    28. "Passenger Lists for American Ports printed in Ire-
    land 1811."

American-Irish Historical Society Journal, New York, volume 29. "Passenger Lists for American Ports printed in Ireland 1815-1816."

Lancour, A. Harold. "Passenger Lists of Ships Coming to North America, 1607-1825; A Bibliography." (New York Public Library *Bulletin,* 41; No. 5, pp. 389-410.)

New England Historical and Genealogical Register:
1. "Two Early Passenger Lists, 1635-1637."
2. "List of Emigrants from England, 1773-1776."
3. "List of Emigrants to America from Liverpool, 1697-1707."
4. "Irish Passenger Lists; Ireland to the U. S. A., 1803-1806." (Copy by Fothergill from British Museum Add. MSS. No. 35932.) Vols. 60, 61, 62, 66.

Recorder, The: (Bulletin of the American-Irish Historical Society, Boston, vol. 3.) "Early Irish Emigrants, 1803-1806" (additions to No. 4 above).

NOTE: Six typed leaflets, deposited in The National Archives Library, contain the names of persons who emigrated, 1833-1835, from various parishes in County Londonderry, Ireland, chiefly to the United States and Canada. These were a gift of the Public Record Office of Northern Ireland, Belfast. For details of the lists see section below on Emigration Records in that repository.

EMIGRATION RECORDS IN THE PUBLIC RECORD OFFICE OF NORTHERN IRELAND, BELFAST:

1. The first three lists published by the New England Historic Genealogical Society, in its *Register* (see Nos. 1, 2, 3, above), were presented by this Society to the Public Record Office of Northern Ireland, Belfast, in 1925.

2. *Emigration from Ulster to North Carolina, etc., from Papers of the late W. C. Houston.* Philadelphia, U. S. A., 1736-1737.

3. *The Drumgooland Vestry Book, 1789-1828,* published in 1892. Being notes of Ulster emigration to America, 1789-1828.

4. Lists of passengers for New York and Philadelphia, etc., sailing from Newry (Co. Down) and Warrenspoint (Co. Down), 1791-1792.

5. A photostat of lists of persons, including many from Northern Ireland, naturalized in New York, 1802-1814.

6. Manuscript copies of Ordnance Survey Documents, deposited in the Royal Irish Academy, Dublin, being lists of persons who emigrated, 1833-1835, from various parishes in County Londonderry, Ireland, chiefly to the United States and

Canada. These lists of names, arranged by parishes, were extracted by the Public Record Office of Northern Ireland from the Ordnance Survey Documents of County Londonderry. The names of the emigrants are arranged under the name of the parish from which they emigrated. The lists show the name of the emigrant, his age, the year of his emigration, the name of the townland (usually his farm) where he lived, his religion (Protestant or Roman Catholic), and the city or state of his destination in America. The parishes for which the emigration lists are made are: Aghadowey, Aghanloo, Agivey, Arboe, Artrea, Ballyaghran, Ballynascreen, Ballyrashane, Ballyscullion, Ballywillin, Balteagh, Banagher, Bovevagh, Clondermot, Coleraine, Desertlyn, Desertmartin, Desertoghill, Drumachose, Dunlo, Dungiven, Enigal, Kilcronaghan, Kildollagh, Killowen, Kilrea, Magilligan, Tamlaght Finlagan. As stated above, The National Archives Library has typed copies of these lists.

NATURALIZATION RECORDS:

Naturalization proceedings will usually furnish the date when an immigrant, petitioning for naturalization, arrived in the United States. This date will serve to locate the passenger list of the ship in which he came to America. The papers will also show, for each applicant, his full name, age or date of birth, the country from which he emigrated, the port of his arrival and, in some cases, more detailed information showing his exact place of origin. The 19th Century naturalization proceedings for the District of Columbia are in The National Archives. Records of the 19th Century for other areas of the country will be found in the Federal, state, or county courts. The petitioner's records will usually be located in the court nearest his place of residence at the time he made application. To avoid a lengthy search, consult any list of voters in the county in which the man was naturalized, which will name the court in which this occurred. Inventories of the records of many counties in the United States of America were compiled by the Work Projects Administration and published. These volumes are in The National Archives and in many large libraries. For information concerning the Naturalization Records of New York State, and City, consult the *Guide to Genealogical and Biographical Sources for New York City (Manhattan), 1783-1898,* by Rosalie Fellows Bailey, F. A. S. G., New York, 1954. This is a thoroughly informative guide to all classes of New York records which will assist in preliminary research in this area.

IRISH PUBLISHED RECORDS AND MICROFILMS IN THE UNITED STATES:

Many of the important published Irish records necessary for the compiling of Irish family histories may be found in the larger American genealogical libraries. If the searcher will familiarize himself with the published Irish sources mentioned in this two-volume GUIDE, which pertain to the Irish locality and to the classes of records which interest him, and will then locate and study as many of the published records as are presently deposited in one or more of the following libraries, he will develop many possibilities for further research by correspondence with Irish repositories. The published sources will be fully discussed and described in the forthcoming chapters, and will be listed in VOLUME II.

The microfilms of Irish manuscript records, located in the United States of America, are listed in the accompanying bibliography, VOLUME II, PART FOUR, under REPOSITORIES OF MICROFILMS, with locating key (see Table of Contents, PART FOUR, 2nd item).

The following libraries have the larger collections of Irish published materials:

The American-Irish Historical Society, 991 Fifth Ave., New York, N. Y.

The Genealogical Society of the Church of Jesus Christ of Latter-Day Saints, Salt Lake City, Utah.

The Huntington Library, San Marino, California.

The Library of Congress, Washington, D. C.

The Newberry Library, Chicago, Illinois.

The New England Historic Genealogical Society, Boston, Massachusetts.

The New York Public Library, New York, N. Y.

The State Libraries, State, County and local historical societies, and the large Public Libraries of all states in which early settlements of the Irish and Scotch-Irish were made. Many of these repositories have accumulated Irish published records, as well as some manuscripts relating to Irish settlers.

CHAPTER II

THE GEOGRAPHICAL ORIGIN OF THE ANCESTOR

In all genealogical work the first and most important step is to establish the geographical origin of the ancestor, in as much detail as possible. This is particularly true in Ireland, because of the variety of ways in which source materials are classified, calendared, and indexed by specific territorial arrangement, according to the source and purpose of the records, while the individual documents further define and identify the geographical location of the people named.

When beginning Irish research, the genealogist may know the name of the county in which the ancestor lived, and be puzzled over a place-name given as the place of his birth or residence, which he cannot locate on a modern map of Ireland. This leaves him uncertain of the nature or meaning of the strange name, the extent of its area, relationship to the county, or location within it. He wonders whether the unidentified name is that of a farm, tiny village unmarked on the map, or is that of a larger place but misspelled beyond recognition. In all probability, the place-name is that of a townland. But even if, in his own record, it is defined in this way, he may not know the meaning of the word townland.

The reference books listed in this chapter, if consulted, will identify the territorial structure of any large or small subdivision of the country and define the relationship of each to the other. Full tables, lists, and descriptions of all territorial units are given by place-name in this manner. Thus, the names of the ancestor's province, county, barony, diocese, parish, and city, town or townland of origin can be determined, and the relationship of each to the other will be clear. This will prepare the genealogist for an efficient and intelligent choice of the records to be searched. The following illustrations of the territorial units by which the various classes of records are arranged will serve to emphasize the necessity for knowing the full details of the place of residence.

From early times, Irish deeds, leases, and other records transmitting land, identify the grantor and grantee by city, town, or townland, and county. The property is described by county, barony, and town or townland, or by county, city and street or district. Records of dates earlier than 1708 are in special collections in various repositories. They are sometimes calendared as units of large estates and in other cases of small ownership by county. They are card indexed by names of the principals, including notations of identifying place-names. Recorded records of this nature from all over Ireland, dated from 1708, were deposited in the Registry of Deeds, Dublin. These included deeds, leases of over three years, assignments, mortgages, marriage settlements involving land, and many memorials (copies or detailed abstracts) of wills submitted with estate settlement papers concerning land. The principals and the property were identified by the same territorial description employed in the earlier records. All original documents in this repository are numbered, deposited in the vaults after a legal copy was made, and both are listed by number, ledger and page, in two indexes. One is a name index, by name of the grantor. The other is a land (or place) index, by place-name of the smallest territorial unit of transmittal. This is usually a townland or piece of city property. The place-names are alphabetically indexed and arranged in volumes by city in which the property is located and by county for land outside the cities. This is an invaluable index for those who know the exact location wherein an ancestor lived. The history of all ownership or leases of a townland or other small piece of property can thus be traced and often will reveal the relationships in several generations. Extensive collections of unrecorded documents of the same nature as those in the Registry of Deeds, Dublin, which are dated both before and after 1708, are in various repositories where they are calendared and indexed by names of the principals in the instruments, with identifying information as above.

Early tax records such as the *Hearthmoney Rolls*, so valuable for locating a man in the period *ca.* 1665, listed an individual by county, parish and city or townland. The existing records or transcripts are in collections by county. Ecclesiastical jurisdiction over testamentary matters was abolished in 1857. All wills dated before 1858 identified the testator by diocese, parish, and city, town, or townland. Wills fell in one of two classes. If a man owned property of more than five pounds in value, in more than one diocese, the will was proved in the Prerogative Court over which the Arehbishop of Armagh, Primate of all Ireland, presided. These Prerogative Wills were calendared and indexed as a class and the existing original records (very few), transcripts, a complete collection of abstracts from 1535 to 1800, and pedigree charts compiled from all of the abstracts, are in special collections, indexed by name of the testator who is identified by city, town, or townland, and by county. The second class of wills, the Diocesan Wills, were those of individuals who owned property of no more than five pounds value in more than one diocese. Such wills were proved in the Consistorial Court of the diocese in which the testator resided, which court was under the jurisdiction of the bishop of the diocese. These wills were indexed by name of the testator under the diocese wherein the will was proved. The original wills (few probated ones exist), a wealth of transcripts and legal copies, abstracts, and a very large number of original wills never probated have been collected in various repositories where they are calendared by diocese and indexed by name of the testator, identifying his city, town, or townland, and county. Several published indexes of the Diocesan Wills, compiled before the destruction of original records, are published by diocese, with names of the testators, alphabetically arranged, and with identifying information as above. The intestate administrations, and administrations with wills annexed, of the Prerogative and Consistorial Courts, are indexed in the same manner.

Registers of baptism, marriage and burial of the Established Church of Ireland, and Roman Catholic Registers of baptism and marriage were kept by parish. These are further identified by diocese, county, and name of the city or town where the parish church was located. The records of the individual within the registers of any parish were often further identified by the city, town, or townland of residence.

Existing Presbyterian Church registers of baptism and marriage (not including death or burial records) are calendared in an index, by name of the congregation or church, identified by the town and county wherein the church was located. Records of the individual are identified by the name of the city, town, or townland of residence.

Quaker records were kept by Provincial and Monthly Meetings which included the areas of specified districts. Individual records of baptism, marriage and burial, copies of marriage certificates, and other miscellaneous records pertaining to individuals, were identified by the county, city, town, or townland of residence.

Government religious surveys, the lists of dissenters at various dates, the 1740 Householder's lists, and various lists of Catholics for specific purposes, placed people by county, barony, parish, and city, town, or townland.

Marriage Bonds, under the jurisdiction of the Established Church of Ireland, were classified and calendared by diocese; the individual records identifying the persons by parish and city, town, or townland.

Land surveys, such as the "Books of Survey and Distribution," being abstracts of various surveys and instruments of title, 1636-1703, contain some genealogical information, history of ownership, etc. Property was listed by county and townland, while the people identified with the records were recorded by county, barony, parish and townland. This collection of records is arranged by county.

Later land valuations, such as "Griffith's Valuation," *circa* 1850, are arranged under Poor Law Unions. These list the townland occupiers and immediate lessors of the land. The records are calendared by county and union.

This brief review of the methods of recording and indexing the various classes of records illustrates the importance of understanding the territorial structure of the divisions and subdivisions of Ireland. These will be defined and further explained below.

TERRITORIAL STRUCTURE OF IRELAND:

Ireland is divided into four provinces. Each province is divided into counties; each county into baronies; each barony into parishes; and each parish into townlands. *Philips' Atlas and Geography of Ireland*, 1883, states, "There are in all of Ireland 32 counties; 325 baronies; 2,447 parishes; and about 64,000 townlands." The dioceses were early ecclesiastical divisions, there being 28 in all of Ireland, the parishes being subdivisions; 2,447 in number.

THE DIVISIONS AND SUBDIVISIONS OF IRELAND:

PROVINCE: Ireland was in ancient times divided into five provinces, or "fifths" of Ireland. In order of their creation, they were Leinster, Munster, Connaught, Ulster, and Meath; the latter having been formed in the second century. Each was ruled by a succession of kings, and some one of the provincial kings was also King of Ireland; Ulster claiming the longest line of supreme monarchs or "over-kings." These provinces continued to be recognized after the Norman Invasion and not until the English and Anglo-Irish jurisdiction over Ireland was accomplished was there a change, at which time the Province of Meath was parcelled out among the older provinces. At this time, also, the provinces were divided into counties; two of them, Meath and West Meath, comprising some of the territory which was earlier a portion of the ancient province of that name. The present provinces and their counties are as follows:

1. *Connaught*, the western province of Ireland, includes the counties of Galway, Leitrim, Mayo, Roscommon, and Sligo.

2. *Leinster*, the middle and south-eastern portion of Ireland, includes the counties of Carlow, Dublin, Kildare, Kilkenny, Leix (Queen's County), Longford, Louth, Meath, Offaly (King's County), West Meath, Wexford, and Wicklow.

3. *Munster*, the southernmost province, includes the counties of Clare, Cork, Kerry, Limerick, Tipperary, and Waterford.

4. *Ulster*, the northern province of Ireland, was divided into

the nine counties of Antrim, Armagh, Cavan, Donegal, Down, Fermanagh, Londonderry, Monaghan, and Tyrone. In 1920, Cavan, Donegal, and Monaghan joined the Republic of Ireland.

COUNTY: The provinces of Ireland were, under English and Anglo-Irish jurisdiction, divided into the thirty-two counties listed above. By the Government of Ireland Act of 1920, six of the nine counties of Ulster, namely Antrim, Armagh, Down, Fermanagh, Londonderry, and Tyrone, remained under the dominion of Great Britain, while three counties came under the government of the Republic of Ireland, namely Cavan, Donegal, and Monaghan. Thus, twenty-six of the counties of Ireland are now a part of the Republic of Ireland. The names of two of the counties of the Province of Leinster were also changed. These were King's County, which became Offaly, and Queen's County which became Leix.

BARONY: This is an ancient division of land, but now comprising a section of a county, corresponding nearly to the English "hundred." Originally, it was the district of an Irish chieftain who held his lands from an ancient king of one of the provinces *in capite* or as a lessor or by lease, for which he paid an annual tribute in tithes and military service. While then under tribal military jurisdiction, it came in the course of time to be used for fiscal and administrative purposes only. The name of the barony is used in land, military, tax and some other government records as descriptive of the district or section of the county. The "Down Survey Maps," 1655-1659, made by Sir William Petty, covering all of Ireland, showed the country divided into 216 baronies.

Philips' Atlas and Geography of Ireland, 1883, shows 325 baronies, indicating further subdivision of some baronies. At that time, the six counties, which now comprise Northern Ireland, contained 59 baronies.

The *Topographical Index, Census of Population of Northern Ireland*, 1926, shows at that time there were 58 baronies in the six counties, the name of the barony of Carrickfergus not being listed. In 1883, the baronies were listed as they lie on the maps, taking them as far as possible from left to right and from top to bottom of each county, as follows:

Antrim, 15: Lower Dunluce; Upper Dunluce; Cary; Kilconway; Lower Glenarm; Upper Glenarm; Lower Toome; Upper Toome; Lower Antrim; Upper Antrim; Carrickfergus; Lower Belfast; Upper Belfast; Lower Massareene; Upper Massareene.

Armagh, 8: Oneilland West; Oneilland East; Tiranny; Armagh; Lower Fews; Upper Fews; Lower Orior; Upper Orior.

Carlow, 7: Carlow; Rathvilly; Idrone West; Idrone East; Forth; St. Mullin's Upper; St. Mullin's Lower.

Cavan, 8: Tullyhaw; Tullyhunco; Lower Loughtee; Upper Loughtee; Tullygarvey; Clankee; Clanmahon; Castlerahan.

Clare, 11: Burren; Corcomroe; Inchiquin; Ibrickan; Islands; Upper Bunratty; Lower Bunratty; Upper Tulla; Lower Tulla; Moyarta; Clonderalaw.

Cork, 23: Duhallow; Orrery and Kilmore; Fermoy; Condons and Clangibbon; West Muskerry; East Muskerry; Barretts; Barrymore; Kinnatalloon; Imokilly; Bear; Bantry; Kinalmeaky; Cork; Kerrycurrihy; Kinalea; West Carbery, West Division; West Carbery, East Division; East Carbery, West Division; East Carbery, East Division; Kinsale; Courceys; Ibane and Barryroe.

Donegal, 7: Kilmacrenan; East Inishowen; West Inishowen; Boylagh; Raphoe; Banagh; Tirhugh.

Down, 14: Lower Castlereagh; Upper Castlereagh; Dufferin; Lower Ards; Upper Ards; Lower Iveagh, Lower Part; Lower Iveagh, Upper Part; Upper Iveagh, Lower Part; Upper Iveagh, Upper Part; Kinelarty; Upper Lecale; Lower Lecale; Lordship of Newry; Mourne.

Dublin, 9: Balrothery West; Balrothery East; Nethercross; Castleknock; Coolock; Newcastle; Uppercross; Dublin; Rathdown.

Fermanagh, 8: Lurg; Magheraboy; Tirkennedy; Clanawley; Magherastephana; Knockninny; Coole; Clankelly.

Galway, 18: Ballynahinch; Ross; Dunmore; Ballymoe; Moycullen; Galway; Clare; Tiaquin; Killian; Aran; Dunkellin;

Athenry; Kilconnell; Clonmacnowen; Loughrea; Longford; Kiltartan; Leitrim.

Kerry, 9: Iraghticonnor; Clanmaurice; Corkaguiny; Trughanacmy; Iveragh; Dunkerron North; Dunkerron South; Magunihy; Glanarought.

Kildare, 14: Carbury; Clane; Ikeathy and Oughterany; North Salt; South Salt; West Offaly; East Offaly; Connell; North Naas; South Naas; Kilcullen; Narragh and Reban West; Narragh and Reban East; Kilkea and Moone.

Kilkenny, 10: Galmoy; Fassadinin; Crannagh; Gowran; Callan; Shillelogher; Kells; Knocktopher; Iverk; Ida.

King's County (now County Offaly), 12: Kilcoursey; Garrycastle; Ballycowan; Geashill; Lower Philipstown; Upper Philipstown; Warrenstown; Coolestown; Eglish; Ballyboy; Ballybritt; Clonlisk.

Leitrim, 5: Rosclogher; Drumahaire: Leitrim; Carrigallen; Mohill.

Limerick, 14: Kenry; Pubblebrien; Limerick, North Liberties; Clanwilliam; Owenybeg; Coonagh; Shanid; Glenquin; Lower Connello; Upper Connello; Small County; Coshma; Killmallock; Coshlea.

Londonderry, 6: Liberties of Londonderry; Tirkeeran; Keenaght; Coleraine; North-east Liberties of Coleraine; Loughinsholin.

Longford, 6: Longford; Granard; Moydow; Ardagh; Rathcline; Shrule.

Louth, 6: Upper Dundalk; Lower Dundalk; Louth; Ardee; Ferrard; Drogheda.

Mayo, 9: Erris; Tirawley; Gallen; Burrishoole; Murrisk; Carra; Clanmorris; Costello; Kilmaine.

Meath, 19: Fore; Lower Kells; Upper Kells; Morgallion; Lower Slane; Upper Slane; Lune; Lower Navan; Upper Navan; Skreen; Drogheda; Lower Duleek; Upper Duleek; Upper Moyfenrath; Lower Moyfenrath; Lower Deece; Upper Deece; Ratoath; Dunboyne.

Monaghan, 5: Trough; Monaghan; Dartree; Cremorne; Farney.

Queen's County (now County Leix), 11: Tinnahinch; Portnahinch; Upper Woods; Maryborough West; Maryborough East; Stradbally; Clandonagh; Clarmallagh; Cullenagh; Ballyadams; Slievemargy.

Roscommon, 9: Boyle; Frenchpark; Castlereagh; Ballymoe; Roscommon; Ballintober North; Ballintober South; Athlone; Moycarn.

Sligo, 6: Carbury; Tireragh; Leyny; Corran; Tirerrill; Coolavin.

Tipperary, 12: Owney and Arra; Lower Ormond; Upper Ormond; Ikerrin; Upper Kilnamanagh; Lower Kilnamanagh; Eliogarty; Slieveardagh; Clanwilliam; Middlethird; Iffa and Offa West; Iffa and Offa East.

Tyrone, 8: Lower Strabane; Upper Strabane; West Omagh; East Omagh; Upper Dungannon; Middle Dungannon; Lower Dungannon; Clogher.

Waterford, 7: Glenahiry; Upper Third; Middle Third; Gaultiere; Coshmore and Coshbride; Decies without Drum; Decies within Drum.

West Meath, 12: Moygoish; Fore; Corkaree; Delvin; Kilkenny West; Rathconrath; Moyashel and Magheradernon; Farbill; Brawney; Clonlonan; Moycashel; Fartullagh.

Wexford, 9: Gorey; Scarawalsh; Bantry; Ballaghkeen; Shelburne; Shelmaliere West; Shelmaliere East; Bargy; Forth.

Wicklow, 8: Lower Talbotstown; Upper Talbotstown; Rathdown; Ballinacor North; Ballinacor South; Newcastle; Arklow; Shillelagh.

PARISH: While the parish was in early times a purely ecclesiastical subdivision of the diocese, it became also an area for civil or government purposes and, as such, could be said to be a subdivision of the barony. Further discussion of the parishes will be given in relation to the dioceses.

CITY AND TOWN: The names of the cities and towns have changed little in the last 300 years and are to be found on a modern map of Ireland. The "General Alphabetical Index to the Townlands and Towns, Parishes and Baronies of Ireland," published with the *Census of Ireland*, 1861, 1904, 1913, and also the "Topographical Index," published with the *Census of Northern Ireland*, 1926 (reprint, 1947), contain tables listing the baronies, parishes, towns, and townlands, which will, for the area of the census, place every barony in its county; every parish in its barony; every town in its parish, and the townlands included in it; also every townland in its parish. Some towns embrace as many as four or five townlands, and cities have spread over the original areas of a larger number. Some cities also include more than one parish. Twenty-four of the thirty-two counties in all of Ireland contain a city or town of the same name; the exceptions being the counties of Down, Fermanagh, Kerry, Leix (Queen's County), Meath, Offaly (King's County), Tyrone, and West Meath. County Donegal has the city of Donegal. Counties and cities of like name are identified as such.

TOWNLAND: From early times this was a unit of land which, in multiples, formed the larger territorial divisions; province, county, barony, parish, city, and town. In size, the townlands vary considerably, on the average containing about 350 acres each. These were from early times family holdings, being farms in the rural areas, and were mostly under lease from large estates for periods of time varying from "in perpetuity or 900 years"; "61 years or three lifetimes, whichever lasted longest"; 21 years; and for shorter periods of three years, more or less. Townlands were also subdivided to lessees. The names of the townlands, after their translation from Gaelic and the adoption of uniform spelling during the *Down Survey, 1655-1659*, have remained much the same. *Philips' Atlas and Geography of Ireland*, 1883, estimates there are "about 64,000 townlands." The *Census of Northern Ireland*, 1926, showed 9,521 townlands in the six counties.

POOR LAW UNIONS: Poor Law Unions, established for poor relief by *Poor Relief Act* (1), 1838, were multiples of townlands, usually with a large market town as a center, within a radius of about ten miles. Some are situated wholly in one county; others extend into two or three counties. *Griffith's Valuation*, begun in 1844, evaluates the land by townlands and gives the names of occupiers and immediate lessors, grouping them under Poor Law Unions and Counties. This survey is valuable for tracing tenants. The records are being indexed by the National Library of Ireland, Dublin.

ECCLESIASTICAL DIVISIONS:

DIOCESE: There are 28 dioceses or ecclesiastical divisions in all of Ireland, dating from early Roman Catholic jurisdiction. The boundaries were little changed when the Established Church of Ireland became the State church in the time of Henry VIII, at which time (and from then on, with the exception of the brief reign of Philip and Mary), a Protestant was appointed by the Crown to fill the place of the Archbishop of Armagh, Primate of all Ireland. Protestant bishops were also appointed by the Crown, each to hold ecclesiastical jurisdiction over a diocese and the parishes within the area. The boundaries of the dioceses have little or no relation to those of the counties, the latter having been created long after the dioceses and the parishes within their areas were established. Each diocese embraces parts of from one to six counties and, conversely, each county falls into from one to several dioceses. Thus, the area of the county in which a man lived determined the diocese which exercised ecclesiastical jurisdiction over his parish records, probate matters, etc.

THE DIOCESES AND PARTS OF COUNTIES INCLUDED IN EACH DIOCESE:

Diocese	*Parts of Counties Included In Each Diocese*
Ardagh	Cavan, Leitrim, Roscommon, Sligo, West Meath.
Ardfert & Aghadoe	All of Kerry, part of Cork.
Armagh	Armagh, Londonderry, Longford, Louth, Meath, Tyrone.
Cashel & Emly	Limerick, Tipperary.
Clogher	Donegal, Fermanagh, Louth, Tyrone, all of Monaghan.
Clonfert	Galway, King's, Roscommon.
Cloyne	Cork.
Connor	Antrim, Down, Londonderry.
Cork & Ross	Cork.
Derry	Antrim, Donegal, Londonderry, Tyrone.
Down	Antrim, Down.
Drogheda	Louth.
Dromore	Antrim, Armagh, Down.

Diocese	Parts of Counties Included in Each Diocese
Dublin	Dublin, Kildare, Queen's, Wexford, Wicklow.
Elphin	Galway, Roscommon, Sligo.
Ferns	Wexford, Wicklow.
Kildare	Kildare, King's, Meath, Queen's.
Killala & Achonry	Mayo, Sligo.
Killaloe & Kilfenora	Clare, Galway, King's, Limerick, Tipperary.
Kilmore	Cavan, Fermanagh, Leitrim, Meath.
Leighlin	Carlow, Kilkenny, Queen's, Wicklow.
Limerick	Clare, Limerick.
Meath	Cavan, King's, Longford, Meath, West Meath.
Newry & Mourne	Down.
Ossory	Kilkenny, King's, Queen's.
Raphoe	Donegal.
Tuam	Galway, Mayo, Roscommon.
Waterford & Lismore	Tipperary, all of Waterford.

THE COUNTIES AND PARTS OF DIOCESES INCLUDED IN EACH COUNTY:

County	Parts of Dioceses Included in Each County
Antrim	Connor, Derry, Down, Dromore.
Armagh	Armagh, Dromore.
Carlow	Leighlin.
Cavan	Ardagh, Meath, Kilmore.
Clare	Killaloe & Kilfenora, Limerick.
Cork	Cork & Ross, Cloyne, Ardfert.
Donegal	Clogher, Derry, Raphoe.
Down	Connor, Down, Dromore, Newry & Mourne.
Dublin	Dublin.
Fermanagh	Clogher, Kilmore.
Galway	Clonfert, Elphin, Killaloe, Tuam.
Kerry	Ardfert.
Kildare	Dublin, Kildare.
Kilkenny	Leighlin, Ossory.
King's	Clonfert, Kildare, Killaloe, Meath, Ossory.
Leitrim	Ardagh, Kilmore.
Limerick	Cashel and Emly, Killaloe, Limerick.
Londonderry	Armagh, Connor, Derry.
Longford	Armagh, Meath.
Louth	Armagh, Clogher, Drogheda.
Mayo	Killala and Achonry, Tuam.
Meath	Armagh, Kildare, Kilmore, Meath.

County	Parts of Dioceses Included in Each County
Monaghan	Clogher.
Queen's	Dublin, Kildare, Leighlin, Ossory.
Roscommon	Ardagh, Clonfert, Elphin, Tuam.
Sligo	Ardagh, Elphin, Killala.
Tipperary	Cashel, Killaloe, Waterford and Lismore.
Tyrone	Armagh, Clogher, Derry.
Waterford	Waterford and Lismore.
West Meath	Ardagh, Meath.
Wexford	Dublin, Ferns.
Wicklow	Dublin, Ferns, Leighlin.

PARISH: From ancient times, the parish was a purely ecclesiastical subdivision of the diocese. It later became also an area for civil or government purposes and, as such, could be said to be a subdivision of the barony. In the course of the change of ecclesiastical jurisdiction in Ireland, from Roman Catholic to the Established Church of Ireland, governed by the Archbishop of Armagh and the bishops of the dioceses, appointed by the Crown, the territorial structure of the parishes was little changed. The rectors, vicars, and curates of the parish were under the jurisdiction of the bishop of the diocese, Sir William Petty illustrated his *Down Survey, 1655-1659*, with 2,000 parish maps. *Philips' Atlas and Geography of Ireland*, 1883, states, "there are in all 32 counties, 2,447 parishes."

Some important published source materials for reference before beginning Irish research will be listed below. These may be found in the large American genealogical libraries. A more extensive list is provided in the accompanying VOLUME II, PART THREE, under GEOGRAPHICAL SOURCES.

THE GENERAL ALPHABETICAL INDEX OF THE TOWNLANDS AND TOWNS, PARISHES AND BARONIES OF IRELAND, published with the *Census of Ireland*. Edited by Alexander Thom. Dublin, 1861, 1904, 1913. These publications are cross-indexed to show all of the territorial divisions; the counties, baronies, parishes, towns, and townlands; a list of all names of places falling under these headings, and their identity with the name of each other division and subdivision.

TOPOGRAPHICAL INDEX, published with the *Government of Northern Ireland, Census of Population of Northern Ireland,* 1926 (reprint, 1947). This furnishes the same information for Northern Ireland as above.

GOBLET, Y. M., *Ed. A Topographical Index of the Parishes and Townlands of Ireland in Sir William Petty's MSS. Barony Maps (c. 1655-9).* Dublin, 1932. This contains an alphabetical index of every townland entered on the barony maps, placing each by county and parish. An index of all parishes places each in its county and barony. There are 214 manuscript Barony maps which contain some 25,000 place-names, mostly names of townlands, made by Sir William Petty. He actually mapped all of Ireland but three counties in Connaught. These included the names of townlands on about 47½ percent of the total area of Ireland. Petty made some 2,000 parish maps while, in 1883, according to *Philip's Atlas and Geography of Ireland,* there were 2,447 parishes.

JOYCE, P. W. *Origin and History of Irish Names of Places.* 3 vols. Dublin, 1869, 1875 (reprint, 1913).

LEET, A. *Directory to the Market Towns, Villages . . . in Ireland.* 1814.

LEWIS, SAMUEL. *Atlas of the Counties of Ireland.* London, 1837.

LEWIS, SAMUEL. *Topographical Dictionary of Ireland, its Several Counties, Cities, Boroughs, Corporate, Market, and Post Towns, Parishes, and Villages, with Historical and Statistical Descriptions . . .* 2 vols. London, 1837. The large volumes containing 1,412 pages in small print are a gold mine of detail.

THE PARLIAMENTARY GAZETTEER OF IRELAND. 3 vols. Dublin, London, Edinburgh, 1841, 1844, 1846. As in the above, these volumes contain a description of each city, borough, corporate, market and post town, village, and parish; placing each one as to county, barony, diocese, and parish. For each, the history, population statistics, and geographical surroundings including distances from larger towns and cities are given. Also named and described are castles, inns, churches of the various denominations, chapels, meeting-houses, schools and other public buildings, and industries within the area. Thus, a full picture can be obtained of the surroundings of an ancestor.

PHILIPS' HANDY ATLAS OF THE COUNTIES OF IRELAND. Revised by P. W. Joyce. 1881. County maps show baronies, cities, towns, many townlands, etc. It is well indexed. Either this or *Philips' Atlas and Geography of Ireland*, edited by P. W. Joyce, 1883, makes an indispensable tool for the genealogist. These are in the larger genealogical libraries in America.

REPORT OF HER MAJESTY'S COMMISSIONERS ON THE REVENUE AND CONDITION OF THE ESTABLISHED CHURCH (IRELAND), 1868. 2 vols. including Appendix with maps included. One shows the relation between the counties and the dioceses, with the boundary lines of the dioceses superimposed upon the county boundaries. Ordnance Survey Maps show the same detail.

* * * * *

EXAMPLE OF WORK

In CHAPTER I, two deeds were quoted from Washington County, Pennsylvania, Deed Book, 2 C, p. 324, and Deed Book, 2 D, p. 404. These named William Dickson and Hannah, his wife, they being of the townland of Mullaghbane, County Tyrone, Ireland, who signed a land partition granting Hannah Dickson's inheritance of land in Washington County, Pennsylvania, from her deceased brother, James McFarland, to their sons, John and Francis Dickson. James McFarland died intestate without issue, leaving four brothers and three sisters, to wit: Andrew, David, Francis, Hugh, Mary, Sarah, and Hannah. The legal papers were signed by the elder Dickson couple, at the town of Dungannon, County Tyrone, Ireland, before William Murray, Chief Magistrate and Provost, of the town of Dungannon, on 15 October 1818.

From the above information, we have three identifying place-names regarding the geographical origin of John and Francis Dickson who, according to the deeds, came to Wash-

ington County, Pennsylvania.   Their parents, William and
Hannah (McFarland) Dickson, lived in County Tyrone, Ire-
land, at a place with a strange name called the townland of
Mullaghbane, which is not recorded on a modern map of Ire-
land. They signed papers at Dungannon, County Tyrone.
These place-names and other data are found as follows:

In less time than it takes to record the information, the
following facts were found which identify the home location
of William and Hannah Dickson in all detail. Three sources
were consulted. The *Topographical Index*, published with
the *Census of Population of Northern Ireland*, 1926, reprint
1947 (price 10 shillings at Her Majesty's Stationery Office,
Belfast), on page 128, lists the townland of Mullaghbane, comprising 281 acres, 2 roods, 20 perch, in the County of Tyrone,
the County District and Union of Dungannon, Registrar's District of Dungannon, in Barony No. 19, and Parish No.
102. Turning to page vii, on which the baronies are listed,
each with a key number to match the numbers used in the
Townland Index, we find that Barony No. 19, is Dungannon
Middle Barony, in County Tyrone. Then turning to page
viii, for the Parish Index, we find that Parish No. 102 is
the parish of Donaghmore, County Tyrone. Wishing to
locate Dungannon, we turn to the Town Index. It is not
listed as one of the 144 towns of 50 houses or more, in 1926.
It was named in the deed as a town, but possibly by 1926 it
had become a city. Next, we find in the Town Index on page
17, a town of Donaghmore, listed as being in the District of
Dungannon, County Tyrone. The key numbers beside it,
when referred to the Barony and Parish Indexes, show that
the town of Donaghmore lies in the Barony of Dungannon
(Middle Barony), and the Parish of Donaghmore. So William Dickson's townland of Mullaghbane, situated in the Parish of Donaghmore, was not far from the town of that name.

We then turn to *Philips' Handy Atlas of the Counties of
Ireland* (purchased in Belfast for 20 shillings) and find that,
in 1883, Dungannon appeared on the map in large print, indicating it was a city. It is located about two miles south-east
of Donaghmore which appears in smaller print. Both are in

Dungannon Middle Barony. Donaghmore is about 7 miles from the County Armagh line, about 10 miles south of the nearest County Londonderry line and about 9 miles northeast of the nearest line of County Monaghan. So William Dickson and his wife, Hannah, lived in this locality and signed the papers in 1818, in Dungannon, some two miles more or less distant from his home.

Turning to the *Topographical Dictionary of Ireland,* by Samuel Lewis, 1837, Volume I, page 574, for Dungannon, and page 469, for Donaghmore, we find all of the information we need for completing the picture of the locality in which William and Hannah Dickson lived, as follows:

Dungannon, in the barony of Dungannon (note that in 1837, Dungannon Middle Barony had not yet been cut off), Parish of Drumglass, County Tyrone, is recorded in almost three pages as being a spacious, handsome and well-built town on the road from Armagh to Coleraine, containing 3,515 inhabitants. A brilliant history of the town is given; of the castle, churches, schools, public buildings, industries, and the people who played a part in the affairs of the locality. As this place where the Dicksons signed the papers lies so close to his parish, it should be kept in mind during a search of all classes of records.

A lengthy account of the Parish of Donaghmore and the village of the same name within its limits is given on page 469. It is described as a parish situated in the diocese of Armagh, barony of Dungannon, county of Tyrone, and province of Ulster; 2 miles N.N.W from Dungannon, containing 12,144 inhabitants. Then follows a long account of its ancient history, castles, schools, churches, public buildings, industries, and description of its setting. The parish is situated in the diocese of Armagh and in the patronage of the Archbishop of Armagh, Lord Primate of all Ireland. The parish church is a large, plain edifice, situated at Castle-Caulfield. There are three meeting houses for Presbyterians, two for Roman Catholics, and a school house is used as a place of worship by the Independents. The parish school is at Castle-Caulfield (located on the map, about 2 miles from and southwest of ⁺he town of Donaghmore). There are seven other schools of

the parish in which about 870 children are taught, and an
infant's school for more than 70 children; also two private
schools, and six Sunday-schools. There are several ancient
forts in the parish, and some small lakes with artificial islands
on which were castles. The parish is situated on the road
from Dungannon to Omagh and comprises, according to the
Ordnance Survey, 18,410½ acres of which 146 are water
(lakes); about 3,000 acres of bog and mountain, but the
greater part is arable land. From this account we know that
any records of Castle-Caulfield should also be checked during
a search for Dickson records.

The village of Donaghmore is described as having been
built since the year 1796, is very flourishing, comprising 88
well-built and slated houses, mostly in one street. As a matter
of interest for local color, we gather that the activities around
William Dickson included "an extensive brewery of the celebrated Donaghmore ale . . . 10,500 barrels of ale and beer annually brewed; also soap and candle manufacturies; much
business in spirit trade . . . and there are large brick-works
adjoining the village. Near Castle-Caulfield is a small green
for bleaching linen cloth, much of which is woven by the
farmers and cottiers throughout the parish. A fair is held
on the first Tuesday of every month for cattle, sheep, pigs,
etc., and a manor court on the first Monday of every month
in the Primate's manor of Donaghmore . . ."

Thus, from two deeds of Washington County, Pennsylvania,
and three Irish references, we have learned a great deal about
the parentage, relatives, geographical origin, and Irish background of John and Francis Dickson who came to America.
Besides William and Hannah (McFarland) Dickson, who
signed the papers in Dungannon, County Tyrone, there was an
undoubted relative, Mathew Dickson, who witnessed their
signatures. He was probably their son, or possibly a brother
or other relative of William. Therefore, the given names of
the Dickson family which must be noted in the Irish indexes
of County Tyrone records or any nearby locality are William,
John, and Mathew. Francis Dickson was probably named for
his mother's brother, Francis McFarland, and as far as the
two deeds show, she did not have brothers William, John or

Mathew. In addition to her brothers James, Andrew, David, Francis, and Hugh, there was a Robert McFarland, who purchased from John and Francis Dickson all of the property which they received from their mother. He was probably a relative, possibly a son of one of James McFarland's brothers. Probate papers in Washington County, Pennsylvania, may throw more light on the Irish origin of the McFarland family. Often estate settlements, involving a division of property among heirs, will list all of the wives and husbands of the heirs and all of their children. If any of the McFarland heirs besides Hannah Dickson were in Ireland at the time of the settlement, their Irish address would be given. Also, earlier land records of James McFarland's first Washington County property might name his Irish place of origin. Thus, before starting a genealogical search for the McFarland family in Ireland, the Washington County, Pennsylvania, records must be thoroughly searched.

Meanwhile, the known facts regarding the Dickson family are sufficient for anyone to begin a search for their Irish records, as we know that William and Hannah (McFarland) Dickson lived on the townland of Mullaghbane, comprising 281 and a fraction acres, a part or all of which he very probably rented on a long or short term lease; this property being in the county of Tyrone, barony of Dungannon (not subdivided before 1837), diocese of Armagh, parish of Donaghmore, not far from the town of Donaghmore which is two miles from each of the city of Dungannon and the village of Castle-Caulfield.

Their proximity to Dungannon, Donaghmore, and Castle-Caulfield, indicates that all existing church registers for these places, except Roman Catholic, should be searched. All existing church registers are listed in this volume, with instructions for having them searched. When tracing the records of any family of Northern Ireland, the two repositories which hold the best possibilities are the Registry of Deeds, Dublin, and the Public Record Office of Northern Ireland, Belfast. The following chapters will explain the nature and extent of the deposits in these and other important repositories of genealogical source materials.

PART TWO

REPOSITORIES OF RECORDS

CHAPTER I

THE REGISTRY OF DEEDS, DUBLIN

GENERAL INFORMATION

The Registry of Deeds, Henrietta Street, Dublin, is under the direction of Mr. J. P. Kenny, Senior Assistant Registrar, and Mr. P. F. McKeown, Junior Assistant Registrar. It is open to the public, from nine until four o'clock, on Monday through Friday.

It was established by an Act of Parliament (6 Anne, Chapt. 2) in 1708, providing for the opening of one central office in the city of Dublin, "for the Public Registring of all Deeds, Conveyances and Wills, that shall be made of any Honours, Manors, Lands, Tenements or Hereditaments" including the written wills from the time "the devisor or testatrix shall die after the said 25th March, 1708." The registration of deeds, conveyances and wills was not compulsory. The terms of the Act stated that deeds not registered "were deemed and adjudged fraudulant and void." However, in the course of time, the courts modified this decision.

This repository now offers one of the most certain sources of genealogical information concerning families in a wide range of social station and material wealth. Records of tenants in modest circumstances, comfortably established gentry and great landlords, are all represented here.

It is a particularly valuable source in Ireland for revealing the pre-emigration identity and parentage of a first generation American, due to the nature and many classes of records which are recorded among the deeds. Often one document will name members of the family in two or three generations, and lead to a chain of other records which will reveal the forbears, their locations and land records through an earlier period.

As any genealogist knows, families can often be reconstructed through land records when probates and other records fail. This approach is frequently necessary in Ireland, due to the destruction in 1922 of most of the wills deposited in the Public Record Office of Ireland, Dublin. While this circumstance was greatly mitigated by the vast amount of copying of the records; the abstracts of all of the Prerogative Wills, 1536-1800, and the pedigree charts constructed from them; the wealth of transcripts of Diocesan Wills made over many decades; the Memorials of Wills recorded in the Registry of Deeds; the success in gathering a very large number of wills never probated, together with other original wills; the fact remains that the original wills of Ireland and the abstracts or transcripts thereof are incomplete.

The leases of less than three years' duration were never recorded in the Registry of Deeds, Dublin. These were retained in the collections of estate records of the landlords. Source materials relating to estates, and other important collections of documents concerning land, will be described and enumerated in PART THREE, CHAPTER XIV, entitled ESTATE RECORDS.

From 1708, the Registry of Deeds for some time allowed a loose interpretation to be placed on the classing of a legal document as a deed or conveyance. Any written instrument under seal which, by law transferred, conveyed or alienated property, was acceptable. Thus, the classes of records which will be found in this repository are: Deeds which are instruments of the sale of property, deeds creating a trust, mortgages secured by owned land, releases, leases for periods of from three years to nine hundred years or in perpetuity, leases in trust, assignments of leases, transfers of leases by sale, mortgages secured by leaseholds, business proposals including the creation and dissolution of partnerships, marriage settlements, wills, and other miscellaneous documents.

All of these instruments were brought to the Registry of Deeds to be recorded. A written record of each document was made. This was usually a complete copy or a fairly full abstract, containing all of the pertinent information including detail (except in some brief abstracts of wills, averaging one-half to one page). These written records were kept in the

Registry of Deeds as "Memorials." The memorial was witnessed by two or more people qualified for the responsibility, with a seal. Often the family heraldic seal was attached. This memorial then became a legal and binding instrument. All of the memorials dated from 1708 are stored in the vaults of the Registry of Deeds, in lead lined boxes. These may be seen by special permission, under the supervision of a guide, if a specific reason is acceptable. A transcript of each memorial was made in the Registry of Deeds and, from 1708 to the present time, these have been bound in date order in large heavy books, similar in size and weight to the volumes of records which are preserved in the county court houses in America.

Anyone wishing to consult the transcripts of the eighteenth and nineteenth century memorials may do so upon application at the desk in the main search room, with the payment of a small fee, after examining either of the two series of indexes, which will later be described in this chapter.

The rules and regulations of this office permit the members of the staff to direct strangers to the location of the records but do not allow them to undertake genealogical research or record searching for a client, either in person or by correspondence. Such work must be done by the genealogist himself or an agent. However, an order for a copy of any memorial will be given attention, if the information for locating it is properly taken from the indexes. This can be done either in the Registry of Deeds, or from the microfilms of the indexes which are in the Genealogical Society Library, in Salt Lake City, Utah, U. S. A., and also in the National Library of Ireland, Dublin. The two indexes will be explained below.

DESCRIPTION OF RECORDS

Before beginning a search of the indexes or the transcripts, the genealogist should have an understanding of the records in the Registry of Deeds. He must become familiar with the various descriptive terms employed in defining the instruments which transferred land. He will be inspired to work with the records when he knows what genealogical information he can expect to find. A knowledge of the customs and practices in leasing land, the duration of the various periods of leases and its effects in creating other records is necessary. It is primarily important to recognize that a tenant as well as a landlord could become a grantor. The conditions will be described under which a tenant or lessee of land could become a grantor of his lease, when disposing of it in contemplation of a marriage, death, emigration, or for other reasons. When he became a grantor of a lease, the instrument of transmittal, by law, was registered in the Registry of Deeds, under his name, which was listed in the grantor "Names Index." It was common practice for tenants as grantors to dispose of their leased land, as well as for landowners to sell land before emigrating to America. These records provide one of the most certain ways of locating and identifying an emigrant, the place-name of his Irish residence, the names of his forbears and other relatives, their locations and circumstances, as revealed in their land transactions. Thus, the records will be described below.

The word "conveyance," mentioned in the Act of Parliament, which established the Registry of Deeds in 1708, was used in the sense that, by law, it was an instrument which transferred title to property, or the right to hold it, from one or more persons to one or other people, by deed, mortgage, trust, lease, release, assignment, marriage settlement, creation or dissolution of a business partnership, or otherwise.

To save repetition in the following description of the records, it is sufficient to say that all instruments recorded in the Registry of Deeds identify the principal contracting parties with their place of residence by city, town, townland with parish or barony, and county. Their station in life (title, Esq., or Gent.) or occupation is stated. Usually this identifying information also accompanies the names of trustees, witnesses at the signing of the original instrument, and witnesses to the memorial.

DEEDS OF SALE: In law, a writing on parchment or paper, authenticated by the seal of the person whose mind it purports to declare, specifically for the purpose of conveying real estate. Deeds are not as numerous as leases, releases, etc., but many plots of land were sold by people in modest circumstances as well as by the great landlords. Land which was transferred by deed had, in many cases, come into the owner's possession by inheritance from father to son over a long period of time. The right of possession was frequently reviewed, including the names of forbears who had previously owned it. People of Scottish lineage in Ireland, as well as the Irish, used heraldic seals if they were entitled to a coat of arms to seal the memorials of their deeds and any other conveyances in the Registry of Deeds.

MORTGAGES: Mortgages placed on land by the owner sometimes recite about the same information as in a deed. In other cases, they are quite uninformative, except as they give the names of the grantor, grantee, and a description of the property, by townland, barony or parish, and county, or by city and street or district. The name of the townland or city location can be traced through the "Land Index" in the Registry of Deeds, and previous possessors in the family who created any record of the land can be found.

DEEDS IN TRUST: A Deed in Trust is a conveyance to one person of property to be by him held in trust for others. The wife of the owner who created the trust occasionally signed away her dower rights. The relationship of the trustee to the owner is often stated. The beneficiaries of the trust are named in order of their right of inheritance, according to age, sex, and survival of issue. Thus, children and grandchildren are identified in this way. A father wishing to name all of his children, might mention a son, "gone to America," being excluded, or with provision for him "if he returns from America." Sometimes the grantor reserved the right of occupancy of the property for himself and wife for their lifetimes. An allowance for an eldest son, in lieu of possession of the property, was occasionally granted, to vary according to his single or married state and residence at home or elsewhere. Provision, past or future, for younger sons was often stated. Marriage portions for daughters were reviewed in the same manner as an element in the trust. These documents were usually witnessed by some member of the family, a married daughter or relative of the grantor, and a close friend or neighbor.

RELEASE: A release was either one of two entirely different acts of transmittal of property.   (1) A release was the signed relinquishment by one person to any further legal claim of ownership of lands, tenements, hereditaments, the rights to a leasehold, etc., previously in his name alone or with others, conveying the right of possession or, in the case of a lease, the privilege of holding it, to another person or persons already having some claim, in such form as to stop the grantor from asserting any rights in the future.   A release could be made for or without a consideration.   This type of release also appeared in a land transaction if the wife signed away her dower rights.   (2) A release was an instrument which renewed a lease.   Although the law did not require it to be recorded in the Registry of Deeds, Dublin, it was sometimes done.

LEASE AND RELEASE: The term "Lease and Release" is encountered in Irish land records.   It was a form of conveyance now disused, but in common use in the sixteenth to nineteenth centuries.   It was devised to avoid the statute of enrolments which then required conveyances to be recorded, by taking advantage of the rule that a tenant in possession could take a release (renewal) without notorization being required.   Thus, a tenant who held a leasehold by a lease which had been renewed, perhaps by his forbear for a lengthy period, claimed the right to it by "lease and release."   The history of the original lease can be traced through the "Land Index."

LEASE: Leases are much more numerous documents in the Registry of Deeds than are deeds of sale, mortgages, deeds of trust, etc., as Ireland was largely occupied by tenants.   A lease is almost always more informative for the genealogist than a deed of sale.   From early times, according to law, a lease was a written instrument in which a leasehold estate was created.   The leasehold was a tenure by lease.   The duration and conditions of the lease varied.   It was usually made in consideration of a periodic compensation, in modern times payable in money.   In addition to the regular rent, a double payment at stated intervals was sometimes required.   In some cases, the compensation was a share of the produce, and in former times frequently in services.   Also a fine (fee) for any transfer of the lease to another person was paid to the landlord. The grantor or landlord was the lessor, the grantee the lessee. The act of the grantor was called a demise. The right of the grantee was called a term. This was the duration of tenure by lease, hence the terminable time or period of the lease, subject to various conditions. The holding of the lessee or grantee was called a tenancy. The right of the lessor or grantor to have possession of the land again at the end of the term, or sooner in case of forfeiture, was called the reversion. If the lessee, holding a leasehold during a term, grants his rights to the remainder of the term to another person or persons, the lessee then becomes a grantor. The contract is not technically a lease, but even if in the form of a lease, is deemed only an assignment. If the lessee as the grantor of a term (the leasehold for the remaining time of the lease) retains any reversion privileges even for a single day, the contract is then a lease. A contract not transferring the right of possession, but merely contemplation that such right shall be transferred in the future, is not a lease, but an agreement for a lease. A contract transferring such a right to commence in enjoyment at a future day, for instance, one executed in January to give possession in June, is a lease; but the right of the lessee for the intervening period before the term is an "interesse termini."

Leases were of three types. In the first, the grantor or lessor named the grantee or lessee, and fixed the duration or term for a definite period, usually from three years to twenty-one years, during which time the tenant or his heirs could hold the land. The second type of lease concerned the lives of the lessee and his heirs. It was usually for sixty-one years or three lifetimes, whichever lasted longest or, as was quite common practice in Ireland, it was a lease in perpetuity, renewable at the fall of each life (death of the current lessee). In the third type of lease, the grantor made the condition of time dependent upon the life or lives of his own heirs. He might fix the term of the lease to include the natural life of his own son and heir, so named, and from his death for the remainder of the period of sixty-one years. The grantor frequently made the lease for a duration to include the life of the last survivor of two or more of his own heirs, the names mentioned being those of his grandchildren.

In any lease the grantor frequently reviewed his right of ownership, by inheritance, giving the names of two or more forbears. Thus, a lease might reveal several generations including the ancestors of the grantor, as well as his children and grandchildren. Or the lease could state the names of the grantee and certain of his children and grandchildren, specified in the terms, who were to enjoy the leasehold.

During the period of the lease, the transfer of it, upon the death of the lessee, to another person presumably an heir, required a review of the history and terms of the lease. A small fee (fine) was paid to the landlord for the trouble of registering the change in his records. As in "lease and release," this was not recorded in the Registry of Deeds. Nor was a release, under the rule, recorded if the deceased was the last in line of three generations, etc., to enjoy a leasehold, the lease expiring with his death, at which time his heir renewed the lease in order to retain the leasehold.

Much trouble developed over the leases for 900 years or in perpetuity, by lives renewable forever. *The Condition and Prospects of Ireland and the Evils Arising from the Present Distribution of Landed Property*, by Jonathan Pim, Dublin, 1848, pp. 260-61; 332-33, gives an explanation of perpetual leases and a "Description of the Tenure by Lives Renewable for ever." He states that this is "a species of tenure, scarcely known elsewhere which prevails . . . one seventh of Ireland . . . held under it. We allude to the tenure by lease for lives, with a covenant of perpetual renewal on payment of a fine, sometimes merely nominal, on the fall of each life." "Forfeitures of the right to enforce a renewal daily occur, through the neglect of tenants or the dexterous management of landlords." ". . . almost every abstract" shows "it became necessary to file a bill in equity." These provide much genealogy.

ASSIGNMENT: The assignment of a lease from one person to another was common practice. The lessee became a grantor when, in contemplation of his death, a marriage in the family, his emigration, or for other reasons, he assigned his right or term of the entire remaining duration of a lease, to another person. The contract was drawn in the form of a lease. The lessee-grantor retained no reversion privileges. Thus, a lessee could grant his remaining term of a leasehold before his death, to his heirs in order of age, sex, and survival of issue, according to his wishes. He could assign it to a trustee for such purposes. He often included an assignment in a marriage settlement for a son or daughter, to take effect upon marriage. The lessee could sell his remaining term of a lease, making a deed of assignment in the form of a lease to a stranger for its full value or to a relative for a small consideration, in preparation for emigration. While retaining no reversion privileges, he could stipulate that the remaining term or duration of the lease was to include the lifetimes of his named son, the son of a brother, etc., and their issue. He could also, by deed of assignment, sell his right to a perpetual lease. In all cases, a fee (fine) was paid to the landlord for making the transfer. As the lessee making the assignment became a grantor, his instrument of transmittal was, by law, recorded in the Registry of Deeds, and thus his name was listed in the grantor NAMES INDEX. Genealogical information regarding the grantor of an assignment is almost always found in such an instrument. The lease has usually been inherited by the lessee who has become the grantor. The names of forbears are frequently given to show his right to make the assignment. The names of heirs whose lifetimes were to determine the duration of the lease under assignment were also named. If no forbears are mentioned, nor the names of heirs, then at least, the name of the townland, or city property in the leasehold can be traced and the history of the leasehold can be discovered by means of the LAND INDEX in the Registry of Deeds. Many first generation Americans disposed of their Irish property in the form of leasehold estates, in preparation for leaving Ireland, by assigning their rights to others.

MARRIAGE SETTLEMENT: Marriage settlements were numerous and common forms of agreement, from early times through the nineteenth century. The broad term, "Marriage Settlement," is used in Ireland to denote any contract which embodied the pre-nuptial agreement between the parties to a contemplated marriage, or between their representatives. A marriage settlement technically secured a jointure to the wife, and in many instruments it provided portions to the children of the marriage in the event of the husband's death. The marriage contract was often termed "Marriage Articles" or "Marriage Agreement," as either one set forth the terms agreed upon between the parties to a contemplated marriage, respecting the rights to property and succession. This often changed the resulting effects of the law regarding the rights of married people.

Marriage settlements were employed by families in modest circumstances, as well as by the wealthy. In the former cases, the consideration was often insignificant, but of importance to the contracting parties. In either case, the purpose was to secure the safekeeping of property, as well as to establish the young people with land, etc., at the time of marriage.

Whether the instrument should be called a Marriage Settlement, Contract, Agreement, or Articles, the embodied genealogical information is of the same nature, and is found in the formal legal instrument which was prepared and recorded in the Registry of Deeds, under the names of the contracting parties.

The pre-nuptial agreement, for the transfer of property to a bride and groom upon their first marriage, was usually entered into by their fathers or the father of one and a representative or two of the deceased father of the other. In the latter case, the bride or groom might be represented by one or more trustees of the deceased father's estate, named in his will. They could be any unrelated trustees or one or more members of the family as named, i. e., the mother, brother, brother-in-law, or uncle, etc.

Particular care was taken to secure the rights of the bride and her issue by the marriage if her father or the trustee of his estate was transferring the larger portion of the property agreed upon in the marriage settlement, thus insuring a specific amount for the bride and her unborn children, and with provision for a portion to her legal heirs, other than her husband, in the event of her death without issue. If the larger portion of property was in the groom's family, a specified amount was frequently agreed upon for the bride and her issue by the marriage, thus securing the property for the children in the event of her second marriage.

In most cases, except when the bride was an heiress without brothers, her portion of the family estate was settled upon her at marriage in the form of money, particularly if the family held little land. If a substantial amount of money was to be transferred from the bride's family, or from her inheritance, to the groom's keeping at the time of marriage, its continued safekeeping and ultimate disposal was secured by a pledge of the groom, or in case he was a minor, by his father or guardian, usually as in a mortgage with their own property insuring safety.

In all cases, the property was either transferred upon marriage or a clear statement in the written agreement guaranteed a later inheritance or a promise of property in the future at a stated time. Frequently, however, a parent qualified the amount of an expected inheritance from himself, naming elder children who had prior claims. The promised portions of elder sons and daughters, yet unmarried, were sometimes mentioned with their names.

Marriage contracts between older adults constituted mutual agreement upon the eventual disposal of presently owned property, including the portion to be held as the dower right of the wife. The older bride was usually represented in the contract by members of her family or a legal agent. The names of her deceased parents were sometimes mentioned in relation to an inheritance. In case she was a widow, her deceased first husband and any children by that marriage were usually mentioned in connection with property in her keeping from this source. Security for its safety and the ultimate division of her first husband's estate might be mentioned.

Thus, marriage settlements almost always furnish much genealogical information about the bride and groom. The names of the contracting parties are entered in the NAMES INDEX of the Registry of Deeds. The marriage settlement for a couple, contracted years before they emigrated to America, often provides the necessary identifying information regarding their parentage, and opens the way to all other records of the families in the Registry of Deeds, as well as in other repositories.

BUSINESS AGREEMENTS: One common business agreement recorded among the records in the Registry of Deeds was the establishment or dissolution of a partnership. In the latter, the person or persons who sold their interests became grantors. Sometimes a history was stated. In other cases, only the facts of the sale of interests were mentioned, together with the names and addresses of the people concerned. Three or four brothers might be included or other relatives named, showing them alive at that time.

WILLS: Only a small fraction of the wills in Ireland were recorded in the Registry of Deeds. These were little known until recently, as they were in effect lost when the memorials and transcripts thereof were filed among those of the other land records. Over 2,000 wills were recorded, 1708-1800, for the purpose of registering the transfer of land by will to the heirs, thus making a written record of the rights of the heirs to possess it. As in the case of land records, the recorded will is called a "Memorial." The original will was taken to the Registry of Deeds to be registered, usually by the executor, trustee, or a witness to the testator's signature. The will was then recorded in one of three ways, each being a "Memorial." Some were copied in the testator's own words. These averaged in length from one to three pages. A large number were recorded in the third person, giving all names and information about them as mentioned in the will. Bequests were described and specified for each person. Unimportant details were included. These averaged in length from one to three pages. The third form was an abstract, usually from one-half to one page in length. This form seems to have been adopted when fewer heirs and beneficiaries were named and the distribution of the estate was made more simple. Information regarding heirs, beneficiaries, trustees, executors, and witnesses was stated as in other forms. Property was described in the briefest identifying way. Among the first two hundred memorials of wills registered between 4 June 1708 and 20 November 1718, forty-three were recorded in the first form, seventy-two in the second, and eighty-five in the third form. The memorial was, at the time of registration, witnessed by two or more people, signed by the executor, or one of the witnesses of the original will, and sealed by the signer, often with the family heraldic seal. These memorials of the wills were filed among all other memorials of deeds, leases, etc., in date order, in the vaults of the Registry of Deeds. Each document is given a number, in sequence, regardless of the class of the record. These numbers are recorded, together with the page number and the volume number in which the transcript of the memorial is preserved. In the NAMES INDEX all three references appear beside the name of the person to identify his record.

One of the finest contributions to Irish genealogy in recent years is the monumental work of Miss P. Beryl Eustace. She located all wills in the Registry of Deeds, 1708-1800, and first made a special manuscript index of them, including over 2,000 items. She then made abstracts of all of the transcripts of the wills; in any case of doubt referring to the original memorial, and checking the names of places and relationships with other authorities. In doing this work she searched over 83,000 recorded records of all kinds, dated 1708-1745, to find the wills, and with 1746-1785 searches, did a greater work. For the lasting benefit of genealogists, her abstracts of the wills, 1708-1785, were published by the Irish Manuscripts Commission in two volumes, entitled *Registry of Deeds, Dublin, Abstracts of Wills, 1708-1745; 1746-1785*, edited by P. Beryl Eustace, Dublin, 1954, 1956. These can be purchased through the Stationery Office, Dublin, or any book shop in Dublin. In these volumes 1,464 of the more than 2,000 wills appear in abstract. The number affixed to the memorial, the volume and page numbers of the transcript of the memorial, together with all names and pertinent information, are recorded in each abstract.

The original memorials and the transcripts give the name of the testator, his title, station in life (such as Esq., Gent.), or occupation; the names and relationship of principal heirs; the wife's surname before marriage, including a surname by an earlier marriage; the names and relationship of other heirs, with careful identification of any grandchildren, parents, brothers, sisters, nephews, nieces, friends, servants, mostly with their addresses in cases of adults. Except in the third class of memorials of wills, by which a few principal heirs are bequeathed all of the property, lands are listed for each heir who is a beneficiary of real property, naming the city with street or district, town, or townland and county. The date of the testator's signing, his name, the names of witnesses with their title (etc.), occupation and addresses, appear in the memorial, together with the date of registration of the memorial, the names of witnesses to the memorial and the name of the executor or witness who signed and sealed it.

The management and arrangement of the records in the Registry of Deeds is much the same as in any county court house in the United States. The transcripts of all memorials are bound in volumes averaging in size, 22" x 17". The transcripts of recent date are kept on shelves in the main search room on the second floor, where the staff central desk is located. Anyone wishing to consult the eighteenth and nineteenth century records (transcripts of the memorials) may do so upon application at the staff desk, and the payment of a small fee before a request to examine certain volumes of either of the two indexes to the records. Having located items of interest, the visitor will be escorted to the floor above, and will be shown the arrangement of the volumes in the rooms, to which both indexes refer. There are desks to which the volumes can be carried for inspection and copying any of the records.

INDEXES

The two series of indexes are the key to all work in this repository.

I. THE NAMES INDEX: This is the index of the Grantors, compiled from 1708 to the present day. It is arranged alphabetically, in periods of years, the entire alphabet being covered within each period. This makes it, in effect, many distinct grantor indexes. The periods, each separately indexed, are:

1708-1729; 1730-1745; 1746-1758; 1758-1768; 1768-1776; 1777-1785; 1786-1793; 1794-1799; 1800-1809; 1810-1812; 1813-1815; 1816-1818; 1819-1821; 1822-1824; 1825-1827; 1828-1832; 1833-1839; 1840-1849; 1850-1859; 1860-1869, and so on to the present day.

This NAMES INDEX lists the principal for whom the instrument was drawn. Within each indexed period, the surnames were arranged alphabetically, by groups of the same surname, and the listings appear with the given names under the surname, in alphabetical order, irrespective of the date within the period or the class of the record. Thus, all Clark entries within the period, 1708-1729, are grouped together in order of the given names from A-Z. These are the names of the Clark family grantors of deeds of sale, deeds of trusts, mortgages, releases, leases, assignments, business agreements, marriage settlements, wills, etc. This arrangement of the NAMES INDEX, in periods, makes it possible for a genealogist to check the indexes during any short time when a marked change in a family occurred, due to marriage, emigration, death, etc., in a quick and easy way. Within each index, the surname of the grantee follows that of the grantor, after which the volume and page number of the transcript of the memorial, and the registered number of the original memorial appear. No description or location of the property, or exact date of the instrument, is entered in this index until the period of 1833-1839. From then on the NAMES INDEX of each period shows the grantor, grantee, first denomination (given names), county, city or town, barony or parish, year of registration, volume and page number of the transcript of the memorial, and the registration number of the original memorial.

It has been stated, "a disadvantage of the NAMES INDEX is that, while the records of people bearing uncommon surnames are few enough to make it safe to examine or order copies of all records of a certain surname without the loss of time or money, difficulty arises when dealing with a common surname" such as Clark, Holmes, or Wilson, due to the lack of identifying place-names. Thus, the records ex-

amined or copies ordered might prove to concern transactions in scattered locations all over Ireland which have no
connection with the immediate family under study. It has
also been stated that a further difficulty lies in the fact that
the NAMES INDEX deals only with grantors of deeds, leases,
etc., while the American genealogist is usually trying to
trace the descendants of grantees of leases, as most of the
emigrants were, with their forbears, previously tenants.

The seventeen examples of the records of one emigrant
family, given in abstract at the end of this chapter, disprove
this. They are included in an illustration of work with the
Dickson family records of Ballymena and Belfast, County
Antrim, and their earlier holdings in County Londonderry,
from 1747 through 1819, when one branch emigrated, and
1824, when family property was sold. There were numerous Dickson families, most of them unrelated within many
generations before 1800. They were located in the counties
of Antrim, Armagh, Cork, Donegal, Down, Fermanagh,
Kildare, Limerick, Londonderry, Meath, Monaghan, Tyrone,
Waterford, and Wexford. Furthermore, they used many
duplicate given names. The William, Francis, and John,
of Counties Londonderry and Antrim, were only remotely
related to the William, Francis, and John, of County Tyrone of the same period. These seventeen records are chosen
as examples because they are representative of the many classes of land records in the Registry of Deeds, and the data
in them were pieced together to reconstruct the family.
Among the seventeen records there are seven leases (one
for 21 years, two for 61 years, two for the term of the original lease, and one in perpetuity), two assignments of long
term leases, three marriage settlements (one assigning a
lease held in perpetuity), two trust accounts, two mortgages, and one dissolution of partnership. The first records
were located in the NAMES INDEX, within the periods of
1800-1821, before the 1819 emigration took place. These
gave the clue to the records, 1747-1800. All led to the finding of earlier documents for this family and allied families

in other repositories. In all cases, the grantor had been either an owner of the property or a lessee disposing of the lease. The fact that the NAMES INDEX is divided into complete indexes for short periods made it possible to order copies of the Dickson records dated within the short time previous to emigration. Of twenty-four copies of documents ordered, seventeen concerned the one Dickson family being studied.

As in the above case, many men, both single and married, who left Ireland, had been engaged in some business such as shopkeeping, linen manufacture, woolen manufacture, as well as farming. The number of weavers who came to America was cause for concern in the Irish Parliament in 1750. Many of these sold property they owned, leased owned property, or assigned or sold leases, before emigrating. Thus, they became grantors who were careful to have their transactions recorded in the Registry of Deeds. In addition, as stated above, the marriage settlements, business agreements and wills, concerned many of the emigrants. Thus, the NAMES INDEX for the period including the date of emigration, and the index for the previous period, should be examined for any entry of the emigrant's name, and all entries of known given names in the family which might reveal records of his father.

The NAMES INDEX is arranged in several series of volumes. The first series of 279 volumes includes the periods between 1708 and 1849. The second series of 54 volumes includes the periods between 1850 and 1900. The third series begins with 1900, etc. Previous to 1950, the Registry of Deeds had the only list of these volumes. This list showed for each index volume, its number, the first letter of the surnames included and the period of years covered in the volume. Thus Volume I, A, 1708-29, included all surnames beginning with the letter "A" during the period 1708-29. This list was consulted in the Registry of Deeds when anyone requested a volume of the NAMES INDEX covering a certain surname within a given period. From the list, the volume could quickly be located.

In about 1950, the entire contents of all volumes of the

NAMES INDEX, 1708-1904, and the LAND INDEX for the same years were microfilmed by representatives of the Genealogical Society of Salt Lake City, Utah. In order for anyone to consult the microfilms, it was necessary to compile lists of all index volumes which had been microfilmed, showing which ones appeared on each film. The volumes were listed in number order, thus making the lists similar to those in the Registry of Deeds. Hence, these lists became available outside this repository. The National Library in Dublin and the Genealogical Society in Salt Lake City, Utah, each have copies. They make an important reference tool for the genealogist, and so are included in this chapter.

II. THE LAND INDEX, of which there are 320 volumes, 1708-1849 (the period which interests most genealogists), has been continued to the present time. It was compiled to make possible the tracing of the history of each unit of land recorded in the original memorials of all documents registered in the Registry of Deeds, and in the transcripts thereof. These units of land were the townlands in the rural areas and the residence or business property in the cities and towns. All memorials referring to these units, and the transcripts of the memorials, are thus indexed according to the lands mentioned in the original document. The LAND INDEX is arranged in volumes by counties and some cities. The townland property in any transfer is alphabetically indexed in the county volume under the barony in which it is located (except when the omission of baronies is noted). The town property is indexed under the towns included in the county volumes. The city property is indexed by street or district in the volumes for some cities, beginning at various dates. The indexes in all volumes are arranged in date order, each volume covering an allotted period of time. Thus, Volume I of the LAND INDEX covers Counties Antrim and Armagh, 1708-38. Dublin was the only city separately indexed for the period 1708-39. From 1739-1810, the indexes for the City of Dublin were arranged according to "Dublin Liberties" or Dublin districts, in one volume. The index for the City of Londonderry was included in that for the County of Londonderry until 1739. From 1739-1810, the index for this city is separately listed, but is bound in two volumes containing also the indexes for County Londonderry and County Fermanagh. Also some indexes for the City of Londonderry, 1780-1810, are bound in one volume for the City of Kilkenny and Drogheda Town. The City of Cork indexes, 1708-39, were included in the County Cork index, 1708-39. This city is separately indexed for the periods 1739-1779; 1779-1810; 1810-1819; 1820-28. For the period 1828-32, the City of Cork index is bound with those for the City of Belfast, Drogheda Town, and Kilkenny City. In the period 1833-35, one volume of the index includes the City of Belfast, City of Cork, Drogheda Town, and the cities of Kilkenny, Limerick, and Londonderry. The City of Belfast is not separately indexed until 1828, as shown above. Before that date, the items for Belfast were included in the period indexes for County Antrim.

Thus the LAND INDEX was compiled in a variable arrangement, which makes it necessary to consult a list of the contents of the index volumes. As stated in the description of the NAMES INDEX, this former index list was available only in the Registry of Deeds, before 1950. In order to consult the microfilms of the LAND INDEX, it was necessary to compile a list of the volumes which had been microfilmed, showing which volumes were filmed on each reel. Hence this list also became available outside the Registry of Deeds, as noted above. It also is an important reference tool for the genealogist and so is included in this chapter.

MICROFILMS

Shortly before 1950, representatives of the Genealogical Society of the Church of Jesus Christ of Latter-Day Saints, Salt Lake City, Utah, realizing the great genealogical value of the records in the Registry of Deeds, Dublin, obtained permission to microfilm both indexes to the records, 1708-1904. They filmed the entire contents of the NAMES INDEX on 122 reels and the LAND INDEX on 283 reels. Copies of the films were deposited in the National Library of Ireland, Dublin.

These microfilms make it possible to discover any memorial deposited in the Registry of Deeds, Dublin, dated within the years 1708-1904, without having to consult the original indexes in this repository. The collection of the 405 original microfilms of the two indexes is in the Genealogical Society Library in Salt Lake City. It is undoubtedly one of the most valuable aids to Irish genealogical research in the United States.

As stated in the descriptions of the NAMES INDEX and the LAND INDEX, it is impossible to use the microfilms without consulting the lists of their contents. Therefore, the subject matter in the microfilms of both indexes, as far as the year 1850, will appear below. The entire list is too lengthy to present. In these lists, the Negative and Positive numbers of the films, heading the contents of each microfilm, are the ones affixed by the National Library of Ireland to their copies of the films. If the Genealogical Society of Salt Lake City has now adopted a different number system for their Negative and Positive films, the contents of each microfilm will, however, be the same as the National Library of Ireland copy. As the Society has a record of the latter number system, it can identify its own films with it.

The lists below show the volumes of either index included in a single microfilm. Thus, the first film of the NAMES INDEX, Negative and Positive number 2,001, includes the entire contents of eight volumes. The first six volumes, each for a different period within the years 1708-1785, contain the indexes of surnames beginning with the letter "A". Two volumes, numbered 7 B 1708-1729, and 8 B (i) 1730-1745, contain the indexes of the surnames beginning with the letter "B". Volume 8 B (ii) 1730-1745, appears on the next microfilm as the first item. This completes the index of surnames of the letter "B" for the period, 1708-1745.

Thus, if the genealogist is searching for the records of an emigrant, James Bell, who came to America in 1740, he or an agent should first examine Vol. 8 B (i) 1730-1745 on microfilm (Negative or Positive) number 2,001, before consulting Vol. 8 B (ii) 1730-1745, on film number 2,002. These two volumes contain the indexes to any records of transfer of land or leasehold, or any other record pertaining to James Bell in which he was the grantor previous to his emigration and as early as 1730, as well as the indexes of records of other members of the Bell family grantors in which he might have been named during this period. All items for the Bell family on these two films, including the period 1708-1729 should be copied for possible future use in ordering copies of the memorials. The information which will appear and must be copied in full is: The surname and given name of the grantor, surname of the grantee, volume and page numbers of the transcript of the memorial, and the registration number of the original memorial, for each item of interest.

If the genealogist cannot consult the microfilms himself, he will shorten the time of an agent by choosing the films he wishes examined from the lists given below.

Following the lists of the microfilms and their subject matter, given below, an example of work will be presented to illustrate the procedure of a search and the findings for one family which emigrated to America in 1819.

MICROFILMS OF THE NAMES INDEX—1708-1849

NEGATIVE 2,001. POSITIVE 2,001. Names Index: Vol. 1 A 1708-29; Vol. 2 A 1730-45; Vol. 3 A 1746-58; Vol. 4 A 1758-68; Vol. 5 A 1768-77; Vol. 6 A 1777-85; Vol. 7 B 1708-29; Vol. 8 B (i) 1730-45.

NEGATIVE 2,002. POSITIVE 2,002. Names Index: Vol. 8 B (ii) 1730-45; Vol. 9 B 1746-58; Vol. 10 B 1758-68; Vol. 11 B (i) 1768-85.

NEGATIVE 2,003. POSITIVE 2,003. Names Index: Vol. 11 B (ii) 1768-85; Vol. 12 C 1708-29; Vol. 13 C 1730-45; Vol. 14 C (i) 1746-58.

NEGATIVE 2,004. POSITIVE 2,004. Names Index: Vol. 14 C (ii) 1746-58; Vol. 15 C 1758-68; Vol. 16 C 1768-76; Vol. 17 C 1777-85; Vol. 18 D (i) 1708-29.

NEGATIVE 2,005. POSITIVE 2,005. Names Index: Vol. 18 D (ii) 1708-29; Vol. 19 D 1730-45; Vol. 20 D 1746-58; Vol. 21 D 1758-68; Vol. 22 D 1768-76; Vol. 23 D 1777-85; Vol. 24 E (i) 1708-29.

NEGATIVE 2,006. POSITIVE 2,006. Names Index: Vol. 24 E (ii) 1708-29; Vol. 25 E 1730-47; Vol. 26 E 1748-58; Vol. 27 E 1758-68; Vol. 28 E 1768-76; Vol. 29 E 1777-85; Vol. 30 F 1708-29; Vol. 31 F 1730-45; Vol. 32 F 1746-58; Vol. 33 F 1758-68; Vol. 34 F 1768-76.

NEGATIVE 2,007. POSITIVE 2,007. Names Index: Vol. 35 F 1777-85; Vol. 36 G 1708-29; Vol. 37 G 1730-45; Vol. 38 G 1746-58; Vol. 39 G 1758-68; Vol. 40 G 1768-76; Vol. 41 G 1777-85; Vol. 42 H (i) 1708-29.

NEGATIVE 2,008. POSITIVE 2,008. Names Index: Vol. 42 H (ii) 1708-29; Vol. 43 H 1730-45; Vol. 44 H 1746-58; Vol. 45 H 1758-68; Vol. 46 H 1768-76; Vol. 47 H (i) 1777-85.

NEGATIVE 2,009. POSITIVE 2,009. Names Index: Vol. 47 H (ii) 1777-85; Vol. 48 I-J 1708-29; Vol. 49 I-J 1730-45; Vol. 50 I-J 1746-58; Vol. 51 I-J 1758-68; Vol. 52 I-J 1768-76; Vol. 53 I-J 1777-85; Vol. 54 K 1708-29; Vol. 55 K 1730-45; Vol. 56 K 1746-58; Vol. 57 K 1758-68.

NEGATIVE 2,010. POSITIVE 2,010. Names Index: Vol. 58 K 1768-76; Vol. 59 K 1777-85; Vol. 60 L 1708-29; Vol. 61 L 1730-45; Vol. 62 L 1746-58; Vol. 63 L 1758-68; Vol. 64 L 1768-76; Vol. 65 M (i) 1708-29.

NEGATIVE 2,011. POSITIVE 2,011. Names Index: Vol. 66 M (ii) 1708-29; Vol. 67 M 1730-45; Vol. 68 M 1746-58; Vol. 69 M (i) 1758-68.

NEGATIVE 2,012. POSITIVE 2,012. Names Index: Vol. 69 M (ii) 1758-68; Vol. 70 M 1768-76; Vol. 71 M 1777-85; Vol. 72 N 1708-29; Vol. 73 N 1730-45; Vol. 74 N 1746-58; Vol. 75 N 1758-68; Vol. 76 N 1768-76; Vol. 77 N (i) 1777-85.

NEGATIVE 2,013. POSITIVE 2,013. Names Index: Vol. 77 N (ii) 1777-85; Vol. 78 O 1708-29; Vol. 79 O 1730-45; Vol. 80 O 1746-58; Vol. 81 O 1758-68; Vol. 82 O 1768-76; Vol. 83 O 1777-85; Vol. 84 P 1708-29; Vol. 85 P 1730-45; Vol. 86 P 1746-58; Vol. 87 P 1758-68.

NEGATIVE 2,014. POSITIVE 2,014. Names Index: Vol. 88 P 1768-76; Vol. 89 P 1777-85; Vol. 90 Q 1708-85; Vol. 91 R 1708-29; Vol. 92 R 1730-45; Vol. 93 R 1746-58; Vol. 94 R 1758-68; Vol. 95 R 1768-76.

NEGATIVE 2,015. POSITIVE 2,015. Names Index: Vol. 96 R 1777-85; Vol. 97 S 1708-29; Vol. 98 S 1730-45; Vol. 99 S 1746-58; Vol. 100 S 1758-68.

NEGATIVE 2,016. POSITIVE 2,016. Names Index: Vol. 101 S 1768-76; Vol. 102 S 1777-85; Vol. 103 T 1708-29; Vol. 104 T 1730-45; Vol. 105 T 1746-58; Vol. 106 T 1758-68; Vol. 107 T 1768-76; Vol. 108 T (i) 1777-85.

NEGATIVE 2,017. POSITIVE 2,017. Names Index: Vol. 108 T (ii) 1777-85; Vol. 109 U-Z 1708-29; Vol. 110 U-Z 1730-45; Vol. 111 U-Z 1746-58; Vol. 112 U-Z 1758-68; Vol. 113 U-Z 1768-76; Vol. 114 U-Z 1777-85; Vol. 115 W 1708-29; Vol. 116 W 1730-45; Vol. 117 W 1746-58; Vol. 118 W (i) 1758-68.

NEGATIVE 2,018. POSITIVE 2,018. Names Index: Vol. 118 (ii) 1758-68; Vol. 119 W 1768-76; Vol. 119a W 1777-85.

NEGATIVE 2,019. POSITIVE 2,019. Names Index: Vol. 120 A-B 1786-93; Vol. 121 CA-CU 1786-93; Vol. 122 D-E (i) 1786-93.

NEGATIVE 2,020. POSITIVE 2,020. Names Index: Vol. 122 D-E (ii) 1786-93; Vol. 123 F-G 1786-93; Vol. 124 H-J 1786-93; Vol. 125 KA-LY (i) 1786-93.

NEGATIVE 2,021. POSITIVE 2,021. Names Index: Vol. 125 KA-LY (ii) 1786-93; Vol. 126 M-N 1786-93; Vol. 127 O-Z 1786-93; Vol. 128 A-D 1794-99.

NEGATIVE 2,022. POSITIVE 2,022. Names Index: Vol. 129 E-J 1794-99; Vol. 130 K-Z 1794-99; Vol. 131 A 1800-09; Vol. 132 BA-BE 1800-09.

NEGATIVE 2,023. POSITIVE 2,023. Names Index: Vol. 133 BI-BO 1800-09; Vol. 134 BR-BY 1800-09; Vol. 135 CA-CL 1800-09.

NEGATIVE 2,024. POSITIVE 2,024. Names Index: Vol. 136 CO 1800-09; Vol. 137 CR-CY 1800-09; Vol. 138 DA-DI 1800-09; Vol. 139 DO-DY (i) 1800-09.

NEGATIVE 2,025. POSITIVE 2,025. Names Index: Vol. 139 DO-DY (ii) 1800-09; Vol. 140 E 1800-09; Vol. 141 FA-FI 1800-09; Vol. 142 FL-FY 1800-09; Vol. 143 GA-GL 1800-09; Vol. 144 GO-GY (i) 1800-09.

NEGATIVE 2,026. POSITIVE 2,026. Names Index: Vol. 144 GO-GY (ii) 1800-09; Vol. 145 HA 1800-09; Vol. 146 HE-HI 1800-09; Vol. 147 HO-HY 1800-09; Vol. 148 I-J (i) 1800-09.

NEGATIVE 2,027. POSITIVE 2,027. Names Index: Vol. 148 I-J (ii) 1800-09; Vol. 149 K 1800-09; Vol. 150 LA-LE 1800-09; Vol. 151 LI-LY 1800-09; Vol. 152 Mc (i) 1800-09.

NEGATIVE 2,028. POSITIVE 2,028. Vol. 152 Mc (ii) 1800-09; Vol. 153 MA-ME 1800-09; Vol. 154 ML-MY 1800-09; Vol. 155 N (i) 1800-09.

NEGATIVE 2,029. POSITIVE 2,029. Names Index: Vol. 155 N
(ii) 1800-09; Vol. 156 O 1800-09; Vol. 157 P-Q 1800-09;
Vol. 158 RA-RI 1800-09.

NEGATIVE 2,030. POSITIVE 2,030. Names Index: Vol. 159 RO-
RY 1800-09; Vol. 160 St.-SL 1800-09; Vol. 161 SM-SY
1800-09; Vol. 162 TA-TY (i) 1800-09.

NEGATIVE 2,031. POSITIVE 2,031. Names Index: Vol. 162 TA-
TY (ii) 1800-09; Vol. 163 U.V.Y.Z., 1800-09; Vol. 164 WA-
WE 1800-09; Vol. 165 WH-WY 1800-09; Vol. 166 A-Z 1810-
12.

NEGATIVE 2,032. POSITIVE 2,032. Names Index: Vol. 167 A-J
1813-15; Vol. 168 K-Z 1813-15; Vol. 169 A-D 1816-18; Vol.
169a E-J 1816-18.

NEGATIVE 2,033. POSITIVE 2,033. Names Index: Vol. 170
K-Z 1816-18; Vol. 171 A-D 1819-21; Vol. 172 E-J 1819-21.

NEGATIVE 2,034. POSITIVE 2,034. Names Index: Vol. 173 K-Q
1819-21; Vol. 174 R-Z 1819-21; Vol. 175 A-C 1822-24; Vol.
176 D-J (i) 1822-24.

NEGATIVE 2,035. POSITIVE 2,035. Names Index: Vol. 176 D-J
(ii) 1822-24; Vol. 177 K-P 1822-24; Vol. 178 Q-Z 1822-24;
Vol. 179 A-D (i) 1825-27.

NEGATIVE 2,036. POSITIVE 2,036. Names Index: Vol. 179
A-D (ii) 1825-27; Vol. 180 E-J 1825-27; Vol. 181 K-O 1825-
27; Vol. 182 P-Z (i) 1825-27.

NEGATIVE 2,037. POSITIVE 2,037. Names Index: Vol. 182 P-Z
(ii) 1825-27; Vol. 183 A-Z Jan.-Aug., 1828; Vol. 184 A Aug.
1828-32; Vol. 185 B Aug. 1828-32; Vol. 186 C (i) Aug. 1828-
32.

NEGATIVE 2,038. POSITIVE 2,038. Names Index: Vol. 186 C
(ii) Aug. 1828-32; Vol. 187 D Aug. 1828-32; Vol. 188 E
Aug. 1828-32; Vol. 189 F Aug. 1828-32; Vol. 190 G Aug.
1828-32; Vol. 191 H Aug. 1828-32; Vol. 192 I Aug. 1828-32;
Vol. 193 J Aug. 1828-32; Vol. 194 K Aug. 1828-32; Vol.
195 L Aug. 1828-32.

NEGATIVE 2,039. POSITIVE 2,039. Names Index: Vol. 196 M
Aug. 1828-32; Vol. 197 N Aug. 1828-32; Vol. 198 O Aug.
1828-32; Vol. 199 P Aug. 1828-32; Vol. 200 Q Aug. 1828-32;

Vol. 201 R Aug. 1828-32; Vol. 202 S Aug. 1828-32; Vol. 203 T Aug. 1828-32; Vol. 204 U Aug. 1828-32; Vol. 205 V Aug. 1828-32; Vol. 206 W Aug. 1828-32; Vol. 207 Y Aug. 1828-32; Vol. 208 Z Aug. 1828-32.

NEGATIVE 2,040. POSITIVE 2,040. Names Index: Vol. 209 A 1833-39; Vol. 210 BA-BE 1833-39; Vol. 211 BI-BO (i) 1833-39.

NEGATIVE 2,041. POSITIVE 2,041. Names Index: Vol. 211 BI-BO (ii) 1833-39; Vol. 212 BR-BY 1833-39; Vol. 213 CA-CI 1833-39; Vol. 214 CL-CO 1833-39.

NEGATIVE 2,042. POSITIVE 2,042. Names Index: Vol. 215 CR-CU 1833-39; Vol. 216 DA-DI 1833-39; Vol. 217 DO-DY 1833-39; Vol. 218 E 1833-39; Vol. 219 FA-FI (i) 1833-39.

NEGATIVE 2,043. POSITIVE 2,043. Names Index: Vol. 219 FA-FI (ii) 1833-39; Vol. 220 FL-FY 1833-39; Vol. 221 GA-GI 1833-39; Vol. 222 GO-GY 1833-39; Vol. 223 HA 1833-39; Vol. 224 HE-HI (i) 1833-39.

NEGATIVE 2,044. POSITIVE 2,044. Names Index: Vol. 224 HE-HI (ii) 1833-39; Vol. 225 HO-HY 1833-39; Vol. 226 I-J 1833-39; Vol. 227 KA-KY 1833-39; Vol. 228 LA-LE (i) 1833-39.

NEGATIVE 2,045. POSITIVE 2,045. Names Index: Vol. 228 LA-LE (ii) 1833-39; Vol. 229 LI-LY 1833-39; Vol. 230 Mc-Ma 1833-39; Vol. 231 MA-MI 1833-39.

NEGATIVE 2,046. POSITIVE 2,046. Names Index: Vol. 232 MO-MY 1833-39; Vol. 233 N 1833-39; Vol. 234 O 1833-39; Vol. 235 PA-PH 1833-39; Vol. 236 PI-PY (i) 1833-39.

NEGATIVE 2,047. POSITIVE 2,047. Names Index: Vol. 236 PI-PY (ii) 1833-39; Vol. 237 RA-RI 1833-39; Vol. 238 RO-RY 1833-39; Vol. 239 St.-SH 1833-39; Vol. 240 SI-SO 1833-39; Vol. 241 ST-SY (i) 1833-39.

NEGATIVE 2,048. POSITIVE 2,048. Names Index: Vol. 241 ST-SY (ii) 1833-39; Vol. 242 TA-TI 1833-39; Vol. 243 TO-TY 1833-39; Vol. 244 WA-WE 1833-39; Vol. 245 WH-WY 1833-39; Vol. 246 Q.U.V.Y.Z. 1833-39.

NEGATIVE 2,049. POSITIVE 2,049. Names Index: Vol. 247 AB-AY 1840-49; Vol. 248 BA-BE (i) 1840-49.

NEGATIVE 2,050. POSITIVE 2,050. Names Index: Vol. 248 BA-BE (ii) 1840-49; Vol. 249 BI-BR 1840-49; Vol. 250 BR-BY 1840-49; Vol. 251 CA-CL (i) 1840-49.

NEGATIVE 2,051. POSITIVE 2,051. Names Index: Vol. 251 CA-CL (ii) 1840-49; Vol. 252 CO 1840-49; Vol. 253 CR-CU (i) 1840-49.

NEGATIVE 2,052. POSITIVE 2,052. Names Index: Vol. 253 CR-CU (ii) 1840-49; Vol. 254 DA-DI 1840-49; Vol. 255 DO-DY 1840-49; Vol. 256 E 1840-49; Vol. 257 F (i) 1840-49.

NEGATIVE 2,053. POSITIVE 2,053. Names Index: Vol. 257 F (ii) 1840-49; Vol. 258 G 1840-49; Vol. 259 HA-HE (i) 1840-49.

NEGATIVE 2,054. POSITIVE 2,054. Names Index: Vol. 259 HA-HE (ii) 1840-49; Vol. 260 HI-HY 1840-49; Vol. 261 I 1840-49; Vol. 262 J 1840-49; Vol. 263 KA-KY (i) 1840-49.

NEGATIVE 2,055. POSITIVE 2,055. Vol. 263 KA-KY (ii) 1840-49; Vol. 264 LA-LY 1840-49.

NEGATIVE 2,056. POSITIVE 2,056. Names Index: Vol. 265 McA-McW 1840-49; Vol. 266 MA 1840-49; Vol. 267 ME-MY (i) 1840-49.

NEGATIVE 2,057. POSITIVE 2,057. Names Index: Vol. 267 ME-MY (ii) 1840-49; Vol. 268 N 1840-49; Vol. 269 O 1840-49; Vol. 270 PA-PR (i) 1840-49.

NEGATIVE 2,058. POSITIVE 2,058. Names Index: Vol. 270 PA-PR (ii) 1840-49; Vol. 271 PU-PY 1840-49; Vol. 272 R (i) 1840-49.

NEGATIVE 2,059. POSITIVE 2,059. Names Index: Vol. 272 R (ii) 1840-49; Vol. 271 a Q 1840-49; Vol. 273 St.-SL 1840-49; Vol. 274 S (i) 1840-49.

NEGATIVE 2,060. POSITIVE 2,060. Names Index: Vol. 274 S (ii) 1840-49; Vol. 275 T 1840-49; Vol. 276 U-V 1840-49; Vol. 277 WA-WH (i) 1840-49.

NEGATIVE 2,061. POSITIVE 2,061. Names Index: Vol. 277 WA-WH (ii) 1840-49; Vol. 278 WI-WY 1840-49; Vol. 279 Y-Z 1840-49.

MICROFILMS OF THE LAND INDEX—1708-1849

Negative 2,123. Positive 2,123.

Land Index: Vol.	1.	Antrim, Armagh.	1708-1738.
,, ,, ,,	2.	Armagh, Cavan (i).	1739-1810.

Negative 2,124. Positive 2,124.

Land Index: Vol.	2.	Armagh, Cavan (ii).	1739-1810.
,, ,, ,,	3.	Clare.	1708-1738.
,, ,, ,,	4.	Clare, Kerry (i).	1739-1810.

Negative 2,125. Positive 2,125.

Land Index: Vol.	4.	Clare, Kerry (ii).	1739-1810.
,, ,, ,,	5.	Cork.	1810-1819.
,, ,, ,,	6.	Clare, Kerry, Limerick.	1811-1820.
,, ,, ,,	7.	Antrim, Down (1).	1811-1820.

Negative 2,126. Positive 2,126.

Land Index: Vol.	7.	Antrim, Down (ii).	1811-1820.
,, ,, ,,	8.	Cork.	1780-1809.
,, ,, ,,	9.	Cork, Corporate towns.	1780-1809.
,, ,, ,,	10.	Antrim (i).	1739-1810.

Negative 2,127. Positive 2,127.

Land Index: Vol.	10.	Antrim (ii).	1739-1810.
,, ,, ,,	11.	Down.	1739-1810.
,, ,, ,,	12.	Cork (i).	1820-1828.

Negative 2,128. Positive 2,128.

Land Index: Vol.	12.	Cork (ii).	1820-1828.
,, ,, ,,	13.	Tipperary, Waterford.	1708-1738.
,, ,, ,,	14.	Kerry, Limerick.	1708-1738.
,, ,, ,,	15.	Carlow, Dublin (i).	1708-1738.

Negative 2,129. Positive 2,129.

Land Index: Vol.	15.	Carlow, Dublin (ii).	1708-1738.
,, ,, ,,	16.	Carlow, Queen's Co.	1739-1810.
,, ,, ,,	17.	Clare, Kerry, Limerick.	1821-1825.
,, ,, ,,	18.	Meath, Queen's Co. (i).	1811-1820.

Negative 2,130. Positive 2,130.

Land Index: Vol.	18.	Meath, Queen's Co. (ii).	1811-1820.
,, ,, ,,	19.	Donegal, Sligo.	1739-1810.
,, ,, ,,	20.	Cavan, Down.	1821-1825.
,, ,, ,,	21.	Galway.	1826-1828.

Negative 2,131. Positive 2,131.

Land Index: Vol.	22.	Clare, Kerry, Limerick.	1826-1828.
,, ,, ,,	23.	Down, Cavan.	1826-1828.
,, ,, ,,	24.	Galway.	1811-1820.
,, ,, ,,	25.	Leitrim.	1811-1820.
,, ,, ,,	26.	Cork (i).	1739-1779.

78 IRISH AND SCOTCH-IRISH ANCESTRAL RESEARCH

Negative 2,132.	Positive	2,132.		
Land Index: Vol.	26.	Cork (ii).		1739-1779.
" " "	27.	Kildare, Kilkenny, King's Co.		1708-1738.
" " "	28.	King's Co.		1739-1810.
" " "	29.	Kildare.		1739-1810.
" " "	30.	Kilkenny (i).		1739-1810.
Negative 2,133.	**Positive**	**2,133.**		
Land Index: Vol.	30.	Kilkenny (ii).		1739-1810.
" " "	31.	Kilkenny, Kildare, King's Co.		1811-1820.
" " "	32.	Kilkenny, Kildare, King's Co.		1821-1825.
" " "	33.	Kilkenny, Kildare, King's Co. (i).		1826-1828.
Negative 2,134.	**Positive**	**2,134.**		
Land Index: Vol.	33.	Kilkenny, Kildare, King's Co. (ii).		1826-1828.
" " "	34.	Dublin.		1739-1806.
" " "	35.	Dublin Liberties.		1739-1810.
" " "	36.	Dublin (i).		1807-1819.
Negative 2,135.	**Positive**	**2,135.**		
Land Index: Vol.	36.	Dublin (ii).		1807-1819.
" " "	37.	Dublin.		1820-1828.
" " "	38.	Mayo, Roscommon, Sligo.		1708-1738.
" " "	39.	Mayo, Roscommon, Sligo (i).		1739-1810.
Negative 2,136.	**Positive**	**2,136.**		
Land Index: Vol.	39.	Mayo, Roscommon, Sligo (ii).		1739-1810.
" " "	40.	Mayo, Roscommon, Sligo.		1811-1820.
" " "	41.	Mayo, Roscommon, Sligo, Donegal (i).		1821-1825.
Negative 2,137.	**Positive**	**2,137.**		
Land Index: Vol.	41.	Mayo, Roscommon, Sligo, Donegal (ii).		1821-1825.
" " "	42.	Mayo, Roscommon, Sligo, Donegal.		1826-1828.
" " "	43.	Fermanagh, Londonderry, Monaghan, Tyrone.		1708-1738.
" " "	44.	Fermanagh, Londonderry, Londonderry City (i).		1739-1810.
Negative 2,138.	**Positive**	**2,138.**		
Land Index: Vol.	44.	Fermanagh, Londonderry, Londonderry City (ii).		1739-1810.
" " "	45.	Monaghan, Tyrone.		1739-1810.
" " "	46.	Monaghan, Tyrone.		1811-1820.
Negative 2,139.	**Positive**	**2,139.**		
Land Index: Vol.	47.	Fermanagh, Londonderry.		1811-1820.
" " "	48.	Fermanagh, Londonderry, Monaghan, Tyrone.		1821-1825.
" " "	49.	Fermanagh, Londonderry, Monaghan, Tyrone.		1826-1828.
" " "	50.	City of Cork (i).		1810-1819.

Negative 2,140. Positive 2,140.

		Vol.	50.	City of Cork (ii).	1810-1819.
Land Index:	"	"	51.	City of Cork (ii).	1820-1828.
"	"	"	52.	Cities of Kilkenny, Londonderry and Drogheda Town.	1780-1810.
"	"	"	53.	Cities of Limerick, Waterford.	1780-1810.
"	"	"	54.	Leitrim, Longford (i).	1739-1810.

Negative 2,141. Positive 2,141.

		Vol.	54.	Leitrim, Longford (ii).	1739-1810.
Land Index:	"	"	55.	Galway.	1708-1738.
"	"	"	56.	Galway.	1739-1810.
"	"	"	57.	Galway, Leitrim, Longford (i).	1821-1825.

Negative 2,142. Positive 2,142.

		Vol.	57.	Galway, Leitrim, Longford (ii).	1821-1825.
Land Index:	"	"	58.	Tipperary.	1739-1810.
"	"	"	59.	Tipperary.	1739-1810.
"	"	"	60.	Tipperary, Waterford.	1811-1820.

Negative 2,143. Positive 2,143.

		Vol.	61.	Tipperary, Waterford.	1821-1825.
Land Index:	"	"	62.	Tipperary, Waterford.	1826-1828.
"	"	"	63.	Westmeath, Wexford, Wicklow (i).	1708-1738.

Negative 2,144. Positive 2,144.

		Vol.	63.	Westmeath, Wexford, Wicklow (ii).	1708-1738.
Land Index:	"	"	64.	Wicklow, Waterford.	1739-1810.
"	"	"	65.	Wexford.	1739-1810.
"	"	"	66.	Westmeath.	1739-1810.

Negative 2,145. Positive 2,145.

		Vol.	67.	Wexford, Wicklow.	1811-1820.
Land Index:	"	"	68.	Westmeath.	1811-1820.
"	"	"	69.	Wicklow, Wexford, Corporation Towns: Athlone, Mullingar.	1821-1825.
"	"	"	70.	Westmeath, Wexford, Wicklow.	1826.
"	"	"	71.	Louth, Meath, Queen's Co. (i).	1708-1738.

Negative 2,146. Positive 2,146.

		Vol.	71.	Louth, Meath, Queen's Co. (ii).	1708-1738.
Land Index:	"	"	72.	Meath.	1738-1810.
"	"	"	73.	Louth.	1738-1810.
"	"	"	74.	Carlow, Louth, Meath, Queen's Co. (i).	1821-1825.

Negative 2,147. Positive 2,147.

Land Index:	Vol.	74.	Carlow, Louth, Meath, Queen's Co. (ii).	1821-1825.
"	"	" 75.	Carlow, Louth, Meath, Queen's Co. (ii).	1826-1828.
"	"	" 76.	Limerick.	1739-1810.
"	"	" 77.	Armagh, Cavan (i).	1811-1820.

Negative 2,148. Positive 2,148.

Land Index:	Vol.	77.	Armagh, Cavan (ii).	1811-1820.
"	"	" 78.	Antrim, Armagh.	1821-1825.
"	"	" 79.	Antrim, Armagh.	1826-1828.
"	"	" 80.	City of Cork.	1739-1779.
"	"	" 81.	Carlow (i).	1811-1820.

Negative 2,149. Positive 2,149.

Land Index:	Vol.	81.	Carlow (ii).	1811-1820.
"	"	" 82.	Cavan, Donegal, Down.	1708-1738.
"	"	" 83.	City of Cork.	1779-1810.
"	"	" 84.	Cities of Limerick, Waterford, Londonderry and Drogheda Town.	1811-1820.

Negative 2,150. Positive 2,150.

Land Index:	Vol.	85.	Cities of Limerick, Waterford, Londonderry and Drogheda Town.	1821-1825.
"	"	" 86.	Cities of Waterford, Kilkenny, Londonderry, Limerick, and Town: Drogheda.	1826-1828.
"	"	" 87.	City of Dublin.	1708-1738.
"	"	" 88.	City of Dublin, A-J (i).	1739-1779.

Negative 2,151. Positive 2,151.

Land Index:	Vol.	88.	City of Dublin, A-J (ii).	1739-1779.
"	"	" 89.	City of Dublin, K-Z.	1739-1779.
"	"	" 90.	City of Dublin, A-J.	1780-1792.
"	"	" 91.	City of Dublin, K-Z (i).	1780-1792.

Negative 2,152. Positive 2,152.

Land Index:	Vol.	91.	City of Dublin, K-Z (ii).	1780-1792.
"	"	" 92.	City of Dublin.	1793-1806.
"	"	" 93.	City of Dublin.	1807-1819.

Negative 2,153. Positive 2,153.

Land Index:	Vol.	94.	City of Dublin.	1820-1828.
"	"	" 95.	Antrim.	Aug. 1828-1832.
"	"	" 96.	Armagh (i).	1828.

Negative 2,154. Positive 2,154.

Land Index:	Vol.	96.	Armagh (ii).	1828.
"	"	" 97.	Carlow.	1828-1832.
"	"	" 98.	Cavan.	1828-1832.
"	"	" 99.	Clare (i).	1828-1832.

Negative 2,155. Positive 2,155.

Land Index:	Vol. 99.	Clare (ii).		1828-1832.
" " "	100.	Cork.	15 Aug.	1828-1832.
" " "	101.	Down (i).		1828.

Negative 2,156. Positive 1,156.

Land Index:	Vol. 101.	Down (ii).		1828.
" " "	102.	Donegal.	15 Aug.	1828-1832.
" " "	103.	City of Dublin (i).		1828-1832.

Negative 2,157. Positive 2,157.

Land Index:	Vol. 103.	City of Dublin (ii).		1828-1832.
" " "	104.	Dublin.		1828-1832.
" " "	105.	Fermanagh.	Aug.	1828-1832.
" " "	106.	Galway (i).	"	1828.

Negative 2,158. Positive 2,158.

Land Index:	Vol. 106.	Galway (ii).	Aug.	1828-1832.
" " "	107.	Kerry.	"	1828-1832.
" " "	108.	Kildare (i).	"	1828-1832.

Negative 2,159. Positive 2,159.

Land Index:	Vol. 108.	Kildare.	Aug.	1828-1832.
" " "	109.	Kilkenny.	"	1828-1832.
" " "	110.	King's Co.	"	1828-1832.
" " "	111.	Leitrim.	"	1828-1832.
" " "	112.	Limerick (i).	"	1828-1832.

Negative 2,160. Positive 2,160.

Land Index:	Vol. 112.	Limerick (ii).	Aug.	1828-1832.
" " "	113.	Londonderry.	"	1828-1832.
" " "	114.	Longford.	"	1828-1832.
" " "	115.	Louth.	"	1828-1832.
" " "	116.	Mayo (i).	"	1828-1832.

Negative 2,161. Positive 2,161.

Land Index:	Vol. 116.	Mayo (ii).	Aug.	1828-1832.
" " "	117.	Meath.	"	1828-1832.
" " "	118.	Monaghan.	"	1828-1832.

Negative 2,162. Positive 2,162.

Land Index:	Vol. 119.	Queen's Co.	Aug.	1828-1832.
" "	120.	Roscommon.	"	1828-1832.
" " "	121.	Sligo.	"	1828-1832.
" " "	122.	Tipperary (i).	"	1828-1832.

Negative 2,163. Positive 2,163.

Land Index:	Vol. 122.	Tipperary (ii).	Aug.	1828-1832.
" " "	123.	Tyrone.	"	1828-1832.
" " "	124.	Waterford.	"	1828-1832.
" " "	125.	Waterford City	Aug.	1828-1832.
" " "	126.	Westmeath (i).	"	1828-1832.

Negative 2,164. Positive 2,164.

Land Index:	Vol.	126.	Westmeath (ii).	August.	1828-1832.
"	"	" 127.	Wexford.	"	1828-1832.
"	"	" 128.	Wicklow.	"	1828-1832.
"	"	" 129.	Cities of Belfast, Cork, Drogheda Town, Kilkenny (i).	Aug.	1828-1832.

Negative 2,165. Positive 2,165.

Land Index:	Vol.	129.	Cities of Kilkenny (ii), Limerick, Londonderry.	Aug.	1828-1832.
"	"	" 130A	Towns, A-H.		1828-1832.
"	"	" 130B	Towns, J-Z.		1828-1832.
"	"	" 131.	Antrim.		1833-1836.
"	"	" 132.	Armagh (i).		1833-1835.

Negative 2,166. Positive 2,166.

Land Index:	Vol.	132.	Armagh (ii).		1833-1835.
"	"	" 133.	Carlow.		1833-1835.
"	"	" 134.	Cavan.		1833-1835.
"	"	" 135.	Cities of Cork, Kilkenny, Limerick, Londonderry; Towns of Belfast, Drogheda.		1833-1835.
"	"	" 136.	Clare.		1833-1835.
"	"	" 137.	Cork (i).		1833-1835.

Negative 2,167. Positive 2,167.

Land Index:	Vol.	137.	Cork (ii).		1833-1835.
"	"	" 138.	Donegal.		1833-1835.
"	"	" 139.	Down (Baronies Ards to Newry).		1833-1835.
"	"	" 140.	Dublin (i).		1833-1835.

Negative 2,168. Positive 2,168.

Land Index:	Vol.	140.	Dublin (ii).		1833-1835.
"	"	" 141.	City of Dublin.		1833-1835.
"	"	" 142.	Fermanagh.		1833-1835.
"	"	" 143.	Galway (i).		1833-1835.

Negative 2,169. Positive 2,169.

Land Index:	Vol.	143.	Galway (ii).		1833-1835.
"	"	" 144.	Kerry.		1833-1835.
"	"	" 145.	Kildare.		1833-1835.
"	"	" 146.	Kilkenny.		1833-1835.
"	"	" 147.	King's.		1833-1835.

Negative 2,170. Positive 2,170.

Land Index:	Vol.	148.	Leitrim.		1833-1835.
"	"	" 149.	Limerick.		1833-1835.
"	"	" 150.	Londonderry.		1833-1835.
"	"	" 151.	Longford.		1833-1835.
"	"	" 152.	Louth.		1833-1835.
"	"	" 153.	Mayo (i).		1833-1835.

Negative 2,171. Positive 2,171.

Land Index:	Vol. 153.	Mayo (ii).	1833-1835.
" "	" 154.	Meath.	1833-1835.
" "	" 155.	Monaghan.	1833-1835.
" "	" 156.	Queen's (i).	1833-1835.

Negative 2,172. Positive 2,172.

Land Index:	Vol. 156.	Queen's (ii).	1833-1835.
" "	" 157.	Roscommon.	1833-1835.
" "	" 158.	Sligo.	1833-1835.
" "	" 159.	Tipperary.	1833-1835.
" "	" 160.	Tyrone.	1833-1835.

Negative 2,173. Positive 2,173.

Land Index:	Vol. 161.	Corporation towns.	1833-1835.
" "	" 162.	City of Waterford.	1833-1835.
" "	" 163.	Waterford.	1833-1835.
" "	" 164.	Westmeath.	1833-1835.
" "	" 165.	Wexford.	1833-1835.
" "	" 166.	Wicklow.	1833-1835.

Negative 2,174. Positive 2,174.

Land Index:	Vol. 167.	Antrim to Carlow. No baronies.	1833-1835.
" "	" 168.	Cavan to Cork. No baronies.	1833-1835.
" "	" 169.	Donegal to Dublin. No baronies.	1833-1835.
" "	" 170.	Fermanagh to Kerry. No baronies.	1833-1835.
" "	" 171.	Kildare to King's. No baronies.	1833-1835.
" "	" 172.	Leitrim to Louth. No baronies.	1833-1835.
" "	" 173.	Londonderry to Mayo (i). No baronies.	1833-1835.

Negative 2,175. Positive 2,175.

Land Index:	Vol. 173.	Londonderry to Mayo (ii). No baronies.	1833-1835.
" "	" 174.	Meath, Monaghan, Queen's. No baronies.	1833-1835.
" "	" 175.	Roscommon, Tipperary. No baronies.	1833-1835.
" "	" 176.	Tyrone, Westmeath. No baronies.	1833-1835.
" "	" 177.	Wexford, Wicklow. No baronies.	1833-1835.
" "	" 178.	Dublin city, Waterford city.	1833-1835.

Negative 2,176. Positive 2,176.

Land Index:	Vol. 179.	Antrim.	1836-1839.
" "	" 180.	Armagh.	1836-1839.
" "	" 181.	Carlow.	1836-1839.
" "	" 182.	Cavan (i).	1836-1839.

Negative 2,177. Positive 2,177.

Land Index:	Vol. 182.	Cavan (ii).	1836-1839.
"	"	" 183.	Cities of Belfast, Cork, Kilkenny, Limerick, Londonderry, and Drog- heda Town.	1836-1839.
"	"	" 184.	Clare.	1836-1839.
"	"	" 185.	Cork city (i).	1836-1839.

Negative 2,178. Positive 2,178.

Land Index:	Vol. 185.	Cork city (ii).	1836-1839.
"	"	" 186.	Cork.	1836-1839.
"	"	" 187.	Donegal.	1836-1839.
"	"	" 188.	Down.	1836-1839.

Negative 2,179. Positive 2,179.

Land Index:	Vol. 189.	Dublin City.	1836-1839.
"	"	" 190.	Dublin.	1836-1839.
"	"	" 191.	Fermanagh.	1836-1839.

Negative 2,180. Positive 2,180.

Land Index:	Vol. 192.	Galway.	1836-1839.
"	"	" 193.	Kerry.	1836-1839.
"	"	" 194.	Kildare (i).	1836-1839.

Negative 2,181. Positive 2,181.

Land Index:	Vol. 194.	Kildare (ii).	1836-1839.
"	"	" 195.	Kilkenny.	1836-1839.
"	"	" 196.	King's.	1836-1839.
"	"	" 197.	Londonderry.	1836-1839.
"	"	" 198.	Limerick (i).	1836-1839.

Negative 2,182. Positive 2,182.

Land Index:	Vol. 198.	Limerick (ii).	1836-1839.
"	"	" 199.	Leitrim.	1836-1839.
"	"	" 200.	Longford.	1836-1839.
"	"	" 201.	Louth.	1836-1839.
"	"	" 202.	Mayo.	1836-1839.

Negative 2,183. Positive 2,183.

Land Index:	Vol. 203.	Meath	
"	"	" 204.	Meath.	1836-1839.
"	"	" 205.	Monaghan.	1836-1839.
"	"	" 206.	Queen's.	1836-1839.
"	"	" 207.	Roscommon (i).	1836-1839.

Negative 2,184. Positive 2,184.

Land Index:	Vol. 207.	Roscommon (ii).	1836-1839.
"	"	" 208.	Sligo.	1836-1839.
"	"	" 209.	Tipperary.	1836-1839.
"	"	" 210.	Tyrone (i).	1836-1839.

Negative 2,185. Positive 2,185.

Land Index:	Vol. 210.	Tyrone (ii).	1836-1839.
" "	" 211.	Waterford.	1836-1839.
" "	" 212.	Waterford city.	1836-1839.
" "	" 213.	Westmeath.	1836-1839.
" "	" 214.	Wexford.	1836-1839.
" "	" 215.	Wicklow (i).	1836-1839.

Negative 2,186. Positive 2,186.

Land Index:	Vol. 215.	Wicklow (ii).	1836-1839.
" "	" 216.	Corporation towns.	1836-1839.
" "	" 217.	Antrim to Cork. No baronies.	1836-1839.
" "	" 218.	Donegal to Fermanagh. No baronies.	1836-1839.

Negative 2,187. Positive 2,187.

Land Index:	Vol. 219.	Galway to Leitrim. No baronies.	1836-1839.
" "	" 220.	Limerick to Meath. No baronies.	1836-1839.

Negative 2,188. Positive 2,188.

Land Index:	Vol. 221.	Monaghan to Waterford. No baronies.	1836-1839.
" "	" 222.	Westmeath to Wicklow and cities of Dublin and Waterford. No baronies.	1836-1839.
" "	" 223.	Antrim. Vol. I.	1840-1844.
" "	" 224.	Antrim. Vol. II. (i).	1840-1844.

Negative 2,189. Positive 2,189.

Land Index:	Vol. 224.	Antrim. Vol. II. (ii).	1840-1844.
" "	" 225.	Armagh.	1840-1844.
" "	" 226.	Carlow.	1840-1844.
" "	" 227.	Cavan.	1840-1844.
" "	" 228.	Clare (i).	1840-1844.

Negative 2,190. Positive 2,190.

Land Index:	Vol. 228.	Clare (ii).	1840-1844.
" "	" 229.	Cork. Vol. I.	1840-1844.
" "	" 230.	Cork. Vol. II.	1840-1844.
" "	" 231.	Donegal (i).	1840-1844.

Negative 2,191. Positive 2,191.

Land Index:	Vol. 231.	Donegal (ii).	1840-1844.
" "	" 232.	Down.	1840-1844.
" "	" 233.	Dublin City. Vol. I.	1840-1844.
" "	" 234.	Dublin City. Vol. II.	1840-1844.
" "	" 235.	Dublin (i).	1840-1844.

Negative 2,192. Positive 2,192.

Land Index:	Vol. 235.	Dublin (ii).	1840-1844.
" "	" 236.	Fermanagh.	1840-1844.
" "	" 237.	Galway. Vol. I.	1840-1844.
" "	" 238.	Galway. Vol. II. (i).	1840-1844.

Negative 2,193. Positive 2,193.

Land Index:	Vol. 238.	Galway. Vol. II. (ii).	1840-1844.
"	"	"	239.	Kerry.	1840-1844.
"	"	"	240.	Kildare.	1840-1844.
"	"	"	241.	Kilkenny.	1840-1844.

Negative 2,194. Positive 2,194.

Land Index:	Vol. 242.	King's Co.	1840-1844.
"	"	"	243.	Leitrim.	1840-1844.
"	"	"	244.	Limerick.	1840-1844.
"	"	"	245.	Londonderry.	1840-1844.
"	"	"	246.	Longford (i).	1840-1844.

Negative 2,195. Positive 2,195.

Land Index:	Vol. 246.	Longford (ii).	1840-1844.
"	"	"	247.	Louth.	1840-1844.
"	"	"	248.	Mayo.	1840-1844.
"	"	"	249.	Meath. Vol. I.	1840-1844.
"	"	"	250.	Meath. Vol. II. (i).	1840-1844.

Negative 2,196. Positive 2,196.

Land Index:	Vol. 250.	Meath. Vol. II. (ii).	1840-1844.
"	"	"	251.	Monaghan.	1840-1844.
"	"	"	252.	Queen's	1840-1844.
"	"	"	253.	Roscommon.	1840-1844.
"	"	"	254.	Sligo (i).	1840-1844.

Negative 2,197. Positive 2,197.

Land Index:	Vol. 254.	Sligo (ii).	1840-1844.
"	"	"	255.	Tipperary. Vol. I.	1840-1844.
"	"	"	256.	Tipperary. Vol. II.	1840-1844.
"	"	"	257.	Tyrone.	1840-1844.
"	"	"	258.	Waterford.	1840-1844.
"	"	"	259.	Westmeath (i).	1840-1844.

Negative 2,198. Positive 2,198.

Land Index:	Vol. 259.	Westmeath (ii).	1840-1844.
"	"	"	260.	Wexford.	1840-1844.
"	"	"	261.	Wicklow.	1840-1844.
"	"	"	262.	Waterford city.	1840-1844.
"	"	"	263.	Towns (i).	1840-1844.

Negative 2,199. Positive 2,199.

Land Index:	Vol. 263.	Towns (ii).	1840-1844.
"	"	"	264.	Belfast and Cork cities.	1840-1844.
"	"	"	265.	Drogheda town and cities of Kilkenny, Limerick and Londonderry.	1840-1844.
"	"	"	266.	Antrim to Cork. No baronies.	1840-1844.

Negative 2,200. Positive 2,200.

Land Index:	Vol. 267.	Donegal to Fermanagh. No baronies.	1840-1844.
"	"	" 268.	Galway to Leitrim. No baronies.	1840-1844.

Negative 2,201. Positive 2,201.

Land Index:	Vol. 269.	Limerick to Meath. No baronies.	1840-1844.
"	"	" 270.	Monaghan to Westmeath (i). No baronies.	1840-1844.

Negative 2,202. Positive 2,202.

Land Index:	Vol. 270.	Monaghan to Westmeath (ii). No baronies.	1840-1844.
"	"	" 271.	Wexford, Wicklow and cities of Dublin and Waterford. No baronies.	1840-1844.
"	"	" 272.	Antrim. Vol. I.	1845-1849.
"	"	" 273.	Antrim. Vol. II. (i).	1845-1849.

Negative 2,203. Positive 2,203.

Land Index:	Vol. 273.	Antrim. Vol. II. (ii).	1845-1849.
"	"	" 274.	Armagh.	1845-1849.
"	"	" 275.	Carlow.	1845-1849.
"	"	" 276.	Cavan.	1845-1849.
"	"	" 277.	Clare (i).	1845-1849.

Negative 2,204. Positive 2,204.

Land Index:	Vol. 277.	Clare (ii).	1845-1849.
"	"	" 278.	Cork. Vol. I.	1845-1849.
"	"	" 279.	Cork. Vol. II.	1845-1849.
"	"	" 280.	Cork. Vol. III.	1845-1849.
"	"	" 281.	Donegal (i).	1845-1849.

Negative 2,205. Positive 2,205.

Land Index:	Vol. 281.	Donegal (ii).	1845-1849.
"	"	" 282.	Down.	1845-1849.
"	"	" 283.	Dublin.	1845-1849.
"	"	" 284.	Dublin city, Vol. I.	1845-1849.

Negative 2,206. Positive 2,206.

Land Index:	Vol. 285.	Dublin city. Vol. II.	1845-1849.
"	"	" 286.	Fermanagh.	1845-1849.
"	"	" 287.	Galway. Vol. I.	1845-1849.
"	"	" 288.	Galway. Vol. II.	1845-1849.

Negative 2,207. Positive 2,207.

Land Index:	Vol. 289.	Kerry.	1845-1849.
"	"	" 290.	Kildare.	1845-1849.
"	"	" 291.	Kilkenny.	1845-1849.
"	"	" 292.	King's (i).	1845-1849.

Negative 2,208. Positive 2,208.

Land Index:	Vol.	292.	King's (ii).	1845-1849.
″ ″	″	293.	Londonderry.	1845-1849.
″ ″	″	294.	Longford.	1845-1849.
″ ″	″	295.	Limerick.	1845-1849.
″ ″	″	296.	Leitrim.	1845-1849.
″ ″	″	297.	Louth.	1845-1849.
″ ″	″	298.	Mayo (i).	1845-1849.

Negative 2,209. Positive 2,209.

Land Index:	Vol.	298.	Mayo (ii).	1845-1849.
″ ″	″	299.	Meath. Vol. I.	1845-1849.
″ ″	″	300.	Meath. Vol. II.	1845-1849.
″ ″	″	301.	Monaghan.	1845-1849.
″ ″	″	302.	Queen's. (i).	1845-1849.

Negative 2,210. Positive 2,210.

Land Index:	Vol.	302.	Queen's (ii).	1845-1849.
″ ″	″	303.	Roscommon.	1845-1849.
″ ″	″	304.	Sligo.	1845-1849.
″ ″	″	305.	Tipperary. Vol. I.	1845-1849.
″ ″	″	306.	Tipperary. Vol. II. (i).	1845-1849.

Negative 2,211. Positive 2,211.

Land Index:	Vol.	306.	Tipperary. Vol. II. (ii).	1845-1849.
″ ″	″	307.	Tyrone.	1845-1849.
″ ″	″	308.	Westmeath.	1845-1849.
″ ″	″	309.	Waterford.	1845-1849.
″ ″	″	310.	Wexford. (i).	1845-1849.

Negative 2,212. Positive 2,212.

Land Index:	Vol.	310.	Wexford (ii).	1845-1849.
″ ″	″	311.	Wicklow.	1845-1849.
″ ″	″	312.	Belfast and Cork cities.	1845-1849.
″ ″	″	313.	Corporation towns.	1845-1849.
″ ″	″	314.	Waterford city.	1845-1849.
″ ″	″	315.	Antrim to Cork (i). No baronies.	1845-1849.

Negative 2,213. Positive 2,213.

Land Index:	Vol.	315.	Antrim to Cork (ii). No baronies.	1845-1849.
″ ″	″	316.	Dublin, Donegal to Fermanagh. No baronies.	1845-1849.
″ ″	″	317.	Galway to Leitrim. No baronies.	1845-1849.
″ ″	″	318.	Limerick to Meath. No baronies.	1845-1849.
″ ″	″	319.	Monaghan to Westmeath (i). No baronies.	1845-1849.

Negative 2,214. Positive 2,214.

Land Index:	Vol.	319.	Monaghan to Westmeath (ii). No baronies.	1845-1849.
„	„	„ 320.	Wexford, Wicklow, and cities of Dublin and Waterford. No baronies.	1845-1849.
„	„	„ 321.	Town of Drogheda; cities of Kilkenny, Limerick and Londonderry.	1845-1849.
„	„	„ 322.	Antrim. Vol. I. (i).	1850-1854.

IRISH LAND MEASURES

The Irish measurements of land from early times are encountered in land records well into the eighteenth century. The old Irish acre contained 7,840 square yards, however shaped; 100 acres of the early Irish measurement being equal to 162 statute acres of the nineteenth century and today. A statute acre contains 4,840 square yards.

The *Book of Survey and Distribution, County of Roscommon*, edited by Robert C. Simington, Dublin, 1949 (Introduction xxxviii), gives the following definitions of early land measures used in the Cromwellian period: "From these computations, it would appear that the Quarter contained 120 native acres [of 7,840 square yards each]; the Carton 30 and the Gneeve—a sixth—20 acres. In the Table, however, printed with the *Census of Townlands* the Gneeve is given as being the twelfth of a Quarter. The Gneeve, states Larcom, was a space of 10 acres; but the acres were . . . by estimation only, and differed considerably." Simington *(ibid.)* also states, ". . . it is not easy to say whether a 'Trine' represented a third of a Quarter or a greater measure. As regards 'Ings' the . . . (p. 114) refers to . . . 1 Quarter divided amongst several men into 'Ings'; this denomination is admeasured as containing 200 acres of profitable land and 202 acres unprofitable."

By rough estimate the old measurements previous to the nineteenth century are as follows:

One Gneeve	contained	10 acres		
One Sessiagh	contained	20 acres	or	2 Gneeves
One Carton	contained	30 acres	or	3 Gneeves
One Tate	contained	60 acres	or	2 Cartons
One Ballyboe	contained	60 acres	or	1 Tate
One Quarter	contained	120 acres	or	2 Ballyboes
One Ploughland	contained	120 acres	or	1 Quarter
One Seisreagh	contained	120 acres	or	1 Ploughland
One Ballybetagh	contained	480 acres	or	4 Seisreaghs

One Townland   contained more or less than 480 acres, or 1 Bally-
    betagh.
One Trioca Cead or Barony contained on an average about 30 Ballybe-
    taghs.

* * * * *

The statute acre of today and during the nineteenth century
contains four roods, each equal to 40 square rods or square
poles, or 1,210 square yards. The statute acre also contains
160 perch of 30¼ square yards each. These modern measurements are mentioned in the illustrations given below.

EXAMPLE: SOME RECORDS OF THE DICKSON FAMILY IN THE REGISTRY OF DEEDS, DUBLIN

This is an example of successful work accomplished by correspondence with the Registry of Deeds, Dublin. Information
was first taken from copies of the microfilms of the NAMES
INDEX which are in the National Library of Ireland, Dublin.
Twenty-four copies of memorials of records were ordered,
of which seventeen concerned the family under study.

The problem was to prove the geographical origin of
Francis Dickson, Sr., who emigrated to America in 1819, and
to find his genealogical records. Tradition assumed that his
children were born in Belfast because he emigrated from that
place. This was proved to be untrue.

The indexes of the Public Record Office of Northern Ireland,
Belfast, offered no clue to the identity of Francis Dickson, Sr.
Earlier Dickson and allied family records in this repository
were later recognized as concerning this family. But the
identifying connection was contained in the records of the
Registry of Deeds, Dublin.

Space does not permit the presentation of the full genealogy of this branch of the Dickson family. Therefore, only the preliminary steps in the United States and abstracts of records in the Registry of Deeds, 1747-1824, will be presented with brief notes as they revealed four generations in the abstracts. This information led to earlier material which will be offered as illustrations in the chapter concerning Quaker records and among some other sources, all of which are indexed in this volume.

FAMILY TRADITION: Francis Dickson, Sr., emigrated to the United States from Belfast, Ireland, in 1819. He landed in Philadelphia, Pennsylvania, then going to Vincennes, Indiana; Mt. Carmel, Illinois; Albion, Illinois; Hillsboro, Illinois, where he died. He came with a wife, Jane, sons William and Francis, Jr., who were adult, and a daughter, Jane. A daughter, Martha, married a Kennedy in Ireland and later came to Hillsboro as a widow with children. A daughter, Margaret, married a Seymour in Ireland and went with him to South Carolina, later coming to Hillsboro, Illinois. William Dickson settled in Philadelphia where he and his wife, whom he married in Ireland, soon died leaving children, of whom Henry, the youngest, was put in the care of his uncle, Francis, Jr., who had gone to Indiana and later to Albion, Illinois, with his father. There he married Ellen Clark in about 1830. The two went to Louisville, Kentucky, where she died in about 1842, leaving three children: Edwin, William and Joseph. Francis, Jr., married a second time and moved to Owensboro, Kentucky, where he died in 1850. He and his first wife were buried in Louisville, Kentucky.

PRELIMINARY RESEARCH IN THE UNITED STATES: Deeds, wills, and records of marriage, census, naturalization, and tombstones, as well as county histories, completed the American genealogy of this family. Two county histories provided the clue which served to locate the Dickson family records in the Registry of Deeds, Dublin, with positive identification. Three county histories are quoted:

The History of Edwards, Lawrence and Wabash Counties, Illinois, 1883, p. 224: "DR. HENRY L. DICKSON was born in the city of Philadelphia, Pennsylvania. His father was William Dickson, a merchant of that city. His mother's name was Rebecca Culloden. They were both natives of Ireland and both died when Henry was a small child. Together with a brother Francis, now a book-keeper in Louisville, Kentucky, he was raised by his grandfather and an uncle. In 1820, he was brought to Vincennes, Indiana."

The History of Kentucky, by Johnson. Vol. II, p. 1092: "Francis Culloden Dickson," born in Louisville, Kentucky, May 5, 1857, was the son of Francis William Dickson, who was born in Belfast, Ireland, in 1812, the son of William Dickson, who with his wife, the former Lady Culloden, and father, one brother Francis and the above F. W. Dickson, then an infant, came to the United States about 1819, landing in Philadelphia where the family settled and the elder Dicksons engaged in merchandising. In 1826, after securing a fine education, he left Philadelphia to live with his Uncle Francis . . . and located in Illinois, where the Uncle was in merchandising in Mt. Carmel, Illinois and Vincennes, Indiana."

History of Johnson County, Indiana, 1888. Part II, p. 786: "Francis Dickson, born Aug. 8, 1850, the son of Francis and Maria (Bliss) Dickson, the former of whom was born in Belfast, Ireland, and grew to early manhood in his native country, but emigrated to America at about the age of twenty-four. Reaching this country, he spent some time in Philadelphia, and afterward came west and was married in the state of Illinois to Ellen Clark, who died about 1840. About 1842, he married Maria G. Bliss, the mother of our subject. The father and mother of our subject were married in Louisville, Ky., and the father died in Owensboro, Kentucky, December 26, 1851. The first marriage of Francis Dickson, father of our subject, resulted in three children, Edwin, William and Joseph."

The statement in the above reference, by a child of the second wife of Francis Dickson, Jr., that he was born in Belfast, was confused with the fact that, as the Irish land records show, he lived in Belfast from about age fifteen to twenty-four, when he emigrated from there. The identifying clue which served to place the family with proof in Ireland, was the maiden name of the wife of William Dickson, son of Francis Dickson, Sr., which was Rebecca Culloden. She was so named in the biography of her son, Dr. Henry Dickson. She was not "Lady" Culloden, as claimed by her grandson, Francis Culloden Dickson. Her deceased father was named in her marriage settlement as "farmer."

Francis Dickson, Jr., was, on April 20, 1820, appointed guardian of the four children of his deceased brother, William, of Philadelphia; his wife, Rebecca, having predeceased him. The children were Jemima, Elizabeth, Francis William, and Henry L. (Knox Co., Ind. Deed Book E. p. 63.)

A note about the tombstone records of the Dickson family will serve to clarify the records. Inscriptions on tombstones in Hillsboro, Illinois are:

"Francis Dickson, born Sept. 25, 1759, died Jan. 11, 1834."

"Jane, relict of Francis Dickson, born June 22, 1760, died Jan. 4, 1853."

"Jane Dickson, died Feb. 19, 1878, in her 85th year."

"Margaret Seymour, died July 2, 1877, in her 70th year."

Tombstones in Louisville, Kentucky, show the following inscriptions:

"Francis Dickson, born 1796, died Dec. 26, 1850."

"Ellen Dickson, born May 30, 1812, died Feb. 2, 1842."

The microfilms of the NAMES INDEX of the Registry of Deeds, Dublin, were examined from copies of those made for the National Library of Ireland, Dublin. All items for the Dickson family within the periods between 1746 and 1824 were copied. This was a long list. One item appeared: "Dickson, Francis, to Culloden. Vol. 571, p. 497. No. 387653." This seemed an excellent lead, so all items of Dickson grantors, of the given names, Francis and William, were ordered in certified copies from the Registry of Deeds.

The copies of the memorials which were received have been briefly abstracted to present here in the following order:

1. The record which identified this family in Ireland and placed it geographically.

2. The records which proved earlier generations.

3. Records of land which Francis Dickson, Sr., disposed of before leaving Ireland.

RECORDS OF THE REGISTRY OF DEEDS, DUBLIN

No. 387653. Vol. 571, p. 497.

On 13 Sept. 1805, FRANCIS DICKSON, of Ballymena, Co. Antrim, Gent., of the first part; WILLIAM DICKSON, of Belfast, a minor, eldest son of FRANCIS DICKSON, of the second part; JEMIMA CULLODEN, of Mill Street, Dublin, widow and admx., of MICHAEL CULLODEN, and REBECCA CULLODEN, second daughter of said MICHAEL CULLODEN, of Mill Street, deceased, "farmer," of the third part; PATRICK CULLODEN, of Strand Mills, and JOHN LOVE, of Ballymena, of the fourth part. MARRIAGE AGREEMENT between WILLIAM DICKSON and REBECCA CULLODEN; her portion of her father's estate, 1,000 pounds sterling. 700 pounds sterling advanced to WILLIAM DICKSON. FRANCIS and WILLIAM DICKSON gave 1,000 pound bond to JEMIMA and PATRICK CULLODEN and JOHN LOVE, to insure the safe keeping of the money and its ultimate disposal to the heirs of REBECCA CULLODEN.

NOTE: This marriage was recorded in *Walker's Hibernian Magazine*, Dublin. *Irish Marriages*, being an index to the marriages in this magazine, 1771-1812, by Henry Farrar, 1897, vol. 1, shows: "Dickson, Wm. to Culloden, Miss, Dublin. at Belfast, Jan. 1806." Ballymena, County Antrim, is about forty miles north-west of Belfast.

No. 340917. Vol. 519, p. 440.

On 9 Jan. 1798, FRANCIS DICKSON, of Ballymena, Co. Antrim, "Innholder," and JOHN ALEXANDER, of Ballymena, "Merchant," in trust for and for the use and benefit of MORGAN DICKSON, brother of said FRANCIS DICKSON, Sergeant, 13th Regiment. FRANCIS DICKSON leased to JOHN ALEXANDER, that farm in the town and lands of DERGANAH, in the Proportion of Vintners, County Londonderry, with messuages and tenements, gardens, etc., belonging and formerly in the possession of WILLIAM FLEMMING, MORGAN WILLSON, and then FRANCIS DICKSON and HANNAH DICKSON. Witnessed by NATHANIEL MCCULLAGH, and WILLIAM DICKSON, brewer, 9 Jan. 1798. Also witnessed by PETER AIKEN, of Harryville, Gent.

NOTE: This "town and lands of Derganah" (misspelled) was the townland of Derganagh, containing 341 acres, in the

parish of Termoneeny, barony of Loughinsholin, County Londonderry, also in the district of Bellaghy, which appears in
later land records of Francis Dickson, Sr., who emigrated in
1819. The parish of Termoneeny was about 15 miles west of
Ballymena, County Antrim. The property in the townland
of Derganagh came into the possession of Morgan Dickson
from his mother Hannah (Willson) Dickson, wife of Francis
Dickson, who received it from her father, Morgan Willson,
who appears in their marriage settlement, 1747, below. At
this time (1747), Morgan Willson was living on the townland
of Lemnaroy, in the same parish of Termoneeny, in which
his townland property of Derganagh was located. Thus Morgan Dickson, his brother Francis Dickson, who emigrated in
1819, and William Dickson, brewer, their brother who witnessed the above transaction (as further records will show),
were all sons of Francis and Hannah (Willson) Dickson.

No. 120335. Vol. 180, p. 238.

On 24 Oct. 1747, MARRIAGE ARTICLES, between WILLIAM
DICKSON, of Ballymacombsbeg, Co. Londonderry, "farmer,"
and MORGAN WILLSON, of Lemnaroy, in said county, "farmer,"
for marriage between FRANCIS DICKSON, son of WILLIAM
DICKSON, and HANNAH WILLSON, eldest daughter of MORGAN
WILLSON. MORGAN WILLSON to pay WILLIAM DICKSON im-
mediately upon the marriage, 30 pounds sterling. WILLIAM
DICKSON to convey and assign to his son FRANCIS DICKSON,
all right and title to all of BALLYMACOMBSBEG, held by lease and
lives renewable forever, under RT. HON. WILLIAM CONOLLY,
ESQ., but not to take effect until the death of WILLIAM DICK-
SON. Witnessed by: JOHN DOWNING, of Rowe's Gift, Co.
Londonderry, Esq., and ANDREW SPOTSWOOD, of Bellaghy, of
said county. JOHN DOWNING, Justice of the Peace.

NOTE: The transcript of the will of Morgan Willson naming Francis Dickson will appear among the Quaker records
in the chapter on such records. Also, the Quaker Marriage
Certificate of Morgan Willson and Hannah Gilbert and other
Quaker records will be given. The townland of Ballymacombsbeg is situated in the parish of Ballyscullion, barony of Loughinsholin, and the district of Bellaghy. This parish is directly
east of the parish of Termoneeny, by about four miles, and in

the same district of Bellaghy. Ballymacombsbeg is about 11 miles west of Ballymena, County Antrim. The townland contains 655 acres and 38 perch. This property does not appear among the records of Francis Dickson, Sr., who emigrated in 1819, or his brother, William. It was probably left to one or both of Thomas and John Dickson who were indicated as brothers in the following records. Their property has not been traced. Francis Dickson, Sr., who emigrated in 1819, was in possession of other property out of Ballymena and near his father's home of Mont Alta, which passed to William Dickson and was later in the possession of his son, Francis.

No. 385066. Vol. 568, pp. 576-8.

On 26 Nov. 1802, FRANCIS DICKSON, of Ballymena, Co. Antrim, "Innkeeper," of the first part; ROBERT STEEL, of Bellaghy, Co. Londonderry, "Malster," of the second part, FRANCIS DICKSON for £260: 06: 03, sterling, leased to ROBERT STEEL, all that Park, marked No. 46, late in the possession of George Mulholland (as a lessee), containing 6 acres, with messuages, tenements, etc., being in the townland of DRUMANEE, Proportion of Vintners, County Londonderry, for the natural lives of FRANCIS DICKSON, son of FRANCIS DICKSON, party thereto; FRANCIS DICKSON, son of WILLIAM DICKSON, of Ballymena; FRANCIS WILLSON, son of GEORGE WILLSON, of Bellaghy, and/or survivors, for the term of the lease made by RT. HON. THOMAS CONOLLY, subject to yearly rent of £2: 17: 04, sterling, etc. Witnesses: WILLIAM DICKSON, of Ballymena, and ALEXANDER BROWN, Attorney, Dublin.

NOTE: Francis Dickson, the above grantor, and his son, Francis, Jr., emigrated in 1819. William Dickson who witnessed the instrument was the brother of the grantor. His son, Francis, was so named. As Francis and George Willson were included, this indicates that the property once was in the possession of Morgan Willson and possibly one of his brothers. This has not as yet been traced. William Dickson had not yet inherited his father's property of Mont Alta.

No. 406146. Vol. 594, p. 545.

On 16 Sept. 1807, WILLIAM RYDER, CAPT., Militia Regt., Kildare, eldest son and heir of ABRAHAM RYDER, of Bray, Co.

Kildare, Gent. MARRIAGE ARTICLES between WILLIAM RYDER and ANN DICKSON, spinster, one of the daughters of WILLIAM DICKSON, of near Ballymena, brewer. The exact amount of the settlement of WILLIAM DICKSON on his daughter ANN, not specified but subject to prior claim of a trust, by which WILLIAM DICKSON was to pay or secure to his sons, JOHN DICKSON and FRANCIS DICKSON, 1000 pounds sterling. WILLIAM RYDER to receive lands of GLENDOWN, Co. Kildare, of 80 acres to settle on himself, etc. Witness: WILLIAM YOUNG, of Ballymena, "Merchant," sworn at Harryville, Co. Antrim.

NOTE: This indicates that William Dickson's sons, John and Francis, were yet unmarried and possibly under age.

No. 407045. Vol. 599, p. 113.

On 18 April, 1807, FRANCIS DICKSON of Ballymena, Gent., leased to JAMES MCILROY, of Ballymena, land at Ballymena, called STONE PARK, containing three acres woodland, bounded on the east by the road to Clough and Brogshane, on the west by the road to Glaryford, from 1 Nov. 1806, at the yearly rent of 3 pounds sterling, payable half yearly, with double years rent every twentieth year. Lease forever. First double years rent, 1820. Witnesses: MR. ROBERT DICKEY, HUGH MCNEILL, ALEXANDER MITCHELL, gentlemen, and MICHAEL HARRISON, Attorney, all of Ballymena.

NOTE: This was a part of a larger tract. See No. 478791 and No. 504552.

No. 419653. Vol. 615, p. 134.

On 20 April, 1809, WILLIAM DICKSON, of Belfast, borrowed from FRANCIS DICKSON, of Ballymena, Co. Antrim, 200 pounds sterling, secured by agreement to give him leases on Belfast property; one tenement leased by William Dickson on 1 May, 1804, from Jane Ramage and Isaac Waring, on the south side of Carrickfergus Peters Hill, 18 feet front and 164 feet depth, for sixty-one years, at the yearly rental of £14: 15: 09, and one tenement leased on 26 Feb. 1850, on the south side of Waring Street, for twenty-one years, at the yearly rental of £22: 15: 00. These two leases made over to FRANCIS DICK-

SON, for the 200 pounds sterling; WILLIAM DICKSON to redeem the leases by returning the borrowed money and interest at 6%. Witnessed by WILLIAM BOURKE of Belfast, Gent.

NOTE: According to tradition, the Dicksons were in the linen business in Belfast before they emigrated. This instrument indicates that William Dickson leased these two places before his marriage, for business and for a home. Three years after his marriage in January 1806, he seems to have exhausted his resources, perhaps including the 1,000 pounds sterling which he received in his marriage settlement from his wife, for which his father had pledged a bond as security. Francis Dickson, thus being involved in any business failure of his son, first loaned him money, and then later at some time after 15 June 1810 and before 1 November 1815 (see No. 431345 and No. 478791) he removed to Belfast with his family to go into business with his son, William, and try to save the situation.

No. 425130. Vol. 619, p. 548.

On 4 Feb. 1810, FRANCIS DICKSON, of the Brewry, leased to NICHOLAS DELACHEROIS CROMMELIN, and SAMUEL KATHERNES, both of the Antrim Regiment of Militia, Esquires, all the dwelling, office houses, gardens, and demesne of Mont Alta, then in the possession and occupation of the said FRANCIS DICKSON, containing 170 acres, 1 rood, 17 perch, for twenty one years, beginning 1 Nov. 1809, at the yearly rent of £106: 05: 00, sterling. Witnesses: JOHN DICKSON and JOHN COURTNEY, both of Ballymena, Co. Antrim.

NOTE: This was the father of Francis Dickson, Sr., who emigrated in 1819. He had a large brewery at Mont Alta and was the only Francis Dickson in this business, as was his son, William. At this time, being about eighty years of age, he probably retired and leased his home and offices, etc. This was only a part of the entire property of 443 acres, 8 perch, of Mont Alta (see No. 501553 and No. 541465, which indicate that by 1818 the property was in the possession of his grandson, Francis Dickson, "Gent." son of William). Francis Dickson, brewer, of Mont Alta, was undoubtedly the original partner with the Galt brothers, engaged in malting and brewing at Coleraine (named in No. 431345, below), using them as an outlet for his product. Proof that Francis Dickson, of the brewery, Mont Alta, was the father of William Dickson, brewer, and Francis Dickson, Sr., who emigrated in 1819, is furnished by the only reference given here outside the land records. *A Statistical Account or Parochial Survey of Ireland,* 3 vols, 1814, by William Shaw Mason, gives a description of Mont Alta, located on the two quarter lands of Skerryravil in the barony of Kilconway, about six miles north of Ballymena. Shaw states that Francis Dickson had many years previously planted trees around the place, he being deceased (before 1814) the grounds were presently in disrepair. This Francis Dickson died after 4 February 1810 when he leased the property and probably before 15 June 1810, when his sons, as shown below, dissolved the partnership. John Dickson, who witnessed the above lease was, undoubtedly, the same as the one mentioned below.

No. 431345. Vol. 625, p. 110.

On 15 June, 1810, DISSOLUTION OF PARTNERSHIP, between JOHN GALT, of Coleraine, Co. Londonderry, "merchant," of the first part; CHARLES GALT, of Millbrook, Co. Antrim, "Merchant," of the second part; JAMES GALT, of Coleraine, "Merchant," of the third part; WILLIAM GALT, of Coleraine, "merchant," of the fourth part; JOHN DICKSON, of Ballymena, Co. Antrim, "merchant," of the fifth part; THOMAS DICKSON, of Ballymena, "merchant," of the sixth part; FRANCIS DICKSON of Ballymena, "merchant," of the seventh part: DISSOLVED THE FIRM OF "GALTS AND DICKSONS", as of 1 Nov. 1809, engaged in malting and brewing, in the town of Coleraine, Co. Londonderry. Witnesses: THOMAS CAVAN, JOHN TAGGART, both of Coleraine, Gentlemen.

NOTE: If Francis Dickson of Mont Alta, brewer, had been a party to the above dissolution, he would have been named first among the Dicksons, and as "brewer." Francis Dickson, "Gentleman," does not appear in the records until 1817 (No. 488619) with his brother, John, also "Gentleman," as trustees of their father William's estate, after which, in 1818, this same Francis Dickson, "Gentleman," leased the second part of his grandfather's Mont Alta property which came to him through his father, William Dickson, undoubtedly the eldest son and largest heir. He, being already set up in the brewing business and the largest heir, probably was not left a share in the smaller matter of dissolving the partnership, which was arranged as of the same date, 1 November 1809, on which Francis Dickson, brewer, of Mont Alta, named the beginning of his lease of that place. Francis Dickson, "merchant" of Ballymena, above, was undoubtedly the Francis Dickson "innkeeper" and also a "merchant" as he leased his "Linen Hall" in Ballymena (No. 504552) before emigrating from Belfast where he was also in the linen business. Thus, it seems certain that Francis and Hannah (Willson) Dickson had five sons, William, John, Thomas, Francis, and Morgan, of which Francis, who emigrated, was born 25 September 1759, twelve years after his parents' marriage in 1747. William, Francis and Morgan are positively identified as sons. John Dickson signed the lease of Mont Alta, to begin on the same day, 1 November 1809, as the dissolution of the partnership in which he was named. Thomas Dickson, named in the same instrument, also witnessed the important Deed of Assignment of Francis Dickson before he emigrated (No. 504393). Thomas Dickson was named "merchant" of Ballymena in 1810, and "attorney" of Ballymoney in 1818. He took part in the dissolution as a merchant but witnessed the latter as an attorney. In a small town he could be both.

No. 478791. Vol. 698, p. 50.

On 1 November 1815, LEASE AND RELEASE, between FRANCIS DICKSON, of Belfast, Co. Antrim, and JANE, his wife, of the first part; THOMAS DICKEY, of Hill Head, Co. Antrim, Esq., of the second part; MICHAEL HARRISON, of Ballymena, of the third part; MARY JONES, of CANADA, widow, of the fourth part. MARY JONES paid FRANCIS DICKSON 950 pounds sterling and for other considerations mentioned. They, FRANCIS DICKSON and JANE, his wife, and THOMAS DICKEY, granted, released and confirmed, according to their respective interests, to MICHAEL HARRISON, attorney (see No. 407045), to hold forever in trust for the sole benefit, use and behoof of MARY JONES, property now in the hands of MR. JOHN TRACY, collector of taxes, property lying on the Ballymena road to Brogshane, and adjoining the town of Ballymena, called FARM LODGE, containing 8 acres of woodland, with dwelling house, offices, and gardens. JANE DICKSON released MICHAEL HARRISON from paying her dower in case she should survive FRANCIS DICKSON. Witnesses: JOHN TRACY, of Ballymena, THOMAS MERCER of Birnie, of Dunminning, Co. Antrim; ALEX STEWART, and RICHARD DAVISON, of Belfast.

NOTE: This property, with dwelling house and offices, was a part of a unit of property which included also six parks of land containing in addition to the dwelling, gardens and offices, the "Old Linen Hall," three cabins and the mill race (see No. 407045 and No. 504552). This was probably the home place of Francis Dickson before he left Ballymena, where he carried on his linen manufacture. From here on, Francis Dickson's land transactions disposing of his Ballymena and Co. Londonderry property before leaving Ireland, took place from Belfast.

No. 488619. Vol. 714, p. 284.

On 28 February 1817, RECONVEYANCE OF A MORTGAGE, made between JOHN DICKSON and FRANCIS DICKSON, both of Ballymena, Co. Antrim, Gentlemen, EXECUTORS of WILLIAM DICKSON, deceased, late of Ballymena, of the one part, and THOMAS McPEAKE, of Coleraine, eldest son and heir of THOMAS McPEAKE, late of Coleraine, Co. Londonderry, deceased, of the other part. JOHN DICKSON and FRANCIS DICKSON, were paid £425: 11: 00 sterling by THOMAS McPEAKE for property in his possession, by lease of one year, being all that part of WEST DIVISION OF BALLYMACPEAKE, in the barony of LOGHENSHOLLEN, Co. Londonderry, it now being occupied by SAMUEL EVANS, MARK DOUGHERTY, PATRICK CUSHLY, PHELIMY DIAMOND, JAMES and PATRICK KEENAN, Srs. and Jrs., and that part formerly occupied by JOHN CASHIDY. THOMAS MCPEAKE to be free of the mortgage. Witnesses: THOMAS CASEMENT, Gent., and ROGER CASEMENT, attorney, both of Harryville, Co. Antrim.

NOTE: These two, John and Francis Dickson, "Gentlemen," then residing in Ballymena, were the two sons of William Dickson named in his trust in the marriage settlement for his daughter, Ann (see No. 406146).

No. 501553. Vol. 736, p. 18.

On 20 November 1818, FRANCIS DICKSON of Ballymena, Co. Antrim, Gent., of the one part; NICHOLAS DELACHEROIS CROM-MELIN, of Carrodore, Co. Down, Esq., of the second part; whereby FRANCIS DICKSON did lease to NICHOLAS D. CROM-MELIN, that coarse Heath or Mountain Farm in SKERRYRAVIL, containing 301 acres, 1 rood, 17 perch, also the dwelling house, outhouses, offices, gardens, and demesne of MONT ALTA, in Skerryravil, of 170 acres, 1 rood, 17 perch, and also the land adjoining, containing 27 acres then in the possession of MANUS O'HAMILL, all together, 498 acres, 2 roods, 34 perch, all being in the barony of KILCONWAY, together with all houses, outhouses, gardens, orchards, mills, mill-races, etc., for the rent of 180 pounds sterling, half-yearly, over and above taxes. Witnesses: ALEX. STEWART, and THOS. AINSWORYH, both of Belfast.

NOTE: In this transaction, Francis Dickson, "Gentleman," leased the whole Mont Alta property, of which his grandfather on 4 February 1810, signed the lease beginning 1 November 1809, for 170 acres, etc., including the above dwelling house, etc., to Nicholas D. Crommelin and Samuel Kathernes. This new lease before the 21-year term was expired, replaced the old one, dropping off Samuel Kathernes, and leasing the entire property for about 254 pounds sterling more rent. See No. 425130.

No. 504393. Vol. 740, p. 458.

On 1 November 1818, FRANCIS DICKSON of Belfast, of the

first part; ANDREW WILLSON, of Bellaghy, Co. Londonderry, "carpenter," of the second part: FRANCIS DICKSON, for £68:05:00 sterling, did make DEED OF ASSIGNMENT of the tenement in Bellaghy, marked No. 6, and No. 33, formerly occupied by EZECHAEL SCULLION, being in the Proportion of Vintners, Co. Londonderry, to hold during the lives of FRANCIS DICKSON, son of the said FRANCIS DICKSON, party hereto; FRANCIS DICKSON, son of WILLIAM DICKSON, of Ballymena, deceased, and FRANCIS WILLSON, son of GEORGE WILLSON, of Bellaghy, and the survivors, etc., for the period named. Witnesses: WILLIAM DUFFIN, of Oatlands, and THOMAS DICKSON, of Ballymoney, attorney. Sworn at Belfast.

NOTE: This was Francis Dickson, Sr., who emigrated in 1819, disposing of Willson property, possibly in preparation for emigration after the following May, 1819; setting the terms of the assignment for the lifetimes of his son, Francis, Jr., his brother's son, Francis, and a Willson relative. His brother (no doubt) Thomas Dickson, witnessed the instrument, as attorney, to see that it was properly executed.

No. 504552. Vol. 741, p. 17.

On 16 March, 1819, FRANCIS DICKSON, of Belfast, of the first part; THOMAS DICKEY, of Leghinmore, County Antrim, Esq., of the second part; MICHAEL HARRISON, of Ballymena, Attorney at Law, of the third part: ARCHIBALD TAYLOR, of Ballymena, Esq., of the fourth part. FRANCIS DICKSON, THOMAS DICKEY and MICHAEL HARRISON, granted, leased, etc., all the lands, tenements, namely all six Parks of land together with the Park called STONE PARK, (see No. 407045), containing a total of 25 acres, 3 roods, 4 perch, (save the part called FARM LODGE (see No. 478791, containing 8 acres), situate near Ballymena, on the great road leading from Ballymena to Brougshane, together with the tenement called THE OLD LINEN HALL, and three cabins next north, all situate in Castle Street, in Ballymena; also one lot of ground in the rear, lying between them and the mill-race, and the whole of which were then in the actual possession of FRANCIS DICKSON and his under-tenants, situate in the Lower Half Barony of Toome, Co. Antrim. LEASE to ARCHIBALD TAYLOR, forever, subject to payment of chief rent and conditions in ORIGINAL LEASE, granted by JAMES STEWART. Witnesses: JAMES ALEXANDER and JOHN KILLEN, both of Ballymena. Signed by FRANCIS DICKSON, THOMAS DICKEY, and MICHAEL HARRISON, he of Ballymena.

No. 504194. Vol. 740, p. 257.

On 1 May, 1819, FRANCIS DICKSON, of Belfast, of the first part, LEASED to ANN COURTNEY (see No. 425130) and ANN THOMPSON, both of Ballymena, spinsters, all that tenement, messuage, and premises with back yard, etc., with liberty of passing to the rear, by the gateway in common with MRS. MARGARET SMYTH, property formerly in the possession of JOHN COURTNEY, deceased, and then in the actual possession of ANN COURTNEY and ANN THOMPSON, being in the town of Ballymena, to hold as tenants in common, but not as joint tenants, for and during the natural life of FRANCIS DICKSON the younger (son of sd. FRANCIS), and from his death, for so much of the term of sixty-one years, to be computed from the 1st Nov., 1806, as then remained unexpired, subject to payment of yearly rent stated. Witnesses: PETER AICKIN and MICHAEL HARRISON, both of Ballymena.

No. 504966. Vol. 741, p. 429.

On 24 May, 1819, FRANCIS DICKSON, of Belfast, LEASED to JOHN PORTER, of Gracehill, and ANDREW PORTER, of the same place, Co. Antrim, for 200 pounds sterling, that dwelling house in Bridge Street, in Ballymena, formerly in the possession of MRS. MCKEAN, bounded by the house of MRS. LINDSAY, on the north-east, and on the south-west by the house of MRS. RUSSELL; on the north-west by Bridge Street, together with back yard, garden, and premises, formerly occupied by RICHARD LENDRICK, formerly of Ballymena. JOHN PORTER and ANDREW PORTER, to hold the LEASE for the life of WILLIAM DICK-

SON, eldest son of said FRANCIS DICKSON, or sixty-one years, which ever lasts longest, subject to rent mentioned. Witnesses: ABRAHAM PORTER, and THOMAS SPENCE, both of Ballymena. Sworn at Henryville, Co. Antrim.

NOTE: This was Francis Dickson, Sr.'s last land transaction before he left Ireland, in 1819.

No. 541465. Vol. 802, p. 329.

On 1 November 1824, MORTGAGE, between FRANCIS DICKSON, of Ballymena, Gent., of the first part; WILLIAM REID, Esq., and MARY REID, otherwise ORR, his wife, of Bologne France, of the second part; JAMES ORR, of Belfast, ROBERT ORR, of Belfast, and THOMAS VANCE, of Beechmount, Co. Antrim, Esquires, of the third part. For 1,000 pounds sterling, FRANCIS DICKSON, did grant, bargain, sell, alien, release, and confirm to JAMES ORR, ROBERT ORR, and THOMAS VANCE, in their actual possession, the two quarter lands of SKERRYRAVIL, with houses, and demesne, of MONTALTO (MONT ALTA), of 443 acres, 8 perch, in the barony of Kilconway, Co. Antrim, forever, subject to the sum and interest. Witnesses: NICHOLAS DELACHEROIS CROMMELIN, of Carrowdore Castle, County Down, Esq. and FRANCIS JOHN DOYLE, of Belfast. Sworn at Belfast.

NOTE: Thus, it appears that this "gentleman" son of William Dickson, brewer, was in financial trouble just seven years after he became trustee for his father's estate. An abstract of the memorial of the will of Arthur Willson, brother of Morgan Willson (grandfather of Francis Dickson, Sr., who emigrated in 1819), connects with the Quaker records of this family, which will be given in the chapter covering Quaker source materials.

No. 133004. Vol. 200, p. 238.

ARTHUR WILSON (Willson), Leminaroy, in the Proportion of Vintners, parish of Termaney (Termoneeny), Co. Londonderry, farmer. 11 June 1759. Recorded 23 July 1759. To his wife JANE and his daughters MARGERY and JANE all his

farm or holding in LEMINAROY (Lemnaroy) in three equal
parts. His son THOMAS WILSON. His son-in-law THOMAS
FAUCET. His son-in-law CHARLES McKAGHEY. His brother
MORGAN WILSON. FRANCIS DICKSON and THOMAS KANE, exec-
utors. Witnesses: ADAM DOWNING, Leminaroy, farmer;
DAVIS (?) STEEL, Drumlamph, said county, JAMES DOWNING,
Leminaroy, Gent. Memorial of the Will witnessed by: ADAM
DOWNING, DAVID STEEL. MARGERY WILSON (seal).

CHAPTER II

THE NATIONAL LIBRARY OF IRELAND

The National Library of Ireland, located on Kildare Street, Dublin, is one of the great libraries of the world. Dr. Richard J. Hayes (LL.D.), is the Director. The two posts of Assistant Librarian were filled in 1950-1951 by the appointment of J. Barry, M. A., and D. Kennedy, B. A., B. Comm.

Other scholars of note associated with this library are: Mr. T. P. O'Neill, who is said to be "a walking dictionary of national biography." Mr. Alfred MacLochlainn is an authority on genealogical source materials. Mr. Basil O'Connell is reputed to know more about the genealogy of the families of the Province of Munster from early times than any man living. Mr. Gerard Slevin is the present Chief Herald and Officer of the Genealogical Office (Office of Arms), Dublin Castle. (This repository is now operated as a department of the National Library of Ireland. It is described in a later chapter.) Two other archivists and genealogists who have been closely associated with the library are: Mr. T. U. Sadleir, past Registrar and Deputy Ulster King of Arms, 1913 to March 1943. He accumulated important genealogical manuscript collections. Dr. Edward MacLysaght was Chief Herald and Genealogical Officer from 1943 until about 1948. He has served the National Library of Ireland as Keeper of the Manuscripts, and is the author of *Irish Families,* published in 1957.

The library is open to the public on Monday through Friday, from 10 a. m. to 10 p. m., and on Saturday from 10 a. m. to 1 p. m. It is a pleasure to work there because the service is prompt and efficient.

For many years the objective of Dr. Richard J. Hayes, the Director, has been to discover and acquire, or borrow for microfilming, all original manuscripts and published source materials dated from early times to the present day which are of a historical, literary, genealogical, or social nature relating to Ireland. He and other archivists of Ireland had long been aware of the great accumulation of records pertaining to Ireland, dated throughout the centuries, which are in other public repositories or have fallen into private custody, at home and abroad. English government officials and agents had sent or carried away State Papers, detailed reports, surveys, and letters regarding the people and affairs of Ireland. Many of the powerful and lesser landlords retained public and personal documents in their family archives in Ireland. Absentee landlords removed many documents from Ireland. Some records belonging in the Office of Ulster King of Arms were taken to London. Much historical and genealogical material has been discovered among these public and private sources.

Many such records came to light as the Irish archivists searched for the rare printed materials and manuscripts in all public and known private repositories in Ireland and also in the British Museum, the Library of Lambeth Palace, and the Public Record Office of London; the Bodleian Library, Oxford; Cambridge University Library; the Scottish Record Office, and the National Library, Edinburgh; the National Library of Wales; the libraries of the Continent, and in many private archives of families descended from past government officials in Ireland, or absentee landlords.

The program of acquiring or borrowing manuscripts and rare printed materials for microfilming, and the accessions of Irish published works such as genealogies, early newspapers, directories, periodicals, and histories of county, town and regional nature, has made this library a great central repository and a mecca for genealogists.

Judging from the National Library of Ireland catalogues, the Reports of the Council of Trustees, and from information communicated over the past ten years to this compiler by Dr. Hayes, it is safe to say that this library is a repository of almost all items calendared in the accompanying Bibliography, VOLUME II, PARTS ONE, THREE and FOUR. The Bibliography, in fact, could contain only a partial list of the great accumulation of records of a genealogical nature in this library. With the most helpful materials listed, it is intended for use not only in Ireland but as a guide for a search of sources, many of which can be located in the larger genealogical libraries of the United States. Americans, who do not have access to these records personally, may enjoy directing the search for their own genealogical information through an agent in Ireland.

USE OF LISTS IN VOLUME II AS A GUIDE TO MATERIAL IN THE NATIONAL LIBRARY:

PART ONE, CHAPTER I.—Books of compiled family history and genealogy in this library are noted with the key letter (A).

PART ONE, CHAPTER II.—The published collections of pedigrees, genealogy, and family history are in this library.

PART ONE, CHAPTER III.—The published biographical dictionaries and biographical succession lists are in this library. The latter are published by diocese and subdivided by parishes. They contain the lists of the bishops and the clergy in order of succession by date, from the fifteenth century, with brief notes regarding them.

PART ONE, CHAPTER IV.—There are forty-two Irish historical and genealogical periodicals listed, with a description of each. Most of them are the publications of county, regional or national historical societies. All have for their primary purpose the encouragement of research of a historical, archaeological and genealogical nature. The genealogical work is of high quality, based upon primary records. Much work was the result of research in the Public Record Office, Dublin, before 1922, when many of the records were burned. The genealogical articles range in scope from full pedigrees of several generations, family notes or biography, to records such as transcripts or abstracts of wills, marriage bonds, entries of baptism, marriage and burial from parish registers, tombstone inscriptions (many with sculptured armorial bearings of Scottish, English and native Irish families), abstracts of deeds, lists of inhabitants at a given date, tax payers of many localities, public office holders of various counties and towns or cities, freemen's rolls, and other material of use in compiling genealogy. The National Library of Ireland has, undoubtedly, the most complete collection of these periodicals in the country. Their importance to historians and genealogists is recognized by the fact that this library has prepared both subject and name indexes of the periodicals of each society, except the three largest publications which have maintained their own printed indexes. The library indexes are preserved on microcards. This makes it possible for a record searcher to locate readily items concerning any one family. The more important of these periodicals are in the larger American genealogical libraries.

PART ONE, CHAPTER V.—For the benefit of Americans who may not have access to the Irish periodicals listed in CHAPTER IV, noted above, this compiler has prepared a family index to the more important compiled genealogical material in twenty-four of the periodicals. The list, by family surname, gives the volume and page number with the name of the periodical indicated by a key number. The printed works concern family history, genealogy, pedigrees, biographies, and transcripts of documents for compiling genealogy. Three hundred articles or series of articles are listed. Photostats can be ordered from the National Library. A deposit of $9.00 must be sent with an inquiry.

PART ONE, CHAPTER VI.—This contains a select list of all the important histories of the counties, towns, cities, and regions; the diocesan and parish histories, and a short but representative list of those of national scope. All contain material such as family history, genealogy, pedigrees, or brief genealogical notes. Many have published transcripts of wills, marriage records, cemetery records, early and late tax records, rent rolls, muster rolls, freeman rolls, lists of county officers, etc., copied from original documents. Some are especially rich in family history and all have genealogical value of one sort or another. The National Library of Ireland has the most complete collection of histories of this nature in the country. Several American genealogical libraries have partial collections. The list of these histories total 148 of county, town or city, 92 diocesan or parish, and 20 of national scope.

PART ONE, CHAPTER VII.—The published Irish manuscripts listed were selected for the genealogical content; and such important source materials are described in the Bibliography. Any of these publications can be purchased at a reasonable price from the Stationery Office, 3 College Street, Dublin.

PART THREE.—Published reference materials for genealogical research are listed. These are presented under the following headings: Catalogues of Irish Repositories; Catalogues of English Repositories containing Irish items; Guides to Genealogical Records; Geographical Sources (Atlases and Maps, Place-Names, Topographical Dictionaries); Arms, Heraldry, and Nomenclature; Ancient Genealogy; Church Records (Congregational, Church of Ireland, Huguenot, Methodist, Presbyterian, Quaker, Roman Catholic); Death Records; Directories and School Registers; Government Records (Census, Emigration, Naturalization, Tax, Vital Records); Land Records; Military and Naval Records; Newspapers and Periodicals; Public Offices, Freeholders, and Guilds; State Papers and Court Records (Chancery, Fiants, Patent Rolls); Wills. The National Library of Ireland has all these published sources.

PART FOUR.—The more important microfilms of genealogical material are listed. Location of copies of each is indicated. The National Library of Ireland has the original microfilms or copies of all of the films listed in PART FOUR except perhaps the microfilms of the Quaker records of Northern Ireland (see VOLUME II, PART FOUR), and those of the Sir William Betham collection of thirty-nine volumes of pedigree charts. (As the original Betham manuscript collection is deposited in the Genealogical Office, Dublin Castle, and convenient for reference, the microfilms were sent to the Library of Congress, Washington, D. C. These are described in CHAPTER IV, THE GENEALOGICAL OFFICE.) Microfilms of especial value to genealogists are as follows:

The Annesley Collection: This is fully described by Dr. R. C. Simington, in *Analecta Hibernica,* No. 16, 1946. It comprises 62 manuscript volumes which are at Castlewellan, Co. Down. Among the volumes microfilmed by the National Library of Ireland are the *Books of Survey and Distribution,* for every county of Ireland except Co. Meath. These concern the survey of land and instruments of title, 1636-1703, before and after the forfeiture of Catholic land due to the 1641 Rebellion and the Williamite War of 1688-89. The genealogical information set forth provides the names of the owners in

1641 and earlier, the relationship to the forfeiting owners (father, grandfather, etc.), the names of the new owners later granted each unit of land forfeited and re-granted. The number of profitable acres and various miscellaneous notes of genealogical value also appear. The forfeitures of 1688-1703, after the Catholic uprising for James II, and the Williamite War are also recorded in the 1700-1703 proceedings of the Council of Trustees appointed to dispose of, by sale, the estates forfeited by Catholics in 1688. These are set forth in 32 documents which include "Outlawrys," petitions, depositions, rent rolls, and accounts of valuations of estates, with the names of former owners and purchasers. Further Catholic land forfeitures to 1770 are recorded in documents of the Annesley Collection. The entire collection provides a great aid to genealogists in tracing families during the 17th and 18th centuries.

Directories: Rare directories such as Lucas' *Directory of Cork City, 1787, and for South-East Ireland, 1788* and Pigot's *Directory for the Counties of Ireland, 1820,* list people by station (title, Esq., Gent., etc.), occupation, together with much miscellaneous information. See VOLUME II, PART THREE, for other city and county directories.

Freeman's Journal Index: The *Freeman's Journal,* a Dublin newspaper, 1763-1780, 1783-1786 (some numbers) has been collected by the library and is of such historical and genealogical value due to the news and the personal items and notices of births, marriages, deaths, emigrations, etc., that a subject and name index has been compiled which has been preserved on microcards. For information on important newspaper collections, see the chapter regarding them in PART THREE of this volume.

Genealogical Office, Dublin Castle, Manuscript Collections: The entire collection of 701 volumes and 23 legal size boxes of documents was microfilmed about 1950.

Names Index and Land Index of the Registry of Deeds: These two indexes are described in PART TWO, CHAPTER I.

Roman Catholic Parish Registers: These registers are, for the most part, dated from about 1830 in the rural districts and in the larger cities begin as early as 1700. The National Library of Ireland has, since 1950, pursued a program of microfilming the registers of the 28 dioceses, one diocese at a time, calling in the registers of each parish for filming. By January 1960, sixteen dioceses had been completed. These are as follows: Achonry, Ardagh and Clonmacnoise, Cashel and Emly, Clonfert, Elphin, Ferns, Galway, Kerry, Kildare and Leighlin, Killala, Killaloe, Limerick, Meath, Raphoe, Tuam, Waterford and Lismore. A typescript list of the parish registers showing the inclusive dates of baptisms, marriages and (few if any) burials will be published when the work is completed.

Tithe Applotment Books: This very large collection of Tithe Applotment Books for all parishes, 1824-1840, lists the names of property owners and occupiers. This source is a valuable means of locating people and to some extent mitigates the loss of the great part of the census records in the destruction of the Public Record Office, Dublin, in 1922.

The wealth of microfilms listed in VOLUME II, PART FOUR, should be studied, and the repositories which have copies supply a valuable aid to genealogists. Many of the most important collections are in the United States.

MANUSCRIPTS

Dr. Edward MacLysaght, formerly Chief Herald of Ireland and Keeper of the Manuscripts of the National Library, states in his *Irish Families,* "There is much genealogical information in the manuscripts as yet uncatalogued in the National Library." Some others which are available are as follows:

BETHAM, SIR WILLIAM. Collections of Pedigrees.

BETHAM, SIR WILLIAM AND DR. SAMUEL MADDEN. Collections of Pedigrees.

BOXWELL AND HARVEY Family Papers, 1700-1850.

BUTLER Family of Castlecrine, County Clare. Family papers.

FORFEITURES of 1641:

1. Account of lands set out to transplanted Irish in the Province of Connaught by way of final settlement, received

from the Deputy Surveyor General, 1664 (Ormond MSS., H. M. Com. 3rd Report).

2. Abstract of the Decrees of the Court of Claims for the Trial of Innocents 1662, 1663 (Egerton MS. 789, Cat. Add. MSS. British Museum).

FORFEITURES OF 1688:

1. Forfeitures in the County of Dublin to be exposed for sale at Chichester House, 8 April 1703, "apparently the original" (Cat. Add. MSS. B. M., 1846-7, p. 146. Copy in National Library).

2. A list of the claims as they are entered with the Trustees at Chichester House on College Green, Dublin, on or before the Tenth of April, 1700 (Copy in the National Library with MS. Rulings). These concerned the estates of the Catholics who supported James II against William of Orange. Notes on the court rulings are shown. These contain pedigree information.

3. Rentals, Incumbered Estates Court, Landed Estates Court and Land Judges. (Sets in the National Library and in Kings Inns' Library and Land Commission.)

4. "A List of Such of the Names of the Nobility, Gentry and Commonality of England and Ireland, assembled in Dublin, 7 May, 1689, before the Late King James, Attainted of High Treason." Printed for R. Cavel and J. Watts, 1690. Also extracted lists in the National Library for various cities, towns, and counties.

GREENE MANUSCRIPTS: 5 vols. Indexed. These contain the following:

1. Extracts from Prerogative and Diocesan Wills.

2. Extracts from Grant Books and Parish Registers.

3. Extracts from Prerogative Rule Books; Wills, Prerogative and Diocesan.

4. Castle Dermott Parish Registers, extracts.

HARVEY FAMILY MANUSCRIPT: See Boxwell.

THE HOWARDS OF SHELTON ABBEY, CO. WICKLOW.   A collection of family papers.

LESLIE, REV. J. B., MANUSCRIPTS: Succession Lists for many dioceses of Ireland, similar to those which were published.

LOMBARD FAMILY MANUSCRIPT: This concerns the Lombard family of Lombardstown, County Cork.

MANUSCRIPT REPORTS: Reports of inspectors for the Irish Manuscripts Commission (typed), on manuscripts in private keeping. These cover abstracts of the documents in the following collections of papers: The families of Colclough, Dillon, Doneraile, Mansfield, Nugent, Power O'Shee, Shirley, Smyth, Vigors. The list contains the names of the owners and their addresses.

MARTIN FAMILY: A collection of letters of Maria Edgeworth, concerning the Martin family of Ballenahinch.

SANDES FAMILY PAPERS: Sent from Mrs. O'Kelly of Crecora, County Limerick.

SARSFIELD FAMILY PAPERS: These concern the Sarsfield family of County Cork.

STEWART-KENNEDY NOTEBOOKS: This is a transcript of the original in Trinity College Library. It contains many abstracts of Prerogative and Diocesan Wills.

WYNNE FAMILY ESTATE PAPERS: Account books and documents relating to the Wynne family of County Sligo, 1738-1777.

MISCELLANEOUS

THE "BLUE BOOK" SERIES: This is a series of reports of the Irish House of Commons. They include:

1. "Returns of Persons entitled to carry Arms." "Claims for Compensation in the 1798 Rebellion." "Holders of Government Annuities," *ca.* 1799.

Some of these reports furnish genealogical information about family relationships. "Returns regarding Religion" are also included. Locations of persons are stated.

2. "Parliamentary Returns regarding Manor Courts in Ire-

land." "Returns of Owners of Land, 1876." "Members of Parliament."

3. "Report on Fictitious Votes." 3 vols. 1837. This is a report of the complete list of "Freemen of the Corporate Towns in each County." It contains also the owners of rent-charges on the estates in all counties; owners of houses in the towns of Armagh, Bandon, Coleraine, Dungannon, Galway, Lisburn, Londonderry, Newry and Youghal.

4. A return concerning the rights of Freemen of the different trade guilds. It contains extracts from the Guild registers, for Dublin citizens, etc., showing the rights of freemen, according to descent from father to son, or by right through marriage.

FREEMEN ROLLS: "A Handlist of the Voters of Maryborough Corporation." This was taken from a notebook which forms part of the Drogheda Manuscript, in the National Library of Ireland. It contains a list of the freemen and burgesses of the borough taken for 1 March 1738/9 to 29 Sept. 1754. This was a rough alphabetical list kept up to date by additions and corrections to 1759, with an amended list to 1760 (MS. 1726, Ainsworth Report (typescript), vol. 4).

"Freemen of the City of Dublin, Jan. 1774 - 15 Jan. 1824." An alphabetical list.

"Freeholders of County Limerick, 1776." A printed list.

All of the above freemen's lists are valuable for locating people and many family relationships are set forth. Other lists are given in PART THREE of this volume.

NEWSPAPERS: The National Library of Ireland has an extensive collection of old newspapers. These will be listed with their dates, among the collections of other repositories, in the chapter devoted to the subject, in PART THREE of this volume. These newspapers, including the *Freeman's Journal* which has been indexed by the library, record births, marriages, deaths and, in the seaport cities, contain lists of the people who departed from time to time for America and other places. These are, in effect, emigration records.

GRIFFITH'S VALUATION: Griffith made a survey and valuation of all property in Ireland, 1844-1866. It was made by townlands showing lists of the occupants and immediate lessors. The lists were grouped and arranged by Poor Law Unions which comprised multiples of townlands, usually with a large market town as a center, within a radius of about ten miles. Some Poor Law Unions are situated wholly in one county; others extend into two or three counties. The National Library has a collection of the entire survey. The names of the townland occupiers provide clues for the use of the LAND INDEX in the Registry of Deeds, by which the deeds, leases, etc., of any townland can be located. This Griffith's Valuation is especially valuable as a means of locating people who emigrated shortly after their property was surveyed. These years saw the greatest Irish emigration of all time to the United States.

Dr. Richard J. Hayes stated in 1961, "The National Library is now making an index of the surnames in *Griffith's Valuation of Ireland*. It will be available here in typed form. It contains an alphabet for each parish and then an alphabet for the county, telling how many householders of any name are in each barony of the county. We have completed three counties: Wexford, Wicklow and Carlow, and hope to produce a county every two months." This will be an extremely important source for locating persons at the time of the records of each county.

The National Library of Ireland Bibliography of Irish Philology and of Printed Literature, Dublin, 1913, 1942 (2 vols.), contains references to Irish works in Irish repositories and in many of Great Britain and foreign countries. The preface to the first volume explains the scope of the contents and the purpose which was " . . . to meet the daily needs of students in the National Library . . ." This bibliography contains numerous references of interest to genealogists who are engaged in advanced and exhaustive work.

OTHER IMPORTANT IRISH LIBRARIES

The genealogical material in Irish libraries varies according to the age, purpose, and locality of each repository. The university, college, and church libraries and the special historical libraries place emphasis upon literature, Irish history, and closely allied genealogy. They have a wide range of printed and manuscript source materials relating to genealogy. The county libraries specialize in histories and manuscript material concerning their local areas and families, being comparable to the county historical societies in the United States. Some have excellent collections of published genealogical source material. They vary in importance according to size of the city or town where they are located. The public libraries are subject to the same conditions. They have published works of more general interest but include histories, periodicals of the area and some family histories deposited by donors. The most important libraries of genealogical interest and a few of their special collections are as follows:

ARMAGH:
ARMAGH COUNTY MUSEUM: This very old library is in the Cathedral City of Armagh, seat of the Archbishop of Armagh, Primate of the Church of Ireland. Mr. T. G. F. Paterson is the Curator. Among the records are:

1. A collection of Pedigrees, Leases, Grants (Probates and Intestates), L. E. C. Rentals, Prerogative and Dromore Diocesan Wills, 1685-1896.

2. Lists of Passengers for New York and Philadelphia, etc., sailing from Newry and Warrensport, 1791-1792.

3. Brownlow Estate Survey, 1667; Rental, 1635. Survey of R. Johnston's estate, Co. Down, Co. Armagh, Co. Monaghan, 1731.

4. Freeholder's Book of County Armagh, 18th Century.

5. Griffith's Valuation of County Armagh, 1839. 28 volumes.

6. Hearthmoney Roll, Fews Barony, County Armagh, 1664. Hearthmoney Roll, Orrier Barony, County Armagh, 1664. This was a legal tax of 2 shillings per hearth in a dwelling or other place using fires, levied on every householder, etc., and constitutes a census by county and barony, the lists being compiled by parish and townland, or city and town.

7. Armagh Militia Records, 1793-1908.

8. Muster Roll of Ulster, 1630 (copy).

9. County Armagh Poll Book, 1753.

ARMAGH DIOCESAN REGISTRY OFFICE, MUNIMENT ROOM: This Church of Ireland repository contains a very old and full collection of diocesan histories, manuscripts and records relating to the church.

ARMAGH PUBLIC LIBRARY: This repository, of which Mr. Hamilton is the director, is one of the finest with respect to its unusually large collections of family histories, pedigrees, and other valuable manuscripts. A *Catalogue of the Manuscripts in the Public Library of Armagh*, by J. Dean, was published in Dundalk, 1928. Some entries are as follows:

1. Census of Kilmore, County Armagh, 1821.

2. Corporation Records of Armagh.

3. Court Records: "A List of Indictments and 'Outlawries' in the Counties of Dublin, Meath and Kildare, 1642." "A List of Claims of Innocents to be heard and determined by His Majesty's Commissioners appointed to execute the Act of Settlement of Ireland in the Court of Claims for the Trial of Innocents, from 28 Jan. 1662/63, to 20 Aug. 1663." This concerned the many Catholics who were not in any way active in the Catholic Rebellion of 1641. Their claims to their estates were set forth showing the owners in 1641, and their rights showing two or three generations of inheritance. When proof was established that the owner in 1641 was "innocent" of rebellion, a decree of "Innocence" was passed. "MSS. Pedigrees extracted from the published *Chichester House Claims, 1700*." This concerns forfeitures after the Williamite War of 1688-89.

4. Crown and Quit Rent Ledger, 1793-1799, for estates in Counties Armagh, Tyrone and Monaghan.

5. Some of the family manuscripts are: The Johnston MSS. collection of abstracts of Wills, Pedigrees, etc. The Reeves MSS. collection containing Pedigrees of the families of note in his "Collo-da-Crioch"; also his MSS. collections with papers and genealogies of the families of Blennerhassett, Denny, McCathusaigh, Mitchell, O'Byrne, and O'Hara.

6. Inquisition of Ulster: "Commission and Grand Inquisition regarding the escheated lands of Ulster so far as it relates 'to this See' of Armagh, 1609."

7. The Walter Harris MS.: "A Book of Inscriptions on Ancient Tombstones."

8. John Lodge's MSS.: Tombstone Inscriptions; Succession Lists of the Clergy (Established Church of Ireland); Index to Lodge's Peerage; Grants of Estates in County Armagh.

9. Diocese of Meath MSS. collection. A very large collection of records of the diocese.

10. *Militia Officers of the Counties of Ireland, 1761.* A rare printed volume.

11. Armagh Manor Rolls and Rent Rolls: Armagh Manor Rolls, 1625-1627; Rent Rolls of property of the See of Armagh, 1615-1746, being land covering the town of Armagh; also an estate map with tenants' names of Bangor town and harbour in 1757. Also tenants on Clanbrassil estate, 1625-1675, in an Entry Book relating to Bangor and the north part of the Ards, Holywood, Dundonald and Saintfield district. Another list, "A Rent Roll of all Houses and Lands belonging to the See of Armagh, *circa* 1620," compiled by Lawrence P. Murray, from records in the Muniment room of the Diocesan Registry Office in Armagh. A list of tenants and their holdings, with some biographical sketches of the estate of Castle Dillon, County Armagh.

12. Visitation Books, States of Dioceses, Valuations of Ecclesiastical Benefices, etc.

BELFAST:

THE LINEN HALL LIBRARY: It was founded in 1788, as "The

Belfast Library and Society for Promoting Knowledge," and since then has been known by the above name, due to its location in the old Belfast Linen Hall, located on Donegall Square North. It is undoubtedly one of the finest genealogical reference libraries in Northern Ireland. A *General Catalogue* was published in 1898. In 1917, a *Catalogue of Books in the Irish Section* was published under the founding name above. It lists about 15,000 printed sources of historical, genealogical and literary interest. The genealogical reference material for all of Ireland, as of that date, included a large proportion of the items listed in VOLUME II, PARTS ONE and THREE of this publication. It has an important collection of Belfast newspapers of early date and some early numbers for Dublin, which will be listed in the chapter on the subject. In 1955, this compiler estimated the collection of printed books of family history to be over two hundred.

The Linen Hall Library, Belfast, also has an extensive collection of Presbyterian printed sources, including histories, church records, newspapers and periodicals, which are calendared in the *Catalogue of Books in the Irish Section, 1917.*

THE PRESBYTERIAN HISTORICAL SOCIETY LIBRARY: This library is in Room 20, Presbyterian Historical Society, Church House, Fisherwick Place, Belfast. It is the center for the study of manuscript material concerning Presbyterian families. Much of its development and progress in the past forty years or more may be credited to the interest and scholarship of the Rev. Dr. David Stewart, formerly Secretary and Librarian of the Society and author of many articles and books concerning Presbyterian history and transcribed records. The library is open to the public from 10 a. m. to 3 p. m. Miss Jeannie L. M. Stewart, Assistant Secretary, is in charge, and is interested in genealogy. The library has three card indexes. One is for the excellent collection of published source materials. These include local and regional histories, primarily of Northern Ireland; the *Ulster Journal of Archaeology* which contains much material regarding Presbyterians; the *Proceedings of the Presbyterian Historical Society, in 1938-1939*, containing lists of accessions of manuscripts by the Society, and *Annual Reports* containing appendices consisting of extracts from original manuscripts; Presbyterian histories and periodicals, including newspapers; Belfast and general directories; printed parish records for the Established Church of Ireland, and some Presbyterian congregations; Minutes of the General Synod of Ulster; Fasti of the Presbyterian Church of Ireland; also a good genealogical reference collection. The second index is for the manuscript materials other than Church Registers. Included are the original ancient records of the Presbyterian local Sessions from which important personal memoranda may be obtained. A large file of biographical and family manuscript material is also indexed. Other manuscript material includes the 1740 Householders' List; Lists of Dissenters at various dates; Hearthmoney Rolls of Northern Ireland; Muster Rolls, Army and Naturalization Lists for Northern Ireland of early 17th century dates. The third index is kept for the Church Registers in local custody. This card index contains notes on the inclusive dates of each Register and its location. Copies of the thirty-four oldest Registers, transcribed in full, are in this repository. All Registers, some 367 in number, are listed with inclusive dates under PRESBYTERIAN RECORDS in PART THREE, CHAPTER VII, together with other manuscript items of special interest which are deposited in this repository and elsewhere. Presbyterian newspapers and periodicals are listed under NEWSPAPERS, in PART THREE of this volume. A short list of some Presbyterian printed histories and Church records appears in the accompanying VOLUME II, PART THREE.

THE QUEEN'S UNIVERSITY LIBRARY: This is a progressive library, containing many genealogical source materials, similar in scope to the collections in the Linen Hall Library, Belfast. All of the Quaker records of Northern Ireland were microfilmed here and copies were sent to the Library of Swarthmore College, Swarthmore, Pennsylvania. Dr. J. B. Woodburn has deposited here an interesting manuscript entitled "American Emigrants", which was prepared as his thesis for the degree of Doctor of Philosophy.

CASHEL:

THE CASHEL DIOCESAN LIBRARY: This library, with its collections of early Church records and genealogical source materials is noted in John Ryland's *Library Bulletin.* An article by R. Wyse Jackson, entitled "The Ancient Library of Cashel," which was published in the *Journal of the Cork Historical Society,* vol. 52, pp. 128-34, also described it.

CORK:

THE CORK COUNTY LIBRARY: This library, located in the city of Cork, has a remarkably large and well selected collection of genealogy, local history, historical and genealogical magazines and other genealogical source materials. Mr. P. J. Madden, Librarian, is interested in anything relating to Munster families.

THE CORK PUBLIC LIBRARY: While this library does not specialize in source materials of strictly genealogical interest, it has a good collection of periodicals including the *Journals* of some historical societies, and an excellent selection of local histories and numerous other publications of use to the genealogist. Mr. Foley, Librarian, is most cooperative.

THE LIBRARY OF UNIVERSITY COLLEGE, CORK: Queen's College (later University College) Cork, is situated in the city of Cork. The library ranks among the best genealogical libraries in Ireland, for its large collection of published source materials relating to the entire country. *A Classified Catalogue of the Books contained in the Library of the Queen's College, Cork,* was published with a Supplement, in 1860. A *Catalogue of the Irish Library, University College, Cork,* was published in 1914. Mr. Cahill, Librarian, and Mr. Ahern, Assistant Librarian, will permit a serious student of genealogy to work with the collections in the open stacks on the second floor. A number of early manuscripts are deposited in the vault, including "Apprentice Indentures Enrolling Book, Commencing 17 Jan. 1756, ending 4 Dec. 1801," transcribed alphabetically by Richard Caulfield.

DONEGAL:

THE DONEGAL COUNTY LIBRARY: This Library in Lifford, Co. Donegal, is the center for many who have a strong interest in the genealogy of the area. Two items of importance among the manuscript collections are "The Register of Freeholders of County Donegal, 1767-1768," and the "Donegal Grand

Jurors: Books of Presentments, 1768-1783; 1815-1856." Another manuscript, an "Index of Persons for County Donegal, from the Catholic Qualification Rolls, 1778-1790," was published in the *Journal of the County Donegal Historical Society,* in 1949, by Sean óDomhnaill (Vol. I, No. 3, pp. 204-206).

DUBLIN:

CENTRAL CATHOLIC LIBRARY: Catholic research should include an examination of the many special collections in this library.

CHURCH OF IRELAND REPRESENTATIVE CHURCH BODY LIBRARY: The library is located at 52 St. Stephen's Green. A catalogue of the manuscripts collected by the Ecclesiastical Records Committee was edited by the Rev. J. B. Leslie, 1938. Much has been done by the Ecclesiastical Records Committee to repair the loss of the Church of Ireland records which were deposited in the Public Record Office of Ireland, Dublin, and were lost in the fire of 1922. A wealth of documents relating to every diocese in Ireland has been collected, many being original records which had been retained in local repositories where they had been deposited by historians, church officials and antiquarians. Some transcripts of the records deposited in the Public Record Office had been made by many responsible church historians and by genealogists. The catalogue lists the transcripts from the Armagh and Cashel archives, the Ossory Chapter original records, and the extensive transcripts made from parish registers in the Public Record Office before 1922, by Tenison Groves. Also among the deposits are the Biographical Succession Lists for the dioceses of Achonry, Ardagh, Elphin, Killala, Kilmore, Limerick, Meath, Raphoe, and Tuam, which were collected for the purpose of publication but not printed as were many others. The collections of manuscripts by James Graves in three volumes relating to Ossory; the eighty volumes of transcripts of Hugh Jackson Lawlor; the three volumes of transcripts of the Commonwealth records by the Venerable Archdeacon St. J. D. Seymour; the seven volumes of transcripts by H. B. Swanzy, and the collection of the Rev. Canon H. W. B. Thompson, are all here.

KING'S INNS LIBRARY: Mr. Thomas Ulick Sadleir, Barrister-at-Law, and past Registrar and Deputy Ulster King of Arms, 1913 to March 1943, a genealogist of note, has been active in building and organizing the collections of manuscript material and transcripts of records in this legal library. Records of the members, students in the law school, and supplemental records regarding the parentage, etc., of the students who were required to complete one year of the study of law in London, were gathered from these sources.

MARSH'S LIBRARY: This library has Dudley Loftus' collection of ancient Annals; John O'Donovan's name books for Counties Carlow, Cavan, Clare, Cork, Donegal and Roscommon; also the Poll Money Ordinances used as supplementary material by Séamus Pender for records of 1660-1661, in his *Census of Ireland, circa 1659,* are in this library.

THE ROYAL IRISH ACADEMY LIBRARY: This library at 19 Dawson Street is open from 12 noon until 4 p. m. It is one of the three libraries in Ireland (the others being the National Library of Ireland, and Trinity College Library) which claim the largest and most ancient genealogical manuscript collections, together with seventeenth century government records and much other miscellaneous genealogical source material.

A Catalogue of Irish Manuscripts in the Royal Irish Academy, compiled by Elizabeth Fitzpatrick and Kathleen Mulchrone, assisted by A. I. Pearson, was published in Dublin, 1948 (586 pp.). This institution, established by royal charter in 1786, has been active in the promotion of scientific, and literary studies and the collection and study of the closely allied ancient historical and genealogical manuscripts. From 1786 to 1906, it published the *Transactions,* containing a selection of the papers on the above subjects read before the Academy. In 1836, a new series called the *Proceedings,* was published and has been continued. From 1836-1866, these contained minutes of the meetings and abstracts of the papers read before the Academy. After 1866, the minutes were recorded separately and there was little difference in the purpose of the two publications. Indexes to the publications 1786-1906, and for the *Proceedings,* 1907-32, were published

in 1912 and 1934, respectively. Four early eighteenth century
Army Lists of Irish in foreign service (one casualty list of
1702) were published in the *Proceedings* (1927, 1930).
Among the important manuscript collections are the following:

Genealogical collections: Duald MacFirbis's great genealogical collection transcribed by O'Curry in 1836, the original
of which is in University College, Dublin.   The Wendele
MSS. collection of 190 volumes containing pedigrees of
chiefly Leinster and Munster families; one volume, however,
containing Munster family pedigrees being in the possession
of John T. Collins of the city of Cork at the present time.   The
De La Ponce MSS. on genealogies and military service
of the officers of the Irish Brigades in the service of France
during the 17th and 18th centuries, which leads to many important Catholic family genealogies in Ireland.

Genealogical Manuscript Collections, published by the Irish
Manuscripts Commission from original manuscripts in the
Royal Irish Academy: The "Great Book of Lecan," one of the
most treasured vellum manuscripts in this repository which
is called, "the corpus of historical knowledge regarding Irish
families."   The "Book of Uí Maine," otherwise known as the
"Book of the O'Kellys," the contents being genealogical,
romantic, metrical, etc. "An Leabhar Munimhneach" (The
Munster Book), an ordered collection of many Irish families,
chiefly of Munster, its scope extending also to the leading
Gaelic families of Ireland in general and to many families of
Norman extraction, many pedigrees being brought down later
than the year 1700.   Manuscript collections (including the
above few mentioned) of the Royal Irish Academy cited in
Séamus Pender's "A Guide to Irish Genealogical Collections,"
published in *Analecta Hibernica,* No. 7. The "O'Clery Manuscript" containing the O'Donnell genealogies (13th-17th centuries) also indexed in the above guide and published in
Analecta Hibernica, No. 8. The "ÓCléirigh Book of Genealogies" is a collection of pedigrees of the leading Irish and
Anglo-Norman families of Ireland, the compiler appearing to
have been one of the Four Masters. It was published in
Analecta Hibernica, No. 18. The "Madden Manuscript" being

a chart pedigree of the family of Adam Loftus and all of his descendants to 1700.

Some Public Documents: A printed list of Freeholders for County Tipperary, 1776. The Ordnance Survey Documents relating to the Vintners property and its British inhabitants, 1622. Ordnance Survey Documents, 1833-1835, for the North of Ireland, particularly County Londonderry, showing emigrants to the U. S. A. and Canada, listed by name, from various parishes of County Londonderry (see PART THREE, EMIGRATION RECORDS). The Charlemont Correspondence, 1707-1803. The Castlereagh Letters, 1791. "Strafford's Survey Book of County Mayo," 1635-1637, is of genealogical value, showing in detail the ownership of land in this county before any plantation was effected, and reflects the medieval pattern of ownership (see PART THREE, LAND SURVEYS). The *Books of Survey and Distribution,* 1650-90, which concern the Cromwellian forfeitures of land after the 1641-1649 Catholic Rebellion, are indispensable for 17th century genealogical work, as for each county they show the names of the owners of land before the Rebellion, the extent of each holding, and the names of the subsequent Proprietor grantees. This set was compiled by Thomas Taylor, by order of the Lord Lieutenant, in 1677. While few wills existed of a date previous to the 17th century, some important ones are in this repository.

TRINITY COLLEGE LIBRARY: Trinity College, Dublin, was founded by Royal Charter, under Queen Elizabeth, in 1591. The earliest information about students, their parentage and place of birth, age upon entry, etc., and the names of the graduates, professors and provosts, 1593-1637, was compiled by George Dames Burtchael for this period, from the Patent Rolls, Ecclesiastical Visitations, Fiants of Elizabeth and James I, Calendars of State Papers, Lists of Wards, Chancery and Exchequer Inquisitions, Funeral Entries, and the Particular Book (the earliest College Accounts), as no register previous to 1637 exists. From this date, Mr. Burtchael and Mr. Thomas Ulick Sadleir together used the College Registers, adding many valuable notes from other sources to complete the information about the above lists to 1846, all of which from 1593-1846 was published in their monumental work, *Alumni*

Dublinenses. London, 1924. The great library of this college has rare books and manuscripts accumulated over a
period of more than 350 years, including family genealogies
and other genealogical source materials, dating through
medieval times to the eighteenth century and later. The
*Trinity College, Dublin, Supplemental Catalogue of the
Library,* was published in 1854. A *Catalogue of the Manuscripts in the Library of Trinity College,* was compiled by
T. K. Abbott, and published in Dublin, 1900. A *Short Guide
to some Manuscripts in the Library of Trinity College, Dublin,* was compiled by Robert H. Murray, Dublin, 1920. These
have been listed in the Irish Book Shop catalogues in the past
few years. J. G. Smyly provides installments of his "Calendar
of Old Deeds, in the Library of Trinity College, 1384-1538," in
the periodical, *Hermathena,* vols. 69-74. The library owns a
series of volumes of manuscript pedigrees compiled in the 16th
and 17th centuries by accredited genealogists. O'Hart, in his
various publications of Irish pedigrees, etc., lists many of
these sources. His series is in most of the large genealogical
libraries of the United States. (He has been much criticised
by contemporary Irish genealogists for his careless use of the
pedigree information, his lack of particular documentation of
the individual pedigrees, and obvious mistakes found in them.
However, O'Hart has included considerable source material
in the form of lists, etc., copied from the manuscripts, which
has great value for the genealogist.) The National Library
of Ireland has microfilmed many manuscripts in this library,
some of genealogical interest being: "Papers relating to
Irish Affairs, Plantations, etc., 16th and 17th century"; the
"Pedigrees of Irish Families, 17th century and circa 1700";
the "Pedigrees of English Families, circa 1700, and of Lancashire and Yorkshire families, circa 1700," members of
which came to Ireland; the "Yellow Book of Lecan" which is
a genealogical manuscript. The Library has also photostated
"The Book of Leinster," which is also genealogical in
character. "The Annals of Loch Cé," a manuscript copied in
1588 from earlier documents, for the members of the Mac-
Dermot family, recording events from 1014-1636, was published in Reflex Facsimile, by the Irish Manuscripts Commission, 1939. Other material of genealogical interest in Trinity

College Library, published by the Irish Manuscripts Commission in its periodical *Analecta Hibernica,* includes an account of the "Applotment Books of St. Michan's, Dublin," the original manuscript giving the names of the residents in this parish; also the "Chichester Letter-Book, 1612-1614," which provides information regarding the Plantation of Ulster and the settlers, and other material during the period in which he was lord-deputy in Ireland. The library has a series of manuscript volumes *circa* 1653-1654, containing the Depositions taken from the Protestant settlers or their near descendants in Ireland, in which each person who suffered loss or damage to his property during the 1641 Rebellion, enumerated the extent of the loss. In many cases the depositions gave detailed information regarding their locations and property. Widows of men who died after 1641 in some cases reported the losses in particular detail. These depositions should be checked during the study of any Protestant family of this period. The library has also a "List of Families and Individuals who Fled to Chester (England), in 1688" before the Williamite War. These were all Protestants, indicted for High Treason, or likely to be, by James II. The list gives the details of the number of members in each family, with the value of their estates in Ireland and England. A "Freeholder's List for County Clare" of the early 18th century contains the names of the wealthier freeholders who were rated at 50 pounds sterling per annum rent or more. The library has an outstandingly valuable and extensive collection of early newspapers which will be listed in PART THREE, under NEWSPAPERS. A series of "Regal Visitation Books" of the 17th and 18th centuries set forth the States of the Dioceses, the valuations of the Ecclesiastical Benefices, and information regarding individuals. The library has a "Register of Wills and Inventories of the Diocese of Dublin, 1457-1483." The originals are in Latin. A translation in English appears in the *Royal Society of Antiquaries of Ireland, Extra Volume,* 1898, with an Introduction containing information concerning early Irish Wills. The series of "Stewart-Kennedy MSS. Notebooks" contain abstracts of some 500 Prerogative and Diocesan Wills of many Ulster families, transcribed by H. Stewart-Kennedy from Wills in the Public Record Office of Ireland, before their destruction in 1922. Mr. Edward Phelps compiled a list of these for the two Public Record Offices in Dublin and Belfast. The National Library has a copy of the entire manuscript collection.

UNIVERSITY COLLEGE, DUBLIN: The manuscript collection in this library is included in the catalogue of Irish manuscripts in the British Museum.

FERMOY:

ST. COLMAN'S COLLEGE LIBRARY: The outstanding manuscript collection in this library is a manuscript book containing a collection of rare genealogies for Ulster. These comprise the pedigrees of the chief families of County Fermanagh, set forth in great detail, down to 1700 and later. The ancient and modern spellings of the family names are as follows: Mag Uidhir (Maguire) in many branches, Mac Maghnusa (Mac Manus), Mac Domhnaill (Mac Donnell) of Clankelly, Mac Gothraidh (Mac Corry, Corry), Mac Cába (Mac Cabe), Mac Gafraidh (Mac Caffrey, Caffrey), Ó Flannagáin, Mag Raith (Magrath), Mac Mathghamhna (Mac Mahon, Matthews), Mac an Mhaighistir (Mac Master, Masterson) Mac Moruinn (Morrin), Ó Caiside (Cassidy), Mag Aodha (Magee, Mac Hugh, Hughes), Ó Manacháin (Monahan), Ó Tréasaigh (Tracey), Ó Banáin (Bannon), etc. This collection of family manuscripts has been edited by Eoin Mac Néill and Cormac Ó Cadhla. Their work was published by the Irish Manuscripts Commission in its periodical, *Analecta Hibernica*, No. 3. Members of the above families of Mac Maghnusa and Ó Caiside were concerned with the keeping of the Annals of Ulster from 1300 to 1588, and thus the above genealogies form a valuable supplement.

GALWAY:

QUEEN'S COLLEGE, GALWAY: One *Alphabetical Catalogue of the Library of Queen's College, Galway* was published in Dublin, 1864; another in 1877. A manuscript collection consisting of the "Galway Corporation Minute Books, 1485-1815" is a rich source for notes about the people of Galway. These were considered of sufficient importance for the National Library of Ireland to microfilm.

LIMERICK:

THE CITY OF LIMERICK PUBLIC LIBRARY: The "Catalogue
of the Museum and Reference Library" by R. Herbert, was
published in *The Limerick Leader* (1941), 16 pp., as a reprint from an earlier publication in the *North Munster Antiquarian Journal*, vol. 2. This library has a rare *Limerick
Directory, 1769* by John Ferrar.

LONDONDERRY:

MAGEE UNIVERSITY COLLEGE LIBRARY: Mr. T. MacCallum
Walker, Librarian, is also a member of the committee of the
Diocesan Library of St. Columb's Cathedral, Londonderry.
He is actively interested in collecting all old manuscript
material and rare books for this important library and for
many years it has been one of the repositories of genealogical
source materials concerning the families of the city and county
of Londonderry. The *McCrea-Magee College Catalogue of
the Library of Magee College in Londonderry* was published
in 1870. The library is open to the public on Monday through
Friday, from 10 a. m. to 5:30 p. m. and on Monday through
Thursday, from 6:30 to 9:30 p. m. It is open on Saturday
from 10 a. m. to 1 p. m. The library is closed during all public
holidays and for the last complete week in July. The library
has a lengthy bibliography of materials on the subject of
emigration. Some of the manuscripts containing genealogical
information are as follows: The "Adair Narrative, 1622-
1670" by Patrick Adair, entitled "A true narrative of the rise
and progress of the Presbyterian government in the North
of Ireland ... 1622-1670" (copy of the original). The Minutes
of the Antrim Meeting, 1654-1658; 1671-1691 (Transcript).
Minutes of the Subsynod of Derry, 1744-1802 (Transcript).
Minutes of the Laggan Meeting, 1690-1700 (Transcript).
Minutes of the Route Presbytery, 1701-1706 (Transcript).
Minutes of Aghadowey Session Book, 1702-1761 (Transcript).
Minutes of the Session of Cahans Presbyterian Meeting House,
1751-1802 (Transcript). Typed copy of documents formerly
in the Public Record Office of Ireland, Dublin, dealing with
Protestant Emigrations, 1718 and 1728. This is a copy of
the original transcript made by the Presbyterian Historical
Society, Belfast, from the Journal of the Irish House of Lords,

1719 and later. This library has an extensive collection of old newspapers. These will be listed in PART THREE, under NEWSPAPERS. Word has just come (1961) that Mr. T. Mac-Callum Walker has become Deputy Librarian of the University Library of Glasgow, Scotland.

OTHER IRISH LIBRARIES WHICH CONTAIN SOME GENEALOGICAL SOURCE MATERIAL

ANTRIM, CO. ANTRIM: The Antrim County Council Library.

ATHLONE, CO. WESTMEATH: The Franciscan Friary Library.

BALLINAMORE, CO. LEITRIM: Leitrim County Library.

BALLYMENA, CO. ANTRIM: The Antrim County Council Library Service.

BELFAST, CO. ANTRIM: The Belfast Public Library, Falls Road; The Belfast Public Library, Royal Avenue; The Royal Academical Institution Reference Library.

CARLOW, CO. CARLOW: St. Patrick's College Library.

CASTLEBAR, CO. MAYO: Mayo County Library.

DOWNPATRICK, CO. DOWN: The Carnegie Library; also the Down County Library.

DUBLIN, CO. DUBLIN: Franciscan Library, Killiney; Royal Society of Antiquaries Library; Society of Friends Library; Dublin University College Library.

ENNIS, CO. CLARE: Clare County Library.

ENNISKILLEN, CO. FERMANAGH: Fermanagh County Library.

GALWAY, CO. GALWAY: Galway County Library, The Court House. Galway University College Library.

KILKENNY, CO. KILKENNY: Kilkenny County Library, John Street; St. Kiernan's College Library.

KILMAINHAM, CO. DUBLIN: Dublin County Library.

LISMORE, CO. WATERFORD: Waterford County Library.

LONGFORD, CO. LONGFORD: St. Mel's College Library.

MAYNOOTH, CO. KILDARE: St. Patrick's College Library.

MONAGHAN, CO. MONAGHAN: St. Macartan's College Library.

MULLINGER, CO. WESTMEATH: Westmeath County Library.

NAVAN, COUNTY MEATH: Meath County Library.

NEWRY, CO. DOWN: Newry Public Library.
NEWTOWN LIMAVADY, CO. LONDONDERRY: Newtown Limavady Library.
OMAGH, CO. TYRONE: Tyrone County Library Depot.
PORTLAOIGHISE, CO. LEIX: Leix County Book Repository.
TRALEE, COUNTY KERRY: Kerry County Library.
TULLAMORE, CO. OFFALY: Offaly County Library.
WEXFORD, COUNTY WEXFORD: Wexford County Library.
WICKLOW, CO. WICKLOW: Wicklow County Library.

LIBRARIES OF GREAT BRITAIN WHICH CONTAIN IRISH RECORDS

CAMBRIDGE, ENGLAND:

The Cambridge University Library: See *A Catalogue of the Bradshaw Collection of Irish Books in the University Library, Cambridge.* 3 vols. Cambridge, 1916.

LONDON:

The British Museum: See *Catalogue of Irish Manuscripts in the British Museum.* Vol. I, by Standish Hayes, O'Grady, London, 1926; Vol. II, by Robin Flower, London, 1926; Vol. III, by Robin Flower, revised and edited by Dr. Myles Dillon, London, 1953.   Many of these have been microfilmed by the National Library of Ireland.   (See *National Library of Ireland Report of the Council of Trustees, 1950-1951,* etc.   See also the list of microfilms in VOLUME II, hereof, PART FOUR.)   See also the *British Museum Catalogue of Manuscripts, Books, Pamphlets and Newspapers relating to the Civil War, the Commonwealth, and Restoration, collected by George Thomason, 1640-1661.* London, 1908. 2 vols.   The British Museum has an important collection of newspapers of Belfast, Cork, Dublin, and Londonderry.

Lambeth Palace, Archiepiscopal Library: The outstanding manuscript collection of Irish interest in this library is the 39 volumes of the "Carew Manuscripts, 1515-1624."   A *Calendar of the Carew Manuscripts, 1515-1624,* was edited by J. S. Brewer and W. Bullen, London, 1867-1873.   6 vols. Among these manuscripts are: "Pedigrees of the Mere Irish" (meaning of pure or unmixed Irish origin).   "Pedigrees

wherein most of the descendants either of the mere Irish or
the English families in Ireland are mentioned." "Pedigrees
of most of the Lords and Gentlemen of the Irish Nation." The
entire collection is of great genealogical value.

The Public Record Office, London: M. S. Giuseppi published *A Guide to the Manuscripts Preserved in the Public
Record Office of England.* State Papers of Ireland deposited
in this repository have been transcribed or microfilmed by the
two Public Record Offices in Belfast and Dublin, and also by
the National Library of Ireland. Among the microfilms of
the latter repository are "Irish Applicants for Emigration to
North America, 1827." Also "Irish Exchequer Rolls, nos.
234-239; 540, 547." Many Irish family manuscripts of more
or less importance are here.

The Society of Genealogists, London: The outstanding
manuscript collection is the seventeen volumes of typescript
copies of the W. H. Welply abstracts of about 2,500 Irish
Wills, Administrations, Marriage Licences, Chancery and
Exchequer Bills, bound in chronological order, from 1569 to
1808. Also included are Pedigree extracts from Plea and
Memoranda Rolls (18 Richard II to 15 Henry VIII). This
original Welply collection was given to the Public Record Office of Northern Ireland, Belfast. It is indexed in the 1934
*Report of the Deputy Keeper of the Public Records of North-
ern Ireland.* The copy of this Welply collection was made for
the Society of Genealogists, London, by J. R. Hutchinson, in
1934. It is indexed. The Rev. Wallace Clare has presented
his "Abstracts from some Irish Wills" to this library. It has
a number of published source materials of Irish interest. One
is *Lambeg Churchyard, Lisburn, County Antrim, Inscriptions on Old Tombstones, 1626-1837.*

Somerset House: This repository, which contains the wills
proved in the Prerogative Court of Canterbury, includes many
Irish Prerogative Wills. Other Irish Prerogative Wills proved
in the Prerogative Court of York are deposited in York, England. Many Irish living in England at time of death, whose
property of more than five pounds sterling in value was then
all in one English diocese, made wills which were proved in
the Consistorial Court of the diocese. These will be found

in the various Diocesan Registry Offices in England. Mr. John Ainsworth published a "Calendar of Irish Wills, 1634-1652," which were proved in the Prerogative Court of Canterbury and are now at Somerset House, London. This appeared in the *Journal of the Royal Society of Antiquaries of Ireland*, vol. 78, pt. 2, pp. 24-37. A "List of Irish Wills and Administrations proved in the Prerogative Court of Canterbury, 1751-1775," edited by the Rev. Wallace Clare, was published in the *Irish Genealogist*, Vol. I, No. 5, p. 161.

OXFORD:

The Bodleian Library: The most important Irish collection in this library is the great Ormond Manuscript collection called the "Carte Manuscripts." The National Library of Ireland has microfilmed these manuscripts on eighty microfilms. They are listed with subject matter in the *National Library of Ireland Report of the Council of Trustees for 1950-1951*, pp. 103-106. MSS. Vol. 69, Microfilm No. 155 (Negative), contains the History of the Butler Family (of the 1st Duke of Ormonde) ; the Correspondence of Thomas, Earl of Ormonde, 1577-1612; the Correspondence of James, 1st Duke of Ormonde, 1633-1641, and thereafter through many microfilms to 1689. For calendar of the Rawlinson collection, see *Analecta Hibernica*, Nos. 1 and 2.

SCOTLAND:

Edinburgh, H. M. Register House: Records of Irish interest in this repository have been transcribed by the Public Record Office of Northern Ireland and are calendared in the various *Reports of the Deputy Keeper*, describing and indexing the collections.

Edinburgh, National Library of Scotland: The Public Record Office of Northern Ireland has also transcribed records of Irish interest in this library and reported on them in the same way as above.

WALES:

Aberystwyth: National Library of Wales. Many families of Wales settled in Ireland in the 12th to 18th centuries. Genealogical source materials regarding their origins and genealogy are in this library. See the catalogue of this library.

CHAPTER IV

THE GENEALOGICAL OFFICE
(OFFICE OF ARMS)

The Genealogical Office (Office of Arms) is located in Dublin Castle, Dublin. Mr. Gerard Slevin, who has the rank of Chief Herald of Ireland, is the present Director. He has an able staff of genealogists as assistants.

The Irish Office of Arms was created in 1552, by Edward VI. On 1 June 1552, Bartholomew Butler, by Royal commission, was appointed the first Ulster King of Arms, to open an Office of Arms in Dublin. Previously, he had been commissioned York Herald and member of the College of Arms in London. The Ulster King of Arms was under the jurisdiction of the College of Arms, London, until after 1633, when a separation was made between the two.

On 31 March 1943, the Government of the Republic of Ireland took jurisdiction over the records in the Office of Arms in Dublin Castle. This repository then became known as the Genealogical Office and was made a department of the National Library of Ireland. Mr. T. U. Sadleir, a great Irish genealogist, had filled the position of Registrar and Deputy Ulster King of Arms, from 1913 to March 1943. He was succeeded by Dr. Edward MacLysaght, who became Chief Herald and Genealogical Officer. He has also served as Chairman of the Irish Manuscripts Commission, as Keeper of the Manuscripts in the National Library, and is the author of *Irish Families* published in 1957.

In 1943, when the office of Ulster King of Arms was discontinued in Dublin, it was returned to the jurisdiction of the College of Arms, London. None of the original records of the Ulster Office in Dublin Castle were removed at the time of the change. However, records relating to Irish Arms, Heraldry and early pedigrees, etc., were photostated for the College of Arms, London, where they are deposited and form the following collections: The Visitation of Dublin, 1568, 1607; The

Visitation of Wexford, 1618; The Grants of Arms in Ireland, A-H, 8 vols.; The Knights' Arms in Ireland, 4 vols.; The Record Pedigrees of Ireland, 27 vols.; The Peers' Pedigrees of Ireland and other records, 10 vols.; The Baronets' Pedigrees, 2 vols.; Royal Warrants, etc., concerning Ireland, 13 vols.; The Sir William Betham Pedigree Charts, 1536-1800, made from his abstracts of all Prerogative Wills and Administrations within these dates, 39 vols. Irish collections acquired by the College of Arms, London, at an earlier date are: The John Lodge (who lived 1692-1774) collection of abstracts and extracts from the Public Records of Ireland, made in the course of his work as a great Irish genealogist, 33 vols.; the Sir William Betham abstracts of Funeral Entries and Lords' Entries, from records in the Ulster Office of Arms, comprising several volumes; the Sir Bernard Burke manuscript collection of genealogical records, 33 vols; the A. J. Toppin collection of the H. B. Swanzy manuscripts, consisting of 2 volumes of abstracts of Irish Wills, and 3 volumes of abstracts of Chancery and Exchequer Bills. All of the above collections will be described in this chapter among the original records or transcripts and abstracts in the Genealogical Office, Dublin Castle.

The Genealogical Office makes searches and provides copies of the records for the following: Pedigree searches, Arms searches, Grants and other Patents, Heraldic illustrations, Certificates, Registrations of Pedigrees. The Heraldic Museum is open to the public and attracts many over-sea visitors. The records and collections in this office, due to their age, fragile condition, and irreplaceable value, are not open to the public. However, this is not a handicap to genealogists. Mr. Gerard Slevin, Chief Herald of Ireland, is most anxious to co-operate with anyone who requests a search of the records.

An American must send a registration fee of $9.00 with a request for a search of the records of an Irish family. A four-page pedigree form, with space for information regarding four generations, will be returned to the client, to be filled out with any information in his possession. Also a sheet showing a scale of fees will be sent. The registration fee will be applied on the charges for a search but will not be returned.

If an American wishes to place his case in the hands of this office, requesting that photostats of any records be sent as references, a member of the staff of this office will undertake the work. A general genealogical search through Office Records, and a report thereon, with extracts typed, will cost about $20.00. An additional charge will be made for photostats and any expenses for a search of outside sources. At the end of this chapter, an illustration will be given of the extensive information received by this compiler who sent $20.00 for a report on the records in this repository which concern one family and four other allied families.

There are 701 volumes of manuscript collections in the Genealogical Office, numbered from Volume 1 to Volume 701, A. These are large ledgers, containing on the average from 300 to 600 pages. There are also many legal-size boxes containing collections of original documents, transcripts and abstracts of records, varying in class and subject. Besides the manuscript collections, this Office maintains a library of printed genealogical source materials and published family genealogies, collections of pedigrees, etc.

The records in the Genealogical Office have been filmed on 127 microfilms and an annotated list of the records on each film accompanies the microfilms. This work was done about 1950, for the lasting benefit of Ireland and the United States, by representatives of the Genealogical Society of Utah, in Salt Lake City, Utah. The original negatives and positives are in the library of this Society under the auspices of the Church of Jesus Christ of Latter Day Saints, Salt Lake City, Utah. Copies of the microfilms are in the National Library of Ireland. Microfilms of the 39 volumes of Sir William Betham's Pedigree Charts, which are a part of the Genealogical Office collections, are now deposited in the Library of Congress, Washington, D. C. Thus, Americans are fortunate in that they now have access to the microfilms of all collections and records in the Genealogical Office, Dublin Castle, and can personally examine the filmed records.

An 85-page typed list of the manuscript collections and records in the Genealogical Office, annotated with a description of the contents of each volume and box of records, is deposited in the National Library of Ireland. This library has microfilmed the list and plans to have it printed.

The Genealogical Office also has a complete name index to all records, transcripts and abstracts in the Office.

In 1955, after a previous visit to the Genealogical Office to collect information, this compiler was allowed, by special permission, to work for five days with the original records in this Office and was given the opportunity personally to examine many of the 701 volumes, several boxes of documents, transcripts and abstracts, and also the 85-page typed list of the collections from which the descriptions of many volumes were copied. (This special privilege was allowed this compiler because it was known by Dr. Richard J. Hayes, Director of the National Library of Ireland, and Mr. Gerard Slevin, Chief Herald of Ireland, that the work on this two-volume GUIDE to the Irish genealogical records was in progress.)

The source materials in the Genealogical Office will be described by subject as follows:

ARMS, HERALDRY AND PEDIGREES: Records of this nature may be found all through the collections preserved in this repository. Among the 701 volumes, numbers 1-46 contain "Emblazons of Arms of Irish Peers; Arms of English, Welsh and Anglo-Irish families, identified with Ireland; Arms of created Irish Peers; Arms of Scottish Peers," etc. These records include genealogical information. The ledgers average in size, 13″ by 8″. The emblazons of Arms are in color, painted by heraldic artists between the 16th and 19th centuries, on parchment. The colors are clear and the work is beautiful. These constitute the "Register of Ulster's Grants of Arms from 1552"; "Official Grants of Arms from 1698"; "Knights Arms (Knights dubbed in Ireland) 1565-1687" and miscellaneous records included. Volume No. 20 contains "Papers and accounts relating to ʻfees of honor payable on change of name, grant of Arms, investiture of Knights," etc., with index. Volume No. 26 contains a "List of persons who had assumed other surnames than their paternal names, without Royal Licences or authority, and of persons who bore arms without authority." This list was compiled by Sir William Betham, with additions by Sir Bernard Burke, also indexed. Volume No. 29 contains the "Ordinary of Arms of English, Welsh and a few Anglo-Irish families, treating principally of fields and partitions, compiled circa 1600." Volume No. 32 contains "Emblazons in color, of the Coats-of-Arms of Irish Peers," compiled by or under the direction of Christopher Ussher, Ulster King of Arms, circa 1595-1597. Volume No. 33 contains "Emblazons in color of the Armorial Achievements of Irish Peers. Emblazons in color of the Arms of Kings of Scotland and their wives, and of Scottish Peers," compiled by or under the direction of William Roberts, Ulster King of Arms, circa 1645, with some short notes added in a hand of a late date, with index. Volume No. 34 contains "Emblazons in color of the Armorial Achievements of the Irish Nobility, with some short historical and genealogical notes as to their ancestry," compiled by Daniel Molyneux, Ulster King of Arms, circa 1597-1603, with index. Volume No. 46 contains "Arms of Officers sent to Ireland, 1649, of Sothill's Venables', Sankey's and Lawrence's Regiments, by the House of Parliament, with notes on their descents," compiled by Albon Leveret, Athlone Office of Arms, 1649, and with some later entries certified by Richard Carney, Principal Herald of Arms *circa* 1657, with index.

There are 27 volumes of "Record Pedigrees"; 10 volumes of Irish Peers' Pedigrees since 1707, and other Lords' Entries; 2 volumes of Baronets' Pedigrees from 1789; 13 volumes of Royal Warrants, etc., listing data on changes of names and Arms, 1795. Volume No. 50 contains a "List of Peers, Baronets and Knights created in Ireland, 1558-1727," also with "Precedence Lists of Irish Peers, 1639 and 1641." (314 pp.) Sir William Betham's 39 volumes of Pedigree Charts are described under the subject of Wills.

CENSUS RECORDS: Some extracts from the destroyed Census Records of Ireland are contained in various manuscript collections in the Genealogical Office. Transcripts of Census Records have been procured whenever possible. The *Religious Census* of Ireland, furnished in 1766 to the Irish House of Commons by the Protestant Rectors of each parish, were destroyed in the fire of 1922 in the Public Record Office, Dublin. However, the Genealogical Office has transcripts, made

before the fire, for a number of parishes. They show the head
of each family, his religion (Roman Catholic or Protestant),
and are arranged by county, parish, town or townland, and
were returned by diocese. These are listed in PART THREE of
this volume under this subject.

FORFEITED ESTATES: Volume No. 481 contains the "Chichester House Claims, circa 1700," concerning the forfeited
estates of Catholics after the Williamite War.

FREEHOLDER'S LISTS: These lists are a valuable source for
locating a "freeman." A freeman was listed as in the following
example: "Baker, George, son of the late Richard Baker,
Ballydavid, Co. Tipperary, 6/8/1817." The lists were compiled by townland, town, city and district, for the county. The
Genealogical Office has the lists for counties of Armagh, 1753;
Donegal, 1761-1775; Fermanagh, 1788; Limerick, 1776; Longford, 1830-1835; Meath, circa 1790; Queen's 1758-1775; Tipperary, 1776; Westmeath, 1761. Further lists and explanation of these records will appear under the subject in PART
THREE of this volume.

FUNERAL ENTRIES (CERTIFICATES): The Genealogical Office has seventeen volumes of these entries dating from 1588-
1729. These contain records of the funerals of the gentry and
some of higher rank, as set forth in certificates issued by the
Ulster King of Arms or his deputy who officially attended the
Funeral Ceremony at the request of the relatives of the deceased and, upon receipt of a fee, duly registered the record in
the Office of Arms, setting forth the following information:
The name of the deceased, his residence and rank (such as
"Knight," "Esquire," "Gentleman"), his parentage and residence of parents (often from two to several earlier generations), name of wife and her parentage with residence, names
of children in order of sex and birth, their marriages or condition as minors, the date and place of burial, name of the
person who furnished the above information for the Funeral
Certificate and his relationship to the deceased. The Certificate is accompanied by Armorial and genealogical notes made
by Officers of Arms, concerning the family. Coats-of-Arms
are attached. An Index to the Funeral Entries, 1588-1729, is

contained in volume 386, in this Office. The volumes containing the Funeral Entries are as follows: Vol. 64, "Funeral Entries," (Vol. 1), 1588-1617; Vol. 65, (Vol. 2), 1588-1617; Vol. 66, (Vol. 3), 1604-1622; Vol. 67, (Vol. 4), 1651-1682; Vol. 68, (Vol. 5), 1622-1633; Vol. 69, (Vol. 6), 1633-1636; Vol. 70, (Vol. 7), 1636-1661; Vol. 71, (Vol. 8), 1639-1641; Vol. 72, (Vol. 9), 1640-1641, 1643, 1652; Vol. 73, (Vol. 10), 1629-1723; Vol. 74, (Vol. 11), 1672-1681; Vol. 75, (Vols. 12 and 13), 1682-1687, 1683-1689; Vol. 76, (Vol. 14), 1651-1691; Vol. 77, (Vol. 15), 1662-1698; Vol. 78, (Vol. 16), 1651-1672; Vol. 79, (Vol. 17), 1622-1729. These dates show that there is no single chronological arrangement, nor are they compiled in a geographical arrangement. The Name Index in Vol. 386 covers all entries. An additional volume belonging in this collection was somehow detached from the set and deposited in the British Museum (Add. MS. 4820). This volume contains the Funeral Entries set forth in 817 Certificates, together with 660 Heraldic illustrations of Arms attached to the Certificates. The Funeral Entries and the illustrations of Arms were copied in the British Museum by Mr. C. T. Lamacraft, and were published in the *Journal of the Irish Memorials Association*, vols. 7 and 8. They were later published in a separate volume, with index. A Funeral Entry of average length in this latter British Museum MS. volume, page 304, no. 647, is as follows: "PATRICK WHITE of the Citty of Corke als White of Pardellstown in the County of Corke Gent., eldest Son and Heir of Edmond White of the same Gent., eldest Son and Heir of Vincent White of the same Gent., eldest Son and Heir of Edmond White of Cloghdwa in the said County Gent. The said Patrick married Christian daughter of Sir Walter Coppinger of Corke, Knt., by whom He had 5 Sons and one Daughter viz. Walter eldest son and Heir, married to Ellen daughter of William Cogan of Bearneheale in the said County Gent; Edmund 2nd, Dominick 3rd, —4th, —5th, all young and not married . . . . the said Patrick died at Cork . . . 163—. . . and was Interr'd in Christ Church in the Sd. Citty of Corke. The truith of the premiss's is test'd by Subscription of Walter White, Son and Heir of the deceased, who returned this Certificate into my Office to be there recorded taken by me Thomas Preston, Esq., Ulster King of Armes the 17th February 1640."

Some "Funeral Processions" 1630-1690, give lists of names of the mourners present at the funerals.

HEARTHMONEY ROLLS: This was a tax on every hearth or chimney in Ireland of 2 shillings. It existed under English law from 1662-1689, and was thereafter reimposed for a time. The Genealogical Office has transcripts of the Rolls for several counties, mostly 1664-1666, which are further described and listed under the subject, in PART THREE of this volume.

INQUISITIONS POST MORTEM: These supply genealogical information given as evidence of the heirs of a tenant *in capite* of the Crown, from the time of Queen Elizabeth (a few in the time of Henry VIII) and come down to the restoration of Charles II, at which time the feudal tenure of property was abolished by Act of Parliament. On death of a person having such property, an "Inquisition Post Mortem" was held. These give an account of the deceased person, his property, date of his death, name of his heir and age at time of death of the deceased, and a description of the acreage and location of the property left by the deceased. The Genealogical Office has four volumes of abstracts of the "Inquisitions Post Mortem" 1550-1690, by John Lodge. The Repertories of Inquisitions Post Mortem for Leinster and Ulster, 1603-1649, were printed by the Record Commissioners, 1826-1829. Transcripts of the Munster and Connaught Inquisitions are in the Public Record Office, Dublin.

LAND RECORDS, ETC.: The Genealogical Office has transcripts of the John Lodge manuscript collection containing 14 volumes of extracts of genealogical value concerning Irish items from the Patent Rolls, grants of land, liveries, deeds, leases, wardships, etc., also 9 volumes of "Repertory to Records of the Exchequer." This Office has the *Fifteenth Annual Report on the Records of Ireland*, 1825, which contains Abstracts of Grants under the "Acts of Settlement and Explanation," 1666-1684, and an "Index to the Inrolments for Adventurers Soldiers etc., 1666."

MANUSCRIPT COLLECTIONS: There are several important

manuscript collections in this Office including genealogical records of Sir William Betham, Sir Edmund Bewley, Col. W. O. Cavenagh, Philip Crosslé, J. N. C. Atkins Davis, P. B. Eustace, D. O'Callaghan Fisher, Sir Alfred Irwin, Edmund Festus Kelly, Alfred Molony, T. U. Sadleir, the Very Rev. H. B. Swanzy, and W. H. Welply. These collections all contain transcripts or abstracts of Wills, which are described below. Roger O'Ferrall's *Linea Antiqua*, a manuscript volume of genealogies dated prior to 1709, is transcribed in three volumes with added notes by Sir William Betham.

MARRIAGE RECORDS: This Office has abstracts of the Prerogative Marriage Licence Grants to 1800. Among the Sir William Betham Genealogical Abstracts in the Public Record Office, Dublin, are 20 volumes of abstracts of the Prerogative Marriage Licences, 1629-1801 (58th *Report*, pp. 25, 26). The Genealogical Office also has abstracts of the Dublin Marriage Licence Grants, complete to 1823. The Sir William Betham collection of abstracts in the Public Record Office, Dublin, also includes 54 volumes of Dublin Marriage Licences, 1660-1824 *(ibid.)*. Other printed marriage records in this Office library are listed in PART THREE, under the chapter on this subject.

MILITARY RECORDS: Besides the various printed Military Records in the library of this Office, such as *King James's Irish Army List* containing genealogical information, the Genealogical Office has also a manuscript entitled, "A Return of Regiments Quartered in Ireland, circa 1769-1773," which contains the name, age, and county of birth of each officer. See also Lodge's Manuscripts. See also VOLUME II, PART FOUR.

PUBLIC OFFICE: This Office has many printed and manuscript sources regarding lists, biographies etc., of those who held public office. The Frazer Manuscripts contain a list of "High Sheriffs for Irish Counties, 1302-1862." (Public Record Office, 55th *Report*, p. 142.) See also Lodge's Manuscripts.

VISITATIONS: The extant original Visitations in this Office number only three: Dublin, 1568 and 1607; Wexford, 1618. Copies of Visitations in the British Museum are: Connaught, 1615 (Add. MS. 19836); Leinster, 1615 (Add. MS.

19836) ; Munster, 1615 (Add. MS. 19836).   See also Narbon's
Visitation of Ireland in Add. MS. fo. 40b.

WILLS: A full explanation of the Prerogative and Diocesan Wills, together with information regarding the various
collections, is presented in PART THREE of this volume in the
chapter on this subject.   One of the most outstanding collections in the Genealogical Office is the 39 volumes containing
the Genealogical Charts, made by Sir William Betham from
Notebooks in which he had made abstracts of all of the Prerogative Wills and Administrations in Ireland, 1536-1800.
Betham called these Pedigree Charts his "Genealogical Analysis" of all of his Abstracts.   Betham's Genealogical Abstracts
fill 241 Notebooks which are in the Public Record Office of
Ireland, Dublin (58th *Report*, p. 25).   Of these, 80 volumes
contain abstracts of the Prerogative Wills, 1536-1800, and
56 volumes contain abstracts of the Prerogative Administrations, 1595-1800.   The 39 volumes of Pedigree Charts show
the names, dates, and place names of the testators and names
of members of the family, other relatives, and place names
in some instances.   Betham's charts show from two to many
generations, as in many cases he combined the information in
the Wills and Administrations of testators in several generations of a family to make one chart of from one to several
pages.   Betham's "Will Pedigree Charts" were used after his
term of office as Ulster King of Arms, 1820-1853, by his successors in office.   In the course of time, these later officers
added countless annotations to Betham's charts as they uncovered proven genealogical information.   This has added
value to the charts.   Betham's successor Ulster King of
Arms, Sir Bernard Burke, copied or had copies of all of
Betham's Pedigree Charts made for his private use.   These
are contained in 42 volumes which were purchased by the
Public Record Office of Northern Ireland, Belfast.   These are
described in the chapter concerning this repository (CHAPTER
VI, in this PART TWO).   All of the Wills represented in the
Betham Pedigree Charts (or the Burke copies) are listed in
the *Index to the Prerogative Wills of Ireland, 1536-1810,* edited
by Sir Arthur Vicars (Ulster King of Arms), Dublin, 1897.
This published Index may be found in most of the large gene-

alogical libraries of the United States and serves to indicate the existence of records of a testator before 1800, which will be found incorporated in the Betham charts. Thus, anyone can request a photostat of any Pedigree Chart containing the name of any testator listed in Vicars' "Index." The Genealogical Office also has abstracts of the "Prerogative Grants of Administrations" prior to 1800.

An "Index of Will Abstracts in the Genealogical Office, Dublin," has been compiled by Miss P. Beryl Eustace, who presented it to the Irish Manuscripts Commission for publication in its periodical *Analecta Hibernica* No. 17, Dublin Stationery Office, 1949. This Index to the Will Abstracts, found in the various manuscript collections of the Genealogical Office, lists about 7,500 testators (largely Diocesan Wills) by name, description (title, occupation, etc.) residence, date of Administration, Diocese and collection. These, with a Foreword, are listed in 200 pages of *Analecta Hibernica* No. 17, which can be purchased directly from the Government Publications Sale Office, 3-4 College Street, Dublin, price ten shillings, sixpence, or through any Bookseller in Dublin. The manuscript collections represented are those of Sir Edmund Bewley, Col. W. O. Cavenagh, "Charitable Donations and Bequests" (Short abstracts made by T. U. Sadleir, from the Report of the Commissioners, 1805 and 1814), Philip Crosslé, J. N. C. Atkins Davis, Drought Will abstracts made by Philip Crosslé, P. B. Eustace, D. O'Callaghan Fisher (over 2,000 abstracts of Dublin Diocesan Wills, 16th-18th century, and of Cork and Cloyne Diocesan Wills), Sir Alfred Irwin, Edmund Festus Kelly, Memorials of Wills printed in *Journals of the Irish Memorials Association*, Alfred Molony, T. U. Sadleir, the Very Rev. H. B. Swanzy (863 abstracts, largely of Down, Connor and Dromore Diocesan Wills), W. H. Welply (collection of 500 Will abstracts). These Will abstracts vary in length from a few words to complete copies of Wills. The Bewley collection contains abstracts of Catholic Episcopal Wills.

EXAMPLE OF A GENERAL SEARCH MADE BY THE GENEALOGI-
CAL OFFICE FOR FAMILY RECORDS

In July 1955, this compiler wrote to Mr. Gerard Slevin, Chief Herald and Genealogical Officer, Genealogical Office (Of-

fice of Arms), Dublin Castle, Dublin, asking that a general
search of the records be made for anything pertaining to the
Pomeroy family of County Cork and allied families of Holmes,
Deane, Towgood, and Love, also of County Cork, giving partic-
ular attention to records of Thomas Holmes Pomeroy who
died in 1752, his wife Andriah Towgood, her mother Melian
Deane, daughter of Sir Mathew Deane; the parents of Thomas
Holmes Pomeroy who were William and Martha (Pomeroy)
Holmes, her father Samuel Pomeroy who made her eldest son,
Thomas Holmes, his heir, provided he assume the name
Pomeroy, which he did.   A Deed (Memorial No. 36737,
Registry of Deeds), of Thomas Holmes Pomeroy dated 6th and
7th March 1726, named his wife Andriah and sons Matthew,
Samuel, William and George.   Records in other Irish reposi-
tories and published sources had provided the above names
and relationships, also the names of Samuel Love and Sampson
Towgood who were the first and second husbands of Melian
Deane.   A general search of the records of the Genealogical
Office was requested for all records pertaining to these families and any branches thereof.   A check for $20.00 was sent
to cover the expense.   An extensive annotated list of references was returned, together with a list of the indexes from
which they were taken.   The records were fully enough described for this compiler to know which records should be
photostated.   The report will illustrate the extensive and
satisfactory work which is done for a client in this Office.

A letter from Mr. Slevin, dated 19 August 1955, to this
compiler states:

"I have the pleasure of enclosing a report on the Pomeroy
and Holmes material in the records of this Office.   The principal manuscript sources have been consulted in the case of each
family and also a limited number of printed works.   The report contains a note of the nature and extent of the information available in each record and we trust these notes will be
sufficient to enable you to decide whether the data is relevant
to your query.   We shall be glad to arrange to have photostats made of any entries which are of interest to you.   In
the case of the Love and Deane families the time at our disposal did not permit of so extensive a search or of assembling

of a full account of all information available in our records. The report does, however, include a note of any material which is relevant to your problem."

POMEROY REPORT FROM THE GENEALOGICAL OFFICE

Sources consulted: *Pomeroy.*

Index to Registered Pedigrees _____ G.O. MSS. Vol. 469
Index to Unofficial Pedigrees _____ G.O. MSS. Vol. 470
Index to Prerogative Wills _____ (ed. Vicars).
Index to Wills at the Genealogical Office _____ G.O. MSS. Vol. 429
Index to Funeral Entries _____ G.O. MSS. Vol. 386
Prerogative Administrations Intestate _____ G.O. MSS. Vol. 259
Obituary Notices from Newspapers _____ G.O. MSS. Vol. 550
Marriages from Exshaws and Hibernian Magazines G.O. MSS. Vol. 133
Prerogative Marriage Licences _____ G.O. MSS. Vol. 607
Chichester House Claims, c. 1700 _____ G.O. MSS. Vol. 481
Index to Grants and Confirmations of Arms ____ G.O. MSS. Vol. 422-3

Reports on Records:

G.O. 176. Registered Pedigrees, vol. 22, pp. 75-77. Pedigree of Pomerai of Sandridge, Devon, covering 17 generations. The descent is traced from Joel, or Jocelin, De Pomerai, who married a natural daughter of King Henry I, to the generation of Valentine Pomerai of East Ogwell, 1620.

G.O. 292. Betham Ms. 2nd series vol. 1, pp. 549-50. Narrative account of the Pomeroy or de Pomerai family giving details of various generations from Ralph de la Pomerai (father of Joel who commences the pedigree in G.O. 176, pp. 75-77) to the generations living in the time of Henry VIII.

G.O. 184. Lords' Entries, vol. 2, p. 153. Entry of the Rt. Hon. Arthur Pomeroy, Baron Harberton (cr. 10 Oct. 1783). Details of his marriage and sons are recorded. An addition records the marriages and issue of two of his sons. (Narrative form). Dated 1778 and 1791. Page 155, gives a further entry of the Rt. Hon. Arthur Pomeroy, Baron Harberton, which includes full particulars of his daughters. (Narrative form). Dated 1778.

G.O. 185. Lords' Entries, vol. 3, p. 312. Entry of the Rt. Hon. Arthur Pomeroy, Viscount and Baron Harberton. Details of his parentage, brother, marriage, children and grandchildren are included. This entry in pedigree form embodies all of the details in the entries in G.O. 184, pp. 153, 155. Dated 1792.

G.O. 187. Lords' Entries, vol. 5, p. 123. Entry of John James Pomeroy, 5th Viscount Harberton and James Spencer, 6th Viscount Harberton. Details of the 5th Viscount, his marriage and issue are recorded. Pages 125-130, contain Viscount Harberton's claim to vote in the House of Lords. Copies of relevant certificates of marriage, birth and death together with copies of two statutory declarations. Dated 1863.

Genealogical Office Carton, VII. Copy of the entry in G.O. 185, p. 312. *G.O. 732.* (1) Pedigree of de la Pomerai, als. Pomeroy, commencing with Ralph de la Pomerai and finishing with the grandchildren of Valentine Pomeroy (as in G.O. 176 and G.O. 205). (2) Pedigree showing the descendants of Elizabeth, daughter of Henry Pomeroy of Sandridge, Devon. She married Sir Thomas Harris Knt., of Clotworthy Priory, serjeant-at-law, M.P. The families shown are Greatrakes, Nettles and Jones.

G.O. 205. Will Pedigrees, vol 3, pp. 112-115. Draft pedigree of Pomerai; afterwards Pomeroy. The pedigree commences with Sir Ralph de Pomerai and comes down to the generation of Valentine Pomeroy of East Ogwell, 1620. It corresponds to that in G.O. 176, pp. 75-77, except for the following additional details:

(1) The descendants, for 4 generations, of John Pomeroy, younger son of Sir Thomas Pomerai and Joan Chidleigh, are recorded.

(2) The descendants, for 3 generations, of Sir Thomas Pomeroy, K. B., younger son of Henry Pomerai and Amy Camill, are recorded.

(3) A note regarding the descendants of Amye, sister of Sir Thomas Pomeroy, K. B., is included.

(4) The children and grandchildren of Hugh Pomeroy, 2nd son of Sir Edward Pomeroy, K. B., and Jane Sapcotts are recorded.

In addition, the issue of grandchildren of Valentine Pomeroy of East Ogwell, are recorded and on this is a faint pencilled addition *affiliating "Samuel Pomeroy of the County of Cork" to Edward Pomeroy, brother of Valentine Pomery.* There is also a trick of arms, Pomeroy, quartering Valletort, Bevill, and Collaton. On page 116, is a pedigree (a continuation of that on p. 113), showing the affiliation of Edward Pomeroy (brother of Valentine Pomeroy) to Sir Thomas Pomeroy. A tentative affiliation line *links Samuel Pomeroy,* of Pallice, Co. Cork, to this Edward Pomeroy. Details of Samuel Pomeroy's issue are given, together with particulars of the children of his daughters Martha Holmes and Mary Coakley. Another tentative affiliation line brings in two further Holmes generations. Page 117, gives the pedigree of Pomeroy of Colleton in Devon; five generations, down to William Pomeroy, aged 14 in 1620. It is stated that John Pomeroy (uncle of this William) died in Ireland, having come over (briefly in the military forces) with Arthur Chichester, Lord Lieutenant of Ireland, and that his son Arthur Pomeroy was Dean of Cork.

G.O. 243. Will Pedigrees, vol. 21, pp. 304, 305. Page 304, contains pedigrees based on the will of Samuel Pomeroy, of Pallice, Co. Cork, dated 1703, recording his marriage, children and grandchildren. Page 305, contains a pedigree showing the descendants of Rev. Arthur Pomeroy, Dean of Cork, 1672, for three generations (his grandson Arthur Pomeroy was created Baron Harberton). A line which affiliated the Rev. Arthur Pomeroy to John Pomeroy of Devonshire (son of William Pomeroy and Mary Bevill) has been crossed out as has a line indicating that the Rev. Arthur Pomeroy was a brother of Samuel Pomeroy of Pallice, Co. Cork.

G.O. 289. Fisher Will Abstracts, p. 24. Abstract of the will of Samuel Pomeroy, proved 23 Jan. 1703.

G.O. 139, p. 117. Fisher Will Abstracts. Abstract of the will of Samuel Pomeroy, of Palles (Pallice), Co. Cork, proved 23 Jan. 1703/4. (Much fuller than in G. O. 289, p. 24, and includes details of lands.)

G.O. 552. Welply Will Abstracts. Abstract of the will of Thomas Holmes Pomeroy, of Palace (Pallice), Co. Cork, proved 4th Oct. 1752.

G.O. 259. Prerogative Administrations Intestate, p. 153. Pomeroy, Arthur, Dean of Cork, clk., administration to Rev. John Pomeroy for Elizabeth Pomeroy, the widow, and Richard, Elizabeth and Maria, the children. 12 Jan. 1709. Also for William Holmes Pomeroy (son of

Thomas Holmes Pomeroy), of Charleville, County Cork, Esq., administration to Susanna Holmes Pomeroy, the widow, Dated, 30 Jan. 1776.

G.O. 550. Obituary Notices from Newspapers. William Holmes
Pomeroy, at Charleville, Sept. 1775. Also two entries relating to the
family of Viscount Harberton.

G.O.133. Marriages from Exshaws and Hibernian Magazines. Two
references to the family of Viscount Harberton (p. 70 & 72).

Printed Sources: References to Pomeroy are noted in the following:

Index to Wills, Diocese of Cork & Ross, 1548-1800 (ed. Phillimore).

Index to Wills, Diocese of Cloyne, 1621-1800 (ed. Phillimore).

Index to Marriage Licences, Diocese of Cork & Ross, 1623-1750 (ed.
Gillman).

Index to Marriage Licences, Diocese of Cloyne, 1630-1800 (ed. Green).

Alumni Dublinenses, 1593-1860 (ed. Burtchaell & Sadleir).

Journal of the Irish Memorials Association.

Fifteenth Annual Report on the Records of Ireland, 1825:
   1. Abstracts of Grants under the Acts of Settlement and Explanation,
1666-1684.
   2. Index to the Inrolments for Adventurers Soldiers etc., 1666.

HOLMES REPORT FROM THE GENEALOGICAL OFFICE

Sources Consulted: *Holmes.*

Index to Registered Pedigrees _____ G.O. MSS. Vol. 469
Index to Unofficial Pedigrees _____ G.O. MSS. Vol. 470
Index to Prerogative Wills _____ (ed. Vicars).
Index to Wills at the Genealogical Office _____ G.O. MSS. Vol. 429
Index to Funeral Entries _____ G.O. MSS. Vol. 386
Index to Prerogative Administrations Intestate ___ G.O. MSS. Vol. 258
Index to Obituary Notices from Newspapers _____ G.O. MSS. Vol. 548
Topographical Notes on Buttevent etc. (Grove-White).
Index to Cork Historical Archaeological Society Journal.

Reports on Records: Holmes.

G.O. 275. Betham Ms. 1st series, Vol. XV, p. 199. Pedigree, covering
five generations, of Holmes of Castlefin, Co. Donegal. The pedigree commences with Robert Holmes who settled in Donegal about 1654, and
concludes with the generation born between 1750 and 1790.

G.O. 386. Index to Funeral Entries. Holmes, Cicely, of Dublin, 1608;
George of Dublin, 1675; Peter, of Dublin, 1675.

G.O. 183. Lords' Entries, Vol. I, p. 150. Entry of Lysaght, Lord Lisle.
Reference to the marriage of Nicholas Lysaght and Grace, youngest
daughter of Col. Thomas Holmes of Kilmallock.

G.O. 385. Bewley Ms., pp. 172-173. Pedigree of Holmes of Belfast and
afterwards of Dublin, covering six generations. The pedigree commences
with John Holmes, died 4 July 1779, and concludes with the generation
born about 1870-1890.

G.O. 384. Donovan Ms., p. 134. Pedigree of Holmes of Castlefin; a continuation of that in G.O. 275, p. 199. The additional material covers
three generations; the descendants of Benjamin Holmes, 1779-1868, and
concludes with a generation born about 1890-1906.

G.O. 576. Sadleir Ms., pp. 110, 111. Pedigree, covering five generations, of Holmes of Johnstown, (als. Peterfield), Co. Tipperary. The pedigree commences with Peter Holmes, of Dublin, died 1675, and concludes with the generation born about 1730. Page 111, contains the pedigree of Holmes, of Belmont, King's Co., and Peterfield, Co. Tipperary, covering four generations. This pedigree is a continuation of that on page 110. It commences with Gilbert Holmes who died in 1810, and concludes with a generation born about 1840.

G.O. 725. A carton containing MSS. in the hand of Atkins-Davis. A pedigree of Holmes of Mallow, Kilmallock, and Pallice. The pedigree covers six generations of Holmes. It commences with the Rev. Thomas Holmes of Lancashire, settled at Mallow, in the time of Queen Elizabeth, and concludes with the generation of Melian Holmes (died, 1755), who married James Roche, of Glynn Castle. Her brothers are also noted. The daughter and grand-daughter of Melian Holmes are also recorded. Also noted are some details of the *Towgood* family, and particulars of *Martha Pomeroy's father;* she married William Holmes.

G.O. 715. Family Record of Holmes and Baldrid. Janette Holmes (1694-1768), daughter of Sir James Holmes (died 1727), by his wife Lady Margaret Jennens, married William Baldrid, June 16th, 1714. The remainder of the record deals with the Baldrid family of Pennsylvania.

G.O. 404. Davis Ms., p. 96. Pedigree notes relating to Holmes of Mallow, Co. Cork, and Peterfield, Co. Tipperary (undated).

G.O. 235. Betham's Will Pedigrees, pp. 305-314. Pedigrees based on the wills of the following:

Page		Probate
305.	Holmes, Sampson, of Crownehorn, Co. Wicklow (2 generations). (On page 307, is a note of the issue of Andriah, daughter of Sampson Towgood, (who married Thomas Holmes Pomeroy, son of William and Martha (Pomeroy) Holmes. Thomas was heir to his grandfather Samuel Pomeroy and assumed the Pomeroy name). A connection with the above abstract is suggested.	1807
306.	Holmes, Mary, of Dublin (3 generations).	1718
306.	Holmes, John, of Dublin, taylor (2 generations).	1721
307.	Holmes, James, of Dublin, merchant (2 generations).	1732
307.	Holmes, George, of Liscloony, King's Co. (2 generations).	1737
307.	Holmes, Isabella, wife of George Holmes (2 generations).	1759
308.	Holmes, Janet, of Belfast (3 generations).	1744
308.	Holmes, Gabriel, of Belfast, mariner (1 generation).	1678
308.	Holmes, William, of Belfast, merchant (nephew & grand-nephew).	1760
309.	Holmes, John, of Ballintobber, Co. Limerick (2 generations). Beside this abstract, p. 309, is a draft pedigree relating to Holmes of Pallice (Thomas Holmes Pomeroy, son of William and Martha (Pomeroy) Holmes), Co. Cork; it covers 5 generations from Thomas Holmes of Kilmallock, living 1675, to Amelia Holmes, wife of Robert Phaire. There is also a note on the Holmes-Pomeroy alliance and issue on p. 314.	1754
309.	Holmes, William, of Donoghmore, Co. Tyrone (3 generations).	1762
310.	Holmes, Hugh, of Antigua, merchant (2 generations).	1762
310.	Holmes, Thomas, of Dublin, merchant (2 generations).	1766

Page   Probate
311. Holmes, John, of Belfast, merchant (3 generations).   1779
311. Holmes, Esther, of Cork (2 generations).   1779
312. Holmes, John, of Athlone, Co. Westmeath (1 generation).   1783
312. Holmes, Elizabeth, of Bollyart, barony of Kilcoursey (2
      generations).   1786
312. Holmes, Launcelot, of Millmount, Co. Roscommon (2 gener-
      ations).   1789
313. Holmes, Samuel, of Kells, Co. Meath (2 generations).   1789
313. Holmes, Robert, of Ballydam, Co. Limerick (2 generations). 1796
314. Holmes, Anne, of Dublin (2 generations).   1796
      There are also some notes of alliances (pp. 305, 306, 310, 311, 312).

G.O. 429. Index to Wills at the Genealogical Office. In the Genealogical
Office are abstracts of Wills of the following:

	Probate	Ms.	No.
Holmes, Allicia, Drogheda, widow.	1775.	512.	S-271
Holmes, Alice, London.	1828.	512.	I-130
Holmes, Elizabeth, Ballyart, King's Co.	1785.	512.	I-124
Holmes, Garner, Joseph, Lisduff, Co. Tipperary.	1845.	512.	I-124
Holmes, George, Lisclooney, King's Co.	1737.	512.	P-85
Holmes, George, Drogheda.	1824.	512.	I-129
Holmes, George, Drogheda.	1843.	512.	I-127
Holmes, George, Arbuthnot, Moorock, King's Co.	1847.	512.	S-245
Holmes, Gilbert, Dean of Ardfert, King's Co.	1847.	512.	S-248
Holmes, Henry Joy, Holywell, Co. Antrim.	1835.	512.	S-156
Holmes, Isabella, widow of George Holmes.	1759.	424.	p. 90
Holmes, James, Antrim.	1752.	512.	S-155
Holmes, John, Belfast.	1626.	512.	I-125
Holmes, Joseph, (Diocese of Clogher).	1785.	512.	S-242
Holmes, Peter, St. Mary's Parish, Oxmantown.	1675.	281.	p. 29
Holmes, Peter, Peterfield, Co. Tipperary.	1803.	512.	S-244
Holmes, Robert, Clongorey, Co. Kildare.	1683.	512.	I-64
Holmes, Sir Robert _____ Dated	1692.	427.	
Holmes, Samuel, Kells, Co. Meath.	1786.	512.	I-125
Holmes, Thomas, Drumnafinchin, Co. Cork, clk.	1718.	530.	
Holmes, Rev. William Anthony, D.D., Templemore, Co. Tipperary.	1844.	512.	S-250
Holmes, William, Cork Hill, Dublin, saddler.	1812.	487.	no. 61

G.O. 258. Prerogative Administrations Intestate. Fourteen entries between 1652 and 1791, but no reference to Holmes of Cork.

G.O. 548. Obituary Notices from Newspapers. Twenty entries between
1753 and 1810, but no reference to Holmes of Cork.

Topographical Notes on Buttevant, Co. Cork, and vicinity (including Kilmallock, Co. Limerick), by Col. James Grove White. There are isolated
references to the name Holmes in: Vol. I, pp. 241, 243, 305; Vol. II,
pp. 22, 215, 218, 249, 267; Vol. III, pp. 148-9, 176, 186. In Vol. IV, on
pages 206-212, are extensive pedigrees and notes on the Holmes family
of Shinnagh and Kilmallock.

Index to the Cork Historical and Archaeological Society Journal. The following references are noted:

Holmes, Peter, M.P. Doneraile, 1797-1800, etc. Vol. I, p. 471.

Holmes, Sir Peter, Vol. IX, pp. 123-4.

Holmes, Sir Peter, inscription on monument of. Vol. XXXIII, p. 34.

Holmes, Sir Peter, statue to (illustr.). Vol. XXXI, f. 68.

DEANE, LOVE AND TOWGOOD FAMILIES, REPORT FROM THE GENEALOGICAL OFFICE

Sources consulted: *Deane and Love, also Towgood.*

Index to Registered Pedigrees _____ G.O. MSS. Vol. 469

Index to Unofficial Pedigrees _____ G.O. MSS. Vol. 470

Index to Prerogative Wills _____ (ed. Vicars).

Index to Wills at the Genealogical Office _____ G.O. Vol. 429

Report on the Deane Family:

G.O. 265. Betham Ms. 1st series, vol. 5. p. 224. Pedigree of Deane, of Dromore, Bart., covering 7 generations. The Pedigree commences with Sir Mathew Deane, Knt., will proved 1717, and concludes with Robert Fitzmaurice Deane (born 1826), eldest son of the 3rd Lord Muskery.

G.O. 231. Betham's Will Pedigrees, New Series, vol. 9, p. 216. Pedigree of Deane, of Dromore, based on the wills of Sir Mathew Deane, Knt., proved 1717 etc. The pedigree covers the same period as that in G.O. Ms. p. 224, but includes additional details. Includes daughter Melian (Deane) Towgood.

Report on the Towgood Family:

G.O. 250. Betham's Will Pedigrees, New Series, vol. 28. Pedigree of Towgood, of Co. Cork, based on the wills of:

Andriah Towgood, widow (sister of John Good). Probate, 1717.

George Towgood, Esq. (son of Sampson and Melian Towgood, nee Deane, and brother of Andriah, wife of Thomas Holmes Pomeroy). Probate, 1720.

Report on the Love Family: Notes on the Love family (in the hand of Atkins Davis) include the following:

1. List of Love entries in Wills in Cork & Ross Diocese.
2. List of Love entries in Prerogative Grants.
3. List of Love entries in Doneraile Parish Register.
4. Isolated abstracts of Love wills and one Love deed.
5. Pedigree, 6 generations (1 name in each) of Love of Gt. Yarmouth.
6. Note from Bill in Chancery and will of Samuel Love; refers to Melian, daughter of Sir Mathew Deane, her husbands, Sampson Towgood and Samuel Love, and her issue by both.

* * *

Very shortly after receiving the above report from the Genealogical Office, this compiler made her third trip to Ireland in five years, to spend six weeks studying the records in all of the principal repositories of genealogical records. With special permission, this compiler was allowed to examine all of the above listed records and other deposits. Many photostats of records which concerned the Pomeroy, Holmes, Towgood, Deane, Love, and other allied families were ordered. These were used in combination with records in other repositories, to compile the genealogies of these families which were published in *The History and Genealogy of the Pomeroy Family and Collateral Lines*, Part One. Cuneo Eastern Press, U. S. A., 1958.

The above report was given space in this chapter to illustrate the fact that the Genealogical Office has a wealth of records which concern the Irish and the Scotch-Irish gentry, as well as the records of titled families. Everyone making a study of a family in Ireland should allow sufficient funds to have a general search made in this repository for all records concerning the family, as soon as the geographical location and some other identifying facts are known. These records must be used in combination with records in other repositories, described in PART TWO, hereof.

CHAPTER V

THE PUBLIC RECORD OFFICE OF
IRELAND, DUBLIN

The Public Record Office of Ireland is located in the Four Courts, Dublin. The Search Room is open to the public from 10:00 a. m. to 4:00 p. m., on Monday through Friday and from 10:00 a. m. to 12:00 noon on Saturday.

Any search for genealogical records of a family in Ireland should be extended to include an examination of the source materials in this repository, as collections representing all of the thirty-two counties are here.

Mr. Diarmid Coffey was appointed Assistant Deputy Keeper of the Records in 1936 and, since October 1944, has carried out the duties of the Deputy Keeper. Mr. James L. J. Hughes was appointed Acting Assistant in 1944 and was confirmed in the office of Assistant in October 1948. Miss Margaret C. Griffith was appointed Assistant in November 1944. Mr. Mac-Giolla Choille was appointed Assistant in 1945. This compiler is indebted to all these archivists for their time and courtesy during three periods of work here in 1951, 1952, and 1955.

A genealogist or record searcher, upon arriving at the Public Search Room, will be directed to the general indexed catalogues, the card indexes in the cabinets, the manuscript volumes of indexes, the printed indexes, and the volumes containing annotated lists of the records in special collections. Records selected from the indexes, etc., will be brought to the Search Room for examination at one of the tables available to visitors. Registration and a small daily fee is required of each record searcher.

Attention will be given to correspondence if accompanied by a registration fee of $9.00. This will cover a reply and an estimate for the photostating of any specific record ordered. A request for a general search of records pertaining to any one family and an annotated report will cost about $20.00. An estimate for this work can be requested. Abstracts of records, or complete copies of documents or photostats, will require an extra charge.

Anyone interested in Irish genealogy should know the history of this repository in order to understand and appreciate the records of a genealogical nature which are presently deposited here.

The Public Record Office of Ireland was established in Dublin, under the provisions of the Public Records (Ireland) Act, 12 August 1867. Its purpose was to establish one central office, and to provide a better custody of the records of the nature belonging in a Public Record Office, which records were then in the keeping of several repositories and had reached the age of twenty years or more.

About two years after this office was established, in 1869, the Search Room and the records were open to the public. Calendars, catalogues, accession lists and indexes of the records were prepared for some collections and were being compiled for others.

The bulk of the collections deposited in the first ten years had been accumulating in other repositories in Ireland during previous centuries. They represented many classes of source materials of genealogical interest. Some of these and other collections acquired before 1922 are noted as follows:

THE TESTAMENTARY RECORDS included the Wills proved in the Prerogative Court, 1536-1858, together with the Prerogative Grants of Administration and the Prerogative Administration Bonds; the Diocesan Wills, proved in the various Consistorial Courts, the Diocesan Grants of Administration and the Diocesan Administration Bonds, all dated from the 16th century to 1858; the Wills, Grants of Administration and the Administration Bonds, 1858-1900, from the Principal and the various District Probate Registries.

THE MARRIAGE RECORDS included the Prerogative and Diocesan Marriage Licence Grants and Bonds, dated from the 17th century to 1845. These were indexed by name of the groom and the bride, the year of marriage, and the volume and page number of the record.

CENSUS AND TAX LISTS, such as the Census Records for all counties, 1813, 1821, 1831, 1851; Parliamentary Returns regarding Religion, 1766, listing Catholic and Protestant heads of families by parish, diocese and county; the 1740 Householders' lists, by parish, barony and county; Tax Rolls such as the Hearth Money Rolls, 1663-1669, listing every man with one or more fire-hearths, by parish, barony and county; Subsidy Rolls, 1663-1668; Poll Money Rolls, 1695-1699; Tithe Applotment Books and lists compiled for tax purposes, 17th-19th centuries.

THE PAROCHIAL REGISTERS of the Established Church of Ireland, from 1,006 of the 1,643 parishes, with entries of marriages previous to 31 March 1845, baptisms and burials prior to 1871.

LAND RECORDS consisting of deeds recited in Chancery and Exchequer Courts; Ecclesiastical deeds; deeds recited in the Incumbered and Landed Estates Court. Other Chancery and Exchequer Court records containing much genealogical information include Wills recited, Affidavits, Inquisitions Post Mortem and on Attainder, Fiants (Warrants, Pardons, Appointments, etc.), Patents, Pipe Rolls, Lists of Crown Rents, Quit Rents, and rentals of undisposed forfeited lands (17th-18th centuries).

THE CIVIL SURVEY, *1654-1656,* made to discover and record by barony, the possessions of proprietors of lands and the tenures and titles of their estates, for all of the Province of Leinster, all of Ulster except the barony of Farney in County Monaghan, all of Munster except County Clare, and only the County of Leitrim in Connaught (then Connacht) ; in all showing the forfeited lands of Roman Catholics, Crown lands, Church lands, the lands of English and of Protestant lands; their owners, and a description, with many genealogical records.

THE BOOKS OF SURVEY AND DISTRIBUTION, *circa* 1658, containing names of proprietors and forfeiting persons of 1641, description of lands and the new owners, and lands not forfeited.

THE EXCHEQUER AND OTHER DOCUMENTS also include records of Catholic forfeitures of 1641, the forfeitures of 1688 and later, with Petitions, Claims, Discoveries, Affidavits, showing from two to three or more generations of Catholic owners, records of the Trustees of the 1688 Forfeited Estates, and a Book of Postings and Sale of Forfeited and other Estates.

AN ALPHABETICAL LIST OF THE CATHOLIC CONVERTS, 1703-1772, and another alphabetical list of the Converts' Certificates, 1709-1773, comprise part of the great "Lodge Manuscripts" in this Office, which will be described among other important manuscript collections presently there.

One of the duties of the Deputy Keeper of the Records was to make an annual *Report* to the government, describing the various collections of records as soon as possible after they were deposited. These were listed by class or subject, source, nature, extent, inclusive dates, with pertinent information regarding the records in each collection. Each *Report* described the care of the records, their arrangement, the progress in indexing, and enumerated the accessions in the library, the number of record searches and documents copied, etc.

These *Reports,* constituting annotated catalogues of the records, were published annually for fifty-two years, from 1869 through 1921, under the title, *The* [number from "First" to "Fifty-Second"] *Report of the Deputy Keeper of the Public Records in Ireland.* After the change in government, in 1922, further *Reports,* under the same title, numbered from the "Fifty-Third" to the "Fifty-Eighth," were published respectively in 1926, 1927, 1928, 1931, 1936, and 1951. These continue the policy of reporting detailed information about the records and program of the Office. The 58 *Reports* range in length from less than one hundred to many hundreds of pages, providing much information for genealogists, historians, the legal profession, and public bodies. A full series of the *Reports* is deposited in each of the important repositories of genealogical records in Ireland, the large genealogical libraries in the United States, and occasionally a partial or full collection may be found in an Irish Book Shop. The use of and the contents of the *Reports* will be described later in this chapter, together with the Indexes, Catalogues, etc., in the Public Search Room. All are guides to the records. The 55th-58th *Reports* are particularly valuable to those who cannot go to the Public Record Office for personal research, as they list the records there today which survived the destruction of 1922, or have been acquired as replacements or new additions.

On June 30, 1922, the buildings of the Four Courts were bombed and fire caused extensive damage. The Public Records had been stored in two buildings. The Record Treasury building which was the principal record repository was all but completely destroyed, together with the records, except for some volumes currently removed, and the contents of the

Treasury vaults which were only partially burned. The Record House escaped the fire, except for some minor damage in the Public Search Room due to heat and water. The indexes, annotated catalogues, calendars and miscellaneous records were in this room. The Library and Strong Room in the Record House were left intact, together with their contents.

Shortly after the fire, when the work of sorting, repairing and calendaring the remaining records was slowly progressing, the officials in this Office adopted a heroic program to replace as many of the destroyed documents as possible and to add many collections of records which had never been sent to the Public Record Office.

The archivists knew that various Government agencies possessed entire collections of several classes of records, of a nature belonging in a Public Record Office. Also among these agencies were deposited copies of some entire series, the originals of which were now destroyed.

Solicitors or legal firms throughout Ireland, and the Bank of Ireland were known to have important collections of original documents consisting of unclaimed Wills, Letters of Administration, Affidavits, Deeds, Leases, Marriage Settlements, etc., which would have added value in the Public Record Office.

The Parochial Records of the Established Church of Ireland had, in 637 parishes, been allowed to remain in local custody, under retention orders or unattached, upon evidence of a proper place of safekeeping. Some Registers had been locally copied before the original records were sent to this Office.

During the fifty-two years before the fire an enormous amount of copying of the records was done in the Public Record Office. Other repositories, historical societies and legal firms sent representatives to obtain official copies of the records from various collections, or to make transcripts, abstracts, and extracts from great numbers of documents. Some famous genealogists, and others who were qualified, spent many years accumulating collections of this nature from all classes of records, for private use. They had compiled numerous family histories, genealogies and pedigrees from these records and other sources. Some were published by or for various families.

Others, together with miscellaneous lists and abstracts or transcripts of documents, were published in historical society journals. The bulk of the work remained in private collections.

Previous to 1867, some great historians, archivists and genealogists, including John Lodge, Sir William Betham, and members of the Record Commission (1810-1830), having access to the records in their earlier repositories, made transcripts and abstracts of several entire series of documents such as Chancery and Exchequer Inquisitions, Decrees, Patents, Fiants, Wills, Administration Grants and Bonds, Marriage Licence Grants and Bonds, and numerous other source materials. In 1922, these manuscript collections were in other repositories or in private hands, except for the famous "Lodge Manuscripts" which were in this Office and survived the fire. A few of the works were published.

Numerous families had preserved their original documents in private archives through many generations. These collections consisted of Wills, Marriage Records, Marriage Settlements, Deeds, Leases, Estate Records, etc., and also extracts from Parish Records, Census Records, and other source materials. Some families possessed important collections of government documents which had come into the hands of an early government official in the family.

Many absentee Irish landlords had carried family records as well as public documents away from Ireland, to England, Scotland and Wales. English Government officials, who had served in Ireland, returned with their papers which concerned the Irish Government and the people. Some of these collections were in private custody and others had been deposited in public repositories such as the British Museum, and other places named in CHAPTER III of this VOLUME I, PART TWO.

Therefore, after the fire, this Office officially requested original documents of a nature appropriately belonging in this repository, and official copies, transcripts, abstracts and notes taken from the records previous to 1922. Every repository in Ireland and abroad, known to have such material, was contacted. In addition, an appeal was advertised throughout Ireland and abroad, for individuals to send or bring in their private collections of records, as gifts, for sale, or to loan them for copying.

The new accessions, other than from Government offices, came slowly at first but, by 1928, the accumulation of replacements and new materials was increasing rapidly.   In the next ten years the acquired collections of a genealogical nature were of great importance.   By 1950, this repository had again become a happy hunting ground for the genealogist.

Libraries, historical societies, and public repositories in Ireland and abroad, responded generously.   Legal firms and individual solicitors in large numbers contributed thousands of unclaimed Wills, other testamentary documents, Deeds, Leases, Marriage Settlements, etc.   One firm, Messrs. Gordon, sent 2,580 original records.   Several extensive manuscript collections of great genealogists were acquired by purchase or gift.   In addition, hundreds of families are represented in the collections acquired from individuals by donation or purchase. These contain a variety of records, including some pedigrees accompanied by documentary evidence, collections of original Wills, Deeds, Leases, Marriage Records, and copies, abstracts or notes taken from the source materials in the Public Record Office before the fire.

Information regarding the records available in this Office is recorded in two ways.   The Public Search Room contains Card Indexes, Manuscript Indexes of various collections, Catalogues, Repertories, and Books of Reference.   The 55th-58th *Reports* also list the records saved from the fire, and calendar all collections acquired since 1922.

For general information, a description of all collections of records in this Office is contained in four main catalogues, located in the Public Search Room.   These list the classes of Testamentary Records; the Chancery, Exchequer, and Common Pleas Court Records; the collections sent from various Government departments, and the special collections acquired by gift or purchase.   The 55th-58th *Reports* also list records calendared in these catalogues, with some pertinent detail.

The most important information about the source materials of a genealogical nature in this Office is presented below.

MANUSCRIPT COLLECTIONS

An alphabetical list of some family collections of documents deposited in this Office has been extracted from the 55th-58th *Reports* and appears in VOLUME II, hereof, PART TWO, CHAPTER II. These collections contain records of various classes ranging from a few to a great many original Wills, Administrations, Marriage Records, Marriage Settlements, Deeds, Leases, etc., and in some cases include pedigrees or compiled genealogy, and transcripts or abstracts of the records. In the above mentioned list are the names of families, the records of which have been the subject of study in the Public Record Office since the fire, according to the lists of genealogical searches recorded in the *Reports*. The list of 537 family surnames is annotated with references to the *Reports* wherein listed.

Perhaps a genealogist or record searcher wishing to locate all records concerning one family or any of its members should next check the larger manuscript collections containing records too numerous to be included in the above mentioned lists. Thousands of records concerning families or individuals are contained in the large manuscript collections. Some contain original documents. Others contain transcripts or abstracts of documents, made from the records in this Office before 1922, representing several classes of source materials. Each manuscript collection is separately indexed.

A visitor in the Search Room may examine the indexes. A genealogist who cannot go to Dublin may, upon sending a fee to this Office, request that a search of the indexes of the manuscript collections be made, and a report on the records of a specified family or individuals be furnished. This will be similar to the report sent to this compiler from the Genealogical Office, Dublin Castle, Dublin, and presented as an example in CHAPTER IV. For this purpose, the most important large manuscript collections will be listed below.

ATHENRY PEERAGE CASE. 7 volumes. Case for the claim of Edward Bermingham to the Athenry Peerage with particulars . . . List of documents presented with schedules of proofs, statements of evidence: History of the Bermingham family; pedigrees, tables of descent and pedigree memoranda of the families of Bermingham (12th Century—1800) and Candler, Carey, Cassan, Chambre, Clare, Cunningham, de Lacy, Leeson, Loftus, Tuite, etc. 16th century to 1800. (56th *Report*, p. 59.)

BELL, ALEXANDER, and Son, Solicitors, Collection. Nearly 3,000 documents (Original, Copy, and Memorials of) dates largely 16th-19th century. Names of principals or families in documents furnished. Documents represent the following classes: Chancery, Exchequer and Common Pleas Courts. Bankruptcy and Insolvency. King's Bench. Recoveries, Exemplifications of. Ecclesiastical Documents. Incumbered Estates Court. Deeds prior to 1700. Deeds, Leases, Conveyances, Assignments, 18th-19th century. Marriage Settlements and Articles. Over 2,000 Deeds, 1703-1901. The lands and premises affected by the deeds are chiefly situated in the counties of Armagh, Carlow, Cavan, Cork, Donegal, Down, Fermanagh, Kildare, Londonderry, Longford, Louth, Meath, Sligo, Tyrone, and the towns of Armagh, Drogheda, Dublin, Londonderry, Lurgan and Newry. (56th *Report*, pp. 20-30.)

BETHAM, SIR WILLIAM, MANUSCRIPTS. The collection of 241 volumes, known as the *Betham Genealogical Abstracts,* was used by Betham to compile his 39 volumes of Pedigree Charts which are in the Genealogical Office, Dublin Castle, Dublin. His *Genealogical Abstracts* contain all genealogical information found in the Prerogative Wills, Administrations, Marriage Licences, etc., 1536-*circa* 1800. The 241 volumes of this collection are subdivided as follows: 80 volumes from Prerogative Wills, 1536-1800. 2 volumes from Kildare Wills, 1661-1826. 16 volumes from Prerogative Marriage Licences, 1629-1801. 60 volumes of which numbers 1-56 are from Prerogative Administrations, 1595-1800, and numbers 57-60 are from Prerogative Marriage Licences, 1629-1800. 54 volumes from Dublin Marriage Licences, 1660-1824. 29 volumes of miscellaneous extracts from court records, pedigrees and memoranda. Besides this collection, there are numerous other volumes, a few of which are as follows: The 8 volumes of papers of Sir William Betham (letters dealing with his genealogical researches and memoranda and extracts on genealogical subjects). A volume of abstracts of Grants of Administration, Prerogative, 1595-1802 (A-C). A volume of abstracts of Marriage Licence Bonds, Prerogative, 1629-1800 (G-Y). A volume of indexes to Clogher Wills, 1658-1849. A volume of indexes to Limerick Wills, 1631-1841. A volume of indexes to Meath Wills, 1635-1838. A volume of indexes to Prerogative Wills, 1641-1811, Waterford Wills, 1659-1838, Cloyne Wills, 1621-1838, Elphin Wills, 1669-1838, and Kilmore Wills, 1682-1838. Copy of Parish Register, St. Peter, Drogheda, 1747-1772. A volume of notes on creations of baronetcies, 1775-1799, pedigrees and miscellaneous genealogical matters. A collection of material on the genealogy of the Wesley or Wellesley family. Another collection of documents of the Hussey family. Some 39 other volumes of miscellaneous subject material are in the collection. (58th *Report*, pp. 25-27.)

CAREW FAMILY MANUSCRIPTS. The Carew family of County Wexford, 8 volumes of records and miscellaneous other documents, 18th-19th century, including estate records of tenants, etc. (57th *Report*, pp. 522-524.)

CARTE MANUSCRIPTS. Transcripts of selected papers (Irish Official) from volumes 1-39, 47-53, 55, 56, 59, 60, of the Carte collection in the Bodleian Library, Oxford, England. Forfeitures of lands by Irish Catholics included. Also a catalogue of the transcripts. (55th *Report*, p. 123.)

CAULFIELD MANUSCRIPTS. 3 volumes: A volume containing pedigrees, arms, memoranda, entries of births, deaths, marriages, etc., of various Jennings families. A volume containing an account of "The French Settlers in Waterford after the Revocation of the Edict of Nantes"; particulars of various families and officials at Waterford and other entries, also a history of the descendants of Mary Sautell, daughter of Major Sautell, and John Roberts of Waterford, including sketches of the families of Roberts, Graham, Makesy, Price, etc. A volume containing extracts of baptisms from the first Registry Book of Waterford, and other miscellaneous memoranda. (55th *Report*, p. 132.)

FERGUSON, J. F., MANUSCRIPTS. 34 volumes. These contain, for the most part, records of the Exchequer Court and contain a considerable amount of genealogical information which will be referred to under COURT RECORDS in PART THREE of this volume. (55th *Report,* pp. 122-123.)

FRAZER MANUSCRIPTS. A collection of some 500 documents dealing largely with the 1798 Rebellion records; some earlier 1796 sketches of persons in custody including Russell, Young, Osborne, Musgrave, Shanaghan, Neilson, Kennedy, Bartley, Teeling and others. There are reports of trials of Ribbon-men, 1840, a list of Sheriffs for the various Irish Counties, also some papers dealing with the disposal of lands assigned to Cromwellian soldiers, etc. (55th *Report,* p. 145.)

FRENCH, E. J., COLLECTION. This is a solicitor's collection of several hundred documents dated 18th-19th century from the courts of Chancery, Exchequer, Common Pleas, King's Bench and Bankruptcy documents; also Testamentary documents including Original Unproved Wills, Grants and Letters of Administration with Wills Annexed; plain copies of Wills, Probates and Grants of Probate; Administrations Wills Annexed, and Administrations Intestate. Also Marriage Settlements and Agreements; Deeds prior to 1700, and later 1710-1881. Names of principals listed and indexed. (56th *Report,* pp. 34-48.)

GREENE MANUSCRIPTS. Copies of the Greene Manuscripts, 5 volumes in the National Library, contain original certified copies of Wills, Baptismal, Marriage and Burial Entries, extracts from 49 Officers' Rolls and Patent Rolls and Abstracts of Wills, Grants and other documents formerly in the Public Record Office, relating to members of various Greene Families and other families connected with the Greenes by marriage. Also a copy was made of a volume of the Greene Manuscripts in the National Library, containing certified copies of Baptismal, Marriage and Burial entries of members of the families of Budd, Croker, Denis or Dennis, Elliot or Elliott, Greene or Green, Hunt, Jones, Lewis, Mackesy, Newport, Poulter, Shearman, etc., families in the parishes of Clonmore, Dunkitt, Fiddown, Kilbeacon, and Macully or Kilculliheen, Diocese of Ossory; parish of Innislonagh, Diocese of Lismore; St. Finnbarr's Parish, Diocese of Cork; and Shanagolden, Diocese of Limerick. (57th *Report,* pp. 54, 56.)

GREVILLE ESTATE PAPERS. Greville Papers, concerning the

Greville family of County Cavan and their estates, early 19th century. "Mr. Cruikshank, Presbyterian Clergyman on the Corronary Estate of this family in County Cavan stated that there is a Congregation in Canada almost exclusively formed of persons who emigrated from this neighborhood and previously belonged to his own congregation." (57th *Report*, pp. 468, 469.)

GROVES, TENISON, MANUSCRIPTS. The Tenison Groves collections consist of the following: Notebooks containing notes and abstracts made in the course of his genealogical searches, with index. Fifteen bundles of abstracts from Wills, Deeds, Court Records, etc., now filed in boxes, with a catalogue of the "Principal Family Names and Associated Names in the Boxes of the Groves Genealogical Abstracts, in the order of their appearance in the abstracts." Several collections containing extracts from Religious Census, 1766, dioceses of Armagh, Clogher, Cloyne, Connor, Derry, Dromore, Down, Dublin, Ferns, Kildare, Kilmore and Ardagh, Ossory, Raphoe, Cork and Ross. Extracts from Hearthmoney Rolls, Subsidy Rolls, Poll Tax Assessments and Accounts, etc. (58th *Report*, p. 20.)

HODGSON COLLECTION. Deeds and other documents, mainly concerning the estates of Sir Hans Hamilton, County Down, late 17th and early 18th centuries; includes Wills of James, Earl of Clanbrassil (d. 1659), James Hamilton (d. 1693) and the Rev. James Hamilton (d. 1721); also Deeds, etc., of estates of William Dongan of Clane, County Kildare; extracts from Census Returns, 1821, 1841 and 1851; a chronological list of Irish students admitted to the Inner Temple, London, 1547-1657, and other miscellaneous records; two volumes of evidence relating to the peerage of Baltinglass, and memoir on the Ormonde family. (58th *Report*, p. 22.)

LODGE'S MANUSCRIPTS. John Lodge (1692-1774) was the author of the *Peerage of Ireland*, edited after his death by Mervyn Archdall and published in 7 volumes, 1789. He was a careful genealogist. His great manuscript collection survived the fire in 1922, and is of especial value now due to the destruction of many series of records which he abstracted and transcribed. Some of the volumes of genealogical interest are:

Patent Rolls, Henry VIII-Charles II.   An alphabetical list of
Catholic converts with dates, places of residence, etc., 1703-
1772, and Converts' Certificates with dates, residence, etc.,
1709-1773.   A list of Protestants, foreign born and inhabitants of Ireland, who took the Oath of Supremacy, becoming
naturalized in Ireland, with their occupations, places of
nativity, dates of oaths, 1662-1737/8.   A list of Certificates
of Conformity enrolled on the Patent Rolls.   Crown Presentations, 1660-1772, 1775, with index.   Naturalization records,
"Denizations" of the Irish, Scots and other foreigners, from
Richard II to George I.   "Pensions," Edward II to George
III.   "Irish Baronage" including lists of created peers by
rank, date, etc.; eldest sons in Upper House of Parliament
(Irish) during the lifetime of their fathers; various surveys
of the Peerage, Henry VII to Queen Anne (1714) ; list of attainted peers (attainders of 1641 and 1689) with dates of
creation of peerages.   A list of members of King's Inns, Dublin, 1607-1771, with dates of admission, some dates of death
and other particulars.   Parliamentary Register with some
14th century records, lists and data mostly 1559-1772.   Patentee Officers, mostly 16th-18th centuries.   A volume of abstracts of Grants of Wardship and Marriage (Henry VIII
-1647, 1660-1661), with Custodies, Liveries, Pardons of
Alienation, Writs of Protection, Assignments of Dower, Pardons of Marriage, etc., included.   A volume of the above
records, Edward II to Henry VII.   (Detailed calendar, 55th
Report, pp. 116-122.)

MONK MASON MANUSCRIPTS.   Among the manuscript collections are the following: A volume of abstracts of "Inquisitions, Counties Dublin and Wicklow" dated from Henry VI
to Charles II.   A "List of Claims as Entered with the Trustees
at Chichester House on or before 10 August, 1700."   This is
printed in two volumes, with manuscript notes by W. Monk
Mason, stating decisions on claims.   The claims were made by
Catholics for their property and as to their innocence in the
1689 Rebellion (before and later).   (58th *Report,* p. 25.)

MOLYNEUX MANUSCRIPTS.   Daniel Molyneux, Ulster King of
Arms, 1809, compiled a volume of extracts from the records
illustrating the history of the earldoms of Ulster (De Lacy

and De Burgo), Kildare, Louth, Ormond, Desmond, Tyrone, Thomond and Clanricarde and the viscounties of Buttevant, Gormanstown and Fermoy, with other miscellaneous notes and extracts of genealogical interest. (58th *Report*, p. 25.)

PRIM COLLECTION: This very extensive collection of original documents, transcripts, abstracts, lists and notes was gathered by J. G. A. Prim, for a history of Kilkenny. It includes much genealogical material consisting of pedigrees, arms, genealogies, family histories, notes, wills, marriage records, and other documents of individuals, the principal families represented being (in order as listed) : O'Shee, Shee, Roth, Colles, O'Grady, Purefoy, Scull, Banastre, Langton, Knaresborough, Bibby, Archer, Cowley or Colley, Fitzmaurice, Comerford, Cantwell, Frayne and Shearman. Individual documents of many other people are included. The collection also contains all manner of public documents and lists, including several lists of Catholic and Protestant inhabitants of various parishes, aged from 16-60 years, dated early 18th century. (58th *Report*, pp. 50-70. Calendar of items with index.)

PRESS COPIES OF CERTIFIED COPIES. This is a 6-volume collection of press copies of certified copies of records, made before the fire of 1922, of the following classes of records: Chancery and Exchequer Inquisitions, Fiants, Grants, Christ Church Deeds, Statutes, Extracts from Plea, Close, Memorandum and Hearth Money Rolls, Decrees of Innocents, etc. (List in Search Room.) (55th *Report*, p. 123.)

SADLEIR MANUSCRIPTS. The collection contains 58 Deeds, 57 Testamentary documents and 70 miscellaneous papers of the Eyre family of Galway city and county, the White, Hedges and Eyre families in County Cork, and the Pearse family in Limerick city, 1663-1819, also Adventurers Certificates to James Reed and others of the lands of Longford, Castlefleming, etc., Queen's County, 19 Oct. 1666. Also a collection relating to the Wolfe family of Forenaghts, County Kildare, 18th century. Extensive collections of transcripts include: Diocese of Ossory (Probate) Administrations, 1738-1804. Eight notebooks containing lists of Army Commissions, 1736-1744 and 1757-1761. List of Freeholders, County Meath, 1781.

Hearth Money Rolls, County Wicklow, 1668. Poll Book, County Westmeath, 1761. Register of Burials, St. Paul's Dublin, 1719-1820. Parish Register, Killeigh, diocese of Kildare, 1808-1835. Burial entries from Parish Register of Carne, diocese of Ferns, 1815-1876. Same for Kilpatrick, diocese of Ferns, 1834-1864, and for Churchtown, diocese of Lismore, 1835-1877. All of the above were copied by Thomas U. Sadleir, a noted genealogist. (58th *Report*, pp. 24, 25.)

SARSFIELD—VESEY FAMILY DOCUMENTS. A very extensive family collection of documents of the Sarsfield and Vesey families of counties Dublin, Wicklow, Kildare and Carlow, dated 13th to 19th centuries, the large part of the documents are dated in late 17th and 18th centuries. The 56th *Report* gives a history of the families and description of the documents (pp. 342-355) ; an index of the deeds, 1414-1808, with names of grantor and grantee, their title or occupation, some relationships, description and location of property, year and nature of the record (pp. 356-378) ; notes on correspondence, 1673-1814, and index, with names mentioned therein (pp. 379-394).

SHEE MANUSCRIPT. Mr. Thomas U. Sadleir presented this transcript of the "Extracts from the Cartulary (book) of Sir Richard Shee," records being dated from the 15th to 17th centuries, concerning members of the Shee family in the counties of Kilkenny, Tipperary and Wexford, and many other persons. (57th *Report*, pp. 469-478.)

SWANZY MANUSCRIPTS. Dean Swanzy's Testamentary Notebook contains genealogical abstracts of Wills, Administrations and Marriage Licences for the Prerogative Court, 1681-1846; Clogher Diocese, 1712-1750; Kilmore Diocese, 1694-1770. (58th *Report*, p. 41.)

THRIFT MANUSCRIPTS. The very large collection donated by Miss Gertrude Thrift consists of pedigree charts, abstracts of Chancery, Equity and Revenue Exchequer documents, Wills (Prerogative and Diocesan), Grants of Administration, Marriage Licence Bonds and Grants. The items number almost 4,000. Due to their importance, the items are presented in indexes in the 55th *Report*, pp. 69-90, and in the 57th *Report*, pp. 325-420. Names of the principals are listed; nature and year of the document; Prerogative, Diocesan or Probate Registry named and number of the abstract. Her collection of Ecclesiastical records is indexed in the 55th *Report*, pp. 91-96.

WALSH MANUSCRIPTS. Transcripts of documents range from the 14th to the 19th century and relate to the Walshes of Athlone, Carrickmines, Ballygunner, Kilgobbin, Killincarrig, Shanganagh, etc., the Kellys, Naghtens and other families. Transcripts and abstracts were made from Wills, Chancery and Exchequer Bills, Answers, Decrees, Depositions, Inquisitions, etc., extracts from Communia Memoranda, Patent, Judiciary and Innocents, etc., Rolls; extracts from Transplanters' Certificates, Assignments and Twopenny Books, etc., family pedigrees and descents. One volume. (57th *Report*, p. 55.)

WHITE, COLONEL JAMES GROVE, MANUSCRIPTS. The collection of Colonel James Grove White, a noted genealogist, consists of 33 notebooks containing parish register extracts and 8 other volumes, containing miscellaneous records as follows: Extracts from parish registers of 36 parishes of dioceses of Cloyne and of Cork and Ross, mostly County Cork, consisting of Baptism, Marriage and Burial records dated late 18th and 19th centuries except for Holy Trinity or Christ Church, Cork city (1643-1868). These items are included in the list of Parish Registers of the Established Church of Ireland with dates of records which appears in PART THREE of this volume. The volumes of extracts from other records are as follows: From Petty's Census, 1659; the Book of Survey and Distribution of County Cork, 1657; Subsidy Rolls, County Cork, 1662-1668; Translation Pipe Roll of Cloyne; Jury List of County Cork, 1814; Calendar of Patent Rolls, James I and Field Book of County Cork, 1839-1840. All contain genealogical information.

WYCHE DOCUMENTS. Papers of Sir Cyril Wyche, chief secretary to the Duke of Ormonde, 1676-1682, and Viscount Sidney, 1692-1693; Lord Justice, 26 June 1693-9 May 1695; for some time one of the trustees for sale of Catholic forfeited estates. The papers refer to many persons. (57th *Report*, pp. 479-518.)

CROSSLÉ FAMILY INDEX. This card index relates to the

records of families and individuals not included in the catalogues and indexes of the above manuscript collections, and not recorded in the card indexes of the Testamentary Records, Deeds, etc. It concerns records from Chancery and Exchequer Court documents and many other sources. The cards fill one large cabinet.

* * * * *

Details of the source materials in this Office will be recorded in the chapters of PART THREE in this volume. A chapter is devoted to a description of the nature and extent of each class of records in Ireland. The collections are listed therein, under the repository where they may be found.

The Catalogues, Calendars and Indexes, with some particulars of the records in this Office, and the printed sources in the *Reports of the Deputy Keeper,* are listed below under the subject headings of the various classes of records. This will serve as a guide for work in the Public Search Room and for research by correspondence.

CENSUS RETURNS

The Census Returns of 1813, 1821, 1831-4, 1841, 1851 were almost all destroyed in 1922. The Returns of 1861, 1871, 1881, and 1891 were not preserved by the Government. Thus, the earliest complete and existing collections of Census Returns were taken in 1901.

A list of the Census Returns, 1821-1851, which did escape the fire of 1922, and copies of some which were transferred from other offices, will be found in the 55th *Report,* pp. 109, 110, 146. Further lists of transferred and presented records are in the 56th-58th *Reports.* All will be noted below.

The Returns of 1841 and 1851 have tables of the names of the present and absent members of the family, and also include a third table naming all members of the family who had died within the previous ten years. The Returns thus present in a most convenient form a register of births, deaths and marriages within the periods, showing in one return, in a great number of cases, as many as three and at times four generations.

In the 28th *Report of the Deputy Keeper*, 1896, p. 6, Mr· Latouche says, "The Census Returns of 1813, 1821, 1831-4, 1841, and 1851 are of record here transferred at different times from their places of original deposit. Their accessibility to the public has proved of incalculable value in inquiries concerning title and pedigree and the tracing of next-of-kin and heirs-at-law." Mr. Latouche thus indicates the great amount of copying of Census Returns which had occurred.

For details of Census Returns of townlands, parishes, baronies and counties (saved, or copies transferred to this Office), see chapter regarding CENSUS RETURNS for all of Ireland, in PART THREE of this volume. The following brief list will indicate the extent of the records available in this Office:

COUNTY ANTRIM: 1851 Census Returns, 23 volumes for various townlands in 13 parishes, saved from the fire. (55th *Report*, p. 110.)

COUNTY CAVAN: 1841 Census Returns (complete) of one parish, saved (55th *Report* p. 109). 1821 complete Census Returns of 13 more parishes and part of another, transferred from the County Cavan Sheriff's Office (55th *Report*, p. 146; 56th *Report*, pp. 8, 18, 413; 57th *Report*, p. 18). Parishes and baronies named, with a complete list in the 56th *Report*, p. 413. 1841 Census Returns and 1851 Returns are represented by miscellaneous extracts for various names (58th *Report*, p. 18).

COUNTY CORK: 1821 Census Returns are represented by copies for various names (58th *Report*, p. 33). 1841 Census Returns (26) saved in 1922, represent names in 4 parishes and 3 not identified (55th *Report*, p. 109).

COUNTY FERMANAGH: 1821 Census Returns, complete for one parish and part of another, saved (55th *Report*, p. 109). 1841 Census Returns, 13 Returns for one parish, saved (55th *Report*, p. 109). 1851 Census Returns, complete for one townland, saved (55th *Report*, p. 110).

COUNTY GALWAY: 1821 Census Returns for two baronies (complete), saved (55th *Report,* p. 109). Copies of 1821 Returns for various families (58th *Report,* p. 33).

KING'S COUNTY: 1821 Census Returns for one barony (complete), saved (55th *Report,* p. 109).

COUNTY LONDONDERRY: 1831 Census Returns for the County and City of Londonderry (11 parishes), 45 volumes, transferred from the Ordnance Survey Department (55th *Report,* p. 110; 56th, p. 18).

COUNTY LONGFORD: No original or copies of entire Returns, but there are three Electoral Lists, c. 1790 (58th *Report,* p. 40).

COUNTY LOUTH: 1821 Census Returns, a number of extracts for families of County Louth and Drogheda town, presented (55th *Report,* p. 110).

COUNTY MAYO: 1821 copies of Census Returns for various families, presented (58th *Report,* p. 33).

COUNTY MEATH: 1821 Census Returns for 2 baronies (complete), saved (55th *Report,* p. 109).

COUNTY ROSCOMMON: 1821 Census Returns for various families, presented (58th *Report,* p. 33).

COUNTY SLIGO: 1821 Census Returns for various families, presented (58th *Report,* p. 33).

COUNTY TIPPERARY: List of heads of houses in Clonmel, from 1821 Census Returns (58th *Report,* p. 44).

COUNTY WATERFORD: 1841 Census Returns (4) in one barony, saved (55th *Report,* p. 109).

Collections of extracts of Census Returns for various families appear occasionally among presented materials throughout the 55th-58th *Reports.* This Office has also some certified copies of Returns and extracts from various Returns as well as a number of Reports of Searches made in the Census Returns prior to their destruction in 1922 (55th *Report,* p. 110). Calendars of all Census Returns and records of Returns are arranged under townlands, parishes, baronies and counties.

EXAMPLES OF COPIES MADE FROM CENSUS RETURNS: Certified Copies presented by Messrs. Gore and Grimes, Solicitors, after 1922 (56th *Report,* p. 48).

1. Kennedy families (Population Returns, 1821), townlands of Bowhill, Stephentown, and Balcunnin, County Dublin.

2. Kennedy families (Census Returns, 1841), townlands of Knock, Ballcunnin (spelling different), and Stephentown, County Dublin.

3. Kennedy families (Census Returns, 1851), townlands of Bowhill, Balcunnin, and Stephentown, County Dublin.

Other source materials which provide lists of inhabitants of more or less wide areas in the 17th-19th centuries, will be described in PART THREE of this volume.

CHURCH RECORDS

ESTABLISHED CHURCH OF IRELAND:

The records of the former Established Church of Ireland, now in this Office and of primary interest to the genealogist, are the Parish Registers (originals or transcripts), the Marriage Licence Grants and Bonds (originals, transcripts, abstracts or Indexes), the Wills and Administration Grants and Bonds, represented by some original records, extensive collections of abstracts and transcripts made before the fire, and some incomplete indexes of the records deposited in this Office previous to 1922. The above Marriage Records and Probates were matters under the jurisdiction of the Prerogative and the Consistorial or Diocesan Courts before 1858. These two latter classes of records will be separately reviewed below, each in combination with records from other sources now in this Office.

The most complete indexed list of the Parish Registers was printed in the 28th *Report of the Deputy Keeper* (1896), Appendix II, pp. 57-108. The list, alphabetically arranged by name of the parish, church or chapel, sets forth for each the diocese, county, number of volumes and the inclusive dates of the records of baptism, marriage and burial. The size of the print (large or small) and the use of asterisks denoted their location, that is, whether in the Public Record Office, or in local custody, either unattached or under retention orders.

By this date (1896), the location or deposit of the Parish Registers of the then Established Church of Ireland was well determined. The Parochial Records Act (Ireland), 1875, 1876, required records of baptism and burial prior to 31 December 1870, and marriages prior to 31 March 1845, to become Public Records. However, in cases where evidence could be shown of an adequate place of safekeeping in the parish (usually a vault in the church), record volumes were allowed to remain in local custody, unattached, or under retention orders.

In 1922, the original Registers of 1,006 parishes of all dioceses in Ireland had been deposited in the Public Record Office. The Registers of 637 parishes were retained in local custody and many original Registers were, before being sent to Dublin, copied by or for the local incumbent, to be kept in place of the original records.

After the fire this Office sent inquiries to all parishes in the 26 counties of Southern Ireland (now the Republic of Ireland) which had lost Registers in the fire, to discover how many had been copied. Replies did not come from all parishes, but 124 reported that transcripts of the original Registers were in local custody.

The 55th-58th *Reports* furnish information regarding the original Registers of parishes, the complete transcripts of Parish Registers (printed and manuscripts), and some partial transcripts of Registers; all now in existence in the Republic of Ireland. The records are listed by name of the parish, diocese and county, as follows:

1. A list of original Parish Registers now destroyed, the records of which were printed before 1922. (55th *Report*, p. 140.)

2. The Registers of 4 parishes, saved from the fire. (55th *Report*, p. 99.)

3. The Parochial Returns of 3 parishes, saved from the fire. (55th *Report*, p. 99.)

4. One Parish Register and 7 transcripts of Registers, presented. (55th *Report*, pp. 99-100.)

5. Original Registers of 416 parishes, in local custody and

under retention orders, after 1922.   (55th *Report,* pp. 100-108.)

6. Original Registers of 6 parishes in local custody and unattached, after 1922.   (55th *Report,* p. 108.)

7. A list of transcripts of destroyed Registers of 124 parishes, including those in local custody and/or in the Public Record Office.   (56th *Report,* pp. 416-420.)

8. Transcripts of destroyed Registers of 32 parishes, now in the Public Record Office, including the transcripts listed in (4) and some in (7) above.   (57th *Report,* p. 566.)

9. A complete list (1951) of original Registers, transcripts of Registers, and partial transcripts of Registers, now in the Public Record Office (duplicating some above).   (58th *Report,* pp. 116-119.)

Inclusive dates of the records are noted only for the original Registers and transcripts of Registers now in this Office. The 55th *Report,* p. 100, refers the reader to the 28th *Report* (1896), to ascertain the inclusive dates of the records of baptism, marriage and burial, in the original Registers of 416 parishes which were retained in local custody in the Republic of Ireland.   Also, one must refer to the 28th *Report* to discover the inclusive dates of the Registers which were transcribed before being sent to Dublin prior to 1922, the transcripts now being in local custody.

This makes a total of ten lists, to which one would have to refer in order to trace all information about the presently existing records.

The same situation exists in Northern Ireland, with regard to information about the existing original Parish Registers in local custody, the transcripts of Registers in local custody, also the original Registers and transcripts of Registers now in the Public Record Office of Northern Ireland, Belfast; all being the Registers of parishes in the six counties of Northern Ireland.   Each of the *Reports of the Deputy Keeper* (1924-1953), contain information known at the time of publication. In addition, there are Office Lists, copies of which have been sent to this compiler.   These contain information about the Registers and transcripts of Registers, supplemental to that in the last *Report* (1951-1953).

Because of the confusion resulting from many lists printed by both Public Record Offices, this compiler made a consolidated card index for each in 1955. Noted on each card is the name of the parish, diocese, county, nature of the records (original, transcript, or partial transcript), their present location, and the inclusive dates of the records of baptism, marriage and burial contained in the Registers. These cards were indexed under the name of the parish and were filed: (1) Under the Republic of Ireland. (2) Under Northern Ireland.

It appears that today there are records of 707 parishes (printed Registers, original Registers, transcripts, and partial transcripts of Registers) in the Republic of Ireland, of which there are an estimated 75 parishes for which partial transcripts were made before 1922. In the six counties of Northern Ireland, there appear to be records of 356 parishes, of which 236 parishes have original Registers, 116 have transcripts of entire Registers, while the Registers of 4 parishes have been printed. The latter includes the parish of Templemore, County Londonderry (Londonderry city and outlying districts), the records (1634-1703) being printed in one volume. The later records (1703-present date) were examined by this compiler, in the vault of the Londonderry Cathedral. They have been indexed by name, in the hope that some day they will be published. This compiler also examined the original records (1634-1703) which are in beautiful condition. Thus, the figures above total 1,063 parishes having existing records of some nature, located in the Republic of Ireland or in Northern Ireland.

From her two card-indexes, this compiler has made two indexed lists containing information taken from all sources, and set forth in the form adopted in the 28th *Report* (1896). These lists are presented in PART THREE of this volume, under the chapter concerning records of the late Established Church of Ireland. The present location of the records is indicated by a key number.

These lists do not include many miscellaneous collections of records of baptism, marriage and burial concerning a large number of families, extracted from the records before 1922 and included in various manuscript collections in both Public Record Offices. One such collection containing extensive extracts from the Parish Registers is the Gertrude Thrift collection which includes abstracts from various Parish Registers of the City and County of Dublin, the Counties of Cork, Kerry, Tipperary, Fermanagh, etc. (55th *Report*, p. 100.)

Copies of Registers of the Established Church of Ireland, published before their destruction in 1922, are listed in VOLUME II, pp. 216-218.

The *Biographical Succession Lists of the Clergy* were compiled from records in this Office and other sources. They contain much in the way of personal records and genealogy of some families in brief notes. These printed volumes are listed in VOLUME II, pp. 218-219.

The Church Registers of denominations other than the former Established Church of Ireland were not constituted Public Records by law, and thus there was no requirement for their deposit in this Office.

HUGUENOT CHURCH:

Huguenot Church Registers were copied and published. Three volumes are in the Public Record Office Library. They are listed in VOLUME II, pp. 220-221.

METHODIST CHURCH:

One deposit of Methodist records was presented to this Office. This is "The Register of the Rev. M. Lanktree, Methodist Missionary for County Down, 1815-1849." (55th *Report*, p. 11.)

PRESBYTERIAN CHURCH:

Presbyterian Registers presented to this Office are: "The Registers of the Presbyterian Congregations of Bull Alley and Plunket Street, Dublin." Vol. I, 1672-1765; Vol. II, 1790-1835. (54th *Report*, p. 11.)

Registers of the Presbyterian Church are in local custody save for a few of the oldest, now deposited in the vaults of the Presbyterian Historical Society, Belfast, and the one above. All existing Registers are listed and their location indicated, in the chapter of PART THREE regarding this Church. It is of interest to note here, for those who are studying any Presbyterian families of the 26 counties now in the Republic of Ireland, that of the 367 congregations with existing Registers, 82 are located in 19 of the above mentioned 26 counties.

Following are the counties and the number of churches in each for which Registers exist: Cavan, 8; Cork, 4; Donegal, 24; Dublin, 4; Fermanagh, 4; Galway, 1; Kerry, 1; Leitrim, 3; Leix, 1; Limerick, 1; Longford, 3; Louth, 3; Mayo, 2; Monaghan, 18; Sligo, 1; Waterford, 1; West Meath, 1; Wexford, 1; Wicklow, 1.

Published records of the Church, including some printed transcripts of Registers and extracts, are listed in VOLUME II, pp. 222-225.

QUAKER (SOCIETY OF FRIENDS) :

No Quaker Church records are here except a deposit from the Society of Friends, Dublin of "Relief of Distress Papers, 1845-1865." (57th *Report*, p. 568.) Published Quaker Church records and other related materials are listed in VOLUME II, p. 225.

ROMAN CATHOLIC CHURCH:

No Roman Catholic Church Registers or copies of them are here. All original Parish Registers are in local custody. The National Library of Ireland is microfilming the Parish Registers of all dioceses in the Republic of Ireland. So far, the Registers of all parishes in 16 dioceses have been filmed. For details, see PART II, CHAPTER II, of this volume. In VOLUME II, PART FOUR, these microfilms are listed under the National Library of Ireland.

While there are no Church Registers in this Office, a large proportion of the records of many classes concern members of the Catholic Church, and hold a wealth of genealogical information. This material will be discussed in PART THREE under the Chancery, Exchequer and Common Pleas Court Records, the Land Records including early Deeds, Surveys, Forfeitures, etc., the Religious Census, Tax and other source materials. See also the chapter regarding ROMAN CATHOLIC RECORDS.

COURT RECORDS AND STATE PAPERS

Not enough can be said to emphasize the genealogical value of the records of the Chancery, Exchequer, and Common Pleas Courts, and of the State. Calendars, repertories, abstracts and indexes represent numerous classes of collections and records now in this Office. Because of the various sources and volume of the records and the importance of first understanding their purpose and contents, it seems best to refer the entire subject to the chapter devoted to COURT RECORDS AND STATE PAPERS, in PART THREE of this volume.

LAND RECORDS

Collections of numerous classes in this Office, dated from early times through the 19th century and later, concern the transfer of property or records relating to ownership, and are of great genealogical value. These are Deeds, Leases, Assignments, Marriage Settlements regarding land, Inquisitions Post Mortem and upon Attainder, Patents, Fines, Forfeitures (by Roman Catholics), Recoveries (of forfeited property), Certificates (warrants for confiscated land) to Protestants, 17th Century Surveys (of property of Roman Catholic proprietors), and Survey and Distribution (giving names and lands of forfeiting Roman Catholic proprietors of *ca.* 1641 and new owners), and numerous other source materials.

In the Public Search Room there is a Card-Index of Deeds, etc., dated prior to the establishment of the Registry of Deeds in 1708. It was first arranged as a Topographical Index of Deeds, etc. By 1955, a Name-Index was compiled. There are also Annual Accessions Lists, Classified Catalogues, and Indexes of the special manuscript collections of purchased and presented material and of the collections sent from other repositories since 1922.

Further information regarding these source materials covering many thousands of original documents, transcripts and abstracts is recorded in the *Reports of the Deputy Keeper,* as follows:

1. The classified lists and indexes in the 55th-58th *Reports* set forth single documents contained in various collections, by

names of the principals, year or period, and specified location or area. These include original documents, transcripts and abstracts saved from the fire, transferred from other repositories, or purchased or presented since 1922.

2. Classified lists of collections of land records in Calendars, Repertories, Indexes and Books of Reference (MSS. and some printed) now preserved in this Office. These include original documents, transcripts or abstracts contained in Chancery, Exchequer and Common Pleas Court Records, and other legal sources. They are listed as original collections saved from the fire; collections of duplicate records sent from other repositories; Transcripts of the Record Commissioners made, 1810-1830; MSS. collections of Lodge, Ferguson, Caulfield, Gertrude Thrift, Sarsfield-Vesey documents, etc., and collections sent by numerous solicitors from the vaults of legal offices; collections from private archives and other sources. These are very numerous, and information regarding them is scattered through the 55th-58th *Reports* and *Appendices.*

3. Land records are included in "A List of some Records not saved from the fire, duplicates or copies of which are preserved in the Public Record Office or other repositories or in private custody or of which there are printed or MSS. calendars or repertories," containing transcripts or abstracts of the records. (55th *Report,* Appendix VII, pp. 133-144; 56th *Report,* Appendix V., pp. 406-412.) These include references to some collections in various Government repositories, since transferred to this Office; also some private collections, transcripts of which are now in this Office. All such collections acquired since the publication of the 56th *Report* (1931) are calendared in the 57th and 58th *Reports* of 1936 and 1951.

The scope of the material outlined above is so great that, in order to avoid repetition, the description of the records and details of sources and references not enumerated here will be set forth in PART THREE of this volume, under the chapter regarding LAND RECORDS, in the subdivision concerning the records of this Office.

MARRIAGE RECORDS

There is no consolidated card-index of marriage records in the Public Search Room. However, the Annual Calendars of Accessions, the separately indexed manuscript collections, the Crosslé Family Card-Index (which fills one large cabinet), and the Manuscript Indexes of Prerogative and Diocesan Marriage Licence Grants and Bonds contain information about many thousands of marriage records. Among the purchased and presented collections, received since 1922, are a wealth of transcripts or abstracts of Marriage Licence Grants and Bonds, also transcripts or abstracts of many Marriage Settlements or Agreements concerning Deeds or other instruments relating to transfer of property. These, for the most part, have come from well-known genealogists and from the vaults of solicitors. Reference to them will be found in the Annual Calendars of Accessions, and in the indexes of the various collections.

The 55th-58th *Reports* provide information about the contents of the purchased and presented collections received since 1922, with notes as to their nature, including marriage records. A number of lists of Marriage Settlements or Agreements set forth the names of the groom and bride and the year of the record. Some Appendices to the *Reports* contain indexes of important collections, purchased or presented since 1922, which include listed marriage records (abstracts or transcripts), setting forth the names of both the groom and bride, the year of marriage, Court of Registry, and reference. Also calendared in these *Reports* are the Manuscript Indexes of the Prerogative and Diocesan Marriage Licence Grants and Bonds and Affidavits, saved from the fire, and the purchased or presented collections of Indexes or Abstracts received since 1922.

The Appendices of *Reports*, published before the fire, beginning with the 5th *Report* (1873), contain many abstracts of records showing evidence of marriage. The Appendix of the 26th *Report* (1895) of 1,089 pages, and the Appendix of the 30th *Report* (1899) containing 1,155 pages, each constitute an "Index to the Act or Grant Books and to the Original Wills, etc., of the Diocese of Dublin," covering respectively years from the 17th century to 1800, and 1800 to 1858. Among more than 100,000 entries the Marriage Licence Grants and Bonds predominate. Names of the groom and bride are separately indexed with the same information; year of marriage (all in the Diocese of Dublin) and reference.

Further detailed information concerning Marriage Records of this Office are contained in PART THREE of this volume, under the chapter regarding this subject.

MILITARY AND NAVAL RECORDS

The Lodge Manuscripts contain "Abstracts of Grants of Pensions (Edward II—George III) in consideration of injuries received in the wars of Ireland . . . They comprise pensions to grantee and heirs, for life, pleasure, good behavior, and otherwise provided for." (55th *Report*, p. 119.) Various lists of records in the Lodge, Frazer, Wyche Manuscript collections and other sources are listed in the chapter on this subject in PART THREE of this volume.

NATURALIZATION AND EMIGRATION RECORDS

The Lodge Manuscripts contain records of "Denizations of the Irish, Scots and other Foreigners (Richard II—George I) ; Lists of persons to whom grants of English Livery (Liberty) or Denization were made." Also in this manuscript collection is "A List of Protestants who in pursuance of an Act of Parliament, 13th Charles II, for encouraging Protestant Strangers and others to inhabit and plant ye Kingdom of Ireland, took the Oaths of Allegiance and Supremacy whereby they became liege, free and natural subjects of Ireland . . ." (55th *Report*, pp. 117, 119.)

Some Emigration Records are contained in a series of Letter Books, 1827-1857, sent from the Valuation Office, dealing with (among other subjects) "Emigration of destitute tenants on Crown Estates." (58th *Report*, p. 18.) See chapter on this subject in PART THREE of this volume.

PARLIAMENTARY RECORDS

The original Journals of the Irish House of Lords and Commons were destroyed in the fire. The *Journals of the House of Commons of Ireland, 1613-1800* and the *Journals of the House of Lords, 1634-1752* had been printed. (See VOLUME II, p. 258.) Ancilliary records, save for a small number of Parliamentary Returns regarding Religion, were all destroyed. However, the "1740 Householder's Lists," the "Parliamentary Returns re Religion, 1766" and "Petitions of Dissenters, 1704-1782" for some counties, scattered dioceses, parishes, etc., have been copied in full and in part. These are valuable for locating persons, and, so far as they exist, supplement the Census Records. For details, see the chapter on this subject in PART THREE of this volume.

REGISTERS OF FREEHOLDERS, GUILDS, POLITICAL OFFICE AND SCHOOLS

Various Registers of the above classified groups have been printed and some are in manuscript collections in this Office. For details, see the chapter on this subject in PART THREE of this volume.

TAX RECORDS

The Hearth Money Rolls, 1663-1669; the Subsidy Rolls, 1662-1668; the Poll Tax Rolls, 1695-1699 (a few earlier and later) ; the Tithe Applotment Books, 1823-1838; also a few 17th century Applotment Books, being draft catalogues of names of householders, compiled for tax purposes, all constitute Tax Records which supply valuable genealogical information for locating people and determining their economic condition. To the extent that they may be found as transcripts of the destroyed records, they substitute to some extent for Census Records. The existing records for various counties, baronies, cities, etc., will be enumerated and described in the chapter on TAX RECORDS in PART THREE of this volume.

TESTAMENTARY RECORDS

The 55th Report of the Deputy Keeper of the Public Records in Ireland (pp. 25-31), presents a "List of Testamentary, Matrimonial and Ecclesiastical Records, Indexes and Calendars salved, and of those received, during the period, from the destruction of the Record Office in 1922 to the end of 1927." Some items of particular interest are as follows:

1. Grant Books: Prerogative, 1684-1688, 1748-1751, 1839. Diocese of Cashel, 1840, 1845 (Probates, Administrations and Marriage Licences). Diocese of Derry and Raphoe, 1812-1851 (Administrations). Diocese of Ossory, 1848-1858 (Administrations and Administrations Will annexed). Diocese of Killaloe Court Book, 1707-1845. Miscellaneous Probates and Administrations from the Principal and District Probate Registries, dated after 1858.

2. Administration Bonds (Diocesan), Indexes to. 26 dioceses, 17th-19th century.

3. Grant Books (Probates, Administrations and Marriage Licences), Prerogative Court, Indexes to, 1595-1858.

4. Inventories (Prerogative Court), Index to, 1668-1858.

5. Wills (Prerogative) Indexes to, 1536-1858.

6. Wills (Diocesan), Indexes to, 27 dioceses, mostly dated 17th to mid-19th century.

7. Wills and Administrations, Registry Books: Diocese of Connor, 1622-1858. Diocese of Down, 1785-1858.

8. Wills and Grants of Probate and Administration (Principal and District Registries) Calendars, 1858-1906; Indexes to Calendars, 1858-1877.

9. Wills (Unproved) Prerogative, Index to, 1689-1858.

10. Wills (Unproved) District Registries, Index to, 1858-1905.

11. Wills (Unproved) Principal Registry, Index to, 1858-1899; Lists of, 1904-1906.

12. Index Books, Dioceses of Cashel, Waterford, Lismore, and Ferns: Grants of Probate and Administration, 1847-1858 (with list of Unproved Wills lodged in Cashel Diocesan

Court, 1638-1856). Diocese of Waterford and Lismore, Grants of Probate and Administration, 1650-1788.

13. Index Books, District Registries of Armagh, Cork, Limerick and Waterford: Armagh District Registry (Wills and Administrations), 1862-1877. Cork District Registry (Wills and Administrations), 1874-1879, 1898-1899 (some entries 1897). Limerick District Registry, 1900-1906. Waterford District Registry, General Index to Applications for Grants, Caveats, Unproved Wills, etc., 1889-1901.

14. Inventories (Copy) (Londonderry District Registry), 1858-1859.

15. Wills, Original, Prerogative and Diocesan, 18th and 19th century (pre 1858), and a few copies of Prerogative 19th Century Wills, listed.

16. Wills and Papers leading to Grants of Probate and Administration Will annexed: Court of Probate, Probate and Matrimonial Division and King's Bench Division (Probate), various years after 1858.

17. Will Books, Prerogative: 1664-1684; 1706-1708 (A-W); 1726-1728 (A-W); 1728-1729 (A-W); 1777 (A-L); 1813 (K-Z); 1834 (A-E).

18. Will Books, Diocesan: Connor (Will and Grant Books), 1818-1820, 1853-1858. Down (Will and Grant Book), 1850-1858.

19. Will Books, Principal Registry: 1874 (G-M); 1878 (A-F); 1878 (G-M); 1878 (N-Z); 1891 (G-M); 1896 (A-F).

20. Will Books, District Registry (Principal Registry Copies): 1869 (G-M); 1891 (M-P); 1901 (A-F).

21. Will Books, District Probate Registry; (Wills and Grants of Probate and Administration), 1858—. Cavan District Probate Registry, 1858-1873. Cork District Probate Registry, 1858-1876. Kilkenny District Probate Registry, 1858-1874. Limerick District Probate Registry, 1858-1875. Mullingar District Probate Registry, 1859-1877. Tuam District Probate Registry, 1858-1877. Waterford District Probate Registry 1858-1873.

INDEXES OF EXISTING DOCUMENTS, PRINTED IN THE "REPORTS": The following indexes of Wills, Grants, Bonds, etc., total an estimated number of 21,400 items. The documents are alphabetically listed, by name of the principal, residence, nature of the record, year, and Court of Registry. The dates are mostly of the 18th and 19th centuries. The indexes are as follows:

1. "List of Original Probates, Letters of Administration Will Annexed and Intestate, Marriage Licence Grants and Official Copies of Wills, Grants, etc., presented during the period from the destruction of the Record Office in 1922 to the end of 1927." Estimated 1,400 instruments. (55th *Report*, pp. 33-68.)

2. "List of Original Unproved Wills (never lodged for Probate), Duplicates of Wills and Plain Copies of Wills, Grants, etc., presented 1922-1927." Estimated 840 instruments. (55th *Report*, pp. 69-90.)

3. "List of Original Probates, etc., and Official Copies of Wills, Grants, etc., presented 1928: Wills in salved Prerogative Will Books, and Wills and Grants of Administration in salved Down and Connor Will and Grant Books." Estimated 4,680 instruments. (56th *Report*, pp. 79-197.)

4. "Original Unproved Wills (never lodged for Probate), Duplicates of Wills and Plain Copies of Wills, Grants, etc., presented 1928. List of." Estimated 200 instruments. (56th *Report*, pp. 198-200.)

5. "List of Original Probates, etc., and Official Copies of Wills, Grants, etc., presented 1929, 1930; Grants in salved Prerogative Grant Books, 1748-1751, and 1839; salved Dublin Marriage Licence Bonds, 'A' 1749-1813; salved Dublin Consistorial Cause Papers . . . Grants of Administration, and Administration Will Annexed in salved Ossory Grant Book, 1848-1858; Marriage Licence Grants, 1776-1845, . . . Caveats, 1708-1723/4, . . ." Estimated 10,480 instruments, (57th *Report*, pp. 62-324.)

6. "Lists of Original Unproved Wills (never lodged for Probate), Duplicates of Wills and Plain Copies of Wills, Grants, etc., presented 1929, 1930, . . ." Estimated 3,800 instruments. (57th *Report*, pp. 325-420.)

After the 57th *Report* (1936), the practice of printing indexes (of records acquired after 1930) in the *Report of the*

Deputy Keeper was discontinued so far as the listing of the purchased and presented testamentary items, etc., in a consolidated index was concerned. However, the 58th *Report* (1951), did continue listing the purchased and presented collections, as well as the incremental deposits and the collections acquired from other repositories. Detailed descriptions of the purchased and presented collections provide information about innumerable testamentary items included, with name, residence (or area), and year of the document. Many descriptions simply state the number and nature of the documents, names of the families concerned, county, etc., and inclusive dates. Thus, full information about any of the separate items acquired since 1930 (too numerous to include in the *Reports*) must be sought in the Catalogues, Calendars and Indexes in the Public Search Room.

INDEXED CATALOGUES IN THE SEARCH ROOM: An indexed catalogue of each large manuscript collection lists the volumes, boxes of records, and their contents, including any transcripts or abstracts of testamentary documents. The volumes and boxes of records are self-indexed. Thus, the volumes of the "Betham Genealogical Abstracts," containing about 37,000 abstracts of Prerogative Wills and Administrations, are each self-indexed. The Tenison Groves, Gertrude Thrift and other collections containing testamentary material are also catalogued and self-indexed. Many copies or abstracts of wills and other testamentary documents are found in the collections containing Chancery and Exchequer Court Records.

CALENDARS: Calendars, being annual lists of the accessions, are maintained in the Search Room. These concern the material from all sources, including the purchased and presented collections and those transferred (not required by law to do so) from other repositories, as well as the normal deposits from other government offices and public bodies. Some testamentary records thus recorded are, in addition to those mentioned above, of particular interest:

1. Annual Calendars of Wills and Administrations, compiled by the Principal Probate Registry, after 1858.

2. A collection of some testamentary records from the Of-

fice of Charitable Donations and Bequests, in Dublin. This Office has kept the abstracts of every Prerogative and Diocesan Will, making any bequest of a charitable nature, from 1800 to the present time. The papers contain information from court cases, records of assets and liabilities of the deceased, and many full copies of Wills. It was common practice for a testator to make some large or small charitable bequest. Thus the numerous records, to some extent, bridge the period from 1800-1858, which Sir William Betham did not cover in his abstracts of Prerogative Wills, 1536-1800, and replaces information in many destroyed Diocesan Wills. Indexes to the records in the Office of Charitable Donations and Bequests, 1800-1858, are in the Public Record Office, with one gap, 1829-1839, covered, however, by records listed below now in this Office.

3. The Irish Will Registers, from the 4th quarter of 1828 to 1839, were taken to England by the British Inland Revenue Board. These concern both Prerogative and Diocesan Wills. The volumes contain abstracts showing date of death of the testator, residence, date of Will, estate liable to duty (amount), executor, his or her residence and description (relationship, i.e. widow, etc.), where and when the Will was proved and summary of disposition of property. The collection includes the following: Registers of Wills, 1829-1839; Indexes of Wills, 1829-1879; Administration Registers, 1829-1839; Administration Indexes, 1829-1879. The Registers, 1840-1879, are missing.

4. A list and copies of the abstracts of Wills (about 500) in the Stewart-Kennedy Notebooks, now deposited in the Library of Trinity College, Dublin.

CARD INDEXES IN THE SEARCH ROOM: A card index of the testamentary documents, other than normal increments (received regularly from the Principal and District Probate Registries), is maintained in the Search Room. This covers the miscellaneous testamentary material and non-official (presented or purchased) documents now in this Office, except for the transcripts and abstracts contained in the large manuscript collections such as the abstracts of Wills in the Betham Genealogical Abstracts, which are self-indexed.

Thus the Card-Index refers to the following, save for the exceptions mentioned:

1. Wills, Grants of Administration and Administration Bonds (originals and transcripts) deposited in this Office before 1922, which survived the fire.

2. Original Probates, Letters of Administration Will Annexed and Intestate, acquired since 1922.

3. Original Wills never lodged for Probate, acquired since 1922.

4. Official Copies of Wills, Grants, etc., acquired since 1922.

5. Transcripts of Wills and Administration Papers, made by qualified persons and acquired since 1922.

6. Abstracts of Wills, Grants, etc., made by qualified persons and acquired since 1922.

It must be remembered that only the testamentary records saved from the fire and those acquired 1922-1930 are listed in the Indexes contained in Appendices of the 55th-57th *Reports of the Deputy Keeper*. The 58th *Report* (1951), discontinued the publication of an index of all testamentary records received since 1930. However, numerous Wills, Administrations, etc., are mentioned by name of the testator in lists of collections acquired since 1930.

Detailed information regarding the Testamentary Indexes, Calendars, and Will Books, etc., and the records acquired in some large collections since 1922, will be given in the chapter on Testamentary Records, in PART THREE, hereof, CHAPTER XXIII.

CHAPTER VI

THE PUBLIC RECORD OFFICE OF NORTHERN IRELAND, BELFAST*

The Public Record Office of Northern Ireland is located in the Law Courts Building, May Street, Belfast, Northern Ireland. The Search Room is open to the public daily, from 9:30 a. m. to 5:00 p. m., on Monday through Friday and from 9:30 a. m. to 12:00 noon on Saturday. Inspection of the records is permitted for genealogical, historical or antiquarian purposes, upon application to the Deputy Keeper of the Records. Registration is required and a nominal fee is charged, the amount depending upon the number of documents, collections of records and books searched, and the time spent in the Office.

The most complete and comprehensive accumulation of genealogical materials and historical records of Northern Ireland, dated from early times, is deposited in this great repository, in addition to the normal increments of a nature belonging in a Public Record Office. Among the extensive manuscript collections of noted genealogists are some relating to all parts of Ireland.

Kenneth Darwin, M. A., was appointed Deputy Keeper of the Records in 1954, having served for a number of years as a member of the staff and as Assistant Deputy Keeper. Among the able members of his present staff is Miss Margaret Johnston, who has been with this Office since 1952. This compiler is greatly indebted to both for their time and courtesy during repeated periods of survey of the records in this repository since 1951, and for information sent from time to time, in photostats of Office Lists of deposits, descriptions of recently acquired collections, and many photostats of single documents; all in the course of compiling this GUIDE to the records.

A genealogist or record searcher, upon arriving at the Public Search Room, will be directed to the extensive consolidated Card-Index, the Catalogues, Calendars, and the printed

*Now located at 66 Balmoral Avenue, Belfast BT9 6NY. The staff, of course, has changed since this book was first published.

or manuscript reference materials on the shelves in this room. Records selected from the indexes, etc., will be brought to the Search Room for examination at one of the tables available to visitors.

A person with proper care of the records, may make copies of the whole or part of any one or more, under certain regulations. Certified or uncertified copies or abstracts, either typed or photostatic, will be supplied in response to prepaid orders.

Visitors who require help with genealogical research are referred to the Ulster-Scot Historical Society. Likewise, all written communications of a genealogical nature are referred to this Society.

* * * * *

The Ulster-Scot Historical Society was established in 1957,* and is located in the Law Courts Building on the Chichester Street entrance. One of its main objectives is to assist persons of Ulster ancestry to ascertain facts about their ancestors in Northern Ireland. The officers, trustees and council of the Society are noted and public spirited citizens. Mr. Kenneth Darwin serves as Director. Miss I. Embleton is the Secretary, to whom correspondence should be addressed.

The Society maintains a staff of skilled record searchers who make use of all source materials in the Public Record Office. Thus, in effect, it operates as a genealogical research department of the Public Record Office.

An inquiry regarding a search for the records of any one or more Ulster families or individuals will be answered and a four-generation form or questionnaire will be enclosed. This is to be filled out, so far as possible, regarding the first and earlier generations for which further information is desired. When it is returned with a written request for a search of the records, it must be accompanied with a registration fee of £2 ($6.00), which is not returnable. The relevant records will then be examined and a report will be furnished.**

The four-generation form states that "an average search and report should not exceed £10 ($30.00). A more difficult search will, of course, cost more but in no case will a cost of

---

*Now called the Ulster Historical Foundation, 66 Balmoral Avenue, Belfast BT9 6NY.

**Orders are now quoted for when they have been assessed. A registration fee of $20.00 is required for a genealogical search, providing the search is accepted by the Ulster Historical Foundation.

£20 ($60.00) be exceeded without further consultation." The Society makes it clear that there can be no certainty of success. This is, of course, true of all genealogical research in any country.

Undoubtedly some people, who must handle their problems of Ulster genealogy by correspondence, will prefer to assign their research entirely to the Ulster-Scot Historical Society. However, experienced genealogists would not miss the joy of the search if there is any means of participating in it. They can take an active part, co-operating with this Society, in so far as they become acquainted with the nature and the extent of the source materials in the Public Record Office.

*   *   *   *   *

Research through correspondence with the above Society, the discovery of records and the ordering of photostats, abstracts, etc., is practicable because of the extensive series of the *Government of Northern Ireland Public Record Office Reports of the Deputy Keeper of the Records,* which are, in fact, catalogues of the records. The contents of manuscript collections, family documents, etc., are described in sufficient detail to identify names, dates, locality and subject matter, except in the cases of the very large collections which are self indexed. It is estimated that over 100,000 items of genealogical interest regarding families, named members, and other individuals are indexed in the Appendices of the *Reports.* These printed sources will be further described in this chapter.

For the benefit of those who do not have access to the *Reports,* this compiler has extracted from the above lists and indexes a list of family and individual records, varying in nature from pedigrees, family notes, etc., to wills, deeds, leases, marriage and other records, sometimes in a series of family documents dated over two or more centuries. These are presented under 848 family surnames, in VOLUME II, hereof, pp. 109-166. References to the sources of these records are given. Photostatic copies of any of the records can be ordered through the Ulster-Scot Historical Society at a nominal cost per page, upon payment of the registration fee. An estimate will be furnished upon request and, if no other expenses have been incurred, a considerable number of photo-stats can be furnished for the cost of the registration fee. Thus, if ordered a few at a time, they can be studied and the information in them may lead to a series of new clues for identifying other records of interest. The genealogist can also request the Society to examine various large manuscript collections described in the *Reports,* which are too extensive to be itemized in the indexes, and contain classes of records relating to the particular area of interest.

Anyone interested in Ulster genealogy should first know the history of the Public Record Office of Northern Ireland in order to understand and appreciate the nature and extent of the great genealogical collections which have been acquired.

The Government of Ireland Act of 1920 which, with amend-ments, forms the Constitution of Northern Ireland, gave power to the Province of Ulster to set up a new Public Record Office for the purpose of housing the records of Northern Ireland, of a nature belonging in such a repository. At the time of the destruction of the Public Record Office of Ire-land, Dublin, in June, 1922, almost all of the documents re-lating to Ulster from ancient times were as yet in that re-pository, and most of them were lost in the fire. By the Government Act of 1923, the Northern Government set up its own Public Record Office in Belfast. This was opened in March, 1924. From this date, the work of building the great record collections was begun and has continued to the present time under the direction of the three successive Deputy Keepers of the Records, to whom Ulster and all Americans of Ulster ancestry owe a great debt of gratitude. These are: D. A. Chart, M. A., Litt. D., 1924-1948; Edward Heatly, LL.B., 1948-1954; and Kenneth Darwin, M.A., 1954 onward. But for their archival knowledge, perseverance and deep interest in rebuilding the records of this ancient prov-ince, the Public Record Office might today have held little more than the normal increments, dated from 1900 or some-what earlier.

Mr. Chart had been a member of the staff of the Public Record Office, Dublin, before the fire of 1922. With his knowledge of the Irish records and the manner of their keep-ing, he first assumed the heroic task of trying to replace the loss of the Public Records, so far as it affected Northern Ireland. In this he was assisted by two staff members, who were also from the Dublin Office, including Mr. Heatly.

All knew the nature and extent of the records of the ancient Province of Ulster which had been housed in the Public Record Office, Dublin. They were aware of important collections of original records including wills, deeds, leases, marriage settlements, estate records, etc., then preserved in family archives, the vaults of solicitors, banks, estate offices, and in other repositories in Ireland and abroad. They also knew that duplicates of several entire series of the destroyed collections were deposited with various government agencies. Some important series of original documents were in the private custody of heirs of previous government officials who had carried them away. Others of this nature had been deposited in public and private repositories in England, Scotland and Ireland. It was well known that for half a century genealogists, solicitors, and representatives of other repositories had been copying important documents or making abstracts and taking extracts of the records in the Dublin Office. Extensive collections of such source materials related to many classes of genealogical records. There were also the famous Lodge Manuscripts, compiled in the 18th century, which survived the fire and contained much of Ulster interest among the transcripts of Chancery, Exchequer, and other records. The Record Commissioner's Transcripts, 1810-1830, included among other source materials relating to this province, the Ulster Inquisitions Post Mortem and on Attainder which had been printed. The Betham Genealogical Abstracts made from the Prerogative Wills and Administrations, 1536-1800, concerned all of Ireland. From his abstracts, Betham had constructed genealogical charts ranging in length from two to many generations. These charts, contained in 39 volumes, were deposited in the Office of Arms (now the Genealogical Office), Dublin Castle.

Thus, realizing the great possibilities of making the Public Record Office of Northern Ireland an important repository of Ulster records, Mr. Chart sent appeals throughout Ireland and Great Britain, to every individual and repository known to possess original records or transcripts relating to Ulster.

He also adopted a program of advertising repeated requests for family documents, genealogical collections, estate records, solicitors' papers and any transcripts of the burned Dublin records of Ulster, to be sent to this Office as gifts or for purchase.

The response was gratifying and gathered momentum through the years. The generosity of repositories located in Dublin and other parts of Ireland can be noted as copies of their collections relating to Ulster were acquired and calendared in this Office. Among the Dublin repositories were the National Library of Ireland, the Office of Arms (now the Genealogical Office), the Public Record Office, the Quit Rent Office, Trinity College Library, and the Royal Irish Academy. In Northern Ireland, the Armagh County Museum, the Armagh Public Library; the Presbyterian Historical Society and the Queen's University, Belfast; Friends Society, Lisburn; Magee University College Library, Londonderry, and other repositories allowed original records or transcripts of collections to be copied.

Hundreds of family collections have been acquired; very many containing pedigrees, family notes, wills, deeds, leases, assignments, mortgages, marriage settlements, accumulated during centuries, also transcripts of baptism, marriage and burial records from Parish Registers, extracts from census records, etc. Some very large collections of personal documents of powerful families and extensive records relating to great estates and the personal records of tenants, dating from the early 17th century, have been donated or loaned for copying.

Many solicitors representing localities throughout Northern Ireland, emptied their offices, vaults and storage places of their 17th to late 19th century documents which had been kept to provide legal evidence of inheritance and ownership of property. The original documents and certified copies of records sent to this Office included wills, proved and unproved, probate records, deeds, leases, mortgages, assignments of property, marriage settlements and agreements, extracts from court records, etc. One collection sent from the neighborhood of Larne, County Antrim, weighed about one ton. From this,

2,920 documents of the above nature were selected for preservation.

Great genealogical collections were purchased. One was the 42 volumes of pedigree charts copied by or for Sir Bernard Burke from the 39 volume collection of Sir William Betham, compiled from his abstracts of the Prerogative Wills and Administrations of Ireland, 1536-1800. The Arthur Tenison Groves collection contains over 9,000 items copied from the Dublin Public Record Office before the fire and from numerous other sources, relating to the records and genealogy of many families. The Philip Crosslé genealogical collection was donated, containing many thousands of transcripts and abstracts of the Dublin Public Record Office documents, and extracts from census and other records made before the fire.

One of the first deposits other than normal increments sent from official sources repaired a serious loss of Ulster records in Dublin. This was a collection of 102 Will Books, sent from the Belfast Principal Probate Registry, containing copies of all Wills proved in the Armagh, Belfast and Londonderry District Probate Registries, dated 1858-1900. The copies were made by each of the District Registries before the original records were sent to Dublin.

In 1928, Mr. Chart initiated the policy of systematically searching for documents of interest to Northern Ireland, in repositories particularly of England and Scotland. The work of investigating and copying material of historical and genealogical importance has continued without interruption, except for the war years, to the present date. Extensive collections have been copied, relating to the plantation of Ulster in the early 17th century, containing some particulars of early settlers who came from England and Scotland. Also transcripts have been made of a wealth of other miscellaneous manuscript materials and documents of genealogical and historical interest, dated from early times to the mid-nineteenth century.

A program of transcribing pertinent records has been carried out by representatives from this Office, in the English repositories, namely the British Museum, Lambeth Palace Library, the Public Record Office in London; the Bodleian Library, Oxford; the Cambridge University Library, Cambridge, and the Scottish repositories of Edinburgh, namely the National Library and the Scottish Record Office.

The total accumulation of records to date, from Irish and other sources, has been enormous and has made this Office a happy hunting ground of great importance to the genealogist. Furthermore, it is believed that the discovery of both public and private records of historical and genealogical significance in Ireland is far from exhausted. Accordingly, this Office pursues a policy of continuously watching for evidence of documents and collections of records in public or private keeping.

A *Report* regarding the progress of the work of this Office has been presented annually by the Deputy Keeper of the Records to the Governor of Northern Ireland, as follows:

THE REPORTS OF THE DEPUTY KEEPER OF THE RECORDS*

The *Government of Northern Ireland, Report of the Deputy Keeper of the Records,* has been published in 14 annual volumes dated 1924-1937, and in 5 volumes dated 1938-1945, 1946-1947, 1948, 1949-1950, 1951-1953. They were printed by His Majesty's (now Her Majesty's) Stationery Office, Chichester Street, Belfast. As of November, 1956, the last three *Reports* could be purchased at this publication office, at $1.50 each. An entire or partial collection can sometimes be located in the Cathedral Book Shop, 18 Gresham Street, Belfast, or in one of the Dublin Book Shops.

The full series of the *Reports* may be found in most of the large genealogical libraries of the United States, as well as in the principal libraries and repositories of genealogical records in Great Britain and Ireland.

Not enough can be said to stress the value of these *Reports* to all who comtemplate Ulster genealogical research. Those who enjoy the opportunity of going to the Search Room for independent work will have a better comprehension of the records if they have previously studied the *Reports*. Those who are dependent upon correspondence with the Ulster-Scot Historical Society in the course of their research can use the *Reports* as catalogues from which to order photostats of listed family or individual records. Also, they can direct the attention of the Society to any collection of records which, ac-

---

*Three further *Deputy Keeper's Reports* have been published since Mrs. Falley's work first appeared.

cording to the description of the contents, appears to be relevant to the problem, and request copies of pertinent items.

It is a foregone conclusion that the person closest to the problem is best equipped to recognize clues which may appear in the descriptions and indexes of collections through the names, particular places of residence and dates of the records. This is due to the fact that all manner of half forgotten or entirely forgotten details of the family history, having had no significance, might come to mind with the help of information discovered in the *Reports*.

As of 1960, it is expected that a *Report* following the 1951-1953 volume will soon appear, with information regarding considerable genealogical material of importance which has been acquired since 1953. It is hoped that the new *Report* will follow the previous plan, with descriptions of the contents of the collections acquired since 1953, and will contain the usual consolidated index of the records of as many collections as possible.

Until this new *Report* is published and available, a genealogical search by correspondence cannot be complete without commissioning the Ulster-Scot Historical Society to search the source materials calendared in the Public Record Office since 1953.

The Deputy Keeper of the Records has, since 1924, followed a consistent plan in presenting the information contained in the *Reports*. This precludes the necessity of a table of contents. The work of the Office staff is noted, the collections are calendared and described, and the indexes are set forth as follows:

1. A report on the research, examination and transcribing of aged and important collections in other repositories, and of loaned collections.

2. Particulars of progress in the management of the Office.

3. A calendar of collections of normal increments sent from government agencies and minor courts, having reached the age of twenty years.

4. A calendar of presented collections, arranged alphabetically under the names of the donors. A brief description of the contents of each, sets forth the nature and class of the

records, inclusive years or year of the documents, number of volumes or single instruments, and area of interest. Some very large collections are not further itemized, while others of considerable extent are noted as to the names of families represented and other data of interest. Most small collections are annotated with the names of the families or individuals which appear in the records, their specific place of residence or county wherein stated, together with above information.

5. A calendar of purchased collections, arranged and described as above.

6. A calendar of collections loaned for copying, described as above.

7. A report on the arrangement and preservation of the records in the Office.

8. A report on the work of calendaring and indexing of the above mentioned materials, other than official increments.

9. A report on the Parochial Records; Parish Registers sent for repair, and photostatic copies made for the Office; names of parishes from which were sent reports on the condition of Registers in local custody.

10. A report on the number of searches made in the Office by genealogists, historians, etc., with a list of the subjects, and names of the families studied.

11. A list of donors to the Library, with titles of books and pamphlets, also the number of same purchased for the Library.

12. Appendix A. This contains a report on each of the chief deposited collections of aged and important documents received during the year or period covered by the *Report*. Each is described in from part of one to three pages, as to subject matter, classes of records, nature of the documents, various dates or inclusive dates, size of the collection, principal names in family manuscripts and source of the records.

13. Appendix B. This contains a consolidated index of the records in the collections calendared in the *Report*, except for the very extensive collections, according to the "Principles of Indexing" set forth in the *Report* of 1929, p. 12. Regulations adopted are "(1) that all copies of destroyed records should be indexed, no matter what their date may be; (2) that all

documents of earlier date than 1701 which are, comparatively speaking, scarce, and therefore valuable, should be indexed as fully as possible; (3) that the eighteenth century should be similarly treated, except that discrimination might be exercised in the case of very voluminous or comparatively unimportant collections; (4) that nineteenth century documents concerning families and individuals, particularly those of the latter half of the century, should not be indexed unless of outstanding interest." Under these principles, over 100,000 items concerning families or individuals, appear in the indexes, 1924-1953.

The records listed under 848 family surnames in VOLUME II hereof, pp. 109-166, are extracted from these indexes and the above calendars. A few single items are presented below to illustrate some of the numerous classes of records pertaining to individuals and families, set forth in the consolidated indexes of the *Reports*.

1. Anderson, Chas., Dav., Mary, and Wm., Portaferry, Co. Down. Passage to America, 1805.

2. Andrews Family, Comber, Co. Down. Pedigree, 1698.

3. Allen, Hugh, Kerr, and Eliza, Family of. Carnmoney Parish, Co. Antrim and U. S. A. (McKinney Note Book.)

4. Bigger, Samuel and Jamison, Janet, Family of. Mallusk, Co. Antrim, 1726-1772.

5. Blacker, Eliza, Hannah, John, Letita, Samuel, Sophia, Louisa, Stewart. Moyallan, Co. Down, 1724-1800. (Quaker Records.)

6. Calwell, John, Belfast. Leases, 1747-1784.

7. Campbell, John, Ann, Eleanor, Sarah and Alexander. Omagh, Co. Tyrone. Passage to America, 1805.

8. Cockeran Family Journal, Liverpool to New York (voyage from Ireland), 1833.

9. Davis, Thomas. Armagh Priml. Manor Rolls, 1625-1627.

10. Davis, Henry, Armagh. Armagh Rent Rolls, 1660.

11. Dickson, John and Steel, Jane, Family of. Carnmoney Parish, Co. Antrim. (McKinney Note Book, n.d.—1753.)

12. Dix(s)on, Anty., Hy., Isa., Rose, Thomas, Wm.—Lurgan and Seagoe, Co. Armagh, 1671-1733. (Quaker Records.)

13. Emigration to South Carolina from Co. Antrim. (Chesney Diary, 1755-1800.)

14. Fews, Barony of, Co. Armagh. Hearthmoney Roll, 1664.

15. Gilbert, Ann, Christine, Hannah, Jonathan, Sarah, Stephen and Thomas, of Lurgan, Co. Armagh, 1702-1732. (Quaker Records.)

16. Gordon, Family of (notebook containing Will Extracts, 1659-1846).

17. Gregory, and Jones, Families of. (Notebook containing Will Extracts, 1659-1846.)

18. Hamilton, Rev. William and Patterson, Anna, Family of, Toronto, Canada. (McKinney Note Book, 1807-1899.)

19. Hill Family Wills. Among the 119 extracts of Prerogative and Diocesan Wills of members of the Hill family of various counties of Ulster, listed in the *Report* of 1932, are the following examples:

> Hill, Arthur, Hillsborough, Co. Down. Prerogative Will Extract, 1665.
> Hill, Michael, Hillsborough, Co. Down. Prerogative Will Extract, 1699.
> Hill, William, Hillsborough, Co. Down. Prerogative Will Extract, 1693.
> Hill, Moses, Hillhall, Co. Down. Prerogative Will Extract, 1682.

20. Hughes, John, Coleraine, Co. Londonderry, etc., Rental, *circa* 1620-1641.

21. Jackson, Anne, George, Richard, Col., and Mr., Coleraine, Co. Londonderry. (Merchant Taylors' Transcripts, 1746-1826.)

22. Jackson, Roger, Killultagh, Co. Antrim. Subsidy Rolls Extracts, 1663-1667.

23. Kelly, James, and Kirkpatrick, Agnes, Family of, Carnmoney Parish, County Antrim. (McKinney Note Book, 1801-1845.)

24. Love, Hugh, Ballylagen, Co. Londonderry. Lease, 1695. (Antrim Deeds. Original Document.)

25. McColloch, Henry. Notes regarding Ulster Emigrants to North Carolina, 1736-1737.

26. Murray, John, versus Coles, Mary, and others. Exchequer Bill Extract, 1722.

27. Newton, Andrew, of Coagh, Co. Tyrone. Lease, Bond, Marriage Articles, Prerogative (?) Will, 1778-1825. (Transcripts and Original Documents.)

28. O'Dogherty, Averkagh McShan, Con McDonell and Hugh Boy McCahyir, of Greenecastle, Co. Donegal. Chancery Inquisition, 1603.

29. Parsons, Family of, Birr, King's Co. Notes and Pedigree, 1600-1902.

30. Richardson, Henry and John, Belturbet, Co. Cavan. Chancery Bill, 1760.

Richardson, James and Charles, Magherafelt, Co. Londonderry. Chancery Bill, 1760.

Richardson, John and William, Tillervey, Co. Tyrone. Chancery Bill, 1760.

Richardson, John and the Rev. John, William, James and Henry, Kerockahilt, Co. Londonderry. Chancery Bill, 1760.

31. Read, William, Aghanloo Parish, Co. Londonderry. Muster Roll, 1666.

32. Speer, Alexander, and William, Families of, Achadachor, Co. Donegal. Census Extracts, 1821-1841.

33. Stewart, James, and Mary Blaire. Derry Marriage Licence Extract, 1687-1688.

34. Templeton, Agnes, Alexander, Henry, John, Samuel and Robert, Co. Down. Deed of Partnership, 1761. (Weir Documents.)

Templeton, Alexander, Ballyvally, Co. Down. Mortgage, Assignment of Mortgage, 1764-1765. *(ibid.)*

Templeton, Henry, Kelpike, Co. Down. Trust Deed, 1712; Dromore Will, 1761. *(ibid.)*

Templeton, John, Kilpike, Co. Down. Lease; Trust Deeds; Dromore Will, 1705-1717. *(ibid.)*

35. Vaughan, John, Londonderry. Exchequer Bill Extract, 1677. (Gen. Soc. Docts.)

36. Wilson, Family of. Wilson and Chesney Documents, 1730-1879.

37. Wilson, John, Family of. 1666-1736. (McKinney Note Book.)

38. Young, Robert, Bush Town, Co. Londonderry. Rental (post) 1729. (Merchant Taylors' Transcripts.)

REFERENCE MATERIALS IN THE PUBLIC SEARCH ROOM

The Public Record Office has, as reference materials in the Search Room, the *Reports of the Deputy Keeper,* Catalogues, Descriptive Lists, Calendars, Indexes, and Books of Reference.

1. *The Annual Reports of the Deputy Keeper of the Records,* 1924-1953 (to date), are kept among the reference materials on the shelves against the East Wall.

2. *Catalogues.*

(i) *Crown and Peace Records.* A bound manuscript catalogue for each of the six counties of Northern Ireland (Antrim, Armagh, Down, Fermanagh, Londonderry and Tyrone), contains references to the numerous classes of records. These collections are calendared in the *Reports* also, when received by the Office. They are mostly dated from the last quarter of the 19th century. Among the many classes are Affidavits, Appeals, Civil Bill Books, Convictions, Coroner's Inquests, Crown Files at Assizes, Voter's Lists and Registers, etc.

(ii) *Legal and Miscellaneous.* A bound manuscript catalogue of the High Court records (King's Bench, Chancery, etc.), the Crown Office, Privy Council Office, Cabinet Office, Bankruptcy Petition Files, Diocesan Records, Ministry of Finance Records. These collections, also dated from the last quarter of the 19th century, are calendared in the *Reports,* upon receipt of the records.

(iii) *Parish Registers.* A bound typed catalogue of all the Registers of the Established Church of Ireland, containing records dated prior to 1871 now existing in Northern Ireland. The catalogue contains also lists of the Presbyterian and the Roman Catholic Registers existing in Northern Ireland. All of the Registers itemized in this catalogue are classified as original records or transcripts, and are noted as to their location and the inclusive dates of the records. Registers of the Society of Friends (Quakers) will be noted among some of the Manuscripts of Chief Deposited Collections, below. Lists of all existing Parish or Church Registers, with the location and the inclusive dates of each, are presented in PART THREE of this volume, under Church Records.

(iv) *Deposited Original Documents.* In the Catalogue are listed all records of this class in numerical order as received by the Office. Each deposit is annotated as to date received, name of the donor, and described in some detail or with a reference to a descriptive list or calendar.

(v) *Transcripts.* A Catalogue of all records of this class contains lists of the records in numerical order as received by the Office, with notes regarding the date of deposit, name of the donor, the authentication of the copy, and details of the record or reference to a descriptive list or calendar.

3. *Descriptive Lists.*

(i) *Deposited Original Documents and Transcripts.* The Office compiles a typed summary of each individual item in the smaller collections, with names, dates, etc., in each record; its class, source, and any other pertinent information. These are arranged in numerical order as received. Those which meet "The Principles of Indexing," mentioned above, are indexed in the *Reports.*

4. *Calendars.*

(i) *Calendars of Collections.* A typed Calendar of each of the larger collections gives a brief summary of the individual items of all classes. A typed guide to and list of the Calendars, which are numbered as they are received, is on the shelf with the Calendars. All of these collections are described in detail in the *Reports.* The large collections of a single class of records will be listed in the chapters of PART THREE of this volume, each of which is devoted to a specific class of source materials. The chapters are subdivided according to the repositories in which the records are deposited. Some of the large manuscript collections containing miscellaneous materials of genealogical interest will be listed below.

(ii) *Calendars of Testamentary Records.* These are bound lists of Wills and Grants of Probate and Administration for Northern Ireland arranged alphabetically by years and form an index to the Wills and Administrations from 1900 to date.

5. *Indexes.*

(i) *Bound Indexes.*

(a) *Wills prior to 1858.* Bound printed, manuscript and typed indexes to Wills proved in the Prerogative Court of Ireland and in the Diocesan Courts of Northern Ireland.

(b) *Wills 1858-1900.* The Calendars of Grants in the Principal Probate Registry, Belfast, should be consulted for this period. The only indexes in this Office are the indexes in each Will Book, there being 102 in number. They contain copies of the original Wills proved in the District Probate Registries of Armagh, Belfast and Londonderry; the copies made before the original documents were sent to the Public Record Office, Dublin, where they were destroyed in the fire of 1922. These transcripts of the Wills are especially important to Americans whose ancestors came from Northern Ireland, *ca*. 1830-1870, during the great emigration period, as their parents more often than not remained behind and many died testate after 1858.

(c) *Wills 1900 to date.* Bound typed and printed Calendars, arranged alphabetically by years and forming an index to Wills and Grants of Administration of Northern Ireland.

(d) *Reports of the Deputy Keeper of the Public Records in Ireland, Dublin.* The 55th-58th *Reports*, Dublin, contain Calendars and Indexes of many records deposited in that Office which concern individuals of Northern Ireland, dated from early times. Also in this Office are indexes of records in the Genealogical Office (Office of Arms), Dublin Castle, Dublin. One is an index contained in *Analecta Hibernica,* No. 17, published by the Irish Manuscripts Commission. It represents some 7,500 abstracts and transcripts of Wills in manuscript collections pertaining to all parts of Ireland. Here also is a copy of an index to some 2,000 Memorials of Wills deposited in the Registry of Deeds, Dublin, of dates 1708-1800. The compiler, Miss P. Beryl Eustace, made abstracts of 1,464 of these Wills which were published by the Irish Manuscripts Commission in two volumes: *Registry of Deeds, Dublin, Abstracts of Wills,* 1708-1745; 1746-1785. Dublin, 1954.

(ii) *Card Index.* This is contained in cabinets located against the West Wall of the Search Room. It is a consolidated master card index of all original documents and transcripts of original documents; the records in the Groves and other principal collections which are not self indexed; all items in miscellaneous collections ranging in extent from a few to many hundreds and some thousands. It includes, also, the Index of the Land Purchase Commission Documents and the Library Index. The principal and other names of importance in each record are entered on separate cards which are cross-indexed and annotated as to class (Will, Deed, Lease, Mortgage, Marriage record, Pedigree, Family MSS., etc.) ; the year and place; nature of the record (original, transcript, collection to which it belongs, etc.). A Subject Index is included. Books and pamphlets deposited in the Office Library are also indexed.

6. *Reference Books.* Books on the shelves in the Public Search Room include the following:

(i) *Published Sources* (listed in VOLUME II, PART THREE, pp. 205-207; 229-231; 259-261).

(a) *Atlases, Maps,* i. e., Lewis's; Philips', etc.

(b) *Dictionaries, Topographical; Gazetteers; Indexes,* i.e., Lewis's; Parliamentary Gazetteer; Topographical Index published with the Census of Northern Ireland, 1926, 1947; General Alphabetical Index of Townlands, Towns, etc. (Thom), 1904, 1913.

(c) *Census Reports* (see above).

(d) *Directories, Almanacs,* i.e., Belfast from 1819 (some early volumes missing) ; Dublin from 1744 (some early volumes missing) ; others include the valuable *Pigot's Directory,* 1824.

(e) *State Papers, Calendars of.* Calendars of State Papers (Ireland), in the Public Record Office, London. Calendars of State Papers (Domestic), in the Public Record Office, London.

(f) *Wills Indexes:* Genealogical Office, Dublin Castle, Abstracts (*Analecta Hibernica,* No. 17) ; Phillimore, *Indexes of Irish Wills (Diocesan);* Vicars, *Index of Prerogative Wills,* etc.

(ii) *Manuscript Volumes.* Details regarding indexes of Marriage Licence Bonds, Wills, Administration Bonds, and transcripts of early tax records, etc., will be listed under the various classes of records in the chapters of PART THREE of this volume.

CHIEF DEPOSITED MANUSCRIPT COLLECTIONS

Several collections of particular genealogical interest will be briefly itemized below. They vary greatly in content and extent. They were presented, purchased, loaned for copying, or transcribed in other repositories by representatives of this Office.

Most of the family collections, containing original documents and transcripts of destroyed and other records, were presented to this office for safekeeping. The miscellaneous collections of genealogical materials, relating to many families, represent the work of noted genealogists who, during many years previous to 1922, transcribed the documents in the Dublin Record Office and in other repositories. Some collections represent an entire series of one class of documents which were transcribed previous to the destruction of the original records. The collections presented by solicitors, which had accumulated in their offices over long periods of time, contain both original documents and official copies of records relating to the transfer of property by Will, Deed, Lease, Assignment, Marriage Settlement and Agreement, Mortgage, etc., in all cases indicating the right of ownership.

The principal collections listed below are all calendared in the *Reports* and the family or individual records are briefly described. Many of these, together with a large number of records in the smaller collections, have been listed under the 848 surnames in VOLUME II, hereof, pp. 109-166.

ANTRIM MANUSCRIPTS. Family papers of the MacDonnells, 1603-1842. Patents, James I, 1603-1604; Grants of Tithes, 1639; Leases, 1625; Rentals, 1668; List of townlands in the Antrim estate with areas and rents, 1700; Deed of Partition of Estate, 18 August 1814, giving names of chief tenants; Genealogical notes of the Stuart family in Scotland. (*Report*, 1925, p. 16.)

ANTRIM RENT ROLL. An Antrim Estate Rent Roll, May, 1641. Copied in the British Museum (Harleian MS. 2138). (*Report*, 1935, p. 14.)

ARCHDALE FAMILY PAPERS. Family papers of Lieutenant-Colonel J. B. Archdale, of Castle Archdale, Co. Fermanagh, dated 1537-1909. An account by William Archdale, late Sheriff of Fermanagh for 1667. A Rent Roll of Henry Mervyn, 1719, relating to Trillick and Omagh district, contains some names of tenants. A survey of Glenally Estate in Co. Fermanagh, 1721, with description of holdings and some names. Copies of Wills, Notices of Marriages, etc., relating to the families of Archdale, Price, Blackwood, Mervyn, Dunbar, Humphrys and many others. (*Report*, 1927, p. 24.)

ARMAGH PRIMATIAL MANOR ROLLS. The collection of early 17th century documents loaned by the Armagh Library for copying, comprises Court Leet Rolls of the following manors: Donaghmore, 1625-1627; Artrea, 1626; Arboe, 1626; Armagh, 1625-1627; Termonfeckin, Co. Louth, 1625-1627, also a list of property of the See of Armagh, 27 September 1620. Manor Court Rolls contain many names of individuals, such as jurors, tenants fined for non-attendance, and persons concerned in the suits. Many names are indexed in the *Report*. (*Report*, 1928, p. 13.)

BURKE, SIR BERNARD; TRANSCRIPTS OF PEDIGREE CHARTS. This collection of 42 large volumes of Pedigree Charts, copied by or for Sir Bernard Burke from the 39 volumes of Pedigree Charts compiled by Sir William Betham, from his Genealogical Abstracts made from the Prerogative Wills of Ireland, 1536-1800. The latter Abstracts are contained in the Betham collection of 241 Note Books, now in the Public Record Office, Dublin. The 39 volumes of the Betham Pedigree Charts are in the Genealogical Office (Office of Arms), Dublin Castle, Dublin. The Burke Charts are in more legible handwriting than that of Betham, but the Betham originals have one advantage in that the margins of the charts contain many notes in the handwriting of several who followed Betham and Burke as Ulster King of Arms. These notes contain genealogical information discovered at subsequent dates. Arthur Vicars' *Index of the Prerogative Wills of Ireland, 1536-1810*, Dublin, 1897, contains over 37,000 items and forms a list of the Wills represented in the Betham Charts. The Pedigree Charts range from two to several generations in length and number about 16,000, having been constructed from one to several Wills Abstracts, for one or more lines of a family. In addition, information from about 5,000 Grants of Administration is represented in Pedigree Charts.

Volumes 1 and 2 contain a more or less haphazard arrangement, based probably on notes made in the course of pedigree searches. Volumes 3 and 4 are devoted to information from the abstracts made of the Wills dated prior to 1700, the charts being arranged alphabetically by surname from D to Y. The volumes 5 to 42 concern information mainly from the 18th century Wills, arranged by surname from A to Y, but not in complete order. Each volume is self-indexed as to names of testators and alliances recorded in the Wills, but does not contain Christian names, residences or dates. This Office has compiled a Master Index of Names of Testators and persons whose property was the subject of Grants of Administration, covering the entire collection. The records in this collection are not indexed in the *Reports*, being already represented in the Vicars' published *Index*.

CROSSLÉ MANUSCRIPTS. The collections of Philip Crosslé of Dublin have come as gifts to this Office in three lots. (*Reports*, 1925, pp. 4, 7-8; 1933, p. 10; 1938-45, p. 15.) The first is one of the largest from a great genealogist, containing many thousands of individual records. It contains:

1. 107 copies or abstracts of Prerogative Wills, Grants, etc. (principal names: Andrews, Charley, Law, McCammon, McCance, Murray, Stephenson, Stouppe, Watson, Wilson), 1668-1855.

2. 22 copies or abstracts of Armagh Wills, Grants, etc. (principal names: Hays, Murray, Watson), 1697-1819.

3. 25 copies or abstracts of Clogher Wills, Grants, etc. (principal name: Murray), 1720-1824.

4. 168 copies or abstracts of Connor Wills, Grants, etc. (principal names: Anderson, Andrew(s), Cunningham, Finlay, Hayes, Law, McCammon, McCance, McClelland, Mulligan, Russel, Stinson, Stouppe, Watson, Wilson), 1672-1847.

5. 37 copies or abstracts of Derry Wills, Grants, etc. (principal names: Haslet, Hay, Murray, Torrens, Watson), 1684-1810.

6. 111 copies or abstracts of Down Wills, Grants, etc.

(principal names: Agnew, Andrew(s), Brown, Graham, Law, McCammon, McCance, Napier, Neeper, Stephenson, Watson, Wilson), 1718-1830.

7. 129 copies or abstracts of Dromore Wills, Grants, etc. (principal names: Andrew(s), Blizard, Law, McCance, Murray, Wallace, Waterson, Watson), 1728-1852.

8. Freeholders' Registers: Co. Down (principal names: Agnew, Andrews, McCance, McCandless, Mahaffy, Morrow, Murray, Wallace, Waterson, Watson), 1746-1795. Londonderry (principal names: Cairns, Fleming, Murray, Torrens), 1761-1829.

9. Extracts from Census Returns, 1821. Parkmount, Co. Antrim; Tullylish, Co. Down; Coleraine, Desertoghill, Aghadowey, Co. Londonderry (principal names: Andrew, Cairns, Fleming, Hilton, Morrow, Murray, Torrens).

10. Extracts from Parish Registers and Parochial Returns: Dromore, 1784-1816 (principal names: Watson, Wright); Kilmore, Co. Armagh, 1800-1896 (principal name, Watson); Lisburn, 1641-1753 (principal names: Andrew(s), Houlden, McMurray, Murray); Lurgan, 1691-1757 (principal names: Andrew(s), Houlden, McMurray, Merrow, Murray).

11. Chancery and Exchequer Bills (principal names: Andrew, Boyd, Boyle, Coles, Coulter, Torrens, Watson).

12. Parliamentary Returns, 1740 and 1776. Parishes of Aghaloo, Carnteel, Derryloran, Drumglass, Kildress, Tullaniskan, Co. Tyrone.

13. Poll Tax Returns, 1662 and 1696-1699. Parish of Aghaloo and Barony of Dungannon. (Totals only.)

14. Subsidy Roll (extracts from), Dungannon Barony, 1663-1667.

15. Extract Hearthmoney Roll, 1666, Co. Antrim (McCance and McCandless), and Hearthmoney Roll, Co. Donegal, 1665, principally.

16. Book of Survey and Distribution, Aghaloo, Carnteel, Drumglass, Tullaniskin, Co. Tyrone, 1661.

17. Civil Survey, 1664-1666, same district.

18. Leases, Assignments, etc. (extracts from). (Princi-

pal names: Andrews, Maffett, Murray, Torrens, Wallace), 1747-1801.

19. Mayor's or Recorder's Court Book, Londonderry (Extracts from), 1755-1768. (Principal names: Cairns, Cochran, Culbert, Hay, Kelly, McCracken, Murray, Orr.) (*Report*, 1925, pp. 4, 7-8.)

Crosslé Manuscripts in the second lot contain 325 documents, including Conveyances, Leases, Maps, Marriage Settlements, Mortgages, Notes on Family History, Wills, etc., 1613-1878, in Counties Antrim, Armagh, Down, Dublin, Londonderry, Louth, Tyrone. The larger part of the records are dated after 1800. Families represented number 101. Records are indexed in the *Report* of 1933. Also in the collection are genealogical notes from the following newspapers dated 1766-1831: The *Dublin Chronicle*, the *Dublin Evening Post*, the *Northern Star*, the *Ulster Magazine*. (*Report* 1933, p. 10.)

Crosslé Manuscripts in the third lot contain 119 abstracts of Memorials of Deeds, 1708-1736; Connor Wills of David Frew, 1699; Alexander Frew, 1732; Alexander Frew, 1778. (*Report*, 1938-1945, p. 15.)

DOBBIN FAMILY MEMOIR. A lengthy manuscript dealing with the history of the Dobbin family of Carrickfergus and elsewhere, containing much biographical detail from 17th-19th century copies of original documents now destroyed, including Wills of the Dobbin family and the allied families of Reynell, Edgar and Kane, of much genealogical interest.

DOBBS MANUSCRIPTS. Dobbs Family Papers, 1694-1775. Correspondence of Arthur Dobbs, born 1689, of Castle Dobbs, County Antrim, M.P. for Carrickfergus, County Antrim and High Sheriff, 1720; Governor of North Carolina, 1753. Includes Carrickfergus Papers (Charters of Elizabeth and James I, Oaths of Mayors, Rolls of Burgesses and Freemen, Statistical Account, etc.), 1569-1822. A Rent Roll of Viscount Dungannon's Estate, Co. Down, 1768. Papers relating to the Hudson Bay Company and a Journal of Henry Kelsey of this Company, 1683-1722. Two volumes on a voyage to Hudson's Bay, 1741-1742 and a similar voyage, 1746. (*Report*, 1925, pp. 7, 13.) Also a Dobbs

Family Note Book containing a Family Pedigree Chart and Genealogy beginning with Arthur Dobbs' great-great-grandfather, John Dobbs, Deputy Treasurer for Ulster, who married in 1603. The line is carried down to 1919. (MS. Transcript No. 1075/22.)

GALT DIARY.   The Diary of John Galt concerns Methodists and events in Coleraine, Co. Londonderry, 1796-1837. (*Report*, 1948, pp. 4, 17.)   Indexed in *Report*.

GROVES MANUSCRIPTS.   Tenison Groves, genealogist and record searcher for 40 or more years, left his collection of many thousands of transcripts, abstracts, notes, etc., made from records in the Public Record Office, Dublin, before the fire of 1922, a part of which was acquired by the Dublin Office and the part relating mostly to Northern Ireland which was purchased by the Belfast Record Office, in 1939. This latter collection is so extensive that a separate card-index was originally compiled for it. This now is a part of the Consolidated Master Card-Index.   The items, numbering over 9,000, were first arranged under the following categories: Families, Counties, Military, Ecclesiastical, Religious Returns.   The collection is not indexed as a whole in the *Report* in which it is described but family items appear in the *Report*, 1946-1947, Index, pp. 14-131.   A description of the collection (*ibid.*, pp. 12, 13) is as follows:

Families: These consist almost entirely of copies and notes made in the course of genealogical searches.   The chief sources are Wills and Administrations (Intestacy), Legal Proceedings, Parish Registers, Census Returns, Religious Returns, Hearthmoney Rolls, etc.

Counties: The following notes indicate what matter is available in each county:

Antrim: Subsidy Roll for Baronies of Cary, Dunluce, Glenarm and Kilconway; Collectors' Accounts . . . Glenavy, Antrim and Ballymena Walks, 1683-1690.   Presentments, examinations, etc., . . . 1710-1740.   Notes about the Hearts of Oak and Hearts of Steel, *ca.* 1770-1780.

Armagh: Exchequer Inquisitions extracts, 1603-1608. Examinations concerning the burning of Freeduff or Creggan Presbyterian Church in 1743; Note of Schoolmasters in Armagh, Lurgan, Portadown, Markethill and Tanderagee (extracted from Commonwealth Books, 1657); notes on Tynan Parish, 17th and 18th centuries; depositions as to riot in Armagh City, 1717; extracts from Minute Books of Armagh Corporation, 1738-1818; Poll Book, 1753; list of inhabitants of Armagh City, 1770.

Donegal: Subsidy Roll of Kilmacrenan, Raphoe and Tirhugh Baronies, 1669; Book of Postings and Sales (extracts from), 1703; list of presentments at Assizes under Tory Acts, 1720-1797.

Down: Religious Return of Kilbroney Parish, 1766; Lecale Barony, list of freeholders, 1795-1800; Monastery of St. Patrick, Downpatrick, Exchequer Inquisition extract, 1549; notes of persons presented for trial at Assizes, 1712-1796; Affidavits as to housing of cattle, 1777; short list of Parish Priests, 1712; notes *re* Clonduff Parish, *ca.* 1605-1834.

Dublin: The material relating to this county is much more bulky and earlier than that of any northern county. Memoranda Rolls and Judiciary Rolls (extracts), *ca.* 1300-1500; Plea Rolls (extracts), *ca.* 1250-1350; Pipe Roll (extracts), *ca.* 1270-1320; Receipts and Payments Roll (extracts), *ca.* 1540-1550; Exchequer Inquisition extracts, 16th and 17th centuries; Subsidy Roll, Baronies of Newcastle, Rathdown and Uppercross.

Fermanagh: Exchequer Inquisitions (extracts), 1613-1690; collectors' accounts, . . . Enniskillen Walk, 1692; registered Freeholders, 1747-1768; notes on the setting of tithes in 17 parishes, 1656-1657; list of Commissioners of the Revenue, 1654; list of Justices of the Peace, 1655; Hearthmoney Roll of Lurg Barony, 1665-1666; return showing number of houses and hearths in each barony, 1732-1734; Recovery Book extracts, 1658-1738.

Londonderry: Summonister Rolls extracts, 1615-1638; Report on Parish Priests, *ca.* 1700.

Tyrone: High Sheriffs' Accounts (Pipe Roll extracts), 1615-1625; Summonister Rolls extracts, 1615-1638; Exchequer Inquisitions, 1658; Subsidy Roll extracts, 1662-

1668; notes on Derryloran Parish, *ca.* 1600-1800; on Badoney Parish *ca.* 1603-1766; extracts from Collectors' Accounts, Artrea, Derryloran, Drumglass and Lissan Parishes, 1690-1692.

Mixed Counties: References mainly in Exchequer Inquisitions to Counties Cavan, Monaghan, Carlow, Leitrim, Meath, Limerick, Kerry, Galway, Sligo, Waterford.

Military: Muster Rolls of the following regiments in 1642: Sir Robert Stewart's, Earl of Eglinton's, Life Guards of the Lord Lieutenant, Viscount Montgomery's, Sir James Montgomery's, Viscount Clandeboye's, Col. Arthur Chichester's, Sir John Clotworthy's, Col. Arthur Hill's, Lord Conway's and Col. Mervyn's; of Londonderry Garrison; of the Companies in Counties Londonderry and Donegal; Quarters of the Army in Ireland, 1690, and at various intervals until 1800; and various army lists for that period; list of militia officers of County Antrim, 1691-1693; lists of yeomanry and militia officers, *ca.* 1797-1810; Muster Rolls of Cookstown Cavalry, Lissan Infantry and Loughry Infantry, 1797.

Returns relating to Religion: Returns of Protestant Householders, 1740, for 68 parishes, seven of which are outside Northern Ireland (lists contain names of the householders (Protestant and Roman Catholic), by townlands, parishes, baronies and counties) ; Returns of 1766 for Dioceses of Armagh, Clogher, Derry, Raphoe, Down and Connor, Dromore, Kilmore and Ardagh, giving total number only of persons in each parish according to their religion (names are given in a few parishes) ; list of Parish Priests, Counties Donegal, Fermanagh, Londonderry and Tyrone.

Ecclesiastical: These papers are mainly copies of documents in Armagh Library; most of them consist of Visitation papers and kindred documents; there are also rentals of lands in various dioceses; a list of tithe payers in Drumcree Parish, Co. Armagh, 1737; petitions (giving names of signatories only) from a large number of dissenting congregations mostly in Antrim and Down, 1775.

HAMILTON DEEDS. These Deeds relating to the Hamilton and

other families number 94, and are dated over the period 1638-1841. In the first Deed, 1638, are Co. Wexford and Co. Wicklow names of Byrne, Flatsborough, Walsh, who leased from Sir Henry Tichborne. The 2nd-4th Deeds, 1654, relate to the Tichborne family, mostly for lands of Co. Louth. Former proprietors of Co. Louth who forfeited lands at this time were John White, Christopher Wotton, Lord Taaffe, Patrick Dardes, George Plunkett, Patrick Clynton, Patrick Drumgooland, Richard Barnewell, Anthony Gernon, Christopher Taaffe, Edward Hollinwood, John Hudson, Patrick Waring. Parliamentary soldiers to whom their lands were assigned were Major William Aston, Lieutenant Dawson, George Whitfield, John Ewre, John Leney, John Graham, John Dawlyn. The Hamilton family appear with the 5th Deed, dated 24 November 1674, by Sir Hans Hamilton of Hamilton's Bawn, Armagh, to Sir William Tichborne, of the Wicklow, Wexford and Louth lands above. The 15th Deed, dated 1682, concerns the locality of the main body of the Deeds, in Killinchy and Killyleagh and the vicinity, in County Down. There are a number of Donegal references to the manor of Ray and to the property of the Brazier family in that county and in Co. Limerick, and a lease, 1698, to John Cowan, merchant of Londonderry, and other Deeds concerning Dublin property. (*Report*, 1925, pp. 7, 15.)

HEARTHMONEY AND SUBSIDY ROLLS. Transcripts of the Hearthmoney Rolls, being lists of all who paid a tax of two shillings on each fire-hearth, are complete in this Office for the following counties: Co. Antrim, 1669; Co. Armagh, 1664; Co. Londonderry, 1663; Co. Tyrone, 1666. The Subsidy Roll of Co. Down, 1663, is complete and relates to people who possessed sufficient property to be subject to payment of the subsidies which then formed the chief means of direct taxation. (*Reports*, 1924, pp. 27-29; 1933, p. 5.) See the *Tenison Groves MSS.*, for Co. Antrim Subsidy Roll records and Counties Donegal and Fermanagh Hearthmoney Rolls (partial lists).

HERTFORD ESTATE DOCUMENTS. The Hertford Estate Documents, Lisburn District, 1719-1894, concern the estate which became known as the Wallace Estate. It comprised the whole barony of Upper Massereene, Co. Antrim, and six townlands on the Co. Down side of the River Lagan. The collection includes two Rental Lists, dated 1719-1727; 1728-1730, covering the entire estate. Many volumes of maps of varying dates show the townlands and occupying tenants. (*Report*, 1938-1945, p. 27.)

IRISH GENEALOGICAL SOCIETY, LONDON. Presented extracts of 117 Prerogative Wills; Diocesan Wills of Clogher, Connor, Derry, Down, Dromore, 1715-1855. Indexed in the *Report*, 1938-1945. (*Report*, 1938-1945, p. 16.)

MACDONALDS AND MACDONNELLS MANUSCRIPT. Manuscript history, purchased. The first eighteen pages deal in detail with the genealogy of the Scottish Macdonalds and related clans, bringing the history of the family down to the end of the 16th century. Records concerning the family in the North of Ireland continue into the 17th century. It appears to have been copied from an original manuscript dated 1715. (*Report*, 1934, pp. 20, 21.)

McKINNEY NOTEBOOK. This remarkable notebook of the late John McKinney, of County Antrim, presented in 1948, contains records of nearly 300 people or families of Carnmoney Parish, County Antrim, and nearby towns. The records consist of family notes, items about individuals and some pedigrees. The records are indexed by principal names in the *Report*, 1949-1950. The collection also includes a register of Carnmoney Presbyterian Church, containing records of Baptisms and Marriages, 1708-1807; also a Census of Ballyeaston Presbyterian Congregation, 1813. Many records are of families which emigrated to the United States. (*Report*, 1948, pp. 4, 6.)

McTEAR COLLECTION. Presented by Miss F. M. McTear, Belfast. The collection, largely of original documents, came in two lots; the first being 52 Conveyances, Leases, etc., of premises and lands situated respectively in Belfast and County Monaghan, 1770-1845. The second lot contains Articles of Agreement (Marriage Settlements), Bonds and Leases, Sales of Property, etc. Principal names: Craw-

ford, Dougan, Henderson, Montgomery, Moor, Oliver Mc-
Tear, 1769-1839. (*Reports*, 1927, p. 7; 1928, p. 8; Indexed.)

MARRIAGE LICENCE BONDS, PREROGATIVE. Six Books of extracts, *ca.* 1629-1857. Also in this collection are 121 documents (originals and copies), being Assignments, Leases,
Wills, etc., and extracts from Wills, 1621-1876. (*Report*,
1938-1945, p. 12.)

MATTHEWS MANUSCRIPTS. A collection of F. M. Matthews
containing 308 abstracts of Prerogative Wills, and Diocesan
Wills of Armagh, Cashel, Clogher, Derry, Down and Connor, Dromore, Ossory, and Raphoe; also Administrations,
etc., 1597-1878. Indexed in *Report*, 1934. (*Report*, 1934,
p. 9.)

MILLIN DOCUMENTS. A collection presented by S. Shannon
Millin, containing 440 items dealing with early Belfast
family history; mainly extracts from leases and deeds
dated from 1686. The records are arranged in order of
streets or localities, and are bound in two volumes. They
are indexed in *Report*, 1938-1945. (*Report*, 1938-1945, p.
7.)

MYLES COLLECTION. Presented by the Rev. E. A. Myles, Tullylish, Co. Down. This is a large collection of transcripts and
abstracts of Wills, Exchequer Bills, Rent Rolls, etc., relating
to families mostly in the Parish of Tullylish, Co. Down,
1572-1840. Principal names in the instruments are indexed in *Report*, 1928. (*Report*, 1928, p. 10.)

PATENTS. An Index to the names of persons mentioned in
the Patents referring to the six counties of Northern Ireland, in the printed but unindexed Calendar of the Patents
of James I. An Index, with a key to dates is contained in
Appendix C, in *Report*, 1938-1945, pp. 76-127.

PATERSON COLLECTION. Presented by T.G.F. Paterson, Armagh. It consists of 400 books and papers; mostly short
term leases for lands of Co. Armagh estates, 1709-1914.
As the names of the present and former leaseholders are
given, the documents have genealogical value. Also the
rentals of the Estates of Charlemont, Cremorne, Dobbin,

and Fox, in Counties Armagh, Down, and Tyrone, 1783-1912, are important as a directory for the area. 100 Maps of the Estates show the location and holdings of the tenants. The records are indexed by name of the lessees in *Report*, 1928. (*Reports*, 1928, pp. 9, 20; 1929, p. 17; 1951-1953, p. 16.)

PENSION (OLD AGE) SEARCH FORMS. These Search Forms and some Certified Copies of extracts from Census Returns, 1841 and 1851, for parts of Counties Antrim, Armagh, Down, Fermanagh, Londonderry, and Tyrone, came from the Customs and Excise Stations at the following places: Armagh, Ballycastle, Ballygawley, Ballymena, Ballymoney, Ballynahinch, Belfast, Castlederg, Coleraine, Cookstown, Dungannon, Enniskillen, Irvinestown, Larne, Limavady, Lisburn, Lisnaskea, Londonderry, Lurgan, Maghera, Magherafelt, Newry, Newtownards, Portadown, Strabane. These are copies of the destroyed Census Records made in the Public Record Office, Dublin, before the fire. (*Report*, 1927, p. 6.)

PILLOW MANUSCRIPTS. A book of Robert Pillow of County Armagh, born in 1832, contains printed and manuscript records relating to his family, also manuscript notes on the Jackson family in Co. Armagh, the Graham family of Drumogher, and notes on Castle Dillon. Included is a Rent Roll of the First Company of Armagh Volunteers, and other extracts of records preserved in the Armagh Library. (*Report*, 1934, p. 5.)

PILSON MANUSCRIPTS. Seven MSS. volumes, Diaries, etc., of the late Aynsworth Pilson, of Downpatrick, Co. Down, covering the period of 1775-1863. These contain Pilson's memoirs and notes on local history. (*Report*, 1934, pp. 5, 6.) One volume is entitled *Notable Inhabitants of Downpatrick*, and gives details of the lives of over 75 people. Five volumes contain abstracts of diaries and personal memoirs. Notes concern the people of Downpatrick and the neighborhood during the late 18th and early 19th centuries. (*Report*, 1934, pp. 21, 22.)

PLANTATION COMPANIES OF COUNTY LONDONDERRY, MANUSCRIPT COLLECTIONS. Dr. T. W. Moody of Queen's University, Belfast, contributed the manuscripts on his research regarding the Irish County Londonderry Plantation Records of the London Companies of the Salters, Vintners, Haberdashers, Goldsmiths, Ironmongers, Grocers, Skinners, and Mercers, representatives of which were settled in County Londonderry in the early 17th century. This Office has also obtained the photostats of the records of the Drapers' Company regarding their settlement in County Londonderry, 1613-1738. These were presented by the Drapers' Company of London, which records were photostated for this Office from the original records in the Company archives. An account of them is given in Appendix A, and the records are indexed in Appendix B, *Report*, 1934. This Office has also made extracts from the documents of the Scottish Record Office, Edinburgh, regarding the Haberdashers' Company (*Report*, 1929, p. 16), and the Merchant Taylors' Company which includes some material relating to the Clothworkers' Company (*Report*, 1933, p. 21). This Office has thus obtained the Irish records of eleven of the twelve Companies which relate to their plantation in County Londonderry (*Report*, 1934, p. 4).

PREROGATIVE GRANTS OF ADMINISTRATION ON INTESTACY. This collection of abstracts of Prerogative Grants of Administration on Intestacy, dated from earliest times to 1802, is deposited in the Genealogical Office (Office of Arms), Dublin Castle, Dublin. Copies of the records were presented to this Office. They are arranged in alphabetical order by name of the principal. (*Report*, 1934, p. 5.)

PUBLIC ELEMENTARY SCHOOL REGISTERS. The Ministry of Education, in 1926, deposited a collection of Public Elementary School Registers, of dates ranging from *ca.* 1850-1920, for the following schools: Ardmillan, Aughnacleagh, Aughnamerrigan, Ballerin, Ballycastle, Ballyfinaghy, Ballygilbert, Ballymoney, Ballynagashel, Belfast (Chapel Lane), Belfast (Felt Street), Belfast (Northumberland Street), Carninney, Clinty and Laymore, Coleraine, Crossnacreevey, Culmore, Derryboy, Derrycra, Dromintee, Drumaney, Edenderry, Erganagh, Feystown, Galgorm, Glenarm, Holywood (Sullivan-Infants), Kilclean, Killadeas (Cules), Killyman, Kilrea, Lisburn (Free), Lisburn (Railway Street), Lislooney, Londonderry (Bennett Street), Mallusk, Newmills, Portavogie, Portstewart, Saintfield, Termon Canice, Whiteabbey (Boys), Whiteabbey (Girls). (*Report,* 1926, p. 8.)

QUAKER RECORDS, SOCIETY OF FRIENDS, LISBURN.   Through the auspices of Mr. J. M. Douglas, under whose care the Quaker Records are preserved in Friends Meeting House, Lisburn, a collection of early Quaker Records was loaned to this Office for the purpose of photostating.   It consists of 38 documents and eight volumes.   The documents are principally Wills and Inventories, 1685-1772.   The volumes are the Lurgan Monthly Meeting Record Books, the Ulster Quarterly Meeting Book, the Book of Old Family Records, the Book of Ulster Province Meeting and Grange Monthly Meeting.   These record books contain records of a very large number of Quaker families and individuals, offering references to the English, etc., origins of many early Irish settlers, and giving entries of births, marriages, deaths, and many miscellaneous records regarding individuals.   (*Report,* 1951-1953, p. 20.)   All photostated records are indexed in Appendix A, of this *Report.*   There are thousands of records.   For further details, see the chapter on QUAKER RECORDS, PART THREE of this volume.

SOCIETY OF GENEALOGISTS, LONDON, COLLECTION OF IRISH RECORDS.   This Society loaned about 2,500 abstracts from Prerogative and Diocesan Wills, Administrations, Marriage Licences, Chancery and Exchequer Bills, etc., and some Pedigree extracts; mostly 17th-18th century.   The collection is indexed by names of the principals and embodied in the Index in Appendix B, *Report,* 1934.   (*Report,* 1934, pp. 3, 4.)

SOLICITORS' COLLECTIONS.   A few of the many important collections sent to this Office from the archives, vaults and storage places of various legal offices are as follows:

1. *Belfast:*   J. Bristow, Solicitor.   3,132 documents, including Wills, Administrations, Assignments, Leases, etc., dated 1600-1893.   Indexed in *Report,* 1938-1945, by principal names in the instruments.   Also 154 documents of like nature dated 1602-1903, indexed in the same *Report.*

2. *Belfast:* Johns, Elliot and Johns, Solicitors. 326 documents, including Wills, Assignments, Leases, dated 1705-1896. Indexed in *Report*, 1938-1945.

3. *Belfast:* McIldowie and Sons, Solicitors. 375 documents, including Wills, Conveyances, etc., dated 1789-1883. Indexed in *Report*, 1938-1945.

4. *Belfast:* H. C. Weir, Solicitor. 237 documents, including Wills, Administrations, Assignments, Conveyances, Leases, Mortgages, dated 1695-1912. Indexed in *Report*, 1930. Also 54 copies of destroyed or other documents of the same classes, dated 1756-1918, indexed in the same *Report*. Also over 1,200 Wills, Administrations, Leases, Conveyances, Mortgages, etc., dated 1680-1926, indexed in *Report*, 1935. Also 198 documents of like nature, dated 1694-1921, indexed in *Report* 1934. Also 89 documents of like nature, dated 1731-1858, indexed in *Report*, 1937.

5. *Downpatrick, County Down:* C. W. Wallace, Solicitor. 1,380 documents, including Wills, Administrations, Assignments, Deeds, Leases, Family Settlements, etc., mostly of County Down; some of Counties Antrim, Armagh, and Tyrone, dated 1602-1897. Indexed in *Report*, 1948.

6. *Downpatrick, County Down:* H. K. Worsley of the Downpatrick Estate Office, sent 358 documents, including Indentures of Apprenticeship, Bonds, Leases, etc., dated 1694-1865. Indexed in *Report*, 1933. Also 63 documents, including Agreements, Leases (Ker Estate, Co. Down), 1692-1890. Indexed in *Report*, 1938-1945.

7. *Dungannon, County Tyrone:* Longfield, Kelly and Armstrong, Solicitors. 934 documents, including Wills, Conveyances, Deeds, Leases, Rentals, dated 1587-1908. Indexed in *Report*, 1946-1947. Also 319 documents of like nature, dated 1698-1893, indexed in the same *Report*.

8. *Enniskillen, County Fermanagh:* James Cooper, Solicitor. 156 documents, including Wills, Administrations, Leases, Renewals, etc., dated 1747-1916. Indexed in *Report*, 1928. Also Final Notice to Tenants of the Enniskillen Estate, 1843-1895. Indexed in *Report*, 1929.

9. *Enniskillen, County Fermanagh:* Miss N. Cooper,

Solicitor.   614 documents, including Wills, Assignments, Agreements, Leases, Grants of Administration, etc., dated 1641-1916.   Indexed in *Report*, 1949-1950.

10. *Larne, County Antrim:* J. W. McNinch, Solicitor. He sent 21 sacks of records weighing about one ton, from which 2,920 documents were selected for preservation. These are known as the Killen documents. Included are 670 Wills and Grants of Probate; 720 Court documents and papers related to litigation; 900 Conveyances, Leases and Deeds; 630 Mortgages, Maps, Bonds, etc.   They are mostly related to the Larne district.   About half of them are original documents dated 1736-1917.   The other half are copies of destroyed documents and other records and are dated 1631-1910.   The 2,920 records are indexed by names of the principals, in the *Report*, 1930.

11. *Lisburn, County Antrim:* Joseph Allen, Solicitor. Rent Roll of Pipe Water, Lisburn, 1768.   Indexed by names in the Roll, in *Report*, 1927.

12. *Lisburn, County Antrim:*   R. Johnson Smyth, Solicitor.   110 documents, including Wills, Administrations, Bonds, Agreements, Leases, dated 1634-1863.   Indexed in *Report*, 1949-1950.

13. *Portadown, Co. Armagh:* Mrs. C. Wilson.   325 documents, including Wills, Assignments, Mortgages, etc., dated 1744-1900.   Indexed in *Report*, 1938-1945.

14. *Portaferry, County Down:*   Sir Roland Nugent.   848 documents, including Wills, Agreements, Leases, Rentals, etc., dated 1605-1840.   Indexed in *Report*, 1948.

15. *Seaforde, County Down:* Major T. W. Forde.   635 documents, including Assignments, Conveyances, Leases, dated 1714-1876.   Indexed in *Report*, 1949-1950.

STEWART-KENNEDY NOTES.   The collection of the late H. Stewart Kennedy contains transcripts of Wills, made from records in the Dublin Public Record Office before the fire, representing some 500 instruments.   The collection is now in the Library of Trinity College, Dublin.   It was loaned to this Office and copies of the Wills of Ulster testators were made. The names are embodied in the Index of *Report*, 1935.

SWANZY MANUSCRIPTS. The collection presented by the Very Rev. H. B. Swanzy, of Newry, County Down, came to this Office in the following lots:

1. A collection presented in 1924, containing: Copies or Notes of 196 Prerogative and Principal Registry (Dublin) Wills and Grants (principal names: Armstrong, Beatty, Corry, Cuppage, Fleming, Hamilton, Higinbotham, Johnston, Knipe, Nixon, Noble, Ovens, Richardson, Rogers, Spencer, Stamford, Swanzy, Vincent, Young), dated 1666-1859. Also 63 Clogher Wills and Grants and Marriage Licences (principal names: Crozier, Forster, Hassard, Johnston, Nixon, Noble, Thompson), 1697-1832. Also 38 Kilmore Wills and Grants and Marriage Licences (principal names: Armstrong, Beatty, Burroughs, Harman, Nixon, Young), 1694-1806. Records all indexed in *Report*, 1924. (*Report*, 1924, p. 10)

2. A collection presented in 1930, being a typed copy of extensive extracts made from Public Records since destroyed in Dublin, being extracts from Chancery and Exchequer Bills and Answers, Wills, etc. The collection of records is recorded in 300 pages and deals mainly with the history of prominent families in the Counties of Cavan, Fermanagh, Monaghan, and Tyrone. An index is embodied in *Report*, 1930. (*Report*, 1930, p. 9.)

3. A List of Justices of the Peace for County Fermanagh, 1663-1844, and a List of High Sheriffs, County Armagh, 1664-1681, 1687, 1704. (*Report*, 1930, p. 10.)

TITHE APPLOTMENT BOOKS. This collection of the Tithe Applotment Books, sent in 1944, from the Ministry of Finance, Dublin, concerns the records taken in preparation for the Tithe tax in over 200 parishes of Northern Ireland, 1834-1837 (approximately). These records of property owners and occupiers for the period constitute in effect a census of the parishes. (*Report*, 1938-1945, p. 6.)

WELPLY COLLECTION. W. H. Welply of Greenisland, County Antrim, loaned his large and valuable collection of gene-

alogical notes containing abstracts of 590 Wills, mainly
Prerogative, and Diocesan Wills of Cork and Cloyne, dated
1569-mid-19th century. A duplicate of the collection is in
the Library of the Society of Genealogists, London. Another copy of the collection is in the Genealogical Office
(Office of Arms), Dublin Castle, Dublin. All are indexed in
the *Report*, 1937. (*Report*, 1937, p. 9.) Another collection
presented by Welply consists of extracts from Funeral Entries, Pedigrees, Wills, etc., dated 1617-1805. Indexed in
the *Report*, 1948. (*Report*, 1948, p. 6.)

WILSON AND CHESNEY FAMILY MEMOIRS. These are two collections of family notes loaned for copying, dealing with the
two families which were allied by marriage. The Wilson
family memoirs concern records taken from an old family
Bible; tombstone records of Broghshane, County Antrim;
a written manuscript of the writer's (evidently David Wilson) great-uncle William Wilson of Ballycloughan, County
Antrim, and conversations with the writer's grandmother,
whose husband, John Wilson, is believed to have come from
Scotland in 1684. The family settled in the early 18th
century in the Parish of Skerry or Braid, County Antrim.
The writer's father, Samuel Wilson, fought with the United
Irishmen at Ballymena in 1798, and his brothers Charles,
Alexander and John went to Australia in 1838 and 1841.
The Chesney Memoirs written by Alexander Chesney concern his emigration to America with his parents and nine
brothers and sisters in 1772; their settlement near Jackson's
Creek and later at Packolet; his service during the Revolution with both the Loyalists and with the "Congress Party"
against the Indians; his return to Ireland in 1782, and later
life in Ballymena and elsewhere. Family records are
mentioned, 1322-1872. Records of both families are indexed in the *Report*, 1935. (*Report*, 1935, pp. 5, 19, 20.)
(NOTE: The Crosslé collection contains 112 abstracts of
Wilson Wills of Counties Antrim and Down, and several of
County Londonderry. These represent some Prerogative
and mostly Diocese of Down and Connor Wills, dated in the
18th and very early 19th centuries, concerning various
branches descended from 17th century Scottish settlers. In

combination with other records of this office, it is possible to identify and trace the separate lines.)

WYNNE MILITARY PAPERS. This collection, dated 1689 to about 1750, was gathered by the Wynne family of Hazelwood, County Sligo, and Lurganboy, County Leitrim. It includes a copy of the signed association of the inhabitants of Enniskillen, County Fermanagh, containing 150 signatures under that of Gustavus Hamilton, their commander and governor of the town, 13 February 1688/9. Officers included William Wolseley, Sir Albert Conyngham and James Wynne. Much of the collection relates to the Wynne Dragoons, from 1689, with particulars of cases of disorders of members of Captain Hugh Galbraith's troops; details of troop actions and incidents in various locations; also a list of the officers subsequent to 6 August 1732, with dates of their commissions. Some documents of the Wynne family are included. The collection is indexed in the *Report*, 1938-1945. (*Report*, 1938-1945, pp. 30, 31.)

* * * * *

The volume of source materials of various classes in this repository is so great that, in order to avoid repetition of description, the reader is referred to PART THREE of this volume.

The chapters of PART THREE are each devoted to a separate class of records which are described or explained. Every chapter is subdivided according to the repositories which contain some collections of the particular class of records. Under these subheadings, the collections are listed as to their nature, extent, area of interest, and inclusive dates. This eliminates confusion, due to the fact that various repositories contain collections of the same class of records which, in most cases, differ entirely or partially, but in other cases are duplicate collections. With the arrangement of the important collections of a single class, all listed in one chapter according to their place of deposit, a genealogist can determine the entire scope of the records as a unit.

Every chapter of PART THREE contains a list of records which are deposited in the Public Record Office of Northern Ireland.

PART THREE

THE RECORDS

CHAPTER I

ARMS, HERALDRY, AND NOMENCLATURE

ARMS AND HERALDRY

Printed sources for a study of Arms, Heraldry and Nomenclature are listed in VOLUME II, pp. 208-212. The most recent, authoritative work embracing all three subjects is *Irish Families, Their Names, Arms and Origins,* by Edward MacLysaght, Dublin, 1957, with illustrations (in color) of 243 armorial bearings, by Myra Maguire, Heraldic Artist to the Genealogical Office (Office of Arms), Dublin Castle, Dublin.

This book was prepared with Americans of Irish and Anglo-Irish ancestry in mind. It answers many questions regarding the law and practice of grants of Arms and registration of pedigrees in Ireland; the varieties and synonyms of surnames and Christian names in Ireland, and some anglicised surnames in Ireland. Many American genealogical libraries have acquired it.

Dr. MacLysaght, formerly Chief Herald of Ireland, and Chairman of the Irish Manuscripts Commission, has drawn upon the full range of authoritative manuscript and printed sources to set forth an accurate and comprehensive study of the above related subjects, and to correct some inaccuracies in earlier published works. *Irish Families* does not contain pedigrees and genealogy. It is a study of some 500 Irish septs or families and Anglo-Irish families; their names, changes and transition of names, the principal locations of representatives of the various branches, with some notes about distinguished members.

The matter of sept arms is explained. Such arms are ascribed to families, the ancestors of which are descended from an early armorial member. Identification and their right to claim the family arms is loosely based upon the location of the known ancestors in the territory of the family and the common usage of the arms through the generations. Confirmation of sept arms on such a basis has been allowed in Ireland for centuries, unlike the practice in England and Scotland. The right to claim the arms of an Irish family must be confirmed by proof of descent from a member of the family whose right to the arms was recorded or registered in this Office of Arms. As Dr. MacLysaght states, many of the oldest armorial bearings have no crests. In some cases, different crests were in use by the several branches of a family or sept, while the arms were common to all. A crest, on the other hand, cannot exist except as an apanage of a coat of arms.

A work of related matter for any who are interested in claiming, and with proof of descent registering their right to family arms, is *The Heraldic Calendar: A List of the Nobility and Gentry whose Arms are Registered and Pedigrees Recorded in the Herald's Office Ireland,* by William Skey, Dublin, 1846. At that time, Skey was St. Patrick Pursuivant and Registrar of the Herald's Office in Ireland. He states in a Foreword, "This work professes to supply a faithful transcript of official records, and is strictly confined to that only. In all cases, therefore, where the armorial ensigns have been duly registered, and the pedigrees recorded *to the present time,* the names have been carefully copied from the record in exact seniority and order of birth. Where, however, pedigrees have been registered with the Arms, but as yet not fully written up, all known members of such families have been printed, to proclaim as widely as possible their just claim to Arms. And lastly, where the Arms alone have been recorded, a few leading names are placed without reference to descent, of which the Herald's Office can have no official cognizance whatever."

The responsibilities of the Ulster King of Arms, of the Office of Arms, Dublin, were numerous. A primary duty was the registration of armorial bearings, newly created or claimed by inheritance; their care, preservation and identification with the families whose right it was to bear arms. The original emblazons of Arms in this Office are of Irish Peers; Arms of English, Welsh and Anglo-Irish families, identified with Ireland; Arms of created Irish Peers; Arms of Scottish Peers, etc., who settled in Ireland. The manuscript volumes of the beautiful emblazons in color have been listed in PART TWO,

CHAPTER IV. An illustration of the genealogical information accompanying registered arms is presented here as it appears below the emblazoned Arms of Lysaght on a page, 9″ x 14″, whereon the Arms are painted in size 8″ x 8″, and on two following pages, in large script (G. O. MS. Vol. 183, Lords Entries, Vol. I).

"From the Ancient and Illustrious House of O'Brien in the County of Clare, some of whom being Auxiliaries in the Provincial Wars of Ireland, so distinguished themselves, as to be called Guil Ysaght in the Native Language, lent Men, which being abridged into the Name of Lysaght.

"Was descended John Lysaght the Elder, of Mount North, in the County of Cork, who was Cornet of Horse under Lord Inchiquin, very Active in the Suppression of the Rebellion, in 1641, especially, at the Battle of Knocknenoss, in that County.

"His two sons, Nicholas and James, entered into the Service of King William of Glorious Memory. James the Younger was killed at the Battle of Steenkirk, in Flanders, then a Captain in the Royal Regiment of Foot, and Nicholas the Elder commanded a Troop of Dragoons in the King's own Regiment in many parts of Flanders, England, Scotland and Ireland, particularly at the ever Memorable Battle of the Boyn, and in several Garrisons in Munster, being Dismounted, to supply the place of Foot, then greatly diminished by Sickness.

"He afterwards Married Grace, the youngest Daughter of Col. Thomas Holmes of Kilmallock, and by her had issue, the present John, Anne, who Married Lieut. General Holmes, of the Isle of Wight, Mary, who Married Beverly Usher, Esq., late Knight of the Shire for the County Waterford, Nicholas, Henry, James and Arthur, who, hath left three sons, Nicholas, and Arthur, both Lieutenants, the one, in General Kennedy's Regiment at Quebec, the other in General Holmes's, in Scotland, and Henry, with two Daughters, Jane, and Grace, both Unmarried.

"The said John on the Happy Accession of his present Majesty was chosen Member of Parliament for the Borough of Charleville, and in 1725, Married Catherine the third Daughter, and Co-Heiress, of Joseph Deane of Crumlin, Lord Chief Baron of His Majesty's Court of Exchequer, in Ireland, by Margaret, Sister to the Earl of Shannon, and by the said Catherine, hath issue, John, who is Member of Parliament for Castlemartyr, Joseph, and James, both of the Inner Temple, Margaret unmarried, and Mary Married Kingsmill, the Son of Col. Richard Pennifather, both Members of Parliament for the City of Cashell, who, by her, hath three Sons, Richard, John, and Kingsmill and one Daughter.

"In the Year 1746, the said John the Elder, Married his 2nd Wife, Elizabeth only Daughter of Edward Moore of Mooresfort, in the County of Tipperary, Esq., by Mary Eldest Sister, of Col. Richard Pennifather aforesaid, and by her, hath issue, one Son, Edward, and two Daughters, Elizabeth and Grace, and in the Year 1768, was by Patent, called up to the House of Peers, by the Name, Stile, and Title of John Lysaght the Elder, Esq., Baron Lisle of Mount North, in the County of Cork, in the Kingdom of Ireland. The truth of which is attested by the said Baron Lisle as also of the Arms and Motto, as in the foregoing is Depicted."

"Chief Seats   "Lisle"
Mount North, in the County of Cork.
Lisle or the little Island, in the Harbour of Cork.
At Crumlin near Dublin, and,
at Dawson's Street, City of Dublin."

In the course of keeping the records, representatives from this Office attended the funerals of the nobility and gentry to record the name, place, date of burial, heirs, pedigree and arms of the deceased. In cases where attendance was prohibited by distance or other circumstance, a representative of the family was permitted to register this data in a Funeral Entry or Certificate. Seventeen volumes of Funeral Entries, 1588-1729, are in this Office of Arms, now the Genealogical Office, Dublin Castle, Dublin. An additional volume, 1634-1729, was somehow deposited in the British Museum (Add. MS. 4820). This was copied and published in the *Journal of the Irish Memorials Association,* Vols. VII and VIII (also the 817 Funeral Entries and sketches of 660 Coats of Arms accompanying the Entries are published as a reprint volume with index). Example of a Funeral Entry: Taken from reprint volume, p. 188:

"Patrick White of the Citty of Corke als White of Pardellstown in the County of Corke Gent., eldest Son and Heir of Edmond White of the same Gent., eldest Son and Heir of Vincent White of the same Gent., eldest Son and Heir of Edmond White of Cloghdwa in the Said County Gent. The Said Patrick married Christian daughter of Sir Walter Coppinger of Corke, Knt., by whom He had 5 Sons and one Daughter viz. Walter eldest Son and Heir, married to Ellen daughter of William Cogan of Bearneheale in the Said County Gent; Ed-

mond 2nd, Dominick 3rd,   4th,   5th, all young and
not married . . . the Said Patrick died at Cork . . . 163 . . . and
was Interr'd in Christ Church in the Said Citty of Corke.
The truith of the premisses is testified by Subscription of
Walter White, Son and Heir of the Defunct, who returned this
Certificate into my Office to be there recorded taken by me
Thomas Preston Esq., Ulster King of Armes the 17th of Feb-
ruary 1640." Key number to Arms (647).

Heralds' Visitations were made upon corporate towns,
cities, town Burgesses, the members of the County Grand
Jury, Armorial families, etc., by Royal Commission, for the
purpose of examining and recording Arms, pedigrees and
data in proof of the right to Arms and pedigrees. An exhibit
of the emblazoned Arms of the original Grant, or proof of
descent from the ancestor to whom a Grant of Arms was made,
together with pedigree and current records, were duly recorded by the Heralds. The original records of the Heralds'
Visitations, extant in this Office, number only three: Dublin,
1568 and 1607; Wexford, 1618. Transcripts in the British
Museum are: Connaught, 1615 (Add. MS. 19836) ; Munster,
1615 (Add. MS. 19836) ; also Narbon's Visitation of Ireland
(Add. MS. fo. 40 b).

A record of the Visitation of Wexford is recorded in the
*History of the Town and County of Wexford; the Town of
Wexford, Taghmon, and Harperstown*, by Philip Herbert
Hore, *Ed.*, London, 1906 (p. 233), as follows: "1618. When
Sir Danyel Molyneux, Ulster King at Arms, visited this town
and County on the 15th April, 1618, he returned the arms of
the town as a ship in flames, with the motto, 'Per aquam et
ignem.' [10] " The pedigrees and coats of Arms of the Grand
Jury for the year 1618 are shown at the end of this volume;
those of some of the Burgesses of the town are also shown, viz.,
Furlong, Stafford of the Castle of Stonebridge, with three
others of the same name, and Turnour.

Not all armorial bearings of Irish, Anglo-Irish, and Scottish families were registered in the Office of Arms. This
may have been due to circumstance, carelessness, lack of proof

---

"(10). A visitation begun in the County and town of Wexford, 15 April
1618, by Daniel Molyneux, Ulster King of Arms, throughout the Realm,
by virtue of a Commission to him directed 28 Feb., 1605." Ulster Office,
vol. 3.

of the right to arms, or ignorance of the importance of registered proof. Many Scottish families and others, particularly
those settled in Ulster, did not register their Arms in Dublin,
but did record them on armorial sculptured tombstones.
Francis Joseph Bigger and Herbert Hughes furnished evidence of this by making tracings of over 250 sculptured Arms
and the inscriptions (mostly 18th and 19th century) from
tombstones in County Antrim. Sketches of the Arms, thus
made, and the inscriptions beneath, were published in a series,
in the *Ulster Journal of Archaeology*, 2nd Series, Vols. VI-IX,
1900-1901. They stated (Vol. VI, p. 39) : "During the summer of 1899, we have been able to visit all churchyards of the
county (of Antrim), and to make rubbings of the arms on the
tombstones in each, and at the same time to copy the inscriptions . . . We found they reached over 250." The plan was to
publish all of these and to end with notes of explanation. A
total of 171 were published before the series ceased.

The Ulster-Scot Historical Society can photostat any page
of the above publications which are in the library of the
Public Record Office, Belfast (see PART TWO, CHAPTER VI).
For this purpose, a list of the churchyards and surnames of
the families whose arms and inscriptions were published are
listed below with references to the *Ulster Journal of Archaeology*, 2nd Series, wherein they appear:

LARNE PARISH CHURCHYARD (Vol. VI, pp. 39-53) :

Burney, Burney, Burns, Burns, Campbell, Allen, Allen,
Chichester, Chichester, Calwell, Carley, Fleck, Eccles, Eccles,
Grant, Glasgow, Glasgow, Ferres, Finley, Finley, Houston,
Edsel, Haddan, Hadden, Kelly, Kirkpatrick, Learmor (Lear-
mouth), Manson.

LARNE PARISH CHURCHYARD (Vol. VI, pp. 90-104) :

Manfod, Mearns, Montgomery, Montgomery, Meharg or
MacHarg, Munro, MacMunn, Murdoch, MacNeill, MacTier,
Naesmith, Ogilvie, Paton or Patton, Patrick, Robinson
(Robertson), Rogers, Shutter, Smith, Stuart, Thom, Wate
(Watt), Watt, Watt, Uriel, Woodside, Workman.

RASBEE PARISH CHURCHYARD (Vol. VI, pp. 162-166) :
Allen, Allen?, Kirkwood, Houston, Hume, Alexander, Mac-
lellan, Orr, Orr, Orr, White.

RALOO PARISH CHURCHYARD (Vol. VI, pp. 167-172) :
Blair, Blair, Blair, Craig, Craig, Craig, Crawford, Craw-
ford, Finlay, Gordon, Jaffrey, Knox, Lock, Lock, Nickle, Mac-
Dowell, Robinson.

CARNCASTLE PARISH CHURCHYARD (Vol. VI), pp. 231-244) :
Bailie, Brown, Brown, Caldwell, Callwell, Calwell, Campbell,
Crawford, Crawford, Dale, Dale, Faries, Faries, Faries, Getty,
Linn, Lorimer, Lorimer, Lough, Lusk, Lusk, Lusk, Magill,
McKee, Moore, Moore, Murphy, Neill, Neill, Parr, Paterson,
Shaw, Sherriff, Sherriff, Steele, Steele.

CARNCASTLE PARISH CHURCHYARD (Vol. VII, pp. 58-61) :
Tweed, Tweed, Willson-Caldwell, Wilson, Wylie, Young,
Wharry.

ANTRIM PARISH (Vol. VII, pp. 142-143) :
Adair, Collingwood.

ARMOY PARISH (Vol. VII, p. 144) :
Clark, Dunlop.

BALLINDERRY PARISH (Vol. VII, pp. 145-146) :
Tatnal, McGee.

BALLYLINNEY PARISH (Vol. VII, pp. 146-147) :
Alexander, Barron.

BALLYWILLIN PARISH (Vol. VII, pp. 147-148) :
Boyd, Ross, Stirling.

KILBRIDE PARISH (Vol. VII, pp. 149-150) :
Allen, Blair.

KILRAUGHTS PARISH (Vol. VII, pp. 150-151) :
Brady, Jameson, Moore.

LAMBEG PARISH (Vol. VII, p. 152) :
Wolfenden.

LOUGHGUILE PARISH (Vol. VII, pp. 152-153) :
MacDonnell, McCollum.

MAGHERAGALL PARISH (Vol. VII, p. 154) :
Watson.

MUCKAMORE PARISH (Vol. VII, p. 155):
Waugh.

SHANKILL PARISH (Vol. VII, p. 155):
Carson.

BELFAST, OLD CORPORATION CHURCHYARD, HIGH STREET (Vol. VII, p. 156):
Lennox.

SKERRY PARISH (Vol. VII, p. 157):
McCollum.

BALLYMONEY PARISH (Vol. VIII, pp. 90-93):
Lecky, Hutchinson, Hamilton, Mitchell, Hackett.

CUSHENDUN PARISH (Vol. IX, p. 93):
MacAulay.

DERRIAGHY PARISH (Vol. IX, p. 94):
Seeds.

DONEGORE PARISH (Vol. IX, pp. 95-96):
Ferguson, Scot, Scot.

ARMOY PARISH (Vol. IX, p. 131):
Smith.

KILLEAD PARISH (Vol. IX, pp. 132-133):
Aikin, Montgomery, Shaw.

RAMOAN PARISH (Vol. IX, pp. 133-137):
O'Hagan Boyd, Boyd, Boyd, O'Mullan, MacCambridge, M'Crank.

Four Allen inscriptions indicate the average variety in information and age of the above records. The first two are in Larne Churchyard. The second two are in Rasbee Churchyard. The arms of the first two are identical, while the crests differ slightly and the motto is not the same. The arms of the third are almost identical. The crest is entirely different but the motto is the same as on the second. The arms of the fourth are so similar to the first two that the missing surname is taken to be Allen. The inscriptions are in this order:

1. Erected in Memory of Patrick Allen who died 6th June 1770 aged 47 years. Also his Daughter Jennet who died 11th Janry 1811 aged 47 years. Also Ann his wife who died 11th Dec. 1811 aged 80 years. Also their son Patrick Allen who died 26th Oct. 1828 aged 57 years. Also their Daughter Ann

Allen who died on the 12th May 1832 aged 68 years. Also their Grand Son Patrick Allen who died on the 17th January 1834 Aged 29 Years. Also their Daughter Margaret who departed this Life 21 December 1837 aged 70 years. Also their Grandson John Allen who died 13th April 1849, Aged 42 years. Also Mary C. Nicholson Wife of the above John Allen, who died 17th June 1873, aged 78 years.

2. Here lyeth the Body of Robert Allen Who died 28th Jan. 1781 aged 3 years. Also Elizath Allen who died the 4th Oct. 1784 aged 4 years and Mary died 20th Sept. 1778. William Died 17th June 1796. James   Allen's   Children his wife Jane who died 6th Aug. 1797 aged 44 years also Jane Allen   daughter who died 16th May 1800 aged 6 years also James Allen Senior who died on 9th of (Apr)il 1816 aged 66 years.

3. Here lyeth the body of John Allen Who departed this life Jan 17th 1788 aged 67 years.

4. Here Lyeth . . . of Hugh . . . Who . . . 1734 Aged 78 years. Also his Wife Elizabeth Aresbal Who died Dec. ye 10th 1723 aged 56 years.

Another Allen tombstone in Kilbride Parish, with entirely different sculptured arms is inscribed as follows:

"Herein is deposited the remains of Mr John Allen of Rashee who departed this life the 10th of April 1742 in the 99th year of his age whose Eminent Virtues and Extensive Charities have left a lasting monument of his Charecter. Here also is deposited the remains of Mrs. Mary Allen his Daughter in law who departed this life the 11th of December 1730 aged 35 yrs four of her children who died young. Herein is also interred the remains of Jane Allen alias Smith relict of the above John Allen who departed this life April 24 1712 aged 85 years. Also the remains of her granddaughter Jane Allen who departed this life 15th June 1762 aged 12 years. John Allen of Rashee died 18th May 1784 aged 72 years. Also Christian Allen alias Russell his wife 23rd April 1802 aged 68 years. John Allen of Collin died 26th Sepr 1847 aged 7 years. Mary Allen died 6th Febry 1854 aged 82 years. John Gillian Allen of Collin died 31st July 1861 aged 47 years. Jane Allen alias Gillian relict of John Allen of Collin died 20th March 1864 aged 78 years. Her remains lie in the adjoining grave."

The shortest inscription is on the Jameson tombstone in Kilraughts Parish. A note of Bigger and Hughes states: "The arms on this stone are very much worn, the inscription is almost undecipherable, and the motto is quite so. The name and date alone can be traced with certainty." It reads: "Daniel Jameson . . . 175(3)." The arms are those of a mariner. It is quartered and in each is depicted a ship with three sails. All that remains of the crest is a little fish. A waving line which may have held a motto would seem to depict the sea.

A comparison of all of the above family inscriptions has been made with William Skey's *Heraldic Calendar*, 1846, and some other published sources listed in VOLUME II, pp. 208-211. This indicates that only a small number of families, whose arms were recorded on their sculptured tombstones in County Antrim, had their pedigrees and arms registered in the Office of Arms, Dublin Castle, Dublin. This may have been due to the reasons mentioned above. Undoubtedly, many families of other counties also failed to register their arms and pedigrees when records were brought with the first settler from England or Scotland, but perhaps with insufficient proof of origin. These families, content with their private family records and certain of their unproved authenticity, used and recorded arms and crests on personal possessions and, for their posterity, on sculptured tombstones, at a time when their neighbors knew their family origin.

The records of very many unregistered arms and pedigrees, as well as those registered in the Office of Arms, Dublin, appear among the following sources listed in VOLUME II: Ancient genealogies (pp. 213-215); Irish periodicals containing the records of families and localities (pp. 43-75); books of compiled family history and genealogy (pp. 3-33); county and town histories (pp. 76-94); death records recorded in funeral certificates, inquisitions post mortem, tombstone inscriptions (pp. 227-228); family documents and records (pp. 109-196); published collections of pedigrees (pp. 34-37); some publications of the Irish Manuscripts Commission relating to genealogy and source materials (pp. 95-106); microfilms (pp. 265-286). Arms and pedigrees of families may also be located in manuscript collections and printed works listed in catalogues of Irish repositories (pp. 199-201).

The Irish historical journals and some other periodicals have given attention to the arms of families (registered and unregistered) within each area covered by the periodical. A very rewarding source for records of families of all counties of Ireland is the *Journal of the Irish Memorials Association* (commonly called "The Memorials of the Dead"), the issues of which contain many thousands of tombstone inscriptions and numerous records, descriptions, and sketches of the arms on armorial sculptured tombstones (VOLUME II, p. 228).

There are 227 Fitzgerald tombstone records listed in the consolidated index of the first seven of the twelve volumes (and two numbers of volume 13) of the *Journal of the Irish Memorials Association*. The later volumes also contain many Fitzgerald records. In addition to the tombstone records, copious notes set forth history and data regarding the various branches of this great family. Sketches and descriptions of the tombstones and armorial bearings are detailed and, for some, fill as many as three pages. In the same manner, the records on the tombstones of numerous other important families and notes regarding the members are set forth. All armorial bearings are described together with the inscriptions, regardless of the size of the stone or importance of the family.

Wax seals attached to Memorials of Deeds, Leases, Marriage Agreements, Wills, etc., deposited in the Registry of Deeds, Dublin, are in many cases imprinted with the family crest. Numerous original records of the above nature, deposited in the Genealogical Office (Office of Arms), the National Library of Ireland, the Public Record Offices in Belfast and Dublin, Trinity College Library, the Royal Irish Academy, etc., are also sealed with wax imprinted family crests.

NOMENCLATURE

The study of Irish and Scotch-Irish surnames and Christian names is one of first importance to Americans, most of whom find it hard to believe that their own surnames could have passed through considerable transition in Ireland, or change upon arrival in America. In preparation for searching the Irish indexes, the following sources should be studied:

1. *Irish Families, Their Names, Arms, and Origins*, by Edward MacLysaght, Dublin, 1957. This furnishes a study of clan names and surnames, their history and transition; the

translation of Gaelic surnames to an anglicised form; the dropping of the purely Gaelic prefixes Mac and O during the seventeenth and eighteenth centuries as a matter of expediency and compulsion under English rule, and the resumption of these original prefixes in the late nineteenth century. He deals with the distortion of surnames; their distribution and identification in particular areas; also Christian names and changes of name. He devotes Part Two to a study of 500 principal Irish names of families or septs, the derivation of the Gaelic name, changes to anglicised forms; locations of the family districts, and other identifying data. The book also contains a series of appendices devoted to classified lists of surnames which help to identify their origins.

Thus it can be understood why the Irish colonists who came to America in the seventeenth and eighteenth centuries, with the names of Brian or Brien, Carroll, Connell, Connor, Callaghan, Daly, Donnell, Hagerty, Kelly, Neill, Reilly, Sullivan, etc., were members of families which had dropped the prefix O. Likewise the original prefix Mac, of surnames of MacDermott, MacDonnell, MacDonald, MacCarthy, MacEwen, MacHenry, MacNaughten, etc., was dropped as above and many colonists in America did not resume their prefix, while others chose to do so. The same holds true for those who arrived with anglicised names, translated from the original Gaelic form.

A man named Daly or Daley in America may know that he is descended from the O'Daly sept "said to be the greatest name in our Gaelic literature," according to MacLysaght (p. 110), who continues, "Other septs may have produced one or two more famous individuals, but the O'Dalys have a continuous record of literary achievement from the twelfth to the seventeenth century and, indeed, even to the nineteenth." Together with other Gaelic families, they dropped the prefix O, under English pressure to stamp out Gaelic influence. When the Irish geographical origin of a first generation American named Daly or Daley is known, his family records are sought in the indexes, with a watchful eye for the transition from O'Daly to Daly or Daley.

With regard to the greatest of Irish families, the O'Briens, Dr. MacLysaght states (p. 62), ". . . it may be observed, that though fifty years ago, one third of the people of the name were registered as plain Brien, nowadays it is rarely found without the prefix O." This came gradually with the lightening of government pressure against Gaelic influence. Thus after the mid-nineteenth century, numerous American settlers left Ireland with the name O'Brien, recently resumed with the prefix O, or they resumed it with pride of their ancestry, upon arrival in America. Their earlier Irish records must be watched for under both forms of spelling.

"Charles Carroll, of Maryland fame," according to MacLysaght, "was of the Ely O'Carroll sept of Tipperary and Offaly (King's County), their original Gaelic name ó Cearbhaill, being derived from Cearbhal, Lord of Ely, who was one of the leaders of the victorious army of Clontarf (1014), and thus descended from King Oilioll Olum. Before the advent of the powerful Norman Butlers, they possessed very extensive territory in County Tipperary, but they were later restricted to the district of Birr, County Offaly (King's Co.)." (*ibid.* p. 75.)

Before the O'Carroll family dropped the prefix O, the following Funeral Entry was recorded in 1639:

"Charles O'Carroll of Beahernagh in King's County, Esq., died 2nd son of Mullrony O'Carroll of Moynndrony in County Tipperary, Eldest son and heir of Charles O'Carroll of Moydrony aforesaid. The said Charles married Giles daughter of Brien O'Kennedy of Lackine in County Tipperary by whom he had 3 Sons and 2 Daughters viz. Charles Eldest Son and Heir who married Johan daughter of Daniel MaGrath of Mountaine Castle in County Waterford Gent.; Kean 2nd Son not married; Anthony 3rd Son married to Jeane Daughter of Edmond Butler of Boytonrath in the County Tipperary Gent.; Fenola eldest Daughter married to Charles Butler of Rorane in the County Tipperary; More 2nd Daughter married to Brassell O'Maddin of Phebegg in the County of Gallway Gent. The 1st mentioned Charles died at Behagh in the County of Tipperary the 10th of February 1638 and was interred in the Parish Church of Moydruny aforesaid the 12th of the same month. The truith of the premissis is testified by the Subscription of Charles oge O'Carroll, eldest son and heir of the Defunct who returned this certificate to my office to be here recorded. Taken by me Thomas Preston Esq. Ulster King of Armes the 1st of July Anno Domini 1639."

"Charles O'Carroll."

It would be a pity to miss this record of the family of

Charles Carroll of Maryland, because of a fixed idea that his surname could be no other than Carroll.

Thus the period of the great Irish emigration to America, 1830-1870, brought men whose families had, at some time in the previous two hundred years, dropped the name prefix Mac or O. Some of these resumed the prefix shortly before or after arrival in America. Their identifying records must be sought in Ireland among names in the indexes, with or without the prefix, and source records regarding their immediate ancestors of the eighteenth century as well as a few earlier generations may be expected to appear more possibly without a prefix.

2. The most important hand-book for the use of all genealogists during Irish research is, *Varieties and Synonymes of Surnames and Christian Names in Ireland. For the Guidance of Registration Officers and the Public in Searching the Indexes of Births, Deaths, and Marriage;* by Robert E. Matheson, Dublin, 1890, 1901. Matheson was Registrar General, of the General Register Office, Charlemont House, Dublin. He was in charge of all registration of Births, Deaths, and Marriages, required by law. This affected the registration of marriages after 31 March 1845, and of births and deaths after 31 December 1870. All were recorded in the nearest local registry and the records were then sent to the General Register Office in Dublin.

Along with the reports on vital records, the local registrars sent notices of changes of surname, peculiarities or distortions of surnames in the particular district, inconsistencies or total differences of surname in a single family, notes regarding the registration of some children at birth, of a surname without a prefix Mac or O, while later births in the family were registered with the resumed prefix. A note was sent in if a man signed his brother's death record with the Gaelic form of the family surname and yet recorded his brother's surname in a translated anglicised form, or perhaps the reverse. He reported if a family of Allison chose to spell the name Ellison in his district or within the same family the name was variously registered Allison, Alison, Alleson and Allisson. In every way the local registrars and the General Registrar tried to keep the identification of members of a family as a unit, with cross references leading to differences in spelling and form, changes, and cases of an affix being added to the name to distinguish a particular branch of a sept.

On the subject of the use of an affix, Matheson quotes (p. 12, 1901), as follows:

"The registrar of Castlebar No. 1 District reports: 'Joyce, a very common name, is distinguished by affixing the father's name, e.g. Tom Joyce (Tom), Tom Joyce (Martin).' The Registrar of Kilkeel No. 2 District, remarks: 'Often the grandfather's Christian name is used as an affix as: Charles Cunningham (Dick).' In Sneem District in Kenmare Union, Sullivans are called after the locality they live in, etc., as Sullivan Glanac, Sullivan Brachae, Sullivan Dillough, Sullivan Budoch."

The body of Matheson's book comprises his alphabetical list of 2,091 principal surnames in Ireland. Under each is listed all of the known variations of spelling. A key number is placed beside any spelling or form of the name which is peculiar to a certain district. On page 64 (1901), he lists the local Registrars' Districts and the Unions in which they are located, with the key numbers to which the above numbers refer. In addition, every principal name is numbered and a master index of every principal name and variation of the name refers to these numbers.

Thus if one wished to examine all Irish indexes regarding an ancestor named Jameson, he could quickly locate the name Jameson in the alphabetical list as a principal name, number 957. Under it are the variations of spelling to be watched for in indexes. These are Jameison (James) 409, Jamieson 390, Jamison, Jemison. The key number 409 is that of Newry District Number 1. This indicates that in this district it has been reported that the name has been contracted to James. The key number 390 is that of Mountshannon Registrar's District in the Union of Scarriff, which Union is in County Clare. This indicates that in the district of County Clare, the usual spelling is Jamieson. For method of locating Scarriff (Scarreff) Union, see *Griffith's Valuation*, under LAND SURVEYS, CHAPTER XII.

3. *Special Report on the Surnames in Ireland*, by Robert E. Matheson, Dublin, 1894, 1909. This *Report* was prepared by

Matheson when he was Secretary of the General Register Office (see *Varieties and Synonymes*, 1901, p. 7). In this he presented notes on the derivation of names, varieties of spelling, etc., as in the above work. The body of the *Report* contains a list of all surnames in Ireland having five or more births registered in 1890, as extracted from the Births indexes of the General Register Office, of that year. This *Report* was published as an Appendix to the 29th *Annual Report of the Registrar General,* and presented to Parliament.

Charles A. Hanna extracted the list for Ulster and published it in his second volume of *The Scotch-Irish* (New York, 1902). The list appears in his Appendix Z, entitled "Locations of Scottish Families in Ireland." Actually, it includes all names of the Irish of Gaelic origin and the Anglo-Irish names as well.

Matheson places after each name, the number of births (5 or more) in all of Ireland, and also the number of births which occurred in the counties where the name was principally registered. As later census records show very little shift of family localities, which indicates the same was even more probably true at earlier dates, one can use this list of Matheson's for all of Ireland, to locate quickly the principal counties in which persons of any name resided.

Also the total number of persons of any one name in a specified county, and the total number in all of Ireland, can be determined by the fact that the average birth rate in 1890 was one birth to every 44.8 persons. Thus in trying to locate the counties in Ireland in which the Jamison family lived, this list extracted by Hanna shows that, in 1890, the births in families of that name numbered 52 in all of Ireland. Of these, 41 occurred in Ulster, with 16 in County Antrim and 9 in County Down.

To ascertain the number of Jamisons (shown Jamison in this list but Jameson is the preferred spelling) in Ireland in 1890, the number 52 multiplied by 44.8 indicates roughly that 2,329.6 of the population of all of Ireland are named Jamison, with this spelling or variations known to pertain to it. The number of 41 Jamison births in Ulster, multiplied by 44.8, shows that roughly 1,836.8 Jamisons were living in Ulster. Of these it is shown that 16 births in County Antrim, multiplied by 44.8, equals 716.8 Jamisons living in County Antrim. Likewise for County Down, 9 births times 44.8, equals 403.2 Jamisons in County Down. Finally, the total for both counties equals 1,120 Jamisons, or almost half of the total of that name were living in one of the two counties. The difference between 2,329.6 Jamisons in all of Ireland, and 1836.8 living in Ulster, leaves 492.8 living outside of Ulster. The difference between 1,836.8 for Ulster and 1,120 in Counties Antrim and Down, leaves 716.8 living in the seven other counties of Ulster in 1890.

Thus if an American does not know from which county in Ireland his first Jamison or Jameson came, he could use this information to direct his search. Obviously, all early records pertaining to County Antrim would first be searched, followed by those of County Down.

4. *Some Anglicised Surnames in Ireland,* by Padraig Mac-Giolla-Domhnaigh, Dublin, 1923. This is a history of surnames, arranged in alphabetical order (unindexed). It deals largely with names of Scottish origin, but includes a number of Irish and English origin. On the whole, he makes no attempt to cover the large and intricate field of Gaelic Irish surnames or those of Norman origin. For the names with which he deals, he gives the various interchanges and synonyms of surnames, and the interchanges of the Irish surnames from their Gaelic forms. J. J. Doyle states in a foreword: "I am glad the author has dealt so fully with Ulster and Scottish names."

One of his more brief examples concerns the Jamison surname (p. 33): *Jamison.* This name is the anglicised form of McJames, a McDonald sept. It is also a sept of the Clan Gunn, and is also anglicised Jameson and Jamieson, in Gaelic MacSheumais. M'Keamish is a form found in the West and North of Scotland.

5. *Sloinnte Gaedheal is Gall* (Irish Names and Surnames), by the Rev. Patrick Woulfe, Dublin, 1923. In this monumental work, Woulfe has attempted to provide, in alphabetical order, the Gaelic and English equivalent of all presently existing Gaelic-Irish surnames. He also includes the most common names of foreign origin now in Ireland. He discusses the his-

tory, origin, and the transition of each name, including variations, corruptions of the names, and other points of interest. This is the accepted, standard work on the subject and, according to Dr. MacLysaght, "deserves high praise" (*Irish Families*, p. 10). He goes on to state, "The errors in it are very few . . . Notwithstanding these minor defects, his book is most valuable." Woulfe's work is not well enough known in America. It should be consulted by the genealogist, or by an agent for him, in every study of Irish names and those of foreign origin.

CHAPTER II

CENSUS RETURNS AND RELATED
MATERIAL

The first complete Census Return by Government officials was taken in 1813, followed by others in 1821, 1831-1834, 1841, 1851, 1861, 1871, 1881, 1891, 1901 and, thereafter, every ten years. The Census Returns of 1813, 1821, 1831-1834, 1841, and 1851, were almost all destroyed when the Public Record Office of Ireland, Dublin, was burned in 1922. The Returns of 1861, 1871, 1881, and 1891, were not preserved by the Government. Thus the earliest complete and existing Census Return is that of 1901.

The Census Returns, 1821-1851, which did escape the fire, and the transcripts of some Returns made before the fire, also extracts from Returns for certain counties, will be listed below. In view of this, their genealogical value should be noted. The Returns of 1841 and 1851, have Tables of the names of the present and absent members of the family, and also include a third Table naming all members of the family who had died within the previous ten years. All Census Returns list the people by parish and county, giving the name of the head of the household, the names of all members of the family, present or absent, and for every one their age, birthplace, religion, and occupation of adults. The Returns thus present in family groups a register of births, deaths and marriages within the periods, showing in one Return, in a great number of cases, as many as three and at times four generations.

In the 28th *Report of the Deputy Keeper of the Public Records in Ireland*, 1896, p. 6, Mr. Latouche states, "The Census Returns of 1813, 1821, 1831-1834, 1841, and 1851, are of record here transferred at different times from their places of original deposit. Their accessibility to the public has proved of incalculable value in inquiries concerning title and pedigree and the tracing of next-of-kin and heirs-at-law." Mr. Latouche indicates the great amount of copying of Census Returns which has occurred, and thus has preserved an untold number of family or personal records. Many of these were certified copies obtained by solicitors in the course of their legal work, which have been donated to this Office among other documents. The collections of some noted genealogists, accredited record searchers, and private family papers also contain information copied from the Census Returns. Many such collections have been deposited in this Office for safekeeping. In addition, transcripts of some entire series of Census Returns, kept in County Offices, have been sent in to the Public Record Office, Dublin. A further voluminous source of information contained in the Census Returns is the Old Age Pension Forms, sent by the Customs and Excise Department, to the Public Record Offices in Dublin and Belfast. These "Green Forms" contain proof of age, parentage, and birth place, taken in certified copies of Census Returns, 1821-1851, issued between 1908 and 1922. These were kept by the local agencies of the Customs and Excise Department and finally returned to the two Public Record Offices in, or about, 1928.

The 53rd *Report of the Deputy Keeper of the Public Records in Ireland,* Dublin (p. 4), dated 30 August 1921, explains the immense work of issuing certified copies of the Census Returns for Pension purposes:

"After the passing of the Old Age Pensions Act, 1908, it was found that the main source of documentary evidence of age for the great majority of the applicants was the Returns of the Census taken in the years 1821, 1841, and 1851, which were deposited in this Office. The heavy task of furnishing evidence of the age of applicants to the Local Government Boards of England, Ireland and Scotland, and to the applicants themselves, was entrusted to this Department . . . The Census Returns of 1851 were taken on the 30th March, 1851. Their usefulness for Old Age Pensions' purposes has been rapidly dwindling for some time and will soon be at an end. The only source of evidence of age for Old Age Pensions' purposes now in this Department is the collection of Parish Registers of the (late Established) Church of Ireland."

This throws light on the fact that for pension applicants born after the Census of 1851, the records were copied from the Parish Registers then deposited in this Office, before their destruction in 1922. Thus thousands of records from the Census Returns and the Parish Registers, later destroyed, were in this way preserved.

The *Report of the Deputy Keeper of the Records of Northern Ireland*, 1927, p. 6, states:

"Old Age Pension Search Forms and some Public Record Office (Dublin) Certified Copies of extracts from the Census Returns, 1841 and 1851, for parts of Counties Antrim, Armagh, Down, Fermanagh, Londonderry, and Tyrone, were received from the Customs and Excise stations at the following places:—Armagh, Ballycastle, Ballygawley, Ballymena, Ballymoney, Ballynahinch, Belfast, Castlederg, Coleraine, Cookstown, Dungannon, Enniskillen, Irvinestown, Larne, Limavady, Lisburn, Lisnaskea, Londonderry, Lurgan, Maghera, Magherafelt, Newry, Newtownards, Portadown, Strabane."

Existing source materials which provide information regarding names of residents of specified areas, from the 17th to the late 19th centuries, thus being substitutes for census records, are listed in the following chapters of this volume: Court Records (Inquisitions on Attainder), XI; Directories, X; Naturalization and Emigration, XXI; Estate Records (Muster Rolls, lists of tenants), XIV; Land Surveys, XII; Military and Naval Records (Muster Rolls), XVII; Registers (Freeholders' Rolls), XIX; State Papers (Religious Census, 1740, 1766), XI; Tax Records, XVI.

Existing Census Returns or transcripts of the Records, available in the Public Record Offices of Dublin and Belfast, the Genealogical Office (Office of Arms), also printed Census Records and lists of inhabitants, are presented below. These repositories maintain indexes of their Census Records and of their Old Age Pension Records.

THE PUBLIC RECORD OFFICE OF IRELAND, DUBLIN

COUNTY ANTRIM: 1851 Census Returns, 23 volumes for various townlands in 13 parishes, saved from the fire.   (55th *Report*, p. 110.)

Parish	Barony	Townlands, etc.
Tickmacrevan	Lower Glenarm	Glenarm Town. Altmore St., Toberwine St.
Carncastle	Upper Glenarm	. . . . .
Grange of Killyglen	Upper Glenarm	. . . . .
Kilwaughter	Upper Glenarm	Ballyedward, Drumnadonaghy.
Larne	Upper Glenarm	. . . . .

Parish	Barony	Townlands, etc.
Craigs (Ahoghill)	Kilconway	Craigs.
Ballymoney	Kilconway	Garryduff.
Dunaghy	Kilconway	Artnacrea, Tullynewy.
Rasharkin	Kilconway	Killydonnelly, Tehorny.
Killead	Massereene Lower	Ardmore, Carnaghliss.
Aghagallon	Massereene Upper	Montiaghs, Tiscallen.
Aghalee	Massereene Upper	. . . . .
Ballinderry	Massereene Upper	. . . . .

COUNTY CAVAN: 1821 Census Returns (complete) of one parish, saved (55th *Report*, p. 109). 1821 complete Census Returns of 15 more parishes and part of another, transferred from the County Cavan Sheriff's Office (55th *Report*, p. 146; 56th *Report*, pp. 8, 18, 413; 57th *Report*, p. 18). Parishes and baronies named, with a complete list in the 56th *Report*, p. 413. 1841 Census Returns and 1851 Returns are represented with miscellaneous extracts for various names (58th *Report*, p. 18).

Census Returns, 1841, saved.

Parish of Killeshandra, County Cavan (complete), 1841. Saved from the fire.

Census Returns, 1821, copies of

Parish	Barony
Annageliffe (part of)	Loughtee Upper.
Ballymacue	Clanmahon.
Castlerahan	Castlerahan.
Castleterra	Loughtee Upper.
Crosserlough	Clanmahon, Castlerahan.
Denn	Clanmahon, Loughtee Upper, Castlerahan.
Drumlummon	Clanmahon.
Drung and Larah	Loughtee Upper and Tullygarvey.
Kilbride	Clanmahon.
Kilmore	Clanmahon and Lougtee Upper.
Kinawley	Tullyhaw.
Lavey	Longhtee Upper.
Lurgan and Munterconaght	Castlerahan.
Mullagh	Castlerahan.

MISCELLANEOUS:

Copies of Census Returns, 1851 (Patt Lee, Monesk, Killinagh, Co. Cavan, Phillip McKeown, Coraghy, Maghereross, Co. Monaghan, and Owen Smith, Killinkere, Co. Cavan) and extracts and reports from Census Returns, 1841 and 1851 (names: Abraham, Brady, Farrelly, Gallagher, Larney, Rooney, Slowey, Smith, Smyth and Sullivan).

COUNTY CORK: 1821 Census Returns are represented with copies for families in Counties Cork, Galway, Mayo, Roscommon and Sligo (number of returns and names not mentioned). (58th *Report*, p. 33.) 1841 Census Returns (26) saved in 1922, representing names in 4 parishes and 3 not identified (55th *Report*, p. 109).

Parish	Barony	No. of Returns
Aughadown	Carberry W.E.D.	8
(Not identified)	Fermoy	1
Creagh	Carberry W.E.D.	1
(Not identified)	Carberry W.E.D.	2
Drimoleague	Carberry W.E.D.	1
Drinagh	Carberry W.E.D.	11
(Not identified)	Carberry W.E.D.	2

COUNTY FERMANAGH: 1821 Census Returns, complete for one parish and part of another, saved (55th *Report*, p. 109). 1841 Census Returns, for one parish, 13 Returns, saved (55th *Report*, p. 109). 1851 Census Returns, complete for one townland, saved (55th *Report*, p. 110).

1821 Census Returns, saved.

Parish	Barony
Derryvullen	Lurg.
Aghalurcher (part of)	Magherastephana

1841 Census Returns, saved.

Parish	Barony
Currin (13 Returns)	Coole

1851 Census Returns, saved.

Parish	Barony	Townland
Drumkeeran	Lurg.	Clonee

COUNTY GALWAY: 1821 Census Returns for two baronies (complete), saved (55th *Report*, p. 109).   Copies of 1821 Census Returns for various families (58th *Report*, p. 33).

1821 Census Returns, saved.

Barony

Arran and Athenry (complete).

Copies of 1821 Census Returns for families in Counties Cork, Galway, Mayo, Roscommon, and Sligo.   (58th *Report*, p. 33.)

KING'S COUNTY: 1821 Census Returns saved: Barony of Ballybritt (complete).

COUNTY LONDONDERRY: 1831 Census Returns for the County and City of Londonderry (11 parishes), 45 volumes, transferred from the Ordnance Survey Department (55th *Report*, p. 110; 56th, p. 18).

Parish	*Barony*
Agivey, Macosquin	Coleraine.
Ballyaghran, Killowen	Coleraine Liberties.
Aghanloo, Tamlaght Finlagan	Keenaght.
Templemore	Londonderry City and Liberties.
Arboe, Termoneeny	Loughinsholin.
Banagher, Glendermot	Tirkeeran.

COUNTY LONGFORD: No original or copies of entire or partial Census Returns, but there are three Electoral Lists, *ca.* 1790.   (MSS. 2486-2488.)   (58th *Report*, p. 40.)

COUNTY LOUTH: 1821 Census Returns, a number of extracts for families, principally relating to Drogheda and County Louth.   (55th *Report*, p. 110.)

COUNTY MAYO: Copies of 1821 Census Returns for families in Counties Cork, Galway, Mayo, Roscommon and Sligo. (58th *Report*, p. 33.)

COUNTY MEATH: 1821 Census Returns saved for the two baronies of Upper Navan and Lower Navan (complete). (55th *Report*, p. 109.)

COUNTY MONAGHAN: Copies of Census Returns, 1851 (Patt Lee, Monesk, Killinagh, Co. Cavan, Phillip McKeown, Coraghy, Magheross, Co. Monaghan, and Owen Smith, Killinkere, Co. Cavan) and extracts and reports from Census Returns, 1841 and 1851 (names: Abraham, Brady, Farrelly, Gallagher, Larney, McDonell, McGinley, McGonigle, McKenna, Markey, Murray, Prior, Rooney, Slowey, Smith, Smyth and Sullivan). (58th *Report*, p. 18.)

COUNTY ROSCOMMON: See County Mayo.

COUNTY SLIGO: See County Mayo.

COUNTY TIPPERARY: List of heads of houses in Clonmel, Co. Tipperary, from 1821 Census, etc. (58th *Report*, p. 44.)

COUNTY WATERFORD: 1841 Census Returns saved, parish of Lismore, barony of Coshmore and Coshbride (4 Returns). (55th *Report*, p. 109.)

MISCELLANEOUS:

1. Collections of extracts of Census Returns for various families appear among presented materials occasionally, throughout the 55th-58th *Reports*.

2. Some certified copies of Returns and extracts from Returns, as well as a number of Reports of Searches made in the Census Returns prior to the destruction of the Office (1922), are preserved. These Reports have been arranged under townlands, parishes, and baronies, and have proved of considerable value. (55th *Report*, p. 110.)

3. List of inhabitants of the baronies of Newcastle and Uppercross, Co. Dublin, *ca.* 1652. (MS. 2467). (58th *Report*, p. 20.)

4. Copy Book of a Survey of County Dublin, 1658. (58th *Report*, p. 20.)

5. City of Dublin, Rental of Landgable Rents (ground rent per house), 1665. A list of residents by street, estimated 1,920 names. This Rental of Landgable Rents and other City dues occurs in a book belonging to the City of Dublin written about the year A.D. 1665 (57th *Report*, pp. 526-558). See also, explanation of Landgable Rents (*ibid.*, pp. 569, 570).

6. Kilkenny, 11 April 1676,—List of inhabitants of the parish of St. Patrick liable to quarter horse and foot. Kilkenny, May (16) 94,—List of some of the outlawed, with discovery of properties. List of Protestants in St. Kennis parish out gates (Kilkenny), numbered 268-287, n.d. (1702?). Lists of Papists, St. Canies in gate (Kilkenny), 1702, numbered 476-580, endorsed "Protestants and Catholics." Kilkenny, 27 Aug. 1715,—List of Protestant inhabitants of parishes of St. John within gates and St. John out gate aged 16 to 60 years. List of Protestants of parish of St. Patrick out gate (Kilkenny), n.d. (1715?), enclosed with previous item. (All in Prim Collection, 58th *Report,* pp. 50, 51.)

PUBLIC RECORD OFFICE OF NORTHERN IRELAND, BELFAST

Attention is called to the fact that many volumes of Census Returns for counties in Northern Ireland are deposited in the Public Record Office of Ireland, Dublin. The records are listed on pages 251-256, herein.

The Public Record Office of Northern Ireland, Belfast, has miscellaneous collections of Census Records and related material which will be listed below. Also the family collections listed under 848 surnames (VOLUME II, pp. 109-166), contain various source materials including extracts from Census Returns, 1821-1851.

Several classes of records represented in large collections in this Office serve more or less as substitutes for Census Returns, in that they contain lists of heads of families in various localities, at specified times or within periods of time. All classes of this nature are discussed in later chapters of this volume. (The subject matter and chapter numbers are noted in the introduction to this chapter.)

Of especial importance is a great collection of Estate Records deposited in this Office which represent many Ulster estates. Most of them contain Rent Rolls which list the names of tenants and other data concerning them at specified times or periods. Some of the Rolls are of very early dates, such as the Armagh Manor Rolls, 1625-1627. The Rent Rolls serve as a means of locating the families between the 17th and 19th centuries. Early Muster Rolls, included in a number of Estate collections, list the names and locations of those aged between 16 and 60 years, who were able to bear arms.

The complete collection of Hearthmoney Rolls for Counties Antrim, 1669; Armagh, *ca.* 1664; Londonderry, 1663; Tyrone, 1666, and some parishes in Counties Donegal and Fermanagh, 1665; also the printed Roll for Co. Monaghan, 1663, in the history of that county, by Rushe, all list every householder who was required by law to pay a tax of two shillings on each fire-hearth. These, and a number of other classes of records containing lists of householders, provide the names of residents and an indication of their economic status or their religion. All offer important information to the genealogist.

The Customs and Excise stations in Northern Ireland sent thirty-three bundles containing many hundreds of Census Returns, mostly of dates 1841 and 1851, which were recorded on Old Age Pension Search Forms, and some certified copies of extracts from Census Returns of the same dates which were taken from the records on the Dublin Record Office before the fire. These represented parts of Counties Antrim, Armagh, Down, Fermanagh, Londonderry, and Tyrone. They were sent from the stations at the following places: Armagh, Ballycastle, Ballygawley, Ballymena, Ballymoney, Ballynahinch, Belfast, Castlederg, Coleraine, Cookstown, Dungannon, Enniskillen, Irvinestown, Larne, Limavady, Lisburn, Lisnaskea, Londonderry, Lurgan, Maghera, Magherafelt, Newry, Newtownards, Portadown, and Strabane. (1927 *Report,* pp. 3, 6.)

Miscellaneous representative Census Returns and related material, listed by counties, are as follows:

ANTRIM:

1. Population Return, Antrim Town, 1821 (extract). (*Report,* 1938-1945, p. 15.)

2. Census of Presbyterian Congregation of Ballyeaston, County Antrim, 1813. (*Report,* 1948, p. 4.)

3. Ballymoney, Tenants Names, 1742. List given by the Earl of Antrim. (*Report,* 1928, p. 9.)

4. Belfast inhabitants, 1819. A list compiled by this Office, from the Belfast Directory, 1819. The names of residents are arranged by street. (*Report,* 1931, p. 14.)

5. Larne inhabitants, 1735. Sent by the Earl of Antrim, Glenarm Castle. (*Report*, 1928, p. 9.)

6. Parkmount Census Returns, 1821 (extracts). (*Report*, 1925, p. 8.)

7. Templeton Estate, Rent Roll, 1851. This appears to be the draft for Census Returns of the tenants on the estate, giving information regarding age, relationships, etc., prepared by the estate agent. (*Report*, 1927, p. 5.)

ARMAGH:

1. Armagh Manor Rolls, 1625-1627. (*Report*, 1928, pp. 9, 13, 14.)

2. See of Armagh, Rent Roll, 1615-1746. (*Report*, 1936, p. 4.)

3. List of inhabitants, town of Armagh, 1770. (*Report*, 1928, p. 9.)

4. Census Returns, Kilmore, Co. Armagh, 1821. (*Report*, 1928, pp. 9, 13.)

DONEGAL:

Extracts from Population Return, 1821, Census Returns, 1841, certain townlands in Drumhome Parish, Co. Donegal. (*Report*, 1933, p. 11.)

DOWN:

1. Cromwellian Census of County Down, 1659. (*Report*, 1930, p. 10.)

2. Ballygally, County Down, list of tenants and list of inhabitants, 1742-1800. (*Report*, 1949-1950.)

3. Extracts from Population Return, 1821, and Census Returns, 1841, of Parishes of Bangor, Comber Donaghadee, Drumbo, Killinchy, Killyleagh, Kilmore, Newtownards, Saintfield, Tullynakill, and from Muster Roll, 1842, of Lord Clandeboy's Regiment (name Stewart). (*Report*, 1933, p. 11.)

LONDONDERRY:

1. Extracts from Census Returns, 1821, Coleraine, Deser-

toghill, Aghadowey; principal names, Andrew, Cairns, Fleming, Hilton, Morrow, Murray, Torrens. (*Report*, 1925, p. 8.)

2. Census Extracts relating to Desertmartin Parish, 1821 and 1851. (*Report*, 1934, p. 9.)

TYRONE:

List of heads of families in Parishes of Badoney, Cappagh, and Drumragh, 1699. (*Report*, 1931, p. 13.)

THE GENEALOGICAL OFFICE (OFFICE OF ARMS)

The Genealogical Office has numerous extracts from the destroyed Census Returns, which are contained in various manuscript collections. Transcripts of Census Returns have been gathered from various sources.

PRINTED MATERIALS

Some Census Records and related materials are listed in VOLUME II, pp. 233-234. *A Census of Ireland* (*ca.* 1659), by Séamus Pender, is described in VOLUME II, p. 97.

RECORDS OF THE CHURCH OF IRELAND

This chapter contains some notes regarding the broad field of genealogical source materials related to the Church of Ireland. Primarily, it will be devoted to two complete lists of the existing Parish Registers and transcripts of the Registers which are located in the Republic of Ireland, and in Northern Ireland.

In the study of Parish Registers, and other identifying source materials relating to any family, the genealogist must keep in mind the fact that many persons changed their membership from one church denomination to another, or were descended from a forbear who effected a change in religion. This was the result of economic conditions, political pressure, legal restrictions, conscience, or church discipline. Such matters are often forgotten in subsequent generations and the information is lost, along with the family records.

Documentary evidence supports the occurrence of many conversions. In most cases the genealogist must rely upon the discovery of church records concerning the individual or other personal documents and local material, to reveal a change in religion.

In Ireland, as in England and America, members of the Established Church (Episcopal) became dissenters when and as the spirit moved them. The Irish Baptists, Congregationalists, Huguenots, Methodists, Presbyterians and Quakers, were all classed by the Church of Ireland and the Government as dissenters. For this reason, in all cases of genealogical research, the Parish Registers of the Church of Ireland should be examined in any known area of interest, on the chance that the records of a dissenter from the Church or his earlier family records may thus be found. This holds true even when searching for information about a person known to have been a Roman Catholic for, in many cases, persons who were fundamentally loyal to their faith found it expedient to become converts temporarily, or their families had found it necessary to do so in a previous generation, for a long or short period of time.

All Protestant Church denominations in England and Ireland, except the Presbyterians and Huguenots, broke away from the Established Church at some time during the 17th and 18th centuries. The Huguenot confession of faith and ecclesiastical discipline was derived from the constitution introduced by John Calvin, their early leader in the years of their exile in Germany, and this was also the model for the Presbyterian Church.

The Established Church of England was erected under Henry VIII, when the spiritual supremacy and jurisdiction of the Pope were abolished, and the sovereign declared himself the spiritual head of the Church, in a close union with the temporal power of the State, known as the establishment of the Church.

From this time, except for the reign of Queen Mary, the Established Church of Ireland was under the ecclesiastical jurisdiction of the Archbishop of Armagh, Primate of all Ireland, and the bishops of the dioceses; all appointed by the Crown, with authority over the several ecclesiastical courts, the parishes within the dioceses, and with a representative voice in matters of State.

In Ireland as in England, every effort of the Church and State was directed to break the power of the Roman Catholic Church and its adherents, in the interests of English rule. The tragic events in Ireland, accented by three major insurrections and one revolution, between the time of Queen Elizabeth and the end of the 17th century, resulted in mass confiscations of the lands of Roman Catholic proprietors, the plantations of the English and Scots, the extermination and degradation of the Roman Catholics by the hundreds of thousands. Only to a lesser degree were the dissenters deprived of civil and religious liberty, by means of the Penal Laws and various Acts of Parliament, intended to crush the Roman Catholics and impress the dissenters under the Church rule.

Due to this pressure, some thousands of Roman Catholics and dissenters left their churches or the churches of their ancestors, to espouse the Established Church of Ireland. The causes and the evidence of this will be noted in the following chapters pertaining to the different denominations. It is sufficient to note here that Dr. William King, Bishop of Londonderry after the Revolution of 1689, was himself a Presbyterian by birth, and his great ambition was to convert Presbyterians to the Church of Ireland. He had much to do with attaching the Presbyterians within the sphere of his influence, willingly or otherwise, to his church.

On the contrary, members of the Church of Ireland became dissenters at a greater rate than their places could be filled with new recruits. Those who did become Church of Ireland converts, particularly the Roman Catholics, were in many cases only briefly, for reasons of expediency, away from the church of their birth. In other instances, as the records show, their changes became permanent. In either case, their records of birth, marriage and death, were entered during some period of time in the Parish Registers of the Established Church of Ireland.

The failure in growth of the Church of Ireland, in contrast to the Presbyterian Church, is a matter of history. In 1861, the religious census appeared. It proved that the membership of the Church of Ireland was only one-eighth of the total population of Ireland, after centuries of privilege, during which time every adult householder had been compelled to pay a tithe tax to support the clergy of the Church of Ireland. This led to the disestablishment of the Church of Ireland, by Parliament in the Irish Church Act, on 26 July 1869, and it took effect on 1 January 1871.

At this time the Parish Registers of the Church of Ireland were accounted Public Records and, under the jurisdiction of the Master of the Rolls, were to be sent to the Public Record Office of Ireland in Dublin, unless the local incumbent of the parish could show evidence of a safe place of deposit for their keeping. With disestablishment, the church property was appropriated by the State and the jurisdiction over probate matters was removed from the ecclesiastical courts. Thereafter, testamentary affairs were handled in the Principal or District Probate Registries.

Thus, as numerous conversions of Roman Catholics are reported as having occurred even in the 19th century, which may or may not have lasted any length of time, it would seem that even in searching for records of this period, the Church of Ireland Registers of the locality in which a forbear is known to have lived should be examined for records, regardless of the church affiliation.

There is no evidence that the clergy were obliged to keep Parish Registers in Ireland before the canons of 1634. The oldest extant Registers (original or published), are of the Holy Trinity or Christ Church, Cork, beginning in 1644; the Dublin Registers of St. Andrews, 1636—; St. Brigad's, 1633—; St. John's, 1619—; St. Michan's, 1636—; the Lisburn Registers, 1639—; the Registers of Derry Cathedral (St. Columb's), Parish of Templemore, Londonderry, 1642—.

The 46th Canon of the Irish Church of 1634 required that "in every parish church or chapel within this realm shall be provided one parchment book at the charge of the parish, wherein shall be written the day and the year of every christening and burial," etc. Every parish was required to provide a place of safekeeping (usually in the church) for the Registers, with "one sure coffer with two locks and keys." One key was to be kept by the local incumbent and the other by the churchwardens.

During the time of the Irish Rebellion, in 1644, Parliament ordered that all births and deaths, baptisms and burials be entered in the Parish Registers. In 1647, the English Parliament appointed Sir Charles Coote to command Derry (Londonderry), which he held under the Commonwealth authorities until the Restoration. During his sway the Episcopalian worship was suppressed and Independent or Baptist teachers, probably either officers from the army or itinerants from Dublin, were alone permitted to preach within the city, and marriages were solemnized before the mayor (Ordnance Survey, p. 7). This is noted in the Preface of *The Registers of Derry Cathedral (St. Columb's), Parish of Templemore, Londonderry, 1642-1703*, published by the Parish Register Society, Dublin, 1910, as a factor which influenced the records.

These Derry Cathedral Registers provide a number of interesting facts about the practices in keeping the records, the evident origin and religion of the families whose records were entered, the very wide area represented, which was heavily settled by Presbyterians and less so by members of the Church of Ireland, while Roman Catholics occupied the barren regions. The records of the early period seem to point to the fact that the English Government was keeping informed about the Irish, the Anglo-Irish, and the new settlers from England and Scotland, through the Parish Registers of the Church of Ireland.

In December 1653, a new Register for Derry Cathedral was begun under the Commonwealth Act of that year (*ibid.*, see extract on p. 13), by which it was provided that all births should be recorded, and that where there are small parishes or places not within any parish, or any usual morning exercises on the Lord's Days, the Justices of the Peace shall invite them to another parish and one Register to serve for such parishes (as did the Register of Londonderry Cathedral for many parishes and places, for which there are indexes, pp. 429-431).

In the above Act pertaining to Ireland, baptisms were not mentioned, but they were entered also in the Register. Even illegitimate births were recorded with the names of both parents. Marriages, deaths and burials were also recorded.

Occupations of male adults, condition of a woman if relict or widow, residence in the city or location in the parish were frequently given, and many names of other locations and parishes appear in records of birth, baptism, marriages, deaths and burials.

Concerning marriages, the Act directed that Justices of the Peace should determine any exceptions against contracts and marriages and that, from December 1653, the "Banes" of the contracting parties were to be regularly published either on three several Lord's Days before a parish congregation, or on three market days in the market place, the Act allowing the latter alternative, "if the parties to the marriage shall desire it." The marriage ceremony was to be performed before a Justice of the Peace. While the performance of religious rites was not prohibited, the Act declares that, "No other marriage whatsoever within the Commonwealth of England, after 29 September 1653, shall be accounted a marriage according to the Laws of England."

The first mention in this Register of a marriage by a

minister is in December 1657. After 1660, notices of marriage by licence are found, as well as by publication of banns.

Scottish people were solidly Presbyterian and, as many such names appear, some of them are mentioned as: Alexander, Allison, Bell, Blair, Bruce, Burns, Campbell, Craig, Crawford, Cunningham, Dickson, Douglas, Duncan, Galt, Gordon, Hamilton, Henry, Houston, Jackson, Jamison, Jemison, Kerr, Knox, Linn, McAfee, McAlpin, McClelland, McCormack, McCullagh, McCullogh, McDowell, McDonnell, McKinley, Montgomery, Patterson, Stewart, and Wallace.

An equally large number of Irish Roman Catholic names appear as: Bourke, Flagherty, Gallagher, Hagarty, Kelly, Malone, MccChonell, MccLaghlin, MccO'Brenny, MccSwyne, Murphy, O'Brien, O'Connell, O'Deaghan, O'Doherty, O'Daugherty, O'Donnell, O'Hagan, O'Heggerty, O'Kelly, O'Murray, O'Quigley, O'Reilly, and Sullivan. These are just a few samples. The index of the records contains 87 surnames, all different and with numerous variations, each beginning with the prefix "O". Under each surname there are from one to 129 entries, the latter being for the members of the O'Doherty (O'Daugherty, and 14 other forms of spelling) family. Besides the 129 entries for the principal spelling of the surname O'Doherty and the 14 variations of the name with the prefix "O", one is referred to Doherty (Daugherty, and 4 other forms) for 94 entries, which indicates that some members of the family used the prefix and some did not (see notes on this in CHAPTER II). It is quite probable that this family and many others of Gaelic Irish surnames were Roman Catholics, a few of whom may have become Protestant converts. But the requirements for the registration of vital records in the Parish Registers would explain the appearance of the surnames of Roman Catholics, Presbyterians and other dissenters in the Registers during the 17th century and somewhat later, during the years of the Penal Laws and the Test Act.

The provision of the Commonwealth Act of 1653, whereby the records of small parishes or places not within any parish, or where there was no regular service on Lord's Days, should be entered in the Registers of another parish, is reflected in the Derry Cathedral Registers, as records from the following places and parishes are recorded. In the published Registers, 1642-1703, an Index of the Parishes represented in the records, and an Index of the Places also named (pp. 429-431), show the wide area from which the records were gathered.

Until the year 1809, the Parish of Templemore included the three present parishes of Burt, Inch, and Muff in County Donegal, as well as the present area of 12,611 acres extending 8 miles along the Foyle River and three miles wide at the greatest, including the City of Londonderry.

The indexed names of places in County Londonderry are too numerous to mention. Those outside the parish are scattered through the county as far as Coleraine at the far northeast corner and Magherafelt in the southeast section. The names of places outside of County Londonderry, mentioned by county are as follows: County Antrim: Ballinarite, Belfast, Carnamaddy, Carrickfergus. County Armagh: Acton, Ardmore, and Kilmore (uncertain about county which may have been Armagh, Down, or Fermanagh). County Donegal: Ardee, Aughnish, Ballevagh, Ballymoney, Carrigans, Donegal, Donoughmore, Drumskellan, Fahan, Fort Stewart, Glashagh, Inch, Killevady, Letterkenny, Lifford, Listicall, Manorcunningham, Moneygreggan, Moville, Newtown, Plaster, Roosky, St. Johnstown. County Fermanagh: Soppog, Tully, Ture. County Sligo: Sligo. County Tyrone: Arcame, Donaghedy, Strabane, Tyrone, Dunnalong. Besides the above, are Limerick, Barbadoes, "Bostin," a few places in Scotland and England, and one item for New England (p. 214, "Richard Meade, a strainger out of New England, buried 16 Dec. 1672").

The records in Derry Cathedral Registers, 1642-1703, also name many parishes besides that of Templemore in which the Cathedral was situated. In addition, there are a great many records which give no location, while others name the person or persons as of the city or the parish. Other parishes named in County Londonderry are 15 in number: Aghanloo, Bovevagh, Camus, Clondermot, Coleraine, Cumber, Desertmartin, Desertoghill, Dungiven, Drumachose, Dunboe, Faughanvale, Kilcronaghan, Magherafelt, Tamlaght Finlagan. Parishes in other counties named: County Antrim: Derryaghy. County Armagh: Creggan. County Donegal: Aghanunshin, Aughnish, Clonca, Clondaraddog, Conwall, Donagh, Donaghmore, Fahan, Killegarran, Killea, Leck, Lifford, Mevagh, Moville, Ramullan (now Kilgarvan), Raymochy, Rasphoe, Taughboyne, Tullyfern. County Fermanagh: Magheraculmoney. County Tyrone: Donaghedy, Errigal, Kilskeery, Leckpatrick, Termonamongan.

Thus the published Derry Cathedral Registers, 1642-1703 (1 vol.), and the original Registers now deposited in the vault of the Cathedral, are an important source for early vital records of many parishes and places in Ulster. However, when searching these Registers, certain gaps in the entries and missing pages should be noted. They are mentioned in the Preface of the published volume. They are listed here to show that family records are not entirely complete.

There are gaps in the Register from 1643-1649, and from 1650-1653. The former are, no doubt, due to the violent uprising of the Roman Catholics in Ulster and throughout Ireland, in the Rebellion of 1641-1652. Their purpose was to overthrow English rule, the recovery of their forfeited estates, the extirpation of Protestantism, and the re-establishment of freedom to the Roman Catholics. The cities and towns controlled by Protestants were in a state of siege, particularly in Ulster. The force of the Rebellion fell principally upon the English, especially upon the clergy, and to a lesser degree upon the Scottish Presbyterians. Sir William Petty estimated that 37,000 Protestants were killed in the first year of the Rebellion. Many fled the country or died of privation. The Roman Catholics suffered equally from English and Scottish military attack and from organized reprisals of Protestant citizens. It is little wonder, therefore, that the Registers of Derry Cathedral ceased to be kept during this period. From 1650-1653, Londonderry was in the control of the Commonwealth Officers who were Baptist dissenters. Thus again no records were kept.

Also the following pages are missing from the Registers: Marriages, 14 May—9 September 1658; Baptisms, 24 April—3 November 1661; Baptisms, 27 May—22 February 1664; Baptisms, 21 October—17 March 1671. Gaps in the Marriage records are from 1668-1678, and 1688-1689; the latter, due no doubt to the terrible Siege of Londonderry during the war between James II (Roman Catholic), and William of Orange,

who became William III.   Some pages were cut out from June
1680-February 1681, together with eight other miscellaneous
pages.

The original Derry Cathedral Registers, 1642-1703, and
1703 to the present time, are in the Cathedral vault.   A transcript of the Cathedral Register, 1703-1732, was made by D.
Alexander, Director of Education, who was a graduate of
London University.   These are in two volumes, 1703-1722,
and 1722-1732. They include Baptisms, Marriages and Burials.
A reference Index accompanies them.   All are in the Cathedral vault with the entire collection of original records.

All are of great importance to Americans of Ulster ancestry, as so many people emigrated from Londonderry and the
surrounding counties, especially County Donegal.

The early Dublin Parish Registers, and some miscellaneous
early Registers outside of Dublin, were published together
with the 1642-1703 Registers of Derry Cathedral by the
Parish Register Society of Dublin.   This set of twelve volumes
is listed with other published Registers, later in this chapter.
The published works have been acquired by a number of large
American genealogical libraries and others with Irish collections, and also are in all important repositories of genealogical records in Ireland.

The Dublin Registers do not show a proportionately large
number of surnames of Irish Catholic or Scottish Presbyterian
families, as do the Derry Cathedral Registers.   However, they
do show a generous sprinkling of Irish names with the prefix "O" dropped and a number with it retained.   They also
contain the names of representative families of Norman origin
and a number of clearly Scottish names.

Using the published Registers of St. John the Evangelist,
Dublin, 1619-1699, as an example, we find names with the prefix dropped, of Brian, Carroll, Donald, Dugin, Farrell, Kelly,
Kennedy, Malone, Murphy, Sullivan, etc., as well as O'Caine,
O'Hara, O'Kelle, O'Morran, O'Naughten, etc.   There are also
entries under the names of Fitzgerald, Fitzlaurence, Fitzmaurice, Fitzpatrick, etc., besides the Scottish names which
are quite numerous.

In the Registers of this parish, few place names are given,

while the occupations named are usually in connection with burial records. In the Registers of some other parishes, the Dublin residence is frequently given by street or lane, and other counties of residence are often given, particularly those of the Province of Leinster, in the marriage records.

An especially large number of Irish Catholic names and place names from several counties appear in *The Registers of Provost Winter (Trinity College, Dublin), 1650-1660, and of the Liberties of Cashel (Co. Tipperary), 1654-1657*. Three of the Dublin Parish Registers which have been published contain important lists of people of Dublin at early dates, as follows:

The Registers of St. Catherine, Dublin, 1636-1715, 1908, contain extracts from the "Subsidy Roll, City of Dublin, 1637, showing the Taxation and Assessment of the Inhabitants of the County and City of Dublin ..." The list for "St. Katherine's Parrish" contains 118 entries of names and the amounts of three taxations (pp. 233-235). This tax concerned the more prosperous citizens who were subject to this form of direct taxation. Also "Extracts from the Hearth Money Roll, City of Dublin," 1666-1667, contain the list of every one in this parish who was subject to the tax of 2 shillings for each fire hearth, in his house or on his property. The list, by streets in the parish, is about twice as long as the earlier Subsidy Roll (pp. 236-240).

The Registers of St. John the Evangelist, Dublin, 1619-1699, 1906, pp. 273-275, contain a "List of those rated for Parish Cess in St. John's Parish (Dublin), Feb. 1621," extracted from the Parish Books. This was a Tithe Tax or "Cesse" due the parson of the parish by Act of the State. The names and amount of tax per person are listed by streets and lanes. Another "Cesse for the Parish, 1646," is given (pp. 276-277). The "Cess for Poore of the Parrish, one year ending Easter 1687," is given with the names listed by Wards (pp. 277-279).

The Registers of the Parish of St. Michan, 1636-1700, Dublin, 1909, contain a list of the people assigned seats in the new church, December 1686 (pp. 552-553). Also a list of "Seats named as marking burial places," with page numbers where mentioned in the published Registers (pp. 553-554). Another list of "Tombs and Burial places," with names and page numbers where mentioned (p. 554).

The *Ulster Journal of Archaeology*, 2nd series, 1903 (Special Volume), contains "The Old Enniskillen Vestry Book (1666-1797)," by the Earl of Belmore, pp. 137-187. In this work, the author has used the Parish Vestry Book, together with some notes from the Parish Registers of St. Michan's, Dublin, and of Derryvullan, to combine Birth, Marriage, and Burial entries, tombstone records and miscellaneous source materials, to set forth genealogical records and relationships of County Fermanagh families and their connections in other counties. The families represented, some with brief entries and others with records covering several generations, are those of Armar, Auchenleck, Caldwell, Corry, Cole, Crawford, Dane, Eccles, Gordon, Hamilton, Magee, Smyth, Somerville, with individuals in many allied families also appearing in the records. The names, dates, Arms, etc., on tombstones in the Church and graveyard are listed, with some notes on the families. Members of some who emigrated to Canada or "North America" are mentioned, but not their places of settlement.

An interesting record in the above, touching upon the division of religion in a family, is found in the nuncupative will of John Deane (Dane), made 20 January 1678/9, which includes the following provisional bequests: "And I leave £10 to each of the rest of my children, provided they shall go to church. And to those of my children who goeth to Mass, I leave them only twelve pence apeace." One of the children alluded to "who goeth to Mass" was, no doubt, his daughter Catherine, who died 1733. In her will she left various bequests to named relatives and £3 to Father Edward Maguire, her parish priest . . .; also £2 to the Roman poor of the parish. This entire family is traced.

Before coming to the lists of the Parish Registers in the Republic of Ireland and in Northern Ireland, other records created by the Established Church of Ireland (and some of later dates) are noted below.

Biographical Succession Lists of the Clergy: Published

volumes for various dioceses are listed in VOLUME II, pp. 41-
42; 218-219. These contain lists of the clergy, by diocese and
parish. Some date back to early times. Information varies,
but in numerous instances it contains parentage, birth-place
and date, college matriculation, university degree, dates of
ordination and clerical appointments, marriage, death, as well
as names of wife and children. In some cases genealogical
accounts extending to three or more generations have been
compiled. Notes about each parish are included. Biographical Succession Lists compiled in manuscript for several dioceses, as yet unprinted, are deposited in the Library of the
Church of Ireland Representative Church Body, at 52 St.
Stephen's Green, Dublin. These documents, together with
other materials in this repository, are listed in PART TWO,
CHAPTER III, hereof, under the name of the library. Other
records containing lists of appointments of the clergy, and
descriptions of the parish property, etc., are the "Regal Visitation Books," and the "First Fruit Rolls." These are relatively unimportant genealogical sources. Other libraries containing materials relating to the Established Church of Ireland, with lists of some of their records, will be found in PART
TWO, CHAPTER III, under the names of the Armagh Diocesan
Registry Office, and the Armagh Public Library.

Attention is called to records of the Church of Ireland, which
because of their classification, will appear in later chapters of
this volume and in VOLUME II. These records include some
classes of genealogical materials, relating to adherents of
all church denominations in Ireland, 1536-1858, by virtue of
the ecclesiastical jurisdiction of this Established Church of
Ireland over Probate and Matrimonial matters, in the Prerogative Court and the Consistorial Courts of the twenty-eight
dioceses.

The Wills proved in these courts and also the Administrations of those who died intestate before 1858, so far as the
original records, transcripts, abstracts and indexes exist, will
be described and listed, together with subsequent records, in
CHAPTER XXIII, hereof.

The Marriage Records issued by these courts prior to 1858

will be dealt with, together with other marriage records and vital records, in CHAPTER XXII.

Ecclesiastical Deeds, Leases, and related materials, will be noted among the land records listed in CHAPTER XV.

Records created in the course of obtaining information, for the payment of tithes by the entire population to the Established Church of Ireland, are contained in the Tithe Applotment Books which, pertaining to a Church Tax, will be discussed among other tax records levied for different purposes in CHAPTER XVI.

The histories of the various counties, cities, towns, dioceses and parishes contain a considerable amount of family notes and some more or less extensive compiled genealogies of the families within the area who were important in one way or another. Emphasis on the choice of records varies according to the religious denomination of the authors. Practically all were either members of the Church of Ireland, Presbyterian, or Roman Catholic Church. One of the great and prolific authors of the Church of Ireland wrote the *History of Kilsaran Union of Parishes in the County of Louth* (Dundalk, 1908). The author, the Rev. James B. Leslie, has produced a classic example of a parish history, filled with compiled genealogies and personal records extracted from all classes of original sources, of use in compiling genealogies, dated from early times to the late 19th century. Several of the families whose records are extensive were originally Roman Catholic, and later of the Church of Ireland.

THE PARISH REGISTERS

After the disestablishment of the Church of Ireland took effect on 1 January 1871, the Parochial Records Acts (Ireland), 1875, 1876, required that records of baptism and burial prior to 31 December 1870, and marriages prior to 31 March 1845, should become Public Records. This referred to the records kept in the Parish Registers of the Established Church of Ireland, and did not assume jurisdiction over the Parish Records of the Roman Catholic Church or the Registers of any other church denomination. Thus the above Acts concerned the Parish Registers of 1,643 parishes of the Church of Ireland. All were ordered to be sent to the Public Record Office of Ireland in Dublin, to be under the care of the Master of the Rolls. However, an Amendment to the Acts provided that in cases where evidence could be shown of an adequate place of safe-keeping in the parish (usually a vault in the church), record volumes were allowed to remain in local custody, unattached, or under retention orders.

A complete indexed list of the Parish Registers for all of Ireland was printed in the 28th *Report of the Deputy Keeper of the Public Records in Ireland,* 1896, Appendix II, pp. 57-108. The list, alphabetically arranged by name of the parish, church or chapel, set forth for each the diocese, county, number of volumes of records, and the inclusive dates of the records of baptism, marriage and burial. The size of the print (large or small), and the use of asterisks, denoted their location; in the Public Record Office, in local custody, either unattached or under retention orders.

By this date (1896), the location of deposit of the Parish Registers of the late Established Church of Ireland was well determined, and had changed little, if any, by 1922 when the original Registers of 1,006 parishes of all dioceses in Ireland had been deposited in the Public Record Office, Dublin, and the original Registers of 637 parishes were retained in local custody. Also, it was known in the Public Record Office that many original Registers had been copied in full, by or for the clergy of the various parishes, before the original Registers were sent to Dublin.

In 1922, the great fire destroyed the Registers of all but four parishes of the 1,006 parishes represented by their Registers in this Office. After the fire, this Office sent inquiries to all parishes in the 26 counties of Southern Ireland (now the Republic of Ireland) which had lost Registers in the fire, to discover how many had been copied and had the transcripts in local custody. Replies did not come from all parishes, but 124 reported that full copies of their Registers had been made, and a few others had come to light. Also, it developed that extensive extracts had been copied from a number of other Registers. In addition, the earliest Registers representing 29 parishes had been printed before 1922.

Information regarding all Parish Registers in existence in the 26 counties of the Republic of Ireland, including all original, transcript, and published Registers and collections of extracts taken from Registers, was published as the Public Record Office in Dublin acquired it, in the *Reports of the Deputy Keeper of the Public Records in Ireland*, Dublin, by name of the county, diocese, parish, and dates of the records, as follows:

1. A list of original Parish Registers now destroyed, the records of which were printed before 1922. (55th *Report*, 1928, p. 140.)

2. The Registers of 4 parishes, saved from the fire. (55th *Report*, 1928, p. 99.)

3. The Parochial Returns of 3 parishes, saved from the fire. (*ibid.*)

4. One Parish Register and 7 transcripts of Registers presented. (*ibid.*, pp. 99-100.)

5. Original Registers of 416 parishes, in local custody and under retention orders, after 1922. (*ibid.*, pp. 100-108.)

6. Original Registers of 6 parishes in local custody and unattached, after 1922. (*ibid.*, p. 108.)

7. A list of transcripts of destroyed Registers of 124 parishes, including those in local custody and/or in the Public Record Office. (56th *Report*, 1931, pp. 416-420.)

8. Transcripts of destroyed Registers of 32 parishes, now in the Public Record Office, including the transcripts listed in (4) and some in (7) above. (57th *Report*, p. 566.)

9. A complete list (1951) of original Registers, transcripts of Registers, and Parochial Returns now in the Public Record Office; also collections of extensive extracts from the Registers and similar records from other sources (the complete list duplicating some above). (58th *Report*, 1951, pp. 116-119.)

The inclusive dates of the records in the above *Reports*, 55th-58th, are given only for the original Registers and transcripts of Registers now in this Office. The 55th *Report*, p. 100, refers the reader to the 28th *Report* (1896), to ascertain the inclusive dates of the records of baptism, marriage and burial in the original Registers of 416 parishes which were retained in local custody in the Republic of Ireland. Also one must refer to the 28th *Report* to discover the inclusive dates of the Registers which were transcribed before being sent to Dublin prior to 1922, the transcripts now being in local custody.

This makes a total of ten lists to which one would have to refer, in order to trace all information about the records presently existing in some form in the Republic of Ireland.

The same situation exists in Northern Ireland with regard to information about the existing original Parish Registers in local custody, the transcripts of Registers in local custody, also the original Registers and transcripts of Registers now in the Public Record Office of Northern Ireland, Belfast; all being the Registers of parishes in the six counties of Northern Ireland. Each of the *Reports of the Deputy Keeper* of this Office (1924-1953) contain information known at the time the *Report* was published. In addition, there are Office Lists, copies of which have been sent to this compiler. These contain information about the Registers and transcripts of Registers, supplemental to that in the last *Report*, 1951-1953.

Because of the confusion resulting from many lists printed by both Public Record Offices, the compiler made two consolidated card-indexes; one for the records in the Republic of Ireland, and one for the records in Northern Ireland. Noted on each card is the name of the parish, diocese, county, nature of the records (original, transcript, or extracts), place where deposited, and the inclusive dates of the records of baptism, marriage and burial contained in the Registers. These cards were indexed under the names of the parishes.

The two lists presented below were compiled from the two card-indexes. Thus the existing original Parish Registers, transcripts of Registers, collections of extensive extracts from certain registers, are all listed. In addition, all published Parish Registers are listed at the end of the former, both for the Republic of Ireland and for Northern Ireland. All inclusive dates of the records are taken from information furnished by the Public Record Offices as stated above.

The following lists of the Parish Registers represent the parishes in the 26 counties of the Republic of Ireland, and the parishes of the 6 counties of Northern Ireland. Registers (original, transcript, extracts from, or published) are listed only if they contain entries of baptism and burial prior to 1 January 1871, as by the Act 38 and 39 Vict. c. 59, they were declared to be public records. Registers commenced subsequent to 31 December 1870, were unaffected by the Act, and have all remained in local custody.

A key to the location of the records which will be furnished for each list of the Registers presented below (not published) will make it possible to locate the present place of deposit of the Registers of each parish. Any interested person can personally search the Registers in Ireland, wherever they may be; in local custody, or in one of the Public Record Offices, in Belfast or Dublin. A search of the Registers of any parish may also be commissioned by correspondence.

Mr. Diarmid Coffey, Assistant Deputy Keeper, Public Record Office of Ireland, Dublin, should be contacted for a commissioned search of any Registers deposited in this Office. Instruction for search fees for this Office is given in CHAPTER V, PART TWO, hereof. If the Registers are in local custody and one wishes to commission the local incumbent (rector, vicar or curate) of any parish in the Republic of Ireland to make the search, his name can be acquired from Mr. Coffey, in the Public Record Office, Dublin, for a small fee.

The Ulster-Scot Historical Society, Law Courts Building, Chichester Street, Belfast, Northern Ireland, makes the search of any Registers (transcripts, etc.) in the Public Record Office of Northern Ireland, Belfast. It will also furnish the name of any parish rector, vicar or curate, to whom to write if the Registers are in local custody and no transcripts of them are in the Public Record Office in Belfast.

If anyone wishes to write directly to the local incumbent of a parish, not knowing his name, a letter can be addressed to "The Rector," name of the church, parish, city, town or village, county, Republic of Ireland or Northern Ireland. In this case, one should ask if the incumbent is willing to make the search, give the known names, and ask him to quote his fee for the search. One cannot expect a reply, without a fee, to a question as to whether any records regarding an individual or family, of the right dates, are in his Registers.

This would require a preliminary search on his part and the expense of a reply with no assurance of recompense.

This compiler prefers to obtain the name of the rector, vicar or curate before writing to him. If the inquirer has taken the trouble to obtain his name, it indicates a business-like procedure and not a vague inquiry. This compiler always sends a $5.00 Post Office Money Order with the request for a search. Also assurance is given that if there are numerous records involving much time for the search and report, any necessary additional fee will be sent prior to the time the report is mailed.

Thus, the first rule is to be generous in sending a preliminary fee. The rectors, etc., regard their time as belonging to the people of their parishes. They cannot stand over visitors to guard the Registers while they are being examined, or devote time to research in the Registers and a written report thereof, to please strangers, without some recompense which will be turned over to the parish church. Furthermore, the local incumbents jealously guard their Registers against undue wear from handling.

If a person can go to Ireland, the $5.00 should be sent also, upon making an appointment by letter beforehand with the rector, vicar or curate, to allow a personal examination of the Registers on a specified date and at a certain hour. Otherwise if one arrives unannounced, he might find that the person in authority is away from his home or church. If more than an hour is spent by a visitor in personally examining the Registers, which are seldom indexed, an additional donation should be made at some time during the search, or certainly upon leaving.

Above all, never appear unannounced on a Saturday or a Sunday. This compiler learned this from experience in 1951, when she was denied the opportunity to see the Registers of the Kilcrow Church, in the Parish of Ematris, just out of Rockcorry, Co. Monaghan, on a Sunday. A request for a search of the Parish Registers, dated 1753-1790, and 1811 on, was left, with a fee. It concerned the family of John Clark, a Methodist, who emigrated, at the age of seventeen, in 1832. His Bible record named his parents, two grandfathers, and his town of Rockcorry, Co. Monaghan. Before his emigration, the Wesleyan Methodist Society in Ireland was not yet constituted a church. It was possible the Clark family had belonged to the Established Church. In a month, a written report was received, containing ninety-six entries of baptism, marriage and burial, which concerned four generations, from the time of his great-grandfather's marriage.

In contrast to the above lost opportunity, this compiler profited in 1952 by writing ahead for several planned appointments. Among these was one fixed for a certain day and hour at the rectory of the Rev. R. J. Williamson, Rector of the Church of Clones, County Monaghan. Without delay, this compiler was allowed to accompany him to the church, where he unlocked the vault containing the Registers dating from 1682, and took the beautifully preserved volumes back to his rectory living room. There this compiler was allowed to examine them at her leisure while the Rev. Mr. Williamson engaged in other work near at hand.

Another experience causing much delay occurred when this compiler undertook a plan of research in Ireland in 1955, too late to make a written appointment. In this case, she was in the neighborhood of Ballinrobe, County Mayo, and drove there to see the Parish Registers, only to be told that the Rev. B. D. Willoughby lived 5 miles away, in Hollymount. When his home was located, a wait of over an hour ensued before he returned from a parish call. He then informed this compiler that two keys were necessary to unlock the church vault in Ballinrobe which contained the Registers. The first key was in his possession but the second key was held by a churchwarden in Ballinrobe, who proved to be out of town. A second churchwarden, having access to the key, was finally located after further delay. All of this consumed some four precious hours before the Registers could be seen.

Such time-consuming formalities, which are quite usual for the protection of the records, affect the cost of reports on entries in the Parish Registers, and must be not only understood but taken into consideration when sending a preliminary payment for a search.

In 1955, there were the same formalities with respect to the examination of the Parish Registers of Londonderry Cathedral (St. Columb's), dated 1642-1703, and from that date to the present time. A previous appointment with Mr. T. MaCallum Walker, Librarian of Magee University College Library, and member of the Cathedral Records Commission, paved the way. He received permission from the Rev. L. R. Lawrenson, Dean of the Cathedral, for this compiler to inspect the Registers in his presence and that of a curate. The two sat in an ante-room, next to the vault, and visited while this compiler spent some time over the Registers.

Attention is called to other manuscript and printed sources, concerning parish records of birth, marriage and death (also baptism and burial), for all denominations.

Among the manuscript collections in both Public Record Offices, in Belfast and in Dublin, are numerous ones containing extracts from the Parish Registers regarding the members of a great many families. One such collection is that of Gertrude Thrift, deposited in the Public Record Office, Dublin. It contains extracts from the Parish Registers, made before 1922, of parishes in the City and County of Dublin, and the Counties of Cork, Kerry, Tipperary, Fermanagh, etc. This collection is fully indexed in the *Reports of the Deputy Keeper of the Public Records in Ireland* (see PART TWO, CHAPTER V hereof). *The Government of Northern Ireland Public Record Office, Reports of the Deputy Keeper of the Records,* contain consolidated indexes, alphabetically arranged under surnames and Christian names, listing their documents and records (see PART TWO, CHAPTER VI hereof).

Printed Death Records which contain tombstone inscrip-listed in VOLUME II, pp. 227-228. Attention is especially called to the *Memorials of the Dead: The Journals of the Irish* led to the *Memorials of the Dead: The Journals of the Irish Memorials Association:* formerly the *Association for the Preservation of the Memorials of the Dead in Ireland,* and, in 1937, incorporating the *Dublin Parish Register Society.* Edited by Thomas Ulick Sadleir. Vols. I-XIII, No. 2. 1892-1937. These contain many thousands of tombstone inscriptions throughout Ireland, and include many genealogical notes of from two to several generations. These volumes are deposited in several large genealogical libraries in America, and in all repositories of importance which contain printed or manuscript collections of genealogical records in Ireland.

It is impossible to over-estimate the great resources for genealogical research offered by the Parish Registers of the Church of Ireland, concerning Church of Ireland families, untold numbers of families of dissenters, and numerous Roman Catholic families (mostly converts), from the time of the earliest Registers to the mid-nineteenth century.

LIST OF PARISH REGISTERS OF THE FORMER ESTABLISHED CHURCH OF IRELAND, THE REPUBLIC OF IRELAND

A list of Parish Registers of the parishes of the former Established Church of Ireland, being original Registers, transcripts of Registers, and some extracts from Registers, with the inclusive dates of the existing records.   (This list is compiled with the use of the *Reports of the Deputy Keeper of the Public Records in Ireland,* No. 55 (1928), pp. 100-108; No. 56 (1931), pp. 414-420; No. 57 (1936), pp. 566, 567; No. 58 (1951), pp. 116-119, which *Reports* refer back to the *28th Report,* Appendix II, pp. 57-108, for the inclusive dates of the existing original Registers, now in local custody of the incumbent of the parish, under retention orders.)

Use of the following key will locate the records:

1. Original Registers, now in local custody of the incumbent (rector) of the parish, under retention orders.

2. Transcripts of the Registers, now in local custody of the incumbent of the parish.

3. Original Registers, now deposited in the Public Record Office of Ireland, Four Courts, Dublin.

4. Transcripts of the original Registers, now deposited in the Public Record Office of Ireland, Four Courts, Dublin.

5. Extracts from original Registers, from authoritative sources, now in the Public Record Office of Ireland, Four Courts, Dublin.

Parish	Diocese	County	Baptism	Marriage	Burial
1. Abbeyleix	Leighlin	Leix (Queen's)	1781-1895	1781-1824	1781-1784
2. Abbeymahon	Ross	Cork	1827-to date		
1. Abbeyshrule (see Tashinny)	Ardagh	Westmeath	1821-1875	1821-1848	1821-1875
1. Abbeystrewry	Ross	Cork	1778-1875	1778-1845	1778-1875
1. Abington	Emly	Limerick	1811-1875	1811-1845	1811-1875
1. Achill	Tuam	Mayo	1854-1877		1854-1877
2. Adamstown	Ferns	Wexford	1802-1849 & Registers to date.		
1. Adare	Limerick	Limerick	1804-1875	1804-1875	1804-1875
1, 4. Aghabullog	Cloyne	Cork	1808-1877	1808-1843	1809-1879
1. Aghada	Cloyne	Cork	1815-1875	1815-1845	1815-1875
1. Aghade	Leighlin	Carlow	1740-1877	1740-1856	1740-1877
1. Aghadoe	(Ardfert & (Aghadoe	Kerry	1842-1877	1842-1861	1845-1877
1. Aghadrumsee	Clogher	Monaghan	1821-1870	1821-1851	1822-1870
2. Aghavallin	Ardfert	Kerry		1845-1872	
1. Aghnameadle	Killaloe	Tipperary	1834-1875	1834-1845	1834-1875
1. Aghold	Leighlin	Carlow	1700-1875	1700-1845	1700-1875
2. Ahamplish	Elphin	Sligo	none prior to 1881		
1. Ahanagh & Boyle	Elphin	Sligo	1856-1875 for other entries, see Boyle		
2, 4. Ahascragh	Clonfert, formerly Elphin	Galway	1775-1875	1785-1859	1787-1875
1. All Saints, Newtown Park	Dublin	Dublin	1870-1879		
1. Annagelliffe	Kilmore	Cavan	1804-1875	1804-1845	1804-1860
1. Annagh or Belturbet	Kilmore	Cavan	1801-1870	1801-1845	1801-1870
1. Ardagh	Ardagh	Longford	1811-1875	1811-1845	1811-1875
1. Ardamine	Ferns	Wexford	1807-1875	1807-1868	1807-1875
2. Ardara	Raphoe	Donegal	1829-1877		
1. Ardcanny	Limerick	Limerick	1802-1875		1850-1875
1, 4. Ardcanny & Chapel Russell	Limerick	Limerick	(1802-1848 (1850-1927	(1802-1844 (1845-1920	1849-1940
Vestry book 1852-1867, with entries of births, marriages & deaths					1822-1877
1. Ardcarne	Elphin	Roscommon	1820-1875	1813-1844	1820-1875
1. Ardee	Armagh	Louth	1735-1868	1744-1849	1732-1875
2. Ardfield	Ross	Cork	1835-1881		
2. Ardragh, St. Patrick's	Clogher	Monaghan	1865 to date		1869 to date
1. Ardrahan	Kilmacduagh,	Galway	1804-1892	1804-1857	1804-1888
2, 4. Ashfield	Kilmore	Cavan	1821-1876		
2. Ashfield	Kilmore	Cavan			(1818-1827 (1856-1876
1. Athboy	Meath	Meath	(1736-1748 (1798-1875	(1737-1747 (1799-1845	(1738-1739 (1799-1875
1. Atherny	Tuam	Galway	1796-1877	1796-1846	1795-1877
1. Athlone, St. Mary's	Meath	Westmeath	1746-1875	1746-1845	1746-1849
1. Athy	Glendalough	Kildare	1669-1875	1669-1875	1669-1875
1. Aughagower, (see Westport)	Tuam	Mayo	1825-1875	1828-1846	1828-1875
1. Augher, (see St. Mark)	Clogher	Monaghan	1866-1877		
1. Aughrim	Clonfert	Galway	1814-1875	1814-1844	1814-1875

Parish	Diocese	County	Baptism	Marriage	Burial
3. Baggotrath	Dublin	Dublin	1865-1879		
1. Bailieboro	Kilmore	Cavan	1744-1873	1744-1845	1809-1859
1. Balbriggan	Dublin	Dublin	1838-1875	1838-1871	1821-1871
5. Ballesanona	Cloyne	Cork	1807-1877	1811-1845	1807-1877
(see Mourne Abbey)					
2. Ballinaclash,	Glendalough	Wicklow	1839-1877	1843-1851	1842-1877
1. Ballinacourty,	Tuam	Galway	1838-1874	——	
1. Ballinakill	Tuam	Galway	1852-1875		1852-1875
1. Ballinakill,	Clonfert	Galway	(1766-1875	(1762-1849	(1800-1875
& Lickmolassy			(1775-1874	(1792-1844	(1802-1872
2. Ballincholla,	Tuam	Mayo	1831-1838	1831-1838	1831-1838
(the Neale)					
5, 2, 4. Ballingarry	Cashel	Tipperary	1816-1818		
1. Ballingarry	Limerick	Limerick	1785-1878	1786-1866	1785-1878
1. Ballinrobe	Tuam	Mayo	1796-1875	1796-1845	1796-1875
1. Ballintemple	Cashel	Tipperary	1805-1875	1805-1850	1805-1875
1. Ballintemple	Glendalough	Wicklow	1823-1855	1823-1854	1848
(see Castlemacadam)					
1. Ballybay	Clogher	Monaghan	1813-1876	1813-1845	1813-1876
2. Ballyboy, or	Meath	Offaly (King's)	1796-1883	1796-1845	1800-1883
Frankford					(extracts)
1. Ballycanew	Ferns	Wexford	1733-1875	1733-1859	1733-1875
1. Ballycarney	Ferns	Wexford	1835-1884	1836-1883	1836-1884
5. Ballyclough	Cloyne	Cork	1795-1899	1795-1899	1795-1899
3. Ballyclough	Cloyne	Cork	1831-1900	1831-1848	1831-1900
1. Ballydehob	Cork	Cork	1826-1875	——	
(Chapel of Ease to Scull)					
1. Ballyfinn	Leighlin	Leix (Queen's)	1821-1875	1821-1845	1821-1875
(see Clonenagh)					
1. Ballyhay	Cloyne	Cork	1728-1875	1728-1845	1728-1875
5. Ballyhooly	Cloyne	Cork	1788-1892	1788-1892	1788-1892
1. Ballymacelligot,	Ardfert	Kerry	1817-1875	1817-1875	1817-1875
1. Ballymachugh	Ardagh	Cavan	1816-1876	1815-1847	1816-1875
5, 2. Ballymaglasson,	Meath	Meath	1800-1850	1800-1850	1800-1850
			(notes)	(notes)	(notes)
4. Ballymartel	Cork	Cork	1799-1868		1800-1876
2. Ballymartel	Cork	Cork	1785-1877	1761-1847	1785-1876
2. Ballymascanlon,	Armagh	Louth	1808-1817	1808-1817	1808-1817
1. Ballymodan	Cork	Cork	1695-1876	1695-1845	1695-1876
2. Ballymoney	Cork	Cork	1805-1876	1805-1853	1805-1877
1. Ballymore-Eustace	Glendalough	Kildare	1838-1879	1840-1865	1832-1879
1. Ballynacourty,	Ardfert	Kerry	1803-1877	1803-1845	1803-1877
(see also Kilflynn)					
2. Ballynure	Leighlin	Wicklow	1807, 1815-79	1807-59, '71	1807, '18-'78
1. Ballysax	Kildare	Kildare	1830-1878	1830-1859	1834-1877
1. Ballyseedy	Ardfert	Kerry	1830-1878		1831-1878
1. Ballysakerry	Killala	Mayo	1802-1875	1802-1845	1802-1875
1. Ballysumaghan	Elphin	Sligo	1828-1870	1828-1845	1828-1875
2. Barragh	Leighlin	Carlow	1831-1879	1845-1879	1838-1879
1. Bective	Meath	Meath	1853-1875		1853-1875
1. Belturbet	Kilmore	Cavan	1801-1870	1801-1845	1801-1870
(Annagh)					
1. Berehaven	Ross	Cork	1787-1875	1787-1845	1787-1875
1. Billis	Kilmore	Cavan	1840-1875	——	

Parish	Diocese	County	Baptism	Marriage	Burial
1. Birr	Killaloe	Offaly (King's)	1772-1875	1772-1845	1772-1875
2. Blackrath	Ossory	Kilkenny	1810-1833	1810-1833	1810-1833
1. Blackrock, St. Michael	Cork	Cork	1828-1875	1828-1845	1828-1875
1. Blackrock (see Carysfort)	Dublin	Dublin	1855-1878	———	———
1. Blesinton	Glendalough	Wicklow	1695-1878	1683-1878	1683-1878
1. Booterstown	Dublin	Dublin	1824-1875	1824-1845	———
1. Borrisnafarney	Killaloe	Tipperary & Offaly (King's)	1827-1878	1827-1851	1827-1878
1. Boyle	Elphin	Roscommon	1793-1875	1793-1845	1793-1875
1. Bray	Dublin	Wicklow	1666-1875	1666-1845	1666-1875
2, 4. Bridgetown & Kilcummer, also see Castletownroche	Cloyne	Cork	1856-1871	1856-1871	1856-1871
1. Brigown	Cloyne	Cork	1775-1875	1775-1845	1775-1875
2. Brinny	Cork	Cork	1797-1876	1797-1847	1797-1877
1. Bruff	Limerick	Limerick	1850-1875	———	1859-1875
1. Bunlin	Elphin	Roscommon	1811-1875	1811-1845	1811-1874
1. Burt	Derry	Donegal	1802-1875	1802-1845	1802-1875
2. Buttevant	Cloyne	Cork	———	———	1870-1878
5. Buttevant	Cloyne	Cork	1757-1876	1757-1876	1757-1876
1. Caheragh	Cork	Cork	1836-1875	1835-1845	1835-1875
2. Cahernarry	Limerick	Limerick	1857-1877	———	———
1. Cahir	Lismore	Tipperary	1801-1873	1802-1845	1804-1877
2. Cappamore & Tuogh	Emly	Limerick	1858-1877	———	1859-1877
1. Cappoquin	Lismore	Waterford	1844-1875	———	———
1. Carbery	Kildare	Kildare	1814-1870	1814-1845	1814-1870
1. Carlow	Leighlin	Carlow	1744-1875	1744-1845	1744-1875
5. Carne	Ferns	Wexford	———	———	1815-1876
1. Carnew	Ferns	Wexford	1749-1875	1749-1845	1749-1875
1. Carrick	Lismore	Tipperary	1803-1875	1803-1845	1803-1875
1. Carrickmacross or Magheross	Clogher	Monaghan	1796-1875	1798-1846	1798-1875
1. Carrigaline	Cork	Cork	(1723-1756 (1808-1875	(1723-1756 (1808-1845	(1723-1756 (1808-1875
5. Carrigamleary	Cloyne	Cork	1779-1881	1779-1881	1779-1881
5. Carrig Park	Cloyne	Cork	1779-1881	1779-1881	1779-1881
2, 4. Carrigtwohill	Cloyne	Cork	(1776-1844 (1863-1877	1779-1844	1776-1843
1. Carysfort (Blackrock)	Dublin	Dublin	1855-1878	———	———
1. Cashel (St. John Baptist)	Cashel	Tipperary	———	1654-1657	———
2. Castlane (Whitechurch)	Ossory	Kilkenny	———	1846-1919	———
1. Castleblayney (Mucknoe)	Clogher	Monaghan	1810-1874	1810-1845	1810-1870
1. Castlecarbery (Carbery)	Kildare	Kildare	1814-1870	1814-1845	1814-1870
1. Castlecomer & (Castlecomer Colliery)	Ossory	Kilkenny	1799-1881	1799-1845	1799-1881
1. Castleisland	Ardfert	Kerry	1835-1877	1836-1876	1836-1875
1. Castlejordan	Meath	Offaly (King's)	1823-1874	1823-1845	1823-1874

Parish	Diocese	County	Baptism	Marriage	Burial
1. Castleknock & Clonsilla	Dublin	Dublin	1709-1875	(1710-1740 (1768-1845	(1709-1742 (1772-1875
1. Castlemacadam (Ovoca)	Glendalough	Wicklow	1720-1886	1720-1860	1720-1886
5. Castlemagner	Cloyne	Cork	1810-1906	1810-1906	1810-1906
2, 4 Castlerickard	Meath	Meath	1869-1877	———	———
1. Castleterra	Kilmore	Cavan	1800-1877	1785-1845	1820-1877
1. Castletown	Leighlin	Leix (Queen's)	1802-1876	1802-1864	1802-1876
1. Castletownarra	Killaloe	Tipperary	1802-1875	1802-1846	1802-1875
3. Castletownroche	Cloyne	Cork	1728-1804	1728-1804	1733-1804
2. Castletownroche	Cloyne	Cork	1842-1876	1842-1877	1845-1870
5. Castletownroche	Cloyne	Cork	1727-1844	1727-1844	1727-1844
4. Castletownroche	Cloyne	Cork	1842-1928	———	———
2. Castleventry	Ross	Cork	1872-date	———	———
1. Celbridge or Kildrought	Glendalough	Kildare	1777-1881	1779-1843	1787-1882
1. Chapelizod	Dublin	Dublin	1812-1875	1812-1845	1812-1875
1, 4. Chapelrussell & Ardcanny	Limerick	Limerick	See Ardcanny		
1. Charlestown	Armagh	Louth	1822-1875	1822-1845	1822-1875
1, 5. Christ Church Cathedral, Dublin	Dublin	Dublin	Portion of Acta Capituli, 1574-1591		
1. Christ Church Cathedral, Dublin	Dublin	Dublin	(1740-1838 (1860-1886	1717-1826	1710-1866
1. Christ Church, Kingston (see Kingston)	Dublin	Dublin	1852-1879	———	———
1. Christ Church, Leeson Park	Dublin	Dublin	1867-1879	———	———
5. Christ Church, (see Holy Trinity)	Cork	Cork	1643-1868	1643-1868	1643-1868
1. Christ Church, (Rushbrook)	Cloyne	Cork	1806-1876	———	———
5. Churchtown	Cloyne	Cork	1806-1872	1806-1872	(1806-1872 (1835-1877
1. Clane	Kildare	Kildare	1802-1875	1802-1845	1802-1875
5. Clenore	Cloyne	Cork	1813-1876	1814-1842	1814-1865
3. Clogherny	Armagh	Tyrone	3/13/1859-2/27/1875	———	———
2. Clogran	Dublin	Dublin	1782-1852	1738-1852	1732-1852
4. Clogran	Dublin	Dublin	1782-1870	1738-1839	1732-1870
1. Clonard	Meath	Meath	1792-1880	1793-1876	1793-1880
1. Clonbroney	Ardagh	Longford	1821-1876	1821-1845	1821-1876
1. Clondalkin	Dublin	Dublin	1728-1875	1728-1845	1728-1875
1. Clondevaddock	Raphoe	Donegal	1794-1875	1794-1843	1794-1875
2. Clondrohid	Cloyne	Cork	———	1840-1875	———
1. Clonegal	Ferns	Wexford	1792-1875	1792-1845	1792-1875
1. Clonegam	Lismore	Waterford	1741-1875	1742-1845	1743-1875
1. Clonenagh	Leighlin	Leix (Queens)	1749-1875	1749-1845	1749-1875
1. Clones	Clogher	Monaghan	1682-1873	1682-1860	1682-1873
2. Cloneyhurke	Kildare	Offaly (King's)	(1824-1847 (1868-1878	———	(1834-1847 (1868-1878
5. Clonfert (or Newmarket)	Cloyne	Cork	1771-1875	1771-1844	1771-1875
1. Clongish	Ardagh	Longford	1820-1875	1820-1844	1820-1875
2. Clonmacnoise	Meath	Offaly (King's)	1828-1874	1845-date	1818-1877

Parish	Diocese	County	Baptism	Marriage	Burial
5. Clonmeen & Roskeen	Cloyne	Cork	1764-1881	1764-1881	1764-1850
1. Clonmel (Queenstown)	Cloyne	Cork	1761-1875	1761-1845	1761-1875
1. Clonmel (see St. Mary)	Lismore	Tipperary	1766-1874	1766-1845	1766-1873
2, 4. Clonmore	Ferns	Wexford	1828-1876		
2. Clonmore	Leighlin	Carlow		1845-date	
2. Clonmore	Ossory	Kilkenny	1817-1906	1845-1870	1822-1901
4. Clonmore	Ossory	Kilkenny	1817-1906		1822-1901
1. Clonoulty	Cashel	Tipperary	1817-1875	1818-1841	1817-1875
4. Clonpriest (see Killeagh)	Cloyne	Cork		1851-1870	
1. Clonsilla (also see Castleknock)	Dublin	Dublin	1830-1875	1831-1844	1831-1875
1. Clontarf	Dublin	Dublin	1807-1875	1811-1852	1812-1875
1. Cloonsast	Kildare	Kildare	1805-1875	1805-1845	1805-1875
2. Cloontibret	Clogher	Monaghan	1864-1865		1864-1865
1. Clough	Clogher	Monaghan	1811-1879	1811-1846	1811-1879
1. Cloughjordan	Killaloe	Tipperary	1827-1875	1827-1845	1827-1848
1. Cloyne	Cloyne	Cork	1708-1878	1708-1862	1708-1878
1. Collinstown	Meath	Westmeath	1838-1875	1838-1851	
1. Collon	Armagh	Louth	1790-1875	1790-1845	1790-1875
1. Cong	Tuam	Mayo	1811-1875	1811-1845	1811-1872
1. Coolbanagher	Kildare	Leix (Queen's)	1802-1870	1802-1845	1802-1870
1. Coolock	Dublin	Dublin	1760-1875	1760-1845	1760-1875
1. Cork (Holy Trinity, or Christ Church)	Cork	Cork	(1643-1666 (1708-1877	(1644-1665 (1721-1845	(1644-1668 (1732-1870
1. Cork (St. Luke)	Cork	Cork	1837-1875	1837-1845	
1. Cork (St. Nicholas)	Cork	Cork	1721-1875	1721-1845	1721-1873
1. Corkbeg	Cloyne	Cork	1836-1875	1836-1845	1836-1875
1. Creagh & Taughmaconnell	Clonfert	Galway	1823-1875	1823-1845	1823-1875
1. Croghan	Elphin	Roscommon	1862-1876		1860-1876
1. Crossmolina Records in Diocesan Register	Killala	Mayo	(1768-1777 (1802-1875	(1769-1777 (1802-1844	(1768-1777 (1802-1875
1. Crosspatrick & Kilcommon	Ferns	Wicklow	1830-1879	1830-1867	1830-1867
2, 4. Crumlin	Dublin	Dublin	(8/24/1740- (12/27/1830 (1823-1863	(1764-1827 (1832-1863	(1740-1862 (1831-1862
1. Cullen	Emly	Tipperary	1770-1875	1770-1845	1770-1875
1. Currin	Clogher	Monaghan	1810-1877	1812-1848	1810-1877
1. Currin Drum	Clogher	Monaghan	1828-1875	1828-1845	1828-1875
1. Delgany (see Newcastle)	Glendalough	Wicklow	1666-1876	1666-1845	1666-1876
1. Delvin	Meath	Westmeath	1817-1875	1817-1845	1817-1875
1. Desertsarges	Cork	Cork	1837-1875	1837-1845	1837-1875
1. Dingle	Ardfert	Kerry	1707-1875	1707-1845	1707-1875
1. Donabate	Dublin	Dublin	1811-1875	1811-1845	1811-1875
1. Donagh	Clogher	Monaghan	1796-1876	1796-1845	1796-1875
1. Donegal	Raphoe	Donegal	1803-1875	1803-1845	1803-1875
1. Doneraile	Cloyne	Cork	1730-1876	1730-1845	1730-1875
5. Doneraile	Cloyne	Cork	1731-1904	1731-1904	1731-1904

Parish	Diocese	County	Baptism	Marriage	Burial
1. Donnybrook (see St. Mary's)	Dublin	Dublin	1712-1870	1712-1858	1712-1872
1. Donoghmore	Glendalough	Kildare	1777-1881	1779-1843	1787-1882
1. Donohill	Cashel	Tipperary	1856-1876	————	1859-1879
2, 4. Doon (with genealogical notes)	Cashel & Emly	Limerick	1804-1877	1812-1845	1812-1873
1. Douglas	Cork	Cork	1792-1875	1792-1845	1792-1875
5. Drishane	Ardfert	Cork	1792-1877	1792-1847	1793-1876
1. Drogheda, St. Peter	Armagh	Louth	1654-1875 (1747-1772 Register in P. R. O., Dublin)	1654-1845	1654-1875
1. Dromdaleague	Cork	Cork	1812-1875	1812-1844	1812-1875
5. Dromkariff	Ardfert	Cork	1825-1878	1825-1872	1825-1874
2, 4. Dromod & Prior,	Ardfert	Kerry	————	1827-1842	————
5. Dromtariff	Ardfert	Cork	1825-1878	1828-1872	1828-1879
4. Drumcliff (Baptismal records have 5 gaps of a few days each)	Elphin	Sligo	1805-1887	(1805-1834 (1845-1866	1805-1858
1. Drumcliff	Killaloe	Clare	(1744-1748 (1785-1875	(1744-1748 (1785-1845	(1744-1748 (1785-1869
2. Drumcliff	Killaloe	Clare	1805-1879	(1805-1833 (1846-1879	1805-1858
1. Drumconrath	Meath	Meath	1799-1875	1822-1845	1822-1875
2, 4. Drumcree	Meath	Westmeath	1816-1875	————	1816-1881
1. Drumgoon	Kilmore	Cavan	(1802-1814 (1825-1875	(1802-1814 (1825-1845	1858-1875
1. Drumhoem	Raphoe	Donegal	1691-1873	1691-1846	1691-1869
1. Drumlease	Kilmore	Leitrim	1828-1875	1828-1845	1828-1875
1. Drumsnat	Clogher	Monaghan	1825-1875	1825-1847	1825-1875
1. Drummully	Clogher	Monaghan	1802-1873	1812-1845	1812-1875
1. Drung	Kilmore	Cavan	1785-1875	1785-1845	1785-1875
1. Dugort	Tuam	Mayo	1838-1875	1838-1854	1838-1875
1. Dundalk	Armagh	Louth	1729-1875	1755-1845	1727-1875
2. Dunderrow	Cork	Cork	———— 1811, 1815, 1818 ————		
1. Dunganstown	Glendalough	Dublin	1783-1875	1783-1856	1783-1875
3. Dungarvan	Lismore	Waterford	1741-1875	1778-1845	1823-1875
1. Dunkerrin	Killaloe & Offaly	Tipperary	1800-1875	1800-1845	1852-1875
1. Dunlavin	Glendalough	Wicklow	1697-1879	1698-1844	1698-1879
1. Dunleckney	Leighlin	Carlow	1791-1876	1791-1845	1791-1876
2. Dunmore	Ossory	Kilkenny	————	1857-1875	
2. Dunshaughlin	Meath	Meath	1800-1850 (notes)	1800-1850 (notes)	1800-1850 (notes)
1. Durrow	Meath	Offaly (King's)	1816-1876	1816-1845	1816-1876
5. Durrow	Ossory	Leix (Queen's)	1731-1841	1731-1836	1731-1836
1. Easkey	Killala	Sligo	1822-1875	1822-1845	1822-1875
1. Eastersnow	Elphin	Roscommon	1800-1875	1800-1845	1800-1875
1. Ematris	Clogher	Monaghan	(1753-1790 (1811-1875	(1753-1790 (1811-1844	(1753-1790 (1811-1875
1. Emlafad	Achonry	Sligo	1831-1875	1831-1845	1831-1875
1. Enniscorthy (St. Mary's)	Ferns	Wexford	1798-1872	1798-1852	1798-1875
2. Errigle-Portclare (St. Mary's)	Clogher	Tyrone	1845-1881	————	————
2. Errigle-Trough	Clogher	Monaghan & Tyrone	1809-1879	1803-1848	1802-1877

Parish	Diocese	County	Baptism	Marriage	Burial
1. Ettagh	Killaloe	Offaly (King's)	1825-1875	1826-1868	1826-1875
1. Fahan, Upper	Derry	Donegal	1761-1875	1831-1860	1831-1875
4. Fanlobbus (Dunmanway)	Cork	Cork	1855-1871	———— (1 entry 1872)	1855-1871
5. Farahy (Farrihy)	Cloyne	Cork	1765-1877	1784-1845	1810-1871
4. Fedamore	Limerick	Limerick	1840-1891	————	————
1. Fenagh	Leighlin	Carlow	1809-1875 (few entries, 1796-1800, bapt., m., bu.)	1809-1845	1809-1875
2. Ferbane	Meath	Offaly (King's)	1819-1875	1845-date	1821-1857 1874-1876
2. Fiddown	Ossory	Kilkenny	————	1845-1886	————
1. Fermoy	Cloyne	Cork	1801-1874	1801-1845	1801-1874
1. Ferns & Kilbride	Ferns	Wexford	1775-1878	1775-1876	1875-1878
1. Fertagh	Ossory	Kilkenny	1797-1875	1797-1845	1797-1875
1. Fethard	Cashel	Tipperary	1804-1875	1804-1845	1804-1875
5. Fiddown (Rathkearan)	Ossory	Kilkenny	1686-1877	1686-1875	1690-1870
1. Finner	Clogher	Donegal	1815-1878	1815-1845	1815-1872
1. Forgney	Meath	Longford	1803-1875	1804-1871	1804-1875
2. Gallen	Meath	Offaly (King's)	1842-1869	————	————
1. Galway, St. Nicholas	Tuam	Galway	1782-1876	**1792-1845**	1838-1876
2, 4. Garrane—Kinnefeake	Cloyne	Cork	1856-1882	————	————
5. Gaulskill & Dunkitt & Kilcollum	Ossory	Kilkenny	1753-1870	1753-1860	1764-1877
1. Geashill	Kildare	Offaly (Kings)	1713-1875	1713-1845	1713-1875
1. Glanely	Glendalough	Wicklow	1825-1875	1825-1845	1825-1875
5. Glanworth	Cloyne	Cork	1805-1877	1805-1877	1805-1877
1. Glasnevin	Dublin	Dublin	1778-1875	1778-1845	1778-1875
1. Glascarrigg	Ferns	Wexford	1807-1875	1807-1845	1807-1875
2. Glencolumbkille	Raphoe	Donegal	1827-1876	1845-date	1827-1877
2, 4. Glengariffe (Holy Trinity)	Ross	Cork	1863-1906	————	————
2. Glenties	Raphoe	Donegal	————	1829-1845	1830-1852
1. Gorey	Ferns	Wexford	1801-1876	1801-1845	1867-1876
1. Graigue	Leighlin	Kilkenny	1827-1868	1827-1845	1827-1868
1. Granard	Ardagh	Longford	1820-1875	1820-1844	1820-1875
2. Grangesylvae	Leighlin	Kilkenny	————	1850, 55, 60	————
2. Hacketstown	Leighlin	Carlow	————	1845-1912	————
1. Harristown	Kildare	Kildare	1666-1875	1666-1845	1666-1875
1. Holmpatrick	Dublin	Dublin	1779-1875	1779-1845	1779-1875
2. Holy Cross	Cashel	Tipperary	1784-1875	1784-1845	1786-1876
1. Holy Trinity (or Christ Church)	Cork	Cork	(1643-1666 (1708-1877	(1644-1665 (1721-1845	(1644-1668 (1732-1870
1. Holy Trinity, Rathmines	Dublin	Dublin	1850-1875	————	————
1. Howth	Dublin	Dublin	1804-1877	1803-1871	1807-1875
3. Inch	Glendalough	Wexford	1726-1876	1726-1876	1726-1876
1. Inniscaltra	Killaloe	Galway	1851-1875	————	1851-1875
1. Inniscarra	Cloyne	Cork	1820-1882	1820-1844	1820-1882
1. Innishannon	Cork	Cork	(1693-1764 (1788-1876	(1693-1764 (1788-1845	(1693-1764 (1788-1876

Parish	Diocese	County	Baptism	Marriage	Burial
1. Inniskeel	Raphoe	Donegal	1826-1875	1827-1844	1852-1875
5. Innislonagh	Lismore	Tipperary & Waterford	1801-1877	1800-1846	1805-1878
1. Innismacsaint	Clogher	Fermanagh	Parochial returns, 1660-1866		
1. Innistiogue	Ossory	Kilkenny	1797-1875	1797-1875	1797-1875
1. Inver	Raphoe	Donegal	1805-1871	1805-1845	1827-1875
1. Irishtown (see St. Matthew, Ringsend)	Dublin	Dublin	1812-1876	————	1812-1872
1. Jonesborough	Armagh	Louth	1812-1875	1824-1833	1826-1875
5. Kanturk	Cloyne	Cork	1818-1877	1818-1877	1818-1877
1. Kells	Meath	Meath	1773-1875	1773-1845	1773-1875
1. Kenmare	Ardfert	Kerry	1799-1873	1799-1845	1799-1876
1. Kenure	Dublin	Dublin	1867-1875	————	1867-1875
1. Kilbarron	Raphoe	Donegal	1785-1875	1785-1845	1785-1875
5. Kilbecon	Ossory	Kilkenny	1813-1883	1827-1835	1815-1882
2, 1. Kilbixy	Meath	Westmeath	1843-1928	1848-1928	————
5. Kilbolane & Knocktemple	Cloyne	Cork	1779-1881	1779-1881	1779-1881
1. Kilbride	Ferns	Wexford	1775-1878	1775-1878	1775-1878
1. Kilbride (Tullamore)	Meath	Offaly (King's)	1811-1877	1807-1861	1812-1877
5. Kilbrin & Liscarrol	Cloyne	Cork	1805-1899	1805-1845	1805-1898
1. Kilbrogan	Cork	Cork	1752-1872	1753-1845	1707-1875
1. Kilbryan	Elphin	Roscommon	1852-1875	————	————
2. Kilcar	Raphoe	Donegal	1819-1877	1819-1843	1818-1875
2. Kilcolgan	Kilmacduagh	Galway	1847-date	1850-date	1850-date
5. Kilcollym	Ossory	Kilkenny	1817-1906	1845-1870	1822-1901
1. Kilcolman	Ardfert	Kerry	1802-1875	1802-1845	1802-1875
1. Kilcommick	Ardagh	Longford	1795-1875	1795-1845	1795-1875
1. Kilcommon	Ferns	Wicklow	1814-1879	1814-1864	1814-1879
1. Kilcullen	Glendalough	Kildare	1778-1880	1819-1839	1779-1879
5. Kilcummer	Cloyne	Cork	1856-1871	1856-1871	1856-1871
1. Kilcummin	Tuam	Galway	1812-1876	1813-1845	1814-1876
2. Kildallon	Kilmore	Cavan	1856-1860	————	————
1. Kildare	Kildare	Kildare	1801-1876	1801-1845	1801-1876
2. Kildimo	Limerick	Limerick	1809-1894	1809-1844	1809-1893
1. Kildrumferton	Kilmore	Cavan	1801-1875	1801-1852	1803-1875
1. Kilfergus & Kilmoylan	Limerick	Limerick	1812-1875	1812-1843	1812-1875
1. Kilfinane	Limerick	Limerick	1804-1875	1804-1845	1804-1875
1. Kilflyn & Particles	Limerick	Limerick	1813-1875	1813-1845	1813-1875
2. Kilflynn	Ardfert	Kerry	1878-date	————	————
1. Kilgarvan	Ardfert	Kerry	1811-1875	1811-1845	1811-1875
2, 5. Kilglass	Elphin	Roscommon	1823-1842	1823-1840	1825-1842
1. Kilgobbin	Ardfert	Kerry	(1713-1754 (1806-1875	(1713-1754 (1806-1845	(1713-1754 (1806-1875
1. Kilkeedy	Limerick	Limerick	1799-1875	1799-1845	1799-1875
1. Kilkeevin	Elphin	Roscommon	1748-1875	1748-1844	1748-1875
1. Kilkenny (see St. Canice)	Ossory	Kilkenny	1789-1878	1789-1869	1789-1878
1. Kilkenny	Meath	Westmeath	1783-1875	1783-1845	1784-1875
1. Kill	Kildare	Kildare	1814-1870	1814-1845	1814-1870

Parish	Diocese	County	Baptism	Marriage	Burial
2. Killaghtee	Raphoe	Donegal	1810-1830	1814-1831	1809 (Bans)
1. Killala	Killala	Mayo	1757-1875	1757-1845	1757-1875
1. Killaloe	Killaloe	Clare	1679-1876	1679-1845	1679-1875
1. Killanne	Ferns	Wexford	1771-1875	1771-1845	1771-1875
1. Killanney	Clogher	Monaghan & Louth	1825-1875	1825-1875	1825-1875
2. Killannin	Tuam	Galway	1844-1877	———	
2. Killanully	Cork	Cork	1831-1877		1836-1877
1. Killashee	Ardagh	Longford	1771-1875	1771-1845	1771-1875
1. Killea	Waterford	Waterford	1816-1886	1816-1845	1816-1886
4. Killeagh	Cloyne	Cork	1782-1880	1776-1879 (also see Clonpriest)	1782-1884
1. Killeban	Leighlin	Leix (Queen's)	1802-1875	1802-1864	1802-1875
1. Killeevan	Clogher	Monaghan	1811-1875	1811-1845	1811-1875
1. Killegney	Ferns	Wexford	1800-1876	1800-1845	1800-1876
1, 4. Killeigh	Kildare	Offaly (King's)	(1808-1835 (1835-1875	(1808-1835 (1835-1845	(1808-1835 (1835-1875
1. Killeshandra	Kilmore	Cavan	1735-1866	1735-1840	1735-1875
1. Killesherdiney	Kilmore	Cavan	1810-1876	1810-1845	1810-1876
1. Killeshin	Leighlin	Carlow	1824-1876	1824-1845	1824-1875
1. Killeney	Ferns	Wexford	1788-1875	———	1788-1875
1. Killesk (see Holy Trinity)	Dublin	Dublin	1829-1878	———	1829-1878
3. Killinick Union	Ferns	Wexford	10/16/1804- 7/30/1820	7/23/1804- 8/3/1820	8/24/1805- 9/9/1819
2. Killiskey	Glendalough	Wicklow	1818-1877	1818-1844 (0) 1846-1900	1824-1876
4. Killochonagan	Meath	Meath	1853-1877	1853-1862	1853-1863; 1877
1. Killoughter	Kilmore	Cavan	1827-1875	1827-1845	1827-1875
2. Killowen	Cork	Cork	1833-1875	———	1851-1875
1. Kill St. Nicholas	Waterford	Waterford	1730-1875	1730-1845	1730-1875
1. Killucan	Meath	Westmeath	1700-1874	1787-1856	1700-1875
1. Killurin	Ferns	Wexford	1816-1879	1798-1865	1816-1879
2. Killury & Rattoo	Ardfert	Kerry	1867-date	———	
1. Killybegs	Raphoe	Donegal	(1787-1796 (1809-1875	(1809-1875	(1809-1875
2. Kilmacduagh	Kilmacduagh	Galway	1874-date		
5. Kilmacow	Ossory	Kilkenny	1792-1876	1805-1864	1803-1877
1. Kilmactranny	Elphin	Sligo	1816-1875	1816-1845	1816-1875
1- Kilmainemore	Tuam	Mayo	(1744-1778 (1821-1845	(1744-1778 (1821-1845	(1774-1778 (1821-1875
1. Kilmainham (see St. Jude)	Dublin	Dublin	1857-1876	———	———
1. Kilmallog	Ferns	Wexford	1813-1873	1813-1874	1813-1870
1. Kilmanagh	Ossory	Kilkenny	1784-1875	1784-1845	1784-1875
1. Kilmeadan	Waterford	Waterford	1683-1875	1683-1844	1683-1874
1. Kilmeen	Ross	Cork	1806-1876	1806-1845	1844-1876
1. Kilmoganny	Ossory	Kilkenny	1782-1875	1782-1873	1782-1875
1. Kilmore	Clogher	Monaghan	1796-1875	1796-1845	1796-1874
1. Kilmore	Kilmore	Cavan	1702-1872	1702-1845	1702-1875
2, 5. Kilmore	Meath	Meath	1800-1850	1800-1850	1800-1850

Parish	Diocese	County	Baptism	Marriage	Burial
1. Kilmoremoy	Killala	Mayo	1801-1875	1801-1866	1801-1875
			Earlier entries in Vestry Book, 1768-1792		
1. Kilmoylan	Limerick	Limerick	1812-1875	1812-1843	1812-1875
1. Kilnasoolagh	Killaloe	Clare	1731-1875	1731-1844	1731-1875
1. Kilnaughtin	Ardfert	Kerry	1793-1875	1793-1845	1793-1874
1. Kilnehue	Ferns	Wexford	1817-1875	1817-1845	1817-1875
1. Kilpipe	Ferns	Wexford	1828-1875	1825-1845	1833-1875
2. Kilrosanty	Lismore	Waterford	1838-1877	1838-1877	1838-1877
1. Kilrush	Killaloe	Clare	1773-1876	1773-1845	1773-1876
			Vol. 1, has some entries back to 1741		
1. Kilsallaghan	Dublin	Dublin	1818-1875	1818-1845	1818-1875
1. Kilscannell					
(see Rathkeale)	Limerick	Limerick	(1746-1780	(1746-1780	(1746-1780
			(1804-1875	(1804-1845	(1804-1875
1. Kilshannig	Cloyne	Cork	1731-1875	1731-1845	1731-1875
1. Kilteevogue	Raphoe	Donegal	1818-1879	————	1825-1857
1. Kiltennell	Ferns	Wexford	1806-1875	1806-1875	1806-1875
1. Kiltennell	Leighlin	Carlow	1837-1875	1837-1875	1838-1875
1. Kilternan	Dublin	Dublin	1817-1880	1817-1866	1817-1880
			See Bray, for earlier records.		
1. Kiltoghart	Ardagh	Leitrim	1810-1875	1810-1845	1810-1875
1. Kiltoom	Elphin	Roscommon	1797-1872	1797-1844	1797-1873
1. Kiltullagh	Tuam	Roscommon	1822-1875	1822-1875	1822-1875
1. Kilwatermoy	Lismore	Waterford	1860-1875 (earlier rec. in Tallow Reg.)		
5. Kilworth	Cloyne	Cork	1776-1886	1776-1886	1776-1886
1. Kingstown	Dublin	Dublin	(See Christ Church and Mariner's Church)		
2. Kinneigh	Cork	Cork	1795-1876	1814-1844	1795-1876
2, 5. Kinnitty	Killaloe	Offaly (King's)	1800-1877	1801-1845	1802-1877
1. Kinsale	Cork	Cork	1684-1875	1688-1864	1685-1875
2. Kinsalebeg	Lismore	Waterford	————	1848-date	————
1. Knappagh	Tuam	Mayo	1855-1875		1855-1875
2. Knockavilly	Cork	Cork	1837-date	1844-date	————
1. Knockbride	Kilmore	Cavan	1825-1875	1825-1845	1825-1875
2, 5. Knockmark	Meath	Meath	1825-1874	1837-1874	1825-1875
1. Knocknarea	Elphin	Sligo	1842-1875	————	1842-1875
5. Knocktemple	Cloyne	Cork	(see Kilbolane)		
2. Lackagh	Kildare	Kildare	1830-1882	1830-1864	1829-1879
1. Lea	Kildare	Leix (Queen's)	1801-1875	1801-1844	1801-1875
1. Leixlip	Dublin	Kildare	1669-1875	1669-1845	1669-1875
1. Leskinfere	Ferns	Wexford	1802-1875	1802-1845	1802-1875
1. Lickmolassy &	Clonfert	Galway	1766-1874	(1762-1849	(1800-1875
Ballinakill				(1792-1844	(1802-1872
1. Limerick	Limerick	Limerick	(See St. Lawrence, St. Mary, St. Michael, and Trinity churches).		
1. Liselton	Ardfert	Kerry	1840-1875	————	1840-1875
5. Lisgoold &	Cloyne	Cork	1847-1875	1847-1875	1847-1875
Imphrick					
1. Lislee	Ross	Cork	1809-1890	1809-1844	1823-1890
1. Lismore	Lismore	Waterford	1693-1878	1692-1841	1711-1878
2. Lissadill	Elphin	Sligo	1836-1876	1845-	————
1. Listowell	Ardfert	Kerry	1790-1875	1790-1845	1790-1875
5. Litter	Cloyne	Cork	1811-1877	1811-1877	1811-1877
1. Loughrea	Clonfert	Galway	1747-1875	1747-1845	1747-1875
1. Lurgan	Kilmore	Cavan	1831-1875	1831-1845	1831-1875
1. Lusk	Dublin	Dublin	1809-1875	1809-1845	1809-1875

Parish	Diocese	County	Baptism	Marriage	Burial
3. Macroom	Cloyne	Cork	(1727-1837 (1837-1878	(1737-1835 (1835-1848	(1727-1836 (1836-1878
5. Macully	Ossory	Kilkenny & Waterford	1817-1877	1818-1863	1817-1877
1. Magheraclooney	Clogher	Monaghan	1806-1875	1806-1843	1806-1875
2. Maglass (rec. at Mulrankin)	Ferns	Wexford	1768-1801	1764-1801	1767-1803
4. Magourney	Cloyne	Cork	1757-1876	1765-1844	1758-1876
1. Malahide	Dublin	Dublin	1822-1875	1822-1863	1820-1875
5. Mallow	Cloyne	Cork	1776-1839	1776-1839	1776-1839
1. Mallow	Cloyne	Cork	1780-1875	1780-1845	1780-1875
1. Manorhamilton (Cloonclare)	Kilmore	Leitrim	1816-1875	1816-1845	1816-1875
1. Mariner's Church Kingstown	Dublin	Dublin	1843-1875	————	————
1. Marmullane	Cork	Cork	1801-1873	1802-1845	1803-1873
1. Maryborough	Leighlin	Leix (Queen's)	1793-1875	1793-1845	1793-1875
1. Mayne	Meath	Westmeath	1808-1877	1809-1845	1808-1876
2. Maÿnooth (Larabryan)	Glendalough	Kildare	1872-date	————	1871-date
2. Mealiffe	Cashel	Tipperary	1791-1875	1795-1845	1830-1871
1. Mellifont & Tullyallen	Armagh	Louth	1812-1873	1815-1847	1814-1875
4. Midleton	Cloyne	Cork	1810-1883	1811-1881	1809-1883
1. Miltòwn (see St. Philip)	Dublin	Dublin	1844-1876	————	————
2. Modreeny	Killaloe	Tipperary	1827-1848	1827-1848	1827-1848
4, 2. Mogeesha (see Carrigtwohill)	Cloyne	Cork	1852-1875	————	————
1. Mohill	Ardagh	Leitrim	1785-1875	1785-1845	1785-1875
1. Monaghan	Clogher	Monaghan	1802-1875	1802-1855	1802-1875
5. Monanimy	Cloyne	Cork	1812-1875	1812-1875	1812-1875
1. Monasteroris	Kildare	Kildare	1698-1875	1698-1845	1698-1875
2. Monksland	Lismore	Waterford	1836-1878	1836-1875	1846-1878
1. Monkstown	Cork	Cork	1842-1875	1841-1845	1842-1875
1. Monkstown, Dublin (see also St. John)	Dublin	Dublin	(1680-1785 (1804-1875	(1669-1785 (1804-1845	(1676-1785 (1804-1875
1. Mostrim	Ardagh	Longford	1801-1874	1801-1843	1801-1875
1. Mountmellick	Kildare	Leix (Queen's)	1840-1875	1840-1856	1840-1875
5. Mourne Abbey (Ballesanona)	Cloyne	Cork	1807-1877	1807-1877	1807-1877
1. Moville Upper	Derry	Donegal	1814-1875	1814-1844	1815-1875
2. Moydow	Ardagh	Longford	1794-1896	1796-1848	1795-1896
2. Moygounagh (in reg. of Crossmolina)	Killala	Mayo	1802-	1802-	1802-
1. Moylough	Tuam	Galway	1821-1875	1821-1845	1821-1875
2. Moyrus, Roundstone	Tuam	Galway	1841-1926	1845-1923	1849-1928
1. Mucknoe (Castleblaney)	Clogher	Monaghan	1810-1874	1810-1845	1810-1870
1. Muff	Derry	Donegal	1803-1876	1804-1844	1847-1875
2. Mullaghfad	Clogher	Fermanagh & Monaghan	1836-1878	1837-1847	1850-1878
1. Mullinacuff	Leighlin	Wicklow	1838-1875	1841-1845	1836-1875
1. Mulrankin	Ferns	Wexford	1786-1875	1786-1845	1786-1875

Parish	Diocese	County	Baptism	Marriage	Burial
2. Murragh	Cork	Cork	1754-1877	(1756-1843 (1846-	1754-date
1. Myshall	Leighlin	Carlow	1814-1876	1815-1855	1816-1877
1. Naas	Kildare	Kildare	1679-1870	1679-1845	1679-1870
2. Nathlash	Cloyne	Cork	1844-1868	1848-1870	1844-1863
2. Navan	Meath	Meath	1870-	1870-	1870-
			(Transcripts in Diocesan Registry)		
1. Newbliss	Clogher	Monaghan	1841-1878	————	1837-1877
1. Newcastle	Glendalough	Wicklow	1698-1875	1698-1845	1707-1875
	(Entries from Newcastle in vol. 1, Delgany records)				
2. Newcastle	Limerick	Limerick	1848-date	1845-date	1848-date
1. Newcastle-Lyons	Dublin	Dublin	1773-1875	1773-1845	1773-1875
1. Newport (see St. John)	Cashel	Tipperary	1782-1875	1782-1845	1782-1875
1. Newtownbarry	Ferns	Wexford	1779-1876	1779-1845	1779-1876
3. Nobber	Meath	Meath	1828-1868	1828-1844	1831-1869
1. Nohoval	Cork	Cork	1785-1879	1785-1845	1784-1879
1. Offerlane	Ossory	Leix (Queen's)	1807-1875	807-1844	1807-1875
2. Ogonnilloe	Killaloe	Clare	1807-1865	1807-1856	1836-1875
1. Oldcastle	Meath	Meath	1814-1875	1814-1845	1814-1875
1. Omey	Tuam	Galway	1831-1875	1831-1844	1832-1875
1. Oregan	Kildare	Leix (Queen's)	1801-1875	1801-1871	1801-1877
1. Outragh	Kilmore	Leitrim	1833-1875	1833-1843	1833-1875
1. Ovoca (see Castlemacadam)	Glendalough	Wicklow	1720-1886	1720-1860	1720-1886
1. Owenduff	Ferns	Wexford	1752-1875	1752-1845	1752-1875
1. Painestown & St. Anne's	Leighlin	Carlow	(1833-1874 (1859-1875	1833-1845	1833-1871
1. Portarlington (see St. Paul)	Kildare	Leix (Queen's)	1694-1877	1694-1812	1694-1875
1. Powerscourt	Glendalough	Wicklow	(1677-1726 (1740-1875	(1662-1726 (1740-1853	(1663-1723 (1740-1875
1. Preban	Ferns	Wicklow	1827-1878	1829-1872	1828-1878
4. Prior & Dromod	Ardfert	Kerry	————	1827-1842	————
1. Queenstown	Cloyne	Cork	1761-1875	1761-1845	1761-1875
1. Quivy	Kilmore	Cavan	1854-1875	————	————
5. Rahan	Cloyne	Cork	1773-1870	1776-1869	1773-1871
1. Raheny	Dublin	Dublin	1815-1875	1815-1845	1815-1875
1. Raphoe	Raphoe	Donegal	1831-1875	1831-1845	1831-1875
1. Rathaspick	Ferns	Wexford	1844-1875	1844-1866	1844-1875
2. Rathbeggan	Meath	Meath	1821-1844	1837-1839	1836-1841
2. Rathcoole	Ossory	(no church; Reg. from 1835; 8 bapt.; 1 bu.)			
1. Rathcooney	Cork	Cork	1749-1875	1749-1845	1749-1874
1. Rathcore	Meath	Meath	1810-1875	1811-1835	1810-1875
1. Rathdowney	Ossory	Leix (Queen's)	1756-1875	1756-1845	1756-1875
1. Rathdrum	Glendalough	Wicklow	1706-1875	1706-1845	1706-1875
1, 4. Rathkeale	Limerick	Limerick	1742-1870	1743-1779	1742-1870
1. Rathkeale & Kilscannell	Limerick	Limerick	(1746-1780 (1804-1875	(1746-1780 (1804-1845	(1746-1780 (1804-1875
2. Rathmichael	Dublin	Dublin	1865-1891		
1. Rathmines (see St. Peter's; Holy Trinity)	Dublin	Dublin	1671-1875	1671-1845	1671-1867
2. Rathronan & Ardagh	Limerick	Limerick	1818-date	1845-date	1824-date
1. Rathsaran	Ossory	Leix (Queen's)	1810-1875	1810-1875	1810-1875

Parish	Diocese	County	Baptism	Marriage	Burial
1. Rathvilly	Leighlin	Carlow	1826-1875	1826-1845	1826-1875
1. Rincurran	Cork	Cork	1793-1875	1793-1845	1727-1875
1. Roscrea	Killaloe	Offaly (King's)	1784-1875	1784-1845	1784-1875
1. Ross Cathedral	Ross	Cork	1690-1879	1690-1845	1690-1878
2. Rossdroit	Ferns	Wexford	1802-1828	(1802-1826 (1846-date	1814-1827
2. Rossmire	Lismore	Waterford	(Entries in Preachers books)		
4. Roatellan (see Midleton)	Cloyne	Cork	1810-1883	1811-1881	1809-1883
1. Rotunda Chapel	Dublin	Dublin	1860-1870	——	——
			(Reg. of births, 1745-, with Registrar)		
2. Royal Hibernian Military School	Dublin	Dublin	(Births & deaths, Reg. Castleknock)		
2, 1. Royal Hospital, Kilmainham	Dublin	Dublin	1826-1879	——	1849-date
			(Deaths, 1789-1833)		
1. Rushbrooke (see Christ Church)	Cloyne	Cork	1866-1876	——	——
5. St. Andrew's	Dublin	Dublin	——	1672-1819	——
1. St. Anne, Shandon	Cork	Cork	1772-1782	1772-1845	1779-1782
1. St. Anne's (see Painestown)	Leighlin	Carlow	(1833-1874 (1859-1875	1833-1845	1833-1871
1. St. Audoen & St. Nicholas Within	Dublin	Dublin	1673-1875	1673-1845	1673-1875
1. St. Bartholomew	Dublin	Dublin	1868-1875	——	——
5. St. Brendan's	Killaloe	Clare	(Miscel. families)		
1. St. Canice	Ossory	Kilkenny	1789-1878	1789-1869	1789-1878
1. St. Catherine & St. James	Dublin	Dublin	(Vestry book, 1657-1692)		
1. St. Catherine	Dublin	Dublin	1679-1875	1679-1845	1679-1875
5. St. Fin Barre	Cork	Cork	1752-1881	1752-1845	1753-1881
1. St. George, C. E.	Dublin	Dublin	1794-1876	1794-1845	1817-1870
1. St. James	Dublin	Dublin	1742-1876	1742-1844	1742-1872
1. St. John Baptist	Cashel	Tipperary	1668-1876	1668-1845	1668-1876
1. St. John, Monkstown	Dublin	Dublin	1860-1875	——	——
2. St. John (Cloverhill Church)	Kilmore	Cavan	1861-1876	——	——
1. St. John	Limerick	Limerick	1697-1876	1697-1845	1697-1876
1. St. John, Newport	Cashel	Tipperary	1782-1875	1782-1845	1782-1875
1. St. John, Sligo	Elphin	Sligo	1802-1875	1802-1845	1802-1875
1. St. John, Sandymount	Dublin	Dublin	1850-1876	——	——
1. St. Jude, Kilmainham	Dublin	Dublin	1857-1876	——	——
1, 5. St. Kevin's	Dublin	Dublin	Portion of Vestry book, 1669-1674.		
1. St. Kevin (see also St. Peter)	Dublin	Dublin	1867-1875	——	——
1. St. Lawrence & Trinity Church	Dublin	Dublin	1863-1875	——	——
1. St. Luke	Cork	Cork	1837-1875	1837-1845	——
1. St. Mark	Dublin	Dublin	1730-1874	1730-1860	1730-1875
1. St. Mark, Augher	Clogher	Monaghan	1866-1877	——	——

Parish	Diocese	County	Baptism	Marriage	Burial
1. St. Mary, Athlone (including Willbrooke Church)	Meath	Westmeath	1746-1875	1746-1845	1746-1849
1. St. Mary, Clonmel	Lismore	Tipperary	1766-1874	1766-1845	1766-1873
1. St. Mary, Donnybrook	Dublin	Dublin	1712-1870	1712-1858	1712-1872
1. St. Mary, Drogheda	Meath	Louth & Meath	1811-1875	1811-1845	1811-1875
1. St. Mary, Enniscorthy	Ferns	Wexford	1798-1872	1798-1852	1798-1875
1. St. Mary, Limerick	Limerick	Limerick	1726-1875	1726-1845	1726-1876
2. St. Mary, New Ross	Ferns	Wexford	1763-1876	1764-1862	1764-1876
2. St. Mary, Portclare	Clogher	Tyrone	1845-1881	——	——
3. St. Mary, Shandon	Cork	Cork	1868-1878	1868-1878	1868-1878
2. St. Mary, Shandon	Cork	Cork	1671-1873	1671-1848	1671-1872
2. St. Mary, Kilkenny	Ossory	Kilkenny	(1729-1776 (1815-1828	(1782-1794 (1815-1828	(1785-1814 (1816-1828
1. St. Matthew, Ringsend	Dublin	Dublin	1812-1876	——	1812-1872
1. St. Matthias	Dublin	Dublin	1851-1876	——	——
1. St. Michael, Blackrock	Cork	Cork	1828-1875	1828-1845	1828-1875
1. St. Michael, Limerick	Limerick	Limerick	1801-1875	1801-1845	1835-1858
1. St. Munchin	Limerick	Limerick	(1700-1704 (1734-1768 (1797-1884	(1700-1704 (1734-1768 (1797-1845	(1700-1704 (1734-1768 (1797-1880
5. St. Nicholas, Nathlash	Cloyne	Cork	1812-1876	1812-1876	1812-1876
1. St. Nicholas, Cork	Cork	Cork	1721-1875	1721-1845	1721-1873
1. St. Nicholas, Galway	Tuam	Galway	1792-1876	1792-1845	1838-1876
1. St. Nicholas Without	Dublin	Dublin	1694-1870	1694-1845	1694-1865
1. St. Patrick's Cathedral	Dublin	Dublin	1687-1879	——	1687-1878
1. St. Patrick's, Waterford	Waterford	Waterford	1723-1875	1725-1845	1723-1855
1, 4. St. Paul's, Dublin	Dublin	Dublin	——	——	——
1. St. Paul's, Dublin	Dublin	Dublin	1698-1879	1703-1845	1702-1879
1. St. Paul's, Portarlington	Kildare	Leix (Queen's)	1694-1877	1694-1812	1694-1875
1, 4. St. Peter's, Drogheda	Armagh	Louth	1747-1772	1747-1772	1747-1772
1. St. Peter's, Drogheda	Armagh	Louth	1654-1875	1654-1845	1654-1875

Parish	Diocese	County	Baptism	Marriage	Burial
1. St. Peter's, Dublin	Dublin	Dublin	1671-1875	1671-1845	1671-1867
1. St. Philip, Milltown	Dublin	Dublin	1844-1876	——————	——————
1. St. Stephen, Dublin	Dublin	Dublin	1826-1875		
1. St. Thomas	Dublin	Dublin	1750-1875	1750-1845	1750-1875
1. St. Werburgh	Dublin	Dublin	1704-1875	1704-1843	1704-1876
1. Sandford	Dublin	Dublin	1826-1880		
1. Sandymount (see St. John)	Dublin	Dublin	1850-1876	——————	——————
1. Santry	Dublin	Dublin	1753-1785	1753-1845	1753-1875
5. Shanagolden	Limerick	Limerick	1803-1877	1797-1843	1804-1879
5. Shanrahan	Lismore	Tipperary	1793-1857	1793-1857	1793-1857
1. Shillelagh	Ferns	Wicklow	1833-1875	1833-1875	1833-1875
1. Shinrone	Killaloe	Offaly (King's)	1741-1875	1741-1845	1741-1875
1. Sligo (see St. John)	Elphin	Sligo	1802-1875	1802-1845	1802-1875
1. Stradbally	Killaloe	Limerick	1787-1875	1787-1845	1787-1875
1. Stradbally	Leighlin	Leix (Queen's)	1772-1875	1776-1845	1726-1875
1. Stradbally	Lismore	Waterford	1798-1875	1798-1845	1798-1875
1. Straffan	Glendalough	Kildare	1838-1876	1838-	1841-1877
2. Straid or Templemore	Achonry	Mayo	(A few entries of baptisms, 1755-)		
1. Stranorlar	Raphoe	Donegal	1821-1870	1821-1845	1821-1870
1. Stratford-on-Slaney	Leighlin	Wicklow	1812-1873	1804-1873	1804-1875
1. Street	Ardagh	Longford	1801-1875	1801-1844	1801-1875
1. Swanlinbar	Kilmore	Cavan	1798-1875	1798-1875	1798-1875
1. Swords	Dublin	Dublin	1705-1875	1705-1875	1705-1875
1. Syddan	Meath	Meath	1720-1878	1721-1865	1725-1878
1. Tacumshane	Ferns	Wexford	1832-1889	1832-1889	1832-1889
1. Tallow & Kilwatermoy	Lismore	Waterford	(1772-1809 (1829-1875	(1772-1809 (1829-1845	(1772-1809 (1829-1875
1. Taney	Dublin	Dublin	1835-1875	——————	1857-1875
1. Tashinney & Abbeyshrule	Ardagh	Longford	1821-1875	1821-1848	1821-1875
1. Taughboyne	Raphoe	Donegal	1819-1876	1836-1845	1819-1876
1. Templecarn	Clogher	Donegal	1825-1875	1825-1844	1825-1875
1. Templeharry	Killaloe	Offaly (King's)	1800-1877	1800-1845	1800-1877
2. Templemartin	Cork	Cork	1806-1879	1808-1845	1810-1879
1, 4. Templemichael	Ardagh	Longford	1796-1835	1777-1838	1796-1838
1. Templemichael	Ardagh	Longford	1795-1875	1795-1845	1795-1875
3. Templemichael	Lismore	Waterford	1801-1867	1804-1865	1823-1864
1. Templemichael	Cashel	Tipperary	1791-1875	1791-1845	1791-1875
2. Templeport	Kilmore	Cavan	1873-date	——————	——————
2. Templescobin	Ferns	Wexford	1802-1928	1853-1928	1835-1928
1. Templeshambo	Ferns	Wexford	1815-1875	1815-1875	1815-1875
1. Terryglass	Killaloe	Tipperary	1809-1872	1809-1845	1809-1872
2. Tessauran	Meath	Meath	1819-1877	1845-	1824-1877
1. Timahoe	Leighlin	Leix (Queen's)	1845-1875	1850-1874	1856-1873
2. Timoleague	Ross	Cork	1823-date	——————	——————
1. Timolin	Glendalough	Kildare	1812-1873	1812-1845	1812-1873
1. Tipperary	Cashel	Tipperary	1779-1875	1779-1845	1779-1875

Parish	Diocese	County	Baptism	Marriage	Burial
2, 4. Toem	Cashel	Tipperary	1802-1886	1804-1845	1803-1877
1. Tomhaggard	Ferns	Wexford	1809-1875	1813-1853	1809-1875
1. Tomregan	Kilmore	Cavan	1797-1875	1797-1875	1797-1875
1. Toombe	Ferns	Wexford	1770-1875	1770-1875	1770-1875
1. Tralee	Ardfert	Kerry	1771-1875	1771-1845	1771-1875
1. Trim	Meath	Meath	1836-1875	————	1849-1875
1. Trinity Church	Kilmore	Cavan	1842-1877	————	————
1. Trinity & St. Olave's	Waterford	Waterford	1658-1875	1658-1845	1658-1875
1. Tuam	Tuam	Galway	1808-1875	1808-1845	1808-1875
2. Tullabracky	Limerick	Limerick	1820-1883	1823-1844	1823-1886
1. Tullahobegly	Raphoe	Donegal	1821-1875	1821-1845	1850-1876
1. Tullamelan	Lismore	Tipperary	1823-1875	1823-1845	1823-1875
1. Tullow	Leighlin	Carlow	1696-1875	1696-1845	1696-1875
1. Tullyallen & Mellifont	Armagh	Louth	1812-1873	1815-1847	1814-1875
1. Tullyaughnish	Raphoe	Donegal	1798-1875	1788-1845	1788-1875
5. Tullylease	Cloyne	Cork	1850-1872	1850-1872	1850-1872
1. Turlough	Tuam	Mayo	1821-1875	1822-1851	1822-1875
1. Tydavnet	Clogher	Monaghan	1822-1872	1822-1845	1822-1875
1. Tyholland	Clogher	Monaghan	1806-1875	1806-1845	1806-1875
1. Urglin (Rutland Church)	Leighlin	Carlow	1710-1853	1715-1877	1715-1877
1. Valentia	Ardfert	Kerry	1826-1875	————	1826-1875
5. Wallstown	Cloyne	Cork	1829-1879	1829-1879	1829-1879
1. Westport & Aughagower	Tuam	Mayo	1801-1875	1801-1845	1801-1875
1. Wexford	Ferns	Wexford	(1674-1753 (1778-1875	(1674-1753 (1778-1845	(1674-1753 (1778-1845
1. Whitechurch	Dublin	Dublin	1824-1877	1827-1845	1824-1877
1. Wicklow	Glendalough	Wicklow	1655-1877	1729-1869	1729-1874
1. Willbrooke Church	Meath	Westmeath	1756-1783 (Records with St. Mary, Athlone)	1756-1783	1756-1783
1. Youghal	Cloyne	Cork	1665-1874 (Lacking 1720-1727)	1665-1845	1665-1874

PUBLISHED PARISH REGISTERS OF THE FORMER ESTABLISHED CHURCH OF IRELAND

The Parish Register Society of Dublin became active at about the turn of the century. The purpose of this Society, approved by the Master of the Rolls in Ireland, was to supply the genealogist and the local and family historian with printed copies of the more important and older surviving Registers, beginning with those of Dublin, more especially those not deposited in the Public Record Office. The Registers of the City of Dublin, besides containing the descent of many of the old city families, are of great importance to all investigating the history of scattered branches of English families, as well as the origins of American Colonial settlers. The Registers of other nearby parishes in County Dublin and in Counties Wexford and Limerick, which were also published, serve the same purpose, as well as the Registers of Derry Cathedral, Londonderry, which were included in this series.

In 1921, the Parish Register Society of Dublin, for purposes of publication of Parish Registers, became incorporated with the Irish Memorials Association, formerly the Association for the Preservation of the Memorials of the Dead. These two latter Societies had, from 1888-1920, been publishing a comprehensive and full tombstone encyclopedia, Vols. I-X; a work which was continued through parts of Vols. XI-XIII. The contents of these publications will be reviewed in CHAPTER XXII; a chapter devoted to records which cannot be classified under the church records of any single denomination.

The Journal of the Irish Memorials Association; now incorporating the Dublin Parish Register Society, edited by Thomas Ulick Sadleir, Vol. XI, 1921-1925; Vol. XII, 1931; Vol. XIII, No. 1 and No. 2, 1935-1937, published the following records:

Volume XI. Parish Registers:

No.	1.	St. Michan's, Dublin	Marriages	1700-1800
No.	2.	St. Mary's, Donnybrook	Marriages	1712-1800
No.	3.	St. John's, Dublin	Marriages	1700-1798
No.	4.	St. Nicholas Within, Dublin	Marriages	1671-1800
No.	5.	St. Michael's, Dublin	Marriages	1656-1800
No.	6.	Finglass, Co. Dublin	Burials	1664-1729
No.	6.	St. Nicholas Within, Dublin	Burials	1671-1823

Volume XII. Parish Registers and other records:

No.	1.	St. Audoen's, Dublin	Burials	1672-1692
No.	2.	St. Mary's, Crumlin, Index (A-K)	Deaths	1740-1830
No.	3.	St. Mary's, Crumlin, Index (L-Y)	Deaths	1740-1830
		Visitation Returns; List (A-W) Burials (Crumlin)		1785-1810
		Crumlin Religious Census, 1766 (Protestant and Popish families)		
		St. Mary's, Crumlin, Baptisms and Marriages		1740-1830
No.	4.	The Parish Church of Belfast	Marriages	1745-1799
No.	5.	St. Andrew's, Dublin	Marriages	1801-1819
No.	6.	St. Nicholas Within, Dublin	Burials	1825-1863

Volume XIII. Indexes:

No. 2. Indexes to the Registers printed in Vol. XII, compiled by B. St. G. Lefroy, Dublin, 1939.

Other Registers printed by the Dublin Parish Register Society and the Irish Memorials Association:

1.	St. Catherine's, Dublin	Marriages	1715-1800
2.	St. Andrew's, Dublin	Marriages	1672-1801
3.	St. Anne's, Dublin	Marriages	1719-1800
4.	St. Audoen's, Dublin	Marriages	1672-1800
5.	St. Luke's, Dublin	Marriages	1716-1800
6.	St. Werburg's, Dublin	Marriages	1704-1800
7.	St. Mary's, Dublin	Marriages	1697-1800
8.	Monkstown, Co. Dublin	Marriages	1669-1800
	Monkstown, Co. Dublin	Baptisms	1669-1800
	Monkstown, Co. Dublin	Burials	1669-1800
9.	Aney, Co. Limerick	Baptisms	1760-1802
	Aney, Co. Limerick	Marriages	1761-1803
	Aney, Co. Limerick	Burials	1759-1802
10.	Rathmacnee, Co. Wexford	Burials	1813-1866
11.	Kilpatrick, Co. Wexford	Burials	1836-1864
12.	Templescobin, Co. Wexford	Burials	1835-1864
13.	St. Paul's, Dublin	Baptisms	1698-1820
	St. Paul's, Dublin	Marriages	1703-1820
	St. Paul's, Dublin	Burials	1702-1820

Publications of the Parish Register Society of Dublin; being the printed Registers of Baptism, Marriage, and Burial, of the following parishes:

Vol.   I. The Register of St. John, Dublin, 1619-1699.

Vol.   II. The Register of St. Patrick, Dublin, 1677-1800.

Vol.   III. The Register of St. Michan, Dublin, 1636-1685.

Vol.   IV. The Register of Provost Winter (Trinity College), Dublin, 1650-1660.

Vol.   IV. The Register of The Liberties of Cashel, Co. Tipperary, 1654-1657.

Vol.   V. The Register of St. Catherine, Dublin, 1636-1715.

Vol.   VI. The Register of The Union of Monkstown, Co. Dublin, 1699-1786.

Vol.   VII. The Register of St. Michan, Dublin, Part II, 1686-1700.

Vol. VIII. The Registers of Derry Cathedral, Parish of Templemore, 1642-1703.

Vol. IX. The Register of The Parish of St. Peter and St. Kevin, 1699-1761.

Vol. X. The Register of St. Nicholas Without, Dublin, 1694-1739.

Vol. XI. The Register of St. Bride, Dublin, 1632-1800.

Other published Parish Registers:

1. The Register of the Diocese of Clogher, *Clogher Records,* Vol. 1, pp. 32-37.
2. The Parish Register of Holy Trinity (Christ Church), Cork, 1643-1668, ed. by Richard Caulfield, 1877.
3. Register of the Hospital of St. John the Baptist, without New Gate, Dublin, transcribed and edited from the Bodleian MS., by Eric St. John Brooks. Irish Manuscripts Commission, No. 2794.
4. Register of the Abbey of St. Thomas, Dublin, edited by Sir John Gilbert, 1889.

The publications of the Irish Memorials Association, and the Dublin Parish Register Society, are in many of the large genealogical libraries of the United States.

PARISH REGISTERS OF THE FORMER ESTABLISHED CHURCH OF IRELAND, NORTHERN IRELAND

Since the establishment of the Public Record Office of Northern Ireland in Belfast, which was opened in March, 1924, the Deputy Keeper of the Records has received annual reports from the clergymen of all parishes in Northern Ireland which have original parish records of the Church of Ireland, dated before January 1, 1871. There are 236 parishes which have such records, in the counties of Antrim, Armagh, Down, Fermanagh, Londonderry, and Tyrone. A report on the condition of each Register containing records of baptism, marriage, and burial is made. Any volume of records which requires repair is sent to this office to have the work done under the supervision of the Deputy Keeper of the Public Records. It has been his practice to have a transcript made by photostat or microfilm of each Register which is sent to the office temporarily for repair. Thus, at the end of 1955, some or all of the registers of 116 parishes had been copied.

The Deputy Keeper of the Public Records of Northern Ireland has made a series of reports on the extent of these parish records which exist in Northern Ireland (*Report of the Deputy Keeper of the Records*, 1933, p. 13; 1934, p. 11; 1935, p. 10; 1937, p. 11; 1938-1945, pp. 15-17, 20, 21 (Office records, T. 679, with additional lists not included in T. 679, photostated). These reports tabulate: (1) The name of each of the 216 parishes which have original parish registers of baptism, marriage, and burial, in local custody; the records being dated previous to 1871. The parishes are listed by diocese and county; (2) the lists of the Registers which have been copied, for deposit in the Public Record Office, with the inclusive dates of baptism, marriage, and burial.

The existing original parish registers in Northern Ireland, except that of Clogherny, Diocese of Armagh, County Tyrone, saved from the fire, have always remained in local custody, thus having escaped the fire in the Public Record Office, Dublin, in 1922. The inclusive dates of baptism, marriage, and burial, contained in these Registers which were retained in local custody, were included in a published list (*The 28th Report of the Deputy Keeper of the Public Records of Ireland*, 1896, Appendix II, pp. 57-108). Therefore, the inclusive dates of the existing original records of each parish in Northern Ireland have been extracted from this publication, and will appear in the following list, opposite the name of each parish.

As not all of the volumes of records in each parish have required the repair mentioned above, and thus not all of the volumes of records of each parish have, in every case, been sent to the Public Record Office, Belfast, where a copy could be made, it will be noted that in many cases there is a difference between the inclusive dates of the original records in local custody, and the inclusive dates of the transcripts which are in the Public Record Office. Also it appears that some parishes possessed later records than those listed in the *28th Report*, 1896, the dates of the transcripts proving their existence. In cases where the dates taken from the two sources of reference do not coincide for either cause named above, a double listing of the parish will be made to show what inclusive dates were reported for the original records in 1896, and the inclusive dates of the transcripts.

The original records listed have no key mark before the parish name. The transcripts are indicated with an asterisk (*).

Parish	Diocese	County	Baptism	Marriage	Burial
Aghaderg	Dromore	Down	1814-1875	1814-1845	1814-1875
* "	"	"	1814-1870	1814-1849	1814-1886
				Bans 1826-30	
Aghalee	Dromore	Antrim	1782-1875	1782-1845	1782-1874
* "	"	"	1811-1881	1811-1881	1811-1881
Aghalurcher	Clogher	Tyrone &	1788-1875	1788-1845	1788-1875
		Fermanagh			
* "	"	"	1787-1870	1801-1841	(1802-1841
					(1843-1870
Aghaveagh	Clogher	Fermanagh	1815-1876	1815-1857	1815-1858
* "	"	"	1815-1926	(1815-1858	1815-1926
				(1869-1926	
Aghavilly	Armagh	Armagh	1844-1876		1846-1876
Ahoghill	Connor	Antrim	1811-1875	1811-1839	1811-1875
* "	"	"	(1811-1829	(1811-1829	(1811-1829
			(1839-1870	(1840-1845	(1840-1870
Annaghmore	Armagh	Armagh	1856-1875	———	1862-1875
* "	"	"	1856-1872	———	1867-1870
Annalong	Dromore	Down	1842-1895	———	1857-1879
* "	"	"	1842-date	———	1845-date
Antrim	Connor	Antrim	(1700-1755	(1700-1756	(1700-1754
			(1828-1876	(1828-1861	(1828-1861
Arboe	Armagh	Tyrone	1773-1871	1773-1845	1773-1875
* "	"	"	(1773-1813	(1773-1813	(1773-1813
			(1824-1838	(1824-1838	(1824-1838
			(Bapt. & Confirmation, 1839-1873)		
Ardkeen	Down	Down	1746-1876	1746-1845	1746-1876
* "	"	"	(1745-1830	1745-1875	1745-1875
			(1829-1875		
Ardmore	Dromore	Armagh	1822-1875	1822-1845	1822-1875
* "	"	"	1822-1837	1823-1842	1822-1842
Ardtrea	Armagh	Tyrone	1811-1885	1811-1845	1811-1878
* "	"	"	1811-1829	1811-1829	1811-1829
Armagh	Armagh	Armagh	1750-1875	1750-1845	1750-1875
Aughavilly	Armagh	Armagh	1844-1876	———	1846-1876
(Aghavilly)					
* "	"	"	1844-1871	———	1844-1871

Parish	Diocese	County	Baptism	Marriage	Burial
Badoney	Derry	Tyrone	1818-1875	1817-1845	1820-1877
(See Lower Badoney)					
* Badoney (Lower)	"	"	1812-1875	1817-1845	1820-1875
Ballee	Down	Down	1792-1878	1792-1845	1792-1878
Ballinderry	Armagh	Londonderry & Tyrone	1802-1875	1802-1845	1802-1875
Ballinderry	Connor	Antrim	1805-1870	1840-1845	1805-1870
* Ballintoy	Connor	Antrim	(Vestry books, c. 1712-c. 1790; c. 1791-1843)		
Ballyclog	Armagh	Tyrone	1818-1875	1818-1845	1818-1875
* "	"	"	1818-1848	1818-1841	1818-1871
Ballyclug	Connor	Antrim	1841-1876	1841-1844	1841-1879
Ballyculter	Down	Down	1777-1877	1812-1845	1812-1877
* "	"	"	1838-1870	1838-1845	1838-1870
Ballyeglish	Armagh	Londonderry	1868-1875	————	1868-1875
Ballyhalbert	Down	Down	c. 1852-1876		c. 1852-1876
Belfast	Down	Down	1827-1876	1827-1857	————
(Ballymacarrett)					
* Belfast "	"	"	1827-1869	1827-1857	————
Ballymena (or Kirkinriola)	Connor	Antrim	1815-1875	1807-1845	1780-1875
Ballymoney	Connor	Antrim	1807-1875	1807-1845	1807-1875
Ballymore	Armagh	Armagh	1783-1871	1783-1845	1783-1871
* "	"	"	1783-1831	1783-1831	1783-1831
Ballymoyer	Armagh	Armagh	1820-1875	1820-1845	1836-1875
Ballynascreen	Derry	Londonderry	1808-1877	1825-1845	1824-1877
* "	"	"	1808-1860	1825-1826	1824-1825
Ballynure	Connor	Antrim	1812-1877	1825-1830	1840; 1852-77
Ballyphilip	Down	Down	1745-1875	1745-1844	1745-1875
Ballysillan (St. Mark's, Belfast)	Connor	Antrim	1856-1875	————	————
* "	"	"	1856-1871		
Ballywalter (Whitechurch)	Down	Down	1844-1875	1844-1875	————
Ballywillan	Connor	Antrim	1826-1875	1825-1844	1826-1895
* "	"	"	1826-1880	1825-1844	1826-1895
Banagher	Derry	Londonderry	1839-1875	1839-1845	1839-1875
Bangor	Down	Down	1803-1876	1805-1844	1815-1876
Belfast (Christ Church)	Connor	Antrim	1837-1875	1837-1845	1837-1875
Belfast (Mariner's Chapel)	Connor	Antrim	1868-1875	————	————
Belfast (St. Anne, Shankill)	Connor	Antrim	1745-1871	1745-1845	1745-1865
Belfast (St. George)	Connor	Antrim	1819-1875	1824-1845	————
Belfast (St. John)	Connor	Antrim	1853-1875	————	————
* "	"	"	1853-1892	————	————
Belfast (St. John Malone)	Connor	Antrim	1839-1875	1842-1844	————
* "	"	"	1842-1887	1842-1844	————
Belfast (St. Mark, Ballysillan)	Connor	Antrim	1856-1875	————	————
Belfast (St. Mary)	Connor	Antrim	1867-1872	————	1860-1870

Parish	Diocese	County	Baptism	Marriage	Burial
Belfast (St. Matthew)	Connor	Antrim	1846-1871	————	————
* ,,	,,	,,	1846-1871	————	————
Belfast (Trinity)	Connor	Antrim	1844-1876	————	————
* ,,	,,	,,	1844-1870	————	————
Belfast (Upper Falls)	Connor	Antrim	1855-1871	————	
Belleek	Clogher	Fermanagh	1822-1875	1822-1845	1822-1875
* ,,	,,	,,	1822-1850	————	
Bohoe	Clogher	Fermanagh	1840-1876	1840-1875	1840-1877
* ,,	,,	,,	1840-1879	1840-1879	1840-1879
Brackaville	Armagh	Tyrone	1836-1876	1836-1845	1836-1870
Bantry	Armagh	Tyrone	1844-1875	1845-	1846-1875
Caledon (Aghaloo)	Armagh	Tyrone	1791-1876	1791-1845	1791-1876
Camlough	Armagh	Armagh	1832-1876	1835-1845	1833-1877
Camus (Mourne)	Derry	Tyrone	1803-1874	1825-1845	1825-1875
Cappagh	Derry	Tyrone	1758-1875	1858-1875	1758-1875
* ,,	,,	,,	1754-1786	1752-1787	1752-1783
Carnmoney	Connor	Antrim	1789-1875	1789-1845	1845-1875
Carnteel	Armagh	Tyrone	1805-1875	1805-1845	1805-1875
Carrickfergus	Connor	Antrim	1740-1875	1740-1845	1740-1870
Castledawson	Derry	Londonderry	1744-1877	————	1844-1877
* ,,	,,	,,	1846-1885	————	
Clabby	Clogher	Fermanagh	1862-1875	————	
Clanabogan	Derry	Tyrone	1863-1875	————	1863-1875
Clogher	Clogher	Tyrone	1763-1875	1763-1845	1763-1875
Clogherney	Armagh	Tyrone	1859-1875	————	
Clonduff	Dromore	Down	1782-1876	1786-1845	1782-1876
* ,,	,,	,,	1782-1864	1786-1850	1787-1848
* Clonfeacle	Armagh	Tyrone	Vestry book, extracts, 1763-1831		
Clonoe	Armagh	Tyrone	1824-1875	1812-1845	1824-1875
Clooney	Derry	Londonderry	1867-1876	————	1867-1876
Coleraine	Connor	Londonderry	1769-1873	1769-1845	1769-1875
Comber	Down	Down	1683-1875	1683-1845	1683-1876
Coolaghty	Clogher	Fermanagh	1835-1875	1844-	————
Cooley or Sixmilecross	Armagh	Tyrone	1836-1879	1836-1845	1836-1879
* ,,	,,	,,	1836-1871	1836-1846	1837-1871
Craigs	Connor	Antrim	1839-1875	1841-1845	1841-1871
Creggan	Armagh	Armagh	1808-1875	1808-1839	1808-1875
* ,,	,,	,,	1827-1838	1827-1839	1827-1838
Cumber, Lower	Derry	Londonderry	1804-1875	1804-1845	1804-1875
Cumber, Upper	Derry	Londonderry	1811-1872	1826-1845	1826-1875
Derg	Derry	Tyrone	1807-1875	1807-1845	1839-1875
Derryaghey	Connor	Antrim	(1696-1738 (1771-1875	(1696-1738 (1827-1844	(1696-1738 (1772-1773 (1827-1872
* ,,	,,	,,	1696-1750	1696-1750	1696-1750
* Derrykeighan	Connor	Antrim	Vestry book, 1802-1826		
Derryloran	Armagh	Tyrone	1796-1875	1796-1845	1796-1875
Derrynoose	Armagh	Armagh	(1710-1746 (1822-1875	(1712-1743 (1822-1845	———— 1835-1875
* ,,	,,	,,	1710-1746	1712-1743	————

Parish	Diocese	County	Baptism	Marriage	Burial
Derryvollan, North	Clogher	Fermanagh & Tyrone	1803-1871	1803-1846	1803-1869
* "	"	"	1803-1837	1803-1837	1804-1837
Desertcreat	Armagh	Tyrone	1812-1873	1812-1845	1812-1875
* "	"	"	1812-1834	1812-1835	1812-1834
Desartlyn		Londonderry	1797-1871	1797-1845	1797-1876
Desartmartin	Derry	Londonderry	1797-1875	1797-1845	1797-1875
* "	"	"	(1785-1802 (1827-1847	(1784-1805 (1832-1845	1842-1861
Devenish	Clogher	Fermanagh	1800-1845	1800-1845	1800-1874
Donaghadee	Down	Down	1778-1875	1778-1844	1778-1875
* "	"	"	1771-1845	1772-1844	(1771-1786 (1817-1841
Donaghcloney	Dromore	Down	1834-1875	1834-1848	1834-1875
Donagheady	Derry	Tyrone	(1754-1765 (1826-1874	1826-1845	1826-1875
Donaghendry	Armagh	Tyrone	(1734-1768 (1810-1875	1811-1844	1811-1875
* "	"	"	1810-1831	1811-1844	1811-1843
Donaghmore	Armagh	Tyrone	1748-1875	1741-1845	1741-1875
* "	"	"	(1748-1833 (1826-1870	(1741-1833 (1826-1870	(1741-1825 (1826-1870
Down	Down	Down	1750-1876	1752-1845	1752-1876
* "	"	"	1837-1856	1837-1845	1837-1871
Dromore	Dromore	Dromore	1784-1875	1784-1845	1784-1873
Drumachose	Derry	Londonderry	1728-1875	1728-1845	1728-1875
* "	"	"	1729-1752	1728-1753	1730-1736
Drumballyroney	Dromore	Down	1831-1875	1831-1845	1831-1875
Drumbanagher	Armagh	Armagh	1838-1879	1838-1845	1838-1879
* "	"	"	1838-1850	1839-1844	1841-1850
Drumbeg	Down	Down	1823-1875	1823-1845	1823-1875
Drumbo	Down	Down	1791-1875	1791-1845	1791-1875
Drumcree	Armagh	Armagh	1780-1875	1780-1845	1780-1875
* "	"	"	1784-1854	1802-1845	1804-1827
Drumglass	Armagh	Tyrone	1665-1875	(1677-1766 (1823-1848	(1677-1767 (1814-1855
* "	"	"	1665-1754	1677-1754	1677-1754
Drumgooland	Dromore	Down	1779-1870	1779-1845	(1779-1791 (1839-1841 (1860-1873
Drumkeeran	Clogher	Fermanagh	1801-1875	1801-1845	1801-1876
* "	"	"	1801-1870	1801;1813-1840	1842-1869
Drummaul	Connor	Antrim	1823-1875	1823-1846	1823-1877
Drumragh	Derry	Tyrone	1800-1876	1800-1845	1800-1875
* "	"	"	1801-1867	1804-1845	1830-1895
Dundela	Down	Down	1864-1879	——	
Dundonald	Down	Down	1811-1880	1811-1844	1823-1881
Dungiven	Derry	Londonderry	1778-1875	1778-1845	1823-1875
* "	"	"	1795-1826 (Vestry book, 1778-1827)	1795-1826	——
Dunluce	Connor	Antrim	1809-1875	1826-1845	1826-1875
Dunseverick	Connor	Antrim	1832-1870	1833-1845	1833-1872
* "	"	"	1832-1895	——	——
Edenderry	Derry	Tyrone	1841-1875	——	1849-1875

Parish	Diocese	County	Baptism	Marriage	Burial
Eglish	Armagh	Armagh	1803-1875	1804-1845	1803-1875
* "	"	"	1831-1844	1831-1845	1831-1844
Errigal-Keerogue	Armagh	Tyrone	1812-1875	1812-1848	1812-1875
Faughanvale	Derry	Derry	1802-1865	1802-1845	1802-1837
Findonagh or Donacavey	Clogher	Tyrone	1777-1878	1800-1850	1800-1878
Finvoy	Connor	Antrim	1811-1880	1812-1845	1811-1878
* "	"	"	1811-1880	1812-1845	(1811-1825
					(1828-1852
					(1856-1885
Fivemiletown	Clogher	Tyrone	1804-1875	1804-1845	1804-1875
Galloon	Clogher	Fermanagh	1798-1873	1798-1844	1798-1875
Gilford	Dromore	Down	1869-1875		
Glenavy	Connor	Antrim	1707-1875	1708-1845	1707-1873
* "	"	"	(1707-1812	(1708-1813	(1707-1828
			(1852-1864		(1852-1864
Glendermot	Derry	Londonderry	1810-1875	1810-1875	1828-1875
Glynn	Connor	Antrim	1838-1875	1838-1845	1838-1875
Grange	Armagh	Armagh	1780-1876	1780-1845	1780-1875
Grey Abbey	Down	Down	1807-1875	1807-1845	1807-1873
Hillsborough	Down	Down	1777-1875	1782-1845	1823-1875
Holywood	Down	Down	1806-1873	1806-1845	1806-1875
Inch	Down	Down	1767-1878	1764-1791	1788-1878
Innishargy	Down	Down	1783-1875	1783-1845	1783-1875
Innishmacsaint	Clogher	Fermanagh	1813-1876	1813-1845	1813-1876
* "	"	"	(1813-1825	1813-1825	1813-1825
			(1836-1885		
Inver & Larne	Connor	Antrim	1806-1871	1817-1845	1826-1875
* "	"	"	(1806-1826	(1817-1819	1839-1850
			(1836-1851	(1831-1845	
Keady	Armagh	Armagh	1780-1871	1780-1845	1813-1881
* "	"	"	(1780-1809	1780-1809	1827-1870
			(1852-1861		
Kilbroney	Dromore	Down	1814-1871	1818-1845	1814-1877
Kilclooney	Armagh	Armagh	1832-1875	1835-1845	1837-1875
Kilcoo	Dromore	Down	1786-1879	1828-1845	1828-1879
* "	"	"	1786-1829		
Kilcronaghan	Derry	Londonderry	1749-1875	1749-1845	1831-1875
Kildress	Armagh	Tyrone	1749-1875	1799-1844	1864-1875
Kilkeel	Dromore	Down	1816-1870	1816-1845	1816-1875
Killaney	Down	Down	1858-1877		1865-1877
Killesher	Clogher	Fermanagh	1798-1876	1798-1856	1798-1876
* "	"	"	1798-1827	1798-1826	1800-1823
Killinchy	Down	Down	1819-1875	1819-1845	1819-1875
* "	"	"	1820-1877	1825-1845	1824-1876
			(Vestry book, 1716-1779).		
Killowen	Derry	Londonderry	1824-1875	1824-1845	1824-1875
Killylea	Armagh	Armagh	1845-1875		1845-1875
Killyleagh	Down	Down	1830-1872	1830-1844	1836-1875
Killyman	Armagh	Tyrone	1741-1875	1741-1845	1741-1875
Kilmegan	Dromore	Down	1823-1879	1823-1845	1823-1879
Kilmood	Down	Down	1822-1880	1822-1845	1793-1879
* "	"	"	1822-1862	1822-1845	1793-1862

Parish	Diocese	County	Baptism	Marriage	Burial
Kilmore	Down	Down	1820-1873	1820-1845	1820-1875
"	"	"	1820-1856	1822-1868	1822-1856
Kilrea	Derry	Londonderry	1801-1875	1801-1845	1801-1875
"	"	"	1801-1863	1801-1863	1801-1863
Kilskerry	Clogher	Tyrone	1772-1872	1772-1845	1772-1875
Kiltumon	Clogher	Fermanagh	1861-1864	——————	——————
Kinawley	Kilmore	Fermanagh	1761-1875	1761-1845	1761-1875
Knockbreda	Down	Down	1784-1873	1784-1845	1784-1875
Knockna-muckley	Dromore	Down	1838-1875	1838-1845	1853-1875
"	"	"	Registers, 1841-1857		
Lambeg	Connor	Antrim	1810-1875	1810-1846	1810-1875
Larne & Inver	(See Inver)				
Layde	Connor	Antrim	1826-1875	1826-1845	1826-1875
Learmount	Derry	Londonderry	1832-1875	1833-1842	1832-1875
Lisburn, Blaris	Connor	Antrim	(1639-1646 (1661-1873	1661-1845	1661-1879
"	"	"	(1661-1739 (1820-1848	(1661-1739 (1820-1848	(1661-1739 (1820-1848
Lisburn Christ Church	"	"	1849-1873	——————	——————
Lislimnaghan	Derry	Tyrone	1862-1875	——————	1864-1875
Lisnaskea	Clogher	Fermanagh	1804-1875	1804-1845	1804-1872
"	"	"	1815-1836	1815-1836	1815-1836
Lissan	Armagh	Tyrone	(1753-1795 (1804-1875	(1752-1793 (1817-1842	(1753-1795 (1805-1875
"	"	"	(1753-1795 (1804-1844	(1744;1749 1794) (1805-1844	(1753-1794 (1805-1816
Londonderry Cathedral (Templemore)	Derry	Londonderry	1642-1875	1642-1845	(1642-1776 (1829-1874
Londonderry (Christ Church)	Derry	Londonderry	1855-1869	——————	——————
Loughgall	Armagh	Armagh	(1706-1729 (1779-1875	(1706-1729 (1779-1845	(1706-1729 (1779-1875
"	"	" Vestry book, 1774-1809; 1788-1830; 1831-1885			
Loughgilly	Armagh	Armagh	1804-1875	1804-1845	1804-1875
Loughlin Island	Down	Down	(1760-1806 (1821-1875	(1760-1806 (1821-1845	(1760-1806 1821-1875
"	"	"	1760-1806	1760-1806	1760-1806
Maghera	Derry	Londonderry	1785-1875	1798-1860	1813-1875
"	"	"	1785-1860	1798-1860	1813-1860
Magheracross	Clogher	Fermanagh	1800-1876	1800-1839	1800-1876
"	"	"	1840; 1846-1890	——————	——————
Magheracul-money	Clogher	Fermanagh	1767-1875	1767-1845	1767-1875
Magherafelt	Armagh	Londonderry	1718-1875	1718-1845	1718-1875
Magheragall	Connor	Antrim	1772-1875	1772-1845	1772-1875
"	"	"	1825-1842	1825-1842	1825-1842
Magheralin	Dromore	Down	1692-1875	1692-1845	1692-1875
"	"	"	1692-1782	1692-1782	1692-1782
Maguires Bridge	Clogher	Fermanagh	1840-1879	1840-1845	1840-1879
Milltown	Armagh	Armagh	1840-1875	1840-1845	1845-1875

Parish	Diocese	County	Baptism	Marriage	Burial
Moira	Dromore	Down	1845-1871	————	1845-1875
* "	"	"	Miscel. Trans., 1784-1860		
Moyntags (Ardmore)	Dromore	Down	1822-1875	1822-1845	1822-1875
* "	"	"	Miscel. Trans., 1789-1863		
Muckamore	Connor	Antrim	1847-1871	————	1847-1871
* "	"	"	1847-1871	————	1847-1871
Mullaghbrack	Armagh	Armagh	————	1767-1811	————
* "	"	"	————	1767-1811	————
Mullavilly	Armagh	Armagh	1821-1874	1821-1845	1821-1875
* "	"	"	1821-1864	1821-1864	1821-1875
Newcastle	Dromore	Down	1843-1875	————	————
Newry	Dromore	Down	1822-1875	1784-1845	1824-1872
Newtown-hamilton	Armagh	Armagh	1823-1826	————	————
* "	"	"	1823-1826	————	————
Portadown & St. Saviour's	Armagh	Armagh	1826-1876	1827-1845	————
* "	"	"	1858-1863	————	————
Rathlin	Connor	Antrim	Vestry book, 1769-1795		
* "	"	"	" " "		
* "	"	"	1845-1941	————	1845-1941
Saintfield	Down	Down	(1724-1757 (1798-1878	(1724-1750 (1798-1845	1798-1878
Sankill	Dromore	Armagh	1681-1767	1676-1767	1675-1753
Seagoe	Dromore	Down	(1672-1731 (1735-1865	(1676-1731 (1735-1845	(1691-1731 (1735-1881
Seapatrick	Dromore	Down	1802-1876	1802-1845	1835-1876
Skerry	Connor	Antrim	1805-1892	1826-1845	1828-1891
Stoneyford (Derryaghey)	Connor	Antrim	1845-1887	————	————
Tamlaght	Derry	Londonderry	1858-1870	————	————
Tamlaghtard	Derry	Londonderry	(1747-1775 (1820-1875	(1747-1775 (1820-1845	(1747-1775 (1820-1875
Tamlaght-finlagan	Derry	Londonderry	1796-1875	1796-1845	1796-1875
Tartaraghan	Armagh	Armagh	1824-1875	1824-1845	1828-1875
* "	"	"	1825-1828	1824-1827	————
Templecorran & Kilroot	Connor	Antrim	1848-1875	————	1856-1875
* "	"	"	————	————	1856-1872
Templemore	(See Londonderry Cathedral)				
Templepatrick	Connor	Antrim	1827-1875	1827-1845	1827-1875
Tempo	Clogher	Fermanagh	1836-1875	1836-1845	1836-1875
Termona-mongan	Derry	Tyrone	1812-1875	1812-1846	1825-1875
* "	"	"	1812-1825	1812-1825	————
Termoneeny	Derry	Londonderry	1821-1875	1821-1833	1823;1846-75
* "	"	"	1827-1839	1828-1838	1823-
Tickmacrevan or Glenarm	Connor	Antrim	(1788-1824 (1845-1876	1788-1824	1826-1876
Trory, St. Michael	Clogher	Fermanagh	1779-1875	1779-1867	1835-1875
Tullylish	Dromore	Down	1820-1875	1820-1845	1849-1875
Tullyniskin	Armagh	Tyrone	1794-1890	1794-1845	1809-1890

Parish	Diocese	County	Baptism	Marriage	Burial
Tynan	Armagh	Armagh	(1686-1724	(1683-1723	(1683-1723
			(1806-1875	(1808-1845	(1808-1875
* "	"	"	1686-1725	1683-1723	1683-1723
Tyrella	Down	Down	1839-1876	1844-	1839-
Urney	Derry	Tyrone	1813-1877	1814-1844	1815-1877
Warrenpoint	Dromore	Down	1825-1875	1826-1846	————
* "	"	"	1835-1871	1835-1846	————
Whitehouse	Connor	Antrim	1840-1875	————	————
Woods Chapel	Armagh	Londonderry	1800-1873	1808-1845	1808-1875

PUBLISHED PARISH REGISTERS OF THE FORMER ESTABLISHED CHURCH OF IRELAND, NORTHERN IRELAND

I. Publications of the Parish Register Society of Dublin and the Irish Memorials Association:

Vol. VIII, The Registers of Derry Cathedral, Parish of Templemore, 1642-1703.   (See pp. 298-299.)

Vol. XII, No. 4, The Parish Church of Belfast, Marriage Register *(Journal of Irish Memorials Association, 1931)* :

Book I, 1745-1761; Book II, 1761-1766; Book III, 1767-1784; Book IV, 1784-1799.

CHAPTER IV

RECORDS OF THE FRENCH HUGUENOT CHURCHES AND SETTLEMENTS IN IRELAND

Some Americans, descended from French Huguenots who settled in Ireland, are under the impression that their ancestors fled from France directly to Ireland, shortly after the Massacre of St. Bartholomew's Eve, in 1572. They believe their families remained in Ireland from about this date until the time of emigration to America. In such cases, it is highly probable that tradition has become confused. With very few exceptions, early refugees did not remain in Ireland. Permanent settlements developed later than in England or in the Protestant countries of Europe.

Thus, for those who do not have access to published and manuscript sources, a brief review of the Huguenot movement in relation to Ireland seems in order. An understanding of the causes, timing, conditions and places of the Huguenot settlements in Ireland will help in directing searches of church records and other Irish sources. It will also point to the possibility of family records existing in England or other places, dated during an interval between the flight from France and arrival in Ireland.

The following notes are drawn from sources listed in VOL-UME II, pp. 220-221. The most important sources will be described later as to their genealogical value, with some lists of surnames appearing in the records of various areas of settlement. An explanation of the nature and extent of the church records will also be given.

The persecution of the Huguenots in France began with intensity in 1525. They were regarded as a heretical sect, disloyal and dangerous to the Crown. Their growing strength resulted in the formulation of a confession of faith and an ecclesiastical discipline which led to a first National Synod of fifteen churches at Paris on 25 May 1559. They derived their inspiration from the constitution earlier introduced by John Calvin at Geneva, which has since become the model for all

Presbyterian churches. Hence, in doctrine, they were disciples of John Calvin and their faith was essentially Presbyterian in form. This is significant in relation to the church affiliations of the refugee Huguenots in Ireland during the seventeenth century and later.

In the latter years of Henry VIII and during the reign of Edward VI, before 1553, French Huguenots had come to England in great numbers to avoid the persecutions which had steadily increased after 1525. Thomas Gimlette, author of *The Huguenot Settlers in Ireland,* states (pp. 119, 124), "When Mary ascended the throne, England was full of foreign Protestants. Several were also settled in the English Pale in Ireland. In no part of Europe was there such freedom from molestation. During the five years of her reign, few remained in any part of her dominions." "Proclamation was made in the seaports of both England and Ireland, that all foreigners should depart without let or hindrance, and the permission was speedily availed in both countries."

With Queen Elizabeth's encouragement, a little colony of Flemish Protestants was established at Swords, County Dublin. Jealousy of foreign Protestants and the religious disturbances discouraged any permanent settlement, and it was not a success. In 1569, some Huguenots, believed to have come from Flanders, appeared in Cork. On 12 July of that year, a petition to the mayor demanded their exodus. Nothing more is heard of the settlement.

Gimlette goes on to state that "after the fearful massacre of St. Bartholomew's Eve, men, women and children fled to the southern shores of England . . . and after a little while, not a few were sojourners in some of the garrison towns of Ireland." Their stay was short because of the Edict of Nantes proclaimed in 1598, by Henry IV. This granted security to the French Protestants, perpetually and irrevocably, with limited religious freedom, complete freedom of conscience, civil equality, guarantees of justice, and a state subsidy for Huguenot troops and ministers, and invited the refugees to return, declaring their children born abroad should become French citizens. Thus, with few exceptions, those who had come to Ireland disappeared.

The privileges and protections granted in the Edict of Nantes allowed the Huguenots to reach a height of power in 1621, when their General Assembly appealed to the Courts of Europe for support of a declaration of independence. Their leaders were accused of high treason, and their political power was broken. While they were still allowed a restricted freedom of worship and civil rights, the pressure and persecution to compel conversions steadily increased.

Thus England, followed by Scotland, welcomed a new wave of refugee Huguenots who came fearful of further trouble in France. They began filtering into Ireland from this time until 1641, at which time the Roman Catholic Rebellion broke out and Protestants fled for their lives, back to England, Scotland, and the Continent. A high percentage of those who did remain, suffered death from murder and privation. At this time the Huguenots had no settled communities of their own. Unprotected except within the Pale, their exodus was general.

In 1649, Cromwell came to Ireland with his army of 20,000 men. He brought a number of Huguenots from the eastern counties of England, employed as officers and soldiers. With the aid of English and Scottish Protestant forces previously there, the last fighting ceased in 1652 and the Roman Catholics were completely crushed. The Commonwealth Government paid the officers and soldiers with debentures for a stipulated number of acres of Irish land, according to their rank and service. Also, funds were raised to finance the war, by the sale of Irish land warrants in England. It is estimated that 11,000,000 acres belonging to Roman Catholic proprietors and Protestant Royalists were confiscated. The Cromwellian "Act of Settlement" set the program by which the land in twenty-six counties, formerly owned by Irish Catholics, etc., was granted to the Protestant army and purchasers who held warrants, government officials and others of influence. At this time many Huguenots received large and small acreage.

Between 1659 and 1682, numerous Edicts were issued in France, attacking the Huguenots on all sides with increasing pressure. The loss of civil and religious liberty became more evident and the persecutions to force conversions to the Roman Catholic faith became intolerable. During the first decade this resulted in a Huguenot emigration of such proportions that France attempted to stop it by an Edict in 1669. This did not prevent the stream of emigration.

The exodus which brought many thousands to England and some organized colonies to Ireland was encouraged by the offer of Charles II after the Restoration, to give the Huguenots protection and civil as well as religious freedom.   In 1662, the Duke of Ormonde, Lord Lieutenant of Ireland, introduced in the Irish Parliament, an "Act for Encouraging Protestant Strangers and Others to Inhabit Ireland." This Act, which received Royal sanction, provided that all Protestants who were foreign born could, within seven years, come to any part of the Kingdom with their stocks and families to inhabit, upon taking the Oaths of Allegiance and Supremacy, whereupon they "shall be reputed the King's Natural Born Liege Subjects," and gave them the privileges, with the payment of fees and certain regulations, of becoming freemen, members of any Guild, etc., in any city, borough or incorporated town, with rights of trading, buying, selling, and working as freemen, but each restricted to no more than six apprentices.

Following the Act, the Duke of Ormonde established colonies in Dublin and Cork cities where they introduced glove making, silk weaving, lace making and the manufacture of cloth and linen.   He also settled linen weavers at Chapelizod in County Dublin, and woolen manufacturers at Carrick-on-Suir and Clonmel in County Tipperary, where they joined some who had received large land grants from the Commonwealth Government following the Rebellion.   Others went to County Waterford where earlier Commonwealth settlers were established.

The refugees were growing prosperous with their trade, and because of additional privileges granted by Charles II in 1674 and 1681 which provided free passports, naturalization and free passage of refugee goods into the country, as well as freedom of occupation and religious protection.

In 1685, the Edict of Nantes was finally revoked and the Huguenots were deprived of their last vestige of civil and religious liberty.   Thousands escaped, risking penalties of imprisonment, death, torture and slavery in the French galleys.

The brief reign of King James II of England, 1685-1688, was followed by three years of war in Ireland, 1689-1691, after he fled to France when, on 13 Feb. 1689, his daughter Mary and her husband William, Prince of Orange, were crowned in London. The struggle of the two monarchs for the Crown brought both to Ireland. The entire populace arose to take sides. The Roman Catholics, in a last stand to keep the civil, religious and military liberty recently granted by James II, who had embraced their faith, saw in him their only hope of regaining their forfeited lands and further liberties. The Roman Catholic military commanders appointed by James II during his reign led a great army, aided by arms and funds from France.

William III, supported by the Protestants, sent his commander, Marshal Schomberg, to Ireland where he landed at Bangor with 20,000 men in August, 1689. One entire regiment of horse was made up of Huguenots raised in England. William landed at Carrickfergus in June, 1690, with forces including Huguenots who had enlisted under him and at his expense in Holland. They formed three regiments of foot under La Melonière, Du Cambon and La Caillemotte Ruvigny. A fifth regiment of dragoons under Miremont eventually became entirely made up of Huguenots.

In gratitude after his victory in 1691, William III declared "that all French Protestants that shall seek their refuge in our Kingdom shall not only have our Royal protection for themselves, families and estates . . . to support, aid and assist them in their several trades and ways of livelihood as to that their living . . . in this realm may be comfortable and easy to them." Shortly thereafter a large number of Huguenots who served in the army were granted Irish lands forfeited by the Roman Catholic proprietors.

The Marquis de Ruvigny was created Earl of Galway and granted the Portarlington, Queen's County estate, which he let on easy terms to Huguenot settlers including some army pensioners. Rene De La Fausille was appointed Governor of Sligo, while the third Duke of Schomberg was created Duke of Leinster, and Ruvigny was made the Lieutenant-General of the Army in Ireland.

Huguenots placed on the Pension List of 1702 numbered 590, including officers, enlisted men and a few civilians. Their names and their statements with lists of their private property and information regarding their families, declared to the Auditor-General, show them settled mostly at Belfast, Dublin, Waterford, and Youghal. The information was abstracted from the volume of records and printed in the *Proceedings of the Huguenot Society of London,* Volume VI. The original records were destroyed in the Public Record Office fire in Dublin, 1922.

After the war, King William favored the Huguenots and benefited Ireland by bringing many from Holland. Strong settlements of linen manufacturers were established at Lisburn, Kilkenny and Waterford. In Dublin they wove silk and poplin and, by 1728, opened a Linen Hall. In Cork they made sail-cloth, and at Dundalk and Lurgan they made cambric. Some 600 families came from Holland and refugees were also sent from Switzerland. Following this era of planned Huguenot colonization, numerous individuals, families and small allied parties continued to arrive in Ireland during the first half of the eighteenth century and somewhat later.

The principal published sources regarding the Huguenots in Ireland are listed in VOLUME II, pp. 220-221. These consist of documented history of the entire Huguenot movement and their settlements in Ireland; also the existing French Church Registers. The histories are a rich source of biographical and genealogical notes taken from town, city or church records, state papers and some private family manuscripts, etc. In many cases information includes some or all of such data as the parentage of the refugee, his origin and further records in France, notes as to the previous English or foreign residence, time or date of arrival in one or more places of settlement in Ireland, occupation, civic or religious activity, marriage and family alliances, names and data about children, their marriages and alliances, further descendants, and some few notes regarding families or members of which emigrated to America. Individual and family history varies in length from one sentence to twelve pages. Most accounts are confined to one or a few paragraphs and scattered notes relating to their activities.

These notes show that in numerous cases the refugees or their children removed from one community to another. A good many came to Dublin from the less strong settlements in the southern interior and western regions as well as from Cork, Portarlington, Waterford and Youghal. The Chapelizod settlement failed early in the eighteenth century as did those of Clonmel and Carrick-on-Suir. This latter colony and that of Wexford seem to have merged with the Dublin settlement, where the Huguenots grew wealthy and had their choice between the two French Churches which conformed to the liturgy and ecclesiastical jurisdiction of the Established Church, or could join one of the two Non-Conformist French Calvinist Churches. Some Belfast settlers are found later in Dublin, while other refugees or their children removed from the strong Lisburn colony to Belfast or Dublin. Also, some members of families in Belfast and Dublin went to Cork and Waterford. They moved about, not only for religious reasons, but also to better their working conditions for they were a thrifty and industrious people who prospered.

It is remarkable that the migrations of so many individuals and families have been traced by the historians. However, there are names and records of Huguenots noted in the later years of the settlements, without mention of a previous place of residence. Some of these surnames are found in earlier records of different localities. In some cases the records of better known allied families may furnish clues to lost identities.

The historians have made no attempt to compile completed genealogical works. However, their well documented information regarding the colonies, smaller settlements, and the data concerning the refugees and their descendants so far as it goes, will furnish a guide to the genealogists in the searching of wills, deeds, leases, and other materials relating to their work.

In the course of time, descendants of the refugees ceased to cling to their own people. While at first even the scattered

Huguenots could be identified by their French names, these in many cases became anglicized. Intermarriage with people of English, Scottish or Irish origins gradually absorbed them. These changes caused all French colonies and settlements to lose their identity.

As it is important for the genealogists to keep in mind the locations of early and later distinctive French settlements, described or noted by the historians, these place-names are listed below, by province, county, and city or town.

ULSTER: *Antrim:* Belfast, Lambeg, Lisburn. *Armagh:* Lurgan. *Down:* Dromore. *Monaghan:* Castleblaney.

LEINSTER: *Carlow:* Carlow. *Dublin:* Dublin, Chapelizod. *Kilkenny:* Kilkenny. *Louth:* Collon, Dundalk. *Meath* and *Westmeath:* Miscellaneous. *Queen's:* Portarlington. *Wexford:* Enniscorthy, Wexford. *Wicklow:* Wicklow.

MUNSTER: *Cork:* Bandon, Cork, Innishannon, Kinsale, Youghal. *Limerick:* Limerick. *Tipperary:* Carrick-on-Suir, Clonmel. *Waterford:* Tallow, Waterford.

CONNAUGHT: *Clare:* Killaloe. *Galway:* Galway. *Mayo:* Killala. *Sligo:* Sligo.

HUGUENOT CHURCH RECORDS

As stated early in this chapter, the French Huguenots were disciples of John Calvin from the early part of the sixteenth century and in doctrine their faith was essentially Presbyterian in form.

The historian, Samuel Smiles, states in *The Huguenots, their Settlements, Churches and Industries in England and Ireland,* 1867 (pp. 128-129), "An attempt was indeed made by Bishop Laud, in the reign of Charles I, in 1622, to compel the refugees, who were for the most part Calvinists, to conform to the English liturgy. On this, the foreign congregations appealed to the King, pleading the hospitality extended to them by the nation when they had fled from papal persecution abroad, and the privileges and exemptions granted to them by Edward VI, which had been confirmed by Elizabeth and James, and even by Charles I, himself. The utmost concession the King would grant was, that those who were born aliens might still enjoy the use of their own church service; but that all their children born in England should regularly attend the parish churches. Even this small concession was limited only to the congregation at Canterbury, and measures were taken to force conformity in other dioceses."

The decisions of the English Government and the influence of the Established Church which was strongly represented by its bishops in the Parliament and in matters of State, extended to Ireland which was under its ecclesiastical jurisdiction. Thus the early printed Parish Registers of Dublin, and of Christ Church in Cork, contain some records of refugees.

Throughout the period of the Commonwealth and the Protectorate, when the Established Church was powerless, more religious freedom and protection was granted the Huguenots. After the Restoration, Charles II expressed particular sympathy for the Huguenots because of his earlier observations of their persecution while he was an exile in France. Thus, when the Established Church again came into power under his reign, it trod lightly with the Huguenots, especially in Ireland, after the Royal sanction was given to the Act of the Irish Parliament of 1662, introduced by the Duke of Ormonde, "for Encouraging Protestant Strangers to Inhabit Ireland," and granted them civil and religious liberty.

Following this the Established Church, with Government sanction and financial aid, benevolently extended its influence by providing churches for French Protestant worship in the strongest Huguenot colonies. They were allowed to choose ministers of their own Calvinistic faith to preach in the French language but, as clergy, they were necessarily ordained by the bishops of the Established Church which extended ecclesiastical jurisdiction over all affairs of the French Churches thus created. They were also provided with the Book of Common Prayer, translated into the French language, as it had been from the time of Edward VI.

The earliest French Church was established in Dublin in 1665. The Huguenots, who settled there before this date, attended the Established Church of their parish. Some of their records of baptism, marriage and burial are found in the early (now published) Parish Registers, both before they acquired a French Church of their own, and afterward in some cases due to intermarriages with people of English origin. In 1700, a second French Conformist Church was opened. Meanwhile, in 1692, a French Non-Conformist Church was opened and, in 1697, a part of this congregation formed another branch Church. As the Registers of all four Dublin French Churches have been published, these will be described later.

In 1667, some five hundred families were invited from Canterbury, England, to settle in Carlow. They brought their own French minister and, by 1696, had their own Conformist Church. The historian, D. C. Agnew, stated that the Church Registers from this date to 1744 were lost.

The refugees were early settlers in the City of Waterford and, as indicated by the Established Church Registers, were scattered through the seven parishes. By 1693, they were provided with a French minister and a place of their own for worship.

The early Huguenots of the City of Cork worshiped in Christ Church and the Registers of this parish from 1642 to 1694 contain a few records of various families. Their first French congregation with their refugee minister was organized in 1694. The second French Church in Cork was founded by a group of new refugees in 1745.

Shortly after the Portarlington colony was established, it was provided with a French Church and minister in 1694. The Registers of this Church have also been printed and will be described.

A large group of Huguenots were invited to come from Holland and settle at Lisburn where they were given their own French Church and minister in 1697. The Registers of this Church have not been preserved, but much has been written about the settlers which will be noted later.

The size of the settlements in all provinces but Ulster can roughly be judged by the fact that the Established Church also provided ministers for fifty or more Huguenots in any one place, who furnished a congregation under the ecclesiastical jurisdiction of the bishop of the diocese. Ministers were sent to Clonmel, Dundalk, Innishannon, Kilkenny and Wexford. The group in Wexford was allowed to worship in St. Mary's Church with a French minister who came to them in 1684. Kilkenny opened French services in 1694, Clonmel in 1699, Dundalk in 1737, and Innishannon for a brief time beginning in 1760.

In the provinces of Leinster, Munster and Connaught, wherever the Huguenot settlements were smaller or only a few families resided, they had no church or minister of their own. Their records should be sought in the Established Church Registers of the parish in which they resided.

Ulster offered a strong attraction for the Huguenots. They tended to seek refuge with the Scotch Presbyterians who worshiped according to their own faith. Many removed from scattered southern communities to northern counties and towns where, except for Lisburn, they did not have French Churches or ministers of their own. It is hard to tell how many Huguenots settled in Belfast, Castleblaney, Dromore, Lambeg, Lurgan and other places besides the strong colony at Lisburn, for where there were no French Churches of their own they did not live unto themselves in a community.

PUBLISHED CHURCH REGISTERS

The Huguenot Society of London has published the existing Registers of the French Churches in Ireland which are five in number. A few notes of explanation will clarify their contents.

In 1665, the Established Church of Ireland provided St. Mary's Chapel in St. Patrick's Cathedral, Dublin, for a Huguenot congregation. In 1700, St. Mary's Abbey was also opened to them for a French Church. These two churches united in 1716. The two churches and later the united congregation conformed to the Episcopal liturgy under the ecclesiastical jurisdiction of the Established Church.

The Registers of the French Conformed Churches of St. Patrick and St. Mary, Dublin. Edited by J. J. Digges La Touche. Printed for the Huguenot Society of London, Volume VII. London, 1893.

	Baptisms.	Marriages.	Burials.
St. Patrick's	1668-1687	1680-1716	1680-1716
St. Mary's	1705-1716	1705-1715	1705-1715
United Churches	1716-1818	1716-1788	1716-1830

Two French Non-Conformist Calvinist Churches were organized in Dublin, after the war of 1689-1691, when William III granted renewed and increased protection and privileges to the Huguenots. Information taken from the Introduction to the published *Registers of the French Non-Conformist Churches of Lucy Lane and Peter Street, Dublin,* shows that the first Calvinistic Non-Conformist Church was formed in 1692, and at first met in a house in Bride Street, after which from 1701-1711, they met in a house in Wood Street. Ground for a cemetery was acquired in a location near Newmarket on the Coombe. In 1711, this congregation built a church on Peter Street, with a cemetery attached. In 1697, a second Non-Conformist group, an offshoot of the Bride Street congregation, acquired an ancient chapel on the west side of Lucy Lane, otherwise Mass Street, and now Chancery Place. Its cemetery was established in Merrion Row, off St. Stephen's Green. In 1707, this Lucy Lane congregation was reunited with that of Wood Street, in its church government, under one consistory. The Lucy Lane congregation continued its Church until 1773, when it was sold to a congregation of Seceding Presbyterians of Skinner's Alley, and was in their hands for fifty years. The Peter Street congregation closed its services in 1814.

The Registers of the French Non-Conformist Churches of Lucy Lane and Peter Street, Dublin. Edited by Thomas Philip Le Fanu. Printed for the Huguenot Society of London, Volume XIV. Aberdeen, 1901. The original Registers consist of two volumes, containing entries as follows:

Volume One: Baptisms, 1701-1731; Burials, 1702-1731; Marriages, 1702-1728; Reconnaissances, 1716-1730.

Volume Two: Burials, 1771-1887 (published to 1831). Vandals burned the Registers in 1771, containing Baptisms, Marriages, Burials, 1732-1771. The Registers of Baptisms and Marriages, after 1771, are missing.

The Portarlington colony in Queen's County established a

French Church in 1692. They adhered to their native form of worship with their own French minister, supported by Lord Galway who built their church and school, and by subscriptions of the congregation. By 1702, they had two churches and schools when, by order of the English Parliament, all were conveyed to the Bishop of Kildare who consecrated the churches and provided his ordained ministers for the two congregations; one being English Protestant and the other French Protestant. Whereupon the congregations conformed and worshiped under the ecclesiastical jurisdiction of the Established Church of Ireland.

The Registers of the French Church of Portarlington, Ireland. Edited by Thomas Philip Le Fanu. Printed for the Huguenot Society of London. London, 1908. The original Registers consist of two volumes, containing entries as follows:

Volume One: Baptisms, Marriages, Burials, 3 June 1694-8th October 1728.

Volume Two: Baptisms, Marriages, Burials, 14 August 1729-20 September 1816.

The Introductions to the three volumes, published by the Huguenot Society of London, contain history of each colony with mention of the ministers and some other men of importance. Biographical notes mention their marriages and children in a few cases. All Registers were kept in the French language.

Copies of these Huguenot Society of London publications may occasionally be found in the Dublin Bookshops, particularly at Hodges Figgis and Company, Ltd., 6 Dawson Street, Dublin, as has been the case since 1950.

HISTORICAL WORKS

The published source materials are listed in VOLUME II, pp. 220-221. Some copies of these may be found in the larger genealogical libraries of the United States. The Irish Bookshops have also acquired various works from time to time. The National Library of Ireland has all Huguenot publications of Irish interest, as do the other large historical libraries. The Linen Hall Library in Belfast has all except perhaps the works of Agnew and Carre. Some notes on the most helpful published sources are as follows:

AGNEW, D. C. *Protestant Exiles from France in the Reign of Louis XIV;* or the Huguenot refugees and their descendants in Great Britain and Ireland. This extensive work of three volumes describes the causes of the Huguenot emigration, the timing, conditions and places of their settlements in Great Britain and Ireland. Information is given concerning hundreds of families; their origins, biographical notes of individuals, their various places of settlement, alliances, occupations, descendants, etc. Agnew was highly regarded by later writers and has been liberally quoted.

He divides the refugees into three groups and, in his third volume, gives the names in Tables; the first is a list of names of settlers prior to the reign of Louis XIV, of France; the second gives the names of those who settled during the reign of Louis XIV; the third contains the names of the refugees who were naturalized by Letters Patent.

Some families in the first group coming to settle in Ireland were: Beauford, Bonnell, Chamberlaine, Dombrain, Langlais (Langley), La Tranche (Trench), Lefroy (Loffroy), Bailleux.

Information is provided on the more important families in the second group of the following names: Abbadie, Barré, Bailleux (Bayley), Belcastel, Beranger, Blaquiere, Boileau, Bouherau, Brocas, Burgeois (Burges), Cambon, Carle, Champagné, Chenevix, Dargent, De La Cheroie, De Laval, De Lavalade, Des Voeux, D'Olier, Drelincourt, Du Bédat, Dubourdieu, Dury, Gaussen, Geneste, Gosset, Gually, Guillot, Guyon, Labat (Labatt), Labouchere, La Roche, La Trobe, Layard, Le Fanu, Le Tablére, Mangin, Mathy, Maturin, Mercier, Misson, Morell, Perrin, Raboteau, Reynet (De Reynet), Roche, Rocheblave, Teulon (Tholan), Vignoles.

GIMLETTE, THOMAS. *The History of the Huguenot Settlers in Ireland.* This work of 296 pages, with Appendices and maps, was not finished as the author planned, due to his death. Thus it is not indexed and stops after the campaign of William III, as far as the general history is given. He devotes 41 pages to the Huguenot colony of Dublin and evidently planned to continue with more detail about the other important colonies. As an appendix, his 22 pages on the Waterford settlement is added, which is a reprint of his articles written for the *Ulster Journal of Archaeology*. His first 108 pages are devoted to a history of the Huguenots in France, and some families later represented as refugees in Ireland are included. His 188 pages bearing on the Irish records are presented in periods of time under the various reigns and the Commonwealth. His work is primarily historical but with the records of individuals included. He offers some biographical notes, family origins, alliances, and three important lists:

1. A list of 42 foreign Protestants who were refugees, or their descendants, who obtained grants of lands under the Commonwealth Government, with the location and number of acres acquired by each grantee. Also a few houses in Dublin were granted. The smallest acreage was granted to Mathew De Renzie, of 115 acres in Queen's County, while the two largest grants were made to Andrew Ricard who received 3,435 acres in Counties Waterford and Tipperary, and to Thomas Guyllyms who was granted 3,667 acres in County Cavan.

2. A list of 66 foreign Protestants with their county of residence who were attainted by James II. Some of these surnames are in the above list.

3. A list of 185 French Huguenot officers who served with Schomberg in the war in Ireland, 1689-1691, several of whom were afterward settled in Dublin, Portarlington, Cork, Youghal, Waterford and Lisburn.

LEE, GRACE LAWLESS. *The Huguenot Settlements In Ireland*. This book published by Longmans, Green and Co. in London, New York and Toronto, 1936, is not only the most easily available but is the most helpful to the genealogist. The author's intention is to trace the Huguenot families, their origins, time of arrival in Ireland, places of settlement, activities, alliances, removals from place to place, and the records of individuals, their children, marriages, and a few records of emigration to America. The information in this 281 page work is well documented and contains an index of over 1,000 items, mostly surnames. The emphasis is on personal history of the Huguenots in the various colonies, smaller settlements and some scattered locations. A bibliography of sources includes most of those in this compiler's list, from which many quotations and references are made. Information has also been taken from general history, local history, biography, contemporary publications of manuscript materials, historical society journals, newspapers and unpublished manuscripts. The following settlements have been described together with the refugee residents:

1. The Colony of Cork City and other settlements in Bandon, Innishannon, Kinsale and Youghal, County Cork.

2. The settlements in Waterford and Wexford cities and smaller places in the counties.

3. The Ormonde group and Colony at Carlow.

4. The Settlement at Portarlington.

5. The Colony at Lisburn and other Settlements at Belfast, Castleblaney, Lambeg, Lurgan, etc.

6. The Huguenots of Dublin and its environs.

7. The Western Settlers of Killaloe, Limerick, Galway, etc.

SMILES, SAMUEL. *The Huguenots: Their Settlements, Churches and Industries in England and Ireland.* The author devotes only one chapter (XVI, pp. 357-388) to Huguenot settlements in Ireland. However, there are numerous personal references throughout his 521 pages relating to Huguenots who were important in the Irish settlements. His Appendix III, pp. 496-521, contains brief sentence notes or a paragraph relating to each of 39 men who went to Ireland, giving some family information. He devotes several pages to the Cork Colony and the family history of its first French minister, Fontaine, and his descendants. He briefly describes the colonies of Dublin, Lisburn, Portarlington, Waterford and Youghal, together with their churches and principal men including their activities and some origins.

The names of the refugees, which he mentions with more or less brief information, are as follows: Abbadie, Bacquencourt, Barré, Blosset, Blaquiere, Boileau, Bonnell, Bouhérau,

Champagne, Chaigneaus, Chenevix, Collet, Crommelin, De La Chervois, De Laval, De Lavalade, De Ruvigny, Des Voeux, Drelincourt, Droz, Dubourdieu, Fleury, Fontaine, Geneste, Goyer, Gualy, Guillot, Hazard (Hasaret), Larochefoucauld, La Touche, La Tranche, Layard, Lefroy, Logier, Majendiu, Maturin, Maziers, Pechell, Perrin, Raboteau, Roche, Saurin, Teulon (Tholon), Thorius, Vignoles, Villette.

THE ULSTER JOURNAL OF ARCHAEOLOGY. First Series, vols. 1-4, 1853-1856; vol. 9, 1861-1862. A series of articles regarding "The French Settlers in Ireland," concerns the Colonies at Lisburn, Youghal, Portarlington, Waterford, and Belfast. Some notes regarding these colonies and the names of the principal families are as follows:

1. "The Huguenot Colony of Lisburn, County of Antrim." By Charles Nicholas De La Cherois Purdon. Vol. 1, pp. 209-217; 286-294; Vol. 2, pp. 167-179.

Lisburn was settled shortly after 1697 when an Act was passed by the English Parliament for the encouragement of the Irish growth of flax and the manufacture of linen cloth. William III, knowing the proficiency of the Huguenot refugees in Holland in the art of linen, silk and poplin manufacture, invited Louis Crommelin, to become "Overseer of the Royal Linen Manufacture of Ireland." Crommelin's experience and leadership in the industry in which his family had engaged for over 400 years in France, fitted him to plant and guide the new settlement at Lisburn (then called Lisnagarvey) and rebuild the old town which had been destroyed with war. Crommelin brought 1,000 looms and spinning-wheels from Holland and a large colony of refugees. These Lisburn families closely adhered to each other, preserved their language and intermarried among themselves for two or three generations. They were granted their own French Church and minister. No Register of this Church exists. However, the author states that many attended the Established Church of the parish, the records of which contain their lists of baptism, marriage and burial as these Registers date from 1661.

The author devotes a page, more or less, to the records of each of the following families of Crommelin, Mangin, Dubourdieu, Goyer, Dupre, Bulmer, Dubourdieu (additional data), De Lavalade, Roche, Geneste, De Blaquiere, Perrin, Guillot, and De Saurin (Saurin).

Some 59 other families are represented in the old Vestry Books and Parish Registers, namely: Brethet, Bulroy, Birrel, Bonace, Burto (Bourto), Blosset, Bonley, Comière, Colbert, Covart (Quavert), Chartes (Chaters), De Berniere, Druet (Drewet, Drued, Druid), Drufan, Defou, Darele, Dufore, Dela Hyde, Deluze, Driffet (Treufet), De Armine, Duliez, Duard, Denmar, Dalton, Domville (Dumvill, Dumbill), De Lap (Dulap), De Vanny, Foguy, Gornal, Garran, Gothard, Higuet, Labady (L'Abbadir?), Lefevre, La Briol (Labrel), Ledrue, Languel, Lascelles, Leroy, Maskue, Marret (Merret), Morrell, Merron, Martine, Maslin, Nebur, Nois, Noblet, Prorié, Petticrew, Purdee, Purdue, Rothell, Réné, Stalliard, Touchamp, Trimullete (Tremmule), Treufet, Taverner, Vandas, Vagieux, Valentin. The author protects himself with the statement that "There is a possibility that several of the above names may not be French."

2. "The French Settlement at Youghal, County Cork." By the Rev. Samuel Hayman. Vol. 2, pp. 223-229. In 1693, about fifty French Huguenots who were retired military officers and soldiers, following the war of 1689-1691, were invited to settle in Youghal by the mayor and corporation of the town. Being a small group of families they early ceased to exist as a distinctive unit in the town. They conformed soon to the Established Church of their parish and their marks of military rank appear in the Parish Registers. The principal families of this group were as follows: Boisrond, Chaigneau, Coluon, D'Anvers, Dehays, Delappe, Desieres, Duclos, Falquiere, Guin, Labatte, Legardere, Lampriere, Marvault, Maziere, Perdu, Ricard, Roviere. The author gives brief notes on the families and states that their names of French origin are still common in the town.

3. "The Huguenot Colony at Portarlington, in the Queen's County." By Sir Erasmus D. Borrowes. Vol. 3, pp. 56-67; 213-231. Portarlington was founded as a Huguenot colony by the Marquis de Ruvigny, created Earl of Galway, to whom William III granted it as an estate. The 267 refugees who settled there were largely noblemen and gentlemen who had

served as officers and soldiers under Schomberg, La Melonnière, La Caillemotte, Cambon and others, in the forces of William, Prince of Orange, in Ireland. Ruvigny leased the land to the settlers on easy terms and helped establish and maintain a French Church which was organized in 1694 with their own French minister. By 1696, the Church was erected, also an English Church, and two schools were established. They had introduced all the amenities of culture when, in 1703, Parliament revoked the grant of the Portarlington estate to the Earl of Galway and took the property for the Government, threatening ruin to the settlers. The Hollow Sword Blade Company of London came to the rescue by purchasing the estate of 8,312 acres from the Government at a sale in Dublin, and allowing the Huguenots to continue to hold their leases. The Government retained the two churches and the schools which were made property of the Established Church of Ireland, under the Bishop of Kildare who required the churches to conform with his ordained ministers, and controlled the schools.

Among the noblemen and gentlemen of the early colony were the Marquis of Paray, the Sieur de Hauteville, Louis le Blanc, Sieur de Percé, Charles de Ponthieu, Captain d'Alnuis and his brother, Abel Pelissier, David d'Arripe, Ruben de la Rochefoucauld, the Sieur de la Boissière, Guy de la Blachière de Bonneval, Dumont de Bostaquet, Franquefort, Châteauneuf, La Beaume, Montpeton du Languedoc, Vicomte de Laval, Pierre Goulin, Jean la Ferriere, De Gaudry, Jean Lafaurie, Abel de Ligonier de Vignoles, Anthoine de Ligonier and numerous others. The Church Registers also show, by occupation, the Fouberts as linen manufacturers, the Blancs as butchers, the Micheaus as farmers, La Borde as a mason, Capel the blacksmith, Gautier the carpenter, and in addition there were other tradesmen and laborers.

4. "The Settlement in Waterford." By the Rev. Thomas Gimlette. Vol. 4, pp. 198-221. The French refugee colony at Waterford was large and important. The town being situated for trade on the river Suir, it was especially named in the Act of Parliament, 1662 and 1672, as chosen for French Huguenot merchants and traders to settle. In 1693, the Cor-

poration of Waterford, wishing for the disbanded Huguenot
officers and soldiers to settle and also those skilled as manufacturers of linens, silks, woolens, etc., provided habitations
for fifty families. The Choir of the old Franciscan monastery
was assigned to them for worship and a pastor was given support for the French Church over which the bishop of the diocese claimed jurisdiction.

From the Parochial Registers it is indicated that they did
not settle in a colony in any distinct part of the city and, while
they lived within the walls, they were scattered throughout
the seven parishes. They preserved the French language in
worship in their own French Church and were also listed in
the Registers of the other parishes. Church wardens in St.
Patrick's Parish were Henri Blanche, Alexander D'Maison,
John D'Maison, Tobias Linnegar, Samuel Oderoft, Anthoine
Harerein, Hector Boisrond, Marquis Guillard, Germain Lune.
In St. Peter's, and St. John's, among the last churchwardens
appointed before the union with St. Patrick's, appear Charles
L'Maistre, Nicholas Spusson, Peter Duclà, John Shelmadine,
Capt. Sautelle, and Francois Spurrier. In St. Olave's, were
James H. Reynette, Thomas Latrobe, and Jean Vinson. In the
Cathedral (Trinity), were Messrs. Gayott and St. Legere.

Being in a port city, the manufacture of sail cloth was introduced by the Huguenots, promoted by Louis Crommelin of
Lisburn, who applied for and received a Crown subsidy for
increasing the linen trade and establishing a sail cloth factory
in Waterford. This trade continued for many years and its
Guild became wealthy. Among those who prospered, there
were represented in the City Council the names of Chaigneau,
Gayott, Vashon, Ayrault. In 1707, John Espaignet was sheriff
of the city. In 1709, Jeremy Gayott was sheriff. Vashon was
alderman in 1719, and mayor in 1726. Peter Vashon was
sheriff in 1735, and in 1738, 1739, Simon Vashon, Jun., was
mayor. Two representing the medical profession were Dr.
Peter De Rante, and Dr. Jacques Reynette.

The Appendix to the *Journal of the Irish House of Commons*, 1719, contains a return of Theophilus Desbrisac, of the
different pensions which had "fallen in" from the French
troops, and also of those who were placed upon the pension

list. Among those settled in Waterford were James D'Augier, who died in Waterford on 11 September 1718. Others were Peter Chelar, Capt. Abraham Franquefort, Capt. John Vaury, Capt. Louis Belafaye.

The Parochial Registers, from 1708, contain the names of Deliz, Duschenne, Belafaye, Delaville, De Lamaindre, Major Sautelle, D'Maison, Blanche, Coquin, Denis, Latrobe, Dermozan, Dugay, Marcel, Chenevix, Fleury.

Other names mentioned in the city records are Vaury, Sandos, Chelar, Perrin, Ponseaux, Petipres, Roquet, Frank, Latour, Tournere, Adderle, Martel.

5. "The French Settlers in Belfast." By C. D. Purdon. Vol. 9, pp. 142-147. Purdon does not make the statement which Agnew did, that the settlement of Huguenots in Belfast was made up largely of the rank and file of disbanded men from Schomberg's army. However, several did arrive shortly after 1691. Among the earliest settlers before 1685 were Le Byrtt (Byrt), and de Lolme. The Currell family is descended from the private secretary of Mary, Queen of Scots. Richard Curle was sworn a freeman on 25 Oct. 1666.

French officers in King William's army who died in Belfast were the Chevalier De Champagné, and one Balquière. The Chartrès family trace their royal descent through the Viscount de Lavalle of Portarlington. This family settled in Bandon, County Cork, then Lisburn and Belfast. The name Gillan became well known after 1700. The Gaussen family of County Londonderry, descended from a refugee in England, is represented by a branch in Belfast. The Godsell family came from County Cork. The Dolling family is descended from the Count of Thoulouse and one who took the name Dolling when he escaped to England about 1580. Thomas Pottinger, the first "sovereign" of Belfast, was the father of another Thomas who was High Sheriff of County Antrim and raised the county in favor of William III. The Sueter family is descended from a French clergyman. Individuals from Lisburn families were of names Saurin and Goyer. Forcade was a physician.

Huguenot families settled in Belfast in the 18th century whose names appear in the Parish Registers are: Bruet, Culbert, Dumay, Juret, Lisle, Luney, Nipe, Pimblet, Prynault, Pettigrew, Sandal, D'Alton, Ayres, Lackney, Guest, Floyer, Latimer, Hugart, Godsell, Cuney, Morrin, Mallard, Bey, Jamphrey.

Others of French or Norman origin who are known to have come from Scotland and England, but not Huguenots, are: Charters, Dunville, Weir (De Vere), La Mont, Suffern (Souverain), Tomb, Montgomery, Sinclair (St. Clair), Telfair (Taille-fer), Joy, Lesquier, Mereci. A more recent French name, not Huguenot, is Burdot.

THE CITY OF CORK COLONY: The records of the Huguenots who came as refugees to the City of Cork are written with considerable detail by Agnew, Gimlette, Lee, and Smiles. Lee devotes 40 pages to this colony and 22 more to other County Cork colonies. Documents quoted by the historians are: The Council Book of the Corporation of Cork, the Vestry Books of Christ Church, the Freemen's Register, the Court of D'Oyer Hundred Book, and the Apprentice Indenture Enrolment Book, the latter three being transcribed by Richard Caulfield. Other miscellaneous references are numerous and include State Papers, Journals of the Irish House of Commons, The Huguenot Society of London Publications, Personal Documents, etc. Another careful historian who has given attention to Huguenot records, including them in his published work, is Charles Smith, author of *The Ancient and Present State of the County and City of Cork*, 1750. (New ed., 1893-4.)

Huguenots served as mayors, sheriffs, representatives in the City Council, members of the Goldsmith's Guild, and appear as tradesmen in the Freemen's Registers. They were professional men, merchants, manufacturers of sail-cloth, distillers, sugar refiners, etc.

The Goble and Robinette families are represented among the Cork goldsmiths of 1656, and several others were members of this Goldsmith's Guild at later dates. The Parish Registers of Christ Church show that the Huguenots were members of this Church in some numbers before 1690. They organized a French Church which met for a time in the County Courtroom and, after 1694, in the home of their first French minister, James Fontaine, who escaped France in that year. Smiles devotes 12 pages to the *Memoirs* of Fontaine, which include the records of his eight children and his wife's family. His sons Peter, Francis, James, John, and a daughter who married Matthew Maury, all emigrated to the American Colony of Virginia. Fontaine also gives data concerning the refugees Roussier, Bonnet, Abelin, De La Croix, Marcomb, Caillon, Renue, Cesteau, Ardouin, Hanneton and Renue (Renew), the latter being sheriff in 1691 and mayor in 1694.

The Register of Cork Freeman, 1685, shows the names of Huguenot refugees: Peter Rogue, John James Ribet (or Riblet) Vigié, Peter Billon and Samuel Ablin, and later that year appeared Mathew Savory, Zacharia Trebuseth and Peter Segan.

Charles Smith states, "On the Revocation of the Edict of Nantes, a number of French Protestants came to Cork, and Godsel's Lane off St. Paul's Church was entirely inhabited by them. Their Church is now occupied by a congregation of Wesleyan Methodists, and attached to it is a graveyard belonging exclusively to their descendants. The congregation must have been numerous and wealthy. Among the emigrants settled in Cork were Arnaud, Allinette, Besnard, Belesaique, Blaquire, Boileau, Cossart, Daltera, De La Cour, Demijour, Hardy, La Touche, Laulie, Laniellier, Lavitte, Maziere, Malet, Perdriau, Pothet, Perrier, Pigne, Rouviere, Teulon." Miscellaneous records of these settlers are noted throughout the work.

The Rev. C. B. Gibson, author of *The History of the County and City of Cork*, 1861, states, "There is another Wesleyan chapel in French Church Street, off Patrick Street, which originally belonged to the French Protestants who settled in Cork after the Revocation of the Edict of Nantes."

The Huguenot Settlements in Ireland, 1936, by Grace Lawless Lee, provides the greatest amount of information about residents of the City of Cork, with some mention of their activities and, in addition, the origins, biographical data and family records of many. Their names came up in the following order: Carré, Quarry, Robinette, Goble, Rogue, Ribet (or Riblet) Vigié, Billon, Ablin, Savory, Trebuseth, Segen, Semerat (Simroe, Semirot), Dean, La Roque, Laroque, Savery,

Dupond, Dela Croix, Ardouin, Guillot, Caillon, Pineau, Fontaine, Boursiquot, Maury, Leserve, Maziers, Roussier, Bonnet, Marcomb, Renue, Cesteau, Hanneton, Lavit, Lasarre, Jagualtz, Lasarre, Massiot, Besnard, Hardy, Perrier, Pique, Madras, Pick, de Mont Cenis, Goetval, Vesian, Foucault, Pantaine, Codier, Toulon, Tolekin, Gayott, Beteilhe, Dumas, Laulie, Cossart, Perdriau, Mathis, Jappie, Plaincé, Bonbonous, Verdille, d'Altera, Malet, Arnaud, Belesaigne, Mazière, Jacques, Le Grand, Le Febre, De La Cour, De La Main, Lamellière, Boileau, Demijour, Pothet, Journeaux, Bussy, Boneval, Pelion, Cazalette, Lorie, Robbins, Ferray, Langlois, Lavitte, de Vitte, Lavit, Allenette, Augée, Laulie, Cossort, Mathis, Jappie, Daunt, Plaincé, d'Altera, Bombenan, Verdailles.

THE CITY OF DUBLIN COLONY: The historians describe the Huguenot colony in Dublin as the largest, most diversified in interests and doubtless the wealthiest and most influential in Ireland. Dublin attracted all classes of refugees. They filled Government positions and local public offices, retired there as pensioners, engaged in silk and poplin weaving, merchandising and export business, provided a large proportion of the members of the Goldsmith's Guild, represented the clergy and professions as well as the banking interests. The Registers of the four churches indicate that they were about equally divided between Conformist and Non-Conformist worship.

Many refugees or their descendants arrived in Dublin before the Rebellion of 1641, from England and the Continent. Some of their records are entered in the early Parish Registers. However, almost none of these families are represented in the Registers of the French Churches from 1668 onward. The more permanent settlers began arriving in 1661 and, by 1682, the numbers greatly increased.

One who did remain, together with his descendants for generations, was John Pue (Pugh), who was Sheriff of Dublin and became Mayor in 1648. Ralph Marlande, who was there in 1645, established a family which was there in later generations. Descendants of LeConte, Le Grand, Liennar, Goughter, Cassels, who came with Cromwell, appear to have records in the French Church Registers.

The names of Huguenots who were settled in Dublin or came afterward are mostly found in the Registers of the French Churches. A few are recorded in the other Parish Registers of Dublin. The historians offer the following names as residents after 1661, together with some biographical and genealogical information: St. Ledger, Carré, Granier, Boileau, Hierome, de Ruinat, Herault, Fontaine, Margeston, Desmynieres, Le Roy, de Massas, La Pierre, Chabrier, La Nauze, Jerome, Abbadie, Séverin, Saurin, Dubourdieu, Durand, Pons, De Bostaquet, Darassus, Lagacherie, Gillet, de St. Ferreol, De La Dousse, Caillard, Pollard, Des Voeux, Pelletriau, Ostervald, Hobler, Subremont, Camperdon, Bessonet, Viridet, Rossel, Barbier, Severin, De La Sara, De La Roche, Quartier, Degalinière, Rocheblave, De La Mothe, de Susy Boan, Boquet, Fleury, Scoffier, Droz, Villette, Beaufort, Pelletreau, Lescure, Letablère, La Touche, Larowe, Lattore, Dezouch, Lartigue, Ozier, Angier, Soret, Racine, Pallet, Vialas, d'Olier, de Limarest, Onge, Vidouze, de Landre, Voisin, La Roch, Moussoult, Malbon, Bovet, Gerrard, Ruchant, Paturle, Fourreau, Boové, Delile, Lorthe, Mondet, Jolly, Desinards, Lapier, Beringuier, Boucher, Goodeau, de Glatigny, Darquier, Soubiran, Pineau, Audouit, Le Clerc, Guyon, Pennete, Duplaix, Daulnis, Raboteau, Barre, Le Fanu, Barbe, Du Bedat, Tardy, de Questebrune, de L'Isle, Seve, La Ramière, La Primaudaye, Belrieu, de Pechels, Gualy, Ligonier, du Poncet, de Romagnac, Bouhéreau, Logier.

Smiles (pp. 395-396), notes the large number of "refugees and their descendants who threw aside their French names and adopted them in an English translation." He is speaking of the Huguenots in England but, as many of these people came to Ireland and the same translated names are recorded in the published Registers of the French Churches, they are noted as follows with the original names and the translations: L'Oiseau became Bird; Le June, Young; Le Blanc, White; Le Noir, Black; Le Maur, Brown; Le Roy, King; Lacroix, Cross; Le Monnier, Miller; Dulau, Waters; Lefevres, Smith; Jolifemme, Pretyman; Momerie, Mummery; Planche, Plank; Villebois, Willamise; Taillebois, Talboys; Le Coq, Laycock; Bouchier, Butcher or Boxer; Coquerel, Cockerill; Drouet, Drewitt; D'Aeth, Death; D'Orleans, Dorling; Sauvage, Savage and Wild; Conde, Cundy; Chapuis, Shoppe; De Preux, Diprose; De Moulins, Mullins; Pelletier, Pelter; Huyghens, Huggins; Huyghens, Higgins; Beaufoy, Boffy; Brasseur, Brassey; Letellier, Taylour; Batchelier, Bachelor; Lenoir, Lennard; De Leau, Dillon; Pigou, Pigott; Breton, Britton; Dieudonné, Dudney; Baudoir, Baudry; Guilbert, Gilbert; Koch, Cox; Renalls, Reynolds; Merineau, Meryon; Petit, Pettit; Reveil, Revill; Saveroy, Savery; Gebon, Gibbon; Scardeville, Scharwell; Levereau, Lever.

CHAPTER V

METHODIST RECORDS

The history of the Wesleyan Methodist Society as it grew to great strength in Ireland is unique, in that its adherents from the beginning in 1747, maintained their memberships in the Churches of their ancestors, until well after the opening of the nineteenth century.

The majority were members of the Established Church. As long as they observed the ecclesiastical jurisdiction of the Church regarding the sacraments of Baptism and Holy Communion, were married in the Church and were buried by the clergy in the parish burial ground, their records were entered in the Parish Registers.

The Wesleyan Methodist Society appealed almost equally to Presbyterians. When they joined the Society, they also remained members of the Presbyterian Church until after 1816 when they began to assert their independence. Before this time their practices regarding baptism, marriage and burial were influenced by their ministers, subject to the laws regarding dissenters, and varied according to individual choice, as in the case of other Presbyterians.

Sources contained in VOLUME II, p. 221, and others listed below, provide the annals of Methodism as recorded in the journals of the Rev. John Wesley and the preachers, minutes of the yearly meetings, Methodist periodicals, and various other materials. These set forth much information about the people who were converted and became active members. The National Library, Dublin, and the Linen Hall Library, Belfast, have full collections of published works, many of which may also be located in other libraries. In recent years, several of the listed items have been located in the bookshops of Belfast, Cork, Dublin, and other places.

ARTHUR, W. Life of Gideon Ouseley. 1876.

CAMPBELL, W. G.   The Apostle of Kerry: the life of the Rev. Charles Graham. 1868.

COKE, T.   Extracts of the journals comprising . . . a tour through part of Ireland. 1816.

COLE, REV. R. LEE.   The Wesleys came to Dublin. Epworth Press: London, 1947.

DONEGALL SQUARE METHODIST CHURCH.   Second Annual Report of the Sunday School Committee. Belfast, 1922.

HAIRE, ROBERT.   Wesley's One and Twenty Visits to Ireland. Epworth Press: London, 1947.

HENDERSON, J. W.   Methodist College, Belfast, 1863-1938. 2 vols.

HUSTON, R.   Sketches from my Notebook: Methodism and Ministerial Life in Ireland. n. d.

LANKTREE, MATTHEW.   Biographical Narrative and Historical Notices on Methodism in Ireland. 1836.

LUMLY, WILLIAM.   Methodist Church, St. Stephen's Green, Dublin, 1843-1893. n. d.

LYNN, J. M.   History of Wesleyan Methodism on the Armagh Circuit. Belfast, 1887.

M'AFEE, D.   O'Connell and the Wesleyans. 1839.

METHODISM: A History of Methodism in Coleraine: from its introduction till about the year 1820, with notices of early Methodists . . . extracts from MSS. Journals of John Galt. By J. M. ca. 1880.

METHODISM IN ENNISKILLEN, COUNTY FERMANAGH. 1917.

METHODIST MINISTERS: Minutes of several conversations between the preachers in connexion established by Rev. John Wesley. Dublin, 1823-1824.

PRIMITIVE WESLEYAN SOCIETY: Primitive Wesleyan Methodist Society and the Irish Church. By a member of the Primitive Methodist Conference. Belfast, 1873.

ST. STEPHEN'S GREEN DUBLIN METHODIST CENTENARY CHURCH, 1747-1943.

SERMONS AND JOURNALS OF JOHN WESLEY.

SMITH, W.   Consecutive History of Wesleyan Methodism in Ireland. 1830.

THOM'S IRISH ALMANAC AND OFFICIAL DIRECTORY. Dublin, 1847. Contains an Alphabetical List of Wesleyan Methodist Ministers with the year in which they began to travel, the earliest date being 1788; also a list of appointments in 1846. Also a List of the Primitive Wesleyan Methodist Ministers, 1846 (pp. 348-350).

ORIGINAL DOCUMENTS: John Galt's Diary concerning Methodists and events in Coleraine, 1796-1837 (Public Record Office of Northern Ireland, Belfast). Methodist Register of the Rev. M. Lanktree, County Down, 1815-1849 (Public Record Office of Ireland, Dublin).

MISCELLANEOUS: Several County and Town Histories contain information about the early Methodist Societies, Meeting-Houses, etc., with lists of the preachers or ministers. *The History of Enniskillen*, by W. C. Trimble, Vol. III, pp. 950-961, is devoted to a history of the Methodist Church, with notices of active members and a list of all Ministers, 1769-1920. This is an unusually full account, but in many local histories some notes can be found. In all cases the *Memorials of the Dead* (listed in VOLUME II, p. 228) should be consulted. These volumes contain many thousands of tombstone inscriptions throughout Ireland.

* * * * *

Methodism was a term given to the studies of a little group of Oxford students who banded together before 1730, under the leadership of John Wesley for spiritual fellowship and an awakening of personal religion.

John Wesley, his brother Charles, and George Whitfield, were all ordained and loyal clergymen of the Established Church, and ever remained so. As they preached throughout England, arousing the multitudes to spiritual heights, they enlisted the services of godly laymen as disciples and preachers to spread the word. By 1740, Wesleyan Methodist Societies were being formed to enhance religion but in no way interfere with the loyalty and duties of the people to the Church of England.

The first word of Wesleyan Methodism came to Ireland soon after 1730 through one of the Oxford group, William Morgan, of Dublin.   In 1738, the Rev. George Whitfield came briefly to Ireland and preached in St. Mary's Cathedral, Limerick, as the guest of Bishop Burscough.   He also preached in St. Andrew's Church and St. Werburg's Church, Dublin, as the guest of Dean Patrick Delany.

On August 7, 1747, the Methodist movement began in earnest in Ireland upon the arrival of the Rev. John Wesley, who was first invited to conduct services in St. Mary's Church, Dublin.   He then traveled for months and preached to the multitudes in the fields, the market places and in some public buildings.   In 1748, his brother Charles spent five weeks in and around the city of Cork, and returned to Ireland again. Whitfield came also a few times.

The Rev. John Wesley furnished the consistent motivating force and leadership which carried Methodism throughout the length and breadth of Ireland.   He made twenty-one extended preaching tours between 1747 and 1789, enduring great hardships and inspiring the people while he gathered disciples, organized Societies and chose qualified laymen of the Protestant Churches to become preachers.

People of all denominations were attracted by curiosity to attend the mass meetings, but it was largely the members of the Established Church and Presbyterians who formed the local Wesleyan Methodist Societies.   The work of many Societies was carried on by appointed leaders while the preachers traveled throughout an organized Circuit to minister to several Societies.

The activities of the members of the Societies and the preachers did not detract from fulfilling their duties as members of the Established Church, the Presbyterian and other Protestant Churches.   Various histories listed above show that the Wesleyan Methodist Society members attended their own churches regularly on Sunday.   The clergymen and ministers of their churches administered to them and their families the sacraments of Baptism and Holy Communion, performed their marriages and buried their dead.

The *History of the Church of Ireland,* by Johnston, Robinson and Jackson, Dublin, 1953 (p. 245), quotes Wesley's two rules which he, as a strong clergyman of the Established

Church, repeatedly impressed upon his followers: *"Keep to the Church.* They that do their best, prosper most in their souls. I suffer no meetings under any pretext to be held during Church hours. When Methodists leave the Church, God will leave them." *"Lose no opportunity of receiving the Sacrament.* All who have neglected this have suffered loss. Most of them are dead as a stone."

Wesley soon established "Yearly Conferences" of the preachers, to study organization procedures and discipline. While Wesley stressed the positive purpose of the Society to enrich the Church through the spiritual awakening of the people, the probabilities are that their need of their Churches declined as they poured their emotions and religious exhaltation into helping each other and seeking new converts. Thus the number and size of the Societies increased to the joy of the Methodists and the alarm of both the Established Church and the Presbyterians.

Almost from the beginning, the zeal of Wesley and his disciples antagonized the bishops, the clergy, and the churchmen who adhered formally to the Established Church. Its doors were closed to meetings of the Societies while it demanded church attendance of its members, and to all Protestants it proclaimed the right, empowered by Acts of Parliament, to administer the sacraments of Baptism and Holy Communion, the performance of marriage and the ritual of burial, regardless of the denomination of their Church, as the exclusive prerogative of the clergy of the Established Church. Fear of the new influence was reflected in attempts to break up the meetings, riots, injury to the persons, homes and character of the members of the Society and people who attended the gatherings. Most of all, the preachers and leaders suffered persecution. When Wesley and his disciples first came to strong Presbyterian towns in Ulster they met the same opposition and fear of losing adherents to the new manner of worship. In Ulster, as in other provinces, violent demonstrations everywhere only strengthened the interest and eventually promoted the growth of the Societies.

Some interesting figures regarding the progress of Methodism from the early days until 1789 when Wesley made his last tour, and from then until 1859, are given in the *History of Methodism in Ireland*, by C. H. Crookshank (Vol. II, pp. 463, 465; Vol. III, pp. 525-526). He states that in all of Ireland, "Its Societies from being mere auxiliaries to other Christian bodies gradually developed into a distinct, well organized, and scripturally constituted Church. Its ministers increased from sixty-five in 1789, to one hundred and seventy-two in 1819; its membership from fourteen thousand and ten, to thirty-four thousand six hundred and eighty-three . . ."

"Although Ulster was the last province in Ireland into which Methodism obtained access, and its progress here at first was exceedingly slow; yet after a few years, the Society began to extend with such rapidity as enabled it soon to outstrip all the rest of Ireland put together. Thus, in 1760, there were one thousand members in Leinster alone, and only two hundred and fifty in Ulster. Fifty-nine years later, the membership in the three southern provinces amounted to about eleven thousand five hundred, while in the north it was more than twice that number. Thus it was in Ulster that Methodism proved most successful. We have before us the names of the leading Wesleyan families, numbering upwards of eight hundred, who at this period resided in the province. Taking from these all whose religious denomination we have been able to ascertain, and assuming that they give an approximate view of the relative proportion of the number of Methodists connected with the different Churches, we find that about forty per cent were Presbyterians."

Regarding the number of Methodists who emigrated with their families between 1819 and 1859, Crookshank states, "Although deprived by emigration of more than thirty-five thousand members, or about one hundred and forty thousand adherents, and in a country the population of which was reduced from upwards of eight million to less than six, the membership rose from thirty-four thousand six hundred in 1819 to about forty thousand in 1859."

The *History of the Church of Ireland*, by Walter A. Phillips (Vol. III, pp. 312-315, 327-330), relates the following information regarding the division of the Wesleyan Methodists into two Societies and their position in the Census of 1834. The

Methodist preachers, in their General Conference of 1814, discussed a number of petitions that the itinerant preachers be allowed to administer the sacraments of Baptism and Holy Communion. The majority favored this innovation but others strongly opposed it and the decision was delayed. The Conference of 1816 brought several preachers to trial for breach of discipline, because they had responded to a petition of a number of Presbyterians who were members of Methodist Societies, openly to administer the sacraments. This breach of discipline also brought a threat from the Attorney-General, regarding proceedings against those who failed to observe the Chapel Trusts.

In 1816, the Methodists were divided over the sacramental issue. Those who adhered to Wesley's insistence on loyalty to the Established Church, agreed on the principle that no Methodist preacher should under any circumstances administer the sacraments of Baptism and Holy Communion to any members of the Societies and refused to allow that "Wesleyan ordination" would permit this. The group which was of this opinion met in a Conference at Clones, County Monaghan, in October of 1816, and formed themselves into the "Primitive Wesleyan Methodists in the Church of Ireland", which in 1817 consisted of 6,136 members and 18 preachers. In 1835, this group numbered 17,738, and retained 66 preachers, with 21 scripture readers and missionary school-masters (Ordnance Survey of Ireland, Dublin, 1837, Vol. I, p. 75). For thirty years or more, the Rev. Adam Averell, a strong clergyman of the Established Church, was their president.

The majority of the "Wesleyan Methodists" of the original Society retained their present organization under this name, and from 1816 allowed their preachers to administer the sacraments of Baptism and Holy Communion. Matthew Lanktree was one of the leaders of the Wesleyan Methodist Society and wrote an account of his ministry and experiences from 1794 to 1833. This was published and is listed above. The "Methodist Register of the Rev. Matthew Lanktree, County Down, 1815-1849" is deposited in the Public Record Office, Dublin. Except for this one Register, no collection of Registers regarding the Societies of this group is available.

The records of baptism for members of the Primitive Wesleyan Methodist Society will, until 1878, be found in existing Parish Registers of the Established Church, due to the close adherence of this Society to the Church. *A History of Banbridge,* by Capt. R. Linn; edited by W. S. Kerr, 1935 (p. 92), states, "In 1878 the Primitive Wesleyan Methodist Society united with the Irish Wesleyan Methodist Church. Most of the preachers of the Primitive Methodist Society were received into the ministry of the Methodist Church; a few accepted ordination in the Church of Ireland."

Methodists were not regarded by the Government or the Established Church as constituting anything more than two Societies until after the Government of Ireland Census of 1834.   This Census listed the Church denomination of the people and none were accounted Methodists.   Thus, in 1834, the members of the two Societies were included among the members of the Established Church, the Presbyterian or any other Protestant Church in which they were enrolled.   The Censuses of 1841 and 1851 omitted any record of religious denomination, but the Census of 1861 listed the membership of the "Wesleyan Methodist Church" as a distinct Church body, enumerated at 45,399 members.

Thom's Irish Almanac and Official Directory for the Year 1847 (pp. 348-350), contains an *Ecclesiastical Directory* which includes a section for *The Methodist Church,* and one for the *Primitive Wesleyan Methodist Society,* with lists of the ministers for each.   These lists are of considerable value for identifying the location of these families in 1846-1847, and establishing the length of service of the preachers previous to this date.   Therefore the two lists of names, the year when each "began to travel" and the number of years each had been appointed to his present position, will be presented later in this chapter.

The marriage and burial records of members of the Primitive Wesleyan Methodist Society will, in most cases up to 1878, be found in the Parish Registers of the Established Church, due to the close adherence of the Society to the Church.

As for the marriage and burial records of the members of the "Wesleyan Methodist Society," they were subject to the conditions and laws which are set forth in the following CHAPTER XXII. It is sufficient to say here that, previous to the passing of the Dissenters Marriage Bill in 1782, the marriages of all Protestant dissenters in Ireland were accounted legal only if performed by a clergyman of the Established Church, except during the period of the Commonwealth and Protectorate. Further laws declaring mixed marriages illegal unless performed by the clergy, were not repealed until 1842 and 1844. Nevertheless, Presbyterian ministers and Quakers from early times, never doubted their right to celebrate marriages of their own members, and their Registers prove that the practice was common. Exceptions are mentioned by a Presbyterian Church historian, the Rev. Dr. David Stewart, in his *The Seceders in Ireland,* 1950 (p. 412), "The wealthier Presbyterians who had property to settle, often submitted to be married in the Episcopal Church [the Established Church of Ireland until 1870; later the Church of Ireland] for the better security of title by conforming to the prescribed law."

There seems to have been no universal practice regarding burial in the cemetery of the Church to which one belonged. Records will be cited in CHAPTER XXII, to show that in Enniskillen, some Presbyterian ministers, and preachers of the Wesleyan Methodist Society (named as such on tombstones or memorial tablets), were buried in the cemetery of the Established Church of the parish or honored with memorial tablets within the Church. These were dated mostly between 1830 and 1858; one being dated as late as 1874. Certainly members of either Society were buried in any family burial plot of any Protestant Church burial ground, beside their ancestors as a general practice.

Usually one who is searching for the records of a Methodist who emigrated to America, does not know to what Church he belonged at the time he was a member of one of the Wesleyan Methodist Societies. Thus the genealogist, realizing the many cross-currents of legal requirements, Church regulations, and individual practice within, or regardless of the law, can only simplify a genealogical search for the records of baptism, marriage and burial of Methodists, by examining or commissioning a search of any existing Parish Registers of the Established Church, as well as of the Presbyterian Church Registers and those of any other religious bodies in the area of interest.   In all cases where one suspects or knows of a Quaker connection these Registers should be examined first. However, even when searching for Quaker records, the Parish Registers of the family locality should be examined, for many cases of discipline are recorded in the Quaker Quarterly or Provincial Minutes regarding marriage by a "priest" of the Established Church.   There is no general rule that all people of Scottish origin were Presbyterians.   The county and town histories and other sources show that many were members of the Established Church.   This fact and the earlier inclusive dates of most Parish Registers compared to the Presbyterian Registers of the same locality, would make it advisable to give first choice to the former but not omit the latter, if the inclusive dates of the records cover the period of interest.   Instructions for personally arranging to examine the Registers, and for commissioning a search by letter, are given in CHAPTER III, of this PART THREE.

This compiler located in two parishes, the records of four generations of the family of her Methodist emigrant ancestor who, with his sister, came to America in 1832.   Their own statements provided the only clues; the name of the town of residence, Rockcorry, County Monaghan; the Kilcrow burying ground, and "the Church of the Clock" where baptisms were performed.

Attention should in all cases be given to the county, town, diocesan and parish histories as well as the historical journals and any other publications regarding the area of interest. Several of these give lists of the clergy, the ministers, and the preachers of the Methodist Societies, with the dates of service. In some cases brief biographies and genealogical notes are included.   Many have published the tombstone inscriptions copied in the parish and other burial grounds, and much material from other sources.

Therefore, in commissioning a search of manuscript materials by the Genealogical Office in Dublin Castle, Dublin, or the Ulster-Scot Historical Society, Belfast, it is well to request a search of the above sources also, and report on any individual records or information regarding the family of interest in a specified area. An American can make his own choice of published materials to be searched, from items listed in the accompanying VOLUME II. In all cases, the *Memorials of the Dead,* listed in VOLUME II, p. 228, should be searched. The *Ulster Journal of Archaeology* should always be examined to discover possible records of any Ulster family.

This research will be done at an average cost of $1.00 per hour. Instructions regarding a request for the search will be found in PART TWO, CHAPTERS IV and VI, of this volume. The reader can make a fairly long list of published sources which can be searched in a day. The Genealogical Office personnel have access to everything in the National Library, and the Ulster-Scot Historical Society personnel have access to the Library of the Public Record Office (as well as its manuscript materials) in Belfast; also the published works in the Linen Hall Library and materials in the Presbyterian Historical Society, Belfast.

Among the Methodist published works listed above, the one which contains notes on the largest number of people is the *History of Methodism in Ireland,* by C. H. Crookshank. 3 Vols., 1885-1888. Crookshank has compiled a running account of the activities of the Rev. John Wesley, all of the preachers, the people who were most active in the Society to 1817, and later in both Societies from 1747 through 1859. He has drawn his information from many unpublished Manuscripts; the Journals of Wesley, published in several volumes; the diaries, journals and letters of preachers; also various Methodist magazines, etc., dating from 1785. He gives no genealogies, but numerous notes can be pieced together resulting in information regarding two or more generations in a number of cases, and usually he gives the year or more particular date of death of each preacher in addition to his appointments and activities in each locality.

As an illustration of running notes on one family, this compiler was attracted to the name Cather which appears in all three volumes. All notes refer to members of three generations of one family. This is a rare name with a dearth of records in Ireland. Therefore the notes quoted by Crookshank will be presented below, followed by a few references gleaned from considerable search through published sources. The following notes are taken from Crookshank (Vol. I, p. 333; Vol. II, p. 369; Vol. III, pp. 133, 257, 263, 280-282, 307, 312, 344, 358, 478, 491, 498, 503):

Mr. and Mrs. Robert Cather, of Carnony, were present at a field meeting in 1779, at the place of Lieut. Scott who resided in the Derg country. Mr. and Mrs. Robert Cather were converted. They then opened their house to entertain the preachers. Mr. Cather gave up tobacco and any use of intoxicating drinks. He died in 1827, having been for forty-eight years a consistent and devoted member of the Society. A note states that he was the grandfather of the Rev. William and Dr. R. Cather. (Vol. I, p. 333.)

Before going further, this compiler located the Cather residence in Carnony. The *Topographical Index,* published with the *Census of Population of Northern Ireland,* 1926 (Reprint, 1947), p. 50, shows that Carnony is a townland of 185 acres, 3 roods, 19 perch, in the County of Tyrone, County District and Union of Omagh, Registrars District of Omagh (No. 1), Barony of Upper Strabane, Cappagh Parish. Lewis's *Topographical Dictionary of Ireland,* Vol. I, 1837 (pp. 240-241), shows that Cappagh Parish is partly in the Barony of Omagh but chiefly in that of Strabane, Union of Omagh, County of Tyrone, two miles north of Omagh, containing with the district parish of Mountfield, 13,300 inhabitants. The living is a rectory in the Diocese of Derry and in the patronage of the Provost and Fellows of Trinity College, Dublin. This latter furnished a clue for research after Crookshank's further notes:

Mr. Gabriel Cather, son of Mr. Robert Cather of Carnony, lived in Omagh, County Tyrone, where he was chiefly instrumental in erecting the first chapel of the Wesleyan Methodist Society in this town, according to notes for the year 1813. He was also active in the Sunday School and in other charitable works.

William Cather, of Omagh, was one of four admitted as preachers on trial, by the Wesleyan Conference held in Cork, in July of 1829. Messrs. Crook and Cather were named as preachers in Tullamore. The Rev. William Cather of Tullamore in 1838 was mentioned as being of Omagh ten years previously. In 1839, the Rev. William Cather completed a term of three years on the Tullamore circuit.

Robert G. Cather, who lived in Tullamore in 1839, became converted in that year. Robert G. Cather became a tutor in Bandon in 1839, while the Rev. William Cather was appointed to the Roscrea circuit in that year. At the annual meeting of the Wesleyan Methodist Conference held in Cork in June of 1841, Robert G. Cather was one of seven admitted as a preacher on trial. The Rev. William Reilly of Portadown, in 1841, had the Rev. Robert G. Cather as his colleague whom he described as "a kind, tender young man . . ." The Rev. Robert G. Cather, A. B., in 1844, in Portadown, became interested in promoting a Methodist school. He went to a meeting in Belfast on May 16, 1844, for the purpose, and became the secretary. On the Belfast South circuit, the labours of the Rev. Robert G. Cather were so successful with many conversions that at the close of his labours on the circuit he was presented with a handsome gold watch in 1845. In 1856, the Rev. Robert G. Cather, A.M., was appointed to take charge of the Coleraine circuit. An account of his successful work in Coleraine is given. He opened a school there and, in 1857, drew an audience of 1,400. In 1858, the Rev. Robert G. Cather, A. M., was present and preached at Donegal. In 1858, at the Wesleyan Methodist Conference in Dublin, the Rev. William Cather was elected as Representative to the British Conference.

Lewis's mention above of Trinity College, Dublin, in connection with Cappagh parish where the elder Robert Cather lived which was near Omagh where Gabriel Cather lived, and the Rev. William Cather and Dr. R. Cather being named as grandsons of the elder Robert Cather, led to a search of the list of alumni and students of Trinity College, Dublin, with the following results:

Alumni Dublinenses, edited by G. D. Burtchaell and T. U. Sadleir, Dublin, 1935, contains a list of students and graduates, etc., from 1593. All listed as "pensioners" paid a fixed sum per year for tuition. Their tutors before entering are

listed in parentheses. The Cathers are entered on page 142 as
follows: The first date is the date of entry. The description
"Mercator" means "Merchant."   The abbreviation "AEst."
is for "Summer" and "Vern." is for "Spring." "s" is for "son"
and "b" is for "born in." "Pen." indicates "Pensioner."

CATHER, JOHN, Pen. (Mr. Smith), Jan. 20, 1831, aged 17;
s. of Gabriel, Mercator; b. Tyrone. B. A. Vern. 1836. M. A.
Vern. 1852. (Archdeacon of Tuam.) See *Boase (Supp.)*.

CATHER, ROBERT GEORGE, Pen. (Mr. Smith), Nov. 21, 1837,
aged 17; s. of Gabriel, Mercator; b. Derry. B. A. Vern. 1842.
M.A. AEst. 1845. LL.B. and LL.D. AEst. 1860.

CATHER, THOMAS, Pen. (Mr. Irwin), Nov. 7, 1825, aged 16;
son of David, Mercator; b. Derry. B.A. Vern. 1830. (Irish
Bar 1837.)

The Wesleyan Methodist records give meaning to the
Trinity College entries of the Cather family and together they
furnish names in three generations which suggest relationships to other Cathers in fragmentary items listed below.
The Names Index and Land Index of the documents in the
Registry of Deeds, Dublin, should be checked for any Cather
items dated from 1708. (See PART TWO, CHAPTER I.)   The
deeds, leases, assignments, marriage settlements, etc., in this
repository may reconstruct the family through several generations of one or more branches. It is possible that a very early
lease or other record may refer to persons living previous to
1708 and might even connect with the David Cather of 1659
and *ca.* 1649.

So far, the above cited Cather records establish Robert
Cather as the father of Gabriel Cather of Omagh, County Tyrone, who had sons John Cather and Robert George Cather
who were graduated from Trinity College, Dublin. John was
born in 1819 in County Tyrone, but Robert George was born
in 1820 at a time when his parents were living, or were for
some reason in County Londonderry. William Cather is named
as the grandson of Robert Cather and appears to have been an
older son of Gabriel Cather as he lived in Omagh and when
he later was stationed in Tullamore, Robert George Cather
also lived there or spent some time there.

The fragmentary records of later and earlier dates are as follows: A John and George Cathers (Cather) of Dernagh, Co. Tyrone, obtained a lease in 1798 (Deputy Keeper's Report, Public Record Office of Northern Ireland, 1948, p. 35). Dernagh is recorded in the *Townland Index* quoted above, as a townland of 274 acres, 20 perch, in Clonoe parish, Dungannon Middle Barony, County Tyrone. Judging from the year (1798) and the given names, it seems safe to guess that John and George Cather were either brothers of Robert Cather or more probably his sons, which would make them brothers of Gabriel Cather who named known sons John and Robert George Cather.

The Cathers found in East Omagh Barony, County Tyrone, listed as renters, 1777-1786, are Dav. (David) and James of Cullagh and Six Mile Cross (*ibid.* 1951-1953, p. 71). This is about six miles southeast of Cappagh parish where Robert Cather lived in 1779. They may have been brothers of Robert, or his father and brother. A David Cather of Gabriel Cather's generation, who had a son George, seems to suggest a relationship with Gabriel who named a son Robert George. This record is found in *The Book of the Royal Belfast Academical Institution*, 1913 (p. 266), which lists a student George Cather who entered in 1833, son of David Cather, of Newtown Limavady, County Londonderry. This George Cather was probably a brother of Thomas Cather who entered Trinity College, Dublin, Nov. 7, 1825, aged 16, born in Derry (Co. Londonderry), son of David Cather. In 1845, Dav. (David), Thomas and William Cather of Limavady, Co. Londonderry, entered into a marriage settlement, and Jane Cather is also listed for the Marriage Settlement at Limavady at this date (Deputy Keeper's Report, Public Record Office of Northern Ireland, 1948, p. 35).

A William Cather of Lissneal, Liberties of Londonderry, parish of Clondermot, made a will proved in the diocese of Derry in 1808, and a Francis Cathers of the same place, left a will proved in the diocese of Derry in 1821 (*Index to Irish Wills, Derry and Raphoe Dioceses*, Vol. V, ed. by Gertrude Thrift. Phillimore, London, 1920 (p. 20)).

All of the above members of the Cather family, mentioned

so far, are no doubt related to or descended from the Cather men listed in the *Parliamentary Returns Regarding Religion, 1740 Householder's List.* (See PART THREE, CHAPTER XI.) These are as follows:

WILLIAM CATHER, no. 2010, living in the parish of Cumber, town of Kilgort, barony of Tyrkeering, County Londonderry.

FRANCIS CATHER, no. 2239, living in the parish of Glendermot (Clondermot), barony of Tyrkeering, County Londonderry.

JAMES CATHER, no. 2441, living in the parish of Glendermot (Clondermot), town of Ardlogh, barony of Tyrkeering, County Londonderry.

FRANK CATHER, no. 2447, living in the parish of Glendermot (Clondermot), town of Lisneal (Lissneal), barony of Tyrkeering, County Londonderry.

* * * * *

A Census of Ireland, c. 1659, edited by Séamus Pender (p. 54), lists just one person by the name of Cather. This is entered as "Dauid [David] Cather gent., and Michaell Harvy Esq., Tituladoes, of townlands of Bellioghogan quarter, Finwer and Downemore quarter, with a total of six people resident; 5 English and Scotts and 1 Irish." The property is situated in the "Parrish" of Mevagh, barony of Kil McCrenan, County Donegal. This barony is the north barony in County Donegal, its east border being about fifteen miles west of Newtown Limavady, County Londonderry; about three miles west of the Liberties of Londonderry, and about twenty-five miles northwest of Omagh, County Tyrone.

The list of *The "Forty-Nine" Officers* (O'Hart, *Irish Gentry When Cromwell Came to Ireland,* Dublin, 1884) contains (pp. 372-411) the "Inrolments of the Adjudications (arrears of payments) in favor of the (A.D.) 1649 Officers (formerly denominated "The '49 Lots") : Preserved in the Office of the Chief Remembrancer of the Exchequer, Dublin." This is a list of Commissioned Officers who served Charles I, in the Wars of Ireland, before the 5th day of June, 1649. On page

378 are listed Lieut. David Cather and Ens. Bernard Cather. Most of these officers received their land for past services, after the Restoration, under Charles II.

The Plantation in Ulster, 1608-1620, edited by the Rev. George Hill, Belfast, 1877 (pp. 322-330), shows a survey of all of the grants of lands in "The Precincts of Doe and Fawnett (now Kilmacrenan), County Donegal. In Pender's Survey above, this Kilmacrenan is listed as Kil McCrenan. The townlands of Bellioghogan quarter and Downemore quarter are included (p. 325), as a part of 1,128 acres granted on 18 May 1611, to Sir Ralph Bingley, Knt. He received the quarter of Bellioghogan (Balleoghegan) and Downedavanmore (Downemore) with the stipulation that he was to plant the land within four years by twenty English or Scotch persons. At the same time, 30 Nov. 1610, William Stewart (p. 322), was granted 1,000 acres in the same barony of Kilmacrenan, County Donegal; also he, as Sir William Stewart, purchased from George Arundel of Omagh, in 1638, extensive lands in the barony of Omagh, County Tyrone. This may explain how David Cather, who leased lands of Bellioghogan and Downemore in the barony of Kil McCrenan, in 1659 or thereabouts, may have acquired leases from Sir William Stewart in the barony of Omagh, County Tyrone, where later Cathers are found.

This lengthy illustration of the Cather records is given to show what can be done with running notes regarding Methodists or people named in records regarding other denominations, to reconstruct some generations and relate them to earlier fragmentary records, all of which can serve as clues in searching the Indexes and documents in the Registry of Deeds. Any existing documents in this repository regarding a family offer the best possible chance of providing a proven line when there are no other genealogical works concerning the family (see PART TWO, CHAPTER I). If an American cannot search the microfilms of the above Indexes, deposited in the Genealogical Society Library, Salt Lake City, Utah, and order copies of any existing family documents himself from the Registry of Deeds, Dublin, he can commission the Genealogical Office, Dublin Castle, Dublin, to do it for him.

Thom's Irish Almanac and Official Directory for the Year 1847, Dublin, 1847 (pp. 348-350), provides two lists of ministers who are mentioned in running notes by Crookshank and other authors of Methodist works, in some cases showing earlier generations of a family. As these names are valuable for locating people, the following two lists are presented:

1847 ALPHABETICAL LIST OF WESLEYAN METHODIST MINISTERS

"The figures at the beginning of the line show the year in which each Minister began to travel; and those at the end denote his first, second, etc., annual appointment to his present Circuit.   The term Super. means Superannuated."

1834	Appelbe, William Parker	Coleraine	3
1816	Armstrong, John	Brookborough	1
1805	Armstrong, William	Lisburn (Super.)	
1838	Atkins, John H.	Castlebar	1
1841	Bagley, John	Newtownbarry	1
1818	Ballard, Thomas	Waterford	2
1831	Bamford, Robert	Longford	1
1834	Banks, Edward M.	Kilkenny	1
1792	Banks, Robert	Carlow (Super.)	
1846	Bass, James	Dungannon	1
1832	Bayley, Benjamin	Lurgan	2
1845	Beale, Henry M.	Portadown	1
1833	Beamish, Thomas	Dublin, South (Super.)	
1824	Beauchamp, Robert	Moira and Dromore	3
1842	Bell, Robert	Lowtherstown	1
1837	Black, James	Lowtherstown	1
1836	Black, Robert	Carrickfergus	3
1839	Boyd, John H.	Lucan and Trim	2
1839	Brown, William	Ballymena and Antrim	2
1810	Bruce, Robert	Wexford	3
1830	Burnside, William	Boyle	1
1809	Burrows, George	Moira, etc.	2
1805	Burrows, Michael	Carrickfergus (Super.)	
1844	Butler, William	Downpatrick	2
1824	Byrne, Claudius	Dungannon	1
1797	Campbell, Archibald	Dublin, South (Super.)	
1812	Campbell, John	Belfast, South (Super.)	
1845	Campbell, Robert	Brookborough	1

1831	Campbell, William G.	Tullamore	1
1810	Carey, John	Londonderry	1
1808	Carson, Robert	Omagh (Super.)	
1841	Cather, Robert George, A.M.	Drogheda	1
1829	Cather, William	Donaghadee	2
1796	Clendinnen, J.	Bideford, England (Super.)	
1810	Cobain, Edward	Ballyycastle	2
1843	Collier, James	Castlebar	1
1832	Cowdy, Samuel	Athlone and Tullamore	1
1814	Cornwall, William	Tuam	2
1804	Crook, William	Maryborough	1
1795	Crozier, Robert	Enniskillen (Super.)	
1834	Darby, William A.	Belfast, South	1
1844	Deery, George	Omagh	1
1799	Deery, Henry	Dublin, North (Super.)	
1840	Devers, Robert A.	Ballyclare	1
1837	Donald, James	Carrickfergus and Larne	1
1838	Donald, John	Mayborough	2
1796	Douglas, William	Lowtherstown (Super.)	
1808	Downing, Samuel	Newtownbarry	1
1840	Duncan, John	Bandon	1
1843	Elliott, Frederick	Kerry, etc.	1
1821	Feely, John	Killaloe	3
1846	Ferguson, Samuel	Kilkenny	1
1790	Ferguson, William	Dublin, South (Super.)	
1808	Ffrench, Patrick	Dublin, South (Super.)	
1810	Finley, William	Strabane (Super.)	
1833	Foster, John	Manorhamilton	3
1843	Foster, Thomas	Tipperary	1
1808	Foote, William	Castleblaney and Monaghan	1
1832	Geddes, Henry	Lucan and Trim	3
1840	Gilbert, John	Erris	1
1834	Giles, Henry J.	Tanderagee	3
1823	Gillman, James B.	Cork (Super.)	
1846	Grant, Charles Lynn	Magherafelt	1
1835	Grant, George	Armagh (Super.)	
1826	Greer, John	Dublin, North	3
1821	Guard, William	Cavan	3
1789	Hamilton, Andrew	Bandon (Super.)	
1836	Hamilton, Robert	Strabane	2
1810	Harman, Joshua	Cork (Super.)	
1828	Harper, Edward	Newtownlimavady	1
1826	Harrington, John	Armagh	1
1840	Hay, John	Dublin, South	2
1809	Hazelton, Edward	Dungannon and Moy (Super.)	
1845	Hazelton, John	Armagh	1
1841	Henderson, Anketell M.	General Missionary for the South	

1826	Henry, James	Cloughjordan	3
1838	Hewitt, Robert	Wicklow	3
1835	Hickey, Thomas	Limerick	1
1842	Higgins, John	Carlow	2
1815	Hill, John	Tullamore	1
1822	Hobart, Nathaniel	Rathmelton, etc.	2
1831	Hoey, William the 1st	Magherafelt	3
1840	Hoey, William the 2nd	Castleblaney and Monaghan	1
1820	Holmes, John	Drogheda	3
1830	Hughes, James	Clones	1
1835	Hughes, John	Wicklow	2
1840	Huston, Andrew	Strabane (Super.)	
1829	Huston, Robert	General Missionary for the South	
1845	Hutchison, James	Donaghadee	1
1806	Irvine, John C.	Pettigo (Super.)	
1815	Jebb, John	Pettigo and Ballyshannon	2
1827	Jessop, Robert	Newry	1
1809	Johnston, Edward the 1st	Dungannon (Super.)	
1845	Johnston, Edward the 2nd	Strabane	1
1808	Johnston, James	Lurgan	3
1846	Johnston, Joseph	Killashandra	1
1840	Jones, Robert Gibson	Dublin, North	2
1846	Keys, James	Cootehill	1
1806	Keys, William	Longfield (Super.)	
1806	Kyle, Samuel	Pettigo (Super.)	
1794	Lanktree, Matthew	Belfast, South (Super.)	
1844	Lebert, William	Wexford	1
1825	Le Maitre, Frederick	Roscrea	1
1834	Liddy, John	Galway	1
1827	Lindsay, Robert H.	Enniskillen	2
1846	Long, Mortlock	Ballina	1
1845	Lough, William	Skibbereen	1
1801	Lougheed, Thomas	Tullamore (Super.)	
1828	Lupton, William	Waterford	3
1808	Lynch, James	Leeds, England (Super.)	
1827	M'Afee, Daniel	Belfast, North	1
1845	M'Clintock, James	Manorhamilton	1
1807	M'Cormick, Charles	Kilrush and Tarbet (Super.)	
1802	M'Cutcheon, James	Omagh and Newtownstewart (Super.)	
1808	M'Dowell, Samuel	Kilrush	1
1806	M'Elwaine, George	Kingstown (Super.)	
1831	M'Garvey, William	Cootehill	1
1840	M'Kay, Joseph W.	Cork	2
1845	M'Lorinan, Thomas	Pettigo and Ballyshannon	1
1838	M'Millen, Gibson	Dublin, South	1
1841	M'Mullan, Wallace	Enniskillen	1

1844	Macdonald, Thomas M.	Dublin, North	1
1812	Masaroon, Robert	Dublin, South	3
1818	Mathews, John F.	Bandon	3
1846	Maxwell, Richard	Clones	1
1845	Meredith, Samuel	Lisburn	1
1828	Meredith, Thomas	Lisburn	2
1837	Meyer, Robert J.	Killeshandra	2
1835	Moore, Hugh	Downpatrick	2
1844	Morrow, Francis	Cavan	1
1829	Mulloy, William	Tralee	1
1790	Murdock, Archibald	Dungannon (Super.)	
1833	Murdock, James	Ballina	1
1824	Nash, John	Newry	3
1809	Nelson, John	Limerick	1
1801	Nesbitt, John	Enniskillen (Super.)	
1810	Noble, Arthur	Dublin, North (Super.)	
1841	Oliver, John	Tanderagee	2
1824	Patterson, James	Kinsale	2
1808	Pratt, James	Enniskillen (Super.)	
1823	Price, Henry	Belfast, South	1
1808	Price, Richard	Longford (Super.)	
1810	Reilly, William	Cork	3
1815	Richey, William	Youghal	2
1789	Ridgeway, Thomas	Belfast, North (Super.)	
1837	Robinson, David	Longford	1
1803	Rogers, John	Cloughjordan (Super.)	
1802	Rutledge, James	Clones (Super.)	
1826	Saul, John	Cove	1
1835	Scott, Robinson	Dublin, South	2
1830	Starkey, William	Fermoy	3
1814	Stephens, Francis	Omagh	1
1845	Stephens, Frederick	Londonderry	1
1800	Stewart, William	Belfast, North	1
1843	Storey, John C.	Coleraine	1
1824	Sullivan, James	Ballinasloe	1
1822	Tackaberry, Fossey	Sligo	1
1829	Tobias, James	Portadown	2
1817	Tracy, Richard T.	Carlow	3
1845	Twiss, Alexander	Dingle, etc.	2
1835	Vance, George	Belfast, North	2
1836	Wallace, Robert	Kingstown	1
1838	Walker, John	Donegal	2
1800	Waugh, David	Tanderee and Banbridge (Super.)	
1840	Waugh, James S.	Sligo	2
1808	Waugh, John	Aughnacloy	2
1808	Waugh, Thomas	Bandon	1

1837	Whitaker, Thomas K.	Roscrea	1
1832	Wilson, Jeremiah	Donegal	2
1828	Williams, John	Skibbereen	2

OFFICERS OF THE WESLEYAN METHODIST CHURCH

The Rev. Jacob Stanley, President. The Rev. William Stewart, Secretary.
The Rev. Walker Oke Croggon, General Superintendent of Irish Missionary Schools.
The Rev. Robinson Scott, Governor and Chaplain of the Wesleyan Connexional School.

DISTRICT CHAIRMEN

Dublin District: The Rev. Robert Masaroon.

Waterford District: The Rev. Robert T. Tracy.

Cork District: The Rev. Thomas Waugh.

Limerick District: The Rev. John Nelson.

Tullamore District: The Rev. William Crook.

Sligo District: The Rev. Fossey Tackaberry.

Clones District: The Rev. John Waugh.

Enniskillen District: The Rev. John Armstrong.

Londonderry District: The Rev. John Carey.

Belfast District: The Rev. William Stewart.

Newry District: The Rev. Claudius Byrne.

1847 ALPHABETICAL LIST OF PRIMITIVE WESLEYAN METHODIST SOCIETY MINISTERS

APPOINTMENTS AT THE ANNUAL CONFERENCE, DUBLIN, JUNE, 1846

Abraham, Thomas. Newtownstewart.

Addy, Edward. Antrim, etc.

Bowes, Edward. Maguiresbridge (Super.).

Brown, William. Newtown Butler (Super.).

Browne, James G. Cootehill.

Burns, William. Queen's County.

Campbell, Alexander. Belfast.

Campbell, Robert. Downpatrick.

Carlisle, John. Dublin.

Clendinning, James. Ballyjamesduff.

Connell, Arthur L. Dublin.

Craig, William. Enniskillen.

Cullen, John. County Wicklow.

Dawson, Abraham. Aughnacloy.

Dawson, Richard J. Clonmel, etc.

Dobbin, Abraham L. Longford.

Edwards, John. Fintona.

Flaherty, William. Athlone.

Ford, Adam. Springfield, etc.

Ford, Adam L. Clones.

Graham, Charles. Mallow.

Graham, John. Belfast.

Graham, William. Downpatrick.

Graham, William H. Waterford.

Griffin, James. Belfast.

Gunne, William. Newry.

Hamilton, George. Lurgan.

Harvey, James. Clones (Super.).

Heather, Dawson D. Dublin.

Heatley, John. Maguiresbridge.

Henderson, Daniel. Lowtherstown.

Henning, John. Newtownbutler.

Herbert, William. Maguiresbridge.

Herbert, William, jun. Clones.

Irwin, George H. Skibbereen.

Johnston, John. Cavan.

Jones, Thomas A. Kinsale.

Kane, Robert. Boyle, etc.

Kerr, Robert. Ballyshannon.

Kingsborough, Robert. Dublin.

Larminie, Samuel. Roscrea.

Lendrum, William. Springfield, etc.

Lindsay, William. Tanderagee.

M'Cormack, Joseph. Sligo.

M'Fann, Thomas. Cork.

M'Gowan, R. Armagh (Super.).

M'Ilroy, John. Armagh.

Maguire, Thomas C. County Kerry.

Mervyn, William H. Limerick.

Milligan, John. Lowerstown (Super.).

Moffit, James. Ennishowen.

Noble, John. Fintona (Super.).

Pattyson, William. Cootehill, etc.

Payne, Joseph. Ballyshannon.

Ramsey, John. Dublin.

Reid, Charles. Banbridge.

Revington, George. Dublin. (Super.).

Robinson, James. Lowtherstown.

Robinson, James, 2nd. Kells.

Robinson, Richard. Manorhamilton.

Robinson, William. Tanderagee.

Scott, William, 1st. Newry.

Scott, William, 2nd. Roscommon.

Sewell, Robert. Armagh.

Skuse, Charles. Athlone.

Skuse, William P. Charlemont.

Stephenson, John. Lisburn.

Stewart, Alexander. Maguiresbridge.

Stewart, George. Ballyconnell.

Stokes, William. Queen's County.

Sullivan, Edward. Youghal.

Taylor, Henry. Bandon.

Taylor, John. Cookstown.

Thompson, Joseph. Londonderry.

Thompson, John. Omagh.

Wherry, John. Charlemont.

White, John. Cork.

Whittle, Edward. New Ross, etc.

Wilson, John. Enniskillen.

Wilson, Robert. Newtownbutler.

Wilson, Thomas. Cloughjordan.

OFFICERS OF THE PRIMITIVE WESLEYAN METHODIST SOCIETY

The Rev. Adam Averell, President.

The Rev. Alexander Stewart, Vice-President.

The Rev. Richard Robinson, Secretary.

The Rev. George Revington, Resident Missionary Secretary, Dublin.

The Rev. Dawson D. Heather,
Traveling Secretary to the Mission, Dublin.

The Rev. John Ramsey, Book Steward.

DISTRICT CHAIRMEN

Dublin District: The Rev. John Carlisle.

Cork District: The Rev. Thomas M'Fann.

Limerick District: The Rev. William Henry Mervyn.

Athlone District: The Rev. Abraham L. Dobbin.

Clones District: The Rev. William Herbert, jun.

Enniskillen District: The Rev. Alexander Stewart.

Ballyshannon District: The Rev. Richard Robinson.

Londonderry District: The Rev. James Herbert.

Charlemount District: The Rev. John Wherry.

Belfast District: The Rev. James Griffin.

Some genealogists might doubt family tradition regarding a first generation American settler of a German name, who is said to have come from Ireland. This tradition could be true. *A History of the Church of Ireland,* 1953, by Johnston, Robinson and Jackson (p. 231), contains a paragraph on "The Palatine Newcomers," containing the following information: During the summer of 1709, some three thousand German-speaking Protestant refugees from the Palatine of the Rhine, landed in Dublin, to be settled in County Limerick and a few other parts of Ireland. The Established Church of Ireland handled them as it did the Huguenots; provided the Prayer Book in German, received them into the Church and, in 1712, the first German-speaking clergyman was ordained. This history states, "To-day Palatine blood is to be found in practically every Church of Ireland congregation in the dioceses of Limerick, Ardfert, Killaloe and Cashel." "John Wesley worked among them and from the Methodist connection created by him there came Barbara Heck and Philip Embury, founders of the Methodist Church in America."

Crookshank, in his *History of Methodism in Ireland*, 3 volumes, gives details of John Wesley's work among Palatines which began in 1749, in County Limerick. Settlements created for the Palatines were those of Court-Matrix, Killiheen, Pallas, and Ballingran which was about three miles from Rathkeale where numbers were located.

The History of Limerick, Dublin, 1866, by Maurice Lenihan (pp. 383, 710-711, 737), states that a large number of the Palatines, of the 3,000 sent on from England, were brought in 1709 by Lord Southwell and settled on his estates around Rathkeale. They also settled around Castlematress, and at Croom, about six miles east of Rathkeale. The names of some of the families of these early settlements were: Baker, Banolier, Bonner, Bethel, Bowen, Bowman, Boviniyer, Brothower, Cole, Coach, Cronderg, Dobe, Embury, Figgle, Grunse, Gruer, Heek (Hech, Hick), Hoffman, Glozier, Lawrence, Lowes, Ledwick, Long, Mich, Modeler, Neizer, Reinheart, Rose, Rodenbucher, Ruckle, St. Ledger, Strange, Sleeper, Shoemaker, Shunwire, Switzer, Tesley, Tettler, Usbenlaugh, Williams, and Young.

Palatines were settled in the Adare estate about six miles northeast of Rathkeale, in 1777-1778. Principal names were: Barkman, Corneil, Dulmage, Figgle, Hiffle, Heavener, Miller (Millar), Piper, Ruckle, Switzer, Sparling, Stark, St. John, Shier, Shoultare. Other Palatines were scattered in the counties of Carlow, Kerry, Queen's, Tipperary, and Wexford.

The most detailed account of the Palatines in Ireland, relating to Methodism, is contained in *Ireland and the Centenary of American Methodism*, by the Rev. William Crook. London, 1866. The first eighty-four pages contain chapters on the Palatines of Ireland, including a brief account of Philip Embury and Barbara Heck who emigrated in 1760 with a party of Palatines, and brought Methodism to New York City. In 1765, several relatives and neighbors followed them to New York. The balance of this work of nearly 300 pages relates to the founding of Methodism in several of the American colonies from *circa* 1760, and in Canada during the time of the American Revolution. The story is told chiefly with emphasis on the part played by the Wesleyan Methodists who emigrated from Ireland, with details of their names, origins, and activities.

CHAPTER VI

BAPTIST AND CONGREGATIONAL (INDEPENDENT) RECORDS

Records of the Baptists and Congregationalists (Independents) are treated as a unit in this chapter due to the fact that their religious, political, and military history was identical during the period of the Commonwealth and Protectorate, after they first came to Ireland in great numbers. They constituted a large part of the army in Ireland, 1649-1655. They rose to positions of power in the Government, filled the political offices, controlled the new State Church, and became proprietors of estates forfeited by the Roman Catholics as well as some Protestant Royalists. After the Restoration, the Baptists and Congregationalists (Independents) were subject equally to changes brought about by the return of Charles II to the throne, and the new Government.

Many left Ireland to settle in America before the Restoration, but they emigrated in greater numbers during the following two or three decades. If they appeared in one of the colonies in 1655 or shortly thereafter, they probably had been soldiers in Oliver Cromwell's army in Ireland, who received debentures for Irish land following their services and, rather than settle in Ireland, sold their rights to their officers who were eager to acquire large estates. The new landed class prospered in Ireland for a decade or more, but shortly after the Restoration in 1660, feared for their religious freedom as well as the safety of their estates. Thus the older emigrants from Ireland were mostly the Cromwellian proprietors and the younger ones their sons. Those who departed later in the century were more certainly sons or grandsons of the first proprietors who had been deprived of part of their new estates and entirely lost their religious freedom. Some information regarding their background will serve as a guide to their records and explain their predicament.

Historically, the two terms Congregationalist and Independent have been used interchangeably in Ireland since about 1700.   Previously they were separate sects, although not far apart in the interpretation of their doctrines.   They and the Baptists traced their earliest beliefs as Non-Conformists to Robert Brown who, in the last quarter of the sixteenth century, advocated a repudiation of the ecclesiastical authority of Queen Elizabeth and a separation from the Established Church.

All maintained one common view that any congregation of private persons had the right to meet for worship without ceremony, vestments or the use of the Book of Common Prayer prescribed by the Established Church.   They further claimed independence of any duty in a religious way, to civil authority or the ecclesiastical jurisdiction of the Established Church, the Presbyterian Church, or other exterior regulations.   Each congregation maintained itself as a separate unit for devout worship.

There is little mention of any of these sects in Ireland before 1649.   The *Ordnance Survey of the County of Londonderry*, 1837 (p. 70), relates under the section regarding Presbyterians that, at the time of the Plantation of Ulster under James I, 1608-1620, the London Companies sent some Puritans, who were Calvinistic in their views, to the town of Londonderry.   These might have been Independents who were closely related at the time.   However, they associated themselves with the Presbyterians who were also settled there and all worshiped in common with members of the Established Church.   This was due to the fact that the bishops in Ulster, before 1625, welcomed the Presbyterian ministers because of the scarcity of Church clergy, and allowed them to preach in the parish churches.   The Plantation records including those of Londonderry are discussed in the following CHAPTER XIII.

The Adair Manuscript, entitled *A True Narrative of the Rise and Progress of the Presbyterian Government in Northern Ireland . . .*, written by the Rev. W. Adair, *circa* 1694, mentions only one settlement of some Separatists in the town of Antrim, *circa* 1635-1638, who were ignored by the Presbyterians and held themselves aloof.

No doubt, some individuals who were Baptists, Congregationalists and Independents came to the larger centers, particularly the seaport towns and cities, before 1641, where they could profit as merchants. Soon after the outbreak of the devastating Roman Catholic Rebellion, all Protestants of English birth, lately arrived in Ireland, as well as the settled English families, were pressed to return to their country on account of the food shortage as well as the danger to their lives. All who could, escaped.

The great wave of these Non-Conformists arrived in Ireland between 1649 and 1659, during the period of the Commonwealth Government and the Protectorate. They came in the army of Oliver Cromwell, also as Government officials, and as new land owners. At that time the term "Independents" was somewhat loosely applied, in a political sense, to all three sects.

Cromwell was a strong and devout leader of the Independents, being a member of this particular sect. His army during the Civil War in England was largely recruited and staffed with carefully disciplined members of his own religious persuasion and the closely related Baptists and Congregationalists. He, as Lord-Lieutenant and General of the army, was determined to end the Irish Rebellion which had dragged on to no conclusion since 1641, and then confiscate the land of every Roman Catholic, as well as that of any Protestant Royalist who opposed the new Government. On 14 August 1649, he landed at Ringsend near Dublin, with some 22,000 men and was joined by 8,000 sent ahead.

After victory was firmly established in 1652, the army was stationed in the garrisons as occupying forces throughout Ireland until 1655. They were issued debentures for Irish acreage, in lieu of long overdue pay for their services. Rank and length as well as place of service, including consideration for time in England, determined the amount of land each was to receive.

Some 11,000,000 acres were confiscated for the Cromwellian settlement, in twenty-six counties of the provinces of Leinster, Munster, and Ulster. Besides this, the northeast portion of County Mayo and all of County Sligo were taken. In addition to land reserved for the army, the Government owed a previous promise of 2,500,000 acres to the English "Adventurers" who subscribed money between 1642 and 1646, to support an army independent of the king, to end the Irish Rebellion in its early years and take part in the spoils. The funds were not used as intended except for a small token force sent briefly to Ireland. Mainly the funds supported the Parliamentary army in England which evolved eventually under Cromwell's leadership and defeated the Royalists. Thus the Adventurers or their descendants, in 1653, were finally granted tracts of Irish land, the size and location of the assignments being determined by the amount of the 1642-1646 subscription and a drawing by lot.

The Government confiscated property in all the cities and towns, all of the Established Church lands, and kept the forfeited property in the counties of Dublin, Kildare, Carlow, and Cork, to repay public debts, and to satisfy favorites of Cromwell or his Parliament, as well as the new officials and public office holders in Ireland. The two baronies of Kinalea and Kerricurrihie in County Cork were reserved for the Lord Protector's Regiment of Foot, two loose Companies under Captains Jordan and Markham, one under Captain Dutton, and two Companies of Colonel Hewson under Captains Turner and Hincham. Thus the settlers in these areas were distinguished as special favorites or purchasers.

In 1655, the assignment of land to the army began when the regiments were marched to stipulated counties under command of the officers, where the men drew lots for their portions and were disbanded. Many soldiers previously in need of funds, and those who did not wish to settle in Ireland, sold their debentures to their commanding officers or other parties who in this way acquired large estates.

Further details and sources regarding the Commonwealth Settlement are contained in the following CHAPTER XIII. The source of the names of the 1,360 Adventurers who subscribed money, 1642-1646, is given which, in most cases, includes the occupation, and English residence, or position as a member of Parliament, before each received Irish land. The counties in Ireland set aside for their assignments, wherein they received one half of the land of each county, are identified. The counties which the army shared equally with the Adventurers and the counties assigned entirely to the army are named, together with one county set aside entirely for the security of enough land for the Adventurers. Thus with the full list of the Adventurers, one can in these counties identify a new proprietor who was of the army by process of elimination, due to the fact that if an Adventurer assigned his land to another it was also recorded. There is another list of the counties and baronies in Munster, where various Companies of sixteen Regiments disbanded and the officers and soldiers received their land, showing the names of the Captains and their superior officers. A further list provides the names of some 200 Adventurers (in a few cases the names of their assignees included) who settled in County Tipperary with the acreage each received, its location in the county, and the amount of the money subscribed by each in 1642-1646.

With these lists, a wealth of other information regarding individuals is provided in the Settlement sources. These materials, in combination with the Census of c. 1659; the *Books of Survey and Distribution* of the next decade and later, showing to whom certificates of title were granted; the Hearthmoney Rolls of the same decade showing the county, barony, and parish of occupants of various counties; the Wills, etc., together with the records set forth in local histories, offer many sources for tracing the families of Baptists, Congregationalists and Independents of this period.

In all cases of search for the records of an English family of the Commonwealth period and later, the histories of any county, town, diocese and parish of the area of interest should be examined, as well as the historical journals and other publications relating to the period and the county wherein any members of the family were established.

The diocesan and parish histories contain much material regarding the local families regardless of their religion, as do the county and town histories. An illustration is taken from *An Ancient Irish Parish, Past and Present, Being the Parish of Donaghmore, County Down.* By J. Davison Cowan. London, 1914. This parish is situated in the southwest end of County Down. The history is a rich source for records of all of its families. The second manor of the parish was the manor of the ancient Magenis family. This history is set forth on pages 66-77, and in other notes. The following records relate to the Hawkins family history (pp. 75-78) : "The following were the ancient residences of the Magennises: New Castle (chief residence), built by Felix Magennis (1558), subsequently owned by Viscount Magennis, forfeited in the Rebellion of 1641, and granted to William Hawkins of London, great-grandfather of Robert Hawkins Magill; Castlewellan (known formerly as Castle-Vellen and subsequently as Castle-William), the seat of the Earl Annesley; Green Castle on Carlingford Bay, of which the Bagnal family deprived them; and Rathfriland Castle, forfeited in the Rebellion, and granted to William Hawkins."

"By Certificate, dated 7th July 1668, William Hawkins, Merchant, London, became the owner of the forfeited estates in this parish of the Lord of Iveagh and of Aughuly Magenis [name spelled both ways]. The property of the Lord of Iveagh comprised the townlands of Tullymore *alias* Ballyreigan (and *alias* Ballymenagh), Tullymore *alias* Killassonne (Killysavan), and Ballymanisbeg (Ballymacrattybeg) ; while that of Aughuly Magenis consisted of the townland of Knocknarney (Knocknanarney). These townlands, although in the parish of Donaghmore, formed, after 1688, [a] portion of the manor of Rathfriland, which was owned by the Hawkins family, having been forfeited by the Lord of Iveagh."

"These townlands passed to John, son and heir of William Hawkins, and from thence to Lord Clanwilliam, and other members of the Meade family—with the exception of Knocknanarney, which subsequently became the property of the Brookes of Brookeborough. It will be seen that the original grantee was William Hawkins. He was succeeded by his son John (High Sheriff of Down, 1675). His son John, of Rathfriland (High Sheriff of Down, 1700), was the next possessor."

"Robert Hawkins (son of John Hawkins of Rathfriland by his wife Mary, sister of Sir John Magill, Bart.—formerly Johnston—daughter of Lieutenant William Johnston of Gilford, Co. Down) assumed the name Magill and became Robert

Hawkins Magill of Gill Hall (High Sheriff, Co. Down, 1718, M. P. for Down 1725-45). He married, as his second wife, Lady Anne Bligh, daughter of John, first Earl of Darnley, and of her (who married secondly, Bernard Ward, first Viscount Bangor) had a daughter, Theodosia, who married, August 29, 1765, John, 1st Earl of Clanwilliam."

This history (p. 69) contains records taken from the *Book of Survey and Distribution* of County Down (copied at that time in the Royal Irish Academy), which show that W. Hawkins received a Certificate of Title dated July 7, 1668 for 221. 1. 00 acres of Tullymore *alias* Ballymanisbeg, forfeited by the proprietor of 1641, Lord of Iveagh. Also on the same date W. Hawkins received a Certificate of Title to 158. 2. 32 acres of the land of Knocknarney, forfeited by the 1641 proprietor, Aughuly Magenis.

The Cromwellian Settlement of Ireland, by John P. Prendergast, Dublin, 1875 (pp. 240, 401, 427) shows that William Hawkins was one of the English Adventurers who subscribed money to support the army to be sent to Ireland, independent of the king, and was to receive Irish land. He received Certificate number 709, and was listed among 1,360, as "William Hawkins, of London, Merchant." An order of the Council of State of 1 June 1653 was made, regulating the method to be pursued by Adventurers in proceeding to obtain satisfaction by lot for their adventures. A Committee was appointed consisting of several aldermen of London, authorized to settle the distribution of the land to the Adventurers by lot. William Hawkins was a member of this Committee, thereby showing he was a trusted public servant during the Commonwealth. It also explains the exceptionally good allotment of property which he received.

Following the Restoration, Charles II made numerous changes in the amount of land earlier granted to the army, in order to reinstate Royalists in Ireland, upon the lands they had forfeited under Cromwell. He also returned some land to many "innocent" Roman Catholics. But he could not deprive the Adventurers of any part of their Irish land, as they were protected by the Act of Parliament of 1642, during his father's reign, which established the Adventurers fund and its purpose as well as the amount of land to be received according to the subscription.   Thus after the Restoration, Charles II made a Declaration in November 1660, laying down the details of a second Act of Settlement by which the Adventurers' lands were confirmed to them but the army allotments were to be revised.   After the Act of Settlement and Explanation, passed by Parliament in 1663, each person holding land in Ireland was to receive a new Certificate of Title. William Hawkins received his two Certificates, dated 7 July 1668, to confirm possession he had enjoyed since about 1655.

The *History of the County Down,* by Alexander Knox, Dublin, 1875 (pp. 358, 388-389), gives further information about William Hawkins as follows: The town of Rathfryland, County Down, "was founded, soon after the Restoration, by Alderman Hawkins, of London, to whom the whole of the extensive manor was granted by Charles II . . ."   "On the summit of a hill, adjoining the town, stand the ruins of an old castle, anciently one of the mansions of the Magennises, Lords of Iveagh.   The castle was pulled down by Mr. Hawkins, the first proprietor of the town, after the rebellion of 1641." "The extensive properties of the Earl of Clanwilliam, in this parish, were originally granted to Mr. Hawkins, an alderman of the city of London, by Charles II, as a recompense for his great and charitable exertions on behalf of the distressed Protestants, during the Civil War."   The author goes on to tell about 30,000 English pounds raised to support 5,000 Protestants who fled from Ireland to England for refuge during the Rebellion, and 45,000 English pounds collected to send to Ireland for those who did not escape.   He then traces the Hawkins property in the parish to the possession of Robert Hawkins who assumed the name Robert Hawkins-Magill, whose daughter Theodosia was married to Sir John Meade, who was created Earl of Clanwilliam, in 1776.   This author missed the Adventurers' records including the records of William Hawkins, published by Prendergast in 1875, the same year in which Knox himself published the *History of the County Down.*

Nenagh and its Neighborhood, by E. H. Sheehan, published about 1905, is a history of the town of County Tipperary, and

its residents there and in the surrounding country in the
upper and lower baronies of Ormond. This little paper bound
book of 98 pages does not appear to be important but it is
filled with genealogical notes and personal information. Some
single paragraphs contain a family line of four or more
generations. A summary of the names of settlers during the
Commonwealth period is given on page 79, as follows: "The
first Cromwellians actually to come to Ormond otherwise than
as actual fighting men are to be found in Nenagh as traders.
In 1659 Edward Hutchinson is there issuing coin of his own as
a medium of exchange. He was a clerk. The tituladoes were
John Stokes, William Moore, James Colman and Cesar Free-
man. The soldiers who were grantees in Ormond were Col.
Henry Prittie, Col. Thos. Sadleir, Col. Finch, Col. Daniel Ab-
bott, Col. Jas. Harrison and Col. Solomon Cambie. Col. Nicho-
las Toler of Ballintotty, was Quarter-Master General in the
Cromwellian forces. Prittie was at one time Governor of
Carlow, but before that had seen much service against the
Royalists in England. He was granted 3,642 acres in Upper
Ormond and Owney-and-Ara including the Silver Mines.
Eventually he settled on the old freeholds of Col. Sean O'Ken-
nedy at Dunaille and founded a family which still endures.
Col. Thomas Sadleir came to Ireland in 1649 and later settled
down at Kilnahalagh, the old chief seat of the Brehon Mc-
Egans in Lower Ormond, now known as Sopwell Hall. Col.
Abbott came over with Cromwell and was Governor of Nenagh
at one time. He had the Manor lands of the Duchess of Ormond and the ancient Manor of Weyperous or Ballinaclogh.
Sir William Flower, acting for the Duchess of Ormond, prevailed on Abbott to withdraw from the Castle of Nenagh and
installed Col. Finch who was Governor in these parts, in his
place. Col. Abbott was finally a grantee of land in and
around Nenagh and in Ara, including the three ploughlands
of Tyone, anciently the property of the Augustinians."

"Simon Cambie drew the Annagh property in Lower Ormond, later this passed by purchase to the Minchin family
who still hold it. Col. Simon Finch had his grants in Aradh
and settled at the ancient McIbrien seat of Kilcoleman. He
had fought at Worcester for Parliament. He brought rein-

forcements to Sir Hardress Waller in Ireland in 1652. Later he supported the Restoration and thus was able to retain his estate."

"Other lesser figures who came to settle in Ormonde were Captain Stopford, Col. John Cole, Thomas Poe, Thomas Peacock, John Gayson, Ri. Andrews, Joseph Fox, Samuel Wade, Ben. Barry and John Briggs."

"Stopford was allotted the entire town of Borrisokane and introduced a number of English tenants in the course of time. Col. Fleetwood was assigned Traverston. There was a John Cole of Castlelough (Prob. 1724); Dancer was probably a '49 officer, was Mayor of Waterford in 1660. His son, Sir Thomas Dancer, came to reside at Modreeny in Lower Ormond where the family remained for some generations. He received 729 acres under the Act of Settlement, 1666. Wade was an officer in Sadleir's Regiment; he settled at Derrycastle, Killaloe. Before the end of the century an only daughter married one Head, a wool buyer of Waterford in whose name the property there descended to our own time."

"Joseph Fox came to Annabeg where later in the century his property there was sold to Captain John Minnitt, Cromwellian Master of the Horse, of Mount Minnitt, Limerick. Lieut. Thomas Poe had a grant in Upper Ormond; Nicholas Poore (Power), Ballyrush in and Knocknabohilly; Lieut. Richard Waller, Cullymore; John Otway in Upper Ormond; John Dawson in Toome, 1,791 acres; John Gayson, Killeen and Drumcask; Captain Stephen Allen, 403 acres, part of Killowning."

"The following are signatures to an address prepared at Nenagh and presented to the Duke of Ormond in London by a number of the Ormond grantees, mostly Cromwellians. The new holders were becoming anxious concerning the security of their possessions ten years after the Restoration."

"Your Grace's most humble and obliged servants:—W. Waller, Thos. Sadleir, Jos. Walker, Joseph Fox, Simon Ffynch, Sol. Camby, Jas. Abbott, Joshua Hoyle, T. Briggs, Henry Helsham, Walter Cooper, Stephen Allen, Samuel Wade, W. Sheldon, Mi. Hunt, Sam Barclay, Peter Dalton, Uriah Foxwell, C. Minchin, Ben. Barry, J. Parker, R. Chizers."

"Nenagh, 3rd March, 1670-'71."

Cromwell's plan of governing Ireland provided four Commissioners who arrived in Dublin during January, 1651. One of their principal purposes was to promote the Protestant religion based on the views of the Independents, and at the same time do away with any vestige of ecclesiastical control by the Established Church. The use of the Book of Common Prayer, the surplice and all ceremonies were forbidden. The old diocesan divisions were no longer recognized and all Church property reverted to the Government. The tithes formerly collected from everyone for support of the clergy were now imposed by the Commissioners, and revenue agents controlled the new Church finances. The old parishes were united or divided to form the precincts of Athy, Athlone, Belfast, Belturbet, Clonmel, Cork, Dublin, Galway, Kilkenny, Londonderry, Limerick, Trym, Waterford, and Wexford.

The Commissioners appointed a committee to choose ministers which became known as the "Committee for Approbation or Trial of Ministers." The preachers were selected for their piety and gift of oratory. The large majority were Baptists, Congregationalists or Independents. Many of these were chosen from among the army officers of the garrison forces which held sway over the principal cities and towns. The available Presbyterian ministers were at first held suspect, owing to their earlier loyalty to the Royalist cause. However, very shortly no strong prejudice was evinced against any Presbyterian minister or even the clergy of the Established Church of Ireland, so long as they divested themselves of all formalities and previous ecclesiastical control by the bishops of the Church. The old churches continued in use where needed and new meeting-houses were built in other areas at Government expense, while the tithes supplied quarterly warrants to the ministers in payment for their services. The existing Parish Registers of this period show that the old Registers were continued for the keeping of records of baptism, marriage and burial, and new Registers were begun where none had existed, according to the Commonwealth Act of 1653 which required the keeping of all such records. Thus after the Restoration and the return of the Established Church to its old power as the State Church, many of the Registers continued to be kept by the clergy with little if any break in the records. The Parish Registers of churches in Cork, Dublin, Londonderry, etc., show this.

The Civil List of 1654 sets forth the names of 115 ministers. Civil Lists are in the Commonwealth Council Books (55th *Report*, Public Record Office, Dublin, p. 134). In 1655, this had grown to 146 and the following year there were 302 ministers. In the first list only six were Presbyterians and ten represented clergy of the Established Church while all the remainder were Baptists, Congregationalists or Independents. The list of 302 contained the names of sixty-seven Presbyterian ministers, sixty-five clergy of the Established Church and the balance were Baptists, Congregationalists or Independents.

The Public Record Office, Dublin, at present has a *Calendar of Church Miscellaneous Papers*, 1652-1795. The documents calendared include appointments to dignities and benefices, and of schoolmasters, resignations, certificates of vacancies and acceptances of Church livings, and recommendations for preferment (55th *Report of the Deputy Keeper of the Public Records in Ireland*, p. 130).

Oliver Cromwell died on 3 September 1658. His son Richard was proclaimed Protector on 3 September 1658, and retired on 25 May 1659. His younger brother Henry Cromwell had since 1655, to all intents and purposes, served as the ruler of Ireland. After his brother Richard's retirement, he refused proposals to assist in the restoration of Charles II, and was recalled to England in June 1659.

Immediately the ignored bishops and clergy began some activity, looking to the future for their old places. Charles II was proclaimed king in the city of Dublin, on 14 May 1660. His proclamation of that month betrayed his promise to Scotland when, soon after the death of his father, he was crowned there as Charles II, King of Scotland, Great Britain and Ireland. The terms were that he should impose Presbyterianism on England and Ireland. In 1660, the Established Church was returned to power as the State Church with the old system of ecclesiastical control by the bishops over the dioceses and the clergy of the parishes, while the people were again subject to the laws of the Church and State requiring them to conform. Protestant dissenters and Roman Catholics alike, were regarded as the enemies of the State. The Government returned all Church lands to the Established Church of Ireland, according to the distribution in effect in 1641.

A strange quirk of history, which must be remembered in judging the period of power of the Independents and their closely allied sects in Ireland, is that it was the Cromwellian leaders supported by their army, in England as well as in Ireland, who were responsible for restoring Charles II to the throne, rather than the old Royalists. Thus in Ireland the Independents were not swept out of office immediately. However, in 1661, the Government agents and the clergy broke up the meetings of Papists, Presbyterians, Independents, Baptists and Quakers. The people were fined for non-attendance of the Established Church. The Non-Conformist preachers and the Roman Catholic priests were fined and imprisoned for conducting services. This was enforced severely until the passing of the Act of Toleration in 1689. From then on the active persecution of Protestant dissenters ended, but they were still subject to the civil and legal disabilities imposed by the Penal Laws, the Test Act and the Corporation Act.

Between 1660 and 1670 the Baptists and Independents were for the most part dispersed. Never having built their own Churches into organized units with a central control by representatives of each Church body, they could only carry on in small separate groups, subject to all the disabilities of dissenters, with no power to assert themselves comparable to that of the Presbyterians. The *History of the Church of Ireland,* by W. A. Phillips, Vol. III, p. 130, states, "By far the greater number of the ministers under the Commonwealth had been Independents or Baptists, and yet within ten years of the Restoration Baptists and Independents seem to have disappeared. Some returned to England, some migrated to America, and the Church absorbed the remainder."

Froude, in his history of *The English in Ireland,* Book I,

Chapter III, makes the sweeping statement regarding the Cromwellian settlers, "The few families of Independents which remained were condemned to spiritual isolation. So long as the first owners lived they retained their beliefs; but deprived as they were of school or chapel, they could not perpetuate them. Liturgy and mass were to them alike detestable. To Church they would not go; separate family worship they were unable to maintain; and thus their children were swept into the Irish stream, became Catholics like those among whom they lived and married, and trod in the steps of the generation who had gone before them." "The immense majority left the country."

To a certain extent this was true, as the forfeitures of Roman Catholic lands after the Williamite War of 1689-1691 show some Cromwellian settlers who had become Roman Catholics and at this time lost their property. Certainly many who remained became members of the Established Church and some became Presbyterians. Within the reign of Charles II, some returned to England and others emigrated to America. A few Baptists and Congregationalists (Independents) quietly maintained private places of worship.

Whether the members of these religious persuasions espoused the Established Church or remained loyal, each to his own sect, their records of baptism, marriage and burial are more apt to be found in any existing Parish Registers of the Established Church in their area, due to the prevailing laws of the kingdom. No Baptist or Congregational Church Registers are deposited in the Public Record Offices in Dublin and Belfast, so far as evidenced by the *Reports of the Deputy Keepers*.

Gradually in the 18th century the Baptists and Congregationalists emerged again. *A Century of Congregationalism: The Story of Donegall Street Church,* by James E. Archibald, published in celebration of the founding of the Church in 1801, offers the following information (pp. 1-4) : During the period of the Commonwealth and the Protectorate, the Congregationalist (Independent) ministers in Dublin were: Samuel Winter, Samuel Mather, Thomas Harrison, Stephen Warnock, John Rogers, John Byewater, and Thomas Huggins. The minister in Waterford was Thomas Patient; in Cork, John Murcot; in Youghal, Joseph Eyres; in Carrickfergus, Timothy Taylor; in Limerick, Claudius Gilbert and Edward Reynolds; in Iredagh, one named Jenner. Besides this, there were churches in Kilkenny, Wexford, Galloway, and other places. Daniel Williams, who was born in 1643 and died in 1716, was chaplain to the Countess of Meath, and preached to an Independent congregation at Drogheda. Some of the early Churches merged into Presbyterianism. The oldest existing churches were (in 1901), at Richhill, Co. Armagh, founded in 1721; Cork, 1750; Sligo, 1787; Moy, Co. Tyrone, 1796; Donegall Street Church, Belfast, 1801. The first minister of the latter Church was the Rev. William Brown, who came from Scotland with other Independent ministers in connection with a revival movement. The first trustees of the Belfast Church in 1801 were: Alexander Blackwell, James M'Tier, Joseph Sheriff, William Miller, William Neilson, John Rea, Henry Herman Jansson, Matthew Gray, William Mattear, and John Kennedy. A Thomas Price and James Harper were added in 1804. This volume contains biographies of all of the ministers up to 1901, but no genealogy.

Thom's Irish Almanac and Official Directory for the Year 1847, gives lists (pp. 347, 350), of the names of the ministers in 1846, of the Baptist and the Congregational churches, and their locations. As these lists may help in locating any existing Church Registers of this date or earlier, the information is presented below.

BAPTIST CHURCH: Names of the ministers, cities or towns, and counties:

T. Berry, Abbeyleix, Queen's.

W. Thomas, Athlone, Westmeath.

(No name), Aughavey, Tyrone.

W. Hamilton, Ballina, Mayo.

(No name), Ballymoney, Antrim.

(No name), Ballygawley, Tyrone.

R. Wilson, Belfast, Antrim.

(No name), Blackforth, Tyrone.

S. Jackman, Boyle, Roscommon.

(No name), Brogshane, Antrim.

G. Moore, Carrickfergus, Antrim.

(No name), Carrandasy, Tyrone.

C. Sharman, Clonmel, Tipperary.

M. Mullarky, Cloghjordan, Tipperary.

W. S. Eccles, Coleraine, Londonderry.

D. Mulhern, Conlig, Down.

(No name), Cookstown, Tyrone.
(No name), Coolaney, Sligo.
G. N. Watson, Cork, Cork.
(No name), Crilly, Tyrone.
(Vacant), Dublin, Dublin.
J. Bates, Dungannon, Tyrone.
(No name), Easky, Sligo.
I. M'Carthy, Ferbane, King's.
(No name), Grange, Antrim.
C. Sharman, Kilcooly Hills, Tipperary.
(No name), Knockconny, Tyrone.
(No name), Letterkenny, Donegal.
R. Bentley, Limerick, Limerick.
W. Thomas, Moate, Westmeath.

(No name), Monaghan, Monaghan.
(No name), Mullaghmore, Tyrone.
(No name), Mullycar, Tyrone.
D. Cook, Omagh, Tyrone.
I. M'Carthy, Rahue, Westmeath.
(No name), Siskanore, Tyrone.
R. H. Carson, Tubbermore (1st), Derry.
R. H. Carson, Tubbermore (2nd), Derry.
C. Hardcastle, Waterford, Waterford.
M. Mullarky, Parsonstown, King's.

CONGREGATIONAL UNION OF IRELAND: Station and Pastor or Missionary.

Armagh, J. White.
Aughnacloy, W. Fordyce.
Ballybay, W. Dowgan.
Ballycraigey, A. Bell.
Belfast, J. Hodgens.
Carrickfergus, J. M'Assey.
Castlebar, J. Murray and T. Jordan.
Clonmel, H. Martin.
Coleraine, H. G. Heathcote.
Cork, T. Shelley and J. Cranbrook.
Donegal, H. G. Brien.
Donoughmore, J. Hanson.
Dublin, J. Bewglass, W. Cooper, W. H. Cooper, W. Foley, J. Godkin, J. Hands, W. Urwick, A. King.
Dungarvan (Vacant).

Kilkeel, J. Mallagh.
Limerick, J. De K. Williams.
Londonderry, J. Jennings.
Mallow, C. B. Gibson.
Maryborough, H. M. Torrens.
Mountmellick, S. M. Coombs.
Moy, S. Shaw.
Newport, J. Gibbons.
Newry (No name).
Newtownlimavady, P. Finan.
Richhill, J. Carroll.
Roscommon Co., G. Sampey.
Sligo, N. Sheppard.
Straid, J. Bain.
Tralee, S. Browne.
Waterford, R. Murphy.
Wexford, E. Dillon.
Youghal, J. B. Grey.

CHAPTER VII

PRESBYTERIAN RECORDS

The Presbyterians in Ireland were largely Ulster Scots. During two and a half centuries after the first plantation of Scottish Presbyterian colonies in Ulster, *ca.* 1606, they maintained a close connection with their homeland, while they remained a race apart from their Irish and English neighbors. They were hated by the Roman Catholics of Ulster, whose land they had usurped. They were despised by the English, whose Government and Established Church inflicted persecution upon them due to religious non-conformity.

The Ulster Scots kept their racial strain pure in matters of intermarriage. They sent their sons to Scotland to be educated for the ministry, etc. Many of them married there before they returned to Ulster. Thus they remained under the influence of Scottish religion, philosophy, and family ties in their early and some later generations.

While the Presbyterians who settled in Ulster were almost solidly Scottish, there were many English Puritans of Calvinistic doctrine who settled in Dublin and the South of Ireland. The English type of Presbyterianism lacked the more severe theology and discipline of the Scottish Church. Their congregations in Leinster and Munster were the outgrowth of the English Puritans and Independents of the Commonwealth period, left there without organization after the Restoration. These two sects united in 1696 and developed the Southern Association of the Presbyterian Church. This became the Presbytery of Munster and a part of the General Synod.

Historians of Church and local affairs, and the genealogists, have preserved a wealth of published and manuscript records regarding Presbyterian families and individuals. The sources are listed in VOLUME II, in which they are indexed as follows: COUNTY AND TOWN HISTORIES, pp. 77-87; DIOCESAN AND

PARISH HISTORIES, pp. 76, 87-92; PLANTATION RECORDS, HIS-
TORY AND DOCUMENTS, pp. 240-241; PRESBYTERIAN RECORDS
AND HISTORY, pp. 42, 222-225; FAMILY RECORDS PUBLISHED,
3-33, 34-37, 38-42, 52-75, 76-94, 256-257; FAMILY DOCUMENTS,
109-166, 167-196.

A few points which may puzzle genealogists will be clarified
by a brief review of the history of the Presbyterians and their
problems, due to the laws of the realm regarding dissenters
from the Established Church of Ireland. This will show that
less than half of the Presbyterian families were permanently
settled in Ireland before 1650. The Penal Laws and other
Acts of Parliament, depriving Presbyterians of religious and
civil liberty, were during some periods more rigorously imposed in Scotland than in Ireland, thus resulting in a large
emigration to Ulster. At other times the Ulster Presbyterians were more severely penalized, causing several ministers
and many Church members to return to Scotland. At all times
until well into the eighteenth century, the religious laws and
practices resulted in the entries of many records of baptism,
marriage and burial, in the Parish Registers of the Established Church.

The first wave of Presbyterian settlers came to Ulster
as lessees of the numerous Scottish proprietors who were
granted estates by James I, 1605-1625. By patent of 16
April 1605, the northeast quarter of County Down was granted
to Hugh Montgomery and the northwest quarter was granted
to James Hamilton. This represented two-thirds of the estates forfeited by Con O'Neill, who later was forced to sell his
remaining lands to the benefit of Hamilton and Montgomery.
The southern part of County Down remained in Roman Catholic hands. The new proprietors were required by the Crown
to live on their estates, build houses, churches, and bring English or Scottish settlers as tenants, able to bear arms for the
King, build houses and develop their land. Hamilton and
Montgomery brought emigrants from the Scottish counties
of Ayr, Renfrew, Wigtown, Dumfries and Kirkcudbright.
They began coming in May, 1606. By 1610, Montgomery could
muster 1,000 men for the King and, in 1614, the two pro-

prietors mustered 2,000 men, representing about 10,000 Scots settled in County Down. Sir Arthur Chichester received a large portion in the southern part of County Antrim. In 1603, he was granted the "Castle of Belfaste" and surrounding property. He soon afterward acquired land along Carrickfergus Bay and to the north almost as far as Lough Larne. He at first settled an English colony around Belfast, but before long the Scottish settlers predominated throughout the lower half of County Antrim. The upper half had been in the hands of the Macdonnell clan since about 1580. Soon after 1607, the area was granted to Randall Macdonnell who, in 1620, became the Earl of Antrim. Scottish tenants also spread through his estates, being required to bear arms for the King and develop the land.

The flight of the Ulster Earls of Tyrone and Tyrconnel with their Chiefs who were confederates, on 14 September 1607, gave James I the opportunity to confiscate their lands for past and present treason. The six counties of Armagh, Cavan, Donegal, Fermanagh, Londonderry, and Tyrone, were escheated to the Crown. This great confiscation, of some 3,800,000 acres, led to the carefully planned "Plantation of Ulster" between 1608 and 1620. Of this land, about 1,500,000 acres were only partly fertile and largely bog, forest, and mountain country. This was restored to the Irish Roman Catholic natives. Extensive grants were reserved for the bishops and their incumbents of the Established Church. Trinity College, Dublin, and other Royal Schools received about 20,000 acres. Land was also set aside for the corporate towns, forts, etc. The remaining half million acres of the most fertile land was reserved for colonization by English and Scottish settlers.

King James at first chose fifty-nine Scotsmen of high social standing and influence and nearly as many Englishmen, together with fifty-six military officers or "servitors" and eighty-six natives, as undertakers who were to receive estates of 2,000 acres or less, in all counties but Londonderry which was reserved for the Corporation of the City of London. Eventually, by 1630, some undertakers acquired as much as

3,000 acres, and estates in County Londonderry came into private hands.

There were three classes of undertakers established. The first group was the most privileged. They were charged a Crown rent of £5 6s. 8d. per thousand acres. The second class of "servitors" or military undertakers, assumed a Crown rent of £8 per thousand acres. While the former were required to bring Scottish or English tenants, the latter were permitted to take Irish tenants, but their rent was reduced for acreage let to the Scots or English. Some native Irish of the third class also acquired large estates of two to three thousand acres, but for the most part the land was parceled out to them in plots of less than one hundred to a few hundred acres. Their Crown rent was fixed at £10 13s. 4d. per thousand acres. They were pledged to loyalty to the king in all respects.

The undertakers of the first two classes assumed the same obligations. Those who received 2,000 acres were to erect a castle and a fortress, occupy their land and bring a minimum of forty-eight able-bodied men of Scottish or English descent to settle on the estate and lease small plots. They were to be furnished with arms by the undertaker, mustered periodically for review, and were required to build houses as well as plant the land. The undertakers who received 1,500 acres or less assumed the same obligations except that in place of building a castle, they were each required to erect a strong stone house to live in, while they directed a proportionately smaller number of tenants in developing the land. All were to provide places for worship and conform to the laws of the Established Church.

The Corporation of London, which was granted the greater part of the county of Londonderry, was required to fortify the towns of Londonderry and Coleraine, lay out the property assigned to the London Guilds, build sufficient houses and churches, settle the property of each Guild with tenants who were English or Scottish, able to bear arms for the king and develop the land.

From the beginning the Scottish tenants in County Londonderry, including the towns of Coleraine and Londonderry, outnumbered the English. A colony of English settled in and around Belfast, and along the river between there and County Armagh where they predominated. They also chose County Cavan, and in County Fermanagh the early Scottish settlers gave way to them in many cases. While the Scots quickly joined the English in their places of settlement, they were more solidly settled in the counties of Antrim, Down, Donegal, Londonderry and Tyrone.

By 1618, there was evidence that the undertakers were not fulfilling their obligations. In that year, Captain Nicholas Pynnar was employed by the Government to make a survey of the six escheated counties included in the "Ulster Plantation." He faithfully followed instructions to visit every estate and make a report on the progress of the settlements, the number of occupants, castles and dwelling houses as well as "bawns" either completed or under construction, the number and description of live animals and the condition of development of each estate.

Pynnar's Survey is included in *An Historical Account of the Plantation in Ulster,* 1608-1620, edited by the Rev. George Hill, Belfast, 1877 (pp. 449-590). This entire work was compiled from the *Calendars of the Carew Manuscripts,* collections of *State Papers of Ireland, Patent Rolls, Inquisitions of Ulster,* and other miscellaneous documents of importance. About half of the pages, 449-590, devoted to Pynnar's Survey, are filled with Hill's documented notes concerning the families of the undertakers or personal information. Much genealogy is included. Also the names and some records of the lessees on several of the estates are included.

Further notes regarding the information in *The Plantation in Ulster,* as well as in the published *Hamilton Manuscripts,* the *Montgomery Manuscripts,* and the *Macdonnells of Antrim,* all of which contain equally copious notes filled with genealogical information, will be contained in the following CHAPTER XIII, devoted to PLANTATION AND SETTLEMENT RECORDS.

Pynnar's Survey of 1618 indicates that one-fourth of the lands were not fully occupied, while some 8,000 men of British birth (English or Scottish), capable of bearing arms for defense, were settled in the six counties. These, together with the 2,000 in County Down and others in County Antrim, indicate that the total number of Scottish settlers who were almost solidly Presbyterian, amounted to about 40,000 in all of Ulster in the first ten years.

A rich source of genealogical information regarding Presbyterian ministers and their families is the *Fasti of the Irish Presbyterian Church*, 1613-1840. The records were compiled by the late Rev. James McConnell, and revised by his son, the late Rev. Samuel G. McConnell. The work was published by the Presbyterian Historical Society, Belfast, 1951. The records of 1,276 ministers are arranged within seven periods: 1613-1642; 1642-1661; 1661-1690; 1690-1720; 1721-1777; 1778-1820; 1820-1840. The records of the first two periods were reprinted from *The Genealogists' Magazine*, 1936, 1937. Records of the second, third, and first half of the fourth period were arranged and edited by the Rev. F. J. Paul and the Rev. David Stewart. The balance of the work was arranged and edited by the Rev. David Stewart. In 1943, he compiled *The Fasti of the American Presbyterian Church*, which is included at the back of the volume. This contains the records of 156 ministers who emigrated from Ulster to America. An Addenda (not included in all volumes), contains the records of eighteen other ministers who emigrated.

Information of genealogical value is included in all of the biographical notices. The records of nearly everyone include the date and place of education, the date and place where each was licensed and ordained, places of assignment, and for those who emigrated, the year of arrival and places where they served. Almost all records show the year or the date and place of death, and a large proportion contain the year and place of birth. The name of the father is always given if he was a minister, and often if not. In all cases, a son and a son-in-law are named if they became ministers. This leads to identification of their later biographies. A number of families contributed ministers in each of several generations. In some cases, brothers who were ministers in a second, third, or later generation, establish the records of separate branches of the family. In other cases, the records of only one minister or of a father and son appear. The biographical notes are extremely valuable, due to the fact that a great number of people of Ulster ancestry are descended from one or more Presbyterian ministers who did not leave Ireland, or from one who emigrated.

Some illustrations of the biographies showing the variety, nature, and length of the genealogical information will be presented, following a brief history of the first few periods. This will explain the religious problems of all Presbyterians in Ulster, and particularly those faced by the ministers. It will clarify the reasons for many dismissals from the ministry due to trouble between the Presbyterian Church and the Government, reinstatements when conditions improved, enforced discipline due to religious laws, periods of imprisonment for upholding their principles, emigration, etc.

Through the influence of John Knox, the foundations of the Presbyterian Church were laid in Scotland and the first General Assembly was called in 1560. James VI of Scotland who succeeded to the English throne as James I, in 1603, was determined to strengthen the Established Church in Scotland. Melville, the leading Presbyterian of the time, was imprisoned in the Tower of London, and the General Assembly was forbidden to function. Presbyterian ministers and their adherents alike were severely persecuted by the bishops, to bring them under Church control.

At the same time, King James was anxious for a large settlement of English and Scots in Ireland. The latter came to Ulster for new land but also for religious liberty, attracted by the tolerant attitude maintained there by the bishops. The new Confession of Faith, sanctioned by Parliament for the Plantation Settlements, reconciled the differences between Anglicans and Presbyterians. It was Calvinistic in doctrine and allowed Presbyterian ministers to serve as clergy in the parish churches according to their own practices and beliefs. This encouraged the Scottish ministers to follow their countrymen to Ulster.

In the first period, between 1613 and 1642, the outstanding ministers in Ulster and the dates of their arrival were: Robert Blair, 1623; John Boyle, 1613; Edward Brice, 1613; Henry

Calvert, 1629; Robert Cunningham, 1615; another Robert Cunningham, 1627; George Dunbar, 1624; William Dyal (or Daniel or Dalzell), 1614; James Glendenning, before 1622; James Hamilton, 1625; Robert Hamilton, 1617; ——— Hubbard, 1621; David Kennedy, 1638; John Livingstone, 1630; Thomas Murray, c. 1640; John M'Clelland, after 1629; Hugh Peebles, c. 1633; ——— Pont, c. 1630; John Ridge, 1619; David Row, c. 1615; Samuel Row, c. 1634; John Semple, 1646; Andrew Stewart, 1627; David Watson, 1617; Josias Welsh, before 1630.

The easy co-operation of the bishops in Ulster changed after 1625, and the ministers preached under increasing restrictions. This came about through the influence of William Laud, Archbishop of Canterbury, over Charles I. They were determined to tighten the control of the Established Church and this was reflected in Ireland. Echlin, bishop of Down, who had been co-operative, suspended from the ministry Robert Blair, minister of Bangor, and John Livingstone, minister of Killinchy, in 1631. This Non-Conformist trouble was reported to the king and resulted in the suspension of Josias Welsh, minister of Templepatrick, and George Dunbar, minister of Larne.

To make matters worse, Wentworth (Earl of Strafford) was appointed to the Irish Vice-royalty and arrived in Dublin in 1633. He and his government began a reign of terror for Roman Catholics and Presbyterians alike. He followed Laud's policy to the letter. The earlier "Articles of Religion" were set aside and the ministers were required to adopt a Confession of Faith embodying the Thirty-nine Articles of the Church of England. He further ordered the Act of Uniformity to be enforced against the ministers. This declared that every clergyman or minister celebrating any religious service other than that of the Established Church, every layman assisting at such a service and every person who opposed the liturgy of the Church, was liable on the third offense to confiscation of goods and imprisonment for life.

George Dunbar disobeyed and was excommunicated in 1634. John Livingstone was sentenced to the same penalty in 1635. In 1636 all ministers were required openly to declare their conformity to the Established Church. Five were deposed and sentenced to perpetual silence. These were: Edward Brice, minister of Ballycarry; John Ridge of Antrim; Robert Cunningham of Holywood (who came, 1615) ; Henry Calvert of Oldstone; and James Hamilton of Ballywalter. The latter was the second son of Gavin Hamilton, merchant of Coleraine, and grandson of Hans Hamilton, minister of Dunlop, Ayrshire. John M'Clelland, of Newtownards, was deposed but continued to preach, and was therefore excommunicated. Samuel Row was banished and escaped to Scotland.

In 1636, Robert Blair, Robert Hamilton, John M'Clelland and John Livingstone organized a group of 140 Scottish settlers to emigrate to New England. They set sail in September, 1636, and when half way across, were driven back by storms. The ministers, to escape arrest, fled to Scotland, accompanied by many of their adherents. At this time Scotland had become a safe refuge.

The crowning blow to Ulster came in 1639 when the "Black Oath" was imposed. The clergy were required to read it from their pulpits and the people were forced to swear on their knees, if over age sixteen, to obey the King's commands and to abjure and renounce the Covenant. The clergy were ordered to report on every Presbyterian in each parish. Some conformed. Landed proprietors such as the Hamiltons and the Montgomerys betrayed their faith and joined the persecutors. Great numbers, who could re-establish themselves in Scotland, returned there. As many as 500 at a time returned to Scotland for the Communion season.

This persecution and departure of many Scots from Ulster saved hundreds of lives during the Rebellion which broke out in 1641. The Roman Catholics, determined to exterminate the English, also hated the Presbyterians for settling on their forfeited land. They tortured and murdered thousands and drove others out of their homes to die of privation. Reprisals by the settlers, and a Scottish army sent to Ulster, were equally devastating.

The biographies of the ministers in the *Fasti of the Irish Presbyterian Church*, give the time and place of death of the ministers who served during the first period, 1613-1642, and in some cases later, with some records of their issue:

Ministers who died in Ireland before 1639: Edward Brice died at Templecorran, just after August, 1636. He left two sons, Robert and Edward, and two daughters; a grandson, Randal Brice, became High Sheriff for County Antrim 1675, and for County Down 1676, and was Member of Parliament for Lisburn, 1692. *William Dyal* died at Donaghenry in 1634; no later record. The *Rev. Hubbard*, at Carrickfergus, 1621; died in 1623. *Andrew Stewart* died at Donegore, September 1634. He had four children, of whom Andrew became minister at Donaghadee (1641-1671), and Janet married Thomas Crawford, minister of Donegore (1655-1670); Elizabeth married Lieut. Paul Cunningham. *Josias Welsh* died at Templepatrick, 23 June 1634. His son, John, was minister of Irongray, Galloway, Scotland (1653-1662).

Ministers who died in Ireland after 1639: Robert Cunningham (who came 1627), died at Taughboyne, County Donegal, June 1654. He married Frances, sister of Hugh Cunningham, minister of Ray, and had issue, Hugh, William, Elizabeth (married John Craig, Londonderry); widow living 27 April 1659. *James Glendinning*, conformed to the Established Church; living 1662; his son, James, executed as a Royalist. *David Kennedy* fled to Scotland, 1638; sentence revoked by the Irish Parliament, 1641. *Thomas Murray*, murdered with two sons during the Rebellion in 1641, at Killyleagh. *John Semple*, in Scotland, 1646-1651; was sometime minister in County Down; died 1677, aged 75. *David Watson*, of Armagh, captured on his way to Scotland, July 1644; died a prisoner in Mingarie Castle, March 1645. He married Isabella Philis Kerk of Drumquin and had issue, three children, of whom Elizabeth married James Hamilton, minister of Ballywalter (1626-1636).

Ministers who died while residents of Scotland: Robert Blair died at Meikle Couston, Aberdeen, 27 August 1666. He married (1) Beatrix, daughter of Robert Hamilton, merchant, Edinburgh, who died 1632, and had issue; (2) Catherine, daughter of Hugh Montgomery, Laird of Busbie, and had issue. He was father of the Rev. David Blair, Old Kirk, Edinburgh, 1691-1710; grandfather of the Rev. Robert Blair, Athel-stanford, 1700-1746; great-grandfather of the Rev. Hugh Blair, Professor at Edinburgh University, 1762-1784. *Henry Calvert*, minister at Paisley, 1 July 1641; died 22 June 1653. *Robert Cunningham* (who came 1615), died at Irvine, 29 March 1637. He married Isabel, daughter of Hugh Montgomery, Laird of Busbie, and had eight children, of whom Robert was minister of Broadisland, 1646-1697; James was minister of Antrim, 1656-1670; Margaret married Patrick Adair, minister of Cairncastle and Belfast; Janet married Archibald Ferguson, minister of Antrim; Isabella married John Law, minister of Campsie, Sterlingshire, and St. Giles, Edinburgh. *George Dunbar*, at Mid Calder, 1638; died December, 1641. He married (1) Jean Crawford, (2) Margaret Wallace, by whom he had issue, Samuel, who inherited his lands of Pollosh; George (died 1641); Margaret and Marian. *James Hamilton* died at Edinburgh, 10 March 1666. He married Elizabeth Watson, daughter of David Watson, minister of Killeavy, County Down, and had fifteen children of whom only Archibald, later minister at Benburb, Armagh and Killinchy; Jane (married her cousin Archibald, minister of Bangor, 1670-1689); Mary; Margaret; Elizabeth, reached maturity. *Robert Hamilton*, minister of Ballantrae, Ayrshire, 1647; died 1659. He married Margaret, daughter of Hugh Montgomery, Laird of Busbie, who died at Kilwinning, March 1659. *John Livingstone*, served on Cromwell's Committee for choosing ministers. Received calls from Antrim, Killinchy, Glasgow, Newtownards, and Killyleagh. Banished 11 Dec. 1662; died at Rotterdam, 9 August 1672. *John M'Clelland*, at Kirkcudbright, 1638; in Ireland, summer of 1644; died in 1650. He married (1) Marion, daughter of Bartholomew Fleming, Edinburgh, who died s.p. 1640; (2) Miss Isobel M'Clelland. *Hugh Peebles*, minister during the Commonwealth, at Aghalow, 1657; died in Scotland, 1691. The *Rev. Pont*, fled Ireland, 1639; died soon after. He was grandson of John Knox; married Isabel Stewart who, in 1639, was arrested by the Bishop of Raphoe and imprisoned in Dublin for three years. *John Ridge* died at Irvine, Ayrshire, 1637. *David Row* returned to Scotland with his wife and five children, *circa* 1640. *Samuel Row* died at Edinburgh, June 1665, aged *c*. 56.

Following the Rebellion, after 1652, the Presbyterians came from Scotland to Ulster in great numbers, owing to the unsettled conditions while Cromwell was attacking the Scottish Royalists. Some, who had fled Ulster during the early years of the Rebellion, returned after Scottish forces made their safety more assured. When peace was established, Cromwell at first held the Presbyterians suspect for having supported the Royalist cause. After a little time they were allowed to flourish and many of their ministers were permitted to preach under ecclesiastical control of the new State Church. By 1658, there were eighty congregations and seventy Presbyterian ministers organized into five Presbyteries and a General Synod.

The Presbyterians who were in Ulster in 1659, if settled in one of the counties of Antrim, Armagh, Donegal, Down, Fermanagh, Londonderry or Monaghan, are listed in *A Census of Ireland, circa 1659*, edited by Séamus Pender, Dublin, 1939. Records for the counties of Cavan and Tyrone are omitted, due to the fact that the original documents were not preserved. At the back of this volume, as Appendices, are the Poll Money Ordinances of 1660 and 1661 for all counties of Ulster. In these, the names of the most important people of each county are given. These were the mayors, sheriffs, titled people, esquires, gentlemen, etc. Also see CHAPTER XVI, following, for information regarding the Hearthmoney Rolls, 1663-1669, and the Subsidy Rolls.

Following the restoration of Charles II, in 1660, he who had pledged his loyalty to the Presbyterian Church when Scotland crowned him king, soon after his father's execution in 1649, now betrayed his word. He and his Parliament returned the Established Church to power. Its lands and churches, taken by the Commonwealth Government, were restored to the extent they were owned in 1641, and the bishops with their clergy regained their positions.

In 1661, the bishops forced Parliament to pass an amended Act of Uniformity, which required every clergyman or minister, before he could teach, preach, or administer the Sacraments, to profess before his congregation his assent to every word of the Prayer Book, and to make a declaration that a subject, under no pretense, may bear arms against the King. Furthermore, in 1661, the House of Commons condemned the Covenant (the oath of Presbyterian ministers before ordination, to the Solemn League and Covenant to the parent Church of Scotland) as seditious and treasonable. The House of Lords declared that anyone who by word or deed defended the Covenant shall be deemed an enemy to his sacred majesty and the public peace and the Church.

In 1660-1661, there were sixty-eight Presbyterian ministers in Ireland, all but one located in Ulster. Of these, sixty-one were forced to leave their churches, while seven betrayed their faith and conformed to the Established Church. The seven congregations found it necessary to conform or go without a minister. The others met in little groups in private houses secretly or in the open fields, to hear their ministers. For this crime of preaching, Thomas Kennedy, John Law, John Lithgow, Anthony Shaw, and James Simpson were imprisoned, while a warrant was issued for the arrest of John Will, in 1661.

In 1663, some members of the past Cromwellian faction, in Dublin, organized a plot to overthrow the restored Royalist Government, the most active instigator being Colonel Thomas Blood, who involved his brother-in-law, the Rev. William Lecky, one of the sixty-one deposed Presbyterian ministers. One minister being guilty, the Government considered all of his Presbyterian colleagues were actively plotting with him and made wholesale arrests. William Lecky was executed. Some ministers were let off because of influence in high places. Thomas Crawford, John Crookshank, John Fleming, Robert Hogsyard and Andrew MacCormick escaped from Ireland to Scotland, but nineteen others were imprisoned for years, for the crime of being unable to prove themselves innocent. These were Patrick Adair, John Cathcart, James Cunningham, John Douglass, John Drysdale, James Gordon, John Greg, Thomas Hall, Robert Hamilton, Alexander Hutcheson, William Keys, Henry Livingstone, Gilbert Ramsey, William Richardson, William Semple, James Shaw, Andrew Stewart, Adam White, and

Hugh Wilson. Thomas Drummond was imprisoned 1664-1670. Five others were imprisoned between 1670 and 1681 for Non-Conformity. These were Robert Campbell, Robert Landass, James Taylor, William Trail and William Weir. The latter two went to prison for observing a day of fasting and prayer with other Presbyterians. These records are all included in the brief biographies contained in the *Fasti of the Irish Presbyterian Church*, references included.

In Sir William Petty's *Survey of Ireland*, he calculates that in 1672 there were 800,000 Irish, 200,000 English, and 100,000 Scots, indicating that regardless of oppression by the Church of Ireland, the Scottish Presbyterians had come to Ulster in great numbers. He divides the 200,000 English into 100,000 legal conformists and the rest distributed between the Presbyterians, Independents, Anabaptists and Quakers.

During the war between James II and William of Orange on Irish soil, 1689-1691, the Presbyterians strongly supported the latter, who became William III. James II proclaimed in 1690 that no more than five Protestants could meet together, on pain of death.

The Presbyterians expected some recognition of their loyalty from the new king whom they had supported, if only relief from persecution, but he could not sufficiently influence the Parliament and their cause was defeated by the bishops. They enjoyed less liberty than during the brief two years, 1687-1688, when James II, hoping for support of the Non-Conformists and Roman Catholics alike, published a "Declaration of Indulgence" without the consent of Parliament. It suspended the Penal Laws against all, but attracted only the Roman Catholics, of whom he was one.

Two Toleration Bills of 1692 and 1695 were defeated, and the Church began persecution anew. Presbyterians were refused burial for their dead except when the clergy officiated. Ministers were heavily fined for performing marriages according to the ritual of the Scottish Church. Schoolmasters and Presbyterian ministers were forbidden to teach. Some people in Ulster, pressed by William King, bishop of Londonderry, who was a Presbyterian by birth, were compelled to serve as Churchwardens and take oaths against their will. All of these conditions caused reluctant but cautious people to subject themselves to the rites performed by the clergy who entered the records in the Parish Registers.

Regardless of the disabilities of Non-Conformists in Ulster, their numbers grew rapidly. By 1697, there were seven Presbyteries, two sub-synods at Coleraine and Dromore, eighty ministers, eleven probationers, and about ninety congregations.

Queen Anne, daughter of James II, succeeded to the throne in 1702. An intolerant, High Churchwoman, her reign brought the Penal Laws into full force. The Test Act (amended) 1704, required that all persons who held public office or received pay from the Crown, should take the Sacrament of Holy Communion in the Established Church. This forced all Non-Conformist Presbyterians to resign their positions as magistrates, burgesses, customs officials, postmasters, officers in the army or navy, or local judges. Only a few sacrificed their religious principles. Hereafter, they had no representation and were ruled and punished by an alien minority. In Londonderry, ten of the twelve aldermen who were Presbyterians, and fourteen burgesses were removed from office. In Belfast, nine Presbyterian burgesses were ejected. Magistrates throughout Ulster stepped down from the office of mayor and sheriff.

At this time, people married by a Presbyterian minister were hailed into the Consistorial Court of their diocese to be publicly censured by the bishop. *A Short History of the Presbyterian Church in Ireland,* by the Rev. David Stewart, Belfast, 1936 (p. 91), states: "Presbyterian Marriages, 1704: Another grievance that afflicted the bishops was the marriage of Presbyterians by their own ministers. Such marriages were denounced 'licences for sin' and the children of such marriages were treated as bastards. Ministers and people were dragged before the bishops' courts and excommunicated as fornicators" . . . "Appeals were made to the Government to redress this intolerable wrong, but they were heard in vain" . . . "It was not until 1782 that an Act was passed in spite of the opposition of the bishops, declaring the perfect validity of marriages solemnized by Presbyterian ministers." Not until 1842-1844 were mixed marriages performed by a Presbyterian minister, between a Presbyterian and one of another faith, finally declared legal. Further details regarding the conditions and laws affecting marriages and burials will be discussed in the following CHAPTER XXII.

Meanwhile, Presbyterians, as well as all other dissenters and Roman Catholics alike, were obliged to pay tithes for the support of the clergy of the Established Church. This law endured until the disestablishment of the Church of Ireland in July, 1869. From the tithes collected among all Presbyterians, a tiny stipend of £1,200 was paid each year for the support of all Presbyterian ministers as a group. In 1718, this was increased by £800. Thus, in 1717, the tithes of some 200,000 Presbyterians in Ulster went to the Established Church except for what was paid to each of 130 Presbyterian ministers from the "Regium Donum" of £1,200, or an average of £10 or less in salary per year for each minister. Each Presbyterian congregation (there being 140 in 1717) contributed additional support to its minister.

In 1714, "The Schism Act" rendered every Presbyterian schoolmaster, including ministers who taught school, liable to three months imprisonment. Some churches were nailed up at this time.

In 1719, a Toleration Bill passed by Parliament, discontinued the fines levied in the past against all dissenters who failed to attend services in the Established Church. This Bill also permitted Non-Conformist ministers to perform their duties without the £100 penalty. Relief was given only to those who took the oaths of allegiance and abjuration, and made a declaration against transubstantiation. Even so, dissenting services were not to be held in a locked room or closed building. The "Sacramental Test Act" which had the effect of removing all dissenters from public office or military or naval posts in 1704, remained in force until 1780. These disabilities, including also the Marriage Act which made Presbyterian marriages invalid, were brewing in the minds of all Presbyterians, along with new high rents inflicted by the landlords, and economic troubles caused by the Government placing restrictions upon trade; all causing the urge for emigration which began in earnest in 1718, and by the end of the century had robbed Ulster of hundreds of thousands of its solid citizens.

Between 1719 and 1726 the Presbyterian Church suffered internal troubles of its own, over disagreements in doctrine. A number of the most able ministers broke away and, as Non-Subscribers, formed the Presbytery of Antrim. Among these was the brilliant John Abernethy, founder of the Belfast Society, in which their ideas were formulated. In 1746, another group of ministers broke away from the original Ulster Synod, becoming Seceders. The Seceders soon became divided in principle over issues which arose in Scotland, thus becoming known as the Burgers and the Antiburgers. They reunited as Seceders in 1818. The division between the original Church and the Seceders was not repaired until 1840. *The Seceders*, by the Rev. David Stewart, Belfast, 1950, contains much information concerning the ministers and congregations of this faction and includes notes on many ministers who emigrated with some of their Church members. These records will be more fully discussed, with records of emigration, in CHAPTER XXI.

Some examples of the records of all Presbyterian ministers, set forth in the *Fasti of the Irish Presbyterian Church, 1613-1840*, mentioned above, are as follows:

BRUCE (pp. 7, 58, 91, 192) : Second through Sixth Periods:

> BRUCE, MICHAEL: Youngest son of Patrick Bruce of Newtown, and Janet, daughter of John Jackson, merchant, Edinburgh; great-grandson of Rev. Robert Bruce, Edinburgh, 1587-1600; born 1634; educated Edinburgh; M.A. (Edin.) 1654; recommended to Killinchy by letter from Rev. John Livingstone to Capt. James Moore, Ballybregagh; ordained Oct. 1657; salary from the Commonwealth £100 per annum from 24 June 1658; married 1659, Jean, daughter of Robert Bruce, Kinnaird; deposed for Non-Conformity, 1661; preached in open fields until forced to flee to Scotland; arrested for keeping Conventicles at Airth, Stirlingshire, 1668; imprisoned in London for six months; returned to Killinchy, April 1670; built a church in which he preached till the Revolution; fled to Scotland, where he became minister 1689; was member of General Assembly, 1690;

present at General Synod of Ulster, 1691; died 1693. Had issue of whom only a son, James, reached manhood. He became minister of Killyleagh (1685-1730). Here follows a list of the writings of Michael Bruce, and references for the above data.

BRUCE, JAMES: First son of Rev. Michael Bruce, Killinchy; born 1661; educated Edinburgh, M.A. (Edin.) 1678; licenced Down Presbytery; ordained Killyleagh, 1687; married 1685, Margaret, daughter of Lt. Col. Trail, Tollychin, Killyleagh; removed to Scotland at Revolution; returned in 1691; Moderator of General Synod 1703; called to Derry, 1710; call disallowed; died 17 Feb. 1730; was a moderate Subscriber [did not secede]. William Bruce, founder of Ministers Widows' Fund, Revs. Michael Bruce, Holywood, Patrick Bruce, Drumbo, Kinallen and Killyleagh, were sons. Rev. James Fleming, Lurgan, was a son-in-law. References.

BRUCE, MICHAEL: Eldest son of Rev. James Bruce, M. A., Killyleagh; born 27 July, 1686; educated Edinburgh; licenced Down Presbytery 27 Oct. 1708; subscribed to Westminster Confession of Faith; ordained Holywood, 10 Oct. 1711; member of "Belfast Society." He married, 1716, Mary Kerr. Withdrew with his congregation from the General Synod and adhered to the Non-Subscribing Presbytery of Antrim, 1726; retired, 1731. Died 1 Dec. 1735, interred at Holywood. Rev. Samuel Bruce, M. A., Wood St., Dublin, was a son. References.

BRUCE, PATRICK: 2nd son of Rev. James Bruce, M. A., Killyleagh; born 11 April 1692; educated Edinburgh, M.A. (Edin.), 1711; licenced Down Presbytery, 1717; ordained Drumbo, 12 June 1717; member of the "Belfast Society." He married 1718, Mary, daughter of John Hamilton, Ladyland, and had issue, 3 sons and 4 daughters. Resigned November 1728; admitted Killalan, Renfrewshire, 15 Feb. 1729; resigned 14 Oct. 1730; installed Killyleagh 1730. Died 9 April 1732. Rev. Henry Hervey Aston Bruce, Bart. (1804), Downhill, Coleraine; Sir Stewart Bruce, Dublin Castle; and John Dunn, K. C., M.P. (Irish Parl.), were grandsons. References.

BRUCE, WILLIAM: 2nd son of Rev. Samuel Bruce, Wood Street (Stephen's Green), Dublin; born 30 July 1757; educated Trinity College, Dublin, and at Glasgow and

Warrington; B.A. (T.C.D.), 1776; ordained Lisburn (1st), 3 Nov. 1779; resigned 1782; installed Strand St. (Stephen's Green), Dublin, 1782; member of General Synod, 1783; married 1788, daughter of Robert Hutton, Dublin; resigned 1790; installed 1st Belfast N.S., 1790; Principal of Belfast Academy, 1790-1822; President of Linenhall Library, 1798-1817; retired owing to blindness, 1831; died at Dublin, 27 February 1841. Rev. William Bruce, 1st Belfast N.S., was a son; William R. Bruce, K.C., Master of King's Bench, and James Bruce, D.L., Benbarb, were grandsons. References.

ABERNETHY: (pp. 4, 89, 129): Second through Fifth Periods:

ABERNETHY, JOHN: Born in Scotland, *ca.* 1630; educated King's College, Aberdeen, 1648-1652; ordained Aghaloo (Minterburn), "1659, John Abernethy was Commonwealth Minister here on the tithes" (*Commonwealth Papers*, P.R.O.); 1660 "Desertlyn and part of Lissan was possest by one Abernethie put in by the Presbyterians" (Eccl. Colln., Bundle 40, 75, P.R.O.), cf. Leslie, p. 221; ejected for Non-Conformity in 1661; succeeded Rev. Archibald Hamilton, who died in 1674, in Brigh; in 1684 accepted a call to Moneymore in preference to one from Antrim; deputed to go to London in 1689 to congratulate William, Prince of Orange, on his arrival, and to encourage him in his enterprise; Moderator of the General Synod, 1691-1692; installed at Coleraine, 1 Nov. 1691; died 14 Nov. 1703. He married a daughter of Mr. John Walkinshaw, Renfrewshire, and a sister of Rev. W. Walkinshaw, Benburb (1673-1677). The Rev. John Abernethy (1680-1740), Antrim and Dublin, founder of the "Belfast Society" and author of celebrated sermons, was his son. John Abernethy, the celebrated London surgeon, was grandson of the latter. References.

ABERNETHY, JOHN: Son of Rev. John Abernethy, Moneymore; born 19 Oct. 1680; educated Glasgow and Edinburgh, M.A. (Edin.) 1724; licenced Route Presbytery 1702; ordained Antrim, 18 Aug. 1703. He married: (1) Susanna Jordan, step-daughter of Dominic Heyland, Castleroe, Macosquin, she died 1712; (2) daughter of John Boyd, Rathmore, Antrim. Founder of "The Belfast Society," 1705; and leader of the Non-Subscribers; Moderator of the General Synod, 1715; he and his congregation withdrew from the General Synod, 1726, and adhered to the Non-Subscribers Presbytery of Antrim; installed at Wood Street, Dublin, 1730. Died 1 Dec. 1740. Dr. John Abernethy, F.R.S. (1764-1831) the eminent London surgeon was a grandson, and Rev. Alexander Maclaine, Ballynahinch, was a son-in-law. References.

ABERNETHY, JOHN: [Probably another grandson of the above], born near Templepatrick, County Antrim [which is about four miles from the town of Antrim], 1736; educated Scotland; licenced Templepatrick Presbytery, 1762; ordained Ballywillan, 15 Aug. 1769; resigned 1774; installed Templepatrick, 12 Aug. 1774; author of "Philalethes," a reply to Paine's "Age of Reason," 1795; resigned 2 June 1796; deposed from every part of the ministerial office for celebrating marriages contrary to all orders, 4 May 1802; acquired a considerable landed estate; married Miss Thompson, Antrim; died at Antrim, 8 April 1818; interred at Templepatrick. References.

[On account of the above mentioned "landed estate," it is probable that some record of this man and origin of his property will be found in the Registry of Deeds, Dublin, through the "Names Index."]

JAMISON: (p. 149, and "American Fasti", p. 12): Fifth Period:

JAMISON, ROBERT: Son of John Jamison, Donegore; educated Scotland; licenced Templepatrick Presbytery, 1733; ordained and designated missionary to America, 1734; Lion's Hill, Delaware, 1734. The "American Fasti" (p. 12), states: JAMESON, ROBERT: To General Synod, 1734, Templepatrick Presbytery, report his ordination in May last for America, as he had a call; settled at Duck Creek, Delaware, 26 Dec. 1734; died 1744. [Note the name is spelled both JAMISON and JAMESON.]

MCGREGOR: (p. 115, and "American Fasti," p. 15): Fourth Period:

MCGREGOR, JAMES: Born near Magilligan, 1677; educated Glasgow 1697; licenced Route Presbytery, 1700; or-

dained Aghadowey, 25 June 1701; able to preach in
Irish. He married a daughter of David Cargill,
R. E., Aghadowey. Resigned 1718, and emigrated
with a section of his congregation to America. Prior
to their departure Mr. McGregor preached a sermon
recounting the reasons for their removal. They were
"to avoid oppression and cruel bondage; to shun
persecution and designed ruin; to withdraw from the
communion of idolators; to have an opportunity of
worshiping God according to the dictates of conscience and the rules of the inspired Word." His
first text after landing was Isaiah, 32, 2. Officiated
at Dracut, Mass., 1718-1719; Nutfield (Londonderry), New Hampshire, 1719-1729. Died 5 March
1729. Rev. Matthew Clark (q.v.) married his widow.
Rev. David McGregor (1710-1777), Western Londonderry (1737-1777), was a son. References. The
"American Fasti" (p. 15), states: As a youth was
in Derry during the siege; it was he who discharged
the gun announcing the approach of the relief vessels; ordained Aghadowey, 25 June 1701; tried by
General Synod for intemperance, 1704, but the case
"not proven"; able to preach in Irish; in 1719 trouble
arose in his congregation and when Committee appointed to investigate arrived, it was reported he had
gone to America; a number of families went with
him; he settled at Haverhill, New Hampshire, calling
it Londonderry; his congregation was regarded as
the first Presbyterian congregation in New England;
died 5 March 1729, aged 52. Rev. David McGregor,
Londonderry, U. S. A., 1737-1777, was a son.

CLARK, CLERK, CLARKE: (p. 92, and "American Fasti", p.
6); Fourth Period:

CLERK, MATTHEW: Born near Kilrea, 1659; educated
Glasgow, 1679; took part as lieutenant in the Siege of
Derry; ordained Kilrea (1st) 1697; resigned 29
April 1729, and emigrated to U. S. A.; installed
Londonderry, New Hampshire, 1729. He married
widow of Rev. James M'Gregor, as his 3rd wife.
Died 25 Jan. 1735. He was Clerk of the Route
Presbytery for a period. References. The "Ameri-
can Fasti" (p. 6), states: Licenced Route Presby-
tery 1697; ordained Kilrea 1698; resigned 1729; to
Londonderry, U.S.A.; succeeded Rev. James M'Gre-

gor; married his widow, 1733. Clerk was in Derry during the siege.

*   *   *   *   *

Among the many Presbyterian published works listed in VOLUME II, pp. 222-225, are some of general interest:

Annual Presbyterian Register. 21 vols. 1759-1783.

Fasti of the Irish Presbyterian Church (noted above).

General Synod of Ulster, Records of: 1691-1820. 3 vols. Belfast, 1890-1898.

These records contain the minutes of all annual meetings of the General Synod, from 1691 to 1820. The volumes are not indexed. Records included for each annual meeting contain the names of all ministers and elders present from each Presbytery, together with the names of those absent, with or without excuse. The dozen or so names on the committee from which the Moderator of the meeting was chosen, and the names of those appointed to all other committees are listed, showing who held the responsible positions. Reports from each Presbytery give the date of death of any minister during the past year; widows who received financial aid; names of ministers who emigrated; cases of discipline, etc. These records show that Matthew Clerk (who emigrated to New Hampshire in 1729), for years before 1729, headed the ministers of Coleraine Presbytery and was appointed to serve on the most important committees.

KERNOHAN, J. W. *County Londonderry in Three Centuries.* Belfast, 1921. This is listed among the County Histories (VOLUME II, p. 83), and is noted here as it contains considerable information regarding individuals and their relationships, during the time of the Plantation; some records of the early emigration to New England, 1718; Church records; Diaries; Wills of a few 17th century settlers mentioned, and other miscellaneous records. Kernohan states (pp. 49, 68), that the Rev. James McGregor, who went to New England with part of his congregation in 1718, was probably born in Ireland. His father was Captain McGregor of Magilligan, said to have been a Cromwellian officer. The son, James, served in the Siege of Londonderry. His sister, Elspeth, married Captain Lachlan McCurdy of Magilligan. Some other emigrants (1718) are named, and the towns in the valley of the Lower Bann, from which they originated.

KILLEN, REV. W. D. *History of Congregations of the Presbyterian Church in Ireland, and Biographical Notices of Eminent Presbyterian Ministers and Laymen.* Belfast, 1886. This not only provides biographical material, but aids in locating persons in their Irish congregations, following their emigration when their Certificates from Irish ministers were recorded in American Presbyterian Church Registers, often with the names of the Irish town or Church and the minister spelled incorrectly (see this VOLUME, pp. 13-14).

REID, JAMES SEATON. *History of the Presbyterian Church in Ireland.* 3 vols. London, 1853. His list of early Presbyterian congregations and ministers in Ireland (17th, 18th and some 19th century records), has the name of each congregation in alphabetical order, under which is listed the name of every minister and his dates of service. The *Scotch-Irish*, by Charles A. Hanna, 1902, Volume II, pp. 371-384, contains this valuable list, extracted from Reid's work.

Thom's Irish Almanac and Official Directory, 1847, pp. 340-347, contains the name and residence of each Presbyterian Church officer and minister, 1846-1847, listed under the various divisions of the Church.

WITHEROW, THOMAS. *Historical and Literary Memorials of Presbyterianism in Ireland, 1623-1731.* Belfast, 1879. This contains the biographies of forty-nine ministers with notes on their literary works. These are: Robert Blair, Bangor; John Livingstone, Killinchy; Andrew Stewart, Donaghadee; Patrick Adair, Belfast; Michael Bruce, Killinchy; Thomas Gowan, Antrim; Dr. Williams, Dublin; John Mackenzie, Cookstown; Joseph Boyse, Dublin; Robert Craghead, Derry; Thomas Hall, Larne; Robert Campbell, Ray; John McBride, Belfast; Nathaniel Weld, Dublin; Thomas Emlyn, Dublin;

400 IRISH AND SCOTCH-IRISH ANCESTRAL RESEARCH

John Goudy, Ballywalter; Francis Iredell, Dublin; Dr. Kirk-patrick, Belfast; Thomas Gowan, Drumbo; Dr. Thomas Steward, Dublin; Samuel Henry, Sligo; Various Authors; James Blair, Derry; Robert Craghead, Jr., Dublin; John Aber-nethy, Dublin; William Livingstone, Templepatrick; Robert McBride, Ballymoney; John Malcome, Dunmurry; The Bel-fast Society; Samuel Dunlop, Athlone; Gilbert Kennedy, Tully-lish; Thomas Maquay, Dublin; Matthew Clerk, Kilrea; Samuel Hemphill, Castleblaney; Charles Mastertown, Belfast; Samuel Haliday, Belfast; Thomas Kennedy, Brigh; Thomas Nevin, Downpatrick; Michael Bruce, Holywood; John Elder, Agha-dowey; Alexander McCrackan, Lisburn; Presbytery of An-trim; Robert Higinbotham, Coleraine; Richard Choppin, Dub-lin; Dr. John Leland, Dublin; John Hutcheson, Armagh; James Reid, Killinchy; John Alexander, Dublin; John Hender-son, Dublin.

Published Church Registers

BELFAST: *Historic Memorials of the First Presbyterian Church, Belfast.* 1887.

Contains: Roll of Ministers, 1642-1887; Baptismal Regis-ter, 1757-1790; Funeral Register, 1712-1736; Earliest List of Members, 1760; Earliest Complete List of Con-stituents, 1775; List of Subscribers and Constituents for 1781, 1790, 1812, 1831, 1877. List of Treasurers, Sextons, etc., 1712-1886.

BELFAST: *Rosemary Street Presbyterian Church, Belfast.* Belfast, 1923. Contains: Baptisms, 1722-1760, 1761-1812; Marriages, 1741-1761, 1762-1811.

BURT, COUNTY DONEGAL: *Burt Presbyterian Church Register Book.* Edited by the Rev. James B. Woodburn. Con-tains: Baptisms, 1676/7-1683, 1683-1687/8; Marriages, 1690-1715/16; Elders listed.

MANUSCRIPT RECORDS

MAGEE UNIVERSITY COLLEGE LIBRARY, LONDONDERRY:

Adair Narrative, 1622-1670. By the Rev. Patrick Adair. (Transcript.) This manuscript is entitled "A True Narrative of the Rise and Progress of the Presbyterian Government in the North of Ireland, and of the various troubles and afflictions which ministers and people adhering to that way did meet with from the adversaries thereof, and of their constant adherence thereunto notwithstanding."

Aghadowey Sessions Book, 1702-1761. (Transcript.)

Antrim Meeting, Minutes of, 1654-1658, 1671-1691. (Transcript.)

Cahans Presbyterian Meeting House, Minutes of the Session of, 1751-1802. (Transcript.)

Derry, Minutes of the Subsynod of, 1744-1802. (Transcript.)

Laggan Meeting, Minutes of, 1690-1700. (Transcript.)

Route Presbytery, Minutes of, 1701-1706. (Transcript.)

Ulster, Minutes of the Synod of, 1785, 1787, 1789, 1794. (Transcript.)

Emigrations, Protestant, 1718, 1728. A typed copy of documents formerly in the Public Record Office of Ireland, Dublin, transcribed from an original copy made by the Presbyterian Historical Society, Belfast, of information taken from the *Journals of the Irish House of Lords,* 1719, and later.

PRESBYTERIAN HISTORICAL SOCIETY, BELFAST

The Library of this Society is located in Church House (Room 20), Fisherwick Place, Belfast. The officers are elected annually. Miss Jeannie L. M. Stewart is retained as Assistant Secretary, in charge of the Library, which is open to the public, from 10 a. m. to 3 p. m. A small charge is required of visitors who are not members. Written inquiries are dealt with courteously and expeditiously by Miss Stewart, who is interested in genealogy. A deposit of $6.00 (or £2) must accompany an inquiry and an estimate of the charge for copies of records will be made upon request.

The Library contains much manuscript material concerning Presbyterian families, not otherwise available, as well as an excellent library of printed sources, including local histories, the *Ulster Journal of Archaeology*; all printed Presbyterian historical materials and published documents such as Church Registers, the *Fasti* and the *Records of the General Synod of Ulster* (illustrated above).

The Library has three card indexes. One is for the published sources. The second is for manuscript sources other than Church Registers. The third index covers the existing Church Registers. The *Proceedings of the Presbyterian Historical Society,* 1938-1939, published for members, contains a list of the accessions of manuscript materials prior to that date. A current catalogue is being prepared.

The manuscript sources are very numerous. Included is a file of family records in the form of brief biographical and genealogical notes compiled in the course of various searches. A few of the other sources, more fully described in following chapters are: The Hearthmoney Rolls, 1663-1669, for the counties of Antrim, part of Armagh, Londonderry, Tyrone, and the Subsidy Roll of County Down; the 1740 Householders' List; the 1766 Religious Returns; the 1775 (some earlier and later) Petitions of Dissenters. Other source materials include the *Adair Narrative,* 1622-1670 (described above) ; the late 17th and the 18th century *Minutes of the Presbyteries* of Armagh, Bangor, Coleraine, Derry, Dublin, Letterkenny, Monaghan, Strabane, Templepatrick, and Tyrone; the Antrim, etc., *Sessions Minutes;* and minutes of the various "Fixed Committees," the "Overtures" Committees, the "Select Committees", from all of which some personal memoranda may be obtained.

The third index covers the original Presbyterian Church Registers of the congregations throughout Ireland, which are 367 in number. All are listed below, with the name of the congregation, the town and county, and the inclusive dates of baptism and marriage in each Register. Burials are not included.

Of the 367 congregations, 82 are located in the present Republic of Ireland. Of the 285 congregations in the six counties of Northern Ireland, 249 of these have retained their Church Registers in local custody. Thirty-six of the oldest Registers have been deposited in the vaults of the Presbyterian Historical Society. These are indicated in the following list with an asterisk. The early records contained in the Registers of three congregations are printed, and have been noted above.

Anyone, who wishes to request a search of a Church Register in local custody, may obtain the name of the present minister of the congregation from Miss Stewart, at the Presbyterian Historical Society (a fee should be sent for the time and trouble of an answer), or one may address a letter to "The Minister" of the congregation. Every request of an American for an examination of a Register must be accompanied by a Post Office Money Order for $5.00. One cannot expect a minister to take time from his church duties, or subject the Church Registers to use, without this recompense.

EXISTING PRESBYTERIAN CHURCH REGISTERS

Registers marked with an asterisk are in the Presbyterian Historical Society.

Congregation	Place	Baptisms	Marriages
Aghadowey	Coleraine, Co. Londonderry	1855	None
Ahoghill (Brookside)	Ahoghill, Co. Antrim	1859	1845
Ahorey	Loughgall, Co. Armagh	1838	1845
Albany	Stewartstown, Co. Tyrone	1838	1838
Anaghlone	Annaclone, Banbridge, Co. Down	1839	1838
Anahilt	Hillsborough, Co. Down	1780	1824
Annalong	Annalong, Co. Down	1840	1840
*Antrim (First)	Antrim, Co. Antrim	1674-1733	1675-1736
*Antrim (Millrow)	Antrim, Co. Antrim	1820-1839	1820-1839
Antrim (High St.)	Antrim, Co. Antrim	1850	None
Ardstraw	Ardstraw, Co. Tyrone	1837	1837
*Armagh (First)	Armagh, Co. Armagh	1707-1729	1707-1728
		1797-1803	1796-1809
Armagh (The Mall)	Armagh, Co. Armagh	1837	None
Armaghbrague	Armagh, Co. Armagh	1870	None
Armoy	Armoy, Co. Antrim	1842	1815
Aughentaine	Fivemiletown, Co. Tyrone	1836	None
Aughnacloy	Aughnacloy, Co. Tyrone	1843	None
Bailieborough (First)	Bailieborough, Co. Cavan	1852	1850
Bailieborough (Second)	Bailieborough, Co. Cavan	1863	1845

Congregation	Place	Baptisms	Marriages
Ballina	Ballina, Co. Mayo	1846	1851
Ballindrait	Ballindrait, Co. Donegal	1819	1845
Ballyalbany	Ballyalbany, Co. Monaghan	1802	None
Ballybay (First)	Ballybay, Co. Monaghan	1834	1834
Ballybay (Second)	Ballybay, Co. Monaghan	1833	None
Ballyblack	Newtownards, Co. Down	1854	1845
Ballycairn	Ballylesson, Belfast, Co. Antrim	1860	1845
Ballycarry	Ballycarry, Belfast, Co. Antrim	1832	None
Ballycastle	Ballycastle, Co. Antrim	1829	None
Ballyclare	Ballyclare, Co. Antrim	1857	None
Ballydown	Banbridge, Co. Down	1809	1845
Ballyeaston (First)	Ballyclare, Co. Antrim	1821	1821
Ballyeaston (Second)	Ballyclare, Co. Antrim	1826	1826
Ballyfrenis	Greyabbey, Co. Down	1863	1863
Ballygawley	Ballygawley, Co. Tyrone	1843	None
Ballygilbert	Craigavad, Co. Down	1841	1841
Ballygoney	Coagh, Cookstown, Co. Tyrone	1834	None
Ballygowan	Ballygowan, Belfast, Co. Antrim	1860	None
Ballygrainey	Ballygrainey, Bangor, Co. Down	1838	1838
Ballyhobridge	Clones, Co. Monaghan	1846	1854
Ballyjamesduff	Ballyjamesduff, Co. Cavan	1845	1845
*Ballykelly	Ballykelly, Co. Londonderry	1699-1709	1699-1740
		1805-1819	1805-1811
Ballylennon	Ballindrait, Co. Donegal	1861	None
Ballylinney	Ballyclare, Co. Antrim	1837	1837
*Ballylintagh	(Church dissolved)	None	1872-1883
Ballymena (First)	Ballyment, Co. Antrim	1825	1825
Ballymena (Second)	Ballymena, Co. Antrim	1837	None
Ballymena (West Ch.)	Ballymena, Co. Antrim	1829	1845
Ballymena (Wellington St.)	Ballymena, Co. Antrim	1862	1862
Ballymony (First)	Ballymony, Co. Antrim	1817	1845
Ballymony (St. James)	Ballymony, Co. Antrim	1835	1845
Ballynahatty	Omagh, Co. Tyrone	1843	None
Ballynahinch (First)	Ballynahinch, Co. Down	1841	None
Ballynure	Ballynure, Co. Antrim	1819	1819
Ballyrashane	Cloyfin, Co. Londonderry	1863	1846
Ballyreagh	Ballygawley, Co. Tyrone	1843	None
Ballyroney	Banbridge, Co. Down	1831	1845
Ballyshannon	Ballyshannon, Co. Donegal	1836	1837
Ballywalter (First)	Ballywalter, Co. Down	1824	1845
Ballywalter (Second)	Ballywalter, Co. Down	1820	1845
Ballywatt	Cloyfin, Co. Londonderry	1867	1884
Ballyweaney	Cloughmills, Belfast	1862	1845
Ballywillan	Portrush, Co. Antrim	1816	1846
Balteagh	Limavady, Co. Londonderry	1868	None
Banagher	Feeny, Co. Londonderry	1834	None
*Banbridge	Banbridge, Co. Down	1756-1794	1756-1794
Banbridge (Sarva St.)	Banbridge, Co. Down	1872	1845
Bandon	Bandon, Co. Cork	1842	None
Bangor (First)	Bangor, Co. Down	1852	1808
Bangor (Second)	Bangor, Co. Down	1833	1845
Belfast (Agnes St.)		1868	1868
Belfast (Alexandra)		1840	1840
Belfast (Argyle Place)		1853	1845
Belfast (Ballymacarrett)		1837	1845
Belfast (Ballysillian)		1839	1845
Belfast, (Belmont)		1862	1862
*Belfast, (Cliftonville)		1825-1842	1826-1843

Congregation	Place	Baptisms	Marriages
Belfast, (Crescent)		1831	1831
Belfast, (Fisherwick)		1810	1828
Belfast, (Fitaroy Avenue)		1820	1821
Belfast, (Great Victoria St.)		1860	1860
Belfast, (Malone)		1837	None
Belfast, (May Street)		1850	1845
Belfast, (Mountpottinger)		1867	1869
*Belfast, (Rosemary Street)		1722-1833	1741-1811
Belfast, (St. Enoch's)		1854	None
Belfast, (Townsend Street)		1835	1836
Bellasis	Bailieborough, Co. Cavan	1845	1845
Bessbrook	Bessbrook, Co. Armagh	1854	1854
Boardmills (First)	Boardmills, Lisburn, Co. Antrim	1824	None
Boardmills (Second)	Boardmills, Lisburn, Co. Antrim	1855	None
Boveedy	Boveedy, Kilrea, Co. Londonderry	1841	1842
Bray	Bray, Co. Wicklow	1836	1837
Brigh	Brigh, Stewartstown, Co. Tyrone	1836	1836
Broomfield	Castleblaney, Co. Monaghan	1841	None
Broughshane, (First)	Broughshane, Co. Antrim	1830	1845
Buckna	Broughshane, Co. Antrim	1841	None
Bucrana	Bucrana, Co. Donegal	1836	None
Burt	Burt, Co. Donegal	1834	1838
*Cahans	Cahans, Ballybay, Co. Monaghan	1752-1759	None
Caledon	Caledon, Co. Tyrone	1870	None
*Carland	Castlecaulfield, Co. Tyrone	1759-1799	1770-1802
Carland	Castlecaulfield, Co. Tyrone	1846	1845
Carlow	Mullingar, Co. West Meath	1820	1845
*Carnmoney	Carnmoney, Belfast	1708-1760	1708-1726
*Carnmoney	Carnmoney, Belfast	1767-1809	1731-1758
*Carnmoney	Carnmoney, Belfast	1813-1819	1767-1807
Carnone	Carnone, Raphoe, Co. Donegal	1834	None
Carrickfergus, (First)	Carrickfergus, Co. Antrim	1823	1823
Carrigallen	Carrigallen, Co. Leitrim	1861	None
*Carrigart	Ballymore, Co. Donegal	1844-1881	None
Carrowdore	Greyabbey, Co. Down	1843	1843
Carryduff	Carryduff, Belfast	1854	None
Castleblaney (First)	Castleblaney, Co. Monaghan	1832	None
Castlecaulfield	Castlecaulfield, Co. Tyrone	1855	1834
Castledawson	Castledawson, Co. Londonderry	1835	1845
Castlederg (First)	Castlederg, Co. Tyrone	1823	1845
Castlederg (Second)	Castlederg, Co. Tyrone	1880	1861
Castlereagh	Castlereagh, Belfast	1807	1816
Cavan	Cavan, Co. Cavan	1851	1845
Cavanaleck	Dungannon, Co. Tyrone	1853	None
Cladymore	Mowhan, P. O. Armagh	1848	1845
Claggan	Cookstown, Co. Tyrone	1848	1848
Clare	Tandragee, Co. Armagh	1838	1838
Clarkesbridge	Altnamackin, Newry, Co. Down	1833	1833
Clenanees (Lower)	Castlecaulfield, Co. Tyrone	1840	1845
Clenanees (Upper)	Castlecaulfield, Co. Tyrone	1868	1860
Clogher	Clogher, Co. Tyrone	1819	1819
Clonduff	Drumlee, Banbridge, Co. Down	1842	None
Clones	Clones, Co. Cavan	1856	1859
Clontibret	Clontibret, Co. Monaghan	1825	1827
Clough	Downpatrick, Co. Down	1836	1842
Cloughey	Cloughey, Co. Down	1844	1845
Cloughwater	Cloughwater, Ballymena, Co. Antrim	1852	1845
Coagh	Coagh, Ballygoney, Co. Tyrone	1839	1845

406 IRISH AND SCOTCH-IRISH ANCESTRAL RESEARCH

Congregation	Place	Baptisms	Marriages
Coleraine (First)	Coleraine, Co. Londonderry	1845	1845
Coleraine (Second)	Coleraine, Co. Londonderry	1842	1842
*Coleraine (New Row)	Coleraine, Co. Londonderry	None	1809-1840
Comber (First)	Comber, Co. Down	1847	1845
Comber (Second)	Comber, Co. Down	1849	1845
Conlig	Conlig, Newtownards, Co. Down	1845	None
Connor	Kells, Ballymena, Co. Antrim	1819	None
Convoy	Convoy, Co. Donegal	1822	1822
Cookstown, (First)	Cookstown, Co. Tyrone	1836	None
Cootehill	Cootehill, Co. Cavan	1828	1828
Corvalley	Corboy, Edgeworthstown, Co.		
Corboy	Longford	1839	1840
Cork	Cork, Co. Cork	1832	1832
Corlea	Cortubber, P. O., Castleblaney, Co. Monaghan	1835	None
	Corvalley, Dundalk, Co. Louth	1840	1845
Creggan	Newtownhamilton, Co. Armagh	1835	None
Cremore	Poyntzpass, Co. Armagh	1831	1832
Crieve	Corlea, Cortubber, P. O. Castleblaney	1819	
*Crieve	Corlea, Deaths, 1883-1897		1846-1895
Crossgar	Macosquin, Coleraine, Co. Londonderry	1839	None
Crossroads	Bogay, Co. Donegal	1855	None
Crumlin	Crumlin, Co. Antrim	1839	1846
Cullybackey	Cullybackey, Co. Antrim	1812-1829	None
Cumber (Lower)	Claudy, Co. Londonderry	1827	None
*Cumber (Upper)	Claudy, Co. Londonderry	1834-1874	1834-1845
Cushendall	Carnlough, Co. Antrim	1853	1853
Derramore	Limavady, Co. Londonderry	1825	None
Londonderry (First)	Londonderry	1815	1827
Londonderry (Gt. James' St.)	Londonderry	1838	1837
Londonderry (Carlisle Rd.)	Londonderry	1838	None
Londonderry (Second)	Londonderry	1847	None
Derryvalley	Ballybay, Co. Monaghan	1816	1833
Dervock	Dervock, Co. Antrim	None	1828
Donacloney	Lurgan, Co. Armagh	1798	None
Donaghadee (First)	Donaghadee, Co. Down	1822	1822
Donaghadee (Second)	Donaghadee, Co. Down	1849	1850
Donagheady	Burndennet, Strabane, Co. Tyrone	1838	1838
Donegal	Donegal, Co. Donegal	1825	1845
*Donegore (First)	Templepatrick, Co. Antrim	1806-21	1806-45
Donoughmore	Castlefin, Co. Donegal	1844	None
	Ardaragh, Newry, Co. Down	1804	None
Douglas	Ardstraw, Co. Tyrone	1831	1832
Downpatrick	Downpatrick, Co. Down	1827	1827
Draperstown	Draperstown, Co. Londonderry	1837	1837
Drogheda	Drogheda, Co. Louth	1822	1823
Dromara, (First)	Dromara, Co. Down	1823	1817
Dromara, (Second)	Dromara, Co. Down	1853	1847
Dromore, (First)	Dromore, Co. Down	1834	1845
Dromore, (West)	Ballina, Co. Mayo	1849	1854
Drumachose	Limavady, Co. Londonderry	1838	None
Drumbanagher	Jerrettspass, Newry, Co. Down	1832	1846
*Drumbo	Drumbo, Lisburn, Co. Antrim	1764-1773	1765-1792
*Drumbo	Drumbo, Lisburn, Co. Antrim	1781-1792	
Drumhillery	Madden P. O., Armagh	1829	1834
Drumgooland	Katesbridge, Co. Down	1833	1836
Drumkeen	Newbliss, Co. Monaghan	1856	1845

Congregation	Place	Baptisms	Marriages
Drumlee	Drumlee, Banbridge, Co. Down	1826	None
Drumkeeran	Carrigallen, Co. Leitrim	1835	1845
Drumlegagh	Baronscourt, Omagh, Co. Tyrone	1864	1845
Drumlough	Hillsborough, Co. Down	1827	None
Drumminis	Armagh, Co. Armagh	1859	1846
Drumquin	Drumquin, Co. Tyrone	1845	None
Dublin, (Abbey)	Dublin	1779	1805
Dublin, (Clontarf)	Dublin	1836	None
Dublin, (Ormond Quay)	Dublin	1787	1797
Dunboe, (First)	Castlerock, Co. Londonderry	1843	None
Dundalk	Dundalk, Co. Louth	1819	1819
*Dundonald	Belfast, Co. Antrim	1678-1698	1678-1692
Dundonald	Belfast, Co. Antrim	1819	1819
Dundron	Crumlin, Co. Antrim	1829	1829
Dunfanaghy	Ballymore, Co. Donegal	1897	1846
Dungannon	Dungannon, Co. Tyrone	1790	1789
Dungiven	Dungiven, Co. Londonderry	1835	1839
Dunluce	Dunluce, Bushmills, Co. Antrim	1865	1845
Edenderry	Omagh, Co. Tyrone	1845	1845
Edengrove	Ballynahinch, Co. Down	1829	1820
Eglish	Dungannon, Co. Tyrone	1839	1837
Enniskillen	Enniskillen, Co. Fermanagh	1837	1819
Fannet	Kerrykeel, Co. Donegal	1859	1827
*Faughanvale	Eglinton, Co. Londonderry	1819	None
Fintona	Fintona, Co. Tyrone	1836	1836
Finvoy	Finvoy, Ballymony, Co. Antrim	1843	1843
Fourtowns	Poyntzpass, Co. Armagh	1822	1845
*Frankford	Castleblaney, Co. Monaghan	None	1820-1834
Galway	Galway, Co. Gayway	1831	None
Garvagh, (First)	Garvagh, Co. Londonderry	1795	1795
Garvagh, (Second)	Garvagh, Co. Londonderry	1830	1830
Gilford	Gilford, Portadown, Co. Armagh	1843	1845
Gillygooley	Omagh, Co. Tyrone	1848	None
Gilnahirk	Gilnahirk, Belfast, Co. Antrim	1797	1828
*Glascar	Ballinaskeagh, Banbridge, Co. Down	1780-1844	1781-1798
Glastry	Glastry, Kirkubbin, Co. Down	1728	1728
Glenarm	Glenarm, Co. Antrim	1850	1845
Glendermott	Drumahoe, Co. Londonderry	1855	None
Glenhoy	Augher, Co. Tyrone	1850	None
*Glennan	Glasslough, Co. Monaghan	1805-1820	1805-1820
Glenwherry	Glenwherry, Ballemena, Co. Antrim	1845	None
Gortin	Gortin, Co. Tyrone	1843	None
Gortnessy	Drumahoe, Co. Londonderry	1839	None
Grange	Toomebridge, Co. Antrim	1824	1824
Greyabbey	Greyabbey, Co. Down	1875	1845
Groomsport	Groomsport, Co. Down	1841	1841
Hillhall	Hillhall, Lisburn, Co. Down	1866	1845
Hillsborough	Hillsborough, Co. Down	1832	1845
Holywood, (First)	Holywood, Co. Down	1856	1846
Holywood, (Second)	Holywood, Co. Down	1857	1858
Irvinestown	Irvinestown, Co. Fermanagh	1867	None
Islandmagee, (First)	Islandmagee, Co. Antrim		
Keady, (First)	Keady, Co. Armagh	1838	1838
Keady, (Second)	Keady, Co. Armagh	1819	1819
Kilkeel	Kilkeel, Co. Down	1842	None
*Killaig	Macosquin, Coleraine, Co. Londonderry	1805-1856	1836-1843

Congregation	Place	Baptisms	Marriages
Killala	Ballina, Co. Mayo	1849	1846
*Killeshranda	Carrigallen, Co. Leitrim	1743-1780	1741-1776
		1800-1834	
Killinchy	Killinchy, Co. Down	1835	1835
Killeter	Mournebeg, Strabane, Co. Tyrone	1839	None
*Killyleagh, (First)	Killyleagh, Co. Down	1693-1757	1692-1757
Killyleagh, (Second)	Killyleagh, Co. Down	1840	None
Kilmore	Crossgar, Co. Down	1833	1833
Kilraughts, (First)	Ballymony, Co. Antrim	1836	None
Kilraughts, (Second)	Ballymoney, Co. Antrim	1858	None
Kilrea, (First)	Kilrea, Co. Londonderry	1825	1825
Kingsmills	Whitecross, Co. Armagh	1842	None
*Kirkcubbin	Kirkcubbin, Co. Down	1785-1807	None
Knappagh	Killylea, Co. Armagh	1842	1845
Knowhead	Muff, Co. Donegal	1826	1846
Larne, (First)	Larne, Co. Antrim	1824	None
Leckpatrick	Strabane, Co. Tyrone	1838	None
Lecumpher	Moneymore, Co. Londonderry	1825	1825
Leitrim	Banbridge, Co. Down	1837	None
Letterkenny	Letterkenny, Co. Donegal	1841	None
Limavady, (First)	Limavady, Co. Londonderry	1832	1832
Limavady, (Second)	Limavady, Co. Londonderry	1845	None
Limerick	Limerick, Co. Limerick	1829	None
Lisbellaw	Lisbellaw, Co. Fermanagh	1849	None
Lislooney	Killylea, Co. Armagh	1836	1845
Lismore	Fermoy, Co. Cork	1891	1853
Lissera	Crossgar, Co. Down	1809	1811
Longford	Longford, Co. Longford	1834	None
Loughaghery	Hillsborough, Co. Down	1801	1830
Loughbrickland	Loughbrickland, Co. Down	1842	1842
Loughgall	Loughgall, Co. Armagh	1842	1845
Loughmorne	Loughmorne, Co. Antrim	1848	1863
Loughmourne	Cortubber, P. O., Castleblayney	1847	None
Lurgan (First)	Lurgan, Co. Armagh	1746	1746
*Lylehill	Templepatrick, Co. Antrim	1832-1856	1830-1844
Maghrea	Maghera, Co. Londonderry	1843	1845
*Magherafelt	Magherafelt, Co. Londonderry	1703-1706	1769-1782
		1771-1780	
Magherhamlet	Spa, Ballynahinch, Belfast	1831	1832
Magherally	Banbridge, Co. Down	1837	None
Magilligan	Bellarena, Co. Londonderry	1814	1814
Markethill	Markethill, Co. Armagh	1821	1821
Maze	Hillsborough, Co. Down	1856	1856
Middletown	Glasslough, Co. Monaghan	1829	None
Millisle	Millisle, Co. Down	1773	1838
Minterburn	Caledon, Co. Tyrone	1829	1845
Moira	Moria, Co. Down	1866	1845
Monaghan, (First)	Monaghan, Co. Monaghan	1824	1830
Moneymore	Moneymore, Co. Londonderry	1827	None
Monreagh	Monglass, Bogay, Co. Donegal	1845	1845
Mosside	Mosside, Co. Antrim	1843	1846
*Mountmellick	Montmellick, Leix	1849-1896	None
*Mountnorris	Mountnorris, Co. Armagh	None	1804-1827
Mourne	Kilkeel, Co. Down	1840	None
Moville	Moville, Co. Donegal	1834	1846
Moy	Moy, Co. Tyrone	1851	1852
Myroe	Limavady, Co. Londonderry	1850	None
Newbliss	Newbliss, Co. Monaghan	1856	1845

Congregation	Place	Baptisms	Marriages
Newmills	Portadown, Co. Armagh	1838	1838
Newmills	Dungannon, Co. Tyrone	1850	1846
Newry, (First)	Newry, Co. Down	1829	1830
Newtownards, (First)	Newtownards, Co. Down	1833	1845
Newtownards, (Second)	Newtownards, Co. Down	1834	1845
Newtownards (Regent Street)	Newtownards, Co. Down	1835	1835
Newtowncrommelin	Newtowncrommelin, Co. Antrim	1835	1836
Newtowncunningham	Newtowncunningham, Co. Donegal	1830	1830
Newtownhamilton	Newtownhamilton, Co. Armagh	1823	1823
Omagh, (Second)	Omagh, Co. Tyrone	1821	None
Orritor	Cookstown, Co. Tyrone	1831	1827
Pettigo	Irvinestown, Co. Fermanagh	1844	None
Pomeroy	Pomeroy, Co. Tyrone	1841	None
Portadown, (First)	Portadown, Co. Armagh	1822	1822
*Portaferry	Portaferry, Co. Down	1699-1822	1785-1822
Portglenone, (First)	Portglenone, Co. Antrim	1859	1845
*Portglenone, (Second)	(Dissolved)	1821-1867 1881-1910	1822-1845
Portrush	Portrush, Co. Antrim	1843	None
Portstewart	Portstewart, Co. Londonderry	1829	1846
Poyntzpass	Poyntzpass, Co. Armagh	1850	1846
Queenstown	Queenstown, Co. Cork	1847	1860
Raffrey	Crossgar, Co. Down	1843	1844
Raloo	Larne, Co. Antrim	1840	1840
Ramelton, (First)	Ramelton, Co. Donegal	1838	1838
Ramelton, (Second)	Ramelton, Co. Donegal	1808	1845
Randalstown, (First)	Randalstown, Co. Antrim	1837	1837
Randalstown (O.C.)	Randalstown, Co. Antrim	1853	1845
Randalstown, (Second)	Randalstown, Co. Antrim	1838	None
Rasharkin	Rasharkin, Co. Antrim	1834	1845
Raphoe, (First)	Raphoe, Co. Donegal	1829	1829
Rathfriland, (First)	Rathfriland, Co. Down	1827	None
Rathfriland, (Second)	Rathfriland, Co. Down	1804	1805
Rathfriland, (Third)	Rathfriland, Co. Down	1834	1834
Rathmullan	Rathmullan, Co. Donegal	1854	1845
Richill	Richill, Co. Armagh	1856	1845
Rostrevor	Rostrevor, Co. Down	1851	1851
Ryans	Ardaragh, Newry, Co. Down	1851-1861 1868-1871 1876	None
Saintfield, (First)	Saintfield, Co. Down	1851	None
Saintfield, (Second)	Saintfield, Co. Down	1831	1837
St. Johnston	St. Johnston, Co. Donegal	1838	None
Saltersland	Loup. Moneymore, Co. Londonderry	1847	1845
Sandholes	Cookstown, Co. Tyrone	1844	1845
*Scarva	Scarva, Co. Down	1807-1833	1828-1845
Scotstown	Scotstown, Co. Monaghan	1855	1846
Seafin	Bailieborough, Co. Cavan	1871	1846
Seaforde	Downpatrick, Co. Down	1826	1827
Seskinore	Omagh, Co. Tyrone	1863	1845
Sligo	Sligo, Co. Sligo	1824	1845
Stewartstown	Stewartstown, Co. Tyrone	1814	1845
Stonebridge	Newbliss, Co. Monaghan	1821	1821
Strabane	Strabane, Co. Tyrone	1828	None
Strangford	Strangford, Co. Down	1846	1848
Tandragee	Tandragee, Co. Armagh	1835	1835
Tartaraghan	Portadown, Co. Armagh	1849	1845
Templepatrick	Templepatrick, Co. Antrim	1831	1831

Congregation	Place	Baptisms	Marriages
Toberkeigh	Mosside, Co. Antrim	1831	None
Tralee	Tralee, Co. Kerry	1840	1844
Trenta	Kilmacrennan, Co. Donegal	1836	1838
Tully	Corboy, Edgeworthstown, Co.		
	Longford	1844	None
Tullyallen	Montnorris, Co. Armagh	1795	1868
Tullylish	Gilford, Co. Down	1813	1820
Urney & Sion	Sion Mills, Co. Tyrone	1837	None
Vinecash	Portadown, Co. Armagh	1838	1838
Waringstown	Waringstown, Co. Down	1862	None
Warrenpoint	Warrenpoint, Co. Down	1832	1832
Waterford	Waterford, Co. Waterford	1770-1841	1761-1843
Wexford	Wexford, Co. Wexford	1844	1846

PRESBYTERIAN CHURCH RECORDS IN THE PUBLIC RECORD OFFICE OF NORTHERN IRELAND, BELFAST

Antrim, Records of the Presbytery of, August 1783 to December 1862. Vols. 2-6. Transcript. (*Report*, 1951-1953, pp. 24-25.)

Ballyeaston Presbyterian Congregation, "Census" of, 1813. Transcript. (*Report*, 1948, p. 4.)

Belfast, Rosemary Presbyterian Church Register. Transcript. (*Reports*, 1932, p. 9; 1933, p. 12.) Baptisms, 1722-1760; 1761-1812; 1796-1842; 1823-1867.

Marriages, 1741-1761; 1762-1811; 1811-1846. Pew Register, 1757-1760; 1726-1767.

A typescript list of all existing Presbyterian Church Registers of the counties of Ulster is kept in this Office. The inclusive dates of Baptism, Marriage, and a few Burial records of each Church Register are given. The location of the Registers is indicated; whether in local custody, or deposited in the vaults of the Presbyterian Historical Society, Belfast. Also, the few which have been printed are noted.

PRESBYTERIAN CHURCH RECORDS IN THE PUBLIC
RECORD OFFICE OF IRELAND, DUBLIN

Registers of the Presbyterian Congregations of Bull Alley and Plunket Street, Dublin. Transcript. (*Report*, 54th, p. 11.) Vol. I, 1672-1765. Vol. II, 1790-1835.

CHAPTER VIII

QUAKER RECORDS

The Religious Society of Friends (Quaker) provided for the keeping of records in Ireland, according to the same system and regulations adopted in England and America.

The original documents, records and minutes of Meetings in the Province of Ulster (with the exception of one early volume), are preserved in a vault at the Friends Meeting-house, Railway Street, Lisburn, County Antrim. John M. Douglas, M.A., Headmaster of Friends School, Lisburn, 1929-1952; later of Taunton Avenue, Belfast, has been in charge of the Ulster archives.

All original documents, records, minutes of the Meetings, etc., of the provinces of Leinster and Munster (also one early volume of Ulster), are preserved at Friends House, 6 Eustace Street, Dublin. A historical library is also maintained, in which are deposited numerous family manuscripts, original wills and other records relating to members, as well as many printed local histories, genealogies, and other works of use in tracing the records of Quakers. Included are the materials listed in VOLUME II, hereof, p. 225.

Further information regarding the records in both repositories, the transcripts and microfilms thereof, published wills, etc., will be noted following a brief review of the history, structure, and purpose of the Quaker records.

A well-known source, published in Dublin in 1751, is Wright's and Rutty's *History of the Rise and Progress of the People called Quakers in Ireland from the year 1653 to 1700 . . . to which is added A Continuation of the same History to the Year of Our Lord 1751*. This outlines the dates and establishment of the Meetings throughout Ireland; the names of some of the early and active members with biographical notes regarding a few; a brief account of "Sufferings"; the names of English Quakers who came each year from various localities to promote the work in Ireland; an outline of Quaker discipline, Marriage regulations, etc., as follows:

William Edmundson, founder of the first Friends Meeting in Ireland and one of the most consistent leaders in spreading the faith throughout the country, was born in 1627 at Little Musgrove, Westmorland, England. He was persuaded to the Quaker faith in 1651, through the influence of James Naylor, a disciple of George Fox, after having served in Cromwell's army in Scotland. He followed his brother, John Edmundson, to Ireland in 1653, and settled as a shopkeeper at Antrim. In 1654, he removed to Lurgan, County Armagh, and established the first settled Quaker Meeting, attended by Richard and Anthony Jackson, John Thompson, Richard Fayle, John Edmundson and William Moon. These men and their families removed with William Edmundson to County Cavan, where they all took up land, in 1655. They were joined by other Friends in 1656, namely John Pim, Robert Wardell, William Neale, William Parker, Thomas Lun, Thomas Morris, John Chandley, John Savage, Isabel Acton, and many more.

During the period of the Commonwealth and the Protectorate, the Quaker faith spread rapidly throughout Ulster, Leinster and Munster. Between 1655 and 1660, the following Ulster Meetings were established: In 1655, at Grange, below Antrim, a Meeting was formed in the home of Gabriel Clark and wife. Archibald Scott opened his house at Toberhead, County Londonderry, for a Meeting. A group consisting of William Williamson, Senior and Junior, John Williamson, Mathew Horner, William Brownlow, Francis and Lawrence Hobson, and Margery Atkinson, formed a Meeting at the home of the latter, near Kilmore, County Tyrone. In 1656, at Belturbet, County Cavan, Robert Wardell and his father, William Parker and wife, and William Morris formed a Meeting. In 1658-1659, a new Meeting at Lisnegarvey (later Lisburn), was formed by George Gregson who built a Meeting-house, and Francis Robson, Roger Webb, Peter Ross, Robert Hoope, and several others. In 1659, a Meeting was established at Lurgan, and in that year William Edmundson with his followers, all removed from County Cavan to settle in and around Mountmelick, in Queen's County. In 1660, a

Meeting was established at Charlemont, under the leadership of Robert Turner. Others formed later in Ulster were: Ballynalargey, removed to Balenderry, 1662/3; one near Carrickfergus at this time which was dropped; Coleraine, and Ballynacree near Ballymoney, 1673; Hillsborough, 1682; Coot-hill, 1692; Dunclaudy, at the house of William Henderson in 1692, continued at his widow's until 1739; Moyallon, by reason of increase of Lurgan meeting; Ballyhaise, 1695; Letterkenny, 1699; Grange, new Meeting-house built by Walter Clark in 1704. Other new Meeting-houses in Ulster were: Antrim, 1707; Balenderry, 1714; one near Rathfryland, County Down, 1722; Castle-shane, County Monaghan, 1723; Newtown, County Down, 1726, at the house of James Bradshaw; Hillsborough, 1748.

Leinster Meetings: The first Meeting was formed in or about Dublin in 1655, at the home of Richard Fowkes, a tailor, near Polegate. The first settled Meeting was established at George Latham's near Polegate. In 1657, Stephen Rich and Capt. Allen are noted as members, and in 1669 Anthony Sharp came over from England. About 1657, this Meeting was removed to Bride's Alley. In 1655, a Meeting was formed at Kilkenny by William Mitchel and wife, George Danson and wife and Esther Beaver. In 1656, Nicholas Starkey opened his house to a Meeting, at Athlone, and in 1657 at Ballykibroe. In this year, Thomas Weston and wife, and Henry Rose formed a Meeting at Carlow, while at Edermine, County Wexford, the Meeting opened in 1657 was moved to Lambstown or Forest in 1667. In 1659, Thomas English opened his house to a Meeting near Moate, which later moved to John Clibborn's house in Moate, with members James Wisely, Henry Fuller, Abraham Fuller, Samuel Strangman, Thomas Beale, William Slade (of Athlone). In the same year a Meeting was formed at Drogheda, and William Edmundson removed his Meeting from County Cavan to Mountmelick, Queen's County. In the same county, Christopher and John Raper formed a Meeting at Ballynakill in 1660, and at about this time one at Newgarden, County Limerick, was briefly active but removed to Carlow. In 1668, Meetings were opened at Wexford and at Curraduff in that county. Others were formed at Poolanarrick, near Baltinglass, County Wicklow, at Peter Peisly's in 1668; one at Athlone which continued to 1684; one each at Garrymore, at Thomas Trafford's (later removed to Wicklow) and at Ballycane and Kilmurry, County Wicklow, in 1669; a Meeting at Ballycarney, County Wexford, moved to Ballynabarney in 1671; Atby, 1672; one at William Bancroft's formed at Ballymorane, later removed to John Edmundson's after 1672, and then to Ballynoulart; one at Birr, King's County, and one at Wicklow in 1674 or 1675.

A Six-weeks Meeting for the Province of Leinster was settled in 1676 at Castledermot. In 1678, at Dublin, the Wormwood-gate meeting for Half-yearly Meetings was added to the Bride's-Alley and Bride Street Meetings, and a General Women's Meeting was established to be held in Dublin every third month, at the same time as the Half-yearly Men's Meeting.

In or about 1680, a Meeting was formed at the house of John Watson in Kilconnor; one was sponsored at Mountrath by the Earl of Mountrath; and one was formed near Ballynaclash, County Wicklow, in the house of Thomas Carlton. In 1694, John Clibborn built a Meeting-house and walled-in burying-place at Moate; the Waterstown Meeting moved in 1736 to Ballykeran in the house of William Lightfoot; the Ballynacarrig Meeting was held at William Sandwith's. The Meeting formed at the house of James Ashton in Kilteel, eight miles from Dublin, in 1678, was moved to Castle-Warden at the home of John Lancaster, in 1704-1723, and dropped in 1744. About the year 1726, the Ballinclay Meeting removed to Ballydonnel at the home of Robert Webster and thence to John Wright's about 1736. He built a Meeting-house at Ballinclay in 1743. The Meeting formed in Ballynacarrig, County Wexford, in 1694, was moved to the house of Joseph Williams at Randal's Mills, in 1739. The Meeting at Israel Webster's in Ballinclare, 1697, was moved to John Wright's at Ballinclay, and to Joseph Smithson's at Ballintogher, County Wexford, in 1742. John Wright then built a Meeting-house at Ballinclay, in 1743. The Ballykeran Meeting-house was moved to William Sprowle's in 1750.

Munster Meetings: In 1655, Meetings were settled at Ban-

don, Cork, Kinsale, Limerick, Waterford and Youghal. The
Meeting in Bandon met at the house of Edward Cook and
Lucretia, his wife. He had been a Cornet of Horse in Oliver
Cromwell's own troop. Other members of this Meeting were
Daniel Massy and wife, Sarah, Robert Mallins and wife, Mary,
William Smith, Katharine Smith, Matthew Prin, William
Driver, Joan Frank, Thomas Biss, etc. The members of the
Cork Meeting were Elizabeth Erberry, Alexander Atkins and
wife, Ann, and son, Thomas, Thomas Mitchel and wife, Sus-
anna (who died in Cork, 1672), Philip Dymond, Richard Pike
and wife, Elizabeth, Francis Rogers, William Rogers, Stephen
Harris and wife, George Webber, George Gamble, Henry Fag-
gater, Thomas Ridge. The Meeting in Limerick met at the
home of Richard Pearce and his son, Thomas. Other members were Thomas Phelps, John Love, John Perrot, Robert
Mallins, Humphrey Norton, William Shaw, Thomas Loe, Barbara Blagden, etc. The Meeting at Youghal was established
by Capt. James Sicklemore and Robert Sandham. The latter
died there in his 55th year. He was born at Woodcutt near
Petworth, parish of Grassom, County Sussex, 1620. He came
to Youghal in 1650, in Col. Sander's Regiment. In 1652, he
married Deborah Baker of Youghal, an Anabaptist. Sandham
became a Quaker in 1655. The Meetings were held at his
house until a Meeting-house was built in 1681.

In 1660, a Meeting was formed at Kilcommonbeg, County
Tipperary. In 1666, William Penn, son of Sir William Penn,
Vice-Admiral of England, was sent to Cork on family business and there was converted to the Quaker faith. He, with
other Quakers, was arrested by the Mayor of Cork and thrown
into prison. He wrote a remarkable letter *(ibid)* to the
Earl of Orrery, Lord President of Munster, which brought
his release. In this year, a Meeting was settled at Charleville, where a Meeting-house was built in 1711, which lasted
until 1740. In 1678, the first Meeting-house was built in Cork
and, in 1688, a Meeting was settled at Mallow which met
monthly at Charleville and Moeg. The Mallow Meeting failed.

A Monthly Meeting was settled at Knockgraffan in 1692
which later was moved to Cahir and from thence to Kilcom-
mon and Clonmel. In 1694, a new Meeting-house was built at

Waterford. In 1696, one was built at Skibbereen. This Meeting was dropped in 1729. In 1699, the Clonmel meetings were held at the home of George Collet as they had been for some years. In this year, Stephen and Joseph Collet gave the ground and funds for a building. In 1701, George Baker established a Meeting-house at Cashel. In 1728, a Meeting-house was built at Bandon where the meetings had previously been held at the home of Edward Cook and later at the home of Daniel Massy. In 1731, a new Meeting-house was built at Cork and in 1736 one was built at Limerick.

Connaught Meetings: In 1714, a few Friends formed a Meeting near Sligo. In 1717, this was removed and settled in County Roscommon, at and near Ballymurry, where in 1721 a Meeting-house was built. A Meeting was also settled at Ballyvaughan, alias Newport, in County Mayo. In 1739, the Friends settled at Newport, removed to Ballymurry Meeting in County Roscommon.

STRUCTURE OF THE SOCIETY OF FRIENDS:

Preparative Meeting: A single congregation, at first gathered in a private home. Many of these later acquired Meeting-houses.

Monthly Meeting: An executive body of two or more Preparative Meetings which were located in one district, gathered for conference monthly or less often.

Quarterly Meetings: Also called *Provincial Meetings*, these embraced all *Monthly Meetings* of one Province. These were formed for each of Ulster, Leinster and Munster. A few *Monthly Meetings* of Connaught met with the *Quarterly Meeting* of Leinster at various times.

National Half Year's Meeting of Ireland: This was first organized in 1670, and met semi-annually until 1797, after which this body met but once annually as *The National Yearly Meeting.*

These Meetings of more than a single congregation were at first termed "Meetings for Worship," but later became known as "Meetings for Discipline." The minutes of these Meetings concern the affairs of many people. They include much gene-

alogical information.   The names and earlier data about
people were set forth in the certificates issued, permitting
them to remove in good standing from one Meeting to another,
in Ireland or upon emigration.   Cases of discipline were
brought before the Monthly Meetings.   The minutes included
the "Testimonies" against offenders for any failure to comply
with the rules and regulations of the Society.   Confessions of
guilt and records of refusal to acknowledge guilt, as well as
details of expulsion and reinstatement were carefully kept.
The act of "Marrying out of Meeting" or "Out of Unity" with
a non-member, or submitting to marriage by a clergyman of
the Established Church, constituted a serious offense, punish-
able by loss of membership unless shortly followed by a confession of guilt and request for pardon and reinstatement upon
acknowledgement of faith.

RECORDS OF BIRTHS, DEATHS AND MARRIAGES:

These together with the Minutes of the Meetings were kept
by law of the Society of Friends.   Great value was attached to
all records of this nature.   They were as carefully preserved
in Ireland as they were in England and America, and thus
they are fairly complete.   The Quaker system of recording
births, deaths, and marriages was quite uniform throughout
England, Ireland and America, and provides more certain
genealogical information than any other accumulation of
vital records of Church or State.

The Birth Records list the surname and given name of the
child; the year, month and day of birth; the place of birth;
name of parents, their residence, frequently the occupation of
the father, and name of the Monthly Meeting.   These Birth
Records and also the Marriage and Death Records are arranged in family groups, with a system of page references to
later groups of the children's children, thus making possible
the identification and parentage of all.

Death Records recorded the surname and given name of
the deceased; the year, month, and day of death; the age at
death; residence, description such as "Wife of William," or
"Son of James and Martha," the name of the Monthly Meeting; the year, month, day, and place of burial.

Marriage Records gave the surname and given name of the groom or bride; his or her residence; his or her description such as "Spinster," "Widow of Robert Wilson," "Widower," etc.; the names of the parents; parents' residence; name of person to whom married; his or her residence; place where married; the year, month, and day of marriage, and the name of the Monthly Meeting where the marriage was performed. The Marriage Records were, after 1730, forwarded to the Quarterly Meetings, and there were kept in a separate Marriage Book. Friends House Library, Dublin, has an Index of all Marriages on record, with all information of the nature listed above.

The Registers of the early Monthly Meetings contain the records of Birth, Marriage and Death, more or less in date order. A separate Marriage Book, kept by many, contains copies of the original Marriage Certificates as they were drawn up, with the names of the groom and bride, and the close relatives who attended the wedding, in one or two columns, and the family friends in others.

In addition to these nearly complete and well-indexed vital records of Ulster, Leinster and Munster, preserved in the two repositories in Lisburn and Dublin, the latter has in its historical library, a large file of manuscript pedigrees, compiled from the above records by Thomas H. Webb, of Dublin. The personnel of this library will, upon request, quote the fee for a search for any records or pedigree. Further information regarding the records is set forth below under the headings of the two repositories.

FRIENDS MEETING HOUSE, LISBURN

In 1955, this compiler was allowed the rare privilege of spending an entire day examining the original records in the vault at Friends Meeting House, Lisburn, through the courtesy of Mr. John M. Douglas, Keeper of the Archives.

In 1951, eight volumes of the records and thirty-eight documents were loaned to the Public Record Office of Northern Ireland, Belfast, for the purpose of photostating. The *Report of the Deputy Keeper of the Records*, 1951-1953 (pp. 29-309), contains an Index of accessions (Documents other than Normal Increments) during the years 1949-1952, in which is incorporated the entire personal name index of the Quaker records which were photostated, as well as a subject index of the records.

The Queen's University, Belfast, was later allowed to microfilm these records. Copies of the microfilms (four in number) are now deposited at the Society of Friends Library, Swarthmore College, Swarthmore, Pennsylvania, where they are available to the public. These are listed in VOLUME II, hereof, pp. 276-277.

The thirty-eight documents are principally wills and inventories (1685-1772), and are indexed in the above *Report*. They were also microfilmed.

The eight volumes of records are as follows:

LURGAN MONTHLY MEETING RECORD BOOKS, *ca.* 1650-1789. 4 vols. Vol. I, *ca.* 1650-1710; Vol. II, 1710-1752; Vol. III, 1752-1779; Vol. IV, 1779-1789. These volumes contain records of Birth, Marriage and Burial; many arranged by families. They include records of origin of members who came from England; Certificates of Removal; Testimonies of Members, 1688-1796; List of Members, to 1883.

ULSTER QUARTERLY MEETING BOOK (Ulster Monthly Meeting). This contains Minutes of Meetings; Testimonials; Certificates of Removal; Marriage Certificates, 1731-1786, 1786-1812; Marriage Register, 1812-1848. Some Family Records are included.

BOOK OF OLD FAMILY RECORDS: Marriage Certificates, Baptismal and Burial Registers, 1658-1815.

ULSTER PROVINCE MEETING BOOK: The Province Minutes, dated from Sept. 1693-Sept. 1694, are missing. An earlier *Book of Ulster Province Meeting*, containing records dated from 10 Nov. 1674 to Aug. 1693, has been rebound and placed in Friends Meeting House vault at 6 Eustace Street, Dublin (see p. 412, hereof). This contains the Province Minutes, including Marriage Certificates presented at Meeting, Testimonies, Certificates of Removal, and some Family Records, all dated 1694-1717, 1717-1750.

GRANGE MONTHLY MEETING BOOK: This contains the records of Birth, Marriage and Burial for Grange District, including areas in Antrim, Tyrone and Londonderry. The records, dated *ca.* 1658-1800, are arranged by families.

LISBURN MONTHLY MEETING BOOK (Lisburn and District), *ca.* 1650-1859. This contains records of Birth, Marriage and Burial; Certificates of Removal; Testimonies; and some family records.

* * * * *

The Quaker records in the above volumes and documents have been indexed by subject, in the *Report of the Deputy Keeper of the Public Records of Northern Ireland*, 1951-1953, as follows:

Catechisms and Primers, 1742.

Certificates of Good Character for Removal, Issues of, 1682-1735.

Children, Education of, 1702-1720.

Graveyards, Records of: Ballynalargy, 1692-1711; Carrickfergus, 1694-1725; Lisburn and area, 1675-1711; Maghaberry, County Antrim area, 1730; Cootehill, County Cavan, 1697-1750.

Legacies, 1685-1772.

Marriage Regulations, etc., Quaker Records, 1677-1734.

Meetings: Antrim, 1697-1745; Ballinderry, 1699-1748; Ballyhagan, 1695-1772; Ballyhaise, 1698-1725; Ballymoney, 1699-1709; Castleshane, 1723; Coleraine, 1697-1794; Cootehill, 1697-1750; Dublin, 1677-1711; Grange (Co. Antrim, 1697-1727; Co. Tyrone, 1685-1750); Hillsborough, 1716-1749; Lisburn, 1675-1735; Lisnagarvey, 1697-1709; Londonderry, 1673; Lurgan, 1658-1768; Moyallen, 1698-1719; Oldcastle, 1697-1734; Rathfryland, 1703-1733; Toberhead, 1694-1717.

Orphans and Poor, Quaker Records, 1690-1741.

Records: Wills; Inventories; Accounts; Monthly Meeting
Record Books; Family Records; Marriage Certificates; Baptis-
mal and Burial Registers; Provincial Minutes and Proceed-
ings; Marriage Proceedings, Persons appointed to inquire into
(1681-1731). Records dated over periods 1658-1800.
School and Teachers, 1699-1720.
Teaching of trades to apprentices, 1706.
Tithe Payments, 1697-1750.

* * * * *

EXAMPLE OF FAMILY RECORDS,
LURGAN MONTHLY MEETING RECORD BOOK, VOL. I.

GIBSON FAMILY: (pp. 105, 126, 365, 367, 373).

WILLIAM GIBSON of Lygacory in parish of Sharboll and
MARY CAIN of Drumgor in parish of Sego [Seagoe] Co. Armagh, married on 20th day of 5th mo. (July) 1655. Signed
by William Gibson and Mary Gibson. Robert Gibson, witness.
[This is an isolated item. It is possible that this William Gibson was a brother of the following David Gibson.]

WILLIAM GIBSON, son of DAVID GIBSON, was born in ye
parish of Killinshy in ye County of Down, ye 3 of ye 3 mo.
1662, and took to wife on ye 7th of ye 8 mo. 1685, MARY, dau.
of FERDINANDO CAIN, who was born in ye parish of Kilmore
and County of Armagh, ye 25th of ye 10th mo. 1664, and had
by her children as follows:

1. GEORGE GIBSON, first son of WILLIAM GIBSON and MARY
his wife, was born at Drumgor in ye parish of Sego and
County of Armagh on ye ——— of ye 5th mo. A.D. 1686.

2. DEBORAH GIBSON, first dau. of WILLIAM GIBSON and
MARY his wife was born in Drumgor aforesaid ye 16th of ye
2nd mo. A. D. 1688.

3. JOHN GIBSON, 2nd son of WILLIAM GIBSON and MARY
his wife was born in Drumgor aforesaid ye 15th of ye 2nd
mo. A.D. 1690.

4. HANNAH GIBSON, 2nd dau. of WILLIAM GIBSON and
MARY his wife was born in Drumgor aforesaid ye 20th of ye
2nd mo. A.D. 1692.

5. JACOB GIBSON, 8th of 4th mo. 1694. And upon ye 20th of ye 2nd mo. A.D. 1695, ye above MARY died, and ye sd. WILLIAM took to wife ROAS [Rose] ye dau. of WILLIAM RAY on ye 15th of ye 5th mo. 1697 and had by her children as followeth:

6. SARAH GIBSON, 1st dau. of WILLIAM GIBSON by ROAS his wife was born at Drumgor aforesaid ye 9th of ye 6th mo. 1698.

7. MARY GIBSON, ye 2nd dau. of WILLIAM GIBSON and ROAS born ye 24th of ye 11th mo. 1699.

8. JOSEPH GIBSON, 1st son of WILLIAM GIBSON and ROAS his wife born ye 8th of ye 2nd mo. 1701.

9. RUTH GIBSON, 3rd dau. of WILLIAM GIBSON and ROAS his wife, born at Drumgor aforesaid ye _____.

10. WILLIAM GIBSON, 3rd son of WILLIAM GIBSON and ROAS his wife was born in Drumgor aforesaid ye 9th of ye 2nd mo. 1696 {1706?}.

11. DINAH GIBSON, 4th dau. of WILLIAM GIBSON and ROAS born in Drumgor ye 11th of ye 3rd mo. 1708.

12. ABIGAIL GIBSON, 5th dau. of WILLIAM GIBSON and ROAS, born in Drumgor ye 6th of ye 5th mo. 1711.

* * * * *

The Certificate of Marriage in the above volume (p. 126) shows that WILLIAM GIBSON married ROSE RAY, 2nd daughter of WILLIAM RAY of Seagoe, County Armagh, on 15th of 5th mo. 1697. Witnesses were: William Ray, James Ray, John Gibson, Robert Gibson, George Gibson, Elizabeth Ray, Ann Ray, Margaret Ray, Ann Cain Jr.

* * * * *

Burial entries in the above volume (p. 373) are as follows:

MARY GIBSON wife of WILLIAM GIBSON of Drumgor died ye 20th of 2nd mo. 1695, buried at Monrcervesty [?].

WILLIAM RAY SEN. departed this life ye 5th 1. mo. 1705/6.

SARAH RAY departed this life ye 12 3/mo. 1710.

SARAH RAY JR. departed this life ye 31 5/mo. 1713.

JAMES RAY departed this life ye 21 6/mo. 1713.

WILLIAM RAY JR. departed this life ye 15 6/mo. 1714.

SAMUEL RAY departed this life ye 18 7/mo. 1723.

JOSEPH RAY departed this life ye 23 7/mo. 1723.

* * * * *

Origin of the above FERDINANDO CAIN and his family record (p. 365).

JOHN CAIN son of FERDINANDO CAIN was born at Mask in Cleveland in Yorkshire, in ye Kingdom of England Anno Dom. 1657 and came into Ireland and married in ye year 1691 ANN daughter to ROBERT GILPIN and by her had children as followeth:

1. George, born in ye parish of Sego, County Armagh, 24th 9/mo. 1692.

2. Mary, born in ye parish aforesaid, 14th 6/mo. 1696.

3. John, born in ye parish aforesaid, 1st 11/mo. 1698.

4. Robert, born in ye parish aforesaid, 10th 6/mo. 1700.

* * * * *

LURGAN MONTHLY MEETING TESTIMONIES, 1688-1796 (p. 101, 105).

HANNAH GIBSON, daughter of WILLIAM GIBSON, secretly married to HUGH MCALLAM, not announcing it until she was with child, 2 Jan. 1716/17.

JOHN GIBSON and CHRISTIAN HARLAND his wife, educated in the way of truth as people called Quakers . . . now out of Communion until repentance.   Lurgan, 25 April 1718.

* * * * *

Examples of records in the Registry of Deeds (VOLUME I, hereof, pp. 94-106) concern the Dickson and Willson family, including the Marriage Settlement between William Dickson for his son, Francis Dickson, and Morgan Willson for his daughter Hannah, on 24 October, 1747, previous to the marriage of Francis Dickson and Hannah Willson.   Several abstracts of later records are also given.   The Quaker records of the Willson, Gilbert and other allied families are numerous. A few early examples of the Quaker records of Morgan Willson's family, being photostatic copies of records made by the Public Record Office of Northern Ireland, Belfast, are as follows:

LURGAN MARRIAGE CERTIFICATES, BOOK II, 1715-1811 (p. 8):

Morgan Willson in the Parish of Termony and County of Londonderry and Hannah Gilbert in the Parish of Ahagallan in the County of Antrim having declared their intention of Marriage with each other in several Public Meetings of the People called Quakers whose (several words missing) appeared in the Public Meeting-house in Lurgan on the 15th day of 3rd Mo. called May in 1717.

Morgan Willson

Hannah Willson

Jonathan Gilbert Junior	Jn Walker	
John Kingsbury	Alex Matthew	Ann Gilbert
Stephen Gilbert	Henry Greer	Mary Webb
Thos Gilbert	Ta Bullogh	Ann Wilson
John Therkell	Sam: Francis	Isabel Robson
Thos Bullock	Ben: Shepherd	Mary Bullock
George Whiteside	Jn Mortanson	Bridget Walker
Daniel Backhus	Jn Hoope	Sarah Gilbert
Joseph Robson	Joseph Berry	Sarah Greer
Timothy Kirk	Joseph Fox	Margot Fawcet
Ta Slaret	S Moore	Sarah Barrow
Jn Robson		Margot Matthew
Thos Gregg		Mary Whiteside
Thos Willson Junior		Mary Hoope
Henderson		Mary Greer
Fox		

PROVINCE QUARTERLY MENS MEETING: (Inquiry preceding the above marriage) (P.R.O.: N.I., T. 1062/41/169).

Morgan Willson of Toberhead Meeting and Hannah Gilbert of Lurgan Meeting having appeared and declared their intentions of marriage with each other before this Meeting. Archibald McCoole and Neile O'Mony, Sarah Lyna and Sarah Greer being appointed to make inquiry concerning their clearness, orderly proceedings, consent of parents and relations concerned: have returned answer that they made inquiry and find nothing to obstruct their proceedings but that they may lawfully marry: So its ye appointment of this Meeting that ye said Morgan Willson do publish or cause to publish their said intention in two severall Meetings at Toberhead or Dunllady and Lurgan and if nothing then appear against them they may in a convenient season take each other in marriage. Alen Mathews, Sam Francis and Benjamin Shepherd are desired to see ye said marriage perfected in good order and to get ye certificate recorded in ye Meeting Book and to return a copy thereof to the next Province Meeting.

Were married in Lurgan ye 15th day of ye 3rd month 1717 as ye certificate may appear.

WILL OF MORGAN WILLSON (P.R.O.: N.I. T. 777/13).

Morgan Willson of Lemnaroy, gent. Devises to trustee William Gregg of Coleraine, merchant, the lands of Lemnaroy in the Vintners' Proportion, Co. Derry, for uses as follows, subject to articles of 1 Oct. 1763, made by testator previous to marriage of his daughter Mary Willson with Jervais Johnson, to pay to daughter Hannah Dickson £15. To daughters Sarah Johnson, Elizabeth Gregg, Anne Kirk, £20 each. To Samuel Johnson, son of Jervais Johnson, £5. Failing heirs to daughter Mary Johnson, who by marriage articles has interest in lands, remainder to daughters Hannah, Sarah, Elizabeth, and Anne. Executors, sons-in-law Francis Dickson, George Gregg, Jacob Kirk. Signed 3 Jan. 1771.

Morgan Willson.
Plain seal

Witnesses: William Dickson, Richard Dickson, John McCullagh, Thos. O'Kane. Probate to Francis Dickson, 3 Dec. 1777.

* * * * *

FRIENDS MEETING HOUSE, DUBLIN

The following original records, which are preserved in the vault of the Society of Friends, have been microfilmed by the National Library of Ireland and copies of the microfilms are now deposited at the Society of Friends Library, Swarthmore

College, Swarthmore, Pennsylvania. These are also listed in VOLUME II, hereof, pp. 274, 275.

1. Records of births, marriages, deaths of members of the Society of Friends, Carlow, Cork, to 1859. The birth records begin in 1660; marriages, 1661; deaths, 1670.

2. Records of births, marriages, Dublin, to 1859. The earliest birth records are dated 1634 and marriages begin in 1659.

3. Records of deaths, Dublin, to 1736. Burial records begin in 1668.

4. Records of deaths, Dublin, 1736-1859.

5. Records of births, marriages, deaths, to 1859, for Edenderry, Grange, Lisburn, Limerick, Lurgan, Moate. Limerick births begin in 1653; marriages, 1686; deaths, 1656. West Meath—Moate births begin 1629; marriages, 1647; deaths, 1664.

6. Records of births, marriages, deaths, to 1859, for Mountmellick, Richhill.

7. Records of births, marriages, deaths, to 1859, for County Tipperary, Waterford, County Wexford, Wicklow, Youghal. The earliest records for Waterford are dated for births, 1624; marriages, 1649; burials, 1656. County Wexford birth records of earliest date are 1641; marriages, 1640; burials, 1656. Wicklow birth records begin 1637; marriages, 1637; burials, 1657. Youghal births begin 1685; marriages, 1684; deaths, 1683.

8. Records of births, throughout Ireland, 1859-1949.

9. Records of marriage, throughout Ireland, 1859-1887; 1893-1947.

10. Records of deaths, throughout Ireland, 1859-1909; 1909-1949.

Among the manuscripts preserved by the Society of Friends are six volumes containing Quaker Wills as follows:

1. Carlow Monthly Meeting, Book of Wills and Inventories, 1675-1740.

2. Edenderry Monthly Meeting, Book of Wills, 1628-1763.

3. Mountmellick Monthly Meeting, Book of Wills, 1755-1795.

4. County Wexford Monthly Meeting Book of Wills, 1680-1760.

5. Dublin Monthly Meeting Books of Wills, 2 volumes, 1683-1772.

Quaker Records, Dublin, Abstracts of Wills, edited by P. Beryl Eustace and Olive C. Goodbody and published by the Irish Manuscripts Commission, Dublin, 1957, contains abstracts of the wills contained in the above six volumes. The Introduction (p. v), explains the purpose of keeping books of wills, which appears on the title page of the Dublin Wills, dated 26 of the 6 month 1684: "A Book For the Recordinge the Last Wills of Friends deceased wherein the Trust is Left (by any friend deceased) to Executo[r]s or Trustees of theyrs Personall or Reale Estates Bequeathed to children in theyer Mynority, that such Estates be Well Looked into and Preserved from Loss or Weast, that such children, orphants, be not wronged."

Appendix I of the above volume contains a list of the only wills, 28 in number, which are preserved in the Records of Ulster Quarterly Meeting in "The Will Book of Ballyhagan Meeting." Abstracts of these were made by Lieut.-Col. J.R.H. Greeves and published in *The Irish Genealogist*, Vol. 2, no. 8, October 1950.

Appendix II of the above volume contains a list of some full copies of wills and some notes from wills which are deposited in the historical library at Friends House, Dublin.

The Public Record Office of Ireland, Dublin, has a valuable collection of papers dealing with the work of the Society of Friends in relieving distress during the famine of the 1840's. (58th *Report*, p. 6.)

CHAPTER IX

ROMAN CATHOLIC RECORDS

Of all the genealogical source materials in Ireland, those which concern the Roman Catholics and have accumulated over many centuries, offer the greatest rewards due to the antiquity of the families. The importance of the records is measured by the number of Roman Catholics in Ireland and the many millions in other countries who are alike descended from forbears identified by their Gaelic-Irish, Norman-Irish, or medieval Anglo-Irish surnames, representing the old Roman Catholic aristocracy of the seventeenth century.

There seems to be a wrong impression among Americans that insufficient source materials exist in Ireland to accomplish effective genealogical work for Roman Catholic families. This is no more true than the story which was passed around in 1922 that, after the destruction of the Public Record Office in Dublin, it would forever thereafter be impossible to compile Irish genealogies. The validity of such an argument has been refuted in the six chapters of PART TWO of this volume.

Records of Roman Catholics comprise an important part of the collections listed under the various repositories, described in the six chapters. The classified collections of these repositories are further explained and itemized in this PART THREE, CHAPTERS I, II, and X-XXIII. Published source materials, many family manuscript collections, and microfilms of the records are listed in the accompanying VOLUME II. They are also rich in information concerning Roman Catholics. In order to avoid repetition, all of these chapters may be regarded as supplemental to this one which contains suggestions for research, a review of certain materials, a list of the original Roman Catholic families of the old aristocracy, and a section concerning the Parish Registers.

Roman Catholic research is at once the most complicated, the most far reaching, and the most challenging as well as intriguing, of any other research in Ireland. The genealogist has the most to learn regarding the records before attempting it. He has the widest range of source materials to cover during the course of his work. Every chapter in these two volumes, except for those devoted to the records of dissenting Protestant Churches, will offer information relating to research for Roman Catholics. In the scheme of work, the resources should be examined according to the chronological order of the records, and the area of interest.

Irish history provides a very necessary background for understanding the purpose, nature, and scope of the source materials, and the tide of affairs of the Roman Catholics. From earliest times until the seventeenth century, the history of Ireland is almost completely a history of its families. This is compiled from the ancient and medieval Annals, and from Government records. The Calendars of State Papers and Court Records contribute a great corpus of records of individuals, dating from medieval times to the nineteenth century. By way of explaining them, history elucidates the prevailing conditions, customs, events, and their effects in the way of confiscations, and religious persecution imposed by the Penal Laws. History also furnishes a guiding thread to the continuity of important genealogical source materials.

Innumerable works of Irish historians are available in America and other countries. A few are listed in VOLUME II, pp. 92-94. Two basic histories which are this compiler's constant companions are the works of Edmund Curtis, M.A., Litt.D., published by Methuen & Co., Ltd., 36 Essex Street, N. W., London. These are: *A History of Ireland*, 1952 (reprint of 6th edition), and *A History of Medieval Ireland, from 1086 to 1513*, 1938 (2nd edition). Dr. Edmund Curtis was Lecky Professor of Modern History at the University of Dublin. He employed the great mass of original source materials (from which genealogical records are drawn), with detached interpretative ability and the genius of a novelist. He lists the works of earlier historians of special interest, "Recommended for further reading." He also presents a series of maps of Ireland, showing the tribal and territorial divisions at different periods.

The *Encyclopaedia Britannica* (14th ed., 1929, Volume 12,

pp. 598-615), contains an article on the history of Ireland which serves as an important outline, offering a comprehensive account of the conditions, events, and their effects on the Roman Catholics under English rule. It does not, however, explain the ancient and medieval manuscripts in the light of their genealogical material. Another article (14th ed., 1929, Volume 19, pp. 419-420), entitled "Roman Catholic Church" (Ireland), supplies a significant review of the suppression of this Church and its adherents. The information is important to every Irish genealogist. Thus, with an outline of Irish history and Roman Catholic Church history, so easily available, it is unnecessary to repeat the reviews as a background for genealogical source materials.

Attention is also called to the series of *Irish Historical Studies.* This is a joint journal of the Irish Historical Society and the Ulster Society for Irish Historical Studies. Publication was begun in 1938, and issues have appeared in March and September of each year to the present time. It presents the well-documented work of numerous scholars on many subjects of importance to the historians and genealogists. Every article has enriched this compiler's understanding of Irish records. The genealogist should read and reread every issue from cover to cover, and keep them all for continual reference. Hodges Figgis & Co., Ltd., 6 Dawson Street, Dublin, will supply them at an annual subscription of 20 shillings, post free.

John P. Prendergast's *The Cromwellian Settlement of Ireland,* Dublin, 1875 (2nd and enlarged edition), contains much information regarding the Commonwealth Government confiscation in 1653, of all Roman Catholic and Protestant Royalist estates in twenty-six counties of the provinces of Leinster, Munster and Ulster. The Roman Catholic nobility and gentry, who owned property or held important leases which they forfeited, were ordered to transplant to Connaught and County Clare, by 1 May 1654, where they were to receive a fraction of the amount of their previous holdings. The confiscated property was divided in three ways: Cromwell's officers and soldiers, in lieu of pay for their services, were granted acreage according to their rank and period of enlistment. English Adventurers, who advanced money 1642-1646 to support the army and navy, were granted 2,500,000 acres. The best lands were sequestered for privileged men holding high Government positions.

The *Civil Survey* of 1654 set forth the names of all property owners as of 1641 (except for certain counties covered by the earlier *Strafford Survey*), with a description of their lands by townland, parish, barony, and county. *The Books of Survey and Distribution* contain abstracts of various surveys and instruments of title, 1636-1703. As in the *Civil Survey* of 1654, they show the names of the property owners of 1641, with the names of their townlands, and arranged by county, barony and parish. Information opposite the name of each proprietor of 1641 shows what happened to their lands. This sets forth the names of the Cromwellian grantees and indicates the property (one-third of that held by the Commonwealth officers and soldiers), which was returned to a great number of "Innocent" Roman Catholics and Protestant Royalists after 1660 by Charles II, and other personal grants which he made to Roman Catholics. By key signs, it is shown which of the owners of 1688 lost property in the confiscation after the Revolution of 1689-1691. This last confiscation was accomplished by a Court of Claims at Chichester House, Dublin, and was not completed until 1703, when the lands were sold at public auction. Roman Catholics were left with something over 1,100,000 acres. These records will be described in the following CHAPTER XIII.

Two lists of all who were transplanted to the Province of Connaught or County Clare are printed in *H.M.C. Reports, Ormond MSS.*, Vol. II, pp. 114-176 (1899). In the second list, the county of origin, if not a fuller address, usually follows the name of the transplanted person, together with the date of decree when the new property was assigned, the date of final settlement, and the number of acres. Thus, if a person was not returned to his ancestral estates by Charles II, and was left as a transplanter, his records can be matched with the above sources for details of his ancestral estates.

The Books of Survey and Distribution, Vol. I, *County of Roscommon*, edited by Robert C. Simington, Dublin, 1949 (pp. xxxi-xxxii), states: "In the specification, county by county, of the names of proprietors of land prior and subsequent to the Commonwealth Settlement, the genealogist is provided with details of the losses no less than the gains of countless families. Here emerges the land of Ireland as it was held three centuries ago by Gaels and Gaelicised Normans, by Normans 'the Old English,' and the later plantations and settlements. *The Books of Survey and Distribution* frequently provide the addresses of landholders and always the parishes in which their possessions were located, details which should prove of much help in genealogical research." The *Civil Survey* of 1654 always provides the names of the townlands owned by the proprietor and sometimes his parentage and other details. Thus the two together make a complete picture from 1641 to 1703, except for the added information which is set forth in the Census of 1659.

A Census of Ireland, circa 1659, edited by Séamus Pender, Dublin, 1939, indicates that there must have been very many exceptions to enforced transplantation of important families, for the list of *Tituladoes* (principal men) of each county includes the names of representatives of over half of the old Roman Catholic nobility and gentry, many listed as "Gentlemen", and in all cases the townlands of which they were possessed, together with the number of Irish living upon them (and in each case no English living on the lands).

Thus in the Census of *c.* 1659, for County Cork, among the *Tituladoes* we find the following names (many with their prefixes dropped and others retaining the O and Mac), in all cases with only Irish living on their lands: Teige Hogane, Thomas Murrough, John Murphy, Dommi Thirry, Teige Sweeny, Cnohor Ó Dyeyneene, James Galwey, Patrick Gould, Thomas Fitzgerald, Teige Carthy, Moylemorry Mc Sweeny, John Oge O'Crowley, Teige Mc Shane Crowley, John O'Hea and his son John, John O'Hea Mc Murtagh, Murtagh Mc Sheehy, Owen Mc Sheehy, Dom Mc Tho O'Hea, Meaghlin O'Hart, Mathew Hea, Tho. Hea, James Hea, Daniel Mc Teig, Richard Coursey, Dom Galwey, Patrick Ld. Coursey Baron Kinsale, Dermod Carthy, Dermod Coughlane, Teige Mc Curtane, Edmund Rashleigh and John his son, Dermod Coughlane and John his son, Donogh Carthy, Tho Owgan, Teige Cowly.

Throughout the Census of *c.* 1659, the principal Irish surnames listed under the baronies of each county are very
numerous. Also the Census figures of the number of English,
English and Scots, and of Irish are given for the counties
(sometimes under the baronies). The following representative figures are presented to show the situation regarding
the residence of Irish during the Commonwealth period
(1659), in counties of the provinces of Ulster, Leinster, and
Munster:

County	Number of English	Number of Eng. & Scot.	Irish
Antrim		6,243	8,485
Armagh		2,393	4,355
Donegal		3,412	8,589
Down		6,540	8,643
Dublin	3,323		9,724
Fermanagh	1,800		5,302
Kerry	566		7,824
Kildare	796		13,029
Kilkenny	1,442		16,985
King's	1,225		7,085
Limerick	1,182		20,690
Longford	281		5,111
Louth	837		7,248
Queen's	1,396		9,719
Tipperary	1,924		27,760
Wexford	1,623		12,048

The above Census shows a good proportion of Irish listed as
living on the estates of *Tituladoes* of Irish names who had no
English living on their property. Certainly hundreds of the
Roman Catholic nobility and gentry managed to retain their
property after the mass confiscations of James I, Cromwell,
and William III. A great many more retained some vestige
of property rights by placing their holdings (owned or lengthy
leases) in the hands of great Roman Catholic landlords who
escaped destruction, and also in the hands of sympathetic
Protestants (relatives or otherwise), as trustees. Some cases
noted in county histories and other sources show that certain
Roman Catholics anticipated trouble before the confiscations
and placed their estates in safekeeping in this way, thus sav-
ing them from confiscation. In other cases, the Roman Catholics who were minors at times of confiscation were wards of

Protestants, and their estates were thus saved. The overwhelming majority of Roman Catholics became tenants, mostly on their ancestral estates. Most of the landlords were Protestants but many were Roman Catholics. That the tenants remained on their ancestral estates, made wills, and divided their leased land among their descendants during the time of a lease, generation after generation, is indicated in the following quotations from authorities and by the indexed Prerogative and Diocesan Wills (and many transcripts of wills in the two Public Record Offices in Dublin and Belfast).

The first quotation is from Arthur Young (1741-1820); born and died in Broadfield, Suffolk, England; second son of the Rev. Arthur Young, Episcopal rector of that place; became an authority in England on agriculture and economic conditions, and eventually was appointed Secretary of the Board of Agriculture (*Encyclopaedia Britannica*, 14th ed., Vol. 23, pp. 903-4). When he made a tour of Ireland to analyze conditions there, 1776-1779, he traveled 2,300 miles and interviewed landlords, middlemen and tenants throughout the country, collecting a vast amount of information on the conditions of the people and agriculture. His detached observations are regarded today as one of the most authoritative sources for the period. They are a severe indictment of political, economic and religious mismanagement. His tour resulted in his two-volume work, *A Tour in Ireland with General Observations on the Present State of that Kingdom, made in the Years 1776, 1777, and 1778, and Brought down to the End of 1779.* Dublin, 1780. In Volume II, Part Two, pp. 40-53, he discusses "Oppression", "Emigration", and "Religion." This should be read for a full understanding of the oppression caused by the Penal Laws against Roman Catholics. On pp. 42-44, he states:

EMIGRATION: "The Catholics never went, they seem not only tied to the country but almost to the parish in which their ancestors lived."

RELIGION: "The history of the two religions in Ireland is too generally known to require any detail introductory to the subject. The conflict for two centuries occasioned a scene of devastation and bloodshed, till at last by the arms of King

William the decision left the uncontrolled power in the hands
of the Protestants. The landed property of the kingdom had
been greatly changed in the period of the reigns of Elizabeth
and James I. Still more under Cromwell, who parcelled an
immense proportion of the kingdom to the officers of his army,
the ancestors of great numbers of the present possessors; the
colonels of his regiments left estates which are now [paying
rents of] eight and ten thousand [pounds] a year, and I know
several gentlemen of two and three thousand a year at present
which they inherited from captains of the same service. The
last forfeitures were incurred in that war which stripped and
banished James II. Upon the whole, nineteen-twentieths of
the kingdom changed hands from Catholic to Protestant. The
lineal descendants of great families, once possessed of vast
property, are now to be found all over the kingdom in the
lowest situation, working as cottars for the great-great grandsons of men, many of whom were of no greater account in
England than these poor labourers are at present on that
property which was once their own. So entire an overthrow,
and change of landed possession, is within the period to be
found in scarce any country in the world. In such great
revolutions of property the ruined proprietors have usually
been extirpated or banished, but in Ireland the case was otherwise: families were so numerous and so united in clans, that
the heir of an estate was always known; and it is a fact that
in most parts of the kingdom the descendants of the old land
owners regularly transmit by testamentary deed, the memorial of their right to those estates which once belonged to
their families. From hence it results that the question of
religion has always in Ireland been intimately connected with
the right to and possession of the landed property of the kingdom; and has probably received from this source a degree of
acrimony, not at all wanting to influence the superstitious
prejudices of the human mind."

This is all very mild, compared to his full details of oppression of the Roman Catholics, but the above account is chosen
only for genealogical information.

A full account of the Penal Laws will be found in *The History of Ireland*, by Edmund Curtis, well indexed. Arthur

Young (*ibid*, p. 44) gives some of the Penal Laws including (3) which required that any leased property or personal estate or inherited estate be equally divided among all children according to the ancient law of Gavelkind, to keep any Roman Catholic estate from accumulating to the eldest heir. He sets forth the following Penal Laws, imposed in the reign of Queen Anne, *c.* 1703.

1. The whole body of Roman Catholics are absolutely disarmed.

2. They are incapacitated from purchasing land.

3. The entails of their estates are broken, and they gavel among the children.

4. If one child abjures that religion, he inherits the whole estate, though he is the youngest.

5. If the son abjures the religion, the father has no power over his estate, but becomes a pensioner on it in favor of such son.

6. No Catholic can take a lease for more than thirty-one years. [These could, however, be renewed over and over.]

7. If the rent of any Catholic is less than two-thirds of the full improved value, whoever discovers takes the benefit of the lease. [Protestant Discovery Bills filed in the Courts, by which they acquired the property of Catholics, were very numerous and contain much genealogical information.]

8. Priests who celebrate mass to be transported, and if they return to be hanged.

9. A Catholic having a horse in his possession above the value of five pounds, to forfeit the same to the discoverer.

10. By construction of Lord Hardwick's, they are incapacitated from lending money on mortgage.

Arthur Young states further, "the preceding catalogue is very imperfect but here is an exhibition of suppression fully sufficient." On page 45, he refers to various ways the Roman Catholics had of getting around the Penal Laws, by the help of Protestants in the family or others, etc. "That they have lessened the landed property in the hands of Catholics is certain; their violence could not have had any other effect, but not, however, to such a degree as might have been imagined. There are principles of honour, religion, and ties of blood too powerful for tyrannic laws to overcome, and which have prevented their full effect." When he quoted the above Penal Laws, it was according to their first form under Queen Anne, and not as they were earlier, or after 1771 when they began to be somewhat relaxed.

Jonathan Pim's *Condition and Prospects of Ireland*, Dublin, 1848, is equally an indictment of the conditions imposed on the Roman Catholics including the following (pp. 16, 330-331): "But it may be said the penal laws were never strictly enforced. This is, no doubt, true. The minds of men revolted at their severity, and refused to carry out in times of peace, the oppressive enactments which the Irish Parliament had passed in the heated feelings engendered by war. Some of the most oppressive soon fell into disuse, or the evasion of them was winked at. The Roman Catholic nobility and gentry retained their estates; in many instances, transferring their title-deeds to Protestants, who held them in trust; and to the honor of these be it said, there is no record that the trust was ever broken." "Among many measures professedly for the improvement of Ireland, an act was passed in 1771, which allowed Roman Catholics to take a lease for sixty-one years of not less than ten acres, or more than fifty, of bog, with only half an acre of arable land for the site of a house, but not to be situated within a mile of a town; and if it was not reclaimed in twenty-one years, the lease to be void. In 1777, it was enacted that titles not hitherto litigated should not be disturbed, and Roman Catholics were allowed to take leases for any term under a thousand years. In 1782, they were allowed to acquire freehold property for lives or by inheritance; and in 1793 was passed a further enactment, which materially affected the position of landlord and tenant. The forty-shilling franchise was by that Act extended to Roman Catholics." ". . . in 1793, in which year Roman Catholics were placed on a par with Protestants as regards the elective franchise, although not allowed to become members of either house of Parliament. A lease for lives of a house or land, in which the lessee had an interest worth forty shillings a year, called 'a forty-shilling freehold' entitled the holder to a vote. This low franchise induced the landed proprietors to divide their estates into many small holdings, for the purpose of increasing their influence at elections. A numerous tenantry, having the right to vote, and practically obliged to exercise that right at the dictation of their landlords, was highly prized." "Subsequently, the Act of 1829 [raising the requirements of the franchise] destroyed the political value of the forty-shilling freeholder, and . . . the landlord, in too many instances adopted what has been called the 'clearance system.' " By this means the landlords used every artifice or excuse to cancel leases and the result was a flood of bills of equity, whereby the tenants appealed for the right to retain their leases.

The Indexes of Prerogative and Diocesan Wills of Ireland, discussed in the following CHAPTER XXIII, bear out the fact that Roman Catholics regularly left wills which were probated. Both classes of indexes show the names, addresses, and dates of probate. The Prerogative Index gives the occupation also. The two Public Record Offices in Belfast and Dublin have collections of original wills, Court copies of wills, transcripts and abstracts of wills, a great many wills never probated, and administrations (original, transcript, or indexes). All of these are listed by collection or indexed in the *Reports* of the Deputy Keepers of these repositories. The Registry of Deeds has transcripts or abstracts of wills. These have been published, 1708-1785, and there is a manuscript index which extends to 1800. Then there are the wills proved in the Principal or District Courts from 1858.

Land transactions of Roman Catholics (leases of over three years) are recorded in the Registry of Deeds from 1708, while shorter leases are recorded in such Estate records as exist. Many other collections of land records are in the Public Record Offices. A large proportion of the records of the high courts and local courts concern Roman Catholics who were prosecuted (often only on suspicion), during times of danger. Rushe's *History of Monaghan for Two Hundred Years, 1660-1860*, has a running account of the people involved tragically in prosecutions. Some printed or manuscript calendars or abstracts of Chancery Court cases are noted in CHAPTER XI. Then there are the Hearthmoney Rolls, Religious Returns, Tithe Applotment Books, Griffith's Survey, which give the names and locations of Roman Catholics; also the *Memorials of the Dead* (tombstone records), which include many inscriptions for Roman Catholics. All of these sources and others are noted in following chapters.

The body of materials, beginning in 1641, concerning the confiscations, when combined with the earlier Inquisitions on Attainder, Inquisitions Post Mortem and other early Court records; also the Funeral Certificates (which often supply the records of a few to six or more generations prior to 1636), all serve to connect the seventeenth century Roman Catholic nobility and gentry with their Gaelic-Irish tribes and septs, and their early Norman-Irish or medieval Anglo-Irish families.

National and local histories, historical society journals, and MSS. or published genealogical collections, universally give attention to the earliest families in each area. Most family histories, or notes regarding them, begin with records compiled from the genealogical materials in the ancient Celtic and medieval manuscripts of the tribes and septs, many of which have been translated, edited with copious notes and published. The published works are listed in VOLUME II, pp. 96-97, 103-104, and 213-215. These and others yet unpublished contain the longest pedigrees in Western Europe. Therefore, something should be known about these ancient and medieval records.

The manuscripts contain the Annals of the tribes and septs. They were written by their hereditary historians (Senachies), and their Bards (Filidhe), who were scholars of the highest order, trained from father to son, to incredible feats of memory. Their writings blended the most ancient tradition with their contemporary records which begin *c.* A.D. 432.

Dr. Edmund Curtis opens his work, *A History of Ireland*, 1952 (pp. 1-3), with observations on early recorded tradition and on the opinions of modern scholars which are briefly noted in the following two paragraphs.

The ancient *Leabar Gabala* (the Book of Invasions) preserves the tradition that three sons of Mileadh of Spain, namely Heremon, Heber, and Ir, conquered Erin (Ireland) about the time of Alexander the Great. From these men descended all the royal clans of later Ireland. To be of the old Milesian race is regarded as an honourable distinction, by those who remember the story of "Meela Spaunya." This all concerns tradition.

Dr. Curtis points out that modern scholars agree on the early races in Ireland, including perhaps certain ones named in tradition. The Gaelic Celts came from southern France or Northern Spain about 350 B.C. They eventually became the political masters of Ireland, and though an upper class minority, had, by A.D. 800, imposed their empire, language and law upon the whole of Ireland. In early history tradition and fact are blended together and, not until St. Patrick's arrival in 432, may we regard ourselves on historical ground.

Ireland was then a land of ancient culture. The extensive discoveries of archaeologists have confirmed this. The manuscripts of the fifth century and later periods contain the art, Brehon laws, music, poetry and literature, embodying family history and genealogical records of the tribes and, in medieval times, the branching septs. They show that Ireland was early divided into five provinces or kingdoms, namely Leinster, Munster, Connaught, Ulster, and Meath. Over each province ruled a king, and one of these secured the position of over-king or monarch of all Ireland. Each province was divided into territories or petty states called *Tuatha*. About one hundred had been established by the year A.D. 1000. Each territory was inhabited by one or more tribes and the members were descended from a common ancestor. Eventually various branches of the tribes, being their respective septs or families, were established. Over each territory ruled a petty king or prince, lord, or chieftain; his rank depending upon its size and importance. The chieftains of the septs and smaller tribes were subordinate to the rulers of the larger districts, and each of these princes, lords, or chieftains, paid tribute to their provincial king.

The ancient Brehon laws of Ireland were administered in

each province and locally, within the territories of the tribes and septs, by learned Brehons or judges. According to the Brehon laws of Tanistry, the most able member of the strongest tribe within each province was elected king. The law required that he be descended within four generations from a previous ruler, but not necessarily in direct hereditary succession. The same laws allowing indirect hereditary rights applied in the election of princes, lords and chieftains, who ruled the greater and smaller tribes and septs.

The laws of Tanistry also provided for the allotment of land for life to each related member descended from the common ancestor of his tribe or branching sept. Thus the pedigree of each man was all-important and acted as a sort of title deed to his rights, both in matters of election to office and land tenure. The Bards and hereditary historians of great learning were maintained in positions of highest honor by each tribe for the purpose of recording their affairs, tribal warfare, records of their heroes and various members. This system of elective rulers, tenure of lands, and the methods of preserving pedigrees, were unknown in England.

These manuscripts show that no office was hereditary except as precedence was granted to the most worthy one among the near relatives of a deceased ruler. To place the power in the strongest hands and keep peace in the kingdom, tribe, or sept, the office usually passed to the previously elected Tanist, or successor, who might be an uncle, brother, nephew, or any one of the sons (legitimate or illegitimate) of the ruler of the time. In some cases, a more remote kinsman raised enough support to secure the office. No one under age or having any physical disability was eligible. A dozen or more members of a tribe or sept were always in line for election according to precedence by birth, and strength to command support. Tribal warfare over the official election of a previously elected Tanist, was frequently sudden and violent, and the stronger, more resourceful man usually won. This created more records with the ancestry of each contender named to the third or fourth generation.

Upon death of a ruler or member, there was a reassignment of lands in order of rank and seniority. Certain *mensal* lands were reserved for the king, prince, lord or chieftain and for their tanists. The members of the tribes and septs paid tribute to support them. As no one had any hereditary estate in their lands, this often caused violent contentions, for all were in a sense tenants-at-will. However, there were also the laws of Gavelkind, signifying the equal share of kindred, or heirs of the deceased according to birth or near relationship. This applied to lands or wealth, personally acquired in warfare with other tribes, etc., or inherited from such a source. The sons (legitimate and illegitimate) shared equally. Daughters received a dowry in cattle, money, goods, etc.

For four centuries after the time of St. Patrick (A.D. 390-461), the numerous monasteries established in the tribal territories, or *tuatha,* became great schools of learning and attracted students from foreign lands. That the ancient manuscripts of the heriditary historians and Bards were deposited in monastery libraries for safekeeping and studied by the scholars, is evident from a lovely poem of fifteen stanzas, written by Alfred (*c.* A. D. 680), later king of Northumbria, who came from Britain to Ireland as a student. It is printed in full in *The History of the Church of Ireland,* edited by Walter A. Phillips, 1933 (Vol. I, pp. 220-221). Alfred described all parts of Ireland in terms of highest praise, including, "Long-living men, health, prosperity . . . Learning, wisdom, devotion to God, Holy welcome, and protection . . . the historians recording truth . . ."

The Church, governed by the bishops, and the monasteries with their learned monks, suffered with the natives after A. D. 800, when Norse and Danish invaders came and for 200 years made sporadic attacks, but were mostly interested in the maritime cities where families of their names were established. The independent tribes with their loose political disunion, prevented conquest in Ireland, in contrast to that in England, Scotland and Wales. The monasteries survived and grew wealthy while their schools prospered and their libraries preserved their accumulated manuscripts, save for some which were carried away by the invaders, *c.* A. D. 800-1000. Some of the existing medieval manuscripts or parts of them show evidence of having been transcribed from original records of much earlier date which have disappeared. Perhaps this was for reasons of security when the originals were removed to other places. The same thing happened in the nineteenth century, when over one hundred of the parishes of the Church of Ireland kept copies of their Parish Registers, made before the originals were sent to the Public Record Office in Dublin. All but four of the original Registers in this Office were burned in 1922, and the transcripts are now honored.

Until a little over a century ago, when the first great corpus of ancient Celtic or Gaelic manuscripts and the medieval manuscripts were translated and published with copious historical notes, the public knew little of these sources. Only the most privileged scholars could examine them where they were then, and are now deposited. Great collections are in the Dublin libraries of Trinity College, the Royal Irish Academy, the Franciscan Convent at Merchants' Quay; St. Colman's College Library, Fermoy; in Scotland: the Edinburgh University Library, the Advocates' Library of Edinburgh, and Glasgow University Library; in London: the British Museum, and the Archiepiscopal Library at Lambeth Palace where the Carew MSS. collection of genealogies is deposited; the Bodleian Library, Oxford (Rawlinson Collection, etc.) ; Cambridge University Library; the National Library of Wales; the Bibliotheque Nationale, Paris; the Vatican Archives, Rome; and monasteries, smaller libraries, etc., throughout Europe.

The great transfer of ancient and medieval manuscripts out of Ireland occurred mostly after Henry VIII made the great breach with Rome through his Reformation Parliament, 1529-1536. Under this monarch the Roman Catholic Churches and their lands, together with more than 550 monasteries and other religious houses, with their schools and libraries, were confiscated and destroyed while the lands were divided between the Crown, the new State Church, and Protestant English planters. From 1539, all Roman Catholic relics were burned when discovered. During Elizabeth's reign, the bishops and clergy were ordered out of the country. A price was put on the heads of any who remained with the penalty of imprisonment or death to those who were found. Any who returned were impeached for treason and executed if discovered. Hundreds remained or returned as missionaries to minister to the persecuted people. Bishops and clergy slept in miserable huts or ruined abbeys, traveled by night and met with their adherents in the early dawn at secret places. Many were discovered and were burned, executed, or imprisoned and, in the time of James I, were exiled to the West Indies. Meanwhile, numerous ancient and medieval manuscripts were hidden while others were carried out of the country.

For over a century the historians and archivists of Ireland have been locating the manuscripts of every nature relating to Ireland which are deposited in Great Britain and Europe. A great program of microfilming the material was begun by the National Library of Ireland in 1941, under Dr. Richard J. Hayes, Director. In 1949, the Celtic Department of Harvard University, Cambridge, Massachusetts (established in 1897), joined in the Irish Celtic project by contributing a share of the expense of the microfilming, and thereby has obtained copies of the films. In 1951, the Eire Society of Boston, Massachusetts, made an important grant toward the project.

The microfilmed material includes some 700 MSS. dated prior to A. D. 1200. King John's letters to his "Lords in Ireland" before 1215, are included among the records. There is much material of the 16th century and some are documents of the 17th and 18th centuries, of important Roman Catholic interest. Nearly 700,000 pages of Irish material have been filmed and sent to Harvard's Houghton Library, together with indexed lists of the contents. These include 803 MSS. found in Germany; 347 in Munich alone. France has contributed 370; Switzerland, 352; England and Scotland, 277; Italy, 187; Austria, 132; and Belgium, 112. A few turned up in America, Canada, Holland, Denmark, and Spain, while six were found in Russia. The material of late date is mostly of literary interest and outside the field of genealogy, but the 17th century MSS. include pedigrees registered in foreign countries, 1550-1700, by Roman Catholics forced to leave Ireland. The compiler is indebted to Mrs. Winifred Lovering Holman, F.A.S.G., of Lexington, Massachusetts, for the above figures, which she sent in a clipping from *The Christian Science Monitor,* Boston (Volume 52, No. 165). This was written by Barbara Brooks

Walker, who quotes Mrs. Philip J. McNiff, a Gaelic speaker and recent cataloguer of all Celtic material at the Harvard University libraries. Dr. Hayes' program of microfilming for the National Library of Ireland is further noted in this VOLUME I, pp. 107-108; VOLUME II, pp. 270-286.

The records in the medieval manuscripts deposited in Ireland, many of which have been translated, edited with copious notes and published as stated above, show that a mixture of the races of Ireland and England occurred after the Norman invasion of 1166-1172. Following this, the families of the Irish provincial kings, princes, lords, and chieftians, of the great and smaller tribes and septs, gradually absorbed each succeeding and thinly spread wave of usurpers, through propinquity and intermarriage. The plantation of the Normans who came to conquer, and the later English Crown favorites who were granted great confiscated estates, failed in its purpose. The three races became inextricably blended in their progeny before the Reformation of 1536. They had adopted the native Irish customs, laws, language, and strong Gaelic independence of English rule, except within the Pale, where English rule prevailed in the counties of Dublin, Kildare, Meath, and Louth, protected by military force. Even in these areas, the old Roman Catholic English by blood cast in their lot with the natives of mixed races or the pure Gaelic-Irish when, in the time of Elizabeth, new Protestant English by birth were granted large estates and usurped the political offices. The Gaelic-Irish, Norman-Irish, and Anglo-Irish, occupied distinct territories or places of residence in the various counties, when England's conquest of Ireland was finally completed in 1603, and the old aristocratic Roman Catholic order was well on the way to destruction. A list of the families and the counties where each was located between the eleventh and seventeenth century, will be noted as a valuable source for research.

Of the published ancient and medieval manuscripts (VOLUME II, pp. 96-97, 103-104, 213-215), two are noted as samples of the material as follows:

Annála Rioghachta Eireann (Annals of the Kingdom of Ireland, composed by the Four Masters from the earliest period to 1616), translated and edited with copious notes, by John O'Donovan. 7 vols., Dublin, 1851-1854. This work was compiled in the first half of the seventeenth century by the learned antiquaries called "The Four Masters," Michael O' Clery, Cucogry or Peregrine O'Clery, Conary O'Clery, and Peregrine O'Duigenan. They were assisted by two other eminent antiquaries and chronologers, namely Fearfeasa O'Mulconaire or O'Conery, and Maurice O'Conery. The former group were hereditary historians to the O'Donnells, Princes of Tyrconnel, and the latter two were hereditary historians to the Kings of Connaught.

Michael O'Clery devoted fifteen years to collecting a vast number of ancient documents as he traveled throughout Ireland in search of tribal records. Among these were the Annals of Tigernach, by the learned Abbot of Clonmacnois, and the Book of Clonmacnois; the Annals of Innesfallen, composed by the learned monks of that Abbey; the Book of the MacBruadins, hereditary historians to the O'Briens and other tribes of Thomond; the Annals of Ulster, by Cathal Mac Guire and Roderick O'Cassidy, celebrated antiquaries of the diocese of Clogher; the Book of Conquests; the Book of the Mac Firbises, the learned antiquaries of *Leacan* in Tireragh, County Sligo; the Book of the O'Conrys, hereditary historians to the Kings of Connaught; the Book of the O'Duigenans of Kilronan, in Roscommon; the Book of the Island of All Saints in Loughree; and many others. All of the records were compiled in chronological order down to A. D. 1616. These men were among the last of their honorable and ancient profession of hereditary historians of the tribes. In a changed world of desecrated monasteries and abbeys which once preserved the manuscripts, and among the last representatives of the Gaelic tribes, the safety of the remaining manuscripts was insecure. All that could be gathered together by these learned men were sequestered, translated and transcribed. Thus have the genealogies of some hundreds of ancient and medieval families been preserved. They include the families seated in Ireland before the Norman conquest and continue, including the records of the Norman knights who exploited them. They show the intermarriages of the Gaelic-Irish and the Normans, and carry on with their descendants. They weave in further alliances with colonizing English and the resultant genealogies thereafter. Some of the ancient and medieval Annals from which this compilation has been made, as well as others, have been separately translated and published as a whole with notes.

The Annals of Ireland, Translated from the Original Irish of the Four Masters, by Owen Connellan, with annotations by Philip MacDermott, M.D., and the Translator, Dublin, 1846. Owen Connellan was Irish Historiographer to George IV, and William IV, and author of a grammar of the Irish language. His *Annals of Ireland* embody only that part of the records in the manuscripts compiled by "The Four Masters" dated 1171-1616. This volume contains the historical and genealogical records of the principal members of the tribes and septs. They are set forth chronologically under the reigns of the English monarchs from Henry II through to 1616, in the reign of James I. Men and women mentioned in the text are usually identified by the names of their progenitors to the second, third, or fourth generation.

The work is supplemented by very detailed and copious notes, covering the historical and genealogical records of the tribes, septs, and their rulers, Brehons, Bards, hereditary historians, hereditary officers, members, etc., from earliest times to 1616. Much information about the Normans and their descendants, as well as the English who came to Ireland, is included. The notes (pp. 550-552, 579, 580), contain a review of the rank and titles of the rulers of the tribes and septs, their attendance at the various Parliaments, etc., and their territories.

At the back of the volume is Philip MacDermott's Map, 1846, with the following title and explanation: "Topographical and Historical Map of Ancient Ireland Shewing the Five Kingdoms of the Pentarchy Meath, Ulster, Connaught, Leinster and Munster as they existed under the Milesian Kings with the old Principalities and other Chief Divisions, the Palaces of the Kings, ancient Cities, Bishops' Sees and remarkable Places and the Territories possessed by each of the Irish Princes, Lords, and Chiefs, from the 11th to the 17th

Century; also the possessions of the Danes in the 10th, 11th and 12th centuries, and of the great Anglo-Norman and old English Families from the Reign of Henry II to that of Elizabeth, comprising the Period from the latter end of the 12th to about the middle of the 16th century." He goes on to explain, "On the Printed Sheet accompanying the Map an Account is given of the extent of all the Ancient Territories, and of the Possessions, Rank, Titles and Descent of all the Irish Princes, Lords and Chiefs, and also the Titles and Territories of the Anglo-Norman Lords and great English families. The Milesian Chiefs are all distinguished by O and Mac. The Head Chiefs are placed about the middle of each Barony and others are on their Localities. The Anglo-Irish are placed on some part of their Possessions and the word Danes is marked on the territories which they possessed. The Abbreviations are P. Prince, L. Lord., C. Chief., C^s. Chiefs., B. Baron., V. Viscount, and E. an Earl."

Explanation of the Map (pp. 735-736), gives details of information taken from the Annals; also further sources from which information was taken as follows: "the Maps accompanying the State Papers of the reign of Henry VIII, which were compiled c. 1515-1567, containing the names of the principal Irish and English possessors at that period; also materials collected from numerous sources such as ancient Histories, Topographies, and Genealogies found in Keating; in Cambrensis Eversus; O'Flaherty's Ogygia; the Dissertations of Charles O'Conor; O'Brien's Irish Dictionary; O'Halloran; Mac Geoghegan; the works of Ware, Usher, Valancey, Camden, Hanmer and Champion; Cox's Hibernia; Colgan, De Burgo, Archdall and Lanigan; the Public Records and Inquisitions published from 1825 to 1829, particularly the Books on Ultonia and Lagenia; all the Topographical Dictionaries; ancient Peerages, by Lodge and others; Burke's Peerage and Landed Gentry; and personal information collected from various sources. The Census of 1821 has been consulted, which gives the names of the families in every parish in Ireland, and the many Clans have been collected from it; for where an old tribe name is very numerous at the present day, it may be inferred that they have been located there for centuries."

This last sentence of MacDermott, written in 1846, just at the beginning of the greatest flood of emigration of the descendants of the old aristocratic Roman Catholic families, offers extremely important and significant information from a great authority, supported by his references, to the effect that through the centuries the dispossessed Roman Catholics remained as tenants on or near their ancestral estates, in great numbers. Many local historians and genealogists have compiled the early and later records of the principal families. They have employed the "Annals of the Four Masters" and other early manuscripts which are published with copious notes, together with the records of following centuries. These are listed in VOLUME II. Thus the principal families which are recorded with their locations and rank, in Connellan's and MacDermott's Notes and on the Map, furnish a guide to the families which have mostly received attention in one way or another from the historians and genealogists. For this reason, the names are presented below by their rank and under the counties wherein they were located.

PRINCIPAL FAMILIES IN IRELAND, 11TH TO 17TH CENTURY

ANTRIM:

> *Earls:* De Burgo, De Courcy, De Lacy, Mac Donnell.
>
> *Lords:* Mac Quillan, O'Donnelan, O'Flynn, O'Kane, O'Neill, O'Sheil.
>
> *No title designated:* Bisset, Mac Alister, Mac Clean, Mac Dougall, Mac Nally, O'Eric, O'Furry, O'Hamill, O'Hara, O'Keevan, O'Mulholland.

ARMAGH:

> *Lords:* Mac Cann, O'Hanlon, O'Neill.
>
> *Chieftains:* O'Duvany, O'Garvey, O'Hanrratty, O'Heir, O'Keiran, O' Larkin, O'Neylan.
>
> *No title designated:* Mac Evoy, O'Callan, O'Colgan, O'Donnegan, O'Marron, O'Tierney.

CARLOW:

> *Barons:* Butler, Carew.
>
> *Lords:* O'Cavanagh, O'Moore, O'Nolan, O'Ryan.

Chieftains: Mac Gorman, O'Cahill, O'Doran.

No title designated: Chevers, Coke, Eustace, Fitzgerald, Grace, Lombard, Mac Murrough, Mac Teigue, O'Bolger, O'Doyle, O'Doyne, O'Gorman, O'Kinsellagh, Sarsfield, Strongbow, Tallon, Wall.

CAVAN:

Prince: O'Reilly.

Lords: Mac Gauran, Mac Kiernan, Mac Tiernan.

Chieftains: Mac Brady, Mac Cabe, Mac Gowan (or Smith), Mac Smith, Mac Tully, O'Farrelly.

No title designated: Fitzpatrick, Fitzsimon, Fleming, Mac Gafney, Mac Hugh, Mac Nulty, Masterson, O'Brogan, O'Clery, O'Conaghty, O'Coyle, O'Curry, O'Daly, O'Dolan, O'Lynch, L'Mulligan, O'Murray, O'Sheridan, Plunkett.

CLARE:

Prince: Mac Namara.

Baron: O'Brien.

Lords: MacMahon, O'Conor, O'Grady, O'Quinn.

Chieftains: Mac Donnell, O'Dea, O'Gorman, O'Hehir, O'Howley, O'Kearney, O'Moloney, O'Morony.

No title designated: De Clare, Creagh, Cusack, Mac Brodin, Mac Clancy, Mac Lysaght, Magrath, O'Callaghan, O'Carmody, O'Connell, O'Considine, O'Creagh, O'Cullenan, O'Culligan, O'Curran, O'Daly, O'Davoren, O'Deegan, O'Dermody, O'Drinan, O'Flattery, O'Flynn, O'Griffin, O'Halloran, O'Heffernan, O'Hickey, O'Hogan, O'Honeen, O'Keeley, O'Liddy, O'Loghlin, O'Lynch, O'Mullins, O'Neil (or Nihel), O'Neylan, O'Quinlevan.

CORK:

King: Mac Carthy.

Princes: Mac Carthy, Mac Carthy Reagh, O'Sullivan, O'Sullivan Beare.

Earls: Barry, De Courcy, Fitzgerald.

Viscount: Roche.

Barons: Barry, Condon.

Lords: Barrett, Barry, De Cogan, Fitzgerald, Fitzgerald

(The White Knight), Mac Donough, O'Callaghan, O'Donovan, O'Driscoll, O'Keefe, O'Leary, O'Lehan, O'Mahony.

Chieftains: Mac Auliffe, Mac Clancy, Mac Sheehy, O'Crowley, O'Cullenan, O'Dea, O'Dugan, O'Flynn, O'Hea, O'Noonan, O'Riordan.

No title designated: Barnwall, Barry Oge, De Capel, De Carew, De Cogan, Coppinger, Galwey, Gould, Mac Sherry, Nagle, O'Ahern, O'Bradley, O'Brigan, O'Callanan, O'Casey, O'Claisin, O'Coleman, O'Creagh, O'Crowly, O'Cullen, O'Curry, O'Daly, O'Danaher, O'Deasy, O'Dennery, O'Dinane, O'Dineen, O'Donovan, O'Flavey, O'Fihelly, O'Flynn, O'Griffin, O'Halahan, O'Hartigan, O'Healy, O'Hennigan, O'Herlihy, O'Heyne, O'Hoollaghan, O'Horgan, O'Hurley, O'Kearny, O'Kelleher, O'Lomasey, O'Looney, O'Lynch, O'Morony, O'Murphy, O'Regan, O'Ronayne, O'Scannell, O'Shea, O'Tuohy, O'Tuomey, Sarsfield, Skiddy, Supple, Walsh.

DONEGAL:

Princes: Mac Loghlin, O'Cannanan, O'Donnell, O'Muldorry, O'Neill.

Lords: Mac Sweeney, O'Boyle, O'Dogherty, O'Dooyarma.

Chieftains: Mac Duvan, O'Breslin, O'Brodar, O'Clery, O'Donnelly, O'Forranan, O'Gallaher, O'Gormley, O'Leaney, O'Quinn, O'Darcert, O'Tarcert.

No title designated: Mac Bride, Mac Clean, Mac Closkey, Mac Crossan, Mac Davett, Mac Gettigan, Mac Gilbride, Mac Ginty, Mac Gorigal, Mac Gowan, Mac Hugh, Mac Intire, Mac Nulty, Mac Teige, Mac Ward, O'Begley, O'Coigley (or Quigley), O'Coyle, O'Curran, O'Devir, O'Donlevy, O'Dornin, O'Duffy, O'Early, O'Freel, O'Hagerty, O'Harkan, O'Hugh, O'Kenny, O'Kernaghan, O'Laverty, O'Lynchy, O'Morrison, O'Mulgee, O'Mulvany, O'Murray, O'Rafferty, O'Roddy, O'Sheeran.

DOWN:

Princes: Mac Gennis, O'Donlevy.

Earls: De Burgo, De Courcy, De Lacy.

Lords: Mac Cartan, O'Neill, Savadge.

Chieftains: Mac Rory, O'Garvey, O'Heoghy, O'Hoey, O'Kelly, O'Lawry, O'Moore.

No title designated: Audley, Copeland, Fitzsimon, Jordan, Mac Gilmore, Mac Gowan, Mandeville, Martell, O'Colgan, O'Coltaran, O'Connell, O'Cormac, O'Florry, O'Hanvey, O'Largnan, O'Lawlor, O'Longan, O'Loughnan, O'Lynch, O'Macken, O'Mahon, O'Moran, O'Rogan, O'Rooney, Le-Poer, Riddell, Russell, Smyth, Staunton, White.

DUBLIN:

Prince: O'Kelly.

Earl: Sarsfield.

Viscounts: Fitzwilliam, Preston.

Barons: St. Laurence, Talbot, Tyrrell.

Lord: Mac Giollamocholmoge.

No title designated: Bagott, Barnewell, Burnell, De Courcy, Cruise, Delahoyde, Fagan, Fitz Eustace, Fitzsimon, Plunkett, Segrave, Taylor, Walsh.

FERMANAGH:

Prince: Mac Guire.

Lords: Mac Gilfinnen, O'Devin.

Chieftains: Mac Donnell, O'Cassidy, O'Heaney, O'Keenan, O'Muldoon.

Brehon: O'Breslin.

No title designated: Mac Caffrey, Mac Enteggart, Mac Garrahan, Mac Lennon, Mac Manus, Mac Tiernan, Mac Tully, Magrath, O'Casey, O'Coigley, O'Corcoran, O'Corrigan, O'Donnegan, O'Felan, O'Gorman, O'Hosey, O'Luinin, O'Meehan, O'Mulrooney, O'Tracy, O'Tully.

GALWAY:

Princes: O'Heyne, O'Kelly.

Earls: Be Burgh, Burke, Butler.

Viscounts: De Burgo, Burke.

Barons: Birmingham, Blake, Brown, Burke, Dillon, O'Daly.

Lords: O'Brien, O'Clery, O'Donnellan, O'Flaherty, O'Madden, O'Shaughnesy.

Chieftains: Joyce, Mac Conry, Mac Hugh, Norton (O'Naghten), O'Connell, O'Conor, O'Halloran, O'Haverty, O'Hoollaghan, O'Horan, O'Hynes, O'Kean, O'Manning, O'Naghten (Norton).

No title designated: Bodkin, Burke, Darcy, Deane, French, Hughes (Mac Hugh), Lynch, Mac Gildauff, Mac Gillikelly, Mac Nevin, Mac Tully, Mac Ward, Martin, Morris, O'Cahill, O'Callanan, O'Cashin, O'Coffey, O'Conealy, O'Connolly, O'Cullen, O'Donnell, O'Doyle, O'Duane, O'Duffy, O'Fahy, O'Feeney, O'Gearan, O'Gevany, O'Hynes, O'Kirwan, O'Larkin, O'Leahan, O'Lee, O'Lennon, O'Loman, O'Maginn, O'Moran, O'Mullarky, O'Mulrooney, O'Scurry, O'Sheehan, O'Sullivan, O'Toole, O'Tormey, Skerret, Staunton.

KERRY:

Princes: Mac Carthy More, O'Conor.

Earls: Fitzgerald, Fitzmaurice.

Knight: Fitzgerald.

Lords: Mac Carthy, O'Carroll, O'Conor, O'Flavey, O'Sullivan More.

Chieftains: Mac Fineen, Mac Gillicuddy of the Reeks, Mac Sheehy, Mac Sweeny, O' Connell, O'Harney, O'Mahony, O'Moriarty, O'Mullane, O'Shea.

Brehon: Mac Clancy.

No title designated: Hussey, Joy, Mac Crehan, Mac Elligot, Mac Kenna, Magrath, O'Brennan, O'Brosnaghan, O'Cahill, O'Casey, O'Creagh, O'Cronin, O'Daly, O'Delany, O'Donoghoe, O'Doolin, O'Dunnady, O'Feenaghty, O'Flynn, O'Foley, O'Gallivan, O'Grady, O'Hagerty, O'Healy, O'Kelleher, O'Kennedy, O'Leahy, O'Leyne, O'Moore, O'Quill, O'Quinlan, O'Scanlan, O'Sheehan, O'Slattery, Smerwick, Stack, Trant.

KILDARE:

Princes: O'Connor, O'Murrigan.

Duke: Fitzgerald.

Earl: Fitzgerald.

White Knight: Fitzgibbon, or Fitzgerald.

Baron: Birmingham.

Lords: O'Kelly, O'Toole.

Chieftains: O'Colgan, O'Dunn.

No title designated: Aylmer, Burke, Delahoyde, Fitzgerald, Fitzhenry, Mac Donnell, O'Cullen, O'Dempsey, Wogan.

KILKENNY:

Princes: O'Carroll, O'Donoghoe.

Earls: De Clare, Le Mareschal.

Viscount: Butler.

Lord's: Grace, O'Brennan, O'Brodar.

Chieftains: Mac Breen, O'Delany, O'Gloran.

No title designated: Archer, Cantwell, Comerford, De Montmorency, Mac Gilpatrick, O'Bolger, O'Bree, O'Callan, O'Doyle, O'Hely, O'Keeley, O'Keveny, O'Loughnan, O'Ryan, O'Shea or Shee, Power, Roth, Shortall, Walsh.

KING'S:

Prince: O'Molloy.

Viscount and Baron: O'Dempsey.

Chieftains: O'Bannan, O'Behan, O'Bergin, O'Hennessey, O'Madden, O'Mooney.

No title designated: Fitzgerald, Fitzsimon, Hussey, De Lacy, O'Hoollaghan, O'Mulvany, Warren.

LEITRIM:

Prince: O'Rourke.

Lord: Mac Clancy.

Chieftains: Ford (or Mac Consnava), Mac Shanley, O'Mulvey, O'Rodaghan.

No title designated: Mac Courty, Mac Dorchy, Mac Finnevar, Mac Gilmartin, Mac Gloin, Mac Gowan, Mac Kenny, Mac Keon, Mac Partlan, Mac Rannall (or Reynolds), Mac Teigue, O'Cuirneen, O'Finn.

LIMERICK:

Earl: Fitzgerald.

Viscount: O'Grady, Sarsfield.

Baron: Burke.

Knight: Fitzgerald.

Lords: Fitzgerald, De Lacy, Mac Eneiry, O'Brien, O'Connell, O'Donovan, O'Quinn.

LONDONDERRY:

Prince: O'Kane.

Lords: O'Conor, O'Quinn.

Chieftains: O'Brolchan, O'Carolan, O'Devlin, O'Freel, O'Hagarty, O'Mullen, O'Murray.

No title designated: Mac Connell, Mac Cracken, Mac Donnell, Mac Gilligan, Mac Loughlin, Mac Namee, Maginn, O'Cassidy, O'Criodan, O'Keenan, O'Mulligan, O'Quigly, O'Scullan.

LONGFORD:

Prince: O'Ferral.

Viscount: Fleming.

Chieftain: Mac Gilligan.

No title designated: Mac Conway, Mac Gavan, Mac Gilchrist, Mac Hugh, O'Higgin, O'Mulfinny, O'Ronan, O'Sheridan, O'Slevin, Tuite.

LOUTH:

Prince: O'Carroll.

Earl: Taaffe.

Baron: Plunkett.

Chieftains: O'Colman, O'Kelly, O'Scanlan.

No title designated: Barnwall, Bellew, De Birmingham, Clinton, Fleming, Mac Cann, O'Branagan, O'Coleman, O'Markey, Peppard.

MAYO:

King: O'Conor.

Prince: O'Dowd.

Baron: Browne, O'Hara, Taaffe.

Lords: Bourke, Mac Jordan, O'Hara, O'Malley, O'Murray, O'Tierney.

Chieftains: O'Bannan, O'Cahaney, O'Callaghan.

No title designated: Barrett, Browne, Cusack (O'Cisoghe), Fleming, Joyce, Lawless, Mac Aveely, Mac Costello, Mac Davett, Mac Garry, Mac Gavan, Mac Gereaghty, Mac Gibbon, Mac Greal, Mac Hale (Mac Cail), Mac Nally, Mac Nulty, Mac Phillips, Nagle, O'Birn, O'Bligh, O'Brody, O'Brogan, O'Connegan, O'Connellan, O'Conor, O'Cummin, O'Dogherty, O'Dolan, O'Donnell, O'Duffy, O'Dugan, O'Flannery, O'Gavagan, O'Gormly, O'Grady, O'Kearny, O'Keerin, O'Kerrigan, O'Killeen, O'Larrissey, O'Lavell, O'Lennon, O'Loghnan, O'Loughnan, O'Milford, O'Moghan, O'Moran, O'Mulleeny, O'Mulrenin, O'Mulroy, O'Quinn, O'Roddan, O'Ronan, O'Rothlan, O'Talcharan, O'Toole, Petit, Prendergast, Staunton, Synott.

MEATH:

King: O'Melaghlin.

Princes: O'Hart, O'Kelly, O'Kindellan, O'Regan, O'Rory.

Earl: Plunkett.

Barons: Barnwell, Bellew, Butler, Dalton, Fitz Eustace, Fleming, Hussey, Marward, Missett, Nangle, Netterville, Nugent, O'Scully.

Lords: De Geneville, De Mortimer, O'Connolly, O'Finnelan.

Chieftain: O'Duvan, O'Hea, O'Reilly.

No title designated: De Bathe, Betagh, Chevers, Cruise, Cusack (O'Cisoghe), Darcy, Dardis, Dillon, Dowdall, Drake, DeLacy, Langan, Mac Grane, O'Carolan, O'Flynn, O'Fox, O'Gogarty, O'Halligan, O'Murtagh, O'Traynor, Phepoe.

MONAGHAN:

Prince: Mac Mahon.

Earl: Devereux.

Lords: Mac Kenna, Mac Mahon.

Chieftains: Mac Ardell, Mac Cabe, Mac Donnell, Mac Gilmichael, Mac Oscar, O'Boylan, O'Connolly, O'Duffy.

No title designated: Hughes, Mac Gilroy, Mac Neney, Mac-Quade, O'Cassidy, O'Hoey, O'Marron, O'Neny.

QUEEN'S:

Princes: Fitzpatrick (Mac Gilpatrick), O'Moore.

Earl: Fitzgerald.

Lords: Mac Coghlan, O'Dempsey, De Vesey.

Chieftains: Mac Donnell, Mac Evoy, O'Dowling, O'Duff, O'Dunn, O'Harty, O'Kelly, O'Lawlor, O'Mooney, O'Regan.

No title designated: Grace, Mac Cogan, Mac Colreavy, O'Brogan.

ROSCOMMON:

King: O'Connor.

Princes: Mac Dermott, O'Kelly.

Earl: Dillon.

Lords: Mac Oiraghty, O'Feenaghty, O'Flannagan, O'Flynn, O'Glennon.

Chieftains: Mac Brennan, Mac Keogh, O'Beirne, O'Connelan, O'Hanley, O'Maol Conry, O'Monahan, O'Mulrenin, O'Norton.

No title designated: Conroy, French, MacDowell, Mac Manus, O'Conannon, O'Connor, O'Corr, O'Donnelan, O'Dugan, O'Duigennan, O'Fallon, O'Fihelly, O'Loman, O'Malbride, O'Meany, O'Moran, O'Molloy, O'Mulvihil.

SLIGO:

Princes: Mac Dermott, O'Donnell, O'Dowd.

Lords: Mac Donogh, O'Conor, O'Flannelly, O'Gara, O'Hara, O'Mulclohy.

Chieftains: O'Crean, O'Hart, O'Kernaghan.

No title designated: Mac Conway, Mac Firbis, Mac Geraghty, O'Brogan, O'Coleman, O'Conaghty, O'Delvin, O'Durkan, O'Feeney, O'Finegan, O'Gavagan, O'Howley, O'Keevan, O'Meehan, O'Mongan, O'Moran, O'Morrissey, O'Morrison, O'Moynagh, O'Mullany, O'Mulvany, O'Spillane.

TIPPERARY:

Kings: Mac Carthy, O'Brien, O'Callaghan.

Princes: O'Carroll, O'Donnegan, O'Donohoe, O'Mulcahy, O'Quinlevan.

Earl: Burke.

Barons: Butler, Purcell.

Lords: De Burgo, Burke, Mac-I-Brien, O'Brien, O'Dea, O'Dwyer, O'Kennedy, O'Meagher, O'Meehan, O'Morrissey, O'Ryan, O'Sullivan.

Chieftains: O'Breslin, O'Cahill, O'Corcoran, O'Cullenan, O'Donnelly, O'Hickey, O'Hogan, O'Kean, O'Lanigan, O'Lenahan, O'Lonergan, O'Quinlevan.

Brehon: Mac Egan.

No title designated: Burke, Butler, Cantwell, Fitzgerald, Grace, Mac Cormac, Mac Gilfoyle, Magrath, Mockler, Morris, O'Cuirc, O'Cullen, O'Dinan, O'Dinerty, O'Fogarty, O'Furey, O'Gleeson, O'Heffernan, O'Hurley, O'-Kearney, O'Lynch, O'Mackey, O'Malquiney, O'Quinlan, O'Scully, O'Sexton, O'Shea, O'Slattery, O'Spillan, Walsh, White.

TYRONE:

King, Prince, and Earl: O'Neill.

Lord: O'Laverty.

Chieftains: Mac Intyre, Mac Rory, Mac Shane, O'Connelan, O'Criocan, O'Donnegan, O'Donnelly, O'Duvany, O'Etigan, O'Hagan, O'Hamill, O'Hosey, O'Kelly, O'Lunney, O'Mellan, O'Neney, O'Quinn.

No title designated: Mac Breen, Mac Conmel, Mac Connell, Mac Coskley, Mac Court, Mac Crossan, Mac Golrick, Mac Owen, Mac Taggart, Maguire, O'Cooney, O'Corran, O'Crossan, O'Donlevy, O'Loan, O'Rafferty, O'Teigue, O'Tomalty.

WATERFORD:

Prince: O'Felan.

Baron: Fitzgerald.

Lords: O'Bric, Le Poer.

Chieftains: O'Baire, O'Brien, O'Conran, O'Crotty.

No title designated: Barron, Butler, Comerford, Dalton, Lombard, Magrath, Morris, O'Begley, O'Dennehy, O'Flahavan, O'Flannagan, O'Geary, O'Mullane, O'Mullany, Talbot, Wadding, Wall, Walsh, White, Wyse.

WEST MEATH:

Prince: O'Melaghlin.

Barons: Dillon, Petit, Tuite.

Lords: Mac Auley, Mac Evoy, Mac Geoghegan, Mac Ruarc, Nugent, O'Daly, O'Tolarg.

Chieftains: O'Carbery, O'Coffery, O'Dooley, O'Hanvey, O'Hennessy, O'Higgin, O'Kearney, O'Shiel.

No title designated: Dease, Fagan, Fitzsimon, De Lacey, De Lacy, De Lamaré, O'Casey, O'Corrigan, O'Curry, O'Fay, O'Fox, O'Hanrahan, O'Malone, O'Mulleady, O'Reilly, O'Sionagh, Tyrrell, De Verdon.

WEXFORD:

King: Mac Murrough.

Earls: Le Mareschal, Strongbow, Talbot.

Viscount: Butler.

Lords: O'Cavanagh, O'Larkin, O'Murphy.

Chieftains: O'Cosgry, O'Dugan, O'Garvey.

Brehon: O'Doran.

No title designated: Browne, Butler, Colclough, Devereux, Fitzgerald, Fitzharris, Fitzhenry, Fitzstephen, French, Furlong, Hay, Hore, Keating, Laffan, Mac Keogh, Masterson, Meyler, De Montmorency, Morgan, O'Doyle, De Prendergast, Redmond, Rossiter, Sinnott, Stafford, Sutton, Wadding, Walsh.

WICKLOW:

Princes: Mac Murrough, O'Toole.

Viscount: Fitz Eustace.

Baron: Butler.

Lords: Fitzgerald, Fitzwilliam, O'Byrne, O'Gahan.

Chieftains: O'Cullen, O'Dowling, O'Doyle, O'Kelly.

No title designated: Archbold, Cheevers, Furlong, Hughes, O'Horan, O'Teige, (or Tighe), Talbot, Walsh.

* * * * *

The first book of reference regarding all families of the above period should be the standard and most complete dictionary of nomenclature of 696 pages. This is *Sloinnte Gaedheal is Gall* (Irish Names and Surnames), by the Rev. Patrick Woulfe, Dublin, 1923. His introduction (pp. vii-xlvi), and his explanation in Part I, "The Irish Name-System", have to do with the evolution of Gaelic surnames of tribes and their branching septs (also given names), with notes on Norman and English influence. The dictionary is arranged by family names, under which are presented the origin, evolution, and history of each Gaelic-Irish, Norman, and English surname, with all varieties of spelling, and with brief notes on each family.

For the advanced student, *Analecta Hibernica,* No. 7, published by the Irish Manuscripts Commission (1935), contains "A Guide to Irish Genealogical Collections," by Séamus Pender. This is a coded Index in Gaelic of the principal ancient and medieval manuscripts in Great Britain and Ireland, ranging from the Laud genealogies of the 8th century to the 18th and 19th century collections of transcripts, etc. *Analecta Hibernica,* No. 1, contains "Reports on the Manuscripts in the Bodleian Library, Oxford" (pp. 1-179), which are filled with items of interest to Roman Catholic families. On pp. 118-119 is a description of a collection of 602 coats of arms of Irish families, entitled "A Collection of the Armes of the Ierish Gentrie" of some date prior to 1681. *Analecta Hibernica* No. 2 (pp. 1-92) continues the "Report on Manuscripts in the Bodleian Library, Oxford" (Rawlinson Collection), and presents "Manuscripts of Irish Interest in the British Museum" (pp. 292-329).

Catalogues of records and printed material are listed in VOLUME II, pp. 199-201. *A Catalogue of the Bradshaw Col-*

lection of Irish Books in the University Library Cambridge, 3 Vols., 1916, is a catalogue of 8,743 books printed in Dublin, 1602-1882. These contain a wealth of material of Roman Catholic interest.

The Carte Manuscripts in the Bodleian Library, Oxford, by C. W. Russell, London, 1871, is a catalogue of the Ormonde MSS. dated largely 1641-1689. One collection of letters of Charles II, contains 1,083 items (pp. 199-231), regarding appointments, and grants restoring estates to Roman Catholics, etc.

Some particularly helpful publications are as follows:

Blake-Foster, Charles French. *Irish Chieftains.* Dublin, 1872.

Census of Ireland, 1871: Part I. Area, houses, and population; also ages, civil condition, occupations, birthplaces, religion and education of people. Vol. I, Province of Leinster (1355 pp.) ; Vol. II, Province of Munster (1157 pp.) ; Vol. III, Province of Ulster (1127 pp.) ; Vol. IV, Province of Connaught (745 pp.).

D'Alton, John. *Illustrations Historical and Genealogical of King James's Irish Army List* (1689). 2nd edition enlarged. 2 Volumes, Dublin, 1860. Contains memoirs of 500 families of the ancient aristocracy of Ireland.

Finegan, Rev. Francis. "Irish Catholic Convert Rolls." *Studies,* Vol. 38, pp. 73-82.

Fitzpatrick, J. W. History of the Dublin Catholic Cemeteries. 1900.

Freeman, A. Martin, *ed. The Compossicion Booke of Conought,* Dublin, 1936-1942. 2 Vols. 1585 A.D. records of family property.

Hill, Rev. George. *An Historical Account of the Plantation of Ulster . . . 1608-1620,* Belfast, 1877. Contains copious notes on the early native families, and a list of the natives with details of property granted to them by James I.

Keating, Geoffry. *A General History of Ireland . . .* Illustrated with above One Hundred and Sixty Coats of Arms of the Ancient Irish, with Particular Genealogies of Many

Noble Families . . . Third Edition, London, 1738. See also other works of Keating.

Leadbeater, Mary. *Cottage Biography; being a Collection of Lives of the Irish Peasantry.* Dublin, 1822.

Lecky, W.E.H. *A History of Ireland in the Eighteenth Century.* London, 1892. Five volumes.

McDowell, R. B. "The Personnel of the Dublin Society of the United Irishmen, 1791-1794, with a List of 425 Persons, Addresses and Occupations . . ." *Irish Historical Studies,* Vol. II, No. 5 (March 1940), pp. 12-53.

Madden, Richard R. *The United Irishmen, their Lives and Times.* London, 1842-1846. Seven volumes.

Moran, Patrick, Cardinal. *Historical Sketch of the Persecutions suffered by the Catholics of Ireland under the Rule of Cromwell and the Puritans.* Dublin, 1884. See also Moran's *The Catholics of Ireland under the Penal Laws in the Eighteenth Century.* London, 1900.

Murray, R. H. *Revolutionary Ireland and its Settlement* (the War of 1689-1691, and William III's Reign). London, 1911.

O'Connell, Daniel. "A Dublin Convert Roll: the Diary of the Rev. P. E. O'Farrelly." *Ecclesiastical Record,* Vol. lxxi, pp. 533-535; lxxii, pp. 27-36. 1949.

O'Domhnaill, Seán. "Index of Persons for County Donegal from the Catholic Qualification Rolls, 1778-1790." *Journal of the County Donegal Historical Society,* Volume I, No. 3, pp. 204-206.

O'Donovan, John. *Tribes and Customs of Hy-Many (O'Kelly's Country),* Dublin, 1843.

O'Donovan, John. *Tribes and Customs of Hy-Fiachrach.* Dublin, 1844.

O'Rahilly, T. F. *Early Irish History and Mythology.* Dublin, 1946.

Roman Catholic Directories: See CHAPTER X.

Ronan, Rev. Myles V. *The Irish Martyrs of the Penal Laws.* London, 1935.

Simms, J. G.   *The Williamite Confiscation in Ireland.*   London, 1956.

* * * * *

O'Farrell's *Linea Antiqua,* a great manuscript collection of genealogies compiled from early Annals, is in the Genealogical Office, Dublin Castle, together with Sir William Betham's enlarged edition of O'Farrell's work.

For special collections of Roman Catholic records which are classed under State Papers and Court Records, see CHAPTER XI.

PARISH REGISTERS

All Roman Catholic Parish Registers are in local custody. The National Library of Ireland, since July 1950, has been engaged in microfilming the Parish Registers in the Republic of Ireland, under the direction of Dr. Richard J. Hayes, Director. They are called in parish by parish until all of one diocese are filmed.   So far (January 1960) all Parish Registers of sixteen dioceses are microfilmed.   The dioceses are: (1) Achonry; (2) Ardagh and Clonmacnoise; (3) Cashel and Emly; (4) Clonfert; (5) Elphin; (6) Ferns; (7) Galway; (8) Kerry; (9) Kildare and Leiglin; (10) Killala; (11) Killaloe; (12) Limerick; (13) Meath; (14) Raphoe; (15) Tuam; (16) Waterford and Lismore.   This leaves unfinished only six dioceses in the Republic of Ireland, which are (1) Cork; (2) Cloyne and Ross; (3) Dublin; (4) Kilmacduagh and Kilfenora; (5) Kilmore; (6) Ossory.   A manuscript Index of the microfilmed records is compiled and, when the work is completed, it will be printed.   It is compiled by diocese and contains the list of Registers of each parish with the inclusive dates of the records.   The films are not available to the public. Inquiries for searching the films of any Parish Registers may be sent to Mr. Gerard Slevin (Chief Herald), Genealogical Office, Dublin Castle, Dublin.

In 1953, Dr. Hayes stated, "The dates of the records in the Catholic Parish Registers vary greatly.   I notice that they tend to be earlier in the good farmland areas, like Tipperary, than in the poorer districts.   They are also earlier in towns than in the purely agricultural areas. In the larger towns (about 5,000 population upwards) they generally begin about 1790. In the still larger towns (about 25,000 population upwards) they begin about 1750, and some earlier. In the good agricultural areas, about 1820. In the poorer districts, about 1835-1840. These latter have the more numerous parishes. These are average figures but you don't get a wide variation from them."

The Registers include Baptismal and Marriage records only. The old Parish Registers of parishes in the City of Dublin contain records beginning as follows:

Parish	Baptisms	Marriages
St. Mary's Pro-Cathedral, 83 Marlborough St.	April, 1734	April, 1734
St. Andrew's, Westland Row	January, 1742	January, 1742
St. Audeon's, High St. (old Bridge-Street)	October, 1778	February, 1746
St. Catherine's, Meath St.	May, 1740	May, 1740
St. James's, 86 James St.	September, 1752	September, 1752
SS. Michael and John, Lower Exchange St.	January, 1742	January, 1742
St. Michan's, Halston St. (old N. Anne St.)	February, 1725	February, 1725
St. Nicholas Without, Francis St.	January, 1742	Missing
St. Paul's, Arran Quay	January, 1731	January, 1731

* * * * *

Thom's Irish Almanac, 1847 (4th annual), pp. 318-339, contains an Ecclesiastical Directory of the Roman Catholic Church. Under the provinces and dioceses, all churches are listed with their town locations, names of their parish priests, curates. The names of the archbishops of the provinces and bishops of the dioceses are given with the dates of consecration. The churches number 1,040. This list provides information as to the existing churches at the time of greatest emigration. Until the National Library of Ireland list of Parish Registers is printed, *Thom's Irish Almanac,* 1847, indicates the Registers which were probably in existence. Other Almanacs may serve much the same purpose.

Following is a list of Parish Registers of the Roman Catholic dioceses included in the Province of Ulster, which list is in the Public Record Office of Northern Ireland, Belfast, and is contributed by Mr. Kenneth Darwin, Deputy Keeper.

PARISH RECORDS OF THE ROMAN CATHOLIC CHURCH OF IRELAND PRESENTLY IN LOCAL CUSTODY IN NORTHERN IRELAND

(Listed by Diocese)

These records are from the date listed to the present time except for missing dates.

Parish	Diocese	Town & County	Baptisms	Marriages	Dates Missing
Armagh	Armagh	Armagh	1796-	1806-	bap. 9/29/-12/17/1797. m. Oct. 1810-Jan. 1817.
Ardboe	Armagh	Stewartstown, Co. Tyrone	1827-	1827-	Fairly complete.
Ardee	Armagh	Co. Louth	1763-		Complete to 1802, fairly so to 1812, imperfect to 1815, blank to 1821.
Ardtrea	Armagh	Moneymore Londonderry	1832-	1830-	1843-1854 & 1869-1900.
Ballinderry	Armagh	Cookstown, Co. Tyrone	1826-	1826-	m. Mar. 1839-Sept. 1841.
Ballymore & Mullabrack	Armagh	Tanderagee, Co. Armagh	1843-	1843-	b. Nov. 1856-June, 1859. m. Oct. 1856-July, 1859.
Carlingford	Armagh	Carlingford, Omeath, Co. Louth	1835-	1835-	
Clogherhead	Armagh	Clogherhead, Drogheda, Co. Louth	1744- (Deaths, 1744-1799)	1744-	1777-1780 (bap. & m.) bap. Jan. 12,-May 15, 1783; 1799-1833. m. Feb. 12, 1782- May 18, 1783; 1799-1833.
Creggaun (Upper)	Armagh	Crossmaglen, Co. Armagh	1796-	1796-	(b. & m.)-Jan. 1803- Dec. 1812.
Dundalk	Armagh	Dundalk, Co. Louth	1790- (Deaths, 1790-1802)	1790-	
Donaghmore	Armagh	Donaghmore, Co. Tyrone	1837-	1837-	

Parish	Diocese	Town & County	Baptisms	Marriages	Dates Missing
Dromintee	Armagh	Jonesboro', Newry, Co. Down	1853-	1853-	Entries missing throughout.
Drumcree	Armagh	Portadown, Co. Armagh	1844-	1844-	bap., incomplete in 1845 and last quarter of 1871. m. incomplete in 1844 and 1845, also from Aug. 1871-July 1872.
Dunleer	Armagh	Co. Louth	1798-	1798-	
Errigal, Kieran	Armagh	Ballygawley, Co. Tyrone	1834-	1834-	Incomplete, 1884-1905. for bapt.; no entries 1894-1898, for m.
Killevey, Upper.	Armagh	Newry, Co. Down	1832-	1832-	
Knockbridge,	Armagh	Knockbridge, Dundalk, Co. Louth.	1858-	1858-	Bap. 1869-1882. & 1888-1895. m., same.
Lordship & Ballymascalon	Armagh	Ravensdale, Dundalk, Co. Louth.	1837-	1837-	
Magherafelt	Armagh	Magherafelt, Co. Londonderry	1834-	1834-	Some missing; but for no periods.
Togher	Armagh	Dunlear, Co. Louth.	1791-	1791-	Almost complete.
Tullyallen	Armagh	Tullyallen, Co. Louth.	1821-	1821-	
Aughnamullen	Clogher	Latton, Co. Monaghan	1835-	1836-	Register complete; many names missing.
Carrickmacross	Clogher	Carrickmacross, Co. Monaghan	1858-	1839-	bap. 1873-78. m. 1843-58.
Clontibret	Clogher	Clontibret, Co. Monaghan	1860-	1861-	
Devenish, Derrygonnely	Clogher	Belleek, Co. Fermanagh	1853-	1853-	Some omissions.
Donacavey	Clogher	Fintona, Co. Tyrone	1857-	1857-	
Donaghmoyne	Clogher	Carrickmacross, Co. Monaghan	9/8/1854-1/30/1863		bap. Jan. 9, 1858-May 19, 1863; Jan. 1878-Sept. 16, 1879. m. 11/6/1879-11/7/1863.
Dromore	Clogher	Dromore, Co. Tyrone	1835-	1833-	
Enniskillen	Clogher	Co. Fermanagh	1838-	1838-	Some omissions.

Parish	Diocese	Town & County	Baptisms	Marriages	Dates Missing
Errigal Trough	Clogher	Emyvale, Co. Monaghan	1835-	1837-	bap. 1853-61. m. 1849-62.
Garrison	Clogher	Garrison, Co. Fermanagh	1860-	1860-	
Innismacsaint	Clogher	Bundoran, Co. Donegal	1846-	1846-	
Killanny	Clogher	Ballymacney, Dundalk, Co. Louth	1835-	1824-	bap. 1844-57. m. 1836-62.
Killeevan	Clogher	Newbliss, Co. Monaghan	1851-	1851-	bap. some missing, 1851-1873. m. 1851-73.
Kilmore & Drumsnatt	Clogher	Stranooden, Co. Monaghan	1835-	1835-	
Kilskerry	Clogher	Trillick, Co. Tyrone	1842-	1842-	Practically complete.
Magheracloone	Clogher	Carrickmacross, Co. Monaghan	1836-	1826-	
Muckno	Clogher	Castleblaney, Co. Monaghan	1835-	1835-	
Pettigo	Clogher	Magheramena, Co. Monaghan	1851-	1836-	bap. Occasional omissions. m. 1884-1892.
Tempo	Clogher	Co. Fermanagh	1845-	1845-	
Tullycorbett	Clogher	Ballybay, Co. Monaghan	1862-	1862-	
Tydavnet	Clogher	Scotstown, Co. Monaghan	1835-	1825-	
Badoney, Lower	Derry	Gortin, Co. Tyrone	1865-	1865-	bap. many names missing. m. same.
Burt & Inch	Derry	Lifford, Co. Donegal	1858-	1858-	Fairly complete.
Clonleigh & Camus	Derry	Strabane, Co. Tyrone	1774-	1778-	bap. 1795-1836, & 1837-1853. m. 1779-1843.
Clonmany	Derry	Clonmany, Lifford, Co. Donegal	1852-	1829-	m. 1829-1852; imperfect.
Desertegny & Fahan (Lower)	Derry	Buncrana, Co. Donegal	1864-	1871-	bap. 1864-72.
Desertmartin	Derry	Desertmartin, Co. Londonderry	1848-	1848-	

Parish	Diocese	Town & County	Baptisms	Marriages	Dates Missing
Drumragh (Drumrath)	Derry	Omagh, Co. Tyrone	1846-	1846-	**1848-1858.**
Dungiven	Derry	Dungiven, Co. Londonderry	1825-	**1830-**	
Errigle (Errigol)	Derry	Garvagh, Co. Londonderry	1846-	1872-	
Kilrea	Derry	Co. Londonderry	**1846-**	**1846-**	
Leckpatrick	Derry	Ballmagory, Strabane, Co. Tyrone	1869-	1869-	
Maghera	Derry	Co. Londonderry	1841- (Deaths,	1841- 1841-)	
Termoneeny	Derry	Knockloghrim, Co. Londonderry	1837-	1837-	**bap. Aug. 1839- Apr. 1852. m. same.**
Urney	Derry	Castlederg, Co. Tyrone	1866-	1866-	
St. Peter's	Down	Belfast, Co. Antrim	1866-	1866-	
St. Columbcille	Down	Belfast, Co. Antrim	1906-	1906-	
St. Malachy's	Down	Belfast, Co. Antrim	1858-	1858-	
St. Paul's	Down	Belfast, Co. Antrim	1887-	1887-	
Blaris (Lisburn)	Down	Co. Antrim	1840-	1840-	**bap. July, 1854- March, 1855. m. Same.**
Bright	Down	Killough, Co. Down	1856-	1856-	
Down	Down	Downpatrick, **Co. Down**	1851-	1852-	**m. only one entry, viz. Feb. 16th in 1852.**
Holywood	Down	Holywood, Co. Down	1866-	1867-	
Loughinisland	Down	Co. Down	1806- (Funerals,	1806- 1806)	
Newtownards	Down	Co. Down	1856-	1855-	
Saintfield	Down	Ballygowan, Co. Down	1837-	1845-	**m. 1848-1853.**
Antrim	Connor	Co. Antrim	1873-	1873-	
Carnlough (St. John)	Connor	Co. Antrim	1869-	1869-	**m. 6/21/1878- 10/12/1879.**

Parish	Diocese	Town & County	Baptisms	Marriages	Dates Missing
Cushendall	Connor	Co. Antrim	1837-	1835-	bap. Apr., 1837-Jan., 1858. m. May, 1844-Mar. 1860.
Greencastle	Connor	Belfast, Co. Antrim	1854-	1854-	
Kirkinriola (Ballymena)	Connor	Co. Antrim	1836-	1836-	bap. Aug. 1842-Jan. 1848. m. Same.
Portglenone	Connor	Portglenone, Co. Antrim	1864-	1864-	
Randalstown	Connor	Co. Antrim	1825-	1825-	bap. 1868-Oct. 1872; 8/5/1855-3/24/1856. m. May, 1867-Oct. 1872.
Rathlin Island	Connor	Co. Antrim	1856-	1857-	
Aghaderg	Dromore	Loughbrickland, Co. Down	1816- (Deaths, 1843-)	1816-	bap. 9/23/1817-12/31/1818.
Clonallon	Dromore	Warrenpoint, Co. Down	1826-	1826-	
Drumgoolan (Lower)	Dromore	Gargory, Banbridge, Co. Down	1832-	1832-	
Drumgoolan (Upper)	Dromore	Leitrim, Banbridge Co. Down	1827- (Funerals, 1828)	1827-	
Dromore	Dromore	Co. Down	1822- (Funerals, 1821)	1821-	Practically complete.
Drumgath	Dromore	Barmeen, Rathfriland, Co. Down	1829-	1837-	
Donoughmore	Dromore	Donaghmore, Newry, Co. Down	1835-	1825-	
Lurgan (Shankhill)	Dromore	Lurgan, Co. Antrim	1822-	1849-	bap. 1851-1866. m. 1849-1866.
Seagoe	Dromore	Derrymacash, Lurgan, Co. Antrim	1836-	1836-	bap. Oct. 1837-Dec. 19, 1837.

CHAPTER X

DIRECTORIES AND ALMANACS

Directories provide considerable help in tracing the names and localities of people and, to a large extent, specify their addresses. Within the scope of each directory is presented the names of all who filled Government offices; local political offices; peers of the realm; the nobility and gentry; the clergy of all denominations; professional men, and officers of their organizations; the officers of universities, colleges, and public institutions; officers of the army, navy, militia; masters and mistresses of local schools; publishers, etc.; officers of commercial and miscellaneous institutions; and a full list of merchants, traders, innkeepers, manufacturers on a large or small individual scale within the area covered by the directory. Thus all but the small farmers, apprentices and servants appear to be listed. Almanacs include all of these lists except the local merchants, traders, etc.

Undoubtedly, the most complete collection of directories and almanacs is in the National Library of Ireland. It also has microfilmed copies of the rare works. Numerous miscellaneous directories and almanacs are listed in the *National Library of Ireland Bibliography of Irish History, 1870-1911*, by James Carty, Dublin, 1940, under "Works of Reference," pp. 1-9. Other important libraries described in PART TWO, CHAPTER III, herein, have collections of various sizes and scope. The collections in the Linen Hall Library, Belfast, and the Public Record Office of Northern Ireland, Belfast, will be enumerated below to illustrate this. Some of the more important directories and almanacs are listed in the accompanying VOLUME II, pp. 229-231.

Guides to almanacs and directories are as follows: (1) Dennan, Joseph. "The First Hundred Years of the Dublin Directory," published in the *Bibliographical Society of Ireland Publications*, Volume I, No. 7. (2) Evans, Edward. *Historical and Bibliographical Account of Almanacks, Directo-*

ries, etc., published in *Ireland from the Sixteenth Century*. Dublin, 1897. (3) Guinness, H. S. "Dublin Directories, 1751-1760." In *Irish Book Lover*, Volume 14, pp. 84-86.

*   *   *   *   *

Dublin, south of Ireland, and general directories:

Wilson's *Dublin Directory* is the earliest for this city. It began in 1751 and was issued annually, except for the years 1754-1759, until 1837. *The Gentleman's and Citizen's Almanack*, published for John Watson and later compiled by John Watson Stewart, began publication in Dublin in 1736, and continued to 1844. Wilson's *Directory* and Watson's *Almanack* were also combined in one publication with an *English Court Directory*, called *The Treble Almanack*. These formed a sort of "Who's Who" for Ireland and England, and with more complete lists in the directory for Dublin. They were bound handsomely in red leather for the desks of the nobility, gentry, etc.

A brief description of the information under various subject headings in the three parts of *The Treble Almanack*, 1816 and later (nearly 700 pp.), is as follows:

I. *The Gentleman's and Citizen's Almanack*, compiled by John Watson Stewart. Lists of chief Governors of Ireland from 1711, Archbishops, Marquises, Earls, Viscounts, Bishops, Barons, Peeresses, Index to the Peers of Ireland, Titles usually borne by the eldest sons of peers, Officers of the Office of Arms. Members of Parliament from the several Counties, Cities and Boroughs in Ireland (including many family relationships, and their other offices), followed by an alphabetical list. Baronets of Ireland from the year 1619, and Knights of St. Patrick. State Officers, and Governors of Counties. Officers of the Court of Chancery, King's Bench, Common Pleas, Court of Exchequer, Crown Solicitors, and officers of various minor and local courts, Magistrates and Sheriffs. Assistant Barristers, Clerks of the Crown and Peace, Treasurers, Secretaries to Grand Juries, and Coroners of the several Counties and Towns of Ireland. Commissioners of Affidavits for the high courts listed by their county of office and residence. Members of the Law

Club, instituted in 1791. Judges and Proctors of the Prerogative Court of Dublin. Archbishops, Archdeacons, Deans, Vicars General, and Registers of the several Dioceses in Ireland. Military Department: Governors of Forts and Garrisons, officers of various departments and branches of the service (Artillery, Cavalry, Infantry, Militia, etc.). Revenue Collectors, Bankers in Ireland by Counties and in Dublin. Dublin City Officers; Common Council; Officers of the Guilds (Trinity, Tailors, Smiths, Barbers, Bakers, Butchers, Carpenters, Shoemakers, Sadlers, Cooks, Tanners, Tallow-Chandlers, Glovers and Skinners, Weavers, Sheermen and Dyers, Goldsmiths, Coopers, Feltmakers, Cutlers, Bricklayers, Hosiers, Curriers, Brewers, Joiners, and Apothecaries). Police of Dublin. Commissioners of various Departments. Officers of Trinity College; King's and Queen's College of Physicians; Royal College of St. Patrick, Maynooth; School of Physic; Royal College of Surgeons in Ireland, and School of Surgery. Practicing Physicians in Dublin, and Apothecaries. Officers and members of various historical and other societies. Officers of various schools, hospitals, institutions, charities, and prisons.

II. The *English Registry* (215 pp.) : Includes a collection of lists of Monarchs, Peers, Nobility, Members of Parliament, Principal Officers of State, etc.

III. *Wilson's Dublin Directory* (220 pp.) : Contains an alphabetical list of the Judges, Barristers, Attorneys, Solicitors, Advocates, Proctors, Public-Notaries, Bankers, Physicians, Surgeons, Dentists, etc. with addresses. A list of the Nobility and Gentry of Dublin with their street addresses (pp. 17-39). A list of the Merchants and Traders, with their trades, and street addresses (pp. 39-138). Pawnbrokers, with street addresses (pp. 174-175). King's and Queen's College Physicians, Practicing Physicians, etc. Royal College of Surgeons, and practicing Surgeons with street addresses. Ministers, Curates, and Church Wardens, etc. Masters, Wardens and Clerks of the 25 Guilds. The Common Council of Dublin, including representatives from the 25 Guilds. Licentiates practicing in Dublin (Roman Catholic Clergy), and various miscellaneous lists.

John Ferrar's *Limerick Directory* was published in 1769. A copy is in the Limerick Public Library. Richard Lucas published *Lucas' Directory of Cork, and south-east towns, Youghal to Kinsale,* 1787; 1821.   He also published the *General Directory of Ireland,* 1788.   This covers 27 towns of the south half of Ireland, excepting those in his 1787 *Directory.*   These two directories of Lucas, being rare, are microfilmed by the National Library of Ireland.   James Haly published a *Directory of Cork,* 1795.   John Connor followed with a *Directory of Cork, ca.* 1820-1830.

Ambrose Leet's *A Directory to the Market Towns, Villages, Gentlemen's Seats, and other Noted Places in Ireland,* 1814, was one of the first general directories for all of Ireland. This was followed by Pigot's *Commercial Directory of Ireland, Scotland, etc.,* 1820.   This was continued in 1824, by Pigot and Company, which published *The City of Dublin and Hibernian Provincial Directory,* (enlarged).   Pettigrew and Oulton followed with a *Dublin Directory* (names arranged by streets and houses), 1834.   The *Dublin Almanac and General Register of Ireland* appeared in 1838.   *The New Commercial Directory of Kilkenny,* 1839, includes Waterford, Kilkenny, Clonmel, Carrick-on-Suir, New Ross and Carlow.   Then came MacCabe's *Directory of Drogheda,* 1830.   I. Slater (Late Pigot and Company) published in 1846 and at intervals as late as 1881, *The National Commercial Directory of Ireland.* It includes all cities, and market and post towns of Ireland. This will be described in more detail below.   *The King's County Directory,* 1890, includes some family history.

Thom's Irish Almanac and Official Directory, published from 1844, annually until 1915, lists all members of Parliament, the Irish Peerage, Baronets, Officers of the Army, Navy, Militia.   Members of Government Departments, all County Officers; members of professional organizations and the professions of law, medicine, surgery, bankers, etc.   The clergy of all denominations are listed under the Churches, and the dioceses, towns, and districts, according to the Church ecclesiastical organization.   Officers of universities, colleges, schools, etc., are also named.   In fact, the lists cover all but the gentry who filled no public or professional place, the tradesmen, small farmers, and the lower classes.

I. Slater's *National Commercial Directory of Ireland*, 1846, contains an Index to the Provinces, Counties, and the Cities, Post and Market Towns of Ireland. The *Directory* is arranged under the four provinces. The City of Dublin lists are set forth in the Leinster section (pp. 25-248). Each city, post and market town is represented with a list of its nobility, gentry and clergy. Members of all professions and trades are listed separately except under the smallest towns for which they are grouped alphabetically with their occupations designated. In addition, for Dublin, Belfast, and Limerick, there is an "Alphabetical Directory" of the city and its suburbs, containing the names, occupation and address of every man listed in the classified section. Also included at the back of the volume are classified directories of the principal merchants, manufacturers, and traders of seven English cities and of Glasgow and Paisley, Scotland.

Under the Irish cities and towns, the number and variety of trades is in proportion to the size of each. The market town of Omagh, County Tyrone, having a population of 2,947 in 1841, serves as a good example to illustrate how the people are classified. Following a half page description of the town, the names and addresses of men are listed under Gentry and Clergy (no nobility), Academies and Schools, Agents, Apothecaries, Attorneys, Bakers, Banks, Blacksmiths, Bookseller and Stationer, Boot and Shoe Makers, Builder, Butchers, Cabinet Makers and Upholsterers, Carpenters, China and Glass and Earthen Ware Dealers, Coach and Car Makers, Commissioners (for taking Affidavits), Confectioners, Coopers, Fire and Office Agents, Grocers, Haberdashers, Hotel Keepers, Ironmongers and Hardwaremen, Leather Sellers, Linen and Woolen Drapers, Milleners and Dress Makers, Newspaper (also day of publication, name of the proprietor, editor and publisher), Painters and Glaziers, Pawnbrokers, Physicians and Surgeons, Plumbers, Printers, Saddlers and Harness Makers, Spirit and Porter Dealers, Straw Bonnet Makers, Tailors, Tallow Chandlers, Tanners, Timber Merchants, Tobacco Manufacturers, Watch and Clock Makers, Whitesmiths, Wine and Spirit Merchants, Woolen Drapers. Miscellaneous occupations include Supervisor of Excise, Deputy

Crown Clerk, Linen Manufacturer, Accountant, Architect, Auctioneer, Clothes Broker, Surveyor, Inspector of Weights and Measures, Gun Maker. Five places of Worship are listed with names of the rectors, curates, and ministers. Officers are listed for the Infirmary, Fever Hospital, Union Workhouse, and County Gaol. The day, hour and place of the departure of Coaches and Cars is stated for travel to Dublin, Dungannon, Enniskillen, Londonderry, and Belfast. A total of 320 names are listed.

*   *   *   *   *

Ulster Almanacs and Directories:

Ulster cities and towns are included in the above general works. *A Directory for Sligo, Enniskillen, etc.,* was published in 1839. Charles MacLoskie published a *Handbook or Directory for the County of Fermanagh,* 1848. Otherwise the directories of Northern Ireland are of Belfast alone, or Belfast and the Province of Ulster. Good collections of the existing directories are enumerated in the two following lists:

The Belfast Library and Society for Promoting Knowledge (Linen Hall Library), Catalogue of the Books in the Irish Section, Belfast, 1917 (Donegall Square North), contains its lists of Almanacs and Directories (pp. 5, 18, 20, 68, 73):

Almanacks (p. 5): Eason (C.) Almanac for Ireland for 1877; Evans (E.) Historical and bibliographical account of almanacks, directories, etc. 1897.

Belfast Almanacs (p. 18):
Annual Belfast almanack for 1827-1828. Belfast. n.d.
Belfast almanack for the years 1770-1775; 1777; 1779-1781; 1788-1790; 1803-1817; 1819-1877; 1880-1887; 1889; 1892-1893. Belfast, n.d.
Belfast memorandum book for 1820. Belfast, n.d.
Belfast predictions, 1791. Belfast, n.d.
The Belfast prognostication, 1782, 1783, 1792, and 1794. n.d.
Belfast temperance almanack, 1836. Belfast, n.d.
Belfast town and county almanacks for 1793; 1795; 1803; 1804; 1806-1810; 1813-1815; 1818; 1819; 1822; 1824-1826; 1828; 1829. Belfast, n.d.

The Belfast town and county prognostication, 1813, 1816-1817. Belfast, n.d.

Farmer's pocket companion for 1812. n.d.

Henderson's commercial Belfast almanac, 1850. n.d.

M'Comb (W.) Presbyterian almanack for 1840-1889.

M'Gee's family almanack, 1864. n.d.

The Parent's; or, Sabbath-School Teacher's almanack, 1836. n.d.

Simms and M'Intyre's Northern; or Belfast almanack, 1836-1840. n.d.
Tradesman and farmer's guide; or, Improved pocket-book for 1827. n.d.
The Ulster calendar of persons and events. Edited by A. Riddell. 1911.

Belfast Directories (p. 20) :

Adair (H.) Belfast directory for 1860-1861. 1860.

Belfast and district directory and Ulster guide for 1878. n.d.

Belfast and district trades directory, 1899, 1904, 1907, 1909-1916. 7 vol. n.d.

Belfast and Province of Ulster directory for 1852; 1854; 1856; 1858; 1861; 1863-1866; 1868; 1877; 1880; 1884; 1887; 1892-1915. Henderson, Belfast.

Belfast and Province of Ulster Post-Office directory and official guide, 1870. Newsletter Office, Belfast, 1870.

Belfast and Ulster trades directory, 1905; 1908. n.d.

Belfast directory for 1806-1808, Smyth and Lyons. Belfast, n.d.

Belfast directory for 1831-1832. Donaldson, Belfast, n.d.

Bradshaw (T.) Belfast general and commercial directory for 1819. With a directory and history of Lisburn. Finlay, Belfast, 1819. [Includes a secondary list arranged by trades.]

Business directory of Belfast and principal towns in Ulster, 1865-1866. Wynne, Belfast, 1865.

Henderson's Belfast directory, 1846-1847; 1852.

Martin's Belfast directory, 1839-1842.

Matier's Belfast directory, 1835-1836.

Post-Office Belfast annual directory, 1843-1844. Wilson, Belfast, 1843.

Smyth (J.) Directory to Belfast and its vicinity. 1819.

Directories (p. 68) :
   Commercial directory for Ireland, Scotland, etc. 1820.
   Leet (A.) Directory to the market towns, villages, gentle-
      men's seats and other noted places in Ireland. 1814.
   Slater's directory of Ireland. 1881.
   Thom's Official directory, 1845-1915 (Wants: 1857, 1867,
      1873, 1894).

Dublin (City and County) Almanacs and Directories (p. 73) :
   Dublin almanac and General register of Ireland, 1838.
      Dublin, n.d.
   Eason (C.) Almanac for Ireland, 1885.
   Gentleman's and Citizen's almanack, 1758, 1759, 1760,
      1761, 1765, 1766, 1768, 1778, 1782, 1789, 1790, 1792,
      1795, 1796, 1798, 1805, 1806, 1809, 1812, 1813, 1814,
      1817, 1818, 1819, 1820, and 1822. n.d.
   Irish Merlin; or, Gentleman's almanack, 1796, 1799. n.d.
   MS. Book, 1671, containing information evidently copied
      from the Dublin almanac.
   Wilson's Dublin directory for 1766, 1768, 1778, 1783,
      1789, 1790, 1792, 1796, 1798, 1805, 1806, 1809, 1813,
      1814, 1817, 1818, 1819, 1820, 1822, 1829. n.d.

* * * * *

The Public Record Office of Northern Ireland, Belfast: The
following list of almanacs and directories on the shelves of
the Search Room was obtained by this compiler in October,
1955. The list is arranged according to the publication date,
or the earliest date of a series. Subject matter of dates later
than 1900 is not noted.

   Dublin Almanacs from 1744 (some early volumes mis-
      sing).
   Leet, Ambrose. A Directory to the Market Towns, Vil-
      lages, Gentleman's Seats, and other Noted Places in Ire-
      land, 1814.
   Belfast Directories from 1819 (some early volumes mis-
      sing). Trades, etc., lists included.
   MS. copy of Directory of Armagh, Lurgan, Markethill,
      Portadown, and Tanderagee, 1819.
   Bradshaw, T. Belfast General and Commercial Directory
      for 1819. With a Directory and History of Lisburn.
      2 vols. Belfast, 1819. This includes a secondary list
      arranged by trades, manufacturers, occupation, etc.

Pigot's Provincial Directory, Belfast and Provincial Towns, 1824. Includes lists by trades, manufacturers, occupation, etc., with names and addresses.

Matier's Belfast Directory, 1835. Includes lists as above.

New Directory for Sligo, Enniskillen, etc., 1839.

Martin's Belfast Directory, 1841. Includes lists as above.

Belfast Directories, 1842-1843; 1846-1847; 1849; 1850, with lists as above.

Henderson's Belfast Directory, 1852, with lists as above.

Belfast Directory (Newsletter Office), Belfast 1852, with lists as above.

Belfast and Province of Ulster Directory (Newsletter Office), Vol. 2, 1854.

The Belfast and Province of Ulster Directories, with lists as above, are also for dates of 1858-1859; 1860-1861; 1863-1864; 1865-1866; 1870; 1880; 1884; 1887; 1890; 1892; 1895; 1897; 1899; 1900.

* * * * *

A work which serves as a directory for the 16th century is H. J. Hore's *The Social State of the Southern and Eastern Counties of Ireland in the Sixteenth Century;* being the presentments of gentlemen, commonalty and citizens of Carlow, Cork, Kilkenny, Tipperary, Waterford, and Wexford, made in the reigns of Henry VIII and Elizabeth. Edited by H. J. Hore and Graves. Dublin, 1870.

The Biographical Succession Lists of the Clergy of the Church of Ireland (VOLUME II, pp. 41-42, 218-219) ; the Fasti of the Irish Presbyterian Church, 1618-1840, and the Annual Presbyterian Register, 1759-1783, etc.   (VOLUME II, pp. 42, 222-223) ; and the directories of the Roman Catholic Clergy (VOLUME II, p. 226), also serve as ecclesiastical directories.

Kelly's *Directory: Roman Catholic Parishes and Parish Priests*, 1936, furnishes a complete list to date of publication. An early work is *A List of the Names of the Popish Parish Priests throughout the Several Counties in . . . Ireland . . .* with their number . . . abode: age: parishes . . . time . . . places . . . sureties. Dublin, 1705.

Directories and School Registers (VOLUME II, pp. 229-232) ; Military and Naval Records (VOLUME II, pp. 244-246) ; and Office Holders, Freeholders and Guilds (VOLUME II, pp. 249-252), all serve the purpose as directories and biographies.

CHAPTER XI

COURT RECORDS, STATE PAPERS AND PARLIAMENTARY RECORDS

The COURT RECORDS in Ireland are distinctive from the State Papers and the Parliamentary Records, although some of the latter two are found among the Court Records of early date. The Courts may be broadly classed as temporal or ecclesiastical. The Court Records under discussion in this chapter are those of the temporal Courts of Chancery, Exchequer, King's Bench, Common Pleas, with some mention of local Courts. The Irish Prerogative Court and the Diocesan or Consistorial Courts primarily held ecclesiastical jurisdiction over probate, matrimonial, and Church government matters. The probate and marriage records are discussed in the following CHAPTERS XXII and XXIII. However, these ecclesiastical Courts also held jurisdiction over certain temporal matters concerning their manors or Church temporalities. An example of this is shown in Herbert Wood's edited *Court Book of the Liberty of Saint Sepulchre within the jurisdiction of The Archbishop of Dublin, 1586-1590*. Exeter, published by the Royal Society of Antiquaries of Ireland, Dublin, 1930.

Irish Court Records, State Papers and Parliamentary Records contain a wealth of genealogical material. All collections will have much more meaning if the genealogist has a sound background knowledge of Irish history. Therefore, the following works of Dr. Edmund Curtis, described in this PART THREE, CHAPTER IX, are again recommended. *A History of Medieval Ireland from 1086 to 1513*, London, 1938 (2nd edition) ; and *A History of Ireland,* London, 1952 (6th edition reprinted).

A very brief review of the evolution and purpose of the Courts will give some idea of the nature and value of the Irish records which exist today in one form or another, and are noted in this chapter. The Courts of Chancery, Exchequer, King's Bench, Common Pleas, and the local Courts which were established in Ireland with jurisdiction over temporal matters, beginning in the reign of King John and thereafter, were patterned after the corresponding English Courts.

The Chancery, Exchequer, King's Bench, and Common Pleas Courts evolved in England from the early medieval structure of the *Curia Regis* which comprised the officers of the king's household. These were the chancellor, the treasurer and other officers of the Exchequer, and the judicial body having jurisdiction over a Common Court of Law. Furthermore, matters which could not be determined in this Court were referred to the king or his justicar (who served when the king was out of the country, under age, etc., one also being appointed to govern Ireland), and others of the *Coram Rege*, the highest body for appeal. Out of this body evolved the Court of the King's Bench.

The chancellor, from the time of Edward the Confessor, was an ecclesiastic and combined the functions of the king's royal chaplain, his secretary in secular matters, and keeper of the royal seal. Cases of equity in the judicial department were also, in the course of time, referred to the chancellor. This practice evolved from the handling of petitions addressed to the king which first came through the chancellor's hands, particularly those requiring the royal seal. The equitable jurisdiction of the Chancery Court thus evolved.

The Court of Chancery came to consist of two distinct departments. One was a Court of Common Law (not to be confused with the Court of Common Pleas); the other a Court of Equity. From the chancellor's Court of Common Law were issued all the original writs passed under the great seal, such as the series of enrolled letters, the Patent and Close Rolls. The Letters Patent were open for inspection with the great seal attached, while the Close Rolls or closed letters were sent for private inspection only.

The Chancery Court of Equity originated from the belief in superiority of conscience and equity over strict law. Instead of being incorporated with the Court of Common Law, it provided for a wholly independent group of tribunals. King James I observed, "When the rigor of the law in many cases will undo a subject, then the Chancery tempers the law with equity, and so mixes mercy with justice, as it preserves a man from destruction."

Equity became an established necessity. The judges evolved strict precedents as in the Courts of Common Law. The equitable jurisdiction of Chancery divided cases under three categories; the exclusive, concurrent, and auxiliary. Exclusive jurisdiction was provided when there were no precedents for relief by the law with respect to rights which should be provided for individuals. Trusts came under this classification. Certain rights of married women, minors, etc., were also handled in this way. Concurrent jurisdiction was offered when Common Law did not give adequate relief in cases of accident, fraud, loss of property, irregular performance of contracts, etc. Auxiliary jurisdiction was provided when the necessary evidence required by other Courts was lacking. The records of this court are particularly rich in genealogical material. The depositions, etc., often give names, ages, and relationships in two or three generations of a family.

The Chancery division was organized with a lord chancellor as president, a master of the rolls, and vice-chancellors. The title of chancellor without the predicates "high" or "lord" was also applied to various other officials including the chancellor of the Exchequer. This office originated with the separation of the Chancery from the Exchequer in the reign of Henry III, 1216-1272.

The treasurer and two chamberlains composed the principal officers of the Exchequer. The lower or Receipt department held jurisdiction over royal revenue and income. The upper Exchequer comprised a Court which convened twice yearly to regulate accounts. Some judicial business related to revenue and accounts was also handled. Among the many duties of the sheriffs of the various counties, they were bound as the king's financial agents to collect royal revenues and present accounts of their stewardship twice a year. The Exchequer "viewed" the state of their accounts at Easter, and audited them on the Pipe Roll at Michaelmas. There were two types of revenue, fixed and casual. Fixed revenue included Crown rents from the King's demesne lands within the counties and also certain boroughs which were required to pay annual revenue for the privileges of their liberties. Casual revenue might include returns from various sources such as escheats, wardships of minors, etc., marriages, the collections in local Courts from amercements, being fines of no fixed amount; also property taken from felons or outlaws, fines consisting of payments made to the king for grants of land, various immunities, contributions to influence haste or delay in legal intervention. In addition there were revenues from subsidies, taxes, and assessments on particular occasions. For making accounts of the casual revenue, the Exchequer received copies of all grants made in the Chancery requiring the payment of rents or fines. These documents were called *Originalia*. The profits of justice were at first reported by "estreats" from the justices' records, or for minor affairs the oath of the sheriff was sufficient. Later some sources of casual revenue were determined by inquisitions.

In the 13th century Memoranda Rolls of the Exchequer developed. They contained records of business delayed for subsequent sittings of the officers. From *c.* 1326, the king's remembrancer kept preliminary records of casual charges while the treasurer's remembrancer exacted the "remanets" of old enrolled accounts and was concerned with the fixed revenue, and the collection of all debts which reached record on the Pipe Rolls. From the 13th century there were separate records for legal cases involving revenue. These included bills, answers, depositions, etc., as in the Chancery.

An Exchequer Court of Equity was established in the reign of Queen Elizabeth. Its registrar was the king's remembrancer. Also in this reign an audit department for land revenue was added. Under William IV, the sheriff's accounts and the Pipe Rolls ceased.

The Court of King's Bench evolved from the Court of *Coram Rege* which was originally an undivided part of the *Curia Regis*. By 1272, in the reign of Edward I, the *Coram Rege* Rolls were established, covering cases for criminal action which especially concerned the king or persons of such importance that they were privileged to be tried only before the king. Gradually this Court lost its close connection with the

king and his council; but emerged as a superior Court of
Common Law, with supreme and general jurisdiction over
(1) criminal cases, (2) civil cases, (3) cases of errors of inferior Courts, including those of the Court of Common Pleas.
The English Court of King's Bench also heard appeals from
the Court of King's Bench in Ireland until 1783. These produced the Irish Judgement Rolls including recorded suits between private persons; the Crown Rolls which recorded Crown
business; the Assize Rolls which contained pleas before the
justices of local Courts of Assize. This Court of Assize was
held twice yearly in each county, presided over by two judges
from the High Court of King's Bench. They tried (1) cases
of treason, murders, felonies, serious civil cases, etc., (2) of
gaol delivery, by which every person in gaol was granted a
trial, whatever his offense. Also they tried cases appealed
from the Quarter Sessions Courts, which were the Courts of
the Chairmen of Counties, or Quarter Sessions.

The Court of Common Pleas was the first to emerge from
the *Curia Regis* in early medieval times, as a Court of Common Law, before those of the Chancery and the King's Bench
became independently identified. Henry II appointed five
justices to form a permanent Court to hear pleas and, if any
could not be settled, the matter was referred to the king and
the *Coram Rege.* Few of the early Irish Rolls have survived
and, except as records have been abstracted or transcribed and
exist among miscellaneous collections, the records are mostly
dated from the late 17th century. A considerable number of
individual records have been presented to the Public Record
Offices in Dublin and Belfast. These are Affidavits, Appear-
ances, Decrees, Defences, Judgements, Conformities (Certificates of Conversion), Deeds leading to Fines and Recoveries,
Leases, Outlawries, Pleadings, etc.

STATE PAPERS: Important series of Calendars of State
Papers relating to Ireland have been published. Some of the
more important of these and also a few sources which list
manuscript collections of this nature are presented in VOL-
UME II, pp. 253-258. Included are Court Records and Parliamentary Records.

The State Papers contain many records of genealogical

interest relating to persons who appealed to the Crown for justice, favors, etc. They are particularly valuable for records of people who lost property by forfeiture, and a great many who were regranted part or all of their ancestral estates. The earliest documents relating to Ireland are among the correspondence running from the reign of Richard I to that of Henry VII, filling 61 volumes of English records. For one period, the Irish records were abstracted in a *Calendar of Documents Relating to Ireland, in the Public Record Office, London, 1252-1357*, edited by H. S. Sweetman, London, 5 volumes (1875-1886). Gustavus F. Handcock completed the editing of Vol. V (1302-1307). The most complete Calendar of State Papers is the series of a *Calendar of State Papers Relating to Ireland Preserved in the State Paper Department of Her Majesty's Public Record Office, London*, compiled and edited by various persons as follows:

First Series: 1171-1251; 1252-1284; 1285-1292; 1293-1301; 1302-1307.

Second Series: 1509-1573; 1574-1585; 1586-1588; 1588-1592; 1592-1596; 1596-1597; 1598-1599; 1599-1600; 1600.

Third Series: 1603-1606; 1606-1608; 1609-1610; 1611-1614; 1615-1625; 1625-1632; 1633-1647; 1647-1660 (and addenda 1625-1660). Also 1642-1659 (Adventurers); 1660-1662; 1663-1665; 1666-1669; 1669-1670 (and addenda 1625-1670).

PARLIAMENTARY RECORDS: Printed records are the *Journals of the House of Commons of Ireland, 1613-1800*. (With Appendix and Index to the first eleven volumes. 41 vols.) Dublin, 1763-1800. Also *Journals of the House of Lords, 1634-1752*. (3 vols. Dublin, 1782-1784.) Ancilliary records, save for a small number of Parliamentary Returns regarding Religion, were all destroyed. However, the records for some counties, scattered dioceses and parishes, were transcribed for parts of Ulster and other localities. These concern the *List of Protestant Householders, 1740; Religious Returns, 1766* (Protestant and Roman Catholic); and *Petitions of Dissenters, 1704-1782*. These serve as lists of inhabitants and supplement the Census records. The Presbyterian Historical Society, Belfast, has the transcripts of Ulster which exist.

Numerous lists of Roman Catholics made as Parliamentary Returns have been copied for local histories, etc. They are of scattered dates in the 17th and early 18th centuries and are usually for towns or parts of cities.

* * * * *

The mass of available Court Records, State Papers and Parliamentary Records (both printed Calendars and Manuscript materials) would bewilder the genealogist, but for the Catalogues of the records. These contain the lists of Calendars, Indexes, and Manuscript collections of the various repositories which are described in this PART TWO, CHAPTERS II-VI (also see VOLUME II, pp. 199-201). One can avoid confusion by consulting the Catalogues of the records of one repository after another.

J. Condon's *A Short Bibliography of Irish History*, Brown and Nolan, Ltd., Dublin (n.d., but *c.* 1903-1905), was compiled for the use of history students working in the National Library of Ireland. It is outdated today, but it has a certain value as a guide to source materials published before this time for two reasons: (1) It is brief and yet contains lists of important works of particular value to the genealogist, including the many Calendars of Court Records, State Papers, and Parliamentary Records; published Manuscripts, etc., which were compiled from records in other repositories in Ireland and Great Britain, prior to 1900. Condon also lists many miscellaneous works which contain abstracts, transcripts and information from records of both historical and genealogical interest; (2) after the first two sections of the Bibliography, it is arranged chronologically in periods. Thus the student or genealogist may direct his attention to the principal works of the particular period which interests him at any one time. It is by no means a complete bibliography of all available historical or genealogical material, but its brevity is certainly a virtue, for any but an advanced student. All sections contain records relating to Ireland.

Condon's arrangement of the records is as follows: (1) Annals and other Historical Materials or Sources. (2) General Histories. (3) Early Period. (4) Norman Invasion.

(5) Plantagenet, Lancaster and York. (6) Tudor. (7) Stuart. (8) Hanover. Condon apparently planned but did not complete lists for (9) Nineteenth Century, and (10) County History (Counties to be arranged according to provinces). At the end of each section or period he gives suggestions as to general references.

Condon's work was too early to cover more recent important sources such as the publications of the Irish Manuscripts Commission (listed in VOLUME II, hereof, pp. 95-106). Its journal, *Analecta Hibernica*, No. I (March, 1930), contains a "Report on Recent Acquisitions in the Bodleian Library, Oxford" (pp. 1-11); and "Reports on the Rawlinson Collection of Manuscripts in the Bodleian Library, Oxford" (pp. 12-178). This Calendar indicates a gold mine of information and sources concerning individuals in Ireland. In this issue is also "Miscellanea of the Chancery, London" (pp. 179-218). This is followed by lists of miscellaneous collections in other libraries of England, Scotland, and Wales (pp. 219-228).

Condon includes the printed works of the Irish Record Commission, 1810-1830, such as the Chancery Inquisitions for Leinster, *Inquisitionum in officio Rotulorum Cancellariae Hiberniae asservatarum repertorium*, VOL. I, 1826, and the same for Ulster, VOL. II, 1829. He does not include the Manuscripts compiled by this Commission which comprise principally Calendars, transcripts and abstracts of a large body of Court Records and State Papers, and which now are substitutes for original records destroyed in 1922, and are thus an important deposit in the Public Record Office, Dublin.

In preparation for a study of the surviving Court Records, State Papers, and Parliamentary Records in this Office, and the manuscript materials which represent Calendars, transcripts or abstracts of the destroyed records, every genealogist should read Margaret C. Griffith's article entitled "The Irish Record Commission, 1810-1830," published in *Irish Historical Studies*, VOL. VII, No. 25 (March, 1950), pp. 17-38. She was appointed Assistant Deputy Keeper of the Public Records in Ireland, Dublin, in 1944 (see p. 156, herein). She contributes the history and details of the work of the Irish Record Commission, appointed by the House of Commons,

London, in 1810. This was an important group of Irish archivists who had charge of the great accumulation of records scattered among various Government repositories in Dublin (transferred after 1867, to the new Public Record Office). The Record Commissioner, Sub-Commissioners and numerous assistants were organized in 1810, and charged with their duties: ". . . to examine the existing repositories and to take such measures as they thought necessary in order to . . . 'methodise, regulate and digest' the records, have them repaired where necessary, and make and have printed exact calendars and indexes of them." Their work of sorting, classifying, calendaring, indexing, etc., the records, making reports on the progress of the work, and publishing some of the most important Calendars, was carried on over a period of twenty years, from 11 September 1810 to 1830, when their patent was revoked by the House of Commons. During this period the Government had incurred an expense of almost £100,000. Except for the published records the bulk of the MSS. transcripts, calendars, indexes, etc., were more or less consigned to oblivion in Dublin Castle after 1830. Not until the destruction of the Public Record Office, in 1922, was their value as substitutes for destroyed records recognized. Today they are deposited in the Public Record Office and, as Margaret C. Griffith states: "In the existing circumstances, however, they form one of our most important collections of historical material . . ." Her article is intensely interesting and contains some humor regarding the conflicting personalities and methods of the Commissioner and Sub-Commissioners, while their chief critic was Sir William Betham. In her Appendix A, she contributes an analysis of the work accomplished, under twelve headings as follows: (1) Patent Rolls; (2) Acta Regia; (3) Chancery Inquisitions; (4) Exchequer Inquisitions; (5) Plea Rolls; (6) Calendar of Fiants; (7) Chancery Decrees; (8) Memoranda Rolls of the Exchequer; (9) Statutes; (10) Parliamentary Records; (11) Regal Visitation Books; (12) Catalogue of Trinity College, Dublin, MSS., by Monk Mason. Her Appendix B concerns "Reports and Papers of the Irish Record Commission," which will be later noted for valuable material. The detailed lists of the above materials also are contained in the 55th *Report of the Deputy Keeper of the Public Records of Ireland*, pp. 111-116. However, Miss Griffith's notes make a valuable supplement.

It is impossible for the genealogist to have any conception of the available Court Records, State Papers, and Parliamentary Records, in one form or another, now deposited in the Public Record Office, Dublin, without a study of the *Reports of the Deputy Keeper of the Public Records*, which are in fact catalogues of the Records. Genealogists are strongly urged first to become acquainted with the 1st to 54th *Reports*, which contain in the Appendices beginning with the 5th *Report* (1873), several series of Calendars of records now all or partially destroyed. These contain the basic information in each document. Illustrations will be given below. Furthermore, the value of the 1st to 54th *Reports* is due to the explanation and description of the original records which must be understood on account of the enormous amount of copying and abstracting of material during the course of the years between 1869 and 1922 (see PART TWO, CHAPTER V, herein). Beginning in 1869, and thereafter through the first fifteen *Reports*, the nature and extent (inclusive dates) of each collection of records was described after its deposit in this Office. The records were dated over many centuries. Lodge and others made transcripts and abstracts prior to this period, when the records were in their earlier repositories. Also some duplicate collections, nearly or completely identical to those destroyed in 1922, were transferred from their repositories to this Office after the fire. These will be better understood in the light of information contained in the early *Reports*. Indexes for the first fifteen *Reports* are at the end of the 5th, 10th and 15th *Reports*, respectively.

The 55th-58th *Reports* contain lists and descriptions of the records saved from the fire of 1922, and all calendars, transcripts, repertories, indexes now in this Office, as well as the original presented documents and manuscript collections, and the records transferred from other repositories, and notes on the published records and records in other repositories. The records are listed as follows:

Reports of the Deputy Keeper of the Public Records in Ireland, 55th-58th:

55th Report:

1. "Memorandum on the Destruction and Reconstruction of the Records," pp. 17-24.
2. Early Rolls and Original Inquisitions saved, pp. 97-98.
3. Record Commissioners Transcripts, Calendars and Repertories, pp. 111-116.

   (1) *Acta Regia Hibernica,* 1603-1625. (7 vols.) These contain (a) Transcripts from the Patent Rolls of James I (some printed in full). (b) Commissions. (c) King's Letters. (d) Grants. (e) Instructions, Orders, etc. (f) Inquisitions and Returns to Commissioners. (g) Letters from the Privy Council in England. (h) Licences. (i) Proclamations.

   (2) Charters (copy) of Towns and Boros (includes records of grants to individuals, to various manors, etc.).

   (3) Decrees (Chancery), Repertories to: 28 Henry VIII-1836. (8 vols.)

   (4) Decrees (Exchequer), 1624-1804. (23 vols.)

   (5) Inquisitions (Chancery), Repertories to. (15 vols.) These are for counties in Munster and Connaught, beginning with Elizabeth or James I. Inquisitions for Leinster and Ulster were printed by the Record Commissioners.

   (6) Inquisitions (Exchequer), Repertories to. (17 vols.) These are for all counties except Queen's. They begin under Henry VIII, Edward VI, Elizabeth, or James I, and continue to Charles I, Charles II, of William III. They include Inquisitions *Post Mortem* on Attainder, and on lands, etc.

   (7) Inquisitions, Deeds and Wills in (Chancery). (30 vols.) These are transcripts of Deeds, Wills and other instruments recited in Chancery Inquisitions, and pertain to all counties but Leitrim.

   (8) Inquisitions, Deeds and Wills in (Exchequer). (12 vols.) These are transcripts of Deeds, Wills, etc., in Exchequer Inquisitions, and pertain to Carlow and Dublin County; Dublin City; Galway; Kildare and Kilkenny; Louth and Queen's; Meath and Dublin City; Meath; Westmeath.

   (9) Memoranda Rolls (Exchequer), Calendars of. A. D. 1280-Henry VII. (43 vols.) These also contain Judiciary Rolls and Common Bench Rolls from Edward I, to Edward II, etc.

   (10) Plea Rolls, Calendar of. (12 vols.) A. D. 1252-1306; 1317-1318. These are abstracted from Justiciary Rolls, Rolls of Justices Itinerant, Common Bench Rolls and one Exchequer Roll.

   (11) Statutes of Ireland, Transcripts of. 12 and 13 Edward IV- 8 Henry VII. Those for King John through 11 and 12 Edward IV, have been published by Dr. H. F. Berry, editor.

(12) Visitation Books (Regal, etc.), Transcripts of. 1607, 1615, 1633-1634, 1673 (?). These are copies of regal visitations for various dioceses, which were preserved in the Prerogative Office.

4. Lodge's Manuscripts. This great collection was saved from the fire in 1922. It was compiled from the patent Rolls, Close Rolls, almost exclusively. It is preserved and classified (pp. 116-122) as follows:

(1) *Acta Regia Hibernica*, 2 vols. Vol. I (Henry VIII), contains transcripts from the Patent Rolls, comprising grants of office, appointments to office, grants of English liberty and protection to new settlers, etc. Vol. II (James I, 1st and 2nd years), contains transcripts from the Patent Rolls, as above.

(2) Converts, Alphabetical List of, and Protestant immigrants. (a) An Alphabetical List of Converts, with their additions and places of residence, giving dates of conformity, certificate on conformity and inrolment. *Circa* 1703-1772. (b) An Alphabetical List of Converts' Certificates, giving their additions, place of residence, where oath taken, date of Certificate and date of filing, 1709-1773. (c) "A List of Protestants who in pursuance of an Act of Parliament 13 Charles II, for encouraging Protestant Strangers and others to inhabit and plant in ye Kingdom of Ireland took the Oaths of Allegiance and Supremacy whereby they became liege, free and natural subjects of Ireland in every respect . . . as if born in Ireland, and were free . . . in any City or Corporation . . ." This list gives the occupation of the persons, place of nativity, time of taking the Oaths (1662-1737-1738), and reference to inrolment (Patent Rolls, 14 Charles II to 11 George II).

(3) Crown Presentations, 1660-1772, 1775. A List of all Deanries, Dignities, Prebends, Rectories and Vicarages in Ireland from the Restoration, with the names of incumbents and dates of appointment. Also observations on Church temporalities, including Crown Rents, etc.

(4) Crown Presentations, Index to. An alphabetical index of persons, to the preceding volume (imperfect). These names are also contained in a repertory of "The Royal Presentations remaining of Record on the Patent Rolls of Chancery in Ireland" printed in the *Liber Munerum*, pt. V, pp. 97-171 (1535-1827). See this compiler's VOLUME II, p. 254.

(5) Enrolments (Miscellaneous), Letters, Grants, on the Patent Rolls of King's Letters.

(6) Irish Chiefs (Articles with), Denizations, General Pardons, etc. (a) Articles of Agreement between the Chief Governors of Ireland and several Irish Chiefs (Henry IV-Elizabeth). These concern agreements of Native and Anglo-Irish Chiefs to become liege subjects, hold their lands of the King, etc. (b) "Denizations of the Irish, Scots and other Foreigners."

(Richard II-George I.)   Concerning the Ulster Plantation, only noted settlers were named.
(c) "General Pardons" and "Particular Pardons." (Edward III-George II.)   General Pardons, beginning with Henry VIII, list only ones of note.   (d) "Publick Commissions." (Edward III-George II.)   Abstracts of Commissions for leasing Crown lands, general pardons, remedy of Defective Titles, and regarding the state of transplanted persons.   (e) "Pensions." (Edward II-George III.)   Abstracts of grants of pensions, annuities or annual rents, in alms, for services, in consideration of injuries in the wars of Ireland, for money due, etc., and to ecclesiastics, etc. Pensions are to grantee and heirs, for life, pleasure, good behavior, etc.

(7) Irish Baronage. "The Irish Baronage" (one vol.) contains lists of the Peers of Ireland from Henry II, as far as can be collected from Records and History to 1772. This contains a list of creations of Irish peerages arranged by rank, dignity and date of creation, with names, titles, and authorities. Also lists of eldest sons called to sit in the Upper House of Parliament during their fathers' lifetimes. A view of the Peerage at the end of each reign Henry VII-George II, Baronets from 1619, with name, residence, etc. List of attainted peers (attainders of 1641 and 1689) with names and dates of creation. Records are printed in *Liber Munerum.*

(8) King's Inns, Members of (1607-1771), and of Officers, (1607-1768), etc.

(9) Parliamentary Register. Information was printed in *Liber Munerum* regarding members, 1559-1772. This Register contains also List of Speakers, 1613-1771; Chaplains, 1661-1769, etc.

(10) Patentee Officers, Lists of. (2 vols.) Civil and Military Officers, 1541-1772. Some as early as 1513. Lists printed in *Liber Munerum.*

(11) Patent Rolls, King's Letters, etc., Henry VIII-Elizabeth (1569).

(12) Records of the Rolls. Henry II - George II. (13 vols.) Abstracts of enrolments on the Patent and Close Rolls of grants of manors, lands, inquisitions, pardons of alienation and intrusion, awards, decrees, depositions, recognizances, deeds, leases, wills, etc. In addition to the ordinary series of Patent and Close Rolls, there are here the abstracts of the Act of Settlement, Commission of Grace and Trustees Deeds Rolls under Charles II, and in his second volume are the "Restorees or Persons restored to their Estates, 30 Nov. 1660.

(13) Records of the Rolls. (Vol. XIV.) Repertory of the names of Grantees, place, date, rent, etc., for all Fairs and Markets, to 1773.

(14) Miscellaneous Notes. (2 vols.)

(15) Wardships, Liveries, Alienations. (2 vols.) Abstracts of grants of Wardship and Marriage (Henry VIII-1647; 1660-1661); Liveries (Henry VIII-1641); Pardons of Intrusion (Henry VIII-1615); Licences and Pardons of Marriage (Henry VIII-Edward VI, Charles I). Pardons and Licences of Alienation (Henry VIII-1641). This is a complete set of collections of Wardships, etc., granted in virtue of Tenures *in Capite* and enrolled in Chancery from Henry VIII to the Dissolution of the Court of Wards in the reign of Charles II (all in Vol. I). The second volume contains abstracts of the same series dated prior to Henry VIII.

5. Ferguson (J. F.) MS. Collection. (pp. 122-123.)

   (1) Collections, extracts, notes, from Memoranda Rolls (Exchequer), from Edward I to Anne. (8 vols.)

   (2) Orders Revenue Exchequer, 1592-1666. (2 vols.) Calendar to "Order Books *ex parte* Second Remembrancer."

   (3) Orders Equity Exchequer, 1604-1673. (3 vols.) Extracts from the "Order Books *ex parte* Chief Remembrancer," included in the Revenue Exchequer Collection.

   (4) Memoranda Rolls Exchequer, Repertory to. Edward III-Charles II. (8 vols.)

   (5) Memoranda Rolls Exchequer, Index to. (4 vols.) (Not a complete Index.)

   (6) Originalia and Communia Rolls, Repertory to. (1 vol.) Extracts, 1605-1734.

   (7) Communia Rolls, Index to. (1 vol.) Not a complete Index.

   (8) Inquisitions, Calendar to. (3 vols.) Counties Antrim, and Meath (not complete).

   (9) Inquisitions, Indexes to. (4 vols.) I. Antrim-Mayo. II. Meath-Tyrone. III. Waterford-Wicklow. IV. Dublin and Galway. Index to persons and places, under heads of counties.

   (10) Exchequer Inquisitions, Dublin. (1 vol.) Notes from Inquisitions and Memoranda Rolls, in index order.

   (11) Adventurers' Certificates. (1 vol.) Alphabetical List of persons to whom Certificates were granted by the Court of Claims. Gives the lands set out to each person, with the county, some denominations, etc.

   (12) Decrees to Innocents. An alphabetical list or repertory of the Decrees to Innocents, fuller than above but without the number of acres.

   (13) Exchequer Records. Edward III-Anne. Under names of persons, places, etc., in index order, are entries on the Memoranda Rolls, relating to attainders, creations of peers, custodians, fines, grants, inquisitions etc.

6. Press Copies of Certified Copies. (6 vols.) Machine press copies of Chancery and Exchequer Inquisitions, Fiants, Grants, Christ Church Deeds, Statutes, Extracts from Plea, Close, Memorandum, and Hearth-

money Rolls, Decrees of Innocents, etc.   (List in Public Record Office Search Room.)   (p. 123.)

7. Carte Papers Transcripts of. Transcripts from MS. collection in the Bodleian Library, Oxford, from vols. 1-39; 47-53; 55; 56; 59; 60. (p. 123.)

55th Report; Appendix VI, pp. 124-132.

1. *Calendars, Repertories, Indexes, and Books of Reference, now in the Search Room:*

   (1) Early Plea Rolls, Calendars of Justiciary Rolls (1-11 Edward II), and Calendar of Roll of Justices Itinerant (33-34 Edward I).

   (2) Bankruptcy and Insolvency. Petition Books (Insolvency), Old Series, 1790-1821, give name of insolvent, prison in which he is confined, date and where petition is heard. Petition Books (Insolvency), for Towns (1821-1840) give name of Insolvent, observations, etc. Same in Books for Counties, 1821-1840. Petition Books (Insolvency), 1857-1872, contain name, description and residence of Insolvent, date, etc. Others for Bankruptcy (1857-1891), contain similar detail.

   (3) Chancery.

   (a) Acts of Parliament, Calendar and Index (Private Acts), 1613-1800.

   (b) Answers, Catalogue of, 1618-1622.

   (c) Bill Books and Pleadings, Indexes and Repertories to: Pleadings, Ancient (Bills), Indexes to, 1561-1634; Answers, 1569-1618; Repertories and Indexes, 1627-1630, 1633-1648, 1655-1659; Palatine of Tipperary, 1662-1690. Bill Books, 1633-1640, 1660-1867, 1867-1877; Palatine of Tipperary, 1691-1715.

   (d) Catholic Qualification Rolls Indexes, 1778-1790; 1793-1796 (Connaught) ; 1793-1797 (Leinster) ; 1793-1801 (Munster) ; 1793-1796 (Ulster). These give name, residence, additions, and place where qualified, with date.

   (e) Cause Books, 1878-1900. Petitions, etc., give name, date, cause, etc.

   (f) Convert Rolls and Certificates of Conformities. Calendars, Indexes, 1703-1845.

   (g) Deeds, Catalogue of. Edward III - George II.

   (h) Deeds and Wills in Inquisitions, Index to.

   (i) Disentailing Deeds Rolls: Calendars, 1834-1839 (Printed); 1840-1866 (Manuscript), contain names, dates and place of lands, etc. Indexes 1840-1898.

   (j) Fiants: Printed Calendars in 7th to 22nd *Reports*, for Henry VIII-Elizabeth. Calendars and Repertories for James I-Charles II, see Record Commissioners Reports and Schedules.

   Various other Calendars, Repertories and Indexes which were compiled for the Patent and Close Rolls, Inquisitions, King's

Letters, and Presentations, are those of the Record Commissioners, 1810-1830.

(4) Common Pleas.

(a) Certificates of Acknowledgement of Deeds by Married Women, Indexes to. 1834-1852. Contain names of wife and husband, dates of deed, and certificate; place of land by Parish, Barony or Manor, etc.

(b) Fines, Index to. 1705-1738. Names of Plaintiff and deforciant, by years and terms, under counties, with denomination of land.

(c) Fines, Indexes to. 1738-1835. Name of person levying fine, as above.

(d) Fines Entry Books. 1511-1648; 1655-1835. Contain names of Plaintiffs and Deforciants, with first and sometimes more of the lands and the county. Books arranged by years and terms; from 1774, under counties.

(e) Fines Entry Books, Index, 1511-1834.

(f) Fines and Recoveries, Palatine of Tipperary. MS. Index to Calendar printed in 5th *Report, Deputy Keeper of the Records.*

(g) Judgement Books. 1851-1887. Names of Plaintiffs and Defendants, amount and nature of Judgement, costs, date, satisfactions from 1854.

(h) Recovery Book or Index to Recoveries. 1590-1739. Name of tenant, demandant, by whom recovery suffered, denomination of lands by counties.

(i) Recovery Books. 1684-1834. Same as above.

(j) Recoveries, Indexes to. 1739-1834. Names of persons suffering the Recoveries and first of lands, by year and term, and counties.

(k) Recoveries Remembrance Rolls, Index to. 1746-1796. Same as above.

(l) Recoveries Remembrance Rolls, Indexes to. 1746-1834. Name of tenant and demandant, person suffering recovery, and first lands, by counties.

(m) Indexes to Case and Deed Rolls, Cause Books and Ejectments.

(5) Exchequer (Equity, Revenue, and Law).

(a) Bill Books (Equity Exchequer). 1674-1850. Similar to Chancery Bill Books. Contains also list of Bills, etc., 1634-1674.

(b) Decrees (Equity Exchequer). See Record Commissioners' Repertories.

(c) Decrees (Equity) Indexes, 1624-1850. Serves as Indexes to above.

(d) Deeds Boxes (Equity Exchequer), Indexes to.

(e) Deeds lodged with Chief Remembrancer, etc., Lists, 1777-1863.

(f) Deeds and Proceedings, Miscellaneous Rolls (Revenue Exchequer) Calendar, 1760-1850.

(g) Deeds and Wills in Inquisitions. See Record Commissioners' Transcripts.

(h) Deeds and Wills in Inquisitions, List of.

(i) Inquisitions, Calendars of. Co. Limerick, Chancery and Exchequer. Co. Dublin, Exchequer, Henry VIII, portion missing.

(j) Inquisitions, Repertory to. See Record Commissioners' Transcripts.

(k) Judgement Books. 1851-1898. Similar to Common Pleas Judgement Books.

(l) King's Rents Solicitor. Schedule of leases, etc. (Leases of Tithes, 1782-1821.)

(m) Memoranda Rolls. See Record Commissioners' Calendars, also printed works.

(n) Survey (Desmond). Limerick portion, MS. Calendar (M. J. McEnery). Co. Kerry (printed); also various extracts for Cos. Cork, Tipperary, and Waterford.

(o) Survey (Peyton's), Co. Limerick. MS. Calendar Indexes to Cause Books, Ejectments and Pleadings (Law).

(6) Incumbered Estates Court, Landed Estates Court and Land Judges (Chancery).

(a) Conveyances, Record of, 1850-1881; 1892-1901. Name of purchaser, amount of purchase money, and date; land and premises with acreage (1850-1858); number of Lot on the Rental, thereafter.

(b) Deeds Boxes, Indexes to. Alphabetical and Numerical. Nos. 1-5344.

(c) Petitions, Indexes to. 1849-1888. Name of Owner of Estate and the Petitioner, number and date of filing, etc.

(d) Proceedings, Record of. 1849-1891. Subsequent proceedings of above. Indexes to Accounts (Receiver's), Consents, Declarations of Title, Rentals and Schedules of Incumbrances, etc.

(7) King's Bench.

(a) Judgement Books, 1851-1899. Similar to Common Pleas Judgement Books.

(b) Satisfaction Entry Books, 1821-1853. Date of Satisfaction and date and amount of Judgement.

Indexes to Cause Books, Consents, Defences, Ejectments, Interlocutory and Case Judgements, Pleadings, Posteas, Recognizances and Bails, Records in Error, Replevins, Scire Facias, Writs and Writs Returned.

(8) Record Tower Collection. (Parliamentary, Council Office and Chief Secretary's Office Records):

    (a) Church Miscellaneous Papers. Calendar of, 1652-1795. Includes appointments to dignities and benefices, and of schoolmasters, etc. Addresses of Presbyterian Ministers to Lord Lieutenant, etc. Petitions and Memorials of Ecclesiastical and other persons.

    (b) Miscellaneous King's Letters and Correspondence, etc.

    (c) Military Commissions and Miscellaneous Documents, Index, 1715-1763.

    (d) Military Memorials. Index to, 1752-1815.

    (e) Officers' Widows' Accounts. Index to, 1716-1749.

    (f) Officers' Widows' Certificates. Index to, 1752-1763.

    (g) Parliamentary Records, Indexes to.

    (h) Presentments, Affidavits, Examinations, Informations, etc., Calendar of, 1698-1813.

(9) Registers of Documents Received from the Quit Rent Office:

    (a) Christ Church Deeds, Calendar of (MS.) 1605-1700. A continuation of Calendar printed in 20th, 23rd and 24th *Reports* of the Deputy Keeper.

    (b) Dublin Applotment Book, 1680-1686. Index. Draft Catalogue of names, and residence, of householders in the City and Liberties of Dublin contained in the Applotment Book.

    (c) Statements of French Pensioners, etc., Indexes to. Index Lists giving military rank and town (? in which resident).

    (d) List of Public Record Office Certified Copies preserved in the Quit Rent Office.

The 55th *Report*, Appendix VII (pp. 133-144) contains a "List of some Records not salved (saved from the 1922 fire), duplicates or copies of which are preserved in the Public Record Office, in other Offices or Repositories, or in private custody, or which have been printed, or of which there are printed or manuscript calendars or repertories." This List is continued in the 56th *Report*, Appendix V (pp. 406-412). The items concern Court Records of the temporal and ecclesiastical Courts, State Papers, and Parliamentary Records. Items are collections of records, listed alphabetically by subject. This provides an invaluable check or reminder of the existence and location of the collections up to time of publication of the 56th *Report*, in 1931. The 57th and 58th *Reports* list the numerous and extensive collections which were transferred from Government repositories subsequent to 1931, and are now in the Public Record Office, Dublin.

56th Report contains lists of the following records:

1. Chancery Records:
    (1) Chancery Records saved from the fire (pp. 203-204).
    (2) Chancery documents presented 1922-1928, Record Commissioners' Transcripts of Acta Regia and Lodge's Acta Regia, Official Copies in the Quit Rent Office of Chancery documents and Press Copies, in the Public Record Office of Certified Copies of Chancery documents, List of (pp. 213-300).
2. Equity and Revenue Exchequer Records:
    (1) Equity and Revenue Exchequer Records saved (pp. 301-303).
    (2) Books, Maps, Conveyances and Certificates in the Quit Rent Office (pp. 303-308). The Ware MSS. in the Armagh Library contains Extracts from Memoranda Rolls of the Exchequer. Also MSS. in Trinity College Library, Dublin, and in the British Museum provide substitutes to a certain extent for the destroyed Exchequer Records. These are set forth in the Lists noted above in the 55th *Report*, Appendix VII (pp. 133-144), and in the 56th *Report*, Appendix V (pp. 406-412). The most valuable collection of Equity and Revenue Exchequer Records was preserved in the Quit Rent Office, Dublin. These were transferred to the Public Record Office in 1931-1934 (see 57th *Report*, pp. 568-569).
    (3) Equity and Revenue Exchequer documents presented, 1922-1928; press copies of certified copies in the Public Record Office; Certified and Attested Copies of Equity and Revenue Exchequer Documents in the Quit Rent Office (pp. 309-341). These are listed with the Name of the Person or place, etc., Title of Suit, etc.; Nature of Document; Year; Original Exemplification, Copy, Abstract or Extract; Reference Number.
3. Records sent from the various High Courts and District or County Courts, include numerous collections of dates in the first half of the 19th century but the larger proportion are later records (pp. 11-20).

57th Report contains lists of the following records:

1. Common Pleas, etc., Records:
    (1) Common Pleas Records saved (p. 421).
    (2) List of Common Pleas Documents Presented to the Public Record Office, 1922-1930; Chancery, Equity Exchequer and Revenue Exchequer Documents Presented, 1929, 1930 (pp. 421-467). These are set forth by Name, of the Person or Place, etc., as noted in (3), under Equity and Revenue Exchequer documents, above.

The 58th *Report* continues the lists of collections transferred from other Government Offices, High Courts, local or County Courts, and also the lists of acquisitions from individuals including families of past government officials and genealogists, solicitors, etc. It does not continue the extensive lists of single documents. The 57th *Report*, p. 7, announced the intention of presenting in the next *Report*, a list of the Chancery and Equity and Revenue Exchequer Abstracts in the "Thrift Abstracts" Collection. This was not done, but they may be examined in the Search Room. There also are lists (detailed) for High Court and Supreme Court and other Court documents. Also there are Card Indexes to the Chancery, Exchequer, Common Pleas and other presented documents. This *Report* contains lists of a great many family collections of wills, marriage records, deeds, leases, etc., for which abstracts have also been made of Chancery, Exchequer, Common Pleas, and other Court documents relating to the family or group of families represented in the collection. A few of the general collections transferred and some of those presented are as follows:

1. The remainder of the records of the Quit Rent Office were transferred in 1943, when the Office was closed. This included two sets of *Books of Survey and Distribution*, in which are the names and lands of those who lost property by confiscation after the Rebellion of 1641-1652; the lands returned to many after 1660, and those lost again after the Revolution of 1689-1691; the lands retained by others; and the names and lands of new grantees. These records are further described in the following CHAPTER XIII.

2. A Calendar was made of the series of prisoners' petitions and cases, 1778-1836, down to 1825. Many of these were political prisoners.

3. Schedules of crown rents, quit rents, new patent rents, innocent papists' lands and undisposed lands, 1663-1827. These came from the State Paper Office.

4. From the Quit Rent Office came the crown rental of 1706, and numerous series of letter books, account books, memoranda, etc., 1689-1942.

5. From the Dublin County Council came the Grand jury minute and order books, 1818-1896, and the Grand jury presentment books, 1822-1895. The Dublin Corporation sent the Records of the Dublin Court of Conscience, including the Registers of proceedings, 1845-1918.

6. A collection of Returns from "Religious Census" of 1766, dioceses of Armagh and Cashel, with 2 for Cork and Ross (Ringrone and Rathbarry) and one for Waterford (Killoteran). In the Tenison Groves MSS. are extracts from the "Religious Census" of 1766, dioceses of Armagh, Clogher, Cloyne, Connor, Derry, Dromore, Down, Dublin, Ferns, Kildare, Kilmore and Ardagh, Ossory, Raphoe, Cork and Ross (M 2476-2478). Also a complete copy of the "Religious Census" of 1766 for the Diocese of Cloyne. The 1766 List of Protestant families in Donaghmore, Co. Donegal, and one of Protestant and Catholic families in Donamore, n.d., 1766 ?, came from the

Lyons collection, Trinity College Library (M 207, 208). A complete "Religious Census" of the diocese of Elphin, 1749 (M 2466) was presented. Also there is a List of the Roman Catholic Inhabitants of County Cork, 1654-1655. The "Religious Census" was taken from time to time by order of Parliament (House of Commons), which required the Protestant Rectors of all parishes to furnish a list of residents in the parish and their Church affiliation, with the names of adult male householders. The large proportion furnished this detail but some gave only a numerical tabulation. Various local histories have included lists of the 17th and 18th centuries. The Presbyterian Historical Society has Lists of the 1740 Householders, the 1766 Lists, and the "Petitions of Dissenters" in the 18th century which are noted below.

7. The Prim Collection, relating to the history of County Kilkenny is calendared in this 58th *Report* (pp. 50-70), with Index. This collection contains much genealogical material of the families of O'Shee, Shee, Roth, Purefoy, Scull, Banastre, Langton, Knaresborough, Bibby, Archer, Cowleyor, Colley, Fitzmaurice, Comerford, Cantwell, Frayne, and Shearman. It also contains the "Religious Census" for 1702 (?) and 1715 as follows:
   (1) Protestants in St. Kennis parish out gates n.d. (1702 ?).
   (2) Roman Catholics of St. Kennis parish out gates (1702 ?).
   (3) Protestants, St. Canies in gate (1702 ?).
   (4) Papists, St. Canies in gate, 1702.
   (5) Kilkenny, 27 Aug. 1715. List of Protestant inhabitants of parishes of St. John within the gates, and St. John out gate, aged 16 to 60.
   (6) List of Protestants of parish of St. Patrick out gate (1715 ?).

8. Plain copy of Test Book, 1775-1776, giving about 1500 names of Roman Catholics, mainly resident in Leinster and Munster, who took the Oaths and subscribed the declaration under Act 13 and 14, George III, *c.* 35 (an Act to Enable his Majesty's subjects of whatever Persuasion to testify their Allegiance to him). This sets out each name, address, trade, profession or social status of the subscribers.

9. Volume of abstracts of inquisitions in counties Dublin and Wicklow, Henry VI-Charles II, compiled by W. Monk Mason. (M 2543.)

10. Copy of List of forfeiting proprietors, from the Commonwealth Council Book, No. A 35. (M 752.)

11. Three volumes of copies of petitions, king's letters, bills, acts and correspondence, Charles II-William III. (M 2458-2460.)

12. 29 volumes of the Betham Genealogical Abstracts, containing miscellaneous extracts from Court Records, pedigrees and memoranda. Index in Search Room.

*   *   *   *   *

Several Calendars of Court Records have been published in Appendices of the 5th-54th *Reports of the Deputy Keeper of the Public Records of Ireland.* These provide an important source of genealogical information. Some of these Calendars are short, while others such as the Fiants are very extensive. Various Calendars are noted and illustrated with samples of the records as follows:

5th Report (1873), Appendix 3, pp. 32-81.

1. Abstracts of Fines Levied in the Palatine of Tipperary. These give the Parties' Names (Deforciants or persons levying the fine, and the Plaintiffs) ; the Date; Premises; Consideration (amount of Fine) ; and the Reference. *Example,* Fine No. 35, p. 45:

   "James Hamilton of the City of Dublin, esq., son and heir of James Hamilton, late of same city, esq., decd., and grandson of Revd. William Hamilton, late Archd. of Emly, decd., and sole exor. of the last will of Isabella, mother of the said James; and Judith, his wife, def. Thomas Howell, of the city of Dublin, merchant, pl. 25 Septr. 1694. Premises: North Clonmore and South Clonmore. bar. (barony) Middlethird. Cons. (Consideration), £647. Reference: F. 39."

2. Abstracts of Recoveries in the Palatine of Tipperary. These give the same information as above, with the names of the Demandant and the tenant, in several cases identical with the parties named in the Fines as above. *Example,* Recovery No. 58, p. 76:

   "Rt. Hon. Hester Ffinch, widow of Hon. Symon Ffinch, late of Kilcolman, esq., deceased and William Ffinch, sen. of Slyse, Hertfordshire, esq., and Alice, his wife, and William Ffinch, jun., of the same, gent. Thomas Moore, of Tullamore, King's Co., esq., dem. Pierse Nugent, of Durrow, King's Co., esq., and Dudley Moore, of Gurteenakelly, gent., ten. 28 Aug. 1705. Premises: Same as Fine 112."

   Fine No. 112, shows the same members of the Ffinch family as "def." (Deforciants), and Pierce Nugent and Dudley Moore as "pl." (Plaintiffs). The Consideration is not given, but the Premises are listed as fourteen townlands including Kilcolman and Tullamore. Reference, D., C., 55; F. 87. The Fine was dated 27 February 1705.

6th Report (1874), Appendix 5, pp. 45-88. Records of the Palatine of Tipperary:

1. Cause List of Chancery Pleadings of the Palatine Court of Co. Tipperary, from 1662 to 1690. *Example,* p. 60.

   "Plaintiff: Keating, Ellis, alias Bryan, alias Power. Defendants: John, James, William, Honor, and Joan Keating, and David Power. 1674."

2. The Rolls of the Chancery of the Regalities and Liberties of the County Palatine of Tipperary, containing Fee-Farm Grants from the Duke of Ormond. *Example*, p. 80.

"Deed dated 19 August, 1665.—"William Ward of Little Houghton, Northamptonshire, esq., grants to Thomas Ward, his son and heir, all the personal property of his brother, the late Robert Ward of Derrilascane, in Ireland. Inrolled, 13 October, 1665."

7th Report (1875), Appendix 10, pp. 33-110. "Fiants," Henry VIII (total 548 Fiants), and Index. Abstracts of Fiants, 1521-1547. The term Fiant is derived from the first word of the usual form, "Fiant literae patentes" (Let letters patent be made). Fiants are warrants to Chancery authorizing the issue of letters patent under the great seal. The printed Calendars, Henry VIII-Elizabeth, noted and illustrated below, are warrants under the Privy Seal and signature of the sovereign or chief governor of Ireland, directing letters patent be passed. These contain pardons, leases, grants of English liberty, presentments, grants of office, grants of pensions, licences of alienation, grants in fee, appointments, etc. *Example*, p. 69.

Fiant No. 377. "Livery to John, son and heir of Christopher Bedlowe, by Katherine Flemyng (formerly of Dweleke, widow), his wife; said Christopher having been son of Walter Bedlowe, knight. Fine £50.—16 November xxxv (1543)."

8th Report (1876), Appendix 9, pp. 26-230. "Fiants," Edward VI (total 1257 Fiants) and Index. *Example*, p. 108.

Fiant No. 770. "Livery to Walter Bermyngham, of Dunferthe, gent., cousin and heir of Edward, late Baron of Carbre, being son of John, brother of William Bremegham, father of the said Edward. Fine, £20.—(1551)."

9th Report (1877), Appendix 4, pp. 59-104. "Fiants," Philip and Mary, 1553-1558 (total 276 Fiants), and Index. *Example*, p. 67.

Fiant No. 88. "Grant of English liberty to Donald M'Cartie [McCarthy], otherwise called Lord M'Cartie More; his daughter, Lady Ellen M'Carty More, Countess of Desmond, and his son, Donald M'Cartie More; and their issue. 4 November, ii. and iii. (1555)."

11th through 18th Reports (1879-1886), Appendices. "Fiants," Elizabeth, 1558-1603 (total 6,792 Fiants). *Example, 11th Report*, p. 101.

Fiant No. 619. "Grant to Nicholas Whitte, gent; of the wardship, marriage, and custody of the lands, of James Wisse, kinsman and heir male of Henry Wise, late of Waterford. To hold during minority, at a rent of £25 7s. 4d., and retaining £20 for the minor's maintenance. Provided that on the death of Lady Elizabeth Plunket, widow of William Wisse, knt., father of said Henry, whose dower is valued at £34 0s. 6d., or of Johanna Clerke, widow of said Henry, whose dower amounts to £22 13s. 8d., the rent shall be increased by one of these sums. Consideration £102 1s. 6d.—8 May (1564)."

At the end of the Fiants of Elizabeth are 19 additional Fiants of Henry VIII, Edward VI, Philip and Mary.

21st and 22nd Reports (1889-1890), Appendices, pp. 32-862. Index to the Fiants of Elizabeth.

19th Report (1887), Appendix V, pp. 35-87. Court of Claims: Abstracts of "Decrees of the Court of Claims for the Tryall of Innocents, 13 January, 1662/63 to 21 August, 1663." With Index (820 Decrees). These decrees concerned people who claimed they or their ancestors who owned property in 1641 and during the Rebellion of 1641-1652, were innocent of any participation or disloyalty. These records are further discussed in CHAPTER XIII, hereafter. The abstracts were taken from information in 9 volumes of records containing much personal detail, and set forth "The Pedigree of ye Claimant, how he derived from ye Proprietor or Possessor in Anno, 1641"; the "Qualification of Innocents"; the same for "Nocents"; "The Number of Profitable acres Decreed." *Examples,* pp. 43, 75.

(1) "4 February 1662/63. No. 30. "Richd. son to Henry son to Richd. Brother to Edward who had 2 sons, Tho. and Willm. Ash." "In." Innocent. Property in Counties Dublin, Kildare. Profitable Irish Acres, 335.

(2) "10 August, 1663. No. 673. "Tho. Clinton son of Steph. son of James." "In. p." Property in County Louth. Profitable Acres, 887-3-0.

The 22nd-24th *Reports,* Appendices, contain "Proclamations" issued by the Lord Lieutenant and Council of Ireland from 1618-1875. These provide information about miscellaneous events of importance, including public and private affairs under Government jurisdiction. Proclamations regarding private affairs contain the names of persons who committed outrages including stealing, rape, abduction of unmarried women or widows for forced marriages, murder, etc.,

with the names and places of the ones who suffered the same.
Other Proclamations give only the names of those who suffered
the crime, and notice for apprehension of the guilty. The
records of private persons are numerous after 1703. Illustrations in the 23rd *Report*, Appendix II, pp. 62, 68, 69, 73, are as
follows:

(1) "Proclamation for discovering and apprehending the Persons who
robbed, tortured, and murdered Edward Johnson, of Carroe,
King's county, Quaker, by heating a griddle and placing him
thereon, heaping hot coals upon him, and burning him with a hot
iron on the Palms of his hands, 1725."

(2) "The like against the Persons concerned in the murder and rob-
bery of Francis Howard of Coolatore, county Westmeath, 1746."

(3) "Proclamation against the persons who broke into the house of
Richard Cole, of Belfast, and robbed and murdered the said
Richard Cole, Elizabeth, his daughter, and Mary Maguire, a
maid servant, 1753."

(4) "The like against the persons therein named who forcibly carried
away Margaret M'Clean, the daughter of John M'Clean, Fay-
archaron, in the county Donegal, farmer, 1763."

35th through 54th Reports, Appendices. "Accounts on the
Great Rolls of the Pipe of the Irish Exchequer," 13 Henry
III (1228-1229) to 22 Edward III (1348-1349). In the
55th *Report*, Appendix I, p. 20, a statement is made regarding the Pipe Rolls, as follows: "The wealth of information
which was to be found in the Pipe Rolls is known to
students of the 'Catalogue of Accounts in the Great Rolls
of the Pipe of the Irish Exchequer,' 13 Hen. III-22 Ed.
III, made by Mr. M. J. McEnery, late Deputy Keeper, and
published in the 35th to 54th *Reports* of the Deputy
Keeper. None of the original rolls which came down to
1818 now survive." However, the published Catalogue,
covering the Anglo-Norman period in Ireland, 1228/29-
1348/49, provides considerable information of a genealogical nature. Names of the sheriffs of various counties,
cities, etc., are included in their records of accounts which
contain numerous names of those who owe debts to the
Crown. Accounts for the Archbishopric and some bishoprics are also presented by their clerks or seneschals. Thus
in the Pipe Roll of Henry III (July 22, 1261), is the "Account of County Meath for the entire year xlv. Henry III,

by Henry de Stratton, the seneschal, and Thomas de Champayne, seneschal of J. de Verdon" (35th *Report,* Appendix, p. 40). In this account is the note that "John de Verdon who has married the other heiress of Walter de Lacy owes £1133. 12s. 9½d., various debts as contained in the same roll." From the time of Edward I, the Pipe Rolls contain accounts of "Escheats and Wardships in King's hands," *in capite,* which reveal the name of the deceased who held such property, and the name of the heir. Illustration: 38th *Report,* p. 78, gives "Escheats and Wardships in King's hands," 27th-32nd Edward I—"Dunmor, Co. Waterford, land which belonged to Michael le Flemmeyng, and held of the King *in capite.* He the Accountant answers nothing because the lands were delivered to Thomas le Mareschal and Constance his wife, sister and heiress of Hugh son and heir of the said Michael, by writ dated 14 July *a. r.* xxvii."

*   *   *   *   *

The great collections in the Public Record Office of Northern Ireland, Belfast, are described in this PART TWO, CHAPTER VI, pp. 199-227. Included are many collections of Chancery, Exchequer, King's Bench, Common Pleas, and local Court Records, State Papers, and Parliamentary Records, dated from early times. One of the great advantages offered by the *Reports* of the Deputy Keeper is that the Indexes in the Appendices contain the names of the principals in the documents of various collections, and in each entry the place of residence or county, the nature of the record and its source.

Court Records in the various manuscript collections, concerning people of Northern Ireland, are referred to in the above mentioned chapter as follows:

1. Chancery Court Records: See pp. 205, 209, 212, 219, 222, 225.
2. Exchequer Court Records: See pp. 205, 214, 215, 216, 219, 222, 225.
3. King's Bench: See p. 205.
4. Common Pleas Court Records: See p. 205.
5. Local Court Records: See pp. 205, 210, 213, 215, 224.

State Papers and Parliamentary Records transcribed in

various manuscript collections are referred to as follows: See pp. 205, 208, 212, 213, 214, 215, 216, 220-221.

The Office Library also contains all printed Calendars, Repertories, etc., of the above Court Records, State Papers, and Parliamentary Records, mentioned earlier in this chapter.

* * * * *

The National Library of Ireland, Dublin, has all printed works referred to, including Calendars, transcripts, abstracts and extracts of Court Records, State Papers, and Parliamentary Records. Some microfilms of manuscript collections of this nature are listed in VOLUME II, pp. 270-286. Two of importance are the microfilmed *Annesley Collection,* described in this VOLUME, pp. 111-112, and the Carte Collection in the Bodleian Library, Oxford. This Library has a catalogue and microfilms of the Hore collection of 67 bound volumes of manuscripts, and 64 unbound manuscripts, collected over the lifetimes of Herbert F. Hore and his son, Philip H. Hore. The collection relates to County Wexford and its residents from early times. The original records are now at St. Peter's College, Wexford, in the custody of the President, Father O'Byrne, who permitted the National Library to microfilm the entire collection. A reprint of the Catalogue of the collection is included (pp. 315-321) in the *Civil Survey of County Wexford, A.D. 1654-1656,* edited by Robert C. Simington, and published by the Irish Manuscripts Commission, Dublin, 1953. Therein the Hore collection is described as "forming a mass of material for local history as yet rarely approached in Ireland." The collection contains transcripts of everything in the way of Court Records, State Papers, and Parliamentary Records, and a mass of other sources, from repositories in Ireland and Great Britain; all of which contribute to the compiled records of about 100 families of the gentry of Wexford (one volume of 800 pages), and two other volumes of pedigrees of Anglo-Irish families of the county (900 pages), together with numerous other volumes containing family pedigrees. From this extensive collection Philip H. Hore selected the copies of Court Records, State Papers and other records concerning individuals and affairs of the county, which he published in his 6-volume *History of the Town and County of Wexford,* London, 1900-1911.

Among the records of the county families which Hore published in his above work were the *Inquisitions Post Mortem.* These were taken under commissioners directed to the Escheators of the province whose duty it was to protect the rights of the Crown, and others joined with them who found upon investigation and the oath of a jury, what lands any person died possessed of, by what rents (Crown or otherwise) and services the lands were held, and who was the next heir, also his age, and by what right the Crown could escheat or take the lands or take the wardship of the heir if under legal age. Inquisitions of this nature began in the reign of Elizabeth and ended during the reign of Charles II.

One of Hore's transcripts (abstracts) of *Inquisitions Post Mortem* (Vol. 5, 1906, pp. 197, 198) is as follows: "1592. Inquisition at Wexford, 17 Feb., before Richard Boile, gent., Deputy to Nicholas Kenny, Esquire, General Escheator for the Queen, etc. [Here follow the names of the jury, all county men.] We declare on oath that Thomas Rauceter of Rathmakne, gent., on the day of his death—22 January, 1592—was seised as of fee of—[Here follow his possessions in the County, some held of the Queen as of her Castle of Wexford in free soccage, at the yearly rental of 2s. and others at different tenures and rents.] That John the father of Thomas Rauceter, in consideration of receiving 50 marks, leased to Patrick Cheevers, merchant of Wexford, on 3 July, 1584, the township of Knockengall, etc., for 11 years. That Thomas Rauceter was seised in fee of 13½ Burgages with their gardens in Wexford, by burgage tenure. They are worth yearly 5s. That the said John Rauceter the father of Thomas, now dead, together with James Sherlocke, clerk, and Philip ffurlonge, merchant, the feoffees afterwards to the use of the said John Rauceter and his heirs, by a certain indented Deed, signed by themselves, dated 24 Nov. 1583, demised, and to farm let to Thomas Siggen, gent., one burgage, and garden situated between the burgage of the late Thomas Codd [here follows a description of property rented for 59 years; rents to John Rauceter and his heirs]. And finally they say that John Rauceter [grandson of the above John] is the legitimate son and next heir of the aforesaid Thomas Rauceter, and was of the age of 4 years at the time of his father's death and not married; and that Constance Stafford, the relict of Thomas Rauceter, the grandfather of Thomas Rauceter, now defunct, and Anastatia Synnott, the widow, late the wife of the said Thomas Rauceter, are [the guardians] of the minor by the course of the common law of this kingdom of Ireland. In testimony, etc." Here follows a further inquisition when the heir, John Rauceter, then age 14, by his mother, Anastatia Synnott, who was his nearest relative, came before the jury, etc. Thus we have, in one document, the names in direct line of four generations.

Inquisitions on attainder were similar and were taken in the same manner before a jury, with the purpose to inquire into the possessions of attainted persons whose property, held from the Crown, was due to be forfeited for real or suspected reasons of disloyalty. Inquisitions on attainder also began in the reign of Elizabeth and ended in the reign of William III. These will be further discussed in CHAPTER XIII, hereafter.

Both Inquisitions Post Mortem and Inquisitions on attainder were employed as historical and genealogical source materials by compilers of national and local histories, genealogies, etc., and by contributors to historical journals and genealogical publications. James Frost's *History of County Clare,* Dublin, 1893, is one of several local histories which are compiled largely from Court Records, State Papers, and Parliamentary Records pertaining to the people of the area. It contains four chapters (pp. 267-337) devoted to brief abstracts of all inquisitions of either type concerning county residents, 1585-1667. Other chapters are devoted to family and personal records contained in early Annals, Crown Rentals, the Composition Book of Clare, 1585, the Book of Survey (forfeitures) and Distribution, Funeral Entries, Subsidy Rolls of 1664, etc., Parliamentary Commissioners' Records, Court of Claims Petitions, Parliamentary Returns regarding Religion, Ordnance Survey Papers, etc.

The National Library maintains a series of catalogues of all manuscripts preserved in the Library and of all which have been located and microfilmed in various libraries or archives in Ireland and abroad. Also a descriptive list has been compiled of the contents of many private family collections which were loaned by their owners to be microfilmed and thus made available for research. Most of these collections in public and private hands contain original documents and transcripts or abstracts of personal records relating to the Courts, the State, etc.

The periodical of the Irish Manuscripts Commission, *Analecta Hibernica,* No. 15, (1944), edited by Edward MacLysaght, who was Keeper of the Manuscripts in the National Library, contains a report on surveys made by the Commission, of such collections of manuscripts as still survive in private keeping, with a view to selecting certain ones for microfilming and others for editing and publishing. Numerous ones which have been printed are listed under the Irish Manuscripts Commission publications, in VOLUME II, hereof, pp. 95-100. A recent publication is *The Inchiquin Manuscripts,* edited by John F. Ainsworth. Collections of manuscripts mentioned by Dr. MacLysaght in *Analecta Hibernica* No. 15 concern the O'Grady, O'Callaghan, the Earl of Longford, Lord Doneraile, Lord Farnham, Lord Inchiquin, Lord Louth and the following families: Bowen, Blunden, Brown, Colthurst, Conner, Daly, de Vere, Harold-Barry, Herbert, Lane, Longfield, McLysaght, O'Connell, O'Gorman, O'Neill Daunt, Ridgeway, Roche, Segrave, Ussher, Waters; also a book of Cromwellian Irish State Accounts, and papers of the Old Corporation of Kinsale. *Analecta Hibernica* No. 20, Irish Manuscripts Commission, Dublin, 1958, contains a "Survey of Documents in Private Keeping, 2nd Series," by John F. Ainsworth and Edward MacLysaght. This contains reports on further collections of documents in private keeping. It also contains a list arranged alphabetically under owners' names, of all the collections which have so far been examined. Reports on all may be examined in the National Library. Reports recently printed include the Nugent papers which contain copies or abstracts of many documents in the Public

Record Office, later destroyed in 1922. Other collections include the Power O'Shee papers and the Colclough papers.

* * * * *

The Genealogical Office, Dublin Castle, Dublin, through the efforts of a long succession of officers who filled the position of Ulster King of Arms, has acquired transcripts of records of a genealogical nature, extracted from the Lodge Manuscripts, and from other collections of Court Records, State Papers, and Parliamentary Records. These include abstracts of Chancery and Exchequer Bills, Inquisitions, Forfeitures, Wardship and Marriage, Petitions to the Crown, Grants of Arms and of Office, Pardons, Salaries, Pensions, etc. Details of some of the collections are set forth in PART TWO, CHAPTER IV, pp. 137-155, herein.

Among the many miscellaneous collections of this nature are also some *Religious Returns* of 1766, transcribed from the Religious Census furnished to the Irish House of Commons by the Protestant Rectors, covering the Protestant and Roman Catholic families by parish as follows: Creggan, Co. Armagh; Lurgan and Munster Connaught, and Lavey, Co. Cavan; Castletown Roche, Co. Cork; Castleknock, and Crumlin, Co. Dublin; Ballycommon, King's Co.; Clonagh, Crough, Dondaniel, Kilfinan, Killscannell, and Rathkeale, Co. Limerick; Abbeylara, and Russough, Co. Longford; Ardee, Ballymakinny, Beaulieu, Carlingford, Charlestown, Clonkeehan, Darver, Dromiskin, Kildemoch, Malpastown, Philipstown, Shanlis, Smarmore, Stickillen, and Termonfeckin, Co. Louth; Ardbraccan, Liscartan, Martry, Churchtown, and Ratine, Co. Meath; Edemine, Co. Wexford; Ballynaslaney, Dunganstown, and Rathdrum, Co. Wicklow.

* * * * *

King's Inns Library, Dublin, has a collection of Rentals, Incumbered Estates Court, and Landed Estates records. A set of these is in the National Library, and another set in the Land Commission Office was transferred to the Public Record Office, Dublin. King's Inns Library has the large Prendergast Collection of papers of the late John P. Prendergast, whose work of great importance, *The Cromwellian Settlement of Ireland,* was published in two editions, Dublin, 1870, 1875. His manuscript collection for the most part relates to the Cromwellian Restoration and Revolution Settlements in Ireland, comprising thirteen bound volumes containing copies and extracts of official documents, State correspondence, petitions concerning confiscated property, throughout the 17th century. Several of the volumes have transcripts, abstracts and extracts from the Carte Manuscripts in the Bodleian Library, Oxford. Other records are noted on p. 125, herein.

* * * * *

Trinity College Library, Dublin, manuscript collections and catalogues have been noted herein, pp. 127-129. A few other collections of interest are:

1. "A List containing all the Payments to be made for Civil and Military Affairs with Pensions in Ireland for one year beginning the 1st of January 1687/8." (Original.) MS. 796.
2. Civil Lists, 1629, 1676. Military Lists, 1616, 1622, 1631, 1640, 1676. MS. 672.
3. Minutes of Proceedings of Court Martial in Wexford, 1798-1800. MS. 1471.
4. List of Established Ministers in the several precincts throughout Ireland. MS. 1040.
5. Inquisitions concerning the Six Escheated Counties in Ireland, 7 James I. MS. 595.
6. Grand Inquest of the Province of Ulster, 1610 *(copia vera).* MS. 1046.
7. List of all the Schoolmasters within this Nation (with their salaries). MS. 1040.

* * * * *

Collections in the Royal Irish Academy, Dublin, have been noted herein, pp. 125-127. It has a collection of abstracts of Chancery and Exchequer Inquisitions (see *A Catalogue of Irish Manuscripts in the Royal Irish Academy,* 1948).

* * * * *

Armagh Public Library, Armagh, has a transcript (published in the *Journal of the Armagh Diocesan Historical Society*, Vol. I, No. 1 (1954), of the Text of the Inquisition of 1609, with Introduction and Notes, concerning "The Churchlands of County Armagh."

Transcripts of Forfeiture records are: (1) A List of Claims of Innocents to be heard and determined by His Majesty's Commissioners appointed to execute the Act of Settlement of Ireland in the Court of Claims for the Trial of Innocents, from 28 Jan. 1662/3, to 20 Aug. 1663. (2) MSS. pedigree information extracted from the published "Chichester House Claims, 1700."

The Ware MSS. contain "Extracts from Memoranda Rolls of the Exchequer." Notes on other records are given on pp. 119-120.

* * * * *

The Linen Hall Library, Belfast, has a remarkable collection of published works concerning Court Records, State Papers, and Parliamentary Records. See its *Catalogue of Books in the Irish Section,* 1917. This includes the *Calendar of the Carew Manuscripts at Lambeth, 1515-1624. With the Book of Howth, the Conquest of Ireland, and Miscellany.* Edited by J. S. Brewer and W. Bullen. 6 vols. 1867-1873.

* * * * *

Collections in the Presbyterian Historical Society Library, Belfast, are noted, pp. 121-122, herein. Collections of interest in this chapter are those transcribed before 1922 in the Public Record Office, Dublin, from the Parliamentary Returns regarding Religion, as follows:

1. Parliamentary Returns: "Protestant Householders, 1740," being the names of the Protestant householders in the towns and parishes of the following baronies:
    (1) County Antrim: Baronies of Carey, Dunluce, Kilconway, and Toome.
    (2) County Donegal: Barony of Ennishowen.
    (3) County Down: Barony of Evagh.
    (4) County Londonderry: Baronies of Coleraine, Kenoght, Kilconway, Laughinshillen, and Tyrkeering.

2. Religious Returns of 1766, transcribed from the Religious Census furnished to the Irish House of Commons by the Protestant Rectors, covering the Protestant and Roman Catholic families by parish as follows:

(1) Aghalow and Caranteele, Co. Tyrone. (2) Ahoghill, Co. Antrim. (3) Artrea, Cos. Tyrone and Londonderry. (4) Ballentoy, Co. Antrim. (5) Ballymoney, Co. Antrim. (6) Banagher, Co. Londonderry. (7) Derryloran, Co. Tyrone. (8) Derryvullen, Co. Fermanagh. (9) Desertmartin, Co. Londonderry. (10) Drumachose, Co. Londonderry. (11) Drumglass, Tullaniskan, and Town and Corporation of Dungannon, Co. Tyrone. (12) Dungiven, Co. Londonderry. (13) Inch, Co. Down. (14) Kilbrony (also for 1740), Co. Down. (15) Kildress, Co. Tyrone. (16) Leck, Co. Tyrone. (17) Lurgan, Co. Armagh. (18) Magherafelt, Co. Londonderry. (19) Seapatrick, Co. Down.

3. Petitions of Dissenters to the Irish Parliament or Lord Lieutenant (in Parliamentary Papers), 1775, containing names of Petitioners, from the following places:

(1) Antrim, Borough of, Co. Antrim. (2) Antrim, Co. Antrim. (3) Ardstraw and Newtown-Stewart, Co. Tyrone. (4) Armagh Parish, Co. Armagh. (5) Ballee, Co. Down. (6) Ballyclare, Town and Neighborhood of Ballyeaston, Co. Antrim. (7) Ballymena, Co. Antrim. (8) Ballynure, Co. Antrim. (9) Bangor, Co. Down. (10) Belfast, Town and Parish of, Co. Antrim. (11) Benburb, Town and Neighborhood of, Co. Tyrone. (12) Carnmoney, Parish of, Co. Antrim. (13) Carnmoney, Parish of, Members of the Church of Ireland. (14) Carrickfergus, Co. Antrim. (15) Clare, Congregation, Ballymore Parish, Co. Armagh. (16) Coagh, County Tyrone. (17) Coleraine and Killowen, Parishes of, Co. Londonderry. (18) Comber, Town and Parish of, Co. Down. (19) Cookstown, Co. Tyrone. (20) Donagore, Kilbride and Nelteen, Co. Antrim. (21) Dundonald, Parish of, Co. Down. (22) Dromore, Parish of, Co. Down. (23) Drumaragh, Co. Tyrone. (24) Drumballyroney and Drumgoolan, Parishes of, Co. Down. (25) Drumgooland, Co. Down. (26) Dublin, Co. Dublin. (27) Two for Dungannon, Co. Tyrone. (28) Dunmurry, County Antrim. (29) Killileagh, Town and Parish of, Co. Down. (30) Larne and Raloo, Carncastle and Kilwaughter, Glenarm and Ballyeaston, United Parishes of, Co. Antrim. (31) Lisburn, Town and Neighborhood of, Co. Antrim. (32) Londonderry, City of, Co. Londonderry. (33) Londonderry, members of the Established Church, Co. Londonderry. (34) Newry, Parish of, Co. Down. (35) Omagh, Co. Tyrone. (36) Rathfriland, Co. Down. (37) Rathfriland, Co. Down.

(38) Sea-Patrick, Tullylish and Donochlony, Parishes of, Co.
Down. (39) Strabane, Town and Neighborhood of, Co. Tyrone.

* * * * *

British Museum, London: For Catalogue of Manuscripts,
see p. 133, herein. The *National Library of Ireland Report
of the Council of Trustees for 1950-1951*, p. 5, states, "A list
of the manuscripts and documents relating to Ireland in the
British Museum has also been drawn up from the printed
catalogues and the whole or sections of approximately 3,500
manuscripts have been selected for filming. So far all the
manuscripts of Irish interest in the Additional series up to
Add. MS. 37,000 have been microfilmed." The work has been
carried on steadily since then, including many series of Court
Records. A few samples of these records are listed in VOL-
UME II, under Microfilms, pp. 273, 274, 278, 281, 284, 285, 286.
The entire list is in the National Library of Ireland.

* * * * *

The Public Record Office, London, is one of the greatest repositories of miscellaneous Court Records and particularly
State Papers, carried back to England by Government officials,
who at one time or another served in Ireland. For a Catalogue of this repository, see p. 134, herein. For "Miscellanea
of the Chancery (Ireland)" see *Analecta Hibernica*, No. 1
(1930), pp. 177-218.

* * * * *

The College of Arms, London, has some records of interest
mentioned on pp. 137, 138, herein.

* * * * *

Lambeth Palace, Archiepiscopal Library, London, has the
original Carew Manuscripts, 1515-1624. The printed *Calendar of the Carew Manuscripts, 1515-1624*, was edited by J. S.
Brewer and W. Bullen, London, 1867-1873. 6 vols. Records
of the Irish Courts and State Papers are represented in this

collection, including "Pedigrees of the Mere Irish." See pp. 133, 134, herein.

* * * * *

The Society of Genealogists, London, has an outstanding collection of nearly 2,500 abstracts from Irish Wills, Administrations, Marriage Licences, Chancery and Exchequer Bills, bound in chronological order, from 1569 to 1808. Also included are Pedigree extracts from Plea and Memoranda Rolls (18 Richard II to 15 Henry VIII). For details, see p. 134, herein.

* * * * *

The University Library, Cambridge, England: Printed works concerning many subjects relating to Ireland are listed in *A Catalogue of the Bradshaw Collection of Irish Books in the University Library, Cambridge.* Cambridge, 1916. 3 vols., including Index. This Catalogue contains 8,743 items, including a great many works of interest in this chapter.

* * * * *

The Bodleian Library, Oxford: *Analecta Hibernica,* No. 1 (1930), published by the Irish Manuscripts Commission, contains Calendars of Irish Manuscript Collections in this Library as follows: (1) Recent Acquisitions (pp. 1-12). (2) Rawlinson Manuscripts (Class A), (pp. 12-118). (3) Rawlinson Manuscripts (Class B), (pp. 118-178). On p. 6, is listed the details of one volume containing "Connecting links between the following families:" Here are listed the families of Kenmare, Herbert, Lacy, Hedges, MacCarthy, O'Sullivan Beare, White, Sackville, Sambrooke, Vanacker, Maynard, Zouche, Listowel, etc. The records include many from sources named in this Chapter. The Rawlinson Collection is largely made up of Court Records, State Papers, and Parliamentary Records. One entry on p. 77 (*Rawl. A.* 247) is a "MS. copy of letters patent in Latin, tested at Dublin, 21 June, 10 Car. I (1634), whereby the King granted to Edward Plowden, Knt., John Lawrence, Knt. and Bt.; Bowyer Worsley, Knt., and Charles Barret, Esq., and John Trusler, Roger Packs, William Inwood, Thomas Ribread, and George Noble, the whole island near the continent or firm land of North Virginia, called Plowden Island or Long Island, near or between the 39th and 40th degrees of North Latitude, together with part of the continent or firm land near adjacent, by points rehearsed, and all islands and islets within 10 leagues called Pamonke, Hudsons or Hudsons River 'Isles' or by any other names: to hold as of the Imperial Crown of Ireland in Chief, independent of any other but the King immediately."

The Manuscript (*Rawl. A.* 253), pp. 78-86, has to do with "Copies and draughts of petitions to the House of Commons, 1701-2, about Irish Forfeitures." The petitions concern the estates of adherents of James II, declared to be forfeited under William and Mary, and vested in the Trustees appointed by Parliament. Included is a list of the petitioners.

The Carte Manuscripts in the Bodleian Library, Oxford, A Report Presented to the Right Honourable Lord Romilly, Master of the Rolls, by C. W. Russell and J. P. Prendergast, London, 1871, contains a Catalogue of the Collection of 272 volumes. It is named from its collector, the Rev. Thomas Carte, the well-known author of the "Life of James, Duke of Ormonde." The principal part of the collection consists of the papers, official, private, and miscellaneous; mostly letters to and from James, the first Duke of Ormonde, nearly all dated between 1641 and 1685. They relate to Government affairs, revealing a wealth of information concerning thousands of individuals and many family relationships. Supplemental Illustrations include Minutes of the First and Second Court of Claims, 1662-1663; 1666-1669. Appendix B contains a Catalogue of three volumes of King's Letters of Charles II (pp. 199-231), addressed principally to the Duke of Ormonde. A great many of the 1,083 items are marked as enrolled in Chancery. They have to do with correspondence from 1660 to 1669, and concern appointments to office or favors, patents, pensions, the restoring of forfeited land to the original proprietors or heirs and sometimes naming two or more generations.

On p. 86, *Custodiams* are discussed. An application for a *custodiam* occurred in some cases when a proprietor who had been transplanted into Connaught or Clare by the Commonwealth Government, 1653-1655, was restored to his ancient estate under Charles II, and his Connaught assignment became vacant, to be disposed of by Ormonde as Lord Lieutenant, in whom all forfeited property was vested as trustee representing the King. The disposal was by order to the Court of Exchequer, to grant the applicant a *custodiam* or tenancy at will under the Crown, at a moderate rent until further order or disposition of the land was made. These usually supply some history of the persons involved. Another source of genealogical information is a Bill of Discovery. Any one, Protestant or Roman Catholic, who could discover and report information about concealed or irregular ownership of lands or leases liable to seizure by the King, was rewarded by one-fourth of the holdings reported and sometimes as much as the whole property. These discoverers applied with a Bill of Discovery to the Court of Exchequer for a *custodiam* in their own favor, pending a decision by the Court (p. 88).

* * * * *

Denis C. Rushe, in his *History of Monaghan for two Hundred Years,* Dundalk, 1921, makes use of five claims on petition to the Trustees at Chichester House in the year 1700, and a Bill of Discovery filed in the Court of Exchequer, 18 January 1749, to prove one line of the McKenna family of Trough, County Monaghan. Philip Shirley's *History of the County of Monaghan,* London, 1879 (pp. 140, 141), gives the pedigree of John or Shane McTool McKenna who is descended from the chief of that tribe, of Trough, Co. Monaghan, and is said by Shirley to be the last of his line, having been killed in rebellion in 1689.

Rushe (pp. 7, 8, 17, 97-99, 356-359) challenges Shirley's statement and presents the following records to prove the continuation of this McKenna line: He shows that Major John McKenna, named above, was a Roman Catholic, appointed by James II through his Lord Lieutenant, to be sheriff of County Monaghan in 1689. An uprising of the Protestants against this appointment resulted in the murder of Major John McKenna in 1689. In the year 1694, John McKenna, son and heir of Major John McKenna, who had been murdered near Glaslough in 1689, was adjudged within the Articles of Limerick. These Articles, signed at the close of the 1689-1691 Revolution, secured the personal property of officers who served James II, and their heirs, without being subject to forfeiture. The five claims were made against the estate of Major John McKenna of Trough, Co. Monaghan, on petition to the Trustees at Chichester House in the year 1700. In each case the descent is clearly set forth and the son and heir, John McKenna is named. In 1703 he sold the greater part of his Trough estates and purchased leases. This, and the fact that he had four sons, namely, Nugent, Francis, Felix, and William, are set forth in a Bill of Discovery to the Court of Exchequer, 18 January 1749. This is given in full in Appendix XI, pp. 356-359. It states that John McKenna, a Roman Catholic, died sometime in the year 1746, having made a will, by which he left his leases for two, three, or more lives, to his four sons, Nugent, Francis, Felix, and William McKenna, and that they being Roman Catholics, evaded Acts of Parliament in holding and concealing the leases and their terms. The discoverer, James Duga Protestant, prays the Court for the benefits of the property.

CHAPTER XII

GOVERNMENT LAND SURVEYS RELATING TO OCCUPANTS

Government land surveys concerning owners of the land and lessees of importance began after the Reformation. In the 16th and 17th centuries these records comprised Inquisitions on attainder, the Civil Survey, the Books of Survey and Distribution, and other miscellaneous records, all related to the changes in ownership and occupation, by way of forfeiture of the land, and its regrant for purposes of plantation and settlement. During this period, 85 percent of the land changed from Roman Catholic to Protestant ownership. Owing to the particular nature of these records they are grouped in the following CHAPTER XIII, under PLANTATION AND SETTLEMENT RECORDS.

After the completion of the great confiscations of the 17th century, relatively little change occurred in the established family estates of the new Protestant landlords until the late 19th century. Among the few Roman Catholics who were left in possession of great estates, some, for purposes of preserving ownership of their property, became Protestants. However, during the 18th century, the dispossessed Roman Catholic majority became a settled tenantry, mostly on the lands of their ancestors, excepting in the more choice areas of Ulster which were planted with a Scottish and English tenantry who held long term leases, usually ranging in length from 21 years, 61 years or three lives, to tenures renewable forever.

The following review of extracts from writings on Irish agrarian conditions, presented in CHAPTER IX, hereof, will emphasize the practices which indicate that families occupied their leased holdings for generations, and thus the names of householders with their place of residence as shown in the

19th century surveys serve as clues for tracing earlier generations:

Arthur Young, famous English Protestant authority on Irish agrarian conditions, following some years of study throughout the country, wrote *A Tour of Ireland* (1776-1779). In Volume II, Part II, pp. 17-53, are sections on the Irish Tenantry, the Labouring Poor, on Emigration, and Religion. He states (p. 42), "The spirit of emigrating in Ireland appeared to be confined to two circumstances, the Presbyterian religion, and the linen manufacture. The Catholics never went, they seem not only tied to the country but almost to the parish in which their ancestors lived." He continues (p. 44), "Upon the whole nineteen-twentieths of the kingdom changed hands from Catholic to Protestant [by 1776]. The lineal descendants of great families, once possessed of great property, are now to be found all over the kingdom in the lowest situation, working as cotters for the great great grandsons of men, many of whom were of no greater account in England than these poor labourers are at present on that property which was once their own . . . families were so numerous and so united in clans, that the [dispossessed] heir of an estate was always known; and it is a fact that in most parts of the kingdom the descendants of the old land owners regularly transmit by testamentary deed the memorial of their right to those estates which once belonged to their families." Thus we have evidence of a settled tenantry.

Arthur Young opens his section on Tenantry (p. 17), with the statement, "It has been probably owing to the small value of land in Ireland before, and even through a considerable part of the present century, that landlords became so careless of the interests of property, as readily to grant their tenants leases for ever."

This resolved itself into a numerous Protestant tenantry clinging to perpetual leases. Roman Catholics who, in the 17th century, for safety, sold their property and purchased perpetual leases of the same, for the most part lost them regardless of the precaution during times of confiscation and in the early years of the Penal laws. They did acquire shorter term leases, indicated by Arthur Young (p. 22), as "usually three lives to Protestants and thirty-one years to Catholics." However, all leases were subject to renewal time after time upon good performance of the tenant.

Jonathan Pim, in his *The Condition and Prospects of Ireland,* Dublin, 1848, p. 332, states, "In adverting to the character of the landlords' tenure in Ireland, it is our duty to observe upon a species of tenure, scarcely known elsewhere, which prevails very extensively in that country, one-seventh of Ireland being said to be held under it. We allude to the tenure by lease for lives, with a covenant of perpetual renewal on payment of a fine." He goes on to note the frequency of litigation over the leases, "Forfeitures of the right to enforce a renewal daily occur, through the neglect of tenants, or the dexterous management of landlords."

With respect to the conditions imposed by the Government upon Roman Catholics, Pim states (p. 330), "Among many measures professedly for the improvement of Ireland, an Act was passed in 1771, which allowed Roman Catholics to take a lease for sixty-one years of not less than ten acres, or more than fifty . . . In 1777, it was enacted that titles not hitherto litigated should not be disturbed, and Roman Catholics were allowed to take leases for any term under 1,000 years. In 1782, they were allowed to acquire freehold property for lives or by inheritance; and in 1793, was passed a further enactment, which materially affected the position of landlord and tenant. The forty-shilling franchise was by that Act extended to Roman Catholics; the landlord and middlemen then found the importance of a numerous following of tenantry, and subdivision and sub-letting, being by this law indirectly encouraged greatly increased."

All of the above comments on the extensive times of leases and the privilege of renewing shorter leases explain the practices which give great importance to the 19th century surveys containing the names of occupants and their leased property throughout Ireland. The name of the townland of a tenant thus recorded can be used in searching the *Land Index* in the Registry of Deeds, Dublin, to trace every memorial of a lease of over three years, or other transaction in the history of that townland which may uncover leases in succeeding generations of a family. The Government surveys of the 19th century are the Tithe Applotment Books, the House and Town Books, and Griffith's Valuation, described below:

Tithe Composition Applotment Books, 1823-1837: This series of over 2,000 MS. volumes was transferred from the Land Commission Office to the Public Record Office, Dublin, in 1944, where an Index of the records by parish and county is in the Search Room. The surveys range in date from 1823 to 1837 and concern every parish in Ireland, excepting those of the cities and larger towns. For each parish they contain the names of every tenant of the land, all of whom were liable for the payment of tithes to the Established Church of Ireland, regardless of their religion. Beside the tenant's name was entered the name of his townland, the acreage of his farm, its valuation and the proportion of future tithe for which he was liable. In some cases additional and varied information relates to such matters as earlier tenants or land holders, legal interests of tenants, notes about emigrants and remarks about earlier history.

The immediate circumstances leading to the compiling of these records by parish was brought about by the Tithe Composition Acts (1 Geo. IV, *c.* 40; 5 Geo. IV, *c.* 63; 7 & 8 Geo. IV, *c.* 60; 2 & 3 Wm. IV, *c.* 119; 3 & 4 Wm. IV, *c.* 100; and 6 & 7 Wm. IV, *c.* 95). Beginning in July 1823, the Acts provided for the payment of tithes to the clergy of the parish in money rather than in kind (produce). This change in the nature of tithe payments required a valuation of the land in every parish, under the direction of two district parochial commissioners. One was elected by the parochial rate payers and the other was chosen by the bishop of the diocese. The district commissioners valued the holdings of every tenant according to the yield and average price of wheat and oats within the parish during a seven-year period prior to November 1, 1821. As pasture lands were also rated for the tithe, protests appear in some reports.

The collection of some 2,500 MS. volumes, of which the volumes relating to 273 parishes were sent to the Public Record Office of Northern Ireland, comprises the original compiled books and numerous copies of the originals which were certified and signed by the commissioners and accepted as valid by Parliament. The entire Tithe Valuation comprises a complete national survey of occupants of the land.

R. C. Simington wrote an article on this great collection (published in *Analecta Hibernica* No. 10, pp. 295-298), in which he directs "attention to the exceptional importance of this extensive repertory, and of its value to students and investigators in the spheres of history, economics and genealogy." He points out that the "Tithe Applotment Valuation furnishes a detailed account of the occupiers of the land with the extent and value of their individual farms. It was the first complete register of the people in relation to the working and tenancy of the land . . . the occupation and usage of the land for two decades immediately preceding the upheaval wrought by the famine of '47."

Other details furnished by Simington are that 1,353 of the 2,450 parishes had been surveyed in Applotment Books, 1823-1830. The remainder were completed by 1837. "Each parochial Applotment Book presents in tabular form the particulars of the Tithe apportionment under the captions of Tenants, Townlands, Area, Valuation, and Tithe Payable." In numerous Books, the records of large estates show "the names of the head landlords and owners in fee, the rents per acre, paid by the tenants, . . . returns of each man's sowing of wheat, barley, oats, potatoes and so on . . . the tithe valuation is of exceptional importance as preserving the memory of the people of the soil." He observes, "Where . . . there was a wholesale removal of tenantry to America, or elsewhere, the Tithe Valuation, in the absence of Emigration lists or other particulars, is the only source enabling descendants to establish connection with the land of their transported ancestry." By this he means that this is the only national series of records of the period which accomplishes this end. *Griffith's Valuation,* described below, is equally complete.

The Public Record Office of Northern Ireland, in 1944, received the Tithe Applotment Books relating to Northern Ireland from the Irish Land Commission, Dublin, by way of the Ministry of Finance of Northern Ireland. These represent part of the collection described above. They concern 273 parishes in counties Antrim, Armagh, Cavan, Down, Fermanagh, Londonderry, and Tyrone. As in the records for all of Ireland the names of the tithe payers are usually arranged alphabetically by townlands and by parish and county. For several parishes there are two copies of Tithe Applotment Books and miscellaneous papers, deeds and letters relating to the tithes. In some cases, surveys of 18th century dates are included. A few parishes are not represented except by miscellaneous papers, these being mostly of cities and larger towns. This Office has indexed the records by parish and county.

The *Boundary Survey Maps*, authorized by the Government Act of 1825 and made under the supervision of Richard Griffith, were a preliminary proceeding for the survey of the country then undertaken by the Ordnance authorities. They were constructed to define the boundaries of townlands, parishes, baronies, and counties. Some 5,500 documents made up this collection of original maps, transferred from the Valuation Office to the Public Record Office, Dublin, after 1944. (*Analecta Hibernica*, No. 17, p. 349.)

Another series comprise the *Field Books, Town, House,* and *Rent Books* (originals and duplicates), transferred from the Valuation Office to the Public Record Office, Dublin. These all represent early proceedings in the determination of the Government Valuation of the country authorized in 1826, but not begun until a few years later. They are of dates extending to 1851. The Field Books (4,587), compiled by parish, describe each townland in the parish; the quality of the soil, and its valuation irrespective of buildings or crops in the ground. The House and Town Books (4,262), were also compiled by parish, in both rural and urban areas. They contain the valuations of all houses and other buildings. Data in the valuations include the data and terms of the tenant's acquisition of the property, the rent, and various particulars in cases of business property. The names of the occupiers consistently appear in the records, together with the dimensions of the buildings and the estimated age of each. The Rent Books (470) contain records of tenure giving various particulars of holdings and tenants. (*Analecta Hibernica*, No. 17, pp. 349-350; Public Record Office, Dublin, 58th *Report*, p. 18.)

The Royal Irish Academy, Dublin, has a collection of Ordnance Survey Documents, relating to various parishes. These contain miscellaneous records of antiquities and such information as lists of emigrants, c. 1833-1837. The records for numerous parishes of Northern Ireland have been loaned to the Public Record Office, Belfast, for copying, particularly the emigration records. The names of the parishes and dates of the emigration records are included in the *Reports* of this Office. As the destination of most of the emigrants was Canada or the United States, copies of the lists were sent to The National Archives in Washington, D. C., where they are in the Library adjoining the Central Search Room. Copies were also sent to the Canadian Archives in Ottawa, Ontario. These records will be further noted under EMIGRATION in the following CHAPTER XXI.

Published Ordnance Survey records are *Ordnance Survey Letters Containing Information Relative to the Antiquities of the Counties*, collected during the progress of the Ordnance Survey of 1835-1840; reproduced under the direction of Rev. Michael O'Flanaghan. Bray, 1927. 35 vols. These concern counties Armagh and Monaghan, Carlow, Cavan and Leitrim, Clare (3 vols.), Donegal, Down, Dublin, Fermanagh, Galway (3 vols.), Kerry, Kilkenny, Kildare, Queen's Co., Limerick (2 vols.), Londonderry, Longford, Louth, Mayo (2 vols.), Meath, King's Co., Roscommon, Sligo, Tipperary (3 vols.), Waterford, Westmeath, Wexford, Wicklow. A set of these records is included in the excellent Irish section of the Huntington Library, San Marino, California. Another set is in the Pennsylvania Historical Society Library, Philadelphia, Pennsylvania.

Griffith's Primary Valuation of Rateable Property in Ireland, 1848-1864, of over 200 volumes, was printed as a Government project. The National Library of Ireland, and the Public Record Office, Dublin, each have nearly complete sets of the records. The Public Record Office, Belfast, has the volumes which concern Ulster.

The valuations or surveys in these volumes were compiled

by Poor Law Unions. The *Poor Relief Act* (1), 1838, established the Poor Law Unions as districts within which the local and rateable people were financially responsible for the care of all paupers of the area. The Poor Law Unions embraced multiples of townlands within an average radius of about ten miles, usually with a large market town as a center. The larger cities contained their own Unions. The boundaries of the Poor Law Unions had no relation to those of the counties. Some Unions comprised areas each entirely within a single county, while others were formed to include parts of two, three, or four counties, depending upon the position of the market town established as the center. Some of the largest Poor Law Unions were sub-divided after 1847.

Griffith's Valuation was a survey made by Government order after the Act of 1838, to determine the amount of tax each able person should pay toward support of the poor and destitute within his Poor Law Union. For this purpose the value of all privately held lands and buildings in both rural and urban areas was determined according to the rate at which each unit of property could be rented year after year. The tax was fixed at about 6d. (with variations), for every pound of the rent value.

The *Poor Relief Act* of 1838 required that the occupiers or tenants, and the immediate lessors of all lands, buildings, etc., for private or business use, were liable for the tax. An immediate lessor could be the landlord if he rented directly to the tenant, or the middleman was the immediate lessor if he leased property from the owner and sub-let it to tenants.

The equalization of the Poor Law Rates in each Union moved slowly for some years and thus the complete Valuation of private property became necessary, but did not take place as a national survey until 1848-1864. Some earlier scattered records will be noted. Griffith's completed Valuation provides a census of all who held property in the year or years the survey was made for each Poor Law Union. This gives the name of each immediate lessor of property, each occupier or tenant, the name of his townland or city location, the parish, the area and value of his holding and thus the amount of tax he was required to pay.

The collections within each Poor Law Union were used to pay off a Government 20-year loan advanced to build a "Work House" for the destitute who were homeless, for their support, and to provide food for some other paupers. Government Commissioners supervised the finances while a local board of unpaid Guardians assumed the responsibility for collecting the assessed rates, and administered the affairs of the "Work House" and other matters relating to care of the destitute.

Jonathan Pim's *The Condition and Prospects of Ireland,* 1848 (pp. 192-234), gives details regarding the organization and operation of the Poor Law Unions, the work of the Commissioners and the Board of Guardians, and the problems of collecting the tax. *Thom's Irish Almanac,* 1847 (pp. 162-163, 167-168, 174), furnishes exact data regarding the operation of the Poor Law Unions; the Poor Rates, the definition of taxable property, and persons liable; the names of the Poor Law Unions in existence at that time, numbering 130; the name of the county, any part of which each Union embraced; the area, and population of each in 1841, the number of paupers; and the net annual rent value of each Union.

The set of *Griffith's Valuation* now in the Public Record Office, Dublin, consists of 198 volumes. Those for the parts of County Carlow, and for the Unions of Abbeyleix and Birr, County Tipperary, are missing.

Dr. Richard J. Hayes, Director of the National Library of Ireland, sent his Library List of volumes, which is presented below. The original volumes each contained the records of parts or all of a Poor Law Union. The National Library rebound its set by counties. In order to do this, the records of all Unions, and sections of any Unions which fall in one county, were assembled and bound in one or more volumes under the name of the county. Therefore, in the following list, the name of a Union will appear under all counties in which any part of it is located. Also it is noticeable in the list that Griffith surveyed some parts of a Union in one year and other parts in one or more following years. Some sections of a Union were surveyed more than once and in combination with parts of other Unions.

Thus in the following list, under County Cork, Vol. I, is the Union of Mallow and the Union of Cork, dated 1851. Following this, the Unions of Cork, Fermoy, and Middleton, were valued in 1853. Under County Cork, Vol. III, is the Valuation of the Union of Cork in 1852, while the Union of Fermoy again appears with the Union of Mitchelstown in 1852. Under County Cork, Vol. V, the Valuation of the Union of Cork appears with that of the Union of Kinsale for 1850. Still again, in Vol. VI, the Union of Cork appears with the Unions of Bandon and Macroom in 1852. Thus the Union of Cork or parts of it appear to have been valued in succeeding years, 1850-1853.

As stated above, *Thom's Irish Almanac*, 1847, listed 130 Poor Law Unions then in existence. Following this date several Unions were sub-divided into two or more Unions due to their size. The National Library List contains the names of 34 Unions created after 1847. Upon comparing this list with the 130 names of Unions given in *Thom's Irish Almanac*, 1847, the names of the newer Unions can be determined. It also appears that the National Library List lacks the Valuation for the two Unions of Newtown Limavady, and Magherafelt, in County Londonderry, and the Union of Lowtherstown which lies in the counties of Fermanagh, Donegal and Tyrone. Otherwise the National Library collection is complete.

The genealogical value of *Griffith's Valuation*, 1848-1864, as substitutes for Census Records is evident. It is especially important for identifying emigrants as to their exact place of origin during this period. Emigration statistics, which will be noted in the following CHAPTER XXI, point to the fact that a large proportion of the great emigration following the "Famine" of 1847, did not occur until after 1855, subsequent to the recording of the bulk of *Griffith's Valuation*. The List of the National Library of Ireland (with a few repeated Valuations for some Unions), shows that 9 were dated in 1848 or 1849; 141 were dated between 1850 and 1855; 45 were dated 1856 to 1859, and 34 were dated 1860-1864.

Dr. Richard J. Hayes sent a report on December 17, 1960, as follows: "I thought you would like to know of a new project here. We are making an index of the surnames in *Grif-*

fith's Valuation of Ireland. It will be available here in typed form. It contains an alphabet for each parish and then an alphabet for the county, telling how many householders of any name are in each barony of the county. We have completed three counties; Wexford, Wicklow, and Carlow, and hope to produce a county [index] every two months."

This will greatly facilitate the use of *Griffith's Valuation* for genealogical purposes, to locate the exact place of origin of an emigrant by townland, if he left Ireland after the Valuation of his area was made. If he held a lease of more than three years duration, the records of his property can be traced through the Land Index of Townlands and city property, in the Registry of Deeds, Dublin. All surveys described in this chapter provide identifying information leading to parish records, leases, wills, and indeed all classes of records.

While Griffith's published Valuation contains the surveys made of the various Poor Law Unions for the years 1848-1864 only, some earlier surveys were made. Griffith's Valuation of County Armagh, 1839, comprising 28 MS. volumes, is in the Armagh County Museum. The National Library of Ireland microfilmed the collection (Film Negative 419; Positive, 99). The Public Record Office, Belfast, has 59 MS. volumes containing the Valuation of County Antrim, 1839; County Cavan, 1841; County Down, 1839.

The National Library of Ireland List of *Griffith's Primary Valuation of Rateable Property in Ireland,* 1848-1864, is bound in volumes by counties and dates, as follows:

County			Union	Date
ANTRIM	VOL.	I.	Antrim	1862
			Ballycastle	1861
			Ballymena	1862
	VOL.	II.	Ballymoney	1861
			Belfast	1861
			Coleraine	1859
			Larne	1861
			Lisburn	1862
ARMAGH	VOL.	I.	Armagh	1864
			Banbridge	1863
			Castleblaney	1864
	VOL.	II.	Dundalk	1854
			Lurgan	1864
			Newry	1864

County			Union	Date
CARLOW	VOL.	I.	Carlow	1852
CAVAN	VOL.	I.	Bailieborough	1856
			Bawnboy	1857
			Cavan	1857
	VOL.	II.	Cootehill	1857
			Enniskillen	1857
			Granard	1855
			Kells	1854
			Oldcastle	1856
CLARE	VOL.	I.	Ballyvaghan	1855
			Corrofin	1855
			Ennis	1855
			Ennistimon	1855
	VOL.	II.	Killadysert	1855
			Kilrush	1855
			Limerick	1852
			Scarriff	1855
			Tulla	1855
CORK	VOL.	I.	Bantry	**1852**
			Mallow & Cork	1851
			Cork, Fermoy, Middleton	1853
			Bantry & Castletown	1852
	VOL.	II.	Bandon, Bantry, Clonakilty, Dunmanway, Skibbereen	1852
			Bandon, Clonakilty, Dunmanway, Kinsale	1851
			Skibbereen	1853
			Bantry, Skull, Skibbereen	1853
	VOL.	III.	Fermoy & Mitchelstown	1852
			Cork	1852
			Kinsale	1851
			Kanturk	1852
			Mallow	1852
			Millstreet	1852
	VOL.	IV.	Fermoy, Mallow, Mitchelstown	1851
			Clonakilty	1852
			Youghal & Middleton	1853
	VOL.	V.	Cork and Kinsale	1850
			Bandon & Kinsale	1851
			Bandon	1851
			Fermoy & Middleton	1850
			Kinsale	1852
	VOL.	VI.	Bandon, Cork, Macroom	1852
			Dunmanway, Macroom, Millstreet	1852
			Kanturk, Kilmallock, Mallow	1851
CORK (Municipal Borough)			Cork	**1852**
DONEGAL	VOL.	I.	Ballyshannon	**1858**
			Donegal	1857
			Dunfanaghy	1857
			Glenties	1857

County			Union	Date
	VOL. II.		Inishowen	1857
			Letterkenny	1858
			Londonderry	1858
	VOL. III.		Millford	1858
			Strabane	1858
			Stranorlar	1857
DOWN	VOL. I.		Banbridge	1863
			Belfast	1861
			Downpatrick	1863
			Kilkeel	1863
	VOL. II.		Lisburn	1863
			Lurgan	1864
			Newry	1864
			Newtown Ards	1863
DUBLIN			Balrothery	1848
			Celbridge	1851
			Balrothery & Dunshaughlin	1848
			Balrothery	1852
			South Dublin & Rathdown	1849
			North Dublin & Celbridge	1849
			South Dublin	1850
			South Dublin & Rathdown (Alterations)	1848
DUBLIN (CITY)			South Dublin	1854
			North Dublin	1854
FERMANAGH			Ballyshannon (Portion)	1862
			Clones "	1862
			Enniskillen "	1862
			Irvinestown "	1862
			Lisnaskea	1862
GALWAY	VOL. I.		Ballinasloe	1856
			Galway	1855
	VOL. II.		Loughrea	1856
			Mountbellow	1855
	VOL. III.		Ballinrobe (Portion)	1855
			Portumna	1856
			Tuam	1855
KERRY	VOL. I.		Listowel & Tralee (Portion)	1852
			Dingle & Tralee "	1852
			Kenmare & Cahersiveen "	1852
			Cahersiveen, Kenmare, Killarney "	1852
			Kenmare & Killarney (Portions)	1852
	VOL. II.		Glin & Listowel "	1851
			Cahersiveen & Killarney "	1852
			Killarney "	1853
			Tralee, Killarney & Dingle "	1853
KILDARE			Celbridge	1851
			Edenderry (Portion)	1853
			Naas "	1853

County			Union	Date
			Athy & Baltinglass	
KILKENNY			(Portion)	1852
			Callan	1849
			Kilkenny & Callan	1849
			Castlecomer, Kilkenny,	
			Arlingford	1850
			Kilkenny	1849
			Callan & Carrick-on-Suir	1850
			Carrick-on-Suir, New Ross,	
			Thomastown & Waterford	1850
			New Ross, Thomastown,	
			Waterford	1850
			Castlecomer, Kilkenny,	
			Thomastown	1851
			Carrick-on-Suir, Waterford	1850
			Carrick-on-Suir, New Ross,	
			Thomastown & Waterford	1850
LEITRIM			Ballyshannon (Portion)	1857
			Bawnboy "	1856
			Carrick-on-Shannon	
			(Portion)	1856
			Manorhamilton	1857
			Mohill	1857
LEIX			Athy & Carlow	1851
			Donaghmore & Mount-	
			mellick	1850
			Carlow	1850
			Mountmellick	1851
			Athy & Mountmellick	1850
			Abbeyleix	1850
LIMERICK	VOL.	I.	Croom & Rathkeale	1850
			Limerick	1851
			Limerick & Croom	1850
			Croom, Limerick, Kil-	
			mallock	1851
			Glin, Newcastle &	
			Rathkeale (Portion)	1852
	VOL.	II.	Limerick	
			& Tipperary (Portion)	1852
			Croom, Glin,	
			Rathkeale "	1852
			Kilmallock, Limerick,	
			Tipperary	1851
			Michelstown,	
			Kilmallock (Portion)	1852
			Kanturk, Newcastle,	
			Rathkeale (Portion)	1852
	VOL.	III.	Limerick	1850
LONGFORD			Ballymahon	1854
			Granard	1854
			Longford	1854
LOUTH			Drogheda	1851
MAYO	VOL.	I.	Ballinrobe (Portion)	1857
			Belmullet	1855
			Castlebar	1857

County			Union	Date
	VOL.	II.	Claremorris	1856
			Killala	1856
	VOL.	III.	Newport	1855
			Westport	1855
MEATH (Louth & Meath)	VOL.	I.	Celbridge	1850
			Dunshaughlin (Portion)	1854
MEATH	VOL.	II.	Edenderry (Portion)	1854
	VOL.	III.	Navan	1854
			Oldcastle (Portion)	1854
			Trim	1854
MONAGHAN	VOL.	I.	Carrickmacross	1861
			Castleblayney (Portion)	1861
	VOL.	II.	Clones (Portion)	1861
			Cootehill (Portion)	1858
			Monaghan	1860
OFFALY			Edenderry (Portion)	1853
			Parsonstown	1854
ROSCOMMON	VOL.	I.	Athlone	1855
			Ballinasloe (Portion)	1855
			Boyle "	1858
	VOL.	II.	Carrick-on-Shannon	
			(Portion)	1858
			Strokestown	1857
SLIGO			Boyle	1858
			Dromore, West	1857
			Sligo	1858
			Tobercurry	1857
TIPPERARY	VOL.	I.	(S.R.) Cashel & Tipperary	1851
			Carrick-on-Suir, Clogheen,	
			Clonmel	1850
			Clogheen, Clonmel	
			(Portions)	1852
	VOL.	II.	(N.R.) Cashel, Nenagh,	
			Thurles, Tipperary	1851
			Cashel & Tipperary	1850
			Callan, Cashel, Tipperary,	
			Clonmel	1850
			Callan, Carrick-on-Suir,	
			Cashel, Thurles, Urlingford	1850
	VOL.	III.	(N.R.) Thurles	1850
			Roscrea & Thurles	1851
			Nenagh	1850
	VOL.	IV.	Nenagh	1850
TYRONE	VOL.	I.	Armagh (Portion)	1860
			Castlederg	1860
			Cookstown	1859
			Dungannon	1860
	VOL.	II.	Gortin	1859
			Omagh	1860
			Strabane (Portion)	1858

County			*Union*	*Date*
WATERFORD	VOL.	I.	Lismore & Youghal	1851
			Dungarvan & Youghal	1851
			Dungarvin, Lismore, Kilmacthomas	1851
	VOL.	II.	Waterford	1848
			Clonmel	1850
			Waterford & Kilmacthomas	1850
			Clonmel & Carrick-on-Suir	1850
			Waterford	1851
WESTMEATH			Athlone (Portion)	1854
			Granard "	1854
			Mullingar	1854
WEXFORD	VOL.	I.	Gorey	1853
			Wexford	1853
	VOL.	II.	Enniscorthy (Portion)	1853
			New Ross "	1853
WICKLOW	VOL.	I.	Baltinglass (Portion)	1854
			Naas "	1853
			Rathdrum	1854
			Shillelagh (Portion)	1853
	VOL.	II.	Naas (Portion)	1853
ARMAGH, LOUTH, MONAGHAN			Dundalk	1854
GALWAY & CLARE (GALWAY, VOL. II)			Gort	1855
GALWAY & MAYO			Clifden	1855
			Oughterard	1855
GALWAY & ROSCOMMON			Glenamaddy	1856
LOUTH & MEATH			Ardee	1854
			Drogheda	1854
MAYO & ROSCOMMON			Swineford	1856
MAYO & SLIGO			Ballina	1856
MEATH & CAVAN (MEATH, VOL. II)			Kells	1854
MEATH & WESTMEATH (WESTMEATH, VOL. I)			Castletowndelvin	1854
MONAGHAN & TYRONE (MONAGHAN, VOL. I)			Clogher	1860
OFFALY (KING'S CO.) & WESTMEATH (OFFALY VOL.)			Tullamore	1854
ROSCOMMON & GALWAY (ROSCOMMON, VOL. II)			Roscommon	1857
ROSCOMMON & MAYO			Castlerea	1857

CHAPTER XIII

PLANTATION AND SETTLEMENT RECORDS

The Plantation and Settlement records of Ireland, c. 1540-
1703, comprise a great corpus of Government documents containing personal records of members of the old and new landed
families, extending from one to several generations. They
concern the progressive confiscations and the successive series
of new land grants, until the final distribution placed most of
the acreage of Ireland in the possession of English Protestants.

The purpose of this chapter is to review the causes and results of the great changes in land tenure, thereby defining the
nature of the source materials, and to discuss the available
records in the following order:

I. The Calendars of collections covering all or most of the
entire period, c. 1540-1703.

II. The source materials relating particularly to one reign or
period of the Government.

III. Notes on miscellaneous manuscript collections and published sources.

In a figurative sense the term "Plantation" is applied to the
establishment of new colonies of English, Welsh and Scots in
Ireland, chiefly carried out by Elizabeth and James I. The
preliminary ground work was, however, laid by Henry VIII,
and the first steps were taken during the reigns of Edward VI
and Mary.

The term "Settlement" used in the last half of the 17th century, in relation to the great changes in ownership and occupation of the land, is explained in *The Cromwellian Settlement of Ireland,* by John P. Prendergast, Dublin, 1875 (pp.
xiii-xv): "The term 'Settlement,' of such great import in the
history of Ireland in the seventeenth century, means nothing
else than the settlement of the balance of land according to
the will of the strongest; for force, not reason, is the source
of the law. And by the term Cromwellian Settlement is to be
understood the history of the dealings of the Commonwealth

of England with the lands and habitations of the people of Ireland after their conquest of the country in the year 1652. As their object was rather to extinguish a nation than to suppress a religion, they seized the lands of the Irish, and transferred them (and with them all the power of the state) to an overwhelming flood of new English settlers, filled with the intensest national and religious hatred of the Irish. Two other settlements followed, which may be called the Restoration Settlement, and the Revolution Settlement. The one was a counter revolution, by which some of the Royalist English of Ireland and a few of the native Irish were restored to their estates under the Acts of Settlement and Explanation. The other (or Revolution Settlement) followed the victory of William III, at the Battle of the Boyne. By it the lands lately restored to the Royalist English and a few native Irish were again seized by the Parliament of England, and distributed among the conquering nation. At the Court for the Sale of Estates forfeited on account of the war of 1690, the lands could be purchased only by Englishmen . . . It will thus be seen that these three Settlements are only parts of one whole, and that the Cromwellian Settlement is the foundation of the present settlement of Ireland."

On the whole, the Plantation and Settlement of Ireland carried out the principal object of the Crown and the English Government (including that of the Commonwealth) over a period of one hundred and fifty years, to eventually subjugate Ireland by confiscation, and plant the realm with new landlords, loyal to the State, who would supply revenue to the Government, maintain English law administered by representatives from England, and furnish protection by locally supported military forces. Thus the forfeitures of individual estates by "enemies of the State" are a part of the series of Plantation and Settlement records which set forth the changes in ownership and tenure of Irish lands.

The source materials of this period, c. 1540-1703, have little significance without an understanding of the course of events they represent. Therefore, a very brief outline of the conditions in Ireland prior to 1540, and the following events which led to the changes brought about by England's purposeful reaction, is presented up to the 17th century periods previously explained in earlier chapters.

When Henry VIII came to the throne in 1509, only the small area called the "English Pale" could be counted obedient to English law and the collection of Crown revenue while supporting a small military force. For about two centuries the Pale had embraced the counties of Dublin, Louth, Meath, and Kildare, with the maritime cities of Cork, Waterford, and a few others of less note. The Anglo-Norman conquest of Henry II and King John had covered half the land of Ireland which was parceled out to the conquering lords who professed allegiance to the Crown of England, but for the most part exercised independent feudal authority over their own territories.

The greatest period of legal control was reached under Edward I, but he turned his attention to conquest in Wales, Scotland, and the more costly war with France. This was continued in France by Edward III and his successors while it exhausted England's resources for a century. Control over Ireland rapidly waned from 1327 to 1366. Descendants of many of the Anglo-Norman and English lords having become absentees, some twenty-four were commanded by the Crown to return and garrison their territories but failed to obey. In the following century a further exodus of Anglo-Norman and English landlords and their tenants occurred. The Gaelic chiefs with a series of petty wars recovered two-thirds of their tribal lands. Intermarriage between the three races became common soon after the invasion. The Anglo-Norman and English lords who remained in Ireland and maintained their independence beyond the Pale adopted the Irish language and customs while many allied themselves with the Gaelic-Irish chieftains against the encroachment of the English officials and new settlers.

During the thirty years of English civil "Wars of the Roses" between the houses of Lancaster and York over the Crown, the Government control in Ireland was further weakened. Home rule began there in 1425 and, except for brief intervals, was carried on successively under the great earls of Ormond, Desmond, and Kildare, until Henry VIII destroyed the house of Kildare in 1534. Gerald, son of Thomas, eighth earl of

Kildare, called by the Irish "Garret More" exercised the power of the real king of Ireland from 1477 until his death in 1513. Henry VII said of him, that "since all Ireland cannot rule this man, this man must rule all Ireland." In 1513 his son, Garret Oge, succeeded to the home rule of Ireland until 1534 when Henry VIII imprisoned him. His son, Thomas, and five of his Geraldine uncles were executed in 1537.

Thus Henry VIII acted when he realized Ireland must be subjugated or lost. Meanwhile his Reformation Parliament, 1529-1536, made the great breach with Rome and, in 1541, he was declared King of Ireland in the Irish Parliament. By an Act of the Reformation Parliament against Irish absentees who had deserted their estates, many which had been acquired during the Anglo-Norman conquest were at this time vested in the Crown, including the lordships of Carlow, Wexford, and other fiefs in Leinster. The earldom of Ulster and the lordships of Leix and Connaught were by right of inheritance vested in the Crown, and thus the King's title could be claimed to great areas occupied by lords and chieftains who resisted English rule. Henry VIII and his successors took the view that land acquired by English subjects at any time since the Anglo-Norman conquest was deemed forever thereafter to be illegally held when regained by the Irish.

The Reformation Parliament declared the king the Supreme Head on earth of the Church of Ireland, and dissolved the abbeys within the Pale and near areas of Leinster and Munster, appropriating their lands and wealth. At this time Henry VIII rejected the policy of conquest by war and plantation on any large scale as being too expensive. The State Papers show that he envisioned a complete reduction of the Gaelic-Irish power and other refractory interests by eventually confiscating their estates one after another, and planting them with new English. But he proceeded cautiously. English-born officials were introduced in Dublin. The rich abbey lands acquired by the Crown were granted to loyal subjects, both English by birth and by blood.

The next step instituted the policy of obtaining treaties with the troublesome Anglo-Norman and Gaelic-Irish nobility who had reason to be uneasy over the titles to their lands. Henry VIII left them undisturbed and persuaded forty of the greatest lords and chiefs to surrender their territories to the Crown and accept them back *in capite* by re-grant, under certain conditions which insured revenue and declared the lands forfeited to the Crown in any case of treason or failure to fulfill the contract, such as supplying military force to support the Government. To further cement the ties to the Crown, he created Murrough O'Brien, Earl of Thomond; Conn Bacach O'Neill, Earl of Tyrone; Ulick Burke, Earl of Clanrickard. Various others were created barons, including the Fitzpatricks, barons of Upper Ossory, and Manus O'Donnell, baron of Tyrconnell. But the members of the tribes who jointly owned the tribal property with their chiefs, according to the ancient Gaelic Brehon law, were left as small freeholders or tenants of their chiefs. This fomented trouble and a welter of petty wars when the eldest son of a chief inherited their great estates.

In 1548, under Edward VI, the Government determined to confiscate the territories of Leix and Offaly held by the O'Mores, O'Connors and others who were engaged in insurrection. Under English law treason was just cause for forfeiture, and this furnished the opportunity to plant a new English colony. In this year Walter Cowley was appointed "Surveyor-General and Escheator-General" to receive, value, and re-distribute the forfeited lands. This was done by process of surveys, followed by the appointment of local juries to make inquisitions of the history of the tenure of the lands and those who were in possession, for the purpose of finding the title of the Crown in one way or another. In this case the Crown title to the territories was found for the king, by right of descent and inheritance from the Mortimers who received it from the Lacys. This dated back to the 12th-14th centuries. Following these inquisitions the Parliament in Dublin was required to pass an Act to confirm the attainder of those convicted of treason and others who were implicated. Some were later pardoned but the instigators were forever deprived of all or part of their lands.

Numerous ones who were pardoned in 1550 were named, with their place of residence, in James Morrin's *Calendar of the Patent and Close Rolls of Chancery in Ireland*, Vol. I, Dublin, 1861, pp. 199 (No. 9); 211 (Nos. 124, 125, 127); 236

(No. 17) ; 245 (No. 102), etc. Commissions for survey and twenty-one year leases are indexed. The Calendar of Fiants of Edward VI contains pardons, and twenty-one year leases to Englishmen naming the sections of lands in Offaly and Leix, 1550-1551. Some mention them as formerly in the possession of attainted O'Connors and O'Mores. Others provide that no one of these surnames shall be allowed to live, under any conditions, on the lands of their ancestors, henceforth leased to named Englishmen. Conditions, similar to those in later leases and grants in all parts of the country, require living on the land and providing military arms, and forces at the forts, etc. *(Appendix to the Eighth Report of the Deputy Keeper of the Public Records in Ireland,* Fiants, Nos. 661, 673, 684-688, 690-692, 699-701, 703-704, 709-710, 716, 724, 726, 732-733, 735-736, 741, 765-767, 829-830, etc.)

During Queen Mary's reign, many pardons appear in the Patents and Fiants, also showing confiscations in scattered areas including the territories of Offaly and Leix and others from which King's and Queen's Counties were formed, in which 160 English settlers were planted while the natives were removed to a poor third of the western areas.

Elizabeth's reign, 1558-1603, was beset with growing unrest, insurrections, rebellions and wars throughout most of Ireland, caused by the insecurity of land-titles of the Gaelic-Irish chieftains and numerous great Anglo-Norman and old English families in Leinster, Munster, and Connaught, while in Ulster the Gaelic-Irish chieftains and tribes presented a solid front to block English incursion and to preserve their own independence and support their great leaders O'Neill, O'Donnell and others. All troubles were augmented by the religious issue.

Unrest following the Leinster confiscations and plantation culminated in the great Desmond rebellion in Munster, 1569-1573, and again 1579-1583. The Earl of Desmond, powerful head of the southern branch of the Geraldines, and one hundred and forty of his adherents were attainted in 1586 by the Parliament in Dublin, and 574,628 acres in Counties Cork, Limerick, Kerry, and Waterford, were subject to confiscation, approved by Elizabeth in June 1586, with final "Articles" for the purpose of an English plantation in Munster.

This was followed by a Government survey of all the attainted lands in Munster, by Sir Valentine Brown. Inquisitions (preserved among the Carew Manuscripts in the Archiepiscopal Library of Lambeth Palace, London) taken by local juries named all who were implicated in the rebellion. They set forth the nature of the land tenures, those who died leaving heirs in minority, with the quantity and value of such lands; property alienated without licence; lands concealed which fell to the Crown by escheat, attainder, suppression of abbeys, with the names of those who were in possession and their history; also a list showing how and in what manner the Earl of Desmond's rents were paid, with the names of the tenants and other details. In the final settlement only 210,000 acres were confiscated for the new English settlement or plantation. All forfeited estates were divided into manors and seigniories containing 12,000, 8,000, 6,000, and 4,000 acres or variations thereof. The records of attainder, escheated lands, rents, pardons, grants to English undertakers, etc., appear in the Patents and Fiants of Elizabeth.

Temporary peace was established in Connaught and County Clare in 1585, under terms arranged with the chieftains for secure titles whereby their tribal lands were surrendered to the Crown and re-granted *in capite* by feudal terms and tenure, following the pattern set by Henry VIII. This was recorded in the Composition of Connaught and of Thomond. Future confiscation was inevitable for violating the terms of the agreement which included the penalty of forfeiture for treason or failure to support the Crown. This hung over the restless natives who were never properly provided with their promised Patents which were to be recorded on the Chancery Rolls. This left defective titles and paved the way, in 1635-1637, for Strafford's Survey of their worthless land-titles, in preparation for the Crown to claim their lands and establish a new English plantation over the entire area. This project was stopped only by matters of greater import causing civil war in England and the outbreak of the rebellion of 1641 in Ireland. But the Strafford Survey preserved genealogical records.

The cycle of records of confiscation, inquisitions, pardons, and grants to new planters concerned many thousands and, with increasing English aggression, led to the war of 1598-1603. It was planned and executed by a great confederation of the Irish chieftains of Ulster with the southern chieftains, all of whom were allied with the MacCarthys, Desmonds and others against the Government. Troops and arms were promised by Spain but came too late, landed in the wrong place, and were insufficient. English military forces were cut to pieces but won a decisive victory at a cost of £1,200,000 for the five-year war.

The greatest chieftains, Hugh O'Neill, Earl of Tyrone, and Rory O'Donnell, submitted on March 30, 1603, not knowing of Elizabeth's death six days before. James I received them in London, restored O'Neill to his earldom and created O'Donnell Earl of Tyrconnell, but greatly limited their privileges and resources, and imposed English law and government upon Ulster. After four irreconcilable years, on Sept. 14, 1607, the two earls, Tyrone, Tyrconnell, his brother Caffar, Maguire, and ninety-nine other chieftains sailed away to exile in Italy. Although the earls and their followers had been pardoned in 1603, King James confiscated their lands comprising the six entire counties of Armagh, Cavan, Derry (Londonderry), Donegal, Fermanagh, and Tyrone.

James I was strongly persuaded that a complete new plantation of British subjects was needed in Ulster, and this was begun as usual with Inquisitions regarding the history of the lands, possessors and occupiers, taken by local juries who found the Crown title to the six entire counties. The "Articles of Plantation" of Ulster, issued in May of 1609, threw open 500,000 acres of the most profitable land to English and Scottish "Undertakers" of high degree and "Servitors" of second rank, who were granted estates of 2,000, 1,500, or 1,000 acres each, while 58,000 acres of less desirable land were granted to native freeholders.

County Monaghan was not confiscated for the reigning chieftain, Ross Mac Mahon, had submitted to surrender and re-grant with succession to his brother Hugh and, though he was executed in 1589, the lands of Monaghan were divided and granted by Elizabeth to seven chief Mac Mahons and one Mac Kenna, who received from 5,000 to 2,000 acres each, and were allowed chief rents from the freeholders amounting to ten pounds for every 960 acres; the chiefs to pay quit-rent to the Crown. All remained loyal to the Government and held their lands until after the 1641-1652 rebellion.

Counties Antrim and Down were handled separately by James I soon after he came to the throne. They were claimed for the Crown by rights dating from the Anglo-Norman invasion. The northern part of Antrim was left to the occupying Mac Donnells. The Magennises held letters patent from the Crown for the lower half of Down, by English tenure. A brief outline of the Ulster Plantation under James I and later developments is contained in the preceding CHAPTER VII, PRESBYTERIAN RECORDS, pp. 377-393.

An account of the Anglo-Norman, old English, and Gaelic-Irish families who lost their property c. 1536-1703, is set forth with the sources in the preceding CHAPTER IX, ROMAN CATHOLIC RECORDS, pp. 429-466.

The Cromwellian Settlement and Re-Settlements of Charles II, and William III, showing the causes, methods, and results, are outlined in CHAPTER VI, BAPTIST AND CONGREGATIONAL (INDEPENDENT) RECORDS, pp. 361-376.

An estimate of the magnitude of the plantation program in the first century, after Henry VIII became king of Ireland, indicates that thirty-nine percent of all the land of Ireland was transferred from Roman Catholic to Protestant possession. Only a small part of this change was due to the conversion of individuals from the former to the latter religion. Almost all of the thirty-nine percent lost to Roman Catholics before 1641 occurred as a result of confiscation and the distribution of their property to Protestant planters.

The figure of thirty-nine percent is assumed indirectly from information presented in the article by J. G. Simms, entitled "Land owned by Catholics in Ireland in 1688," published in *Irish Historical Studies,* Vol. VII, No. 27 (March 1951) pp. 180-190. Mr. Simms draws his conclusions from a careful analysis of the *Books of Survey and Distribution* and other authoritative sources, summed up and presented in a table showing the acreage (profitable, unprofitable, and total acres) owned by Catholics which was sixty-one percent in 1641; twenty-two percent in 1688; and fifteen percent in 1703. Thus one hundred percent of the land of Ireland owned by Roman

Catholics in 1541 changed by confiscation or religion of the owners to sixty-one percent, or a loss of thirty-nine percent by 1641, while over the entire period of Plantation and Settlement, 1541-1703, some eighty-five percent changed hands over and over during various reigns, to final Protestant ownership.

The principal collections containing Plantation and Settlement Records (some of the most important will be described in this chapter) are listed in the following sources:

1. Published records and microfilms, listed in VOLUME II, herewith: (1) Local and national historical works, pp. 77-94. (2) Publications of the Irish Manuscripts Commission, pp. 95-105. (3) Ancient Genealogy (including 16th century records), pp. 213-215. (4) Forfeitures, pp. 239-240. (5) Plantation Records, 240-241. (6) Surveys, 241-243. (7) State Papers and Court Records, pp. 253-258. (8) Microfilms, pp. 265-286.

2. Manuscript collections listed in the *55th Report of the Deputy Keeper of the Public Records in Ireland:* (1) Irish Record Commissioners' Transcripts, Calendars and Repertories, pp. 111-117. (2) Lodge's Manuscripts, pp. 117-122. (3) Ferguson (J.F.) MS. Collection, pp. 122-123. (4) Press Copies of Certified Copies (6 vols.), p. 123. (5) Carte Papers, Transcripts of, p. 123. (6) Calendars, Repertories, Indexes and Books of Reference, pp. 124-132. (7) List of collections of records and their location, by subject, pp. 133-144, and continued in the 56th *Report,* pp. 406-412. These records have been listed and described to some extent in the preceding CHAPTER XI.

3. *Irish Historical Studies,* Vol. VII, No. 25. (March, 1950), Margaret Griffith's "Irish Record Commission, 1810-1830," pp. 17-38.

4. Manuscript collections listed in the *Reports of the Deputy Keeper of the Public Records of Northern Ireland, 1924-1953* (personal names of the principals and their records are indexed).

5. National Library of Ireland, Dublin, Catalogues of all manuscripts preserved in the Library and of all which have been located and microfilmed in various libraries or archives in Ireland and abroad. Also a descriptive list has

been compiled of the contents of many private family collections which have been loaned for microfilming.

The following records are discussed in groups according to the plan outlined on the first page of this chapter:

I. CALENDARS AND TRANSCRIPTS OF INQUISITIONS, PATENT AND CLOSE ROLLS IN CHANCERY, AND FIANTS, DATED OVER ALL OR MOST OF THE ENTIRE PERIOD, 1541-1703. These records are contained in various collections mentioned in the preceding CHAPTER XI. Their particular importance for this period, as sources revealing the changes in land tenure, requires emphasis here and a more detailed description of their contents.

1. *Inquisitions:* A description of the Inquisitions Post Mortem and the Inquisitions on Attainder is given by James Morrin in the Preface (pp. xxxiv-xxxv) to his *Calendar of the Patent and Close Rolls of Chancery in Ireland*, Vol. I, Dublin, 1861. He uses almost the wording of James Hardiman which is quoted below from another source. James Morrin concludes his description, "To illustrate the great value of these important documents, independent of their legal and historical value, it frequently occurs that where, from want of accurate information, we are unable to find a particular patent, we can generally satisfy the inquiry suggested, by referring to the Inquisitions of that particular county, and to this extent they supply the want of the patent. Here are also preserved the celebrated Inquisitions finding the title of Charles I to the province of Connaught; they are called 'Strafford's Inquisitions,' having been taken before that nobleman in the years 1635 and 1637. They include all the lands in the province, and the names of the tenants and holders thereof at the time, with the exception of the county of Leitrim, of which county no Inquisition appears to have been taken."

An explanation of Inquisitions is given by the Rev. William Healy in his *History and Antiquities of Kilkenny (County and City)*, Vol. I, 1893, p. 23. He quotes from James Hardiman who was a member of the Irish Record Commission, 1810-1830, and was active in the work of compiling Calendars of the Inquisitions. Hardiman also helped with preparing and indexing, for publication, the Inquisitions of Leinster and of Ulster, under the title, *Inquisitionum in officio rotulorum cancellariae Hiberniae asservatarum repertorium.* 2 vols.

(Vol. I, Leinster, 1826; Vol. II, Ulster, 1829.)   He is quoted as follows:

"The Inquisitions preserved in the Rolls Office of the Court of Chancery of Ireland are records of the highest authority and value.   They may be classed under two distinct heads, viz.— *Inquisitions Post Mortem,* which are the most numerous, and *Inquisitions on Attainder.*   They are divided according to the four Provinces and the several counties of Ireland into Reigns, and generally commence in the time of Elizabeth, few being prior to that period.   The former class ceases soon after the Restoration of Charles II, when the feudal tenures were abolished by Act of Parliament.   The latter extends to the reign of William III.   The *Inquisitions Post Mortem* were taken under commissions directed to the *escheators* of each province and others joined with them, and find by the oath of a jury what lands any person died seized of, by what rents and services they were held, and who was the next heir, and his age, by which the right of the Crown to escheat or wardship was ascertained.   On them were founded all grants of wardships, of body and marriage, liveries of lands, pardons of intrusion, pardons and licences of alienation, etc., in virtue of the tenures *in capite.*   They are the best evidence of the descent of families, and of the transfer and possession of property during the period they embrace.   Numerous family settlements, deeds, wills, leases, and other instruments relating to property in Ireland, are set out in full, or copiously recited, and of the greater number of these there are at present no other traces to be found.   The *Inquisitions on Attainder* were generally taken under commissions directed to the Commissioners in the several counties, and show whether any person was attainted, in which case his lands and other property, which were also found, were seized into the King's hands. These important documents have suffered much injury from time and neglect, but have been carefully arranged, cleansed, and placed in port-folios, by order of his Majesty's Commissioners, on the public records, a process which will tend to secure their future preservation.   Under the same authority a Repertory of their contents has been formed."

The original Inquisitions were lost in the destruction of the Public Record Office, Dublin, in 1922.   The Repertories to the

Leinster and Ulster Inquisitions were published in 1826 and 1829, respectively, as stated above. The manuscript Transcripts of the Chancery Inquisitions Post Mortem and Inquisitions on Attainder (15 volumes), compiled by the Irish Record Commission, 1810-1830, for Munster and Connaught, are now in the Public Record Office, Dublin. In these volumes the records of counties Clare, Cork, Galway, Leitrim, Mayo, Tipperary, and Waterford, date from the reign of Elizabeth, and extend to that of William III, except for Clare which ends with Charles I. The records for Limerick and Roscommon begin with James I, and end with William III. Kerry records begin with James I, and end with Charles I. The records are bound by counties and are compiled by reigns. The two types of Inquisitions are grouped together for each county; no Inquisitions Post Mortem being dated after Charles II. There are also Repertories to the Exchequer Inquisitions Post Mortem and Inquisitions on Attainder, and on the lands of dissolved abbeys, monasteries, etc., for all counties except Queen's (17 volumes). Of these the records for counties Carlow, Galway, Kildare, Kilkenny, Limerick, Meath, Tipperary, Waterford, Westmeath, and Wexford, all begin in the reign of Henry VIII, and extend to that of William III, except for Tipperary, which extends only to Cromwell. Dublin records begin in the reign of Henry VI, and extend to William III. Down records begin with the reign of Edward VI, and end with Cromwell. Louth records extend from Edward VI, to William III. The records beginning in the reign of Elizabeth are for the counties Cavan, Clare, Donegal, Kerry, King's, Longford, Leitrim, Mayo, Roscommon, and Sligo. Except for King's County and Mayo, which extend to the reign of William III, the others end in the reigns of Charles II, or James II. The records for the counties of Antrim, Armagh, Cork, Fermanagh, Londonderry, Monaghan, Tyrone, and Wicklow, begin in the reign of James I, and mostly extend to the reign of Charles II, or James II, except for the Londonderry records which end with Charles I, and those for Cork which extend to William III. (55th *Report of the Deputy Keeper of the Public Records in Ireland,* pp. 114-115.)

The Public Record Office, Dublin, has thirty volumes of transcripts of Deeds and Wills recited in Chancery Inquisitions covering all counties except Leitrim. An index in the Search Room for these records, except for counties Louth and Wicklow, and the missing Leitrim records, gives the names of the parties with the date and nature of the records. Also in the Public Record Office, Dublin, there are twelve volumes of transcripts of Deeds and Wills recited in Exchequer Inquisitions for the counties of Carlow, Dublin, Galway, Kildare, Kilkenny, Louth, Queen's, Meath, Westmeath, and for the city of Dublin. The above index for the Chancery Deeds and Wills in Inquisitions covers this Exchequer series. All of these records were transcribed by the Irish Record Commission, 1810-1830. (55th *Report,* p. 115.)

Numerous Inquisitions of earlier dates than the above have been transcribed from various Court Records, State Papers, and appear in manuscript collections but not in any distinct series. From the time English Courts of law were introduced in Ireland in the 13th century and shire or county government was organized with sheriffs, coroners, escheators, and other officers of the law representing the English form of government where it was in control, the taking of Inquisitions Post Mortem, on Attainder, and for miscellaneous disputes over land, etc., was ordered from time to time by the judiciary, the escheator, or sometimes for smaller matters by the sheriff. The facts of each case and the possessions in question, held by the individual or individuals involved, were reviewed by an appointed jury named in the records, as in the 16th to 18th centuries. These records are contained in the great Lodge and Ferguson collections listed in the preceding CHAPTER XI; also in a volume of abstracts of Inquisitions for counties Dublin and Wicklow, dated from Henry VI to Charles II, compiled by Monk Mason (M 2543) ; and in 6 volumes of "Press Copies of Certified Copies" of Chancery and Exchequer Inquisitions, Fiants, Grants, Christ Church Deeds, Statutes, Extracts from Plea, Close, Memorandum, and Hearthmoney Rolls, Decrees of Innocents, etc., all being in the Public Record Office, Dublin. (55th *Report,* pp. 116-123.)

The National Library of Ireland, Dublin, has microfilms of the great Hore Manuscript Collection of County Wexford, which is rich in Inquisitions. It also has microfilms of the "Pedigrees, Inquisitions, Visitations, etc.," collected by Sir

William Betham, 2 volumes, the original records being in the British Museum, London. (Add. MSS. 26,688-9.) The Genealogical Office, Dublin Castle, Dublin, has abstracts of Inquisitions from the Lodge Manuscripts, the Irish Record Commission Transcripts and Repertories, etc. The Public Record Office of Northern Ireland, Belfast, has the Groves Collection which contains Exchequer Inquisitions extracts for County Armagh, 1603-1608; for County Dublin, 16th and 17th centuries; for County Fermanagh, 1613-1690; for County Tyrone, 1658; and for mixed counties there are references, mainly in Exchequer Inquisitions to Counties Cavan, Monaghan, Carlow, Leitrim, Louth, Meath, Limerick, Kerry, Galway, Sligo, and Waterford. The great collection of Carew Manuscripts in the Archiepiscopal Library, Lambeth Palace, London, is also rich in Inquisitions. Trinity College Library, Dublin, has "Inquisitions concerning the Six Escheated Counties in Ireland, 7 James I (Ulster)", MSS. 595. It also has the "Grand Inquest of the Province of Ulster, 1610 *(copia vera)*", MS. 1046.

2. *The Patent and Close Rolls in Chancery:* These form almost one continuous chain of personal records from the reign of Henry II onward, with the exception of some chasms in the reigns of the three Edwards, and during the first twenty years of the reign of Henry VIII. James Morrin defines their contents in the Preface (pp. xxx-xxxi) to his *Calendar of the Patent and Close Rolls of Chancery in Ireland, of the Reigns of Henry VIII, Edward VI, Mary, and Elizabeth,* Vol. I, Dublin, 1861, as follows: "Upon these Rolls are contained the enrolments of grants in fee or perpetuity, for lives and years; of Crown lands, abbey lands, and escheated lands; patents of creations of honour; grants of charters of incorporation and liberties; grants of offices, denizations, ferries, and fisheries; patents for inventions, and specifications; licences and pardons of alienation; presentations; promotions to bishoprics and deaneries; special licences; grants of wardships; commissions; inquisitions *post mortem* and on attainder; orders of Council; depositions of witnesses in *perpetuam rei memoriam;* deeds; conveyances; grants in *custodiam;* grants of manors and all of their appurtenances, and of fairs and markets; surrenders of lands and offices to the Crown; summonses to Par-

liament; bonds; obligations; replevins; pardons; letters of attorney; licences for officers to treat with the Irish; treaties; Papal bulls; proclamations; letters of protection; writs of *amoveas manus* of possessions taken by the Crown; writs of *ouster lemain*; deeds and conveyances; King's letters; wills; commissions for survey, apportionment, and erection of counties; for remedy of defective titles; for the appointment of Justices and Commissioners, as well civil as military; for the conversion of lands held by the Irish custom of tanistry into the English custom of tenure; and on various other subjects." He also states, regarding the Patent and Close Rolls, "both species of Rolls contain matters of a similar kind . . ."

Of the Fiants which comprise the original instruments under the Privy Seal, directing that Letters Patent be passed, James Morrin says (p. xxxiii), "They were all supposed to be enrolled on the Patent Rolls, but numerous instances occur where the Patent not being found on the Rolls, reference must be made to the original Fiat [Fiant], or in the event of the Roll being lost, or in any portion illegible, the examination of the Fiat serves to supply the deficiency; those records, in consequence, have always been considered of great value."

The above full description of the contents of the Patent and Close Rolls and the Fiants serves to indicate the many occasions which would cause the affairs of a man or woman to appear in the Rolls. Added value is given to the records owing to the careful identification of each person, usually by place of residence or land holdings, parentage, or family relationship, and sometimes earlier generations. The records of numerous families occur in a series of instruments of succeeding reigns, showing several generations when pieced together. In the reigns of Henry VIII, Edward VI, and Mary, the most numerous records are the pardons; grants of escheated or forfeited lands of attainted persons, and of confiscated abbeys, monasteries, etc., to new English by birth or blood, mostly by lease of twenty-one years; grants of English liberty; presentations; grants of office; pensions; grants of lands in fee or in perpetuity; wardships, etc. In Elizabeth's reign the pardons grew to an enormous number. Some instruments concerned one or a few people, but during the latter part of this reign a single Fiant commonly named and identified scores of people who were either pardoned after an insurrection or given a clear record absolving them from participation, while the chief instigators were attainted. The leases increased proportionally while there were many grants of great manors and records of surrender and re-grant. The published Calendars of Patent and Close Rolls, and the Fiants, are listed in VOLUME II, pp. 253-257, herewith. Lodge provides the greatest manuscript collection of these records. Others containing similar records will be noted below.

3. *State Papers and Parliamentary Records:* The published Calendars of the State Papers relating to Ireland, beginning in 1509 and continuing to 1670, are listed in the foregoing CHAPTER XI, pp. 484-485. The Preface to each of these volumes covering a certain period runs about fifty pages, and provides invaluable historical background with explanations of the cause, nature, and results of the events within the particular dates, and calls attention to important documents. Supplemental Calendars of State Papers and transcripts of such documents contained in other representative manuscript collections are also mentioned in the preceding CHAPTER XI, pp. 480-518. Illustrations of the nature of the records within the most important periods will be given below under the various reigns including that of the Commonwealth.

On the whole, the published and manuscript Calendars of State Papers and the transcripts of documents in other collections set forth a very great variety of records concerning many thousands of people of high and lower degree, taken from reports of Government officials in Ireland to the King, to the English Privy Council, to the Irish Commissioners, or from correspondence of various officials, from English Government documents, and from other miscellaneous sources. The abstracts and transcripts concern military matters; plots for and against the Government; reports of spies; insurrections, indictments for treason, imprisonment, executions, attainders, pardons; lists of prominent families in various counties, defined as loyal or disloyal to the Government, with short pedigrees thereof; references to surrender and re-grant; details of Plantations and Settlements, with information regarding grants in fee and leases for lives or years to British "Undertakers" and their affairs such as marriages, wardships, debts, mortgages; a very full collection of the records of English "Adventurers" for land in Ireland, 1642-1659, including the names and English addresses of those who purchased subscriptions to allotments of land to be provided by future confiscation, with their subsequent assignments of their certificates to others soon after purchase, or to heirs as recited in wills; the final lists of grantee "Adventurers" in Ireland, by county and barony; allotments to certain officers and officials; also the records of those who lost land and others who gained it during the Restoration Settlement of Charles II, showing the confusion of interests; with the final records of confiscation, claims of innocents, and sale of estates by the Government to English Protestants following the Revolution Settlement under William III. All through the State Papers there are a multitude of petitions for redress and justice or pardon, giving much personal information regarding hardship and ruin, frequently accompanied by family records in proof of rights or reason for clemency, with some wills or pedigrees recited. All of these records are well indexed by names of the principals, subject material, and as county items. Names in long lists are not all indexed. Thus it is well to read all of the abstracts dated within any particular period of interest. It is a fascinating task for any genealogist.

The records of the Dublin Parliament are contained in the published *Journals of the House of Commons of Ireland, 1613-1800* (41 vols., Dublin, 1763-1800) ; and the *Journals of the House of Lords, 1634-1752* (3 vols., Dublin, 1782-1784). In many respects these records are related to the State Papers. The *Journals* contain the names of the members and show their participation in the business of the Parliament. They give the dates of the return of members and their residences in warrants for new writs. Those in the House of Lords sat by hereditary right. The members of the House of Commons were always chosen from among the landlords or their immediate relatives in their respective counties or boroughs. In numerous cases representatives of a single family held a seat successively in one generation after another. In 1612-1613, the House of Commons consisted of 225 members of whom, at the opening of the session, there appeared 121 Protestants and 101 Roman Catholics. Information is thus provided regarding the new and most important Protestant "Undertakers" or grantees in the Plantation movement, who were not of the peerage but had become powerful in their local areas or with the Government; also the representatives of the old Roman Catholic families who were rapidly becoming a minority influence. The membership of the Dublin Parliament provides a gage of the fluctuating power of families during the periods of the Restoration Settlement of Charles II, the brief reign of James II, and the Revolution Settlement under William III.

The *Journals* contain records of many cases which were brought before the House of Commons and the House of Lords. Miscellaneous cases before the former concerned pensions for military or other past service; disputes or violence over estates, resulting in warrants for taking persons in custody for hearings or prosecution. Acts of indemnity for late crimes were issued. Petitions were introduced for pardons, justice, relief relating to attainders or losses. It was necessary for Parliament to confirm the attainders of persons convicted of treason whereby their lands were confiscated for the Crown, thus providing for new plantations. The Act for inviting Protestant strangers (French Huguenots) to inhabit Ireland, and other provisions for them are mentioned in the preceding CHAPTER IV, among "Records of the French Huguenot Churches and Settlements."

The great collection of Lodge Manuscripts in the Public Record Office, Dublin, contains lists of the Irish peerages, dates of creation, rank of dignity; eldest sons of peers who were called by writ to sit and vote in the Upper House of Parliament in the lifetime of their fathers; the peers in each reign from Henry VII to George II; attainted peers (attainders of 1641 and 1689) ; and a "Parliamentary Register" containing lists of members returned to serve in the Parliaments of Ireland, 1559-1772, with alphabetical lists of members for this period with some death dates, official appointments, etc. These records and a vast amount of other material transcribed by Lodge are contained in *Liber Munerum Publicorum Hiberniae*, for which see VOLUME II, p. 254, herewith.

II. MANUSCRIPT COLLECTIONS (SOME PUBLISHED) RELATING PARTICULARLY TO ONE REIGN, including the Commonwealth, from the time of Elizabeth, listed chronologically:

1. THE REIGN OF ELIZABETH, 1558-1603 : The Public Record
Office, Dublin, has portions of the Desmond Survey, made
after the Desmond Rebellion of 1579-1583, which are listed in
the 55th *Report*, pp. 11, 129, 143, as follows: (1) MS. Calendar of Limerick portion (Mc Enery). (2) Manor of Kilcoleman (official copy). (3) County Kerry portion, printed
translation. (4) Extracts from Counties Cork, Waterford,
and Tipperary in Appendix to House of Lords Blackwater
Fishery Case. This office also has copies of the Inquisitions on the Composition of Thomond, 1585 (58th *Report*, p.
22) ; see also Fiant No. 4761 (15th *Report*). The Compositions of Connaught are printed in Hardiman's *O'Flaherty's
West or H-Iar Connaught*. The Irish Manuscripts Commission published *The Compossicion Booke of Conought* (see
VOLUME II, pp. 98-99, herewith). The Armagh Library has
a MS. Book of Compositions for Connaught, 1585, and for
the Pale, 1599 (Cat. MSS. p. 17). Trinity College Library,
Dublin, has MSS. Papers relating to Irish Affairs, Plantations,
etc., 16th and 17th centuries (MS. No. 672, F. 3. 15) ; the
National Library has photostats. The Chancery Inquisitions
of Ulster, published by the Irish Record Commission, 1829
(see VOLUME II, p. 253, herewith), contain in that volume
also, the Commission for dividing Ulster into shire ground,
with returns, 1591; the survey of County Monaghan, 1591;
the survey of Fermanagh, 1605; the perambulation of Iveagh,
1618. The Carew Manuscripts, which will be described among
other collections, contain much material for this and earlier
reigns and for the reign of James I.

2. THE REIGN OF JAMES I, 1603-1625: This reign is noted
for the Plantation of Ulster and further plantations in Leinster. *An Historical Account of the Plantation of Ulster, 1608-
1620*, by the Rev. George Hill, Belfast, 1877, was compiled
from early *Annals*, the *Calendars of the Carew Manuscripts*,
the *Calendars of Irish State Papers, Patent Rolls, Fiants, Inquisitions of Ulster, Pynnar's Survey, Barony Maps of 1609*
which show how the lands were laid out for Plantation purposes, and many miscellaneous sources including the Lodge
Manuscripts. A history of the Ulster tribes and their chieftains, including genealogy, is presented in Chapter I, pp. 1-59.
"The Grants and Grantees," pp. 259-353, are given including

personal names, property by county, precinct or barony, denomination, acreage, and name of manor erected, with other
miscellaneous notes. A history and plan of "The Londoners'
Plantation" is given by barony, pp. 353-444. Captain Nicholas
Pynnar's Survey is presented, pp. 445-590. This is a survey
of the six escheated counties after the settlement of the
Plantation, Dec. 1, 1618 - March 28, 1619, as contained in
Hibernica; or some ancient pieces relating to Ireland, edited
by Walter Harris, Dublin, 1747. It gives an account of the
progress made by the English and Scottish undertakers, servitors, and natives who were granted lands and subject to fulfill certain conditions for developing their estates of 2,000,
1,500, 1,000 or less acres, with a sufficient castle or stone house,
bawn, cattle, tenants, arms, etc. Pynnar gives the name of
each landlord, his acreage, how he acquired it, a description of
his estate, and in some cases the names of the tenants. The
survey was made by county, barony, and precinct. The body
of the entire work and the notes which fill more than half the
space, contain much family history and genealogy.

The *Ulster Inquisitions* (published by the Irish Record Commission in 1829), were taken by juries in the six escheated
counties of Armagh, Cavan, Donegal, Fermanagh, Derry (Londonderry), and Tyrone, set forth the lands owned *c.* 1609, by
the native families who held it from their ancestors "time out
of mind". Numerous early Scottish settlers are also listed as
landlords and tenants. The *Journal of the Armagh Diocesan
Historical Society*, Vol. I, No. 1 (1954), pp. 67-100, contains
that part of the Inquisitions relating to the See of Armagh
which comprised the Church lands of 81,160 acres, which
shows 39 native septs and their holdings of Church lands over
successive generations as Church wardens.

The Public Record Office of Northern Ireland, Belfast, has
a collection of records of the London Companies which settled
plantations in County Londonderry. Dr. T. W. Moody of
Queen's University, Belfast, contributed the MSS. on his research regarding the Irish Plantation records of the London
Companies of the Salters, Vintners, Haberdashers, Goldsmiths,
Ironmongers, Grocers, Skinners, and Mercers, in the various
sections of County Londonderry. This Office has also obtained
the photostats of the Drapers records of County Londonderry,

1613-1631, etc. These were presented by the Drapers Company of London who had the original records in their archives photostated for this Office. An account is given in *Report* 1934, Appendix A, and the records are indexed in Appendix B. This Office has made extracts from the records of the Haberdashers' Company deposited in the General Register House, Edinburgh (*Report* 1929, p. 16), and of the Merchant Taylors' Company and some material relating to the Cloth-workers' Company (*Report* 1933, p. 21). This Office has thus obtained the Irish records of eleven of the twelve great companies relating to their plantations in County Londonderry (*Report* 1934, p. 4). This Office has a copy of the Royal Irish Academy's Ordnance Survey Documents relating to Vintners property and its British inhabitants, 1622 (*Report* 1935, p. 4).

Analecta Hibernica No. 8 (March 1938), pp. 181-297, contains a Calendar of Ulster Plantation Papers, 1608-1613, from MS. N. 2.2, in the Library of Trinity College, Dublin. Presented by T. W. Moody, Ph.D. His seven-page Introduction places these papers as formerly a part of the MSS. of Archbishop King, who probably had them bound in the one volume after 1688. This came to the library in the Clarke collection in 1840. A "Chronological Table of the Printed Contents of Ulster Plantation Papers" contains the date, nature of each document and its number in the collection. The documents are miscellaneous in nature and content and offer information regarding individuals. No. 21 contains the schedules of the assignments of the proportions in precincts allotted to British undertakers in Ulster, from April to May 1610. The name of the county, precinct, proportion, and the acreage of each allotment is given with the name of the grantee or Undertaker, his degree of dignity (Mr., Gent., Esq., or Sir) or occupation, with an occasional relationship. Thus in the Precinct of Clogher (Co. Tyrone), Mr. Francis Willoughby, son to Sir Perciuall Willoughby, received Fentonaghe of 2,000 acres (p. 223). No. 11 contains the schedules of plantation grants and grantees in 1610-1611 for all six counties. No. 54 contains a schedule of the sums to be paid by the King to the ancient inhabitants of Derry as composition for surrender of houses and lands, dated July, 1611 (pp. 261-263). Thus "Mr. Deane Webb for a house a garden ground and a smale tenement at

18 pounds." The full names are given and all are of English origin as follows: Deane Webb, Wm. Everinge, Edward Blundell, John Bishop, Thoriston Henebery, Anthony Maiehew, Willm. Cooke, Willm. Newtown, John Howton, Ringan Boyde, Robert Miler, Thomas Ridgate, Robte Aires, Fingan English, Willm. Rew, Willm. Taylor, John Woods, Water Talent, Willm. Lowbery, Haniball Harison, Richard Babbington, Humffrey Wale, John Banke, Richard Griffin, Capt. Baxter, Lieut. Jones, Paddy Wardes, Tho. Plumketts, Willm. Buckley, Jo. Barrett, Willm. Cotsmore, Jesse Smith, Richard Babbington, Cornett Wray, Thomas Greene, Sr Oliuer St. Johnes, Captaine John Vaughan, Captaine Henrie Vaughan, Capt. Hart, John Betson, Captaine John and Captaine Henrie Vaughan, Reece Coitmore, John Wray, Willm. Lynne, Richard Birne, Tho. Pendry, Robte Byars, Richard Smith, Sandy Lowry, Griffyn Thomas, The Lo: Byshopp, John Betson, Henrie Sadler, Wybrand Oldfers, Richard Apleton, Richard Smith, Robte Kinesman, Robte Lyppett, Willm. Longe, Andrew Dikes, Humfrey Tuckey, Mr Hubberston, Thomas Parkins, George Reynolds, Thomas Thornton.

The Presbyterian Historical Society, Belfast, in 1952 and 1954, issued three pamphlets, compiled by the Rev. David Stewart, D. D., which contain invaluable lists of the Scots who settled in Ulster, mostly in the reign of James I. The first two pamphlets, entitled "The Scots in Ulster, their Denization and Naturalization, 1605 to 1634" (2 Parts), contain the lists of those who received letters patent of Denization, and those who were Naturalized by Act of Parliament. A denizen paid a fine and took the Oath of Allegiance, whereby he "occupied an intermediate position between an alien and a native born subject." Naturalization "put an alien in the same position as if he had been born a native subject." The names, places of origin in Scotland (with a few exceptions), date of naturalization, and some places of settlement are given in the first pamphlet. The second contains lists of the "Early Scots Settlers" in the Counties of Antrim, Armagh, Cavan, and Donegal. Under each county there is an alphabetical list of names, their locations and dates of settlement. Tenants of the large estates and date are listed by county. The third pamphlet contains the names and dates with the place of settlement in the same arrangement for the Counties of Down, Fermanagh, Londonderry, and Tyrone.

In 1614, James I issued a Special Commission to Lord Deputy Sir Alexander Chichester, to inquire into the title or rights of the Crown in the King's and Queen's Counties, and in those of Longford, Leitrim, and Westmeath. The result was the seizure by the Crown of 385,000 acres. Lands in North Wexford, South Carlow, and the adjoining part of Wicklow, containing 67,000 acres, were also seized. The *Inquisitions of Leinster* (published by the Irish Record Commission, 1826), cover this confiscation and the *Patent and Close Rolls of Chancery* of James I and Charles I (see VOLUME II, p. 255, herewith) contain the grants to new settlers.

3. THE REIGN OF CHARLES I, 1625-1649: In the early years of his reign, Charles I continued granting Crown lands of Leinster, etc., confiscated by James I, as shown in James Morrin's *Calendar of Patent and Close Rolls of Chancery in Ireland, of the Reign of Charles I, 1625-1633.* Dublin, 1863. Meanwhile, since 1615, the London Companies had been under fire of criticism for failure to comply with the terms of their grants in County Londonderry, for which James I, by letter, had directed a special inquiry. Sir Thomas Phillips, who had been appointed to some form of governorship of the county, quarreled with the Londoners over their failure to build sufficient houses, fortifications, and properly remove the natives from the proportions of the Guilds. Copies of the documents and tracings of the maps finally submitted by Sir Thomas Phillips to Charles I in 1629, setting out the conditions of the county and records of the work from the beginning, are published under the direction of D. A. Chart, Deputy Keeper of the Public Records in Northern Ireland, in a volume entitled *Londonderry and the London Companies, 1609-1629, being a survey and other documents submitted to King Charles I, by Sir Thomas Phillips.* Belfast: His Majesty's Stationery Office, 1928. This volume contains thirty-two illustrations of the maps, some in color, showing sketches of the two-story houses of Tudor architecture, built on the settlements of the various Guilds for the principal settlers with their names indicating the occupant of each, and public buildings; also

maps of the various sections with names of the grantees, etc., c. 1622. Of the documents and maps, Mr. Chart states (pp. vii-viii), "The personal detail which they contain will undoubtedly be of great value to those concerned in genealogy . . ."

In this reign new plantations were not accomplished but much was envisioned and preparations were made for the confiscation of the entire Province of Connaught and County Clare, to be laid out for plantation. In 1632, Sir Thomas Wentworth came to Ireland as Lord Deputy and in 1639, as Lord Lieutenant, was created Earl of Strafford. He attempted to make Ireland support its English Government and supply a surplus to the Crown. Land had been practically given away to the English by birth, and taxes were low. He attacked them all on the grounds that new wealthy Protestants were a greater danger to the Crown than the defeated natives. This included the London Companies. He caused their Charter for their plantation in County Londonderry to be forfeited with a fine of £70,000, for failure to fulfill their contract.

In preparation for the confiscation and plantation of Connaught and Clare, Strafford hit on the scheme of attacking the defective titles of all who had submitted to Surrender and Regrant in 1585, but never received properly registered patents as promised. He established a Commission in 1635 at Boyle, and grand juries were summoned for the different counties. He promised the members of the juries three-quarters of their own property in return for finding the King's title to all lands. Only the Galway jury refused to comply and was heavily fined. The planned plantation failed to materialize when Strafford was recalled in 1639, but the celebrated Strafford Inquisitions of 1635-1637 include all the lands of the Province of Connaught (excepting County Leitrim), and County Clare, and show the names and holdings of the owners and tenants. These are included in the manuscripts of the Irish Record Commission concerning the Inquisitions of the various counties of Connaught and County Clare, listed above. *The Strafford Inquisition of County Mayo*, edited by William O'Sullivan, was published by the Irish Manuscripts Commission, Dublin, 1958. It contains an index of names, places, and subjects, and shows also the landowners and description of their lands in 1641, with genealogical information in some notes concerning dowagers, minors, and other details of family relationship. Most names are of old Gaelic families but there are Bourkes, Binghams, Browns, Boyles, etc.

During this reign, many petitions were made to the Lord Deputy for justice or relief, pardons, etc. A manuscript volume of petitions to Lord Deputy Wentworth, June to November, 1638, with decisions of the Council thereon (MS. 2448), is in the Public Record Office, Dublin. The published Calendars of State Papers contain very numerous petitions, including information about the affairs or holdings of individuals, often their parentage and sometimes mention of earlier generations.

4. THE COMMONWEALTH GOVERNMENT, 1649-1660: The source materials of this period, which will be listed below, concern such matters as the treason cases and war records of many who were involved in the Rebellion of 1641-1652; the subsequent forfeiture records of numerous innocent as well as guilty persons, showing the size and location of their estates; the county origins of those who were transplanted in the Province of Connaught or County Clare, and their places of assignment; the petitions for pardon or special dispensation containing notes on personal or family history; cases requiring adjudication for particular reasons, with details of personal affairs; the records of the Adventurers for lands in Ireland, including their English origins, occupations, and in many cases family records; their allotments and locations of the property in Ireland; the allotments to English army officers and their locations; also numerous personal records representing miscellaneous interests.

The most detailed history and explanation of the records is contained in *The Cromwellian Settlement of Ireland*, by John P. Prendergast (2nd edition, enlarged), Dublin, 1875. A great many personal records, presented singly and in lists, illustrate this copious history of the Commonwealth period and prior years of the Rebellion.

The records begin after Feb. 11, 1642, when an Act of the English Parliament "for speedy reducing of the rebels in Ireland," was passed (and followed by further Ordinances of 1643-1646), whereby Adventurers for land in Ireland were promised the spoils of war to the extent of 2,500,000 acres to be confiscated when the Rebellion should be ended, in return for £336,000 which they subscribed, 1642-1646, to support an army and sea forces for service against the rebels, independent of the king. The money was paid to a private fund, administered by a committee, half being members of Parliament and half representative of the subscribing Adventurers. The funds were actually diverted to support the army for civil war in England against the king, while only a token force was sent to Ireland.

The Adventurers were each issued a receipt guaranteeing some future allotment of land for the amount of the subscription, at the rate of 1,000 acres in Ulster for £200, in Connaught for £300, in Munster for £450, or in Leinster for £600. Lands were to be assigned by lot following the Rebellion.

The first object of the Commonwealth Government of England, after the execution of Charles I in January of 1649, was to defeat the Rebellion in Ireland which was involved in a very tangled situation. Roman Catholic war against the Protestants had broken out in Ulster in 1641. The rebels were organized under a Confederate Government in 1642, with which Charles I later treated when in need of aid in the English civil war. Thus by 1647 many of the Protestant royalists joined with the Confederates for the king and against the Parliament. When Cromwell's forces came to Ireland they broke the main strength of the rebels by May of 1650, and his officers and army were left to complete the conquest in 1652.

An "Act for Settling of Ireland," was passed in the House of Commons on August 12, 1652, whereby the entire nation was deemed guilty of rebellion, excepting those who could prove that they had supported the Parliament against the king, and actively demonstrated their loyalty to Cromwell and his army in Ireland. Thus only the Protestant landlords who could prove this "constant good affection" were exempt from confiscation of their estates or some part thereof. Lands totaling 11,000,000 were in due course confiscated to satisfy the Adventurers, to pay arrears of £1,550,000 to army officers and soldiers, to discharge debts of £1,750,000 advanced for army supplies, and to provide for the benefits of Government officials, regicides, private favorites, and supporters of the republican cause in Parliament.

To ascertain the debt owing to the Adventurers, on June 1, 1653, a committee of London merchants was appointed to judge their claims, supported by their receipts and any papers showing the transfer of rights to others by sale, assignment to satisfy debts, or by will of a deceased Adventurer, sometimes followed by a partition of rights among the heirs.

The rebels were classified under eight qualifications of guilt, established by the Act of August 12, 1652. Those in the first five were subject to death or banishment from the country and the confiscation of their entire estates. Included were all who had promoted the rebellion before October 1641 or fought for the Confederate cause before November 10, 1642; all Roman Catholic priests, Jesuits, etc., who had supported the war; over one hundred Royalist and Confederate leaders; all who had killed loyal non-belligerent English in the war in Ireland, and those Irish who had waged war without themselves being in the pay or service of the Confederate Government; and all who refused to surrender within twenty-eight days after the publication of this Act.

To judge and sentence these chief offenders a High Court was set up in Dublin in August 1652, under control of the Commissioners of Ireland, appointed in January, 1651, by Parliament for governing Ireland, namely Edmund Ludlow, Miles Corbet, John Jones, and John Weaver. Only fifty-two rebels were executed by Court order. Over 30,000 rebel officers and prominent leaders of the rebellion and the principal Royalists were given leave to transport themselves to France, Spain, and other countries in amity with the Government. Several thousand of one or another of the five qualifications were shipped to the West Indies to serve as indentured servants or political slaves. The families left with nothing, either escaped to the Continent or were picked up as vagrants and sold as slaves to ships captains who disposed of them in the West Indies and the American Colonies.

Other classes of guilt included the following: The general officers in the civil and military service of the Confederate Government were subject to banishment from the country and two-thirds of their estates confiscated, the remaining third or its equivalent to be assigned to their wives and children elsewhere in Ireland. Pardon was extended to some who submitted within twenty-eight days, and banishment was in such cases commuted to transplanting elsewhere in Ireland, where they were assigned the equivalent of one-third of their forfeited estates. All Roman Catholic laymen in Ireland between October 1, 1641 and March 1, 1650, who had not in every way manifested their loyalty and constant good affection to the Parliament, were subject to confiscation, transplanting, and assignment of lands elsewhere equal to the equivalent of two-thirds of their forfeited estates. It was virtually impossible for a Roman Catholic to prove constant good affection to the Parliamentary party or the Commonwealth Government. Even the act of giving food to a rebel relative or paying taxes to the Crown as late as 1648 was counted against them. Protestants who had not on opportunity shown loyalty and constant good affection to the Parliamentary party and the Commonwealth Government were to forfeit one-fifth of their estates and pay a fine equal to two years rental value of their estates, but not transplant.

Only those who owned no land and no more than £10 value in personal goods were given a free pardon if they surrendered within twenty-eight days of the publication of the Act. This covered the laboring class, most of whom were needed to work on the forfeited estates and thus were allowed to remain and serve the new English proprietors. Boys under fourteen and girls under twelve could remain if taken as servants of the loyal English and trained as Protestants. Thus some thousands of war orphans became laborers on their ancestral estates and for the most part eventually remained Roman Catholics.

The qualifications of guilt are important to keep in mind with relation to following records for the fate of each person was determined by his past degree of importance and the extent of his forfeited lands.

To clear the way for the new settlement of Adventurers, army officers and soldiers, etc., in the provinces of Leinster, Munster, and Ulster, all guilty persons who forfeited their estates in these provinces and were classed as transplanters under the qualifications specified in the Act of August 12, 1652, were ordered to remove to the Province of Connaught or County Clare, by May 1654, on pain of death for refusal to obey. There they were to be allotted land equivalent to the fraction of their former estates, to which they were entitled.

While the Commissioners for Irish Affairs under the direction of General Fleetwood (later Lord Deputy) handled the general direction of the immense program and reviewed special cases, etc., Ireland was finally divided into twelve precincts, each with a military governor and Commissioners of Revenue, for administration of justice and local affairs. In July 1653, all who possessed any right or title to lands in Ireland on 23 October 1641, subject to forfeiture, were required to submit a statement of their claims in writing. In each precinct a Court of Delinquency was established to hear claims and inquire into the behaviour of claimants during the Rebellion. Thereafter a Transplanters' Certificate was issued to each one ordered to remove to Connaught or County Clare. It contained information regarding the transplanter and each member of his family, including also the records of any tenants, servants, and friends or relatives who were to accompany him. It set forth the past abode of each, the name, age, stature, colour of hair, and other distinctive marks, together with the number of their cattle, and other possessions.

The head of the family or transplanting group was required to present his Transplanters' Certificate to the Commission at Loughrea in Galway which was appointed on January 6, 1654, to make conditional allotments to the applicants. A further review of the qualification of guilt of each transplanter was made by a Commission set up at Athlone, after which a final settlement of land was granted.

There were a great many delays in leaving forfeited estates, pending a flood of petitions to the Commissioners of Revenue of the various precincts. Reasons of illness, old age, inability to travel, harvesting of crops, and requests for other special dispensations were submitted. The Commissioners were also empowered to hear the claims of those whose cases were exceptions to the rule and not among those whose land was affected by the qualifications of the Act of August 12, 1652. Some of these were Roman Catholics in Dublin who were loyal and held leases from Protestants, dated between 1647 and

1652, who were left unmolested. Loyal Roman Catholics in the towns of Cork, Youghal, and Kinsale, were also excepted from the rule of transplantation. The mass of claims in some precincts dragged on into 1656.

Difficulties arose because in many cases forfeited lands of Roman Catholics were held by them in trust for Protestants, or Protestants were trustees for Roman Catholic minors. Protestants also held mortgages on Roman Catholic properties which should be honoured by Parliament. On the whole, those considered as proprietors and therefore transplantable, in addition to the property owners, were mortgagors and mortgagees; any in line to become heirs (though never in arms), who might be eldest or younger sons, brothers or their heirs; copyholders of twenty acres or less; lessees for seven years and their children; widows with rights to jointures; wives and children of swordsmen sent out of the country; orphans of transplantable persons; men who married transplantable women and thus became so themselves.

Meanwhile, by Act of Parliament on September 20, 1653, "for Satisfaction of Adventurers for Lands in Ireland, and of arrears due to the soldiery there and other public debts," half of the forfeited lands in the counties of Limerick, Tipperary, Waterford, King's and Queen's Counties, Meath, Westmeath, Down, Antrim, and Armagh, were allotted to the Adventurers and the other half to the army personnel. The division of the counties was by baronies. The allotment of baronies respectively to the Adventurers and to the army was determined by lots drawn by a committee which sat at Grocers' Hall, London.

Parliament set out for additional security to insure enough land for the Adventurers and army, all of County Louth excepting the barony of Ardee which was reserved for the army. In addition to the above lands for the army officers and soldiers, sufficient lands for their arrears were provided in the counties of Cavan, Fermanagh, Kerry, Kilkenny, Londonderry, Monaghan, Tyrone, and Wexford. County Sligo and the northeast portion of County Mayo were eventually taken from the transplanters in Connaught for the army. Counties Donegal, Leitrim, Longford, and Wicklow, were reserved for officers who fought before 1649 in Ireland, after which time they joined Cromwell's forces.

The officers and soldiers acquired their lands by a series of lotteries whereby the regiments drew lots for the province and county, and thereafter the baronies where their companies were to locate. At various times the companies were marched to their respective baronies where they disbanded and the officers and soldiers were assigned their plots according to the amount of land allowed for their arrears of pay indicated on their debentures.

A series of lotteries held at Grocers' Hall, London, determined the allotment of land to each Adventurer, first by a drawing for the province, then county, barony, and subdivision therein, where he was to receive acreage in accordance with the amount of money he had subscribed, and the value placed upon the land. Groups of Adventurers in England customarily gave power of attorney to their county sheriff or some one person in their town, or a friend, to draw lots for them.

All English and Protestants previously living in Connaught or County Clare and having lands there at the close of the Rebellion, who wished to remove to Leinster, Munster or Ulster, were offered in exchange a Parliamentary title to property for twenty-one years or three lives at a reasonable rent.

The baronies of Coolock and Balrothery in County Dublin and the barony of Imokelly in County Cork were reserved for maimed English soldiers and widows with arrears not exceeding £150. Counties Dublin and Cork, excepting the above baronies and the counties of Kildare and Carlow, the fortified towns, forts and castles, were reserved for the Government as revenue producing property or for defense purposes.

The Commissioners for Irish Affairs and the Commissioners of Revenue of the various precincts were faced with a mass of petitions in addition to those of the forfeiting proprietors. Others represented the disagreements of Adventurers and army personnel over boundary lines and other matters. Allotments of their lands sometimes conflicted with the lands of occupying Protestants, or with the interests of Protestants who held mortgages on forfeited Roman Catholic property, or with the rights of Protestants who held Roman Catholic property in trust, etc.

The principal sources of the records created by all of the above procedures of forfeiture, transplantation, the settlement of the new English proprietors, the petitions, claims, etc., are listed below. Additional and very numerous sources containing transcripts, abstracts or notes from miscellaneous records of this nature are found among the local histories, historical society journals, published genealogies, family manuscripts, etc.

(1) *The Cromwellian Settlement of Ireland,* by John P. Prendergast (2nd edition, enlarged), Dublin, 1875, contains running illustrations of personal records all through the work, and the following lists, specimens of records, and maps:

A list of the 1,360 Adventurers for land in Ireland (including those who subscribed toward support of the army and the sea service). Prendergast states that this is evidently the original list, which he compiled from documents in the Record Tower, Dublin Castle. It gives the names, occupations or English places of residence (more often both are specified), and the amount of money subscribed by each one, 1642-1646. The list (pp. 403-448) shows a total of £252,712:4:8 subscribed, which indicates it is not complete, for Parliament acknowledged a debt to the Adventurers of £336,000.

Prendergast gives an "Account of the Adventurers in the County of Tipperary," in the baronies of Middlethird, Iffa and Offa, Clanwilliam, Eliogartie, Illeagh, and Ikerrin. In a table for each barony are the names of the Adventurers, the divisions and subdivisions where each was located, the sums of money paid, and the acreage by Irish and by English measure. There are about two hundred names (pp. 389-400). A folded map of County Tipperary shows how it was divided as to baronies, between the Adventurers and the army personnel.

Prendergast gives a list showing where the companies of sixteen regiments and some "Loose Companies" were disbanded and settled in the counties of Cork, Kerry, Kilkenny, Limerick, Meath, Queen's, Tipperary, Waterford, Westmeath, and Wexford. The names of the baronies of settlement and the assignments under names of the captains and superior officers are set forth (pp. 216-219).

Two folded maps show how the lands of Ireland were allotted. One contains the division by counties marked with key letters to indicate which ones were reserved for the Adventurers and army, for the army entirely, for the transplanters, the Government, and for other interests. The other map is of the Province of Connaught and County Clare. The counties are divided by their respective baronies, each one colored to indicate the county origin (in the other provinces) of the transplanters. Thus the transplanters from the counties of Down and Antrim were assigned lands in the baronies of Carra, Clanmorris, and Kilmaine, in County Mayo.

Some of the miscellaneous records include a list of the names and acreage of the Adventurers in King's County, 1655; examples of petitions for dispensation from transplantation (pp. 110-117, 377-385) ; and specimens of Transplanters' Certificates (pp. 363-376).

(2) The *Calendar of the State Papers relating to Ireland preserved in the Public Record Office. Adventurers for Land. 1642-1659.* Edited by Robert Pentland Mahaffy. London, 1903. This Calendar of documents in the Public Record Office, London, relating to the Adventurers for Land in Ireland, is a goldmine of genealogical records of English families. Regarding the records, the Preface states: "They consist firstly of the receipts given to persons who subscribed money for the support of the Parliamentary cause in Ireland in the years 1642, 1643 and 1647, in return for a promise of land in Ireland; and secondly of the documents by which the heirs, executors, administrators or assigns of these subscribers proved their right to claim lands in Ireland in respect of such subscriptions in the years 1653 and 1654 . . . The papers before us are in effect a list of the names and addresses of subscribers, of the places in which the land was awarded to them or their successors, and of the deeds or transfers by which those who actually received land derived their title from the original subscribers."

The receipts mentioned above, show the name, residence, and usually the occupation or rank of the Adventurer, with the same information concerning all who acquired rights as heirs, assigns, etc., gave power of attorney for drawing their lots as to province, county and barony, and their final assignments. Many of their parents and other relatives are named. Groups of friends and relatives from a single locality in England commonly joined in a large subscription, and their lots or those of heirs or assigns were drawn together. The Index contains the surnames and given names of everyone mentioned in the records; also all English counties and towns, and Irish counties and baronies named in the records of individuals; a list of wills indexed by names of the testators, etc. Thus among the very numerous wills and estate settlements or Administrations recited is the following example (pp. 32-33): On 4 July 1653, the following documents were exhibited for the Winston family, at Grocers' Hall, London: "Agreement by Richard, John, Robert, Dorothy and Elizabeth Winston, and by William and Ann Smith and Mary Underwood. They are all (except Wm. Smith) the children of Richard Winston, late of St. Stephen's Walbrook, London, confectioner, deceased, Mary Underwood being the widow of Richard Underwood, deceased, and Anne Smith is the wife of Wm. Smith. They agree to the division amongst them in equal parts of the late Richard Winston's adventure of £200, which, by his will, dated 27 Feb. 1646/7, he devised, with his other goods, &c., to and among his children." This was signed and sealed by the heirs before witnesses. The will was duly checked at the prerogative office, by Wm. Tibbes, clerk, attending the Committee for satisfying the Adventurers for land in Ireland. Richard Winston's receipts for his payment of the total of £200 in 1642 were also examined. At that time he was listed as a grocer of London. The Irish land which the heirs received was assigned in the barony of Decies, Co. Waterford on 3 May 1654. An amount worth £28/11/5 was assigned to John Wells, of London, merchant, for good consideration. The remaining amount was divided into seven shares, John Winston receiving three parts, and the other named heirs each one share, except Mary Underwood, who assigned her share to her brother, John, citizen and grocer of London, for £17, and Robert Winston, who also assigned his share to John, for £14.

(3) The *Calendar of the State Papers relating to Ireland preserved in the Public Record Office. 1647-1660.* Edited by

Robert Pentland Mahaffy. London, 1903. Pages 41-362 belong to the reign of Charles I, and mostly concern petitions of
people of high rank, revealing personal or Government affairs.
The documents calendared on pp. 394-535 are supplementary
to those in the above volume relating to the Adventurers.
These are the records of power of attorney given by the Adventurers, their heirs or assigns, to draw lots for them at
Grocers' Hall, London, for their location of land in Ireland
by province, county, and barony. Details of their rights to
land are set forth in cases of heirship and assignment or sale
of rights from the original subscriber, all being dated in 1653
or 1654. Documents calendared pp. 536-725 mostly concern
petitions to the Council of State by persons claiming rights to
lands or showing reasons why their estates should not be
forfeited. Other documents relate to miscellaneous personal
and Government matters.

On pp. 655-656 is a "Copy of Petition to the Protector of
Gerald Westley, an orphan, *aet.* 18, by Dr. Henry Jones, his
guardian, showing that:-Petitioner's grandfather, Valerian
Westley, in consideration of the marriage of Wm. Westley, his
son with Margaret Hemp (petitioner's father and mother),
and of a great marriage portion paid, did, by feoffment in
June, 1637, convey the manor of Dengan [Dangan] and all his
other lands, &c., in Meath, to the following use, viz., part of
the lands to Wm. and Margaret for their lives, and the remainder with the residue of all lands to Valerian for life; remainder of the whole to William and the heirs male of his body
with other remainders over. Petitioner's father died in 1637,
. . . and his mother died in 1646." The petition goes on to
state that Gerald Westley was educated by Dr. Jones and at
the College of Dublin. His grandfather, Valerian Westley,
died in May, 1655. Gerald Westley is suing for his estates
which were given to Col. Daniel Axtell by the Commonwealth
Government as a delinquent's estate. Dated 14 Dec. 1657.
Col. Daniel Axtell then petitioned the Protector showing why
he was entitled to the estate, as Valerian Westley was a rebel
and Gerald Westley's mother Margaret married a grand rebel,
Lt. Col. Rochford; all being Papists, etc. Dated 22 Dec. 1657.

Irish Historical Studies, Vol. X, No. 37 (March, 1956, pp.
20-58), contains an article entitled "The Irish Adventurers

and the English Civil War", by J. R. MacCormack. This provides interesting historical background for the Adventurers and their activities. An Appendix contains statistics regarding 136 Adventurers who were members of the House of Commons, alphabetically arranged, showing for each his residence, amount of money subscribed, date of payment, acreage received and place of assignment in Ireland, except in cases of decease or assignment of the rights to others. The references to sources are given, including the State Papers (described above), Prendergast's list of Adventurers (mentioned above), and also a manuscript in Marsh's Library, Dublin (MS. No. Z 2.1.5.), entitled, "An account of adventurers in Ireland in Oliver Cromwell's time, with a list of the lands allotted to each (ex libris Dudl. Loftus) 35 fols."; and *Historical Collections,* by John Rushworth, London, 1731 (Vol. 5).

(4) *Ireland Under the Commonwealth,* by Robert Dunlop. 2 vols. Manchester, 1913. This contains a selection of documents relating to the Government of Ireland from 1651 to 1659, from the Commonwealth Records preserved in the Public Record Office, Dublin. A report on the contents of the entire collection, by Sir Bernard Burke, is in the 2nd Appendix to the 14th *Report of the Deputy Keeper of the Public Records in Ireland.* Dunlop's Preface to Vol. I contains an Historical Introduction of 124 pages, and 23 pages giving a valuable view of the entire process of the Cromwellian Settlement with regard to forfeitures, transplanters, claims and exceptions refused and granted, the army and Adventurers' allotments, the work of the Commissioners of the precincts, the Lord Deputy and Council, special commissions, etc. The selected documents represent reports and letters of these Government officers to each other and to Cromwell, the Council of State in London, Parliament, etc. They contain Government and Settlement matters and also very numerous petitions or reports on them. Volume II, pp. 404-405, contains lists of the baronies in the first ten counties allotted to the army and the baronies in the same counties allotted to the Adventurers. The names of the various officers of the regiments and companies who drew lots for their location of lands are given. Much other information concerning the officers, their work and locations, with personal notes, provides a background for

a great many who became important landlords. However, there is very little in the way of genealogical records.

(5) The Irish Manuscripts Commission published *The Civil Survey, A. D. 1654-1656,* edited by Robert C. Simington. 9 vols., Dublin, 1931-1953. The volumes concern the counties of Tipperary (Eastern and Southern Baronies) ; Tipperary (Western and Northern Baronies) ; Donegal, Derry, and Tyrone; Limerick; Meath; Waterford, Muskerry Barony (County Cork), and Kilkenny City; Kildare; Wexford. In each of the nine volumes, Simington presents an almost identical general Introduction, explaining the history, purpose, and process of the Civil Survey. A further historical Introduction in each volume concerns the work and results of the Survey in the particular county, parts of a county, or more than one county represented.

The Act of 26th September 1653, for the "Satisfaction of Adventurers and Soldiers," directed the Commissioners of Irish Affairs, with instructions, to have a perfect survey made by inquisition, in preparation for the enormous transfer of forfeited lands to the English Adventurers, army personnel, the Government, and other interests. The Civil Survey was begun in June, 1654, and was made in all counties of Leinster, all of Ulster, excepting the barony of Farney in County Monaghan; all of Munster, except County Clare; and County Leitrim in Connaught. In all, twenty-seven counties were surveyed. Strafford's survey of the other five counties of Clare, Galway, Mayo, Roscommon, and Sligo, had been made some fifteen years earlier.

Commissioners of Revenue were appointed to hold Courts of Survey in each county to ascertain the particulars from a jury for each barony, composed of some ten to forty-five members, representing "the most able and ancient inhabitants of the country," whose duties required them to enter and examine the property of all forfeiting proprietors, as well as Crown and Church lands. They were required to provide a description of each barony, parish by parish, as to the profitable and unprofitable lands, their measurements, bounds, the manors, castles, value of tithes, etc. They reported the name of every man who was the proprietor of an estate in 1640, with his rank or designation, his qualification (Roman Catholic "Irish Papist", English Protestant) ; the acreage, bounds, and value of his profitable and unprofitable holdings; his ownership by ancestral tenure, by patent from the Crown, or by purchase. Some juries supplied additional particulars regarding rents received in 1641, bequests by testament, mortgages, marriage settlements, relationships, etc.

The records of each barony were attested by three Commissioners and returned to the Surveyor-General, with a duplicate sent to the Registrar for Forfeited Lands, in Dublin. This Civil Survey was intended as a preliminary work, necessary to the discovery of all lands of forfeiting proprietors, the Church, and the Crown. Abstracts of the records by barony were then supplied to Sir William Petty for the use of his Under-Surveyors, in admeasurement and mapping every barony during the course of the "Down Survey" which included all but those previously in the Strafford Survey.

The original documents were housed in the Surveyor-General's Office which was burned in 1711. In 1817, it was discovered that two sets of the original Civil Survey Barony Books had been prepared. At this time, the duplicates for ten counties were found in Lord Headfort's library at Kells. These books were transferred to the Public Record Office, Dublin, on condition that copies be made for the Quit Rent Office, in 1910. The Headfort books were destroyed in the fire of 1922, and the Quit Rent Office copies were later transferred to the Public Record Office.

The surviving records of the Civil Survey cover the counties of Tipperary, Limerick, Waterford, and part of one barony in Kerry, in the province of Munster; Dublin, Kildare, Meath and Wexford, in the province of Leinster; Donegal, Derry, and Tyrone, in the province of Ulster. Certified copies of the Survey for Kilkenny City, Callan, and Inistioge, in County Kilkenny; and the barony of Muskerry in County Cork were discovered and added to the surviving records. Copies of the Survey of the barony of Louth and extracts from the Survey of County Carlow and of County Kilkenny are among the Ormonde Manuscripts.

Of the nine published volumes, the first two give the text for the baronies of Tipperary. The second volume includes the separate return for Church lands of the entire county.

The third volume containing the records of Donegal, Derry, and Tyrone, shows the ownership established by the Plantation of Ulster and also the names and properties of minor freeholders and lessees of Church lands. The fourth volume gives the records for the county and city of Limerick, including the town of Kilmallock. The fifth volume concerning Meath has a Survey descriptive of the Tithes of every parish of the county, including the names of owners and the value in 1640. The sixth volume, containing the records of Waterford, contains also the records of Muskerry barony in County Cork, and the records of Kilkenny City. Additional features of this volume are the Valuations *circa* 1663-1664, recording the proprietors of houses in Cork and Waterford cities in 1640, and their "tenants or possessors" some twenty years later. The seventh and eighth volumes contain the records of the counties of Dublin and Kildare. The ninth volume of County Wexford records contains in Appendix B (pp. 315-321) a descriptive list of the great Hore Manuscript Collection of 67 bound volumes and 64 unbound manuscripts, compiled by Herbert F. Hore and his son, Philip H. Hore, all of which relate to the records and pedigrees of County Wexford families from early times, a large percentage being of Anglo-Norman or English origin. The original manuscripts are now at St. Peter's College, Wexford, in the custody of the President, Father O'Byrne, who permitted the National Library to microfilm the entire collection. From this extensive collection Philip H. Hore selected the copies of Court Records, State Papers, the Civil Survey, the Books of Survey and Distribution, and all other classes of records relating to the county families which he published in his *History of the Town and County of Wexford*, 6 vols., London, 1900-1911.

A county map showing the baronies with the boundaries of the year of the survey, and the names of the parishes and principal towns, accompanies the records of each county in the nine volumes. At the end of the records of every barony throughout the volumes are the original indexes of the persons and lands. This collection of the *Civil Survey* provides an enormous amount of information for the genealogist. The volumes may be purchased at two pounds ten shillings each,

from the Government Publications Sale Office, G.P.O. Arcade
Dublin, or through any Irish bookshop.

Irish Historical Studies, Vol. IX, No. 35 (March, 1955, pp.
253-263), contains an article on "The Civil Survey, 1654-
1656," by J. G. Simms, in which he presents an informative
analysis of the records, and calls attention to interesting features concerning the history and results of the Survey in the
various counties.

(6) *The Down Survey, 1654-1656.* A first "Gross Survey"
was ordered for producing admeasurements and maps of the
forfeited lands, Crown lands and Church lands, according to
instructions issued to the Commission for Irish Affairs, by
Act of 26 Sept. 1653. Benjamin Worsley, Surveyor-General,
and his Under-Surveyors were appointed and proceeded at
once with the work as outlined in the instructions. The "Gross
Survey" furnished only the "grosse surrounds" of the lands
surveyed. This was hastily attempted, proceeded slowly, and
caused dissension among the army personnel, as it was inaccurate. It was incomplete when Sir William Petty (then Dr.
Petty) proposed a more efficient system of survey. He was
appointed on 11 Dec. 1654, and contracted to map the forfeited
lands set aside for the soldiers in twenty-two counties, within
thirteen months after 1 Feb. 1655. Worsley, who remained
Surveyor-General until January 1657, worked with Petty, who
was further employed on 3 Sept. 1656 to map the forfeited
lands set aside for the Adventurers. Petty's *Down Survey*
was so called because of its topographic details, all laid down
by admeasurement on barony and parish maps.

All counties were thus mapped by barony and by parish, except Galway, Roscommon, and Mayo (in this county he mapped the barony of Tyrawley). In some baronies where there
were no forfeited lands (being inhabited by loyal Protestants),
Petty only produced an outline map of the barony. Abstracts
of the Civil Survey, and the Strafford Survey of 1637, were
supplied to Petty and his surveyors for the details which
they used regarding baronies, parishes, townlands, and the
estimates of the extent of the forfeited lands.

The official maps of the Down Survey, completed in 1659,
were of the baronies, containing their boundaries, the subdivisions of the parishes being marked with their boundaries

and names, with the natural features and principal castles, forts, and churches; the maps of the parishes containing the subdivisions of townlands, their names and other details such as the names of the forfeiting owners and the area of their property and, in many cases, the names of those who did not forfeit their land.

Apparently four sets of the Down Survey maps were produced, representing originals and copies. The first set of the official barony and parish maps was bound in thirty-one volumes, with "Abstracts or Reference Sheets" facing each map. These reference sheets contained information taken from the books of the Civil Survey, describing (1) the parish boundaries and notable features, (2) the numeral given to each denomination (tract of land indicated by boundaries) on the map, (3) the names of the proprietors and usually their qualifications, (4) the place-names of the denominations, (5) their total acreage, (6) the number of profitable and unprofitable acres in each denomination, and (7) their qualities as to arable, meadow, and bog. These thirty-one volumes were deposited by Petty in the Surveyor-General's office, Dublin, where thirteen of the volumes were destroyed by fire in 1711. The barony and parish maps and their reference sheets for twenty-one counties, contained in the remaining volumes, were sent to the Public Record Office, Dublin, and were destroyed in the fire of 1922. Fortunately, copies of the maps and reference sheets were made by Daniel O'Brien, surveyor, in 1786-1787, and assembled in seventeen volumes. These were acquired by Messrs. Reeves, Solicitors, Dublin, who after 1938 deposited fifteen of the volumes in the National Library of Ireland, and two in the Public Record Office of Northern Ireland, Belfast. The volumes in the National Library contain the barony and parish maps and their reference sheets for the following counties: (1) Dublin; (2) Wicklow and Catherlogh (Carlow); (3) (4) Westmeath, 2 vols.; (5) Eastmeath; (6) King's County; (7) Longford; (8) Queen's County and Kilkenny; (9) Wexford; (10) (11) Cork, 2 vols.; (12) Limerick; (13) Tipperary; (14) Waterford; (15) Leitrim. The remaining two volumes in Belfast are for the counties following: (16) Antrim, Tyrone, Armagh, Down; (17) Donegal,

Londonderry. These latter two volumes were photostated for the National Library of Ireland, Dublin.

Analecta Hibernica, No. 8 (March 1938), contains two articles regarding these maps, copied by O'Brien in 1786-1787. One is a report presented by Charles McNeill, containing a full description of representative volumes (pp. 419-427). The second is a discussion of the origin of copies of Down Survey Maps, by R. C. Simington (pp. 429-430).

The second set of the Down Survey Maps was preserved in the archives of Petty's descendant, the marquess of Lansdowne, at Lansdowne House, Bowood, England, after being sent from Dublin in *c.* 1800. These are believed to have been Petty's private but not official set of maps. In 1920, this set consisted of the maps of twenty-four counties, one hundred and three baronies and one map of Ireland.

A third set, entitled *Hibernia Regnum,* was en route from Dublin to London in 1707, when the ship was captured and the maps eventually were deposited in the Bibliothèque Nationale in Paris. This set comprises the maps of two hundred and sixteen baronies (lacking that of Coolvain, Co. Sligo), and others of the provinces and counties. Photographic reproductions were made in 1907 for the United Kingdom Ordnance Survey, and copies of these have been placed on sale at the Government Publications Sale Office, G.P.O. Arcade, Dublin. The barony maps have as much detail, taken from Petty's parish maps, as the space allows.

A fourth set of the Down Survey Maps, comprising eighty-three barony maps, was copied by Sir Thomas Taylor, deputy Surveyor-General, 1660-1667, from Petty's original maps. His descendant, a member of the Headfort family, sold them to the Government in 1837, and they were eventually lodged in the Quit Rent Office. In 1943, eighty-three barony maps were transferred from the Quit Rent Office, to the Public Record Office, Dublin (58th *Report,* p. 18).

The History of the Survey of Ireland, Commonly Called The Down Survey, by Doctor William Petty, A.D. 1655-1656, was compiled from three manuscripts, by Thomas Aiskew Lacrom, Dublin, 1851. Lacrom states that this work contains "copies of all the official proceedings preliminary to and during the employment of Sir William (then Doctor) Petty, in the business of the Down Survey, with a running commentary written by the Doctor" (Preface, p. ii). The 402 pages and Index contain no genealogical records, but present much important information.

Irish Historical Studies, Vol. III, No. 12 (Sept. 1943), pp. 381-392, contains an article entitled, "The Maps of the Down Survey," by Seán Ò Domhnaill. It presents a brief and interesting explanation of the work of Sir William Petty, and a subsequent history of all sets of the maps. An Appendix contains a "List of Baronies and Maps," given in the table of contents of *Hibernia Regnum* (mentioned above). These, as noted, were photographed and copies are sold at the Government Publications Sale Office, G. P. O. Arcade, Dublin.

(7) *Manuscript material in the Public Record Office, Dublin:*

(a) Civil Survey: The transcripts of the Headfort Collection of the Civil Survey, made in 1910, for the Quit Rent Office, were transferred to the Public Record Office in 1943. (55th *Report*, p. 133; 56th *Report*, p. 306; 58th *Report*, p. 18.)

(b) Commonwealth Council Books, transcripts from: Eleven manuscript collections are listed which are in the British Museum, Trinity College Library, the Genealogical Office in Dublin Castle, and the Public Record Office. The third collection contains "Orders of the Parliamentary Commissioners for the Affairs of Ireland, made on Petitions and on General Affairs, 1651-1655, and extracts from the Books of the Council relating to grants of forfeited lands. (Transcribed) (Egerton MS., 1762. Cat. Ad. MSS. B. M.)" (55th *Report*, pp. 134-135.)

(c) List of Indictments and Outlawries in the Counties of Dublin, Meath, and Kildare, 1642. (56th *Report*, p. 409.)

(d) Forfeited Estates: Copy made by or for Sir William Betham, of a list of forfeiting proprietors, 1657, from the Commonwealth Council Book, No. A. 35 (MS. 752) (58th *Report*, p. 21.)

(8) *Manuscripts in Trinity College Library, Dublin:* Thirty-three volumes of Depositions of Protestants, 1642-1654, who claimed redress or compensation, for loss of property due

to robberies and outrages committed from the outbreak of the Rebellion, or deposed as witnesses to the same. These Depositions, duly alphabeted and indexed and made up into books, by province and county, were used by the Commissioners at Dublin and at Athlone, together with the books of the Civil Survey, and the captured books of the late Government of Confederate Catholics, to discover any evidence against the transplanters which could influence the final allotment of land in Connaught or County Clare. These were all termed the "Books of Discrimination (or Black Books)."

5. THE REIGN OF CHARLES II, 1660-1685: The Books of Survey and Distribution, containing the records of landowners of Ireland, 1641-1703, reveal the changes in tenure made during and subsequent to the Cromwellian Settlement. The changes prior to 1660 have been noted but, as redistributions occurred between 1660 and 1703 which require explanation, this series of records is listed and described hereafter.

Following the restoration of Charles II, in June 1660, the many conflicting interests in Ireland caused the King's Declaration of 30 November 1660. This provided that, (1) lands in the possession of Adventurers and soldiers on 7 May 1659, should be confirmed to them; (2) that all commissioned officers of regiments raised in Ireland or in English regiments sent out of the country in the service of Charles I, or his son, the present King, before 5 June 1649, should be paid their arrears; (3) that all commissioned officers, who had received no compensation for services since 1649, should be satisfied with land as above; (4) that forfeiting Protestants should be restored the full amount of their estates, and any occupying Adventurers or soldiers should be reprised with other land of equal value; (5) that Innocent forfeiting Irish proprietors who had been dispossessed merely for being Roman Catholics and had taken land as transplanters in Connaught or County Clare, should be restored to their former estates and give up their transplanter estates; (6) that soldiers from Ireland who had served under the King's ensigns abroad (called "Ensignmen"), should be restored their estates; and (7) some thirty-four Innocent noblemen and gentlemen, duly named, were to be restored their forfeited estates at once.

In April 1661, Commissioners were appointed to sit at Dublin and hear claims. Roman Catholics were required to prove their innocence of initiating or taking part in the Rebellion before 1646, etc., under eleven clauses of qualifications. The thirty-three books of Protestant Depositions, 1642-1654, and other "Black Books" were examined for any evidence against them. The Innocents, who had taken no land in Connaught or County Clare, were to be restored at once.

The Commissioners conducting the Court of Claims were a group of Cromwellians. Only a few of the thirty-four restored by the King actually acquired their former lands. Others waited indefinitely for the Protestant occupiers to be reprised and remove elsewhere. Innocent Catholics refused to appear before the Commissioners. The Adventurers and soldiers, having acquired more land than they were entitled to receive, neglected to present their papers confirming their allotments. Judges decreed that the King's Declaration required confirmation by Act of Parliament which was finally secured in the Act of Settlement of 27 September 1662. This embodied the terms of the earlier Declaration, with alterations and additions, and instructions for its execution.

James, Duke of Ormonde, was sent over as Lord Lieutenant in 1662 (served until 1669, and again 1676-1685), with wide powers over execution of the new Act and supervision of the Court of Claims, set up with Commissioners to hear claims from 13 January to 22 August 1663. About 7,000 claims were presented but six-sevenths were left unheard when the time expired. Over 500 were given decrees of Innocence. These decrees contained details of personal history and of the lands which were owned in 1641, with evidence of title when lands were confiscated. Among the cases heard, preference was given to those who had taken no land as transplanters in Connaught or County Clare. Protestants who were given decrees for restoration of property were required to wait until the Adventurers and soldiers occupying their property could be reprised elsewhere.

The Act of Settlement, 1662, failed to satisfy competing claimants for landed estates. It was disclosed that over 1,000,000 acres of good profitable land had been allotted to the Adventurers and soldiers at the rate of unprofitable land. Immense quantities of concealed land had been acquired by the

Cromwellians, which now rightfully belonged to the Crown. Thus the Act of Settlement was suspended and long negotiations between interests led to the decisions which were embodied in the Act of Explanation, passed by the Irish House of Commons on 23 December 1665. This amplified and amended the former Act, and all lands forfeited after the Rebellion of 1641 were vested in the King except the lands of those already declared Innocent. The redivision was planned as follows: (1) The Adventurers and soldiers to be confirmed in two-thirds of the lands of which they stood possessed on 7 May 1659; (2) certain properties purchased by Protestants in Connaught and County Clare, to be reduced by one-third of that possessed in September, 1663; (3) all adjudged not Innocent under the Act of Settlement could at no future time claim lands. Of the thirty-four whom the King named for restored estates, under his Declaration and under the Act of Settlement, only twenty had actually been restored their ancestral estates. This number was again confirmed and the favor was extended to others, making a total of fifty-four to whom their principal places of residence were returned, with 2,000 acres adjoining. If any greater quantity had been possessed in 1641, it was to be vested in the King for distribution to others.

For these purposes of new distribution, a third Court of Claims was set up with Commissioners, on 4 January 1666, and lasted until 3 January 1668/9. It heard principally the claims of English Protestants and some Anglo-Irish, chiefly of the old royalist families of the Pale and a few living in Munster.

The Lord Lieutenant was authorized and required to grant letters patent upon request to everyone who received a certificate from this Court of Claims, reciting the claimants' names, particulars of lands allotted, location, number of acres, rents reservable, etc. Adventurers and soldiers received 1,767 certificates. Of the "Forty-nine" officers, 100 received certificates. The acreage allotted and confirmed by letters patent was as administered in the Down Survey.

Again under the King's directions of 22 September 1675, a new Court of Claims was set up in pursuance of the Acts of Settlement and Explanation, and Commissioners were appointed for hearing and judging the claims of transplanted persons who as yet had had no hearing. From 20 March 1676, and during two years thereafter, some 580 certificates were issued, which recited the lands set out to the transplanters in Connaught or County Clare, now in the hands of their descendants or claimants, to the point that letters patent be issued for a final settlement.

This was followed by the Commission of Grace, 1684-1688 (36 - 37 Charles II, and 1 - 4 James II), instructed to adjudicate the remaining unsatisfied claims, particularly of deficient Adventurers and soldiers, the Duke of York, the "Forty-nine" officers, and the unreprised Protestants. Some 500 grants direct from the Crown were made.

The existing original records comprising Court or other official documents of the reign of Charles II, arising from sources described above, and the existing abstracts or Calendars thereof, are filled with information regarding persons concerned in the tenure of estates from 1641 to 1685. The various manuscript collections of this nature are listed below under their repositories; the printed Calendars and microfilms of collections are also noted.

(1) *Public Record Office, Dublin.* Collections listed in *Reports of the Deputy Keeper of the Public Records in Ireland:* (a) "Account of lands set out to transplanted Irish in the Province of Connaught by way of Final Settlement received from Deputy Surveyor-General, 1664." (Ormonde MSS., Vol. II (1899), Historical Manuscripts Commission, 3rd *Report*, pp. 114-176.) This contains two lists, concerning the forfeiting proprietors of 1641, whose estates were located in the provinces of Leinster, Munster, or Ulster. Each list is alphabetically arranged, and signed by "Thomas Eliot, Deputy Surveyor-General." In this account the county of origin if not a fuller address usually follows the name of the transplanted person. Three other items are the "Date of the Decree," the "Date of Final Settlement," and the "Number of Acres," of the transplanted person. At the end of the second list it is stated that "Upon search made into the Books of Final Settlement, it was found that the lands set to the transplanted Irish in Connaught contained 717,076 Irish acres or 1,161,544 Eng-

lish acres." (Title and source of the lists in 55th *Report*, p. 137.)

(b) "Abstract of the Decrees of the Court of Claims for the trial of Innocents, 1662, 1663," regarding Forfeitures of 1641. (Egerton MS. 789, Cat. Add. MSS. B. M.) (55th *Report*, p. 137.) Concerns Forfeitures of 1641.

(c) "Abstracts of the Decrees of the Court of Claims for the Trial of Innocents, commencing 13th Jan. 1662, printed in 19th *Report*, D. K. R." (55th *Report*, p. 137.)

(d) "Forfeited Lands Liberties of Galway (Hardiman's Galway)." (55th *Report*, p. 137.)

(e) "Settlement of Clonmel, 1666 (History of Clonmel, Burke)." (55th *Report*, p. 137.)

(f) "Transcripts of selected papers (Irish Official) from volumes 1-39, 47-53, 55, 56, 59, 60 of the Carte Collection in the Bodleian Library." (55th *Report*, p. 123.) This is Carte's Collection of the Ormonde MSS., including letters and petitions to the Lord Lieutenant, Ormonde, containing personal or family information regarding those involved in the redistribution of land, etc. See below under National Library of Ireland.

(g) *Adventurers' Certificates.* (1 vol., Ferguson Coll.) "Alphabetical List of persons to whom Certificates were granted by the Court of Claims. It gives the quantity of lands set out to each person, the county, and sometimes the denominations (boundary locations) of the lands, the persons in whose favour savings were made, and the Roll upon which the Certificate was enrolled." (55th *Report*, p. 123.)

(h) *Decrees to Innocents* (Ferguson Collection). "An Alphabetical list or repertory of the Decrees to Innocents somewhat fuller than the Adventurers' List, except that it does not give the number of acres decreed. It also gives the Roll upon which the Decree was enrolled." (55th *Report*, p. 123.)

(i) *Press Copies of Certified Copies* (6 vols.). Among Machine press copies of Chancery and Exchequer Inquisitions, Fiants, etc., are Decrees of Innocents, etc. (55th *Report*, p. 123.)

(j) *Lodge's Manuscripts.* The MS. Calendars of Patent Rolls of Charles II, supplement and provide records for some years for which there is no other record. His *Records of the Rolls,*

Henry II to George II (13 vols.), contain abstracts of Patent and Close Rolls, of particular importance for this period. (55th *Report*, pp. 116-122.)

(k) "List of Claims of Innocents, to be heard by Act of Settlement Commissioners for Trial of Innocents. (Hearings Book) 28 Jan. 1662/3 - 20 Aug. 1663. (MSS. Armagh Library.)" (56th *Report*, p. 409.)

(l) "A Rentrole of the Forfeited Houses, Landes and Tenements assigned towards satisfaction of the Arrears of the Commissioned Officers who served in Ireland before the 5th June 1649, sett for one year determining the 25th of March 1662, reserved thereon." (In Rawlinson Coll., B. 508, Bodleian Library.) (56th *Report*, p. 409.)

(m) "Schedules of crown rents, quit rents, new patent rents, innocent papists' lands and undisposed lands, 1663-1827." (58th *Report*, p. 17.)

(n) "Three volumes of copies of petitions, king's letters, bills, acts, correspondence . . . 1660 - *c.* 1700. M2458-2460." (58th *Report*, p. 27.)

(2) *Irish Record Commission Reports, 1811-1825* (3 vols.). Volume III, published in 1825, contains the 11th - 15th reports with an appendix to the latter, which contains Lodge's abstracts of grants under the Act of Settlement (1662) ; an index to the certificates of the Court of Claims; abstracts of conveyances by the trustees for forfeited estates; indexes to Adventurers' and soldiers' certificates, Decrees of Innocents, Connaught Certificates, and adjudications in favour of the 1649 Officers, etc. (*Irish Historical Studies*, Vol. VII, No. 25 (March 1950), "The Irish Record Commission, 1810-1830," by Margaret Griffith, p. 35.) (See 19th *Report of the Deputy Keeper of the Public Records in Ireland*, p. 38.)

(3) *Calendar of State Papers relating to Ireland, deposited in the Public Record Office, London, 1660-1662; 1663-1665; 1666-1669; 1669-1670, with Addenda, 1625-1670.* Edited by Robert Pentland Mahaffy, 4 vols., Dublin, 1905-1910. These abstracts of documents relate to the great variety of matters noted above, and include a mass of petitions of individuals to the King or the Lord Lieut., James, Duke of Ormonde, for redress or justice or some favor. They often contain personal

notes or family history of the applicant, covering from one or two to as many as three or more generations.

(4) *Account of the Carte Collection of Historical Papers in the Bodleian Library, Oxford,* by C. W. Russell and J. P. Prendergast. London, 1871. The Carte Collection, named for the Rev. Thomas Carte, the well-known author of the *Life of James, Duke of Ormonde,* is comprised of 272 volumes of documents. The bulk of the collection consisting of the official, private, and other miscellaneous papers of James, the first Duke of Ormonde, is dated prior to and during his periods of office under Charles I, and Charles II. A descriptive catalogue of the volumes is presented, pp. 30-67. A more complete calendar of some of the volumes is given. A great many personal records of individuals are contained in the papers which explain the struggles of the conflicting interests in the settlement of Ireland after 1600. Ormonde, as Lord Lieutenant of Ireland, was the central figure to whom the King, the Adventurers and soldiers, the Protestant and Roman Catholic royalists, the ancient native Irish proprietors, and the Commissioners of the various Courts of Claims had constant recourse. Calendars of the documents contain many examples of petitions, claims, decrees of Innocence or Nocence, and several lists of this nature. Included is a "Catalogue of 1,083 Original King's Letters . . . addressed some few to the Lords Justices, but principally to the Duke of Ormonde, 1660-1669, contained in Volumes 41-43" (pp. 199-231). Subject matter of each letter is noted in a sentence or two. Thus Letter No. 82 is listed as, "Robert Harpool, an infant son and heir of Captn. W. Harpool, is granted restitution of his estate, on the petition of himself and his mother, Martha Harpool, setting forth that said Robert's grandfather, Captain Robert Harpool, were [was] slain in H. M.'s service at the storm of Drogheda, and his father William Harpool executed by Axtel, November 21, 1660."

(5) The National Library of Ireland, Dublin, has microfilmed the entire Carte Collection, MSS. 10,447 - 10,674. (See VOLUME II, p. 286, herewith.) It has also microfilmed the British Museum Additional Manuscripts, Nos. 47,209 - 47,238, containing "Conveyances by the Committee for Claims of lands in King's Co., 1654-1690; in Limerick, 1653-1690; in Meath,

1666; in Queen's Co., 1654-1666; in Co. Waterford, 1654-1666; in Co. Westmeath, 1666." (VOLUME II, p. 285, herewith.)

6. THE REIGNS OF JAMES II, 1685-1689; WILLIAM AND MARY, 1689-1694; AND WILLIAM III, 1694-1702: James II, a converted Roman Catholic, succeeded his brother as king on 6 February 1685. While the fortunes of the Roman Catholics had improved under Charles II, it was shown by Petty's Census of 1672 that they then owned only 3,500,000 of the 12,000,000 profitable acres in Ireland; the new Cromwellian settlers had acquired 4,500,000 acres and the older Protestant proprietors were secure in their possession of 4,000,000 acres. No great changes were made before 1685.

James II rapidly admitted Roman Catholics to legal, political, and military offices in Ireland. Col. Richard Talbot was created Earl of Tyrconnell and Lieutenant-General of the army. He staffed his army with Roman Catholic officers and his object was to establish a Roman Catholic parliament in Dublin, representing the old Anglo-Irish party. In 1687, he became Lord Deputy in Ireland. After James II broke with the Established Church and the Tory party in England, his son-in-law and his daughter, William of Orange and wife Mary, were offered the English Crown on 13 February 1689.

James II fled to France and, on 12 March 1689, arrived in Ireland at Kinsale, escorted by a French fleet with money and arms, to meet Tyrconnell's army. The most loyal of the old English and the surviving lords of the Pale stood with the old Irish gentry for James II, as their only hope, while he looked on Ireland as a stepping stone to the recovery of his throne in England.

His Irish Parliament which met on 7 May 1689, repealed the Acts of Settlement and Explanation, without regard to established legal rights of property owners. An Act of Attainder was passed against some 2,400 Protestant landowners who failed to support James II, most of whom had fled to England. Their property was seized and they were commanded to return and prove their innocence and loyalty or stand trial after fixed dates.

Tyrconnell's army secured the chief garrisons but failed to take Londonderry and Enniskillen. The war commenced with the Siege of Derry which lasted from 17 April to 30 July

1689. On 13 August 1689, William's army landed at Bangor, and he with other forces arrived at Carrickfergus on 14 June 1690, thereby uniting forces of 36,000.

On 1 July 1690, the Battle of the Boyne marked the fall of the old English loyalist aristocracy, comprising mainly Anglo-Normans with some Gaelic survivors and later Elizabethan additions. The Treaty of Limerick, 3 October 1691, secured the victory of William after James had fled to France. It provided that Irish Catholics were to enjoy the degree of religious liberty permitted under Charles II. All inhabitants of the city of Limerick and all officers in arms under James II, in the counties of Limerick, Clare, Cork, Kerry, Mayo, and Galway (by separate articles), and all under their protection in such counties, were promised retention of their estates and civil rights upon taking the oath of Allegiance to the Crown. Any who stood attainted were, if possible, to be restored their estates. Some 7,000 officers and men, who refused to take the oath of Allegiance, were permitted to follow James II to France. This number of exiles increased to a total of 11,000, representing most of the aristocracy who lost their estates.

The Treaty of Limerick was not ratified by the Protestant Irish Parliament until 1697. Some 4,000 landowners were attainted and their property confiscated. By 1700, a Court of Claims was set up at Chichester House in Dublin. About 400,000 acres were regranted to "innocent papists," but finally some 1,000,000 acres were vested in the Crown and sold by the Government at public auction to Protestants. Records covering this period are as follows:

(1) *The Public Record Office, Dublin:* Collections listed in the *Reports of the Deputy Keeper of the Public Records in Ireland:*

(a) Forfeitures of 1688, in the County of Dublin, to be exposed for sale at Chichester House, 8 April 1703, "apparently the original" (Cat. Add. MSS. B. M., 1846-7, p. 146). (55th *Report*, p. 137.)

(b) Forfeitures of 1688: A list of Claims as they are entered with the Trustees at Chichester House on College Green, Dublin, on or before the Tenth of August, 1700. (Copy in the National Library with MS. Rulings.) (55th *Report*, p. 137.)

(c) Forfeitures of 1688: Book of Postings and Sales of

Forfeited and other Estates and Interests in Ireland. (Copy in the National Library.) (55th *Report*, p. 137.)

(d) A printed list of (b) above. (56th *Report*, p. 303.) This came from the Quit Rent Office, and with it were two other items: Claims entered with the Trustees at Chichester House, Dublin, since 10 August 1700 (MS. List) ; and a printed "List of the Several Estates in the County of Cork belonging to the Governor and Company for making Hollow Sword Blades in England, with the quantity of Acres as by the Survey of the late Trustees for Sale of Forfeited Estates. (56th *Report*, p. 303.)

(e) Forfeited Estates, 1688: "A List of the Lands forfeited to the Crown in consequence of the Rebellion of the year 1688 as taken from the Book of Postings and Sales, Conveyances and other Books in the Forfeiture Office at the Custom House containing the Purchaser's names, denominations, extent, situation, amount of purchase money remaining unpaid. (Copy or duplicate of volume formerly in the Record Tower Collection *4P. 27, 55.*)" (56th *Report*, p. 305.)

(f) Forfeitures of 1688: "Copies and draughts of Petitions and Reports to the House of Commons, 1701-2. Bodleian Library, Oxford, "Rawlinson Coll. B. 508 (*Analecta Hibernica,* No. 1, p. 177)." (56th *Report*, p. 409.)

(g) Forfeitures of 1688: "Copies of the books appended to Report of the Parliamentary Commission on Forfeitures, 1699. Book No. 1 to No. 9." (56th *Report*, pp. 409-411.) These nine volumes are filled with lists and information concerning persons who were indicted and outlawed for High Treason; lists of forfeiting persons not restored and of those restored to their estates, with locations and descriptions of their estates; lists of Adjudications at the Council Board and in the Court of Claims, with names of the claimants, rank, place of abode, and rulings or decisions, 1692, 1694, 1697, 1699; Pardons; Grants; Forfeitures; all with particulars of cases.

(h) "Rolls containing Judgements, Deeds, Recoveries of Confiscated Land." Twelve Notebooks containing records dated from 1590 to 1837. Volumes 3 - 7 contain the records from 1656 to 1715. (58th *Report*, p. 27.)

(i) A printed volume by C. Cavel and J. Watts, dated 1690,

containing "A List of Names of the Nobility, Gentry, and Commonalty of England and Ireland, Assembled in Dublin, 7th May 1689, before the Late King James, Attainted of High Treason." This is also in the National Library of Ireland, and has been (1955) listed by Hodges Figgis & Co., Ltd. (No. 1765. £3:3:0).

The Books of Survey and Distribution: This series of records originally comprising a set of twenty manuscript volumes containing abstracts of documents dated from *c.* 1636-1641, to 1701-1703, represents a magnificent work of compiling information pertaining to all landowners in Ireland, the description of their lands, the changes in ownership of each original estate or part thereof, and the rights or instruments of title within this period. The records are now preserved in four sets of *Books of Survey and Distribution.* Each set varies somewhat as to detail according to the purpose of the copies made from the original records. Two sets are in the Public Record Office, Dublin; one in the Royal Irish Academy, Dublin, and a fourth set, representing part of the Annesley Collection now in private custody, has been microfilmed by the National Library of Ireland. All will be noted.

The series originally deposited in the Auditor-General's Office was transferred to the Public Record Office, where the volumes were destroyed in the fire of 1922. It appears that a duplicate of this series of twenty manuscript volumes was made for the Quit Rent Office. In 1943, this set was deposited in the Public Record Office.

These records are compiled parish by parish and barony by barony for all counties of Ireland. They are arranged in columns on wide folios with a series of signs to further indicate references, content and the nature of the records. Within the columns are set forth the names of the owners of the lands of each estate in 1636, 1640 or 1641, showing those who forfeited their property under Cromwell and those who retained their lands; the names of the new proprietors, and for all old and new proprietors, the denominations or place-names of the estates, their location and acreage as to profitable, unprofitable and total extent of each holding. The first recorded changes in ownership were those established by the various Acts of

Settlement and Explanation, the rulings of the Commissioners of the Courts of Claims and the decisions of the King, the Lord Lieutenant, the Commission of Grace, etc., during the period 1660-1685. The names of the proprietors, who forfeited or retained their estates after the Revolution of 1689-1691, are revealed by the names of the owners and description of their lands after the final distribution, 1701-1703.

This great corpus of information represents abstracts of the Strafford Survey of *c.* 1636; the Civil Survey of 1654-1656; the subsequent Down Survey; the rulings of the various Courts of Claims under Commissioners set up by the Restoration Acts; the Certificates and patents, etc., granted under Charles II; the Parliamentary Commission on Forfeitures with rulings on decisions of 1692-1699; the claims, petitions and rulings regarding high treason, outlawries, forfeitures, pardons, etc., by the trustees at Chichester House, Dublin, 1701-1703, and the final Government sales of forfeited estates to English Protestants.

Two volumes of the *Books of Survey and Distribution* for the counties of Roscommon and Mayo, edited by Robert C. Simington, and published by the Irish Manuscripts Commission, 1949, 1956, each contain a forty-page Introduction, describing the full history of the sources and nature of the records of the original and official series in the twenty volumes first deposited in the Auditor-General's Office, and the Quit Rent Office set representing duplicates now in the Public Record Office, Dublin. This latter set is the source (with some particulars from other collections) used for the two published volumes.

It is hoped that the records of Survey and Distribution for all other counties of Ireland will, in time, be edited with the learning and skill of Dr. Simington, and published in the same form by the Irish Manuscripts Commission. In the Introduction to the Roscommon volume, p. xxxi, Dr. Simington states, "For topographical and genealogical research the *Books of Survey and Distribution* are of the utmost importance . . . In the specification, county by county, of the names of proprietors of land prior and subsequent to the Commonwealth settlement, the genealogist is provided with details of the losses no less than the gains of countless families. Here emerges the land of Ireland as it was held three centuries ago by Gaels and Gaelicised Normans, by Normans "The Old English," by "The New English" of the Elizabethan and of the later plantations and settlements. The *Books of Survey and Distribution* frequently provide the addresses of landholders and always the parishes in which their possessions were located, details which should prove of much help in genealogical research."

There are nine columns across the wide pages of the Roscommon volume which illustrate the form followed in the manuscript volumes of the *Books of Survey and Distribution*. The headings of the columns (with original spelling) are listed below:

(1) "Number of reference in ye Alphabett." This is the reference number on the Down Survey parish map, indicating on the Reference Sheet facing each map the forfeited or unforfeited admeasured denomination (estate) with the place-name.

(2) "Proprietors names Anno: 1641." The name of the proprietor, forfeiting or non-forfeiting, is taken from the Civil Survey which shows the proprietor of each estate in 1640 or 1641. For the counties where Strafford's Survey of *c.* 1636 made the Civil Survey unnecessary, the proprietors of *c.* 1636 are shown in this column.

(3) "Denominations." Here is entered the name of the townland or, if more than one, every townland, and the total extent expressed in fractions or more of a quarter of land.

(4) "Number of Acres unproffitable."

(5) "Number of Acres profittable."

(6) "Number of profittable Acres disposed of on ye Acts." These are the Acts of Settlement and Explanation and the changes made by the Commissioners of the various Courts of Claims, the King and Lord Lieutenant by special grant, the Commission of Grace, etc., in the reign of Charles II, thereby redistributing the lands after the Cromwellian settlement.

(7) "To whom soe disposed with their Title whether by Decree, Certificate or Patent, References to ye Record thereof." In this column appears the name of the proprietor es-

tablished by Charles II. The new proprietor was (1) the old forfeiting proprietor or his heir to whom the family estates or part thereof were returned by Charles II, or (2) a proprietor or his heir who was not subject to forfeiture by Cromwell and was confirmed in all or part of his estate by Charles II, or (3) an Adventurer, soldier, officer, purchaser, etc., to whom Charles II granted two-thirds of his Cromwellian estate, or (4) a "Forty-nine" officer who received a grant of land under Charles II. The title to the property and description of the class of the proprietor is defined by a key sign placed beside the name.

(8) "Number of ye Book or Roll of ye Page or Skin." A note at the bottom of the page states, "The particulars which the captions of this and the succeeding column indicate are not furnished by the [Roscommon] text; these last two columns were availed for other purposes—in the present instance, to record the names of the purchasers of lands forfeited in 1688 and number of acres thereof [sold by the Trustees at Chichester House, Dublin, 1701-1703]. This column No. 8, is used to show the number of acres purchased.

(9) "Number of ye profitable Acres remaining undisposed." As stated above, this column is used for the name of the purchaser of the land forfeited after 1688. If these columns are left blank, it indicates that the one who acquired the land under Charles II continued to retain it in 1703. The key sign after the purchaser's name in column No. 9 places him as a purchaser of a forfeited estate of 1688, at the Trustee's sale, 1701-1703.

The key signs called "Markings", used in columns No. 7 and No. 9, are listed in the Roscommon volume, p. lv. They are as follows, numbers being used here in place of the peculiar signs, with the key to their meaning copied exactly:

"Markings in Roscommon Book of Survey and Distribution (extracted from copy of table in P. R. O. Dublin)." A note regarding this table states that "This includes other markings which do not appear in the Roscommon Book of Survey and Distribution."

1. Certificate and Patent Act of Settlement.

2. Certificate Court of Claims or Certificate Adventurers, Soldiers or Transplanters.
3. Decrees of Innocence: Decrees Court of Claims.
4. Commission of Grace 14 March (36 Charles II) to 21 April (1 James II).
5. "In cases examined where this mark appears, and which is not included in the P. R. O. table, the instruments of title; in so far as these can now be established, would appear to have been Decrees of Innocence."
6. Trustees Sale 1688 Forfeitures; sold in 1701-1703, T. D. Trustees Deed Rolls. This last "Marking" is used only in the last column, No. 9, as illustrated in the Roscommon volume.

The two volumes of the *Books of Survey and Distribution* for County Roscommon and for County Mayo, edited by Robert C. Simington, and published by the Irish Manuscripts Commission, should be included in every Irish genealogical library. They can be purchased from the Government Publications Sale Office, G. P. O. Arcade, Dublin, or from Hodges Figgis & Co., Ltd., or other Dublin bookshops, at price £2:15:0 for the Roscommon volume and at £3:3:0, for the Mayo volume, or more, as the volumes become scarce.

The twenty manuscript volumes of the *Books of Survey and Distribution* which comprise the Quit Rent Office set, now in the Public Record Office, Dublin, contain county records by parish and barony as follows: (1) Armagh, Down, Antrim; (2) Kildare, Carlow; (3) Fermanagh, Monaghan, Cavan; (4) (5) Clare; (6) Cork; (7) Derry, Donegal, Tyrone; (8) Dublin, Wicklow; (9) (10) Galway; (11) Kerry, Waterford; (12) Wexford, Kilkenny; (13) King's, Queen's; (14) Leitrim, Sligo, and barony of Tyrawley, Co. Mayo; (15) Limerick; (16) Westmeath, Longford; (17) Meath, Louth; (18) Mayo; (19) Tipperary; (20) Roscommon. (Introduction, Roscommon vol., p. v.)

The four sets of the *Books of Survey and Distribution* vary somewhat as to detail; the Quit Rent Office collection now in the Public Record Office, Dublin, being on the whole the most complete. Space does not permit further description of the other collections which contain some supplemental data. The sources containing information regarding the content of all four sets are as follows: The Introduction to the Roscommon and Mayo volumes, noted above, contains an exhaustive history and description of the original *Books of Survey and Distribution*, a detailed account of the content of the Quit Rent Office set now in the Public Record Office, Dublin, and brief notes regarding the Headfort set in the Public Record Office; the Taylor set in the Royal Irish Academy, and the Annesley set which was microfilmed by the National Library of Ireland. The 56th *Report of the Deputy Keeper of the Public Records in Ireland,* Dublin, contains descriptions of the Quit Rent Office collection (pp. 305-306) ; the Headfort Collection (pp. 307-308) ; the Taylor Collection in the Royal Irish Academy (pp. 406-408). *Analecta Hibernica,* No. 16 (March 1946), pp. 341-354, contains a description of the Annesley volumes of the *Books of Survey and Distribution,* contributed by Robert C. Simington, as part of an article on the entire Annesley Collection deposited at Castlewellan, County Down, and microfilmed by the National Library of Ireland (pp. 341-373).

The Public Record Office of Northern Ireland, Belfast, has complete copies of three volumes of the Quit Rent Office set of the *Books of Survey and Distribution* which relate to Ulster. These are, Vol. I, for Armagh, Down, Antrim; Vol. III, for Fermanagh, Monaghan, Cavan; Vol. VII, for Derry, Donegal, Tyrone. It has copies of numerous manuscript collections described above, or parts thereof relating to Ulster, which are indexed as to individual records by means of catalogues or card indexes in the Search Room, and to some extent they are indexed in the *Reports of the Deputy Keeper of the Public Records of Northern Ireland.*

*   *   *   *   *

III. NOTES ON MISCELLANEOUS MANUSCRIPT COLLECTIONS AND PUBLISHED SOURCES :

Calendar of the Carew Manuscripts, 1515-1624. Edited by J. S. Brewer and W. Bullen. Vols. I - VI (Vol. VI containing the Book of Howth, the Conquest of Ireland, and Miscellany), London, 1867-1873. This is a Calendar of the manuscripts compiled or collected by Sir George Carew and contained in 39 volumes, preserved in the Archiepiscopal Library at Lambeth Palace, London. This Calendar, published by the English Government, represents a rich collection of historical and genealogical material, dated from the 12th century to 1624.

Sir George Carew (created Earl of Totness), born 1558, was heir to his kinsman, Sir Peter Carew, to whom Queen Elizabeth granted the barony of Idrone, County Carlow, claimed by doubtful descent from the Carew family, possessed of vast estates in Leinster and Munster, 1170-1370. Sir George Carew became an officer in Elizabeth's forces against the Desmond rebellion; a Lieut. General of the English Ordnance, 1596; President of Munster, 1600-1602, when he played an important part in the capitulation of the Gaelic confederation forces in Munster. He was appointed Chief Commissioner of the Plantation of Ulster, 1611, by James I, to report on the progress of affairs in Ulster. He had every opportunity and reason to accumulate his vast collection of Gaelic-Irish, Anglo-Norman, and old English family genealogies, Gaelic Annals, Court Records and State Papers representing Inquisitions, Official Letters, Patents, Petitions, Wills, Plantation documents of Munster and Ulster, including the records of Pynnar's Survey, and much historical and genealogical material regarding the Gaelic chiefs and new planters.

The 39 volumes of the Carew Manuscripts at Lambeth Palace include "Pedigrees of the mere Irish" (MS. 599) ; "A Book of Pedigrees wherein most of the descendants of either the mere Irish or the English families in Ireland are mentioned" (MS. 626) ; and "Pedigrees of most of the Lords and Gentlemen of the Irish Nation" (MS. 636). A book (MS. 632) contains early Anglo-Norman family records and documents, including the charter granted to New Ross, Co. Wexford, by Roger Bigod and William Marshall, 1389.

The letters and many other papers of Sir George Carew were bequeathed to Sir Thomas Stafford who, in 1633, published under the title *Pacata Hibernia,* that portion having reference to Carew's administration as President of Munster. In addition to the 39 volumes deposited in the Archiepiscopal Library at Lambeth Palace, 4 volumes were acquired by Archbishop Laud and given as part of his collection to the Bodleian Library, Oxford (catalogued Laud Misc. 526, 610, 641, etc.). A small part of the Carew collection is in Trinity College Library (E 3.3; 3.5; 3.29; 3.30; 4.1). The history of the collection of Sir George Carew is described by the Provost of Eton, in the *English Historical Review*, vol. xlii (1927), p. 261.

The genealogist is further referred to the journals published by the Irish Manuscripts Commission, *Analecta Hibernica*, No. 1 - No. 20, which contain numerous descriptive articles concerning various manuscript collections of Irish historical and genealogical interest, presently deposited in the British Museum, the Bodleian Library and other public repositories and private archives in Great Britain and Ireland. It is important to become familiar with the content of these collections, as the National Library of Ireland has microfilmed most of them and is continuing the program.

CHAPTER XIV

ESTATE RECORDS

A significant outcome of all the confiscations, plantations and settlements of the lands of Ireland, c. 1540-1703, was the survival of some great medieval and later plantation estates, in the possession of the old aristocracy. The final settlement of 1703 also preserved or established some hundreds of new estates, whose owners soon profited with every opportunity for further accumulation of land offered by marriage, inheritance and purchase.

The great family estates were finally broken up in the latter years of the 19th century, under the Land Acts and by the Incumbered Estates Court. Before this occurred, a list of the land owners was compiled, 1871-1876, by Government order and printed in the *Return of Owners of Land of One Acre and Upwards, in the Several Counties, Counties of Cities, and Counties of Towns in Ireland, to which is added A Summary For Each Province and for All of Ireland (Presented to both Houses of Parliament by Command of Her Majesty)*. Dublin, 1876. The "Summary of Ireland" (p. 325), shows the following situation regarding the number of land owners in 1876:

The area of Ireland measured 20,150,612 acres, 2 roods, 20 perch. The number of owners of one or more acres was 32,614. The number of owners of less than one acre was 36,144. An owner was counted as anyone who held title to the property outright or held a lease of more than 99 years, or a lease with the right of perpetual renewal. The total population in 1871, computed from figures given for each county, was 5,309,500. By provinces and under counties are arranged alphabetically, the names of owners, their addresses, the extent of their property (acreage) comprising one acre or more, and its valuation. Under the same headings are given the number of householders, the total number of householders in all counties being 960,410. According to the above figures showing 32,614 owned more than one acre of land and 36,144 owned

less than one acre each, the total number of owners was
68,758. If these were all householders it would leave 891,652
householders owning no land and either holding a lease of less
than 99 years or living in some family habitation or in a house
provided for a servant or laborer.

The most important point brought out by the above *Return
of Owners of Land of One Acre and Upwards* is the small number of individuals who owned the bulk of the land of Ireland.
In the various counties, estates belonging to 19 people, each
contained between 50,000 and 160,000 acres, with a total acreage of 1,670,692. There were 254 estates or parts of estates,
each owned by an individual and located in one county, which
contained between 10,000 and 50,000 acres. Some 418 estates
or parts of estates, each owned by an individual and located
in one county, contained between 5,000 and 10,000 acres.
Thus it is evident that most of the acreage of Ireland was held
in very large estates, each of which was necessarily operated
as a family business. In addition, there were several hundred
estates containing between 1,000 and 5,000 acres which were
handled in somewhat the same manner as the large estates.

The known collections of family estate records mostly concern the holdings of 5,000 acres upwards. The records relate
to the ownership, tenure, management of the land and its occupants. No two collections resemble one another exactly as
to age, content, size or completeness, for each was accumulated
at will and subject to different conditions while preserved in
the family archives from generation to generation.

The principal family records in full collections usually include deeds, long and short term leases and releases, assignments, mortgages, declarations of trust, marriage settlements,
wills, proposals and acceptances dealing with the agents or
other business matters. Personal letters, business or official
correspondence, records of litigation, and private household accounts are not uncommonly found among the estate papers
of a family. The accounts record the expenditures of or for
members of the family, such as school tuition in Ireland or
England, travel, purchase or repair of clothing, personal supplies and other miscellaneous items concerning the operation

of the manor house and grounds including the wages of servants.

Estate accounts contain charges for improvement, planting, reaping, payments for the services of tenants and laborers or notes as to work owed by them, rent charges, and incidental debts of the tenantry, agents, local gentry, etc. The estate ledgers contain records with particulars of rentals, long and short term leases, names of heirs in cases of leases for lives in two or three generations, assignments, and fines upon the fall of a life, the death being noted. There are frequently lists of tenants at will or of those who held leases of less than three years duration. Full rent rolls, dated from time to time, contain the names of the tenants, names of the leased lands (townlands) or parts thereof held by each, the conditions of tenure including valuation of the property, the length of each lease and provisions for renewal, the annual rent and fines due, and the amount of the paid or unpaid balance. Landlords or estate agents often kept tithe lists, voters' lists, 17th century muster rolls, and notes concerning family alliances and character of various tenants. Estate maps usually accompany the records of an estate.

Records of some large estates were kept by families who held their lands by perpetual leases from the owners, dated from the 17th or 18th century. Such leases were granted for nine hundred years, a thousand years or in perpetuity, at low annual rents with provision for the payment of a fine upon the fall of each life (death of the lessee), and renewal of the lease to the heir of the deceased. To all intents and purposes this class of landlords operated as owners and preserved the records of their management of the property.

Jonathan Pim, in his *Condition and Prospects of Ireland,* Dublin, 1848, p. 332, observed that one-seventh of the lands of Ireland were let, usually by absentee owners, to lessees who held tenure by leases for lives with a covenant of perpetual renewal. They were termed middlemen in cases of a lessee subleasing his holding to tenants and managing the property. Other absentee owners and some landlords in residence employed estate agents who performed the duties of management and kept the records.

As old estates were greatly reduced in size or broken up in the latter years of the 19th century, under the Land Acts and by the Incumbered Estates Court, the legal or practical need for the estate records by the families who had owned or operated the lands, and the space for the storage of old documents rapidly disappeared. In some cases, important documents relating to the ownership or tenure of the land, or legal copies thereof, were acquired by solicitors or their legal firms at times of litigation over the property.

The collections of estate records have been eagerly sought by the Public Record Offices in Dublin and Belfast, and by the National Library of Ireland. In recognition of the great historical and genealogical value of these collections, they have been acquired as gifts from the families or have been purchased, or if the owners of important collections wished to retain possession of their records, they in many cases allowed them to be calendared or placed on loan for the purpose of photostating or microfilming the entire contents.

In 1939, the members of the Irish Manuscripts Commission determined to locate and examine important collections of family and estate documents yet in private keeping. Dr. Edward MacLysaght was appointed to make the survey. His findings up to October 1942 were compiled in a report published in *Analecta Hibernica*, No. 15 (1944). This concerns the following collections: "The O'Grady, The O'Callaghan, The Earl of Longford, Lord Doneraile, Lord Farnham, Lord Inchiquin, Lord Louth, and the following families: Bowen, Blunden, Brown, Colthurst, Conner, Daly, de Vere, Harold-Barry, Herbert, Lane, Longfield, MacLysaght, O'Connell, O'Gorman, O'Neill Daunt, Ridgeway, Roche, Segrave, Ussher, Waters." *Analecta Hibernica*, No. 20 (1958), contains a "Survey of Documents in Private Keeping, 2nd series," by John F. Ainsworth and Edward MacLysaght. The report gives an account of the documents in the following collections in private keeping: The Colclough, Dillon, Doneraile, Mansfield, Nugent, Power O'Shee, Shirley, Smith and Vigors papers (pp. 3-310). An Appendix gives a list of the owners of the collections in private keeping with addresses (pp. 311-318). Detailed calendars of the reports concerning all of the above family collections are typed and deposited in the National Library of Ireland. A *Catalogue of Irish Manuscripts in the National Library of Ireland* (103 pp.) is published by the Dublin Institute for Advanced Studies (Paper bound, 21 s.), 1961.

Some estate records published by the Irish Manuscripts Commission are listed and briefly described in VOLUME II, pp. 99-102, herewith. Among these are the *Dowdall and Peppard Deeds; The Calendar of Ormond Deeds, 1172-1603; The Red Book of Ormond; Irish Monastic and Episcopal Deeds from The Ormond Collections;* the *Calendar of the Orrery Papers; The Kenmare Manuscripts; The Shapland Carew Papers.*

The printed Calendar of the *Ormond Deeds, 1172-1603* (6 vols.), and other publications of Ormond records cover a great mass of documents concerning the land transactions of hundreds of lessees and other owners besides the Ormond family. The same is true of the Calendar of the *Dowdall and Peppard Deeds.*

The *Calendar of the Orrery Papers,* edited by Edward Mac-Lysaght, 1941, concerns the management of the farms and estates of the Orrery family in the counties of Cork and Limerick; the rent rolls, wills, marriage settlements, leases, personal family records, etc., which relate principally to the period between the Restoration and the beginning of the Williamite War. The original documents are in the National Library. As late as 1871, the Earl of Cork and Orrery yet owned 20,165 acres in County Cork (*Return of Owners of Land of One Acre and Upwards . . . 1876*).

The Calendar of *The Kenmare Manuscripts,* edited by Edward MacLysaght, 1942, concerns the vast estate of the Earl of Kenmare, located in the counties of Kerry, Limerick, and Cork, which estate was established by Kenmare's ancestor, Sir Valentine Browne (appointed Surveyor General in 1559), and further by his eldest son, Nicholas, who married the daughter of O'Sullivan Beare, and contains also the records of later generations who were allied by marriage with the leading Catholic aristocracy of Munster. The Browne family, heirs of more than 130,000 acres in the one estate, survived the 17th century and later confiscations. Their MSS. relating to pedigrees, etc. (*Kenmare Manuscripts,* pp. 458-468) and the family pedigree chart (pp. 469-475), are given to clarify relationships and identify persons mentioned in the mass of family papers which are calendared. The records of thousands of individuals are set forth in the leases for lives, conveyances, correspondence, rent rolls, hundreds of Chancery Bills, and other family documents. In 1871, the Kenmare estate in County Cork yet contained 22,700 acres and in County Kerry it yet contained 91,080 acres.

The Shapland Carew Papers were edited by A. K. Longfield, 1946, from four volumes of estate rentals of the Carew family of Castleboro, County Wexford, and cover the estate located in the counties of Wexford (1740-1758; 1780-1798; 1811-1837), and Waterford (1744-1763; 1780-1816). Other records consist of Estate Accounts (Miscellaneous and for Woodstown and Castleboro, 1746-1782); Memorandum Book (1672-1677 and 1704-1727); Servants' Book (1780-1793); Dysart Rents (1798-1809); Miscellaneous Documents (1740-1840). The Carew Pedigree, 17th-19th century (p. 210), is set forth to help identify persons mentioned in the documents. Thus only the main branch of the Carew family at Castleboro is mentioned. Hundreds of names are mentioned in the leases for lives, usually covering the life of the lessee and his named heirs. In 1871, Lord Carew yet owned 17,830 acres in County Wexford.

Another collection of estate records calendared by the Irish Manuscripts Commission and published in its journal, *Analecta Hibernica,* No. 10 (July, 1941), pp. 253-286, was edited by Paul Walsh and concerns the Adams family of County Westmeath. It is entitled *The Adams Rental,* and is a transcript of the original manuscript presented to the National Library of Ireland on April 10, 1933. The manuscript appears to have been in the possession of the family since it was compiled in 1697. It contains the record of the formation of a great post-Cromwellian estate in County Westmeath. The lands to which the rental has reference are located in the barony of Moyashel and of Magheradernan principally, and in those of Moyashel and Rathconrath for the remainder. The manuscript includes the brief Adams family history and genealogy for three generations from the first Randall or Randolph

Adams who came to Ireland from Lincolnshire, England, in 1620, he being the son of the Rev. Richard Adams, Rector of Woodchurch, Chester. The estate contained about 3,500 acres. Notes on earlier owners, of the Hope family from the mid-16th century and the Pettit family, concern some four generations. Detailed rental lists of the late 17th and early 18th century give the names of the tenants, names and description of their lands, number of acres, terms of the leases, etc. Other personal family documents, estate papers and maps are included.

The earlier publications of family papers, including their estate records, give further examples of the nature of such documents, a few being as follows: *The Hamilton Manuscripts: Containing Some Account of the Territories of the Upper Clandeboye, Great Ardes, and Dufferin, in the County of Down,* printed from the Original MSS., by Sir James Hamilton, Knight (pre. 1703) ; edited by T. K. Lowry, Belfast, 1867. This collection of family papers, compiled and calendared about the end of the 17th century, contains the genealogy and pedigree of the Hamilton family including the six brothers, their marriages, children, wills, partition of the lands, the rentals of the Clandeboye estate in 1681 with the tenants' names and the denominations of their lands and yearly rent (pp. 108-111), another rent roll of 1688-1691 (pp. 125-130), and miscellaneous records including Patents (1605-1630), Inquisitions (1623-1644, and 1662), and records of occupying families.

Other collections of family history, genealogy and estate records are set forth in publications listed in VOLUME II, pp. 3-106, herewith, and among the unpublished manuscript records listed in VOLUME II, pp. 109-196. A great variety in the nature, age, completeness and extent of the collections is evident. *The Montgomery Manuscripts, 1603-1704,* compiled from family papers by William Montgomery and edited by the Rev. George Hill, Belfast, 1869, supplies a considerable amount of genealogical material regarding the principal Montgomery family, its allied families and others who occupied the lands of the estate, principally in County Down. *An Historical Account of the Macdonnells of Antrim,* edited by the Rev. George Hill, Belfast, 1873, supplies an equally great amount of information regarding the principal Macdonnell and other allied families who occupied the lands of the estate in County Antrim. *The McGillycuddy Papers,* edited by W. Maziere Brady, London, 1867, concern the documents relating to the vast estate in County Kerry, originally belonging to the sept of Donald or Donogh Mc Dermott O'Sullivan, otherwise called McGillycuddy, in the 16th century. He was of the 36th generation, according to ancient Irish genealogies, from Oilill Olum, King of Munster, who died A. D. 234. The family papers concern the survival of the estate in the 16th to 18th centuries. The 1871 records of all estates of one acre and more, show that the McGillycuddy estate yet contained 15,518 acres in County Kerry.

The *Reports of the Deputy Keeper of the Public Records of Northern Ireland,* 1924-1953, contain calendars of all the principal collections of estate records which were deposited in the Public Record Office, Belfast, before 1953, and also those which were copied, photostated or microfilmed prior to that year. The records concern the estates located in the six counties of Northern Ireland, namely Antrim, Armagh, Down, Fermanagh, Londonderry, and Tyrone. Excepting the very large collections which are self indexed, the names of the owners, tenants, and a word of description of each document in the records of an estate are included in the indexes comprising the bulk of each *Report.* The Search Room contains the detailed Calendars, the master card-index, and the estate maps which furnish guides to the estate collections deposited up to the present time. There are now some hundreds of complete or partial collections of estate records which vary in size or extent as well as in the nature and age of the records. Some of the chief deposited collections are:

ABERCORN, DUKE OF, ESTATE PAPERS OF BARONSCOURT (over 1,500 documents) concerning Irish estates of the family in Counties Tyrone and Donegal, from *c.* 1610 to 1900. Patents, fines, conveyances, leases, rent rolls, maps, estate agents' letters, family settlements, wills, administrations, etc. (1951-1953 *Report,* p. 7.)

ANTRIM MANUSCRIPTS, 1603-1842, concern the papers,

loaned for copying by the Earl of Antrim, of the McDonnell or
Macdonnell family. The estate records cover 107,584 acres
and name 900 tenants in the baronies of Cary, Glenarm, Kil-
conway and Dunluce, including the Liberties of Coleraine. The
Manor Court Books of Glenarm, Ballycastle, Dunluce and
Oldstone; 306 documents, 1610-1784, relating to estates in
Counties Antrim and Londonderry (mostly leases); List of
Larne Inhabitants, 1735; Tenants' names in Ballymoney, 1742,
etc. (*Reports*, 1924, pp. 53-54; 1925, pp. 16-18; 1828, pp. 9,
13.)

ARCHDALE PAPERS, 1537-1909. Archdale family estate, of
Castle Archdale, County Fermanagh, including Rent Rolls.
(*Report*, 1927, p. 24.)

ARMAGH PRIMATAL MANOR ROLLS, etc., containing Court
Leet Rolls of manors of Donaghmore, 1625-1627; Artrea,
1626; Armagh, 1625-1627; Termonfeckin, County Louth,
1625-1627 (*Report*, 1928, pp. 9, 13-14). Rent Rolls, See of Armagh, 1615-1746 (*Report*, 1936, p. 4). Estate map with
tenants' names of Bangor town and harbor, 1757, and tenants
on Clanbrassil Estate from Rent Roll, 1625-1675 (*ibid.*).
Rent Roll of See of Armagh relating to the City and Liberties
of Armagh, 1615-1624 (*Report*, 1933, p. 9). Extracts from
the Rent Rolls of the See of Armagh, 1703 (*Report*, 1946-1947,
p. 10).

BELFAST: See Donegall Estate (*Report*, 1928, p. 16).

BELL ESTATE MAPS, Arboe, 1753, Ballynagown (Undated)
(*Report*, 1924, p. 8).

BERESFORD, JOHN GEORGE, PRIMATE, PAPERS, County Londonderry, 1822-1828 (*Report*, 1926, pp. 21-24).

BRETT PAPER: 1685-1711 (*Report*, 1928, pp. 13-14).

BROWNLOW ESTATE RECORDS (Lurgan, County Armagh);
Rentals, Brownlowsderry, 1635-1667; Lease Book, 1667; Es-
tates in Counties Louth and Monaghan, to 1667; Brownlow
Estate Survey, 1667 (*Report*, 1946-1947, pp. 4, 10).

BURGES OR BURGESS ESTATE, County Tyrone, tenants of,
1750-1771 (*Report*, 1949-1950, p. 5).

CALEDON ESTATE RECORDS, purchased with those of Charlemont, Cremorne, M'Kinstry: Account Books, Conveyances,
Leases, Ledgers, Letter Books, Manor Court Books, Rentals,
etc., Counties Armagh, Down, Monaghan, Tyrone, *c.* 1709-
1921. (*Report,* 1928, p. 8.)

CASTLEDAWSON PAPERS, County Londonderry, 1720-1740.
Notes, Transcripts, and Rent Roll. (*Report,* 1938-1945, pp. 18,
39.)

CHARLEMONT ESTATE PAPERS.   Contained in the Paterson
Collection, 1709-1914, County Armagh.   400 books and papers,
mostly short term leases.   Holder of former tenancy given.
Valuable to genealogists.   Rentals of estates of Charlemont,
Cremorne, Dobbin, Fox, in Counties Armagh, Down and Ty-
rone, 1783-1912, forming a directory of the area.   Manor
Court Book, 1839-1859.   100 maps of area give names of some
tenants.   Indexed.   (*Report,* 1928, p. 20.)   30 documents con-
cerning estates of Charlemont, Cremorne, Verner, 1768-1907.
(*Report,* 1930, p. 9.)

CLANBRASSIL ESTATE.   Entry Book of Tenancies, 1615-1678.
Area covered tract from east suburbs of Belfast to Donaghadee and down western side of Strangford Lough to Killyleagh.
Estate Rent Roll, *c.* 1670, Co. Down.   (*Report,* 1938-1945, pp.
7, 36-37.)

CLANEBOY ESTATE MAP, 1625-1626.   (*Report,* 1938-1945, p.
7.)

CLOTWORTHY FAMILY PAPERS.   Deeds, etc.   See MSS. of
Viscount Massereene and Ferrard, 1539-1822.   (*Report,* 1926,
p. 15.)

COLERAINE AND NEIGHBORING MANORS.   17th century Rent
Roll.   (*Report,* 1935, p. 19.)   Tracing of map of Coleraine
among other Estate Maps, 1758.   *(ibid.)*   These show names
and locations of lands of tenants.   Maps of other manors
of Drumaron and Loughans, County Down, 1731; Rathfriland,
County Down, 1776.   (*Report,* 1938-1945, p. 19.)

COLVILLE ESTATE, Rent Rolls, 1712-1715, for parishes of
Newtownards, Greyabbey and Bangor, County Down.   Each

yearly account contains about 400 names. (*Report*, 1937, p. 21.)

CONYNGHAM, LENNOX, family papers, County Londonderry. (*Report*, 1926, p. 20; 1927, p. 25; 1929, p. 17.)

CREMORNE: See Charlemont.

DELAFIELD FAMILY PAPERS. (*Report*, 1924, p. 54; 1934, pp. 5, 17-18; 1946-1947, p. 9.)

DILLON, FAMILY ESTATE. List of tenants and their holdings with some biographical sketches of the estate of Castle Dillon, Co. Armagh, 1617-1722. (*Report*, 1934, p. 45.)

DOBBIN FAMILY MEMOIR: See Charlemont. (*Report*, 1926, p. 25; 1938-1945, p. 15; 1949-1950, p. 78.)

DOBBS MANUSCRIPT: Rent Roll of Viscount Dungannon's Estate. (*Report*, 1925, p. 13; 1927, p. 17; 1936, p. 23; 1951-1953, p. 98.)

DONEGALL ESTATE. Account Books, 1706-1715, relating to Inishowen, Belfast and Carrickfergus. (*Report*, 1928, p. 16.)

DONEGALL FAMILY: See Shaftsbury. (*Report*, 1951-1953, p. 17.)

DOWNSHIRE LETTERS (Hillsborough Collection), of the Marquis of Downshire. Part I, 1746-1783; Part II, 1784-1789; Part III, 1790-1793, etc. (*Report*, 1925, pp. 18-21; 1926, pp. 17-19; 1927, pp. 13-16; 1929, p. 15; 1930, pp. 15-16; 1931, pp. 20-21; 1932, pp. 16-17; 1933, pp. 19-20; 1934, pp. 18-19.)

DRAPERS COMPANY, LONDONDERRY PLANTATION. Catalogue of the Records, 1585-1907. (*Report*, 1929, p. 16.)

DUNGANNON, COUNTY TYRONE, MAP OF THE MANOR OF, 1710. With the names of tenants. (*Report*, 1932, p. 9.) Estate Rent Roll, 1768. (*Report*, 1925, p. 7.) 49 Maps of Dungannon Estate, County Tyrone, 1815. (*Report*, 1938-1945, p. 18.)

ELY ESTATE, COUNTY FERMANAGH, Rent Roll, 1742. (*Report*, 1946-1947, p. 6.)

ENNISKILLEN ESTATE. Final Notice to Tenants, 1843-1895. (*Report*, 1929, p. 10.)

608 IRISH AND SCOTCH-IRISH ANCESTRAL RESEARCH

FOTTRELL PAPERS, (Lenox-Conyngham Collection), 1722-1739. (*Report*, 1926, p. 20.)

FOX: See Charlemont.

GAGE ESTATE, County Antrim, *c.* 1789-1821. 58 documents including conveyances, judgements, memorandum of agreement, wills, etc., 1691-1867. (*Report*, 1936-1945, p. 13.)

HABERDASHERS' COMPANY, Londonderry Plantation, 1613-1616. (*Report*, 1929, p. 16; 1934, pp. 19-20.)

HAMILTON ESTATE PAPERS, County Down, 94 Deeds, 1639-1841. (*Report*, 1925, pp. 4, 15.) Rent Rolls, 1670, with lists of tenants of the parishes of Bangor, Holywood, Dundonald, Ballywalter and Killyleagh, County Down. (*Report, ibid.*)

HAMILTON ESTATE, County Monaghan, Rent Roll Accounts. (*Report*, 1949-1950, p. 5.)

HERTFORD ESTATE DOCUMENTS, 1719-1894. Hertford Estate, later known as the Wallace Estate, comprised the entire barony of Upper Massereene, County Antrim, and six townlands in County Down. The estate was eventually sold to the tenants and the office in Lisburn was closed. The collection includes two maps of 1726 and 1729, showing the names and locations of holdings of tenants of all lands including Lisburn; a Rental List, 1719-1727, for the whole estate; a Rental List, 1728-1730, for the entire estate; some eleven volumes of maps of the estate by parishes, giving the holdings of each tenant by name and with other particulars as of the 1833 survey; four volumes of townland maps giving the rental and valuation of each holding in 1865. (*Report*, 1938-1945, pp. 14, 27, 28.)

IRWIN ESTATE PAPERS, 1737-1888. Some 122 documents in the Paterson Collection relate mostly to the Irwin family and estate at Carnagh, County Armagh; some records concerning the Noble and Strahan families included. (*Report*, pp. 10, 17-18.) Rentals, 1872-1911, include Rent Rolls of the Estates of Bull, Dolling, Irwin, and Mc Intire. (*Report*, 1924, p. 8.)

JOHNSTON ESTATE, COUNTIES DOWN, ARMAGH, AND MONAGHAN. A Rent Roll of the Estate of William Johnston, County

Down, 1725; also Lists of Tenants of the Burges Estate, County Tyrone, 1750-1771, presented by Major Y. A. Burgess. (*Report,* 1949-1950, p. 5.) A Survey of R. Johnston's Estate in Counties Down, Armagh, and Monaghan, in 1731, is in the Armagh County Museum, and has been microfilmed by the National Library of Ireland.

KER ESTATE, COUNTY DOWN, 1692-1890. Sixty-three documents comprising leases, agreements, etc. (*Report,* 1938-1945, p. 15.)

LENNOX-CONYNGHAM PAPERS. Part I, 1630-1759. (*Report,* 1926, p. 20; 1927, p. 25; 1929, p. 17.)

LONDONDERRY DOCUMENTS (Newtownards Estate Office): Estate papers of Robert Stewart, First Marquis of Londonderry, born 1739, son of Alexander Stewart of Ballylawn Castle, County Donegal, and nephew of Sir Robert Cowan, Governor of Bombay. Estate papers loaned for copying comprise some 2,000 documents from the Londonderry estate office at Newtownards. They relate mostly to County Down, covering the "Newtown and Comber" and the "Newtown and Greyabbey" estates which are represented by the Rentals, Moss and Lease Books which start at 1740 and continue at about ten year intervals to 1860. Leases, conveyances, marriage settlements, wills, grants of administration are dated 1650-*c*. 1850. Accounts, 1757-1812. Maps of many townlands, etc., are dated from 1778 on. A Freeholders' and Voters' List for County Down is dated 1790, with notes about the personalities and politics. (*Report,* 1949-1950, p. 11.)

MACDONALDS AND MACDONNELLS MANUSCRIPT HISTORY, written late 17th or early 18th century (copy of original). (*Report,* 1934, pp. 20-22.)

MAGINNISS FAMILY RECORDS, 1629-1831. Some 58 copies of Wills, Extracts from Wills, Grants, Bonds, Chancery Bills and Petitions, Marriage Settlements, Leases and Deeds, all relating to the family of Maginniss. (*Report,* 1924, p. 10.)

MASSEREENE AND FERRARD, VISCOUNT, PAPERS OF, 1539-1822. (*Report,* 1926, pp. 15-16.) Massereene Title Book, 1605-1713. (*Report,* 1929, p. 18.) Massereene Manuscript

(Foster Papers). (*Report,* 1931, pp. 21-22; 1949-1950, pp. 13-17.)

McCANCE COLLECTION, 1689-1798. (*Report,* 1928, p. 17.)

McKINSTRY ESTATE PAPERS. Included among documents of the following Estates: Caledon, Charlemont, Cremorne, McKinstry and many others, consisting of Account Books, Conveyances, Leases, Ledgers, Letter Books, Manor Court Books, Rentals, in Counties Armagh, Down, Tyrone, and Monaghan, *c.* 1709-1921. (*Report,* 1928, p. 8.)

Mc TEAR LEASES, COUNTY ANTRIM, Belfast area, 18th and 19th century. (*Report,* 1927, p. 9.)

MERCHANT TAYLORS' COMPANY, RECORDS OF, 1616-1840, relating also to other London Companies. (*Report,* 1933, p. 21.)

MONTGOMERY: See Nugent Documents.

MONTGOMERY FAMILY OF BLESSINGBOURNE, FIVEMILETOWN, COUNTY TYRONE. Over 1,000 original documents relating to this family. It forms a complete collection of estate records and family papers when combined with miscellaneous Montgomery documents deposited in 1940. (*Report,* 1951-1953, p. 15.)

MOUNT ALEXANDER RENT ROLL, Comber District, 1684, 1771-1780. (*Report,* 1932, p. 24.)

MOUNT ROSS ESTATE, Portaferry, County Down, Rental (Rent Roll), *c.* 1778. (*Report,* 1933, p. 55.)

NOBLE: See Irwin.

NUGENT DOCUMENTS. Some 848 original documents and copies, including 40 wills, over 60 rent rolls, a number of accounts, many maps, leases and agreements (1624-1848); Rent Rolls (5 in the 1640's) beginning 1644, set out the names of tenants, their townlands, acreage, rents, etc. Only the chief tenants named. Area of estate, 3,255 acres in and near Portaferry, County Down. These concern principally the Savage and Montgomery families from 1624 to 1848; plus the claim of Andrew Nugent to the Barony of Delvin, 1814-1817. (*Report,* 1949-1950, pp. 11-13.)

ORRERY, ESTATE OF LORD ORRERY, COUNTY ARMAGH (part of) Rental, 1775; Leases, Rent Books, etc. Verner Estate, 1705-1880; Wills and Grants of Administration and Memorandum of Agreement, 1744-1871 (principal names, Farlow, Gormley, Seaver, Verner). (*Report,* 1927, p. 7.)

PILSON MANUSCRIPTS. Seven manuscript volumes of Downpatrick estate, *c.* 1775-1863. (*Report,* 1934, pp. 21-22.)

RANFURLY AND VERNER ESTATE PAPERS, Counties Tyrone and Down, 1671-1874. The Ranfurly records consist of 200 Deed Books of records and leases relating to tenants and lands in or about Dungannon, County Tyrone. Some earlier records relate to County Down. The Verner records consist of nearly 500 documents and books containing leases, etc., 1705-1780, in Counties Armagh and Tyrone. Most leases were for no longer than one life or 21 years. Eight volumes of rentals and the leases together form a directory to a large area. (*Report,* 1927, p. 26.) Ranfurly Estate Extracts made from Dungannon leases, 1757-1832, and the Rent Roll with maps of 1815 (49 maps of Dungannon Estate, County Tyrone) were loaned for copying. (*Report,* 1938-1945, p. 18.)

SAINTFIELD ESTATE, COUNTY DOWN. Rent Rolls, 1751, 1776. (*Report,* 1928, p. 8; 1938-1945, p. 14.)

SAUNDERS ESTATE, Newtown and Comber, County Down, 1771-1780, Rent Roll. (*Report,* 1932, p. 8.)

SAVAGE: See Nugent Documents.

SHAFTESBURY, EARL OF, ESTATES. About 2,000 documents, mainly leases and conveyances, 1617-1932. These are from the estate office of the Earl of Shaftesbury, but relate also to lands of the Donegall family in County Donegal near Londonderry City and in Antrim town, Carrickfergus, and Belfast areas. The Shaftesbury family acquired the documents by marriage in 1857. Leases of 1770 give the names of the undertenants such as the native Irish Cummins, Dougherty, Kelly, McColgan, McConnell, McCrevan, McLaughlin, McManus, McSweeny, O'Connaghan, O'Donnell, etc. (*Report,* 1951-1953, p. 17.)

SOUTHWELL ESTATE, Downpatrick, County Down.   Rent Rolls, Manor of Down, Parish of Inch, 1700-1865; 1743-1744. (*Report*, 1930, p. 10; 1936, p. 9.)

STEWART FAMILY ESTATE RECORDS: See Londonderry.

STONE DEEDS, 13th Century to 1717.   (*Report*, 1926, p. 26.)

STRAHAN: See Irwin.

TEMPLETOWN RENT ROLLS, Indexed.   (*Report*, 1927, p. 9.)

VERNER ESTATE.   Leases, Rent Books, etc., 1705-1880.   (*Report*, 1927, pp. 7, 26.)

VERNER ESTATE: See Charlemont.

VERNER ESTATE: See Ranfurly.

WALLACE ESTATE DOCUMENTS.   Mostly of Downpatrick, County Down (contents of a solicitor's office).   Wills, Grants of Administration, Leases and family settlements, 1624-1900. Also some documents for Counties Antrim, Armagh and Tyrone.   (*Report*, 1948, p. 16.)

WARINGSFORD ESTATE, County Down.   List of Tenants, Will Extracts, etc., 1727-1828.   (*Report*, 1929, p. 10.)

*   *   *   *   *

The Reports of the Deputy Keeper of the Public Records in Ireland, Dublin (55th to 58th *Reports*), contain calendars of a few of the principal deposits of estate records, and lists of a large number of collections deposited, with the names and county locations of the estates, but no indexes of the names appearing in the records.   Some of the larger collections of estate records are:

BATEMAN PAPERS.   Documents relating to the property of the Bateman family in County Kerry, 1648-1848.   Nearly 500 items, mainly deeds, leases, etc.   (58th *Report*, p. 28.)

CALLAGHAN ESTATE.   Incumbered Estates Court Rental (Rent Roll) of the F. M. Callaghan estate, barony of Fermoy, County Cork, 1853.   (58th *Report*, p. 32.)

CAREW ESTATE PAPERS. The collection of five Rental Books, three other volumes and some miscellaneous papers dating from the 17th, 18th and 19th centuries, are records of the Carew family of Castle Boro, County Wexford. This is the collection calendared by A. K. Longfield and edited as the *Shapland Carew Papers,* published by the Irish Manuscripts Commission, Dublin, 1946. (57th *Report,* pp. 522-524.)

COPPINGER ESTATE RENTALS. Coppinger Rentals of the County and City of Cork, 1768-1773. (58th *Report,* p. 43.)

DUNSANDLE PAPERS. Papers relating to the property of Lord Dunsandle in County Tipperary and town of Thurles, 1665-1911 (deeds, rentals, accounts, cases for counsel, etc.). (58th *Report,* p. 40.)

DWYER ESTATE PAPERS. Dwyer family estate documents (lands in Counties Clare, Leix, Limerick and Tipperary) 267 items including deeds, fines, recoveries, rentals, copies of Act of Settlement Grants and Down Survey traces and reference for Stradbally parish, County Limerick. (58th *Report,* p. 34.)

EDGEWORTH PAPERS. Late 17th to early 19th century documents concerning the family estates in County Longford and the town of Kinsale. Included are 109 items, mainly deeds relating to Edgeworth estates in County Longford, 1671-1847, with a few relating to property in Kinsale, 1693-1695. One volume contains the records of management of the estate. (58th *Report,* p. 31.)

GREVILLE ESTATE PAPERS. Documents relating to the estates of the Greville family in County Cavan, early 19th century. (57th *Report,* pp. 468-469.)

HAMILTON ESTATE PAPERS. Hamilton family papers relating to estates in Counties Armagh and Down, 17th and 18th centuries. (58th *Report,* p. 22.)

HOWLIN ESTATE PAPERS. Howlin family estates of Ballycronigan, County Wexford, 1723-1793; volume of deeds, correspondence, rent rolls, maps, and miscellaneous papers. (58th *Report,* p. 27.)

KING-HARMON PAPERS. Estate papers relating to the King-Harmon family property in Counties Longford (Newcastle, Mosstown, Ballinamuck), Kildare, Queen's County, and Westmeath, mostly deeds, rentals, maps and miscellaneous documents, 1656-1893. (58th *Report,* p. 40.)

LYNCH ESTATE PAPERS. Lynch family estates of Newtown, County Mayo, and valuation of estates of Sir Samuel O'Malley in County Mayo, 1845. List of householders in Aran not having farms, 1838-1839. Rentals, etc., relating to Martin estate, County Galway, 1829-1857. (58th *Report,* p. 39.)

MALONE ESTATE PAPERS. Malone family estates in Counties Dublin and Westmeath, 1700-1855. Deeds and other estate papers. Map of estate in Westmeath, 1852. (58th *Report,* p. 22.)

MARTIN ESTATE PAPERS: See Lynch.

MONTEAGLE ESTATE PAPERS. Nearly 300 documents relating to the Spring and Rice families and their properties in Counties Kerry and Limerick, 1669-1925. Includes Rental Book for the estates of Stephen Edward Rice in County Limerick, 1788-1810, and rental of the manor of Mount Trenchard, estate of Long and Hippisley, 1747, and other miscellaneous documents. (58th *Report,* p. 43.)

NUGENT ESTATE PAPERS. Nugent family documents, deeds, certificates for property in Counties Westmeath, Galway and Dublin City, 1637-1848. Also notebook of Lord Chief Justice Nugent, 1686-1689. (58th *Report,* p. 21.)

O'SHEE, O'SHEA, SHEE, ETC., FAMILY ESTATE PAPERS, and genealogical records. A large vellum book of the period of Queen Elizabeth, containing the records of the property possessed by Sir Richard Shee and acquired by purchase by him and his father in the counties of Kilkenny, Tipperary and Wexford. Calendar of the documents, 15th to 17th century, concerning the O'Shee or Shee estate. (57th *Report,* pp. 469-479.) See also Pedigree of O'Shee or Shee family and other documents relating to the history and lands of the family. (58th *Report,* p. 60.)

POOLE ESTATE. Incumbered Estates Court Rental of the estate of William Poole, Monevane, County Offaly, 1853. (58th *Report*, p. 35.)

PURDON ESTATES. Purdon estates rentals in Counties Clare and Limerick, 1836 and 1853. (58th *Report*, p. 46.)

SARSFIELD-VESEY PAPERS. Family documents of the Sarsfield and Vesey families in counties Dublin, Wicklow, Kildare and Carlow, dated largely late 17th and 18th centuries. Deeds from 1414-1808 (287 items). List of Deeds, Index to Correspondence and some items printed in full including history of the family. (56th *Report*, pp. 342-396.)

STERNE ESTATE PAPERS. Sterne estate, County Tipperary, Judicial Rentals, Deeds, 1760-1860, and map of Gortnabaran, 1859. (58th *Report*, p. 48.)

STYLES ESTATE PAPERS. Styles family estates in Counties Roscommon and Donegal. Collection of documents, mainly deeds and rentals of properties of Corlacky and Glenfin, County Donegal, 18th century. (58th *Report*, p. 21.)

TYRONE, EARL OF, ESTATE. Rental of estate in County Cavan, 1829; maps and surveys, 1729-1884. (58th *Report*, p. 42.)

WALLER FAMILY PAPERS. Waller family, County Meath, 69 documents, 1673-1837, including maps of Waller estates, County Meath, 1716-1770, and deeds affecting lands in Counties Meath, Galway, Mayo, and Monaghan, 1673-1837. (58th *Report*, p. 48.)

MISCELLANEOUS ESTATE PAPERS: 601 documents, 18th and 19th centuries, relating to the following families and estates: Alexander (Co. Antrim), Lord Audley (Co. Cork), Birch (Cos. Dublin and Meath), Earl of Blessington (1846), Burnside (Co. Wicklow), Cameron (Co. Dublin), Campbell (Dublin), Connolly (Co. Donegal), Disney (Dublin and Co. Wexford), Dowdall (Co. Meath), Edgar (Co. Donegal), Ferguson (Co. Tyrone), Findlater (Dublin), Henry (Dublin), Higginbotham (Dublin), Law (Co. Down), Lecky (Dublin), McIntire (Derry City), Madder (Dublin), Earl of Miltown (Dublin and County Kildare), Moorhouse (Dublin), Norris (Co. Tyrone), Ormsby (Cos. Dublin and Roscommon), Pollock (Co. Meath), Riddal (Dublin), Countess of Rosse (Dublin and Co. Wicklow), Spencer-Cowper (Dublin), Stewart (Co. Tyrone), Tiernan (Dublin), Trotter (Dublin and Co. Meath). (58th *Report*, p. 28.)

MISCELLANEOUS ESTATE PAPERS: 2268 documents, mainly 18th and 19th centuries, for the following estates, properties and interests: Armstrong (Cos. Leitrim, Mayo and Sligo), Armstrong (Mealiffe, Co. Tipperary), Bellingham (Cos. Louth and Monaghan), Bianconi (Ardmayle, Co. Tipperary), Blackwood (Meath), Brabazon (Co. Tipperary), Bradshaw (Cos. Kilkenny and Tipperary), Caldwell (Cos. Meath and Dublin), Carroll (Dublin City and Co., and Co. Meath), Cleare (Co. Tipperary), Coote (Leix), Cox (Cos. Cork, Kilkenny and Tipperary), Crofton (Dublin), Croker (Co. Limerick), Duckett (Clonmel), Eccles (Dublin and Co. Wicklow), Fennell (Co. Tipperary), French (Leitrim and Roscommon), Gordon (Cos. Dublin and Louth, Tipperary and Waterford), Grace (Cos. Tipperary and Waterford), Green (Dublin and Co. Tipperary), Hely-Hutchinson (Cos. Dublin, Meath, Tipperary and Wexford and Dublin City), Hickson (Westport and Co. Tipperary), Jones (Dublin City and Counties Meath and Roscommon), Kearney (Dublin), Kemmis (Co. Louth), Larive (Dublin), MacKenzie (Co. Tyrone, Belfast and Armagh), Massey (Co. Dublin), Moore (Cos. Tipperary and Waterford), O'Brien (Dublin), O'Connor (Dublin), Oliver (Cos. Cork, Leitrim and Limerick), O'Neill (Co. Kildare), Osborne (Leix, Offaly, Waterford and Dublin City), Palliser (Cos. Clare, Kildare, Limerick, Tipperary and Waterford), Pennefather (Cos. Dublin, Kildare, Offaly, Wicklow, and especially Co. Tipperary), Prendergast (Cos. Galway and Tipperary), Purefoy (Co. Tipperary), Quin (Co. Tipperary), Reynell (Co. Westmeath), Robinson (Dublin), Ryan (Co. Tipperary), Saunders (Cos. Cavan, Dublin, Tipperary, and Wicklow), Smyth (Dublin), Staples (Derry, Mayo, Offaly, Tipperary and Tyrone), Steele (Louth, etc.), Usher (Cos.

Cork and Waterford), Wall (Co. Waterford), Woodcock (Co. Limerick). (58th *Report,* p. 36.)

Many other collections of hundreds of family estate documents and some hundreds of bundles of such documents relating to families throughout the country are listed in the *Reports.* All such papers are listed in the catalogues, calendars and indexes in the Search Room of the Public Record Office, Dublin, where the documents may be examined.

It must be remembered that the Grantor Names and Land Indexes of the Registry of Deeds from 1708 will lead to the memorials of documents concerning all land transactions which were registered therein. Many of the collections of estate documents are rich in records regarding personal land transactions such as deeds, leases, assignments, mortgages, marriage settlements, trusts, etc., which were of a nature requiring registration in the Registry of Deeds but were never properly submitted. A great many of these documents reached the hands of solicitors, and of recent years have been deposited in the Public Record Offices in Dublin or Belfast. Others retained in family archives are rapidly being acquired by or copied for one of the Public Record Offices or the National Library of Ireland, Dublin.

Both Public Record Offices have deposits of records from the Incumbered Estates Court and Land Judges, dated mid and late 19th century. Sets of these records were acquired by the National Library, King's Inns Library and the Land Commission (55th *Report,* p. 142). Landed Estates Documents from the Valuation and Ordnance Survey Division, Ministry of Finance, consist of original estate maps, reports, rentals, etc., prepared by the Ordnance Survey and printed for use of the court. Several thousand documents, otherwise unobtainable, were sent to the Public Record Office of Northern Ireland, Belfast. (*Report,* 1936, p. 4.)

CHAPTER XV

LAND RECORDS: SPECIAL COLLECTIONS, MEDIEVAL AND MODERN

Aside from the many collections of land records discussed in previous chapters of this VOLUME I, there are numerous miscellaneous collections to which attention must be called. These are principally deposited in the two Public Record Offices in Dublin and Belfast, and in the National Library of Ireland, Dublin, as follows:

THE PUBLIC RECORD OFFICE OF IRELAND, DUBLIN: In the Public Search Room there is a Card-Index of Deeds, dated prior to the year 1708 when the Registry of Deeds, Dublin, was established. It was at first arranged as a Topographical Index of Deeds. By 1955, a Name-Index was compiled. There is also a Catalogue of Deeds, Edward III to George II. There are Annual Accessions Lists and Indexes of the special manuscript collections of purchased and presented material. The records of these miscellaneous collections range in date from medieval to modern times. By 1952, the purchased and presented documents (other than normal increments) concerning the transfer of property numbered 19,500. Some representative collections listed in the 55th-58th *Reports* are as follows:

55th Report: (1) A List of Ecclesiastical Deeds, Leases, Certificates, etc., and Extracts from Ecclesiastical Records, presented 1922-1927. These principally concern the leases of property of the Established Church of Ireland in various dioceses to respective individuals. Thus the "Cashel and Emly See Leases" include one to Richard Pennefather of Newpark, Co. Tipperary, in 1749, and a lease to Major William Pennefather of Newpark, Co. Tipperary, in 1772 (pp. 91-96). (2) A collection in the Public Search Room containing "A Calendar (MS.) of Christ Church Deeds, 1605-1700," by M. J. McEnery. This is a continuation of the printed Calendar of Christ Church Deeds, *c.* 1174-1684, contained in the 20th, 23rd, and 24th *Reports of the Deputy Keeper* (with Index in the

27th *Report*). (See 55th *Report*, p. 133.) (3) Deeds and Wills in Inquisitions, Indexes listed (pp. 114, 123, 129, 138). (4) Chancery and Equity Exchequer Deed Boxes saved from the fire of 1922, a List of, in the Public Search Room (p. 135). (5) Incumbered and Landed Estates Court Deed Boxes saved from the 1922 fire, List of, in the Public Search Room (p. 135). (6) Dublin Applotment Book, 1680-1686, Index, and a Draft Catalogue of the names and residence of the householders in the City and Liberties of Dublin contained in the Applotment Book (p. 132). (7) List of Public Record Office Certified Copies of Documents preserved in the Quit Rent Office (later transferred to the Public Record Office), in the Public Search Room (p. 132).

56th Report: (1) Indexed List of Deeds, 1414-1808, contained in the Sarsfield-Vesey Collection (pp. 356-394). This index contains the names of many people concerned in the documents, representing some hundreds of other families besides Sarsfield or Vesey. (2) A List of Deeds and Leases dated prior to 1700 and contained in presented collections of solicitors. The names of the principals concerned in the instruments, the year, and the location of the property are given (pp. 24-26, 33, 43, 57). (3) A List of Deeds, Leases, and miscellaneous conveyances pursuant to Orders and Decrees of Courts of Chancery, Exchequer, King's Bench, Common Pleas, etc., mostly dated after 1703, presented by solicitors (pp. 26, 29-31, 33, 34, 36, 37, 43, 44, 47, 53, 56, 57). (4) Deeds 1703-1901:—Deeds of Agreement, Appointment, Appointment of Trustees and Assignment, Bonds, Conveyances, Deeds of Covenant, Defeazance, Dissolution of Partnership, Indemnity, Rent Charge and Settlement, Mortgages, Reconveyances, Leases, Renewal Leases, Surrenders, Statements of Title, etc. The collection comprises over 2,000 deeds besides miscellaneous documents. The lands and premises affected by the deeds are chiefly situated in the counties of Armagh, Carlow, Cavan, Cork, Donegal, Down, Fermanagh, Kildare, Londonderry, Longford, Louth, Meath, Sligo, Tyrone, and the towns of Armagh, Drogheda, Dublin, Londonderry, Lurgan and Newry. The principal names in these deeds are: Acheson, Archer, Atkinson, Ball, Barrett, Bell, Bellew, Beresford, Blacker, Bourke,

Brownlowe, Butler, Caldwell, Carhampton, Carpendale, Carroll, Clare, Close, Coates, Cooper, Coote, Cope, Courtenay, Cremorne, Daly, Darley, Dartrey, Dawson, Dobbin, Eden, Ekenhead, Elliott, Faviere, Gervais, Godley, Graham, Greene, Hamilton, Harrison, Harvey, Henzell, Hewison, Howison, Higginbotham, Hodges, Holmes, Hume, Hutchinson, Jackson, Kelly, Kennedy, Kerr, Kidd, Killmorey, Leonard, Magrath, Maxwell, Mayne, McCullagh, McKinstry, McWilliams, Moore, Murdoch, Nunn, Oliver, Owens, Prentice, Richardson, Robinson, Scott, Sample, Semple, Talbott, Tate, Thompson, Tisdall, Turner, Whaley, Whiteston, Wilson (p. 30). (5) Deeds, etc., 1710-1881: Deeds of Annuity, Appointment, Appointment of Trustees, Partition, Trust and Surrender, Conveyances, Fee-farm Grants, Leases, Releases, Mortgages, Reconveyances of Mortgages, Assignments of Leases, Mortgage Charges, Decrees, Judgements, Attornments, Declarations of Trusts, Bonds, Warrants, Copy Affidavits and Certificates of Registry of Judgements, Abstracts and Statements of Title, etc. The principal names are Armstrong, Beecher, Bell, Birch, Blake, Boyle, Bryan, Bunbury, Butler, Callaghan, Callan, Campbell, Carr, Cathcart, Chambers, Dawson, Delacour, Dunn, Eldridge, Fitzgerald, Fosbery, Freeman, French, Fuller, Gabbett, Gardiner, Gaussen, Gormley, Graves, Greer, Hamilton, Harding, Harris, Harrison, Henderson, Hickman, Holmes, Irvine, King, Knox, Lecky, Lloyd, Lopdell, Lowry, Lysaght, Magill, Maxwell, McCarthy, McCausland, McMahon, Montgomery, Moore, Nicholson, O'Brien, Ogden, O'Keeffe, Orr, O'Sullivan, Purcell, Rankin, Richardson, Roddy, Scott, Shadwell, Smith, Stacpoole, Stewart, Stillingfleet, Stuart, Tuthill, Ward, Warren, Westropp, Williams, Young. The lands and premises affected are chiefly in the Counties Armagh, Clare, Cork, Dublin, Limerick, Londonderry, Tyrone, and in the City of Dublin (pp. 47-48). (6) Miscellaneous Bankruptcy and Insolvency Documents and Incumbered and Landed Estates Courts Documents (pp. 27-29, 38, 44-46, 48-49, 56). (7) Marriage Settlements and Articles (Original, Copy, and Memorials of) concerning property conveyances, presented by various solicitors as above. The names of the groom, the bride, and the year of the marriage (with number of the document in the collection) are listed (pp. 27-30, 44-46, 51-52, 58). (8) Crown Rental of 1706, consisting of 33 volumes of records in the Quit Rent Office, transferred to the Public Record Office in 1943, according to the 58th *Report*, p. 18, to replace the duplicate records contained in 25 volumes destroyed in the fire of 1922 (56th *Report*, p. 303). The Quit Rent Office set of 33 volumes is described in the 55th *Report*, p. 135, as follows: "Crown Rental, 1706, in Quit Rent Office (? copy of Rental of 1692 prepared in 1706). 'An abstract of every rent per annum in every Barony in each County in the Kingdom of Ireland as they were given in charge to the several collectors according to their districts by the Chief Commissioners and Governors of Revenue of his Majesty in Ireland at Michaelmas, 1678 (Ad. MS. B.M. 15899)'." (9) Forfeitures 1641—Plus and Undisposed Lands—"A List of such part of the forfeited lands in that part of the United Kingdom called Ireland as come under the description of undisposed and plus lands being the forfeitures of 1641 as they appear in the new Rental in the Auditor General's Office together with the situation, number of acres and the yearly quit rent now payable to or received by the Crown." The new Rental is the 1706 Rental. (Copy or duplicate of volume formerly in Record Tower Collection 4P. 27. 54.) (56th *Report*, pp. 304-305.) (10) Crown Rental, *circa* 1828: For Carlow, Dublin, Dublin City, Galway, Kildare, Kilkenny, King's County, Longford, Louth, Mayo, Meath, Queen's Co., Sligo, Westmeath, Wexford, Wicklow. This Rent Roll of the Crown Estate in Ireland is imperfect and incomplete (p. 304).

57th Report: (1) Miscellaneous Deeds, Leases, and other conveyances dated prior to 1700, acquired in presented collections from solicitors and in some purchased lots from other sources (pp. 24, 31, 42, 43, 44, 48, 49, 50, 51, 52). Miscellaneous Deeds and other conveyances, dated after 1700, are also listed in collections received from various donors or in purchased lots (pp. 24-52). One small listing is as follows: "Deeds (Miscellaneous), etc., 1700-1884. Awards, Conveyances, Fee Farm Grants, Leases, Renewal Leases, Mortgages, Assignments, Deeds of Appointment, Survivorship, Surrender, Powers of Attorney, Cases, Statements of Title, Warrants,

etc. The principal names are: Anketell, Armstrong, Bunbury, Caldwell, Cummin, Denham, Fetherston, Gervais, Hamilton, Irvine, Johnston, McDowal (or McDowell), Mervin (or
Mervyn), Moutray, Palliser, Richardson, Thompson. The
lands and premises affected are in the counties of Cavan, Cork,
Dublin, Galway, Kildare, Kilkenny, King's Co., Longford,
Louth, Meath, Monaghan, Queen's Co., Tipperary, Tyrone
and Wicklow, the city of Dublin and towns of Augher and
Maryborough" (p. 45). The items in this particular collection
presented by Messrs. S. and R. C. Walker and Son, Solicitors,
are part of an accumulation of records relating to several of
the above families, dated from the early 17th century, each
document being listed by full names of the principals, the year
of the record and the county or more particular address (pp.
42-45). The documents include Court Records of the Chancery, Common Pleas, Equity Exchequer, and Incumbered and
Landed Estates Courts and Land Judges; Ecclesiastical
Records; Testamentary Documents; Marriage Settlements;
Deeds, Leases, etc., dated prior to 1700, and Estate Maps.
The families of Anketell, Bunbury, Galbraith, Hamilton,
Mervyn, Moutray and Richardson of County Tyrone and other
counties are allied or related. (2) A volume of "Rental of
Landgable Rents, City of Dublin, c. 1665" contains the names
of residents of Dublin by streets and the amount of the rent
charge for each. Landgable Rent was a quit rent or tax on
land, or ground rent for the site of a house, thus the list sets
forth the residents of Dublin (pp. 526-558). (3) A supplement to this list is given in an account of the number of
houses in the city of Dublin showing the number of hearths,
taken in the year 1664, by street and parish (pp. 559-560).
(4) A list of persons, proprietors of 6 hearths and upwards
(listed by parish), residents of Dublin, 1664 (pp. 560-563).

58th Report: In the period 1936-1950, transfers of records
were made to the Public Record Office from other repositories
as described in previous chapters. Some miscellaneous collections of land records were acquired as follows: (1) The
State Paper Office sent Schedules of Crown Rents, Quit Rents,
New Patent Rents, Innocent Papists' Lands and Undisposed
Lands, 1663-1827 (p. 17). (2) The Crown Rental of 1706

(33 volumes), described in the 55th *Report*, p. 135, was transferred from the Quit Rent Office to the Public Record Office
in 1943, together with some fifteen boxes of copies of Deeds
and Patents dated from the 15th century onward (p. 18).
(3) Collector's account of arrears of quit rent, County Kerry,
1666-1667 (p. 19). (4) Copy of book of postings and sales
of Trustees for Forfeited Estates, 1702-1703 (substitute for
destroyed original), M2578 (p. 20). (5) Volume of extracts
from records illustrating the history of the earldoms of Ulster
(De Lacy and De Burgo), Kildare, Louth, Ormond, Desmond,
Tyrone, Thomond and Clanricarde and the viscounties of
Buttevant, Gormanstown and Fermoy, with other miscellaneous notes and extracts of genealogical interest, compiled
by Daniel Molyneux, Ulster King of Arms, 1809. M2550 (p.
25). (6) Volume of notes of leases by the dean and chapter
of Christ Church, Dublin, and grants by archbishops of Dublin, 1577-1644, by Thomas Howell, chapter clerk. M2534 (p.
26). (7) Account of rents from crown holdings in Dublin
city and in Counties Dublin, Longford, Tipperary, Wicklow,
and Queen's County from Michaelmas 1662 to Michaelmas
1672. M2535 (p. 26). (8) Papers relating to property of
Lord Dunsandle in County Tipperary and town of Thurles,
1665-1911 (deeds, rentals, accounts, cases for counsel, etc.).
D15776-15850 (p. 40). (9) 23 documents, 1666-1827, including 18 deeds, relating to lands in Co. Limerick (Oliver,
Cripps and Ryves families) and in Castletownroche and Newmarket, Co. Cork (Aldworth) (p. 45). (10) Deeds, etc., for
property in Counties Dublin, Kildare, Leix, Offaly and Tipperary and Dublin city, names Butler, Fitzgerald, Hewitt, Sawyer,
and Stoney prominent (p. 46). (11) Documents relating to
Hayden and others, Kilkenny city, 1811-1877 (p. 46). (12) 63
documents, 1713-1870, including 36 deeds relating to Blennerhassett and Marshall property, County Kerry (p. 47). (13)
Testamentary documents, Conran, Kearney, Kelly, Meekings,
etc., deeds relating to property in County Kildare (Mount-
armstrong), Kilkenny (Ballyogan), Offaly, Wicklow (Whites-
town) and Dublin city (Summerhill) in possession of Armstrong and Sherlock families, 1703-1888, and Exchequer
declaration in ejectment, Trinity 1838 (Tenode, Co. Wicklow,

lessees of Hornidge v. ejector) (p. 48). (14) Testamentary documents, deeds and miscellaneous papers relating to property of Ball, Clarke and Vincent families in County Kilkenny, 1827-1905 (p. 48). (15) Papers relating to Sterne estate, Co. Tipperary (judicial rentals, deeds 1760-1860, and map of Gortnabaran, 1859); papers relating to Handy estates in Trim, County Meath, Celbridge, County Kildare and Dublin city, 1734-1921; papers relating to Whittaker trusts (property in Enniskillen and elsewhere in County Fermanagh), viz: 30 deeds, 1824-1923, 37 testamentary documents, various names, 1815-1905, and miscellaneous papers, 151 items in all (p. 48). (16) A Calendar and Index of the Prim Collection containing papers relating to the history of Kilkenny, collected or compiled by the late J. G. A. Prim (pp. 50-70). This is compiled in four parts: (a) Documents concerning the inhabitants of certain parishes, 1702 and 1715; the administration of the mayor and sheriff and municipal matters, 1659-1701; (b) miscellaneous late 17th and 18th century papers relating to the Kilkenny militia, copies of inquisitions, and some court cases; (c) a series of copies and abstracts of corporation leases of city property to inhabitants, 1537-1681, showing the names of various mayors, burgesses, members of the corporation who signed as lessors and other residents as lessees; (d) extensive genealogical material contained in original documents or copies of pedigrees, family history, letters patent, deeds, leases, miscellaneous other conveyances, wills, birth and death records, respectively relating to the families of Shee (or O'Shee), Rothe, Colles, O'Grady, Scull, Langton, Knaresborough, Bibby, Archer, Cowley, Comerford, Cantwell, Frayne and Shearman. The most prominent Shee (or O'Shee) records date from the 14th century to the late 19th century (Shee leases, pp. 53-59; list of O'Shee or Shee pedigrees and other documents, p. 60).

THE PUBLIC RECORD OFFICE OF NORTHERN IRELAND, BELFAST: The great accumulation of land records (Deeds, Leases, Assignments, Mortgages, Marriage Settlements, Crown Rent Rolls) in miscellaneous or special collections, is recorded in various ways in the Public Search Room. The records are entered and described in the Catalogues of Accessions; Descriptive Lists of deposited original documents and transcripts; Calendars of Collections; and under the surnames of the principals in each document the records are alphabetically recorded in the Master Card Index. All land records which are contained in chief deposited collections, and in other presented or purchased collections, are also described or listed in the *Report of the Deputy Keeper* following the year of the deposit. All records which meet the principles of indexing, appear also in the body of the Index of the Report. It is impossible to do more than call attention to the enormous number of miscellaneous land records concerning individuals and families, many collections of which have been listed in the chapter concerning the Public Record Office of Northern Ireland, Belfast, pp. 199-228, herein, and among the family manuscripts listed in VOLUME II, pp. 109-166. It is a simple matter to have the above sources searched in the Public Search Room for evidence of land records concerning a family of a certain county. The Index in each *Report of the Deputy Keeper* should be searched in every case, according to instructions in PART TWO, CHAPTER VI, herein. Two collections not heretofore mentioned are: (1) Crown Rent Rolls, Copies of, 1692, for "Armagh, Belfast, and Coleraine; Donaghadee, Strabane, and Londonderry; Fermanagh, Strangford and Lisburn." (1926 *Report*, p. 8.) (2) Crown and Quit Rent Ledger, 1793-1799. Estates in Counties Armagh, Monaghan and Tyrone (copies). (1936 *Report*, p. 8.)

PUBLISHED LAND RECORDS: Collections of Early Documents are listed in VOLUME II, pp. 238-239, herewith. Further publications, concerning land records, by the Irish Manuscripts Commission are listed among its works in VOLUME II, pp. 95-106. Microfilms of special collections of land records are listed in VOLUME II, pp. 270-285, herewith. A Calendar of "Old Deeds in the Library of Trinity College," by J. G. Smyly, is published in *Hermathena*, Vols. 69-74 (1946-1949). This series of Deeds is dated 1348-1538.

CHAPTER XVI

TAX RECORDS

Irish tax records fall into two distinct series: (1) The records created under the English feudal system, extending from the Anglo-Norman invasion, 1169-1172, under Henry II, to the reign of Charles II, 1660-1661, when the feudal rights of the Crown were abolished in the Irish Parliament of 1661-1666. In this period the tax records are construed to cover the direct or indirect military and pecuniary exactions of the crown, for the support of the various branches of the Government under terms of the early feudal dues, knights' services, fees, licenses, rates, aids, assessments, duties, imposts, military or parish cess, etc. (2) The tax records created after 1660-1661, comprising distinct local taxes, either general and extending over every district, or special and confined to particular portions of the country. The general taxes were Government Subsidies, Hearth Money Tax, Poll Tax, Tithes, Parish Cess, Grand Jury Cess, Poor Rates, etc. The special taxes were assessed in cities or boroughs for local expenses such as lighting, cleaning of streets, pipe water, etc.

The conquering Anglo-Norman barons, in the first few years after the invasion, secured half of Ireland to the Crown as a revenue producing colony. They were consequently granted great fiefs or estates *in capite*, directly from the Crown and became tenants-in-chief of the king. They were charged with a primary duty, according to feudal law, to furnish military aid for the support of their sovereign. They were therefore required to furnish a specified number of knights for service in the field, according to the size of their estates. Their lands, granted by the Crown, were divided by estimation into Knights' Fees. "A Knight's Fee, *Feudum Militare*, is so much inheritance as is sufficient yearly to maintain a knight with convenient revenue, and in Henry III's days was £15 (Camden's Brit. p. 111), in the time of Edward II, £20; a knight's fee contained 12 plough lands, or 5 hides, or 480 acres." (*Limerick, its History and Antiquities*. By Maurice Lenihan. Dublin, 1866, p. 48.)

Each baron or tenant-in-chief, enfeoffed by the king on terms of military support, was required to furnish an exact quota of knight-service. This was one or more units of ten knights each (or a fraction of a unit). The knights were tenants of the baron, each holding land by a system of sub-enfeoffment, and each required to supply at his own expense a certain military following of service in the field, usually for 40 days, more or less, each year, together with certain specified armour and arms. A tenant-in-chief who kept too much of his estate to himself or for other reasons was unable to supply the quota of knight-service required of him, could resort to hiring the necessary number of knights and their military following and equipment for specified pay (scutage), of one sort or another in terms of money. Every knight was, however, sub-enfeoffed by some tenant-in-chief or baron or over-lord, to whom he owed military service and military protection of his lord's castle, and when called upon was required to answer with attendance every *Rising out* or *Hosting* which was a great meeting of the military of a province, county, or district, convened to prepare for service in the field. Details of some of the *Hostings* and their personnel are given in *The Annals of Ireland . . . of the Four Masters*, by Owen Connellan, Dublin, 1846, pp. 656-658, etc.

Scutage was an impost tax by feudal law, or a fine levied upon a knight's-fee in commutation for, or by any reason of default in the render of military service due by reason of holding the knight's-fee. Thus many lords paid scutage to the king for knight-service not available; their lands being insufficiently divided into knights' fees to produce the required units of military service, or having become subdivided or sub-enfeoffed to such small fractions of a knight's-fee that the military obligation could be settled only by scutage. As time went on, the payment of scutage became more and more common until in the time of Henry III, the obligations of tenure were measured by scutage as well as by knight-service. This continued until feudal obligations to the Crown were abolished under Charles II.

The Feudal system imposed also certain pecuniary obligations of a tenant by knight-service to his lord, identical with those of the lord to the king as follows: (1) "Relief": A tax paid at the time of succeeding to inherited lands or knights'-fees. (2) "Wardships": The profits from lands of a ward of the Crown, or heir of a tenant-in-chief during his minority, were vested in the Crown unless the right to the ward and management of his inheritance was purchased or acquired for a fee from a lord or other person appointed by the Crown. (3) "Marriage": A tax or fine paid by a knight or lord for the right of giving in marriage of an heir (if a minor), an heiress or a widow.

These feudal rights of the Crown to fees, dues or taxes, for the privilege of inheriting land, acquiring a wardship and giving in marriage, are discussed in *An Historical Account of the Plantation in Ulster . . . 1608-1620,* by the Rev. George Hill, Belfast, 1877, p. 81, as follows: "Wardship was simply a power vested in the King to plunder minors, which power the King had the right to sell to others, who performed their work of enriching themselves at the expense of their wards without scruple. Marriage meant the right of the King to provide wives or husbands for his wards, as the case might be, if under age. This privilege, also, the King invariably sold to favorites, and the latter, in their own interests, most generally practiced deceptions in providing matches for those thus cruelly handed over to their keeping."

The Lodge Manuscripts in the Public Record Office, Dublin, include two volumes of "Wardships, Liveries, Alienations." This is a collection and complete repertory of the records as follows: Volume I contains the abstracts of grants of Wardship and Marriage (Henry VIII to 1647, and 1660-1661), Liveries (Henry VIII to 1641), Pardons of Intrusion (Henry VIII to 1615), Licences and Pardons of Marriage (Henry VIII to Edward VI, and Charles I), Pardons and Licences of Alienation (Henry VIII to 1641). Lodge has the following note: "This work in two volumes is a complete collection of all the Wardships, Liveries, Licences, and Pardons of Alienation granted in virtue of the Tenures in Capite and inrolled in Chancery, from the Reign of K. Henry 8 to the Dissolution of the Court of Wards in the reign of **K. Charles II.**" Volume II contains "Pardons of Alienation, Wardships, etc., prior to the reign of Henry VIII." These are described as: "Abstracts of grants of Marriage, Wardships, Custodies, Liveries, pardons of alienation, writs of protection, *amoveas manus*, assignment of dower, liberate, licences and pardons of marriage, remittal of arrears of custody rents; of fines for intrusion and outlawry for debt. There are two series, one from the Rolls in the Rolls Office, the other from those in the Bermingham Tower (Edward II - Henry VII). Both volumes are indexed" (55th *Report*, p. 122).

The above revenue producing feudal rights of the Crown caused the making of countless records of interest to the genealogist. All "Scutage" and the fees or fines from "Relief", "Wardship" and "Marriage" were recorded by the Exchequer on the Pipe Rolls, as Crown revenue. The names of the principals, dates, lists of the property and fines, etc., involved, and in the records of inherited property the name of the deceased, his heir, and payments of money owed to the Crown; the names and relationships, in cases of Wardships and Marriages, are all set forth in the abstracts of the Pipe Rolls.

The great genealogical value of the Irish Pipe Rolls is discussed in an article entitled "Norman Ireland in 1212," by H. G. Richardson, published in *Irish Historical Studies*, Vol. III, No. 10 (Sept. 1942), pp. 144-158. This concerns the oldest existing Irish Pipe Roll containing accounts of the Exchequer, "The Irish Pipe Roll of 14 John, 1211-1212", edited by Oliver Davies B. Quinn, in *The Ulster Journal of Archaeology*, Series 3, Vol. IV (Supplement), July, 1941.

A Catalogue of the *Accounts on the Great Rolls of the Pipe of the Irish Exchequer*, 13 Henry III (1228-1229) to Edward III (1348-1349), is published in the Appendices of the *Reports of the Deputy Keeper of the Public Records in Ireland* (35th to 39th, 42nd to 45th, 47th, 53rd, 54th *Reports*). This Catalogue was compiled by M. J. McEnery who was a member of the staff of the Public Record Office, Dublin, from 1882, and Deputy Keeper of the Records from 1914 until his retirement in 1921. These early Pipe Rolls are the best authority for the descent of the Anglo-Norman and English families in

Ireland during the period they represent. The Pipe Rolls contain also a wealth of information about the Government personnel in administrative offices concerned with financial matters of the Crown.

A great series of dues, fees, fines, etc., is recorded in the *Inquisitions Post Mortem*, described in the preceding CHAPTER XIII. The Rev. William Healy, author of *The History and Antiquities of Kilkenny*, 1893, presents forty-four Inquisitions together with family history and other genealogical records of the following Kilkenny families: Bryan, Lincoln, Blanchfield, Comerford, Fitzgerald, St. Leger, Butler, O'Ryan, Walshe (Walsh), Earls of Ormonde, Lawless, Archdeacon, O'Shee (Shee), Roth, Shortal, Purcell, Lord Galmoy, Strange, Grace, Shortall, Rochford, Archer, Preston, Blake, D'Alton, Sweetman, De la Frene, Laffan, Forstall, Montgarret, Rothe, Denn, Fanning.

"Cess" was a term applied to local taxation, levied by town, parish, or county authorities for various purposes: (1) For some degree of support of military forces by local residents. The obligations of the Anglo-Norman and Anglo-Irish of the Pale during Elizabeth's reign to support military forces on the borders of or within the Pale, and in other counties where needed, are recorded in the *Book of Howth;* in the *Carew MSS.;* the *State Papers.* The system of Cess is explained in *Ireland Under the Commonwealth*, by Robert Dunlop, 1913 (Vol. I, pp. xxxviii - xliv). (2) From the time of Charles I the counties were governed by Grand Juries. The Justices of the Peace in their Quarter Sessions, assisted by the Juries (limited in number to 23), established the county rate or "Cess", for the upkeep of the bridges, roads, and other local expenses. "Cess" was levied also by Corporations (incorporated boroughs or towns) by vote of the mayor, burgesses and freemen, for support of local military forces and for assessments for highways, etc. (3) "Cess" was also assessed in the parishes by the Churchwardens and Select Vestry for care of the churches, church property, the poor, etc.

The Town Book of the Corporation of Belfast, 1613-1816, Edited from the Original . . . by Robert M. Young, Belfast, 1892, contains various lists of the freemen, the burgesses and the mayor or "sovraigne" who paid the Cess. A list of the Sovraigne and Burgesses who paid the rate for "fittinge" of the Town Hall was taken on 12th October 1639; lists of the same for 18th October 1640, and 30th January 1642; a list of the "Sovraigne & Burgesses and the Cominalty" taken on the 13th May 1643 who paid the rate for the highways, numbering 239 residents; and several lists of Cess for support of certain numbers of soldiers in 1645 (pp. 11-12, 19-20, 25-28, 35-37, 40-42).

Payments of Cess in the parishes is illustrated in *The Registers of the Parish of St. John the Evangelist,* Dublin, 1619-1699, edited by James Mills, and published by the Parish Register Society of Dublin, 1906. This contains three lists of the Parish Cess, extracted from the Parish Books: (1) A list of the parishioners who on the 24th February 1621, authorized the Cess due the parson according to Act of State. The list of heads of families is arranged by streets, lanes, keys, etc. (2) The same for 1646. (3) A list of householders arranged by wards in the parish, who paid a Cess for the poor for one year ending at Easter, 1687.

The Vestry Records of the Church of St. John Parish of Aghalow, Caledon, Co. Tyrone, 1691-1807, edited with genealogical notes by John J. Marshall, Dungannon, 1935, contains hundreds of names, and notes regarding them as they appear in the accounts (collections and expenditures of the parish. Families whose names are prominent in the records are (chronologically) : Hamilton, Pringle, Petticrew, Allen, Lowry, Moor, Davison, Agnew, Johnston, Campbell, Rutherford, Wye, Harriot, Ambrose, Alexander.

* * * * *

HEARTH MONEY, POLL TAX AND SUBSIDY ROLLS.

Hearth Money Rolls: The following explanation of the Hearth Money tax is given in the 33rd *Report of the Deputy Keeper of the Public Records in Ireland* (pp. 44-45) : "Hearth Money was a tax of 2s. on every hearth and fireplace, established by the Act 14 and 15 Car. II, *c.* 17, and payable at Lady Day and Michaelmas by equal portions. The first portion was payable on Lady Day 1663, and it was to be collected in the different counties by the sheriffs. The persons liable to pay were to be entered in a list which was to be prepared by the Justices of the Peace, and lodged with the Clerk of the Peace; and a duplicate thereof, signed by three Justices, was to be sent to the Exchequer. These lists are known as the Hearth Money Rolls. Returns of any increase or diminution of hearths were to be sent to the Exchequer as in case of the original return. By 17 & 18 Car. II, *c.* 18, the entire sum became payable on the 10th January, yearly. The rolls contain, according to counties, baronies, parishes, &c., the names of the inhabitants liable to the tax, and the amounts they were to pay. So far as the number of hearths with which each person is charged can be taken as an indication of wealth and rank, these lists are a valuable addition to local and family history."

The original Hearth Money Rolls were destroyed in the fire of 1922, as they had been deposited in the Public Record Office. Their value for locating householders or possessors of one or more hearths had long been recognized by the genealogists, and thus much copying of the Rolls had been done. These are as follows:

The Public Record Office, Dublin, was loaned the Hearth-money Roll contained in the original Hearth Money Book for the City of Dublin, 1663, which was afterwards used as a Minute Book by the Committee appointed for the erection of King Charles II's (or the Blue Coat) Hospital. The Governors of the Hospital allowed the transcript of the Roll to be made after the fire of 1922. (55th *Report,* p. 12.) The Phillipp's MS. 17044, purchased by the Public Record Office, containing many miscellaneous records of the City of Dublin, includes "A List of the Houses in the Citty of Dublin and the number of Hearths in each, taken in the year 1664." The list is set forth by parishes and streets, in the 57th *Report,* pp. 559-560. Included in the same MSS. is a "List of Persons in Preceeding Account, Proprietors of 6 Hearths or Upwards." The names of these Dublin residents are set forth with the number of hearths for each, listed by parish, in the 57th *Report,* pp. 560-563. The Tenison Groves Collection contains extracts from the Hearth Money Rolls for County Armagh, 1664 and 1665; County Donegal, 1663, 1665, and some of no date; County Fermanagh, 1665 and 1666 (58th *Report*, p. 20). Transcripts of the Hearth Money Rolls for the Baronies of Tullychonco and Tullycagh, County Cavan, 1664, were presented (57th *Report*, p. 40). Abstracts of the Hearth Money Rolls for the diocese of Cloyne were presented (57th *Report*, p. 55; 58th *Report*, p. 8). The Hearth Money Rolls, Baronies of Iffa and Offa, and Middlethird, County Tipperary, 1734, 1735 (rare ones of the later date), were presented among the J. C. Morrissey MSS. (58th *Report*, p. 44.) The T. U. Sadleir MSS., purchased 1939-1947, include "Copies of Hearth Money Rolls, Co. Wicklow, 1668" (58th *Report*, p. 25). D. J. Liam Price presented an abstract of the County Wicklow Hearth Money Roll, 1669 (58th *Report*, p. 46). A copy of the Hearth Money Roll of 1665, for County Donegal was purchased, 1932-1934, from the collections of Tenison Groves (57th *Report*, p. 569). A miscellaneous collection of records including copies of some Hearth Money Rolls, is entitled "Press Copies of Certified Copies" (6 vols.) (55th *Report*, p. 123).

The Presbyterian Historical Society, Belfast, had secured transcripts of the following Hearth Money Rolls before the Public Record Office, which housed the original records, was burned in 1922, and loaned the transcripts to the Public Record Office of Northern Ireland for copying: The entire Roll of County Antrim, 1669, copied by Mr. J. Adams, in 1912; the Rolls of County Londonderry, 1663 and County Tyrone, 1666, and the Subsidy Roll for County Down, 1663, all copied by Mr. Tenison Groves, *c.* 1912 (1924 *Report*, N. I., pp. 27-29). An interesting description and analysis of these Rolls shows that at the time each was compiled there were 11,800 hearths in County Antrim; 3,178 hearths in County Londonderry and 2,712 hearths in County Tyrone. These three Rolls and the Subsidy Roll for County Down contain a total of about 18,000 names of persons and some 4,000 place-names (1925 *Report*, p. 9). The names of the tax-payers are listed by county, barony, parish, town or townland, with the number of hearths on which each paid two shillings tax per year. Other transcripts of Hearth Money Rolls received by purchase or donation are: Extracts of 1666, County Antrim; County Donegal, 1665 (1925 *Report*, p. 8). County Armagh (Barony of

Fews excepted), 1664 (1932 *Report* p. 7). Barony of Fews, County Armagh, 1664 (1933 *Report,* p. 5). Portadown Parish, County Armagh, 1664; Raphoe Parish, County Donegal, 1665 (1926 *Report,* p. 9). Devenish Parish, County Fermanagh, 1665/7 (1925 *Report,* p. 9). Notes on names in County Armagh Hearth Money Roll, 1664 (1928 *Report,* p. 9). Lurg Barony, County Fermanagh, 1665/6 (1946/47 *Report,* p. 12). This office has an index of the names and places in the Hearth Money Rolls.

Published Hearth Money Rolls (also spelled Hearthmoney) are listed in VOLUME II, pp. 235-237, herewith. Other miscellaneous transcripts for a county, barony or parish, may be found in printed historical society journals (such as that of Dundalk, in the *County Louth Archaeological Society Journal;* that of County Tipperary, in the *Journal of the Cork Historical and Archaeological Society*), and in local histories such as *The History of the Two Ulster Manors of Finagh, in the County of Tyrone, and Coole, Otherwise Manor Atkinson, in the County of Fermanagh,* by the Earl of Belmore, London, 1881. In the latter are the Hearth Money Roll, 1666, for Omagh Barony, County Tyrone; the Subsidy Roll, 1666, and the Poll Money tax of the same period (pp. 304-316). The *Clogher Record,* Vol. XI, No. 1 (1957), began publication of "Hearth Money Rolls, County Fermanagh, 1665-6," contributed by the Rev. P. Ó Gallachair. The *Register of the Union of Monkstown, County Dublin, 1669-1786,* published by the Parish Register Society of Dublin, 1908, pp. 85-88, contains the Hearth Money Roll, 1664 and 1666/7 for this area. The *Registers of St. Catherine, Dublin, 1636-1715,* published by the Parish Register Society of Dublin, 1908, pp. 233-235, contains "Extracts from the Subsidy Roll, City of Dublin, 1637", for this parish (118 names), and also the Hearth Money Roll for the parish, 1666-1667, with 250 names, 8 illegible, and part torn off (pp. 236-240).

The Genealogical Office, Dublin Castle, Dublin, has accumulated copies of transcripts of original Hearth Money Rolls, Subsidy Rolls and Poll Tax Rolls, as far as possible, and has the printed sources containing the Rolls of various localities.

Some microfilms of Hearth Money Rolls, made by the National Library of Ireland, are listed in VOLUME II, herewith.

SUBSIDY ROLLS: The original Subsidy Rolls indicate the taxable wealth in each county from time to time, 1662-1668. They constitute lists of the names and the amount of the tax paid by each person, all of whom possessed sufficient property to be liable to payment of the Subsidy which then formed the principal direct taxation on wealth by the Crown.

The Appendix to the 33rd *Report of the Deputy Keeper of the Public Records in Ireland* (1901), pp. 45-46, contains a Table of the Hearth Money Rolls, Poll Tax Rolls, and Subsidy Rolls, for the 32 counties and the cities of Dublin, Kilkenny and Limerick, with the dates of the Rolls; also the following explanation of the Subsidy Rolls: *"Subsidies* were grants made to the King from a very early date; but with the exception of Co. Armagh, Dublin City, and a few concerning all Ireland, the rolls preserved all relate to the period from 1662 to 1669. Subsidies, both lay and clerical, were granted by the Parliament which commenced to sit in Dublin on the 8th May, 1661 . . . The lay subsidies are as follows: A grant of eight subsidies, payable in 1662-3, . . . four subsidies payable quarterly . . . in 1664 . . . eight subsidies were voted, payable half-yearly, the first payment on Midsummer, 1665, and the last on Christmas, 1668." "These lay subsidies were to be levied off temporalities, lands and goods. Commissioners were appointed to deliver detailed lists of persons taxed to the sheriffs, &c., who were to collect the subsidies, and they were to return gross amounts into the Exchequer as a check on the Collectors' accounts. The Commissioners, in obedience to writs from the Exchequer, returned copies of the lists supplied to the sheriffs, and these are the records styled Subsidy Rolls."

As stated above, all of the original Subsidy Rolls in the Public Record Office, Dublin, were destroyed in 1922. The Subsidy Roll of County Down, 1663, copied in the Public Record Office, Dublin, by Tenison Groves, *c.* 1912, was acquired by the Presbyterian Historical Society, Belfast, and loaned for copying, to the Public Record Office of Northern Ireland, Belfast (1924 *Report*, N. I., pp. 27-29). This latter repository also acquired transcripts of Subsidy Rolls in the purchased collection of the Tenison Groves transcripts, etc., as follows: Baronies of Cary, Dunluce, Glenarm, Kilconway, Co. Antrim; Baronies of Kilmacrenan, Raphoe, and Tirhugh, Co. Donegal, 1669; Baronies of Newcastle, Rathdown and Uppercross, Co. Dublin; and extracts of Subsidy Rolls, Co. Tyrone, 1662-1668 (1946/47 *Report*, N. I., p. 12). This repository also acquired in the collection presented by Philip Crosslé, "Extracts from the Subsidy Roll of Dungannon Barony, Co. Tyrone, 1663-1667 (1925 *Report*, N. I., p. 8). The Tenison Groves collection acquired by the Public Record Office, Dublin, contains extracts from the Subsidy Rolls of Co. Armagh, 1634; Co. Dublin, *c.* 1663-1668; Co. Tyrone, 1667 and 1668; Dublin City, 1634 and 1637 (58th *Report*, p. 20). Some printed copies of Subsidy Rolls have been mentioned above, and should be further sought in county histories and in historical society journals, etc.

POLL TAX ROLLS: The Poll tax was levied from time to time, mainly to provide money for military purposes. The Poll Tax Rolls of all counties, destroyed in the Public Record Office fire of 1922, were dated mostly 1695-1699, with a few earlier and later. The first Poll Money Ordinances, 1660-1661, are explained in the Introduction to *A Census of Ireland, Circa 1659, With Supplementary Material From The Poll Money Ordinances (1660-1661)*, edited by Séamus Pender, published by the Irish Manuscripts Commission, Dublin, 1939 (pp. ii-v). Mr. Pender briefly sums up the Poll Money Ordinances by quoting R. C. Simington (the learned editor of the Civil Survey): "Some four or five months prior to the English Act, Poll-tax was levied in Ireland in pursuance of an Ordinance of the General Convention dated April 24, 1660. It directed that all persons of the ranks and degrees therein mentioned should pay the respective sums of money appointed, viz., 'that every person above the age of fifteen years of either sex . . . under the degree or quality of a yeoman, or farmer yeoman, or farmer's wife or widdow shall pay twelve pence'. The sums payable by gentlemen, esquires, knights, barons, earls, and so on, are then specified in an ascending scale. A second ordinance, passed by the same Convention, dated March 1, 1660, doubled the tax referred to specifically as 'Pole-money'—on those above 15 years of age, and imposed much higher levies on persons of particular ranks and degrees . . . 'Able and discreet Protestants' appointed by County Commissioners, named in the Ordinances, were 'to enquire of all and every person within the respective places limited to their care, of each sex, of and above the age of 15 years', of their ranks, qualities and degrees, and of the dwelling and abiding places of such persons." The material from the Poll Money Ordinances, now in Marsh's Library is, through the courtesy of Newport B. White, M. A., Librarian, printed in the volume edited by Mr. Pender, as an appendix (pp. 609-646). The "Commissioners appointed for putting into execution the Poll Money Ordinance within the Counties, Cities and Buroughs" are listed by name and title under each locality as follows (pp. 638-646): (1) Names of the Commissioners for the Counties of Dublin, Wicklow, Kildare, Catherlogh (Carlow), Wexford, Kilkenny, Queen's County, King's County, Meath, Louth, Longford, Westmeath, Cork, Waterford, Kerry, Limerick, Clare, Tipperary, Roscommon, Leitrim, Sligo, Galway, Mayo, Fermanagh, Monaghan, Londonderry, Armagh, Donegal, Down, Antrim, Tyrone, Cavan. (2) Names of the "Commissioners for the Cities, Buroughs, Corporate Towns": Dublin, Wicklow, Naas, Kildare, Athie, Catherlogh, Wexford, Kilkenny, Callen, Thomas-Towne, Goran, Ennisteige, Marriborugh, Phillips-Towne, Trym, Navan, Kells, Athboy, Dundalk, Drogheda, St. Johns-Town, Mullinger, Athlone, Kilbeggan, Cork, Youghal, Kinsale, Bandon-bridge, Waterford, Dingle, Traly, Ardfert, Limerick, Inish, Cashel, Clonmel, Fetherd, Carrick, Galway, Enniskillen, Carrickfergus, Monaghan, Londonderry, Cavan.

The number of Commissioners named for handling the collection of the Poll Tax was in proportion to the population of the counties, cities, towns, etc. Their names indicate the high proportion of English by birth or by blood who were entrusted with responsibility by the Government. Thus the Commissioners for the "City and County of the City of Dublin" are named as follows: William Davis, Esq., Robert Deey, William Smith, William Bladen, Raphael Hunt, Richard Tigh, Daniel Hutchinson, John Preston, Thomas Hook, Ridgley Hatfield, Thomas Waterhouse, Peter Wibrant, Daniel Wibrant, Robert Mills, George Gilbert, John Cranwel, William Cliff, Richard Cook, John Desmineer, Daniel Bellingham, Mark Quin, John Forrest, Ralph Vizard, Sir William Usher, Sir Robert Newcomen, Sir Robert Meredith, Sir Paul Davis, Sir Wil. Domvile, Sir Hierom Alexander, Wil. Knight, Philip Fernely, Wil. Dixon, Rob. Shapcot, Rob. Kennedy, Doctor Ralph King, Doctor Dudley Loftus, Thomas Richardson, Richard Palfrey, William Sands, Abraham Yarner, Thomas Boyd, Abraham Clements, Enoch Reader, Lewis Desmineer, Samuel Salterson, John Beuchamp, John Smith, Thomas Howard, Thomas Pooley, Robert Hughes, John Povey, John Ket, Thomas Maul, Thomas Kennedy, Patrick Tallant, William Corey, John Moor, John Burniston, Ralph Allen, Thomas Worsop. These were mostly knights and esquires.

The Public Record Office, Dublin, has a copy of the Poll Tax assessments, Barony of Uppercross, County Dublin, 1698, acquired in the Tenison Groves Collection (58th *Report,* p. 20) ; a copy of the Poll Tax accounts, Parish of Donaghedy, County Tyrone, 1693 *(ibid.);* and a copy of the Poll Book, County Westmeath, 1761, acquired as a part of the T. U. Sadleir collection (58th *Report,* p. 25).

The Public Record Office of Northern Ireland, Belfast, has copies of Poll Tax Returns, Aghalow Parish, Co. Tyrone, acquired in the Rev. H. G. Scott collection of records, 1630-1814 (1928 *Report,* p. 9) ; a copy of the Fermanagh County Poll Book, 1788, sent to this Office from the Genealogical Office, Dublin Castle, Dublin, for copying the 3,500 names of freeholders (county electors), their abodes and freeholds, grouped by the initial letter of their surnames (1931 *Report,* p. 5) ; a copy of the Poll Book of County Armagh, 1753, acquired in the Tenison Groves Collection (1946-1947 *Report,* p. 12).

A few scattered lists of Poll Money records appear in local histories, such as the "Original Poll Money Roll, Barony and Liberties of Clonmel," published in the *History of Clonmel,* by William P. Burke. Waterford, 1907.

Some 19th century tax records have been described previously in this volume as follows: *Tithe Composition Applotment Books*, 1823-1837 (pp. 522-524); *Griffith's Primary Valuation of Rateable Property in Ireland*, 1848-1864 (pp. 525-534).

CHAPTER XVII

MILITARY AND NAVAL RECORDS

The earliest records of a military and genealogical nature are contained in the ancient and medieval Annals of Ireland and other Gaelic manuscripts. Some of these have been published and are listed in VOLUME II, pp. 213-215, herewith. The original manuscripts are deposited in various repositories; in the Royal Irish Academy and in Trinity College Library, Dublin; the British Museum and the Archiepiscopal Library of Lambeth Palace, London; the Bodleian Library, Oxford, etc. Microfilms of a vast number of early manuscripts of this nature, located in repositories throughout Europe, have been noted (pp. 440-450, herein), as acquired by the National Library of Ireland, Dublin.

The records of tribal warfare, the invasions, the conquests and military achievements on the countless fields of ancient and medieval battle, preserve the chronicles of the personal exploits and violent conflicts of war between the Irish kings, princes, lords of Anglo-Norman and English origin, Gaelic chieftains and their heirs, constantly challenged by members of cadet branches descended from the respective forbears from whom they derived a common ancestry. The principal reason for following the exploits of these early tribal leaders and their Anglo-Norman or English adversaries is that their every record, set forth in the Annals of the tribal historians, identifies the conquering or defeated hero by his paternal ancestry in the second to third or fourth generations and frequently reveals family alliances by marriage. These records are described herein, pp. 429-450.

Military records of the 16th-19th centuries are found in a wide range of manuscript and printed source materials. They provide valuable lists of officers and soldiers in local armed forces; accounts of military activity including officer personnel; local incidents and names of rebellious persons; the various records often accompanied with biographical and genealogical notes.

The *Calendar of the Carew Manuscripts, 1515-1624*, Vols. I-VI, London, 1867-1873, is a calendar of the 39 volumes of the original manuscripts of Sir George Carew (created Earl of Totness) who, as an officer in the Desmond rebellion and later as a Lieut. General, 1596, accumulated military records, pedigrees, and other materials described (pp. 594-596) herein.

The Ormonde Manuscripts, a calendar of the manuscripts of the Marquis of Ormonde preserved at Kilkenny Castle, was published by the Historical Manuscripts Commission, Old Series, Vols. 1-2, 1895-1899; New Series, Vols. 1-8, 1902-1920. The two volumes of the Old Series are full of matter of military interest, dating from the time of Henry VIII. Included are numerous lists of Army records. Volume two (Old Series) has a copious index. The second or New Series is also a very fruitful hunting ground for the biographer and genealogist. The editors, Sir John Gilbert and Caesar Litton Falkiner, state that these Manuscripts "are the richest of all extant manuscript materials of modern Irish history." The Petitions during and following the periods of war are replete with personal information. The documents extend from the 16th to the 18th centuries, but relate mainly to the period from Charles I to James II, during most of the time (except the period of the Commonwealth and Protectorate) when James, 1st Duke of Ormonde, served as Lord Lieutenant of Ireland. The records continue with those of James, 2nd Duke of Ormonde, who became Lord Lieutenant of Ireland under Queen Anne and served during most of that reign.

From the 17th century the sources are greatly increased. The 33rd *Report of the Deputy Keeper of the Public Records in Ireland*, Dublin, pp. 52-53, calls attention to the "vast quantity of books dealing with military accounts . . . Containing a great many names, and connected incidentally with a great many events, they throw some light on family and general history." The 55th *Report*, p. 136, calls attention to the duplicates or copies of destroyed records of a military nature now deposited in the following two repositories:

TRINITY COLLEGE LIBRARY, DUBLIN: The MSS. listed in the above 55th *Report:*

(1) Copy Establishment, year ending 31 March 1601 (T.C.D. Ms. 1218 (2)).

(2) Military Establishment to commence 1 April 1618 (T.C.D. Ms. 808 (10)).

(3) The Civil Lists for Easter, 1618, 1623, 1629. Civil and Military Lists, 1666, 1669 (T.C.D. Ms. 808 (11)).

(4) Civil Lists, 1629, 1676. Military Lists, 1616, 1622, 1631, 1640, 1676 (T. C. D. Ms. 672).

(5) An Establishment or List containing all the Payments to be made for Civil and Military Affairs with Pensions in Ireland for one year beginning the 1st of January 1687/8 (original) (T.C.D. Ms. 796).

(6) Military Establishment for 1689-90 (T.C.D. MS. 851 (6)).

(7) An Establishment, Anne R. (T.C.D. Ms. 756).

(8) Establishment, 1719 (T.C.D. Ms. 591).

(9) Establishment, 1721 (T.C.D. Ms. 1179 (28)).

THE PUBLIC RECORD OFFICE, LONDON: The above 55th *Report*, p. 136, lists the following records entered in the *Guide to the Manuscripts Preserved in the Public Record Office* (London), by M. S. Giuseppi:

(1) Lists of the Civil and Military Establishment, Ireland, 1604-1629 (Vol. II, p. 77).

(2) Irish Military Establishment, 42 Elizabeth to 21 James I (Vol. I, p. 195).

(3) Civil List Establishment, Ireland, 1709-1715 (Vol. I, p. 186).

(4) Register of Civil and Military Establishments in Ireland, 1700-1720 (Vol. II, p. 18).

(5) See also the *Calendars of State Papers Domestic (Ireland)*, which are a rich source for the genealogist.

(6) The records of the "Irish Volunteers," 1776-1783; the "Yeomanry Corps of Ireland," 1823-1834; Dillon's Regiment,

1796-1815; Irish Brigade, 2nd Regiment, 1796; 3rd Regiment, 1796; 6th Regiment, 1795-1798; 1st Ulster Regiment, 1782-1896; Militia of Ireland, 1793-1896; Irish Fusiliers (provincials) 1783.

(7) Records of Irishmen who had served in the Royal Navy are included in the following sources: (a) Naval Board Registers: Bounty Papers, 1675-1822, supply a certificate of baptism of the deceased and often a certificate of marriage for himself and parents, and the name and address of person to whom bounty is to be paid (widow, parent, child, etc.). (b) Bounty Applications: Application Papers, 1798-1821, contain the name, place of residence, and other information concerning the widow, children, parents, etc., accompanied by marriage certificates, baptismal certificates, of the applicants and minor children. (c) Seamen's Effects Papers: Contain marriage certificate of parents, baptismal certificate, will and administration papers of the deceased.

THE PUBLIC RECORD OFFICE OF IRELAND, DUBLIN: Military records in this repository are listed as follows:

55th *Report of the Deputy Keeper of the Public Records in Ireland:* Lodge's Manuscripts include a volume of Enrolments (Miscellaneous), containing enrolments on the Patent Rolls of King's Letters, Grants, etc., including Military Matters: Writs to reside on lands to keep guard against the hostile Irish, etc. (55th *Report*, p. 118). Two volumes of Lodge's Manuscripts contain: (1) "Lists of Patentee Officers in Ireland, Civil and Military, from the 33rd year of the reign of King Henry VIII and the year of Our Lord 1541 . . .," and (2) "Lists of such Patentee Officers before the Reformation as are now remaining of Record." Some lists in point of date belong in Vol. 1, such as the Judges of the Admiralty, 1591, 1677-1701; Admirals of Ireland, 1335-1670 (55th *Report,* p. 121). Lodge's *Parliamentary Register* includes an alphabetical "List of Members," giving in some cases the date of death and official and military posts held by members. (55th *Report*, p. 120). The Frazer MSS. comprising some 500 documents deal with the 1798-1800 Rebellion period; one item contains the Minutes of Proceedings of Court Martial in Wexford, 1798-1800, from MS. 1471, in Trinity College Library (55th *Report,* pp. 12, 145). The Entry Books of the Muster Master General of Ireland, 1709-1823, deposited in the Public Record Office, London, are noted in the 55th *Report,* p. 139. Indexes in the Public Search Room include (1) Index to Military Commissions and Miscellaneous Documents, 1715-1763; (2) Military Memorials, 1752-1815, Index to; (3) Index to Officers' Widows' Accounts, 1716-1749; Index to Officers' Widows' Certificates, 1752-1763 (55th *Report,* p. 131).

The 57th *Report of the Deputy Keeper of the Public Records in Ireland,* Appendix III. C., pp. 479-517, contains a Calendar of the Wyche Documents: Papers of Sir Cyril Wyche, chief secretary to the Duke of Ormonde, 1676-1682; of Viscount Sidney, 1692-1693; and the papers of his own office as Lord Justice, 26 June 1693-9 May 1695, and as one of the trustees for the sale of forfeited estates. The papers relate to forfeitures, military affairs and the administration generally. A detailed catalogue is in the Public Search Room.

The 58th *Report of the Deputy Keeper of the Public Records in Ireland,* contains notices of the following deposits in the Public Record Office, Dublin: The T. U. Sadleir MSS. include eight notebooks containing lists of Army Commissions, 1736-1744, and 1757-1761 (p. 25). A volume contains lists of officials on the civil and military establishment and ecclesiastical dignitaries with miscellaneous notes, 1688-1729 (p. 26). Two volumes of copies of warrants of Lords Justices & Council to Vice-treasurer, petitions, acquittances, etc., relating chiefly to army affairs, 1642-1643 (p. 27). A volume of copies of petitions and memorials, with reports of the Attorney General thereon, and miscellaneous material, 1702-1706, including a list of officers of the French regiment who are to have their pensions restored, 1706 (p. 27). A number of volumes dealing with Army records, including seven volumes regarding the County Sligo Militia, 1855-1857 (Mss. 2558-2563).

THE ROYAL IRISH ACADEMY, DUBLIN: The de la Ponce MSS., compiled by Amadie de la Ponce, of Paris, France, contains the military records and genealogies of the officers of the Irish Brigades in the service of France during the last half of the 17th and throughout the 18th centuries. Among the miscellaneous military records is the "Muster Roll, Newtown Limavady, County Londonderry, 1666."

THE GENEALOGICAL OFFICE, DUBLIN CASTLE, DUBLIN: Among the records of this Office are the registered Arms of many who were created peers following distinguished military service. The emblazoned Arms of Lysaght accompanied by military and genealogical information presents an excellent illustration (pp. 233-234, herein). Miscellaneous records include a MS. "Return of Regiments Quartered in Ireland, *c.* 1769-1773," showing the age of each officer and the county of his birth.

THE NATIONAL LIBRARY OF IRELAND, DUBLIN: The descriptive lists of deposited manuscript collections (originals and transcripts) should be consulted. The list of microfilms in this repository should also be examined for military and naval records. Some microfilms noted in VOLUME II, herewith, are: Army Lists, pp. 277, 279, 280; Militia Records, p. 270; Muster Rolls, pp. 270, 278, 281. Military and Naval records are contained in a vast number of published sources available here. Records are noted in this VOLUME I, and in VOLUME II as follows:

1. The "Blue Book" Series (p. 115, herein).

2. The Carte Manuscripts in the Bodleian Library, Oxford (pp. 585-586, herein).

3. The *Calendar of the Carew Manuscripts, 1515-1624,* 6 vols. (pp. 594-596, herein).

4. Biographical Dictionaries (Vol. II, pp. 38-40).

5. Directories (Vol. II, pp. 229-231).

6. Plantation and Settlement Records (Vol. II, pp. 240-241).

7. Military and Naval Records (Vol. II, pp. 244-246).

8. County, Town, and Regional Histories (Vol. II, pp. 76-94).

9. Historical and Archaeological Society Journals (Vol. II, pp. 43-51).

10. State Papers and Court Records (Vol. II, pp. 253-258).

A few works of note among the published materials are as follows:

John D'Alton's *Illustrations, Historical and Genealogical, of King James's Irish Army List (1689)*, Dublin, 1855, and 2nd edition, enlarged, 1860. The first edition (one volume) of 975 pages "embraced the Memoirs of 500 families, the aristocracy of Ireland." The second edition (two volumes), of which Volume I, of 462 pages, concerns the members of the Cavalry, and Volume II, of 808 pages, concerns the members of the Infantry. Valuable genealogical information about the Irish families is contained in this work.

The Pedigrees and Papers of James Terry, Athlone Herald at the Court of James II in France (1690-1725) Together with Other Pedigrees, and Naturalisations from the MSS. d'Hozier and other Sources in France. By Charles E. Lart, Exeter, 1938. James II, after his defeat by William III in Ireland in 1690, was accompanied or followed to France by many thousands of his Irish officers, soldiers and gentry, to share his exile and join the French Army. As the King was creating peerages and titles and required a Herald for matters of genealogy and arms, he in 1690 appointed James Terry, of Limerick, Athlone Herald. His services were also needed as many of the Irish gentry flocked into the French army, and as the Laws of Noblesse required an applicant for a commission to give proof of three generations of the rank of esquire or more, the services of a Herald were required to produce sufficient proof of descent. The Foreword indicates the numerous and important sources of records of a genealogical nature in the repositories of France, concerning the mass of English, Scots and Irish who followed James II to France, of whom the Irish were by far the most numerous. The pedigrees in this volume, marked Volume I, serve as only a suggestion of the wealth of records concerning Irishmen, deposited in France. These pedigrees are brief and relate to certain branches of the families of D'Arcy, De Cusack, Higgins, Keating, O'Keefe, Lynch, MacCartan, MacDonald, Macnamara, Maguire, Magenis, Middleton, Oglethorpe, O'Mahony, Porter, Power, Ryan, Sandilands, Williamson, with brief notes on the Terry family (pp. xvi-xvii).

The National Library of Ireland has acquired a great collection of microfilms of the military records of the Irish in France, documents relating to Irish persons in France, and genealogical records concerning "Preuves de noblesse de familles irlandaises," and many other records of interest to the genealogist. The microfilms are of records deposited in Paris in the Archives Nationales, the Bibliothèque De L'Arsénal, and the Bibliothèque Nationale, and are listed in many pages of the *National Library of Ireland Report of the Council of Trustees* (3 vols.), 1949-1950; 1950-1951; 1951-1952.

Richard Hayes has compiled five important works concerning Irish officers, soldiers, and gentry who fled to France, and whose genealogical and personal records contribute to Irish genealogy. These works are: *Ireland and Irishmen in the French Revolution*, Dublin, c. 1930; *Irish Swordsmen of France*, Dublin, 1934; *The Last Invasion of Ireland*, Dublin, 1937; *Old Irish Links with France*, some echoes of exiled Ireland, Dublin, 1940; *Biographical Dictionary of Irishmen in France*, Dublin, 1949. The latter work contains several hundred biographies setting forth places of birth in Ireland and, in most cases, parentage and other genealogical information. The repositories of unpublished sources which contributed to these biographies are listed and their collections briefly discussed, pp. 319-326. Irish noble families in France are listed, pp. 327-332.

The Ancient and Present State of the County and City of Cork, by Charles Smith (edited and revised), 2 vols., Cork, 1893-1894, contains extensive military lists of the "Volunteers" of the several Counties of Munster, 1782, and of the "Yeomanry of Ireland, 1796-1834," with a list of the corps in County Cork and the records of the Doneraile Yeomanry.

The *Cork Historical and Archaeological Society Journal*, Vol. 34, pp. 76-90, contains "The Galway Prisoners . . ." contributed by W. H. Welply. This work sets forth the names, history, and some genealogical notes regarding the 197 Protestant men of Munster who were taken prisoners in March 1688/9, when on their way to join forces at Sligo, and thereafter were held prisoners at Galway; later in May 1690, transferred to confinement in Dublin until the Battle of the Boyne, July 1, 1690, set them free.

The *Journal of the Kilkenny Archaeological Society*, Vol. III (later reorganized as the *Journal of the Royal Society of Antiquaries of Ireland*), contains "Documents Connected with the City of Kilkenny Militia in the Seventeenth and Eighteenth Centuries," by John G. A. Prim (pp. 231-274). This contains the names on the Muster Rolls of the Militia, extracted from documents of the Kilkenny Corporation in the Evidence Chamber of Kilkenny Castle. The Muster Rolls are set forth with lists of the non-commissioned officers and soldiers of the following dates: 8 April 1667; 21 Sept. 1681; 5 Oct. 1685; 2 Feb. 1690; 19 June 1691; Mar. 1702; 19 Mar. 1707; 1715; 1719.

The *Cork Historical and Archaeological Society Journal*, Vol. 32, pp. 1-7, contains "Militia Commissions, Co. Cork, 1727-56," copied by Rev. Henry B. Swanzy, from the Book of Entries, Militia, formerly preserved in the Public Record Office, Four Courts, Dublin.

Enniskillen Parish and Town, by W. H. Dundas, 1913, pp. 146-147, contains the "Names of the Townsmen of Eneskilen and their Armes," from the Muster Roll of the County of Fermanagh, about 1631 (Add. MSS., British Museum, 4770).

The Munster Military Journal and Cork District Directory, published monthly, began its New Series, Vol. 1, No. 1, in January, 1888. A map (pp. 2-3) in this and later issues shows the Cork Military District comprising Counties Clare, Cork, Kerry, Kilkenny, Limerick, Tipperary, Waterford and Wexford. The Military Stations were at first indicated by key numbers. In September, 1888, the "Garrison Towns and Stations" were indicated "in Red," and thereafter they were shown on the maps in this way. A Cork Military District Directory of Officers of the eight counties is set forth alphabetically with their addresses. Names of the Officers by rank, and news of the various Military Stations, social and otherwise, is a feature of each issue. A series of "Our Regimental Historiettes" gives the date of the formation of each regiment, the names, dates and places of service of each officer; thus the names and places of service of all officers in regiments, sent to America during the Revolution, show the officers who commanded troops at Bunker Hill, Brandywine, etc. Births, marriages and deaths of officers, soldiers and members of their families are posted. A series of articles entitled "Old Corks," published in the issues from August 1888, to December 1890, contain history of the area from the time of the Anglo-Norman invasion, including some genealogy.

The History of Enniskillen With References to Some Manors in Co. Fermanagh, by W. Copeland Trimble, 3 vols., Enniskillen, 1919, contains (Vol. I, pp. 200-221) the Muster Roll of Co. Fermanagh, *c.* 1631, copied from MSS. 4770 in the British Museum. The list is set forth by baronies and the names of the various "Undertakers", the number of acres each was granted (5,000 to 1,000), with the lists of the men and arms on each estate. There are 971 names which occur in order of the number of times as follows: Johnston (55); Armstrong (41); Beaty (Beatty, Bayty, Baetye, Baiteye) (36); Ellot (33); Graham (29); Little (25); Irwin (17); Nixon (10); Smith, Wilson (9); Brown, Hall, Moore, Thomson (8); Sympson (7); Anderson, Bell, Clarke, Michell, Ossenbrooke, Rogers (Roger), West (Wayst), Wiggan, (6); Barton, Carleton, ffayre, Henderson, Maxwell, Mophat (Moffet), Scot, Trotter (5); Allen, Atkinson, Crawford (Craford), Ewat, Greg, Montgomery (Mungomery), Murray, Noble, Notley, Portis, Rennick, Walker (4); Amerson, Burney, Brock, Black, Burse (Birs), Car, Cooke, Duffyn, ffrizell, ffoster, Gibson, Good, Goodfellow, Hayes, Harrison, Hemiston, Hogg, Hume, Knowells, Middlebroke, Ogle, Pageot, Presby, Readman, Robinson, Souage, Spence, Steele, Wallis, Westby, Widson, Williamson, Warrall (3). Most of these were Scottish. A number of English names were: Aston, Addison, Barefoot, Beard, Barton, Boots, Bridghowse, Bucket, Carver, Carnaby, Cottingham, Caps, Cranley, Cooke, Emery, Glover, Kettle, Hall, Hollywood, Little, Middlebrook, Newborne, Savage, Skales, Slater, Wyndsor, Westby, Wiggan, Wiggans, Woods. The natives of Gaelic stock, not being Protestants, did not obtain land from the Undertakers as armed tenants who were mustered periodically by the Muster Master.

The above *History of Enniskillen*, Vol. III, pp. 684-702, contains the list of Militia Officers of 1689, and at various times thereafter in 1698, 1702, 1708, 1715, 1716, 1727/8, and 1756.

The Fighters of Derry, their Deeds and Descendants; being a Chronicle of Events in Ireland during the Revolutionary Period 1688-1691, by William R. Young, with an Introduction by Thomas U. Sadleir, London, 1932, contains extensive lists, biography and genealogical information both as to the progenitors and descendants of a great many of the "Fighters," while others are noted only by name and county of origin (a few with no identification). There were a total of 1,660 "Defenders," of Londonderry who are listed, and 344 of the Jacobite Army. A considerable amount of information about these men, contained in other sources, has been omitted, perhaps for lack of space, and a few names of "Defenders" were also overlooked.

The above printed source materials have been noted as examples of the various types of published records which are available in the National Library of Ireland, Dublin, and in other genealogical libraries.

THE ARMAGH COUNTY MUSEUM, ARMAGH: The library has a manuscript copy of the Muster Roll of Ulster, 1630; also the Armagh Militia Records, 1793-1908. The National Library of Ireland has microfilms of both collections.

THE ARMAGH PUBLIC LIBRARY: Among its many genealogical works and MSS. or printed source materials is a rare printed volume containing the names of the Militia Officers for the counties of Ireland, 1761.

THE PRESBYTERIAN HISTORICAL SOCIETY, BELFAST: The library of this Society has manuscript copies of the Muster Rolls of 1631. One of the conditions of the Plantation of Ulster was that the Undertakers should muster their tenants periodically and parade them before the Government Muster-Master who set down the name, age (between 16 and 60 years), and the arms borne by each person capable of bearing arms. All were Protestants and, for the nine counties, numbered over 12,000. (*Strafford's Letters and Despatches*, Vol. I, p. 199). "They were distributed as residents of the counties in numbers as follows: Co. Antrim, 1618; Co. Armagh, 902; Co. Cavan, 495; Co. Donegal, 1225; Co. Down, 4,045; Co. Fermanagh, 923; Co. Londonderry, 1950; Co. Monaghan, 95; Co. Tyrone, 1,538. There was also a yeomanry of about 2,600 enrolled from all the counties and a permanent garrison at Carrickfergus, just above Belfast. The latter may account for the fact that no list of Chichester's men appears in the Antrim Muster (see Pynnar's Survey of the Plantation, made in 1618-1619, and published in Harris's *Hibernica*). Ten years after the aforesaid Muster, the men were mustered for active service in the suppression of the Rebellion begun in October, 1641. The Rolls of each regiment are extant, giving the companies of each regiment, officers and men, thus forming a sequel to the Muster of 1631. The Presbyterian Historical Society possesses a copy" (The Rev. Dr. David Stewart, Belfast, 1952).

THE PUBLIC RECORD OFFICE OF NORTHERN IRELAND, BELFAST: Under the direction of D. A. Chart, Deputy Keeper of the Public Records of Northern Ireland for some years, the two MSS. volumes of Sir Thomas Phillips (1609-1629), and a volume of tracings from the original maps of the London Companies, deposited in this office in 1926 (1926 *Report*, pp. 3-4), were edited, transcribed, and published under the title, *Londonderry and the London Companies, 1609-1629, being a survey and other documents submitted to King Charles I*. By Sir Thomas Phillips. Belfast (His (now Her) Majesty's Stationery Office), 1928. On pp. 52-53, is a "Muster . . . of all the Inhabitants with their Servants residing in the County [City?] of Londonderry, with their several Arms. 1622, Sept. 20." The names of 110 masters and servants are listed. This is followed by a list of "The Names of such as were Mustered for the Town of Coleraine the 20th Sept. 1622," all of which numbered 100 (pp. 53-54).

The Muster Rolls of the following regiments in 1642 and some later records were acquired by this Office in the Tenison Groves collection of transcripts (1946-1947 *Report*, p. 13) : "Sir Robert Stewart's, Earl of Eglinton's, Life Guards of the Lord Lieutenant, Viscount Montgomery's, Clotworthy's, Col. Arthur Hill's, Lord Conway's and Col. Mervyn's; of Londonderry Garrison; of the Companies in the Cos. Londonderry and Donegal; Quarters of the Army in Ireland, 1690, and at various intervals until 1800; and various army lists for that period; list of militia officers of Co. Antrim, 1691-1693; lists of yeomanry and Militia officers, *circa* 1797-1810; Muster Rolls of Cookstown Cavalry, Lissan Infantry and Loughry Infantry, 1797."

A transcript of a Muster Roll of County Down, 1642, was presented to this Office by the Rev. David Stewart (1932 *Report*, p. 8). A list of the "Officers of the Green Howards (19th Foot), 1688-1931," was presented by Maj. M. L. Ferrar. (1931 *Report*, p. 15.)

The Wynne Military Papers, 1689 to about 1750, acquired by this Office, are a collection of the Wynne family of Hazelwood, Co. Sligo, and Lurganboy, Co. Leitrim. Among the papers is a copy of the signed association of inhabitants of Enniskillen, Co. Fermanagh, containing 150 signatures under that of Gustavus Hamilton, their commander and governor of the town, 13 Feb. 1688/9. Much of the collection relates to the Wynne Dragoons from 1689, with particulars of cases of disorders of members of Capt. Hugh Galbraith's troops, and details of other incidents and actions in various locations. There is a list of officers subsequent to 6 Aug. 1732, with dates of their commissions. Documents of the Wynne family are included in the collection. The contents of the entire deposit have been indexed and printed in Appendix B, 1938-45 *Report*, pp. 30-31.

The Findlay and Williams collections deposited in this Office contain: (a) Records of the Down Militia Regiment, 1803-1863. (b) Court Martial Book, 1800-1814. (c) Irish

Army List of 1737, believed to be the earliest in existence. (d) Irish Commission Registers, 1737-1760, 11 vols., containing several thousand appointments. (1929 *Report*, p. 18.)

Some other miscellaneous collections in this Office are: 1. A "Revenue and Army Account Book of William III, 2 June 1690 to 11 March 1691," compiled when he was in Ireland with several regiments, gives the lists of officers of the various regiments (but incomplete lists for the Fermanagh and Londonderry contingents). (1935 *Report*, p. 22.) 2. The following documents were purchased: (a) Irish Commission Registers, 1727-1760. (b) Irish Half-Pay Lists, 1715 and 1748/9. (c) Irish Army List, 1737 (copy). (d) Quarters of the Army in Ireland, 1739; Regimental Lists of 3rd Horse, 5th, 14th and 17th Dragoons, reviewed in Presentments, Co. Antrim, 1888-1897; Presentments, Co. Down, 1841-1894. (1929 *Report*, p. 9.) 3. Muster Rolls, Review Returns, etc., of the Armagh Militia, 1793-1791. (1926 *Report*, p. 8.) 4. A List of the Armagh Militia, 1808. (1931 *Report*, p. 13.)

During the past two centuries or more the historians and genealogists have employed the original sources and have made transcripts, extracts and abstracts of the records for family genealogical purposes, and for compiling and publishing local, regional or general history concerning military records of particular sieges, battles, local incidents, distribution of troops, Muster Rolls, lists of the "Volunteers," *c.* 1782, etc. The county records of Courts of Assize, of Grand Juries, and of High Sheriffs, etc., include local incidents involving criminal proceedings against various opposing leaders of the Tories, and the secret Patriot Clubs; the "Whiteboys", "Oakboys", "Hearts of Steel". Later the "Orangemen", "Defenders", and "United Irishmen" were involved in riots and the 1798 Rebellion. All cases contributed information regarding families and individuals. Local military lists and affairs, Court Records, legal proceedings including punishment for violence or slight offenses against the militia, serve to locate people, often with genealogical information. These accounts are set forth in various county, town, parish, and regional histories.

The *History of Belfast*, by D. J. Owen, 1921, contains an explanation and history of "The Patriot Clubs, the Rise of the Volunteers, and the Hearts of Steel, 1751-1772" (Chapter X, pp. 92-104); "The Period of the Volunteers, 1773-1791" (Chapter XI, pp. 105-120); "The United Irishmen, the Orangemen, and the Rebellion of 1798" (Chapter XII, 121-137).

The "Volunteers," numbering ultimately in 1782, some 100,-000 armed officers and men, were organized locally in the cities, towns and villages of every county, to defend the county against foreign invasion at a time when England was engaged in war with France and later during the American Revolution when France united with the American Colonies and threatened to invade the British Islands.   The "Volunteer" movement raised a powerful army under volunteer Field Officers and Officers of the several corps of Cavalry, Artillery, and Infantry.   The men were self equipped with uniforms and arms, etc., unpaid, and disciplined by their own efforts under their volunteer officers.   They served their purpose to their own and England's benefit during the period of danger, to 1783.   After this their organized strength was turned to the political reform of the Irish Parliament, to make it truly representative of the people; to achieve Roman Catholic emancipation; to relieve Protestant dissenters from disadvantages; to open the ports of Ireland to all nations not at war with the King.   The "Volunteer" leaders among the peers and gentry saw danger and fell away from association with this political aftermath.   The English Government had kept careful records of all enlistments in the "Volunteer Army."   Its extinction gave rise to the "United Irishmen," the origin of the "Orangemen," the "Defenders," and the Rebellion of 1798. Anarchy, rebellion (particularly in the south of Ireland) gave rise to the enlistment of 37,000 "Yeomen," mostly cavalry, who were equipped, armed, and paid by the Government to drill two days a week, to defend the land by co-operating with the militia, etc., against rebellion.   In addition they were often on duty for long periods when needed to put down riots.   All of this activity caused many records which are preserved in MSS. and printed local history and family records.   The *History of*

Monaghan for Two Hundred Years, 1660-1680, by Denis Carolan Rushe, Dundalk, 1921, is told from this viewpoint. The
Foreword states: "In recent years the descendants of many
Monaghan men resident abroad have been making unsuccess-
ful efforts to find their family history; in these pages the
names of as many Monaghan people are given as may assist
all pedigree seekers."

CHAPTER XVIII

PENSION RECORDS

Pension records could quite properly be included among the "Military and Naval Records," set forth in the previous CHAPTER XVII, except for the fact that there were Civil as well as Military Pensions granted in Ireland. Collections in various repositories are as follows:

THE PUBLIC RECORD OFFICE OF IRELAND, DUBLIN:

1. Among the Lodge MSS. deposited in this Office is a volume containing abstracts or references under the heads below to entries on the Patent Rolls: (1) "Indentures or Articles of Agreement between the Chief Governors of Ireland and several Irish Chiefs" (Henry IV - Elizabeth). (2) "Denizations of the Irish, Scots and other Foreigners" (Richard II - George I). (3) "General Pardons" and "Particular Pardons" (Edward III - George II). (4) "Public Commissions" (Edward III - George II). (5) "Pensions" (Edward II - George III). This latter section contains "Abstracts of grants of pensions, annuities or annual rents, in alms, for services, in consideration of injuries received in the wars of Ireland, in composition for money due, etc., pensions to ecclesiastics upon the dissolution of Abbeys, etc. They comprise pensions to grantee and heirs, for life, pleasure, good behaviour, until otherwise provided for. For Charles II, there are separate heads for Pensions and Grants of Money". (55th *Report,* p. 119.)

2. This Office has a collection of records sent from the Record Tower, representing Parliamentary, Council Office and Chief Secretary's Office Records. Among these are: (1) "Index to Officers' Widows' Accounts, 1716-1749." (2) "Index to Officers' Widows' Certificates, 1752-1763." (55th *Report,* p. 131.) The Appendix to the 2nd *Report of the Deputy Keeper of the Public Records in Ireland* (1870), p. 54, contains the following explanation of the records which were sent from the State Paper Department, and were indexed: The

"Collection of Certificates Respecting Officers' Widows, made before Justices of the Peace, for the Purpose of their obtaining payment of their pensions, containing 2,265 documents, has been arranged, numbered, and placed in cartons, and a comprehensive Index made to it. This collection gives not only the Widows' Affidavits, but also the Certificates of Ministers and Churchwardens as to identity and existence. Each Affidavit states the fact of marriage, the name of the deceased husband, his rank in the Army, and the Regiment in which he served. These Widows' Certificates, which commence in 1752 and end in 1763, supply a link in the chain of evidence of marriages and deaths, and may be found of importance in legal investigations." The "Officers' Widows' Accounts" consisted of one bundle giving information of the above nature. The Appendix to the 5th *Report*, p. 30, explains the latter collection further: "Officers' Widows' Accounts, 1716-1749 (carton 42). The Index to this collection, referred to in my last [fourth] *Report* (p. 25), has been completed. The documents give the names of the Widows' husbands, their rank, and the Regiments to which they belonged. In some cases the date of the death of the Widow is given." The Indexes contain the pertinent information, sufficient to identify the contents of each document; the names, places, dates, etc. The original documents were destroyed in the 1922 fire.

3. "Indexes to Statements of French Pensioners, etc." (1) "Index List giving military rank." (2) "Index List giving town (? in which resident)." (55th *Report*, p. 132.)

4. A volume of copies of petitions and memorials, with reports of the Attorney General thereon, and miscellaneous material, 1702-1706, including a list of officers of the French regiment who are to have their pensions restored, 1706. M2461. (58th *Report*, p. 27.)

5. Volume marked "Civil and Military Establishment of Ireland," 1743, containing list of salaries and pensions payable, as on 26 Oct. 1727. M2480. (58th *Report*, p. 24.)

6. In this Office is a series of old age pension records (the Green Forms) listed in the Miscellaneous (Fourth General

Index) based on the Census Returns of 1841 and 1851. Information on these forms is taken from the Census Returns in proof of the age of applicants for Old Age Pensions and thus supplies records of age and relationship in various families. After the original Old Age Pension Forms were destroyed in the 1922 fire, some collections of certified copies of extracts from Census records made for applicants were sent in from the Customs and Excise stations. The 53rd *Report*, p. 4, explains these records as follows: "After the passing of the Old Age Pensions Act, 1908, it was found that the main source of documentary evidence of age for the great majority of the applicants was the Returns of the Census taken in the years 1821, 1841 and 1851, which were deposited in this Office. The heavy task of furnishing evidence of the age of the applicants to the Local Government Boards of England, Ireland and Scotland, and to the applicants themselves, was entrusted to this Department . . . The Census Returns of 1851 were taken on the 30th March, 1851. Their usefulness for Old Age Pensions' purposes has been rapidly dwindling for some time and will soon be at an end." This was written and dated 30 August 1921 (published, 1926), before the 1922 fire and indicates that for every destroyed record there was a copy for the Local Excise Station, and a copy for the applicant. Hence many have been deposited as legal evidence of the age of recipients of pensions.

THE PUBLIC RECORD OFFICE OF NORTHERN IRELAND, BELFAST:

1. This Office has the printed works containing various lists of civil and military pensions; also copies of MSS. lists of pensions such as the Lodge collection mentioned above.

2. The *Report of the Deputy Keeper of the Public Records of Northern Ireland,* for the year 1927, p. 6, contains a list of the following records transferred to this Office from H. M. Customs and Excise, in 1927: "Old Age Pension Search Forms and some Public Record Office (Dublin) Certified Copies of extracts from the Census Returns, 1841 and 1851, for parts of Counties Antrim, Armagh, Down, Fermanagh, Londonderry, and Tyrone, were received from Customs and Excise

stations at the following places:-Armagh, Ballycastle, Ballygawley, Ballymena, Ballynahinch, Belfast, Castlederg, Coleraine, Cookstown, Dungannon, Enniskillen, Irvinestown, Larne,
Limavady, Lisburn, Lisnaskea, Londonderry, Lurgan, Maghera, Magherafelt, Newry, Newtownards, Portadown,
Strabane."

TRINITY COLLEGE LIBRARY, DUBLIN: Among the military records in this repository, listed in the previous chapter herein,
is a collection, "An Establishment or List containing all the
Payments to be made for Civil and Military Affairs with
Pensions in Ireland for one year beginning the 1st of January
1687/8 (Original) (T.C.D. Ms. 796)."

PRINTED SOURCES: Among the printed sources are the fol-
lowing: *A Catalogue of the Bradshaw Collection of Irish
Books in the University Library, Cambridge*, 1916, Vol. II (p.
744), contains item No. 4526: "Lists of the Pensions on the
Civil and Military Establishment as they stood the 26th of
October, 1763."

*Liber Munerum Publicorum Hiberniae ab an. 1152 usque
ad 1827* . . . London, 1852 (see VOLUME II, herewith for further details (p. 254)), contains numerous lists of pensions, as
shown in the Index to this work, by subjects, contained in the
9th *Report of the Deputy Keeper of the Public Records in Ireland*, pp. 21-58.

Various county, town, diocesan, and miscellaneous histories
contain Pension Lists. The *Historical Notices of Old Belfast
and its Vicinity,* edited with Notes by Robert M. Young, Belfast, 1896, contains (pp. 101, 106), two lists of Pensioners,
Precinct of Belfast, 1655, 1657.

CHAPTER XIX

RECORDS OF PUBLIC OFFICE,
FREEMEN, FREEHOLDERS, GUILDS, SCHOOLS

The most recently published work regarding persons who held public office prior to the 19th century is *Patentee Officers In Ireland, 1173-1826*, edited by James L. J. Hughes and published by the Irish Manuscripts Commission, Dublin, 1960. This is a list of individuals who held Crown appointments to offices in Ireland, secured by Patent and recorded on the Patent Rolls or among the Fiants. The names are alphabetically arranged, in each case giving the office or nature of the appointment, the date, place (county, etc.), and the reference to the record in that part of *Liber Munerum Publicorum Hiberniae* from which the information was taken. The offices range from that of Lord Lieutenant or Lord Deputy, through the entire galaxy of Crown appointments; of Judges, Members of Parliament, Army and Navy Officers, the succeeding officers appointed Ulster King of Arms, the Ecclesiastical appointments, High Sheriffs, Governors of Counties, Clerks of the Crown and Peace, Constables of Crown Castles, numerous other officers and pensioners, in so far as any records of this nature were preserved in existing Patent Rolls or Fiants. The editor, James L. J. Hughes has included a list of "Other Printed Sources" containing information regarding the holders of various Patentee Offices.

The above work was compiled to fill the need for an annotated Names Index of *Liber Munerum Publicorum Hiberniae ab an 1152 usque ad 1827; or, The Establishment of Ireland from the Nineteenth of King Stephen to the Seventh of George IV* (2 vols.), London, 1852. This latter work was compiled by Rowley Lascelles while he served as a member of the Irish Record Commission which was established by Patent from 1810 to 1830. He extracted his material from that portion of the Lodge MSS. known as "Lodge's Patentee Officers," compiled by John Lodge from his transcripts of the Patent Rolls made while he was Deputy Keeper of the Rolls, and Keeper of the Records in Bermingham Tower, prior to 1774. Lascelles added the records extracted from later Patent Rolls, Fiants, and other sources dated prior to 1826. An explanation of this work of two volumes containing 1,757 pages, finally published by the English Government in 1852, without an index, is presented in the 9th *Report of the Deputy Keeper of the Public Records in Ireland* (p. 6). The Appendix to this 9th *Report* (pp. 21-58), contains a Subject Index of the work. A brief history of Lodge's MSS. is contained in the 26th *Report* (pp. 7-8).

RECORDS OF PUBLIC OFFICE HOLDERS: Published sources containing the records of this nature are listed in VOLUME II, herewith, as follows:

1. Biographical Dictionaries and Biographical Succession Lists (pp. 38-42).

2. County and Town Histories; Diocesan and Parish Histories; Histories of Ireland (pp. 77-94).

3. Various works of the Irish Manuscripts Commission in addition to the above noted *Patentee Officers in Ireland, 1173-1826, Dublin, 1961*, contain a large collection of abstracts and extracts forming a calendar of the O'Brien family papers which concern many military and political figures of the 16th and more particularly the 17th to the 19th centuries. The journal, *Analecta Hibernica,* Nos. 1-22, carries various calendars of MSS. collections. The Rawlinson Collection in the Bodleian Library, Oxford, is calendared in *Analecta Hibernica,* No. 1 (pp. 12-178) ; No. 2 (pp. 1-92). These calendars are full of information concerning public officers in all branches of the Government in Ireland. Journal No. 1, pp. 37-38, contains "A List of the Names of such Persons as are to be Sheriffs in the several Counties of Ireland for the Ensuing yeare."

4. Directories and school Registers (pp. 229-232). Also the more detailed account of the Directories and Almanacs contained in this VOLUME, pp. 471-479, indicates the amount

of information compiled about the personnel of the various public offices of all branches of the Government. *Thom's Irish Almanac and Official Directory*, published from 1844 onward, contains many lists of office holders by Government appointment with the dates of office, some of which are earlier than 1800. A list of the "Militia of Ireland," contained in the 1847 issue (pp. 243-249), sets forth the names of all regimental and company officers in all counties of Ireland, with the date of appointment in each case.

5. Records of Public Offices, Freeholders and Guilds (pp. 249-252).

6. State Papers and Court Records (pp. 253-258).

7. Historical and Genealogical Periodicals (pp. 43-51). The Family Index to Articles in Irish Periodicals (pp. 52-75) lists 299 articles concerning the important county families, most of which contributed members to public office. In addition, these periodicals contain various lists of public office holders. The historical and archaeological society journals of county, regional and national scope should be searched for such lists and for the biographical and genealogical notes regarding public office holders. The *Cork Historical and Archaeological Society* published in its *Journal* a long series of articles or notes regarding the Cork Members of Parliament. The Index of the *Journal*, 1892-1940, published in 1943, contains a list of the items under "M.P.s," followed by the personal name and the references. "A List of the Justices of the Peace in the Several Counties of Ireland in 1797-8," is contained in *The Gentlemans' and Citizens' Almanack*, compiled by John Watson Stewart, 1797-98. The names of the Justices of the Peace for the Counties Antrim, Cavan and Fermanagh, extracted from the above *Almanack*, are published in the *Ulster Journal of Archaeology*, 2nd Series, Vol. VII (1901), p. 138.

8. A few other miscellaneous works are: (a) *Parliamentary Memoirs of Fermanagh County and Borough from 1613 to 1835*. By the Earl of Belmore. Dublin, 1885. This contains biographical and genealogical records of the Members of Parliament from Fermanagh County and Borough. (b)

Members of Parliament, 1213-1874. 3 vols. London, 1878. This contains a return of the names and brief notes regarding each member of the Lower House of the Parliaments of England, Scotland and Ireland. (c) "The Chief Secretaries of Ireland, 1566-1921," by James L. J. Hughes, published in *Irish Historical Studies,* Vol. VIII, No. 29 (March 1952), pp. 59-72. (d) *The Viceroys of Ireland,* by C. O'Mahony. London, 1912. (e) A "List of Aldermen of Corporations in Ireland, 1689," in Ware's *Life of William III.*

The county and town histories are particularly rich in records concerning the families and members thereof who served in some capacity as public officials. *A History of the City and County of Cork,* by M. F. Cusack, Dublin, 1875, contains a list of the "High Sheriffs of the County Cork (alphabetically arranged), "with the years of office, from 1319 to 1873 (pp. 554-561) ; and the list of "Mayors of the City of Cork (alphabetically arranged)" with the years of office, from 1326-1873 (pp. 562-567). *The Ancient and Present State of the County and City of Cork,* by Charles Smith (edited by Robert Day and W. A. Coppinger), 2 vols., Cork, 1893, 1894, contains lists of Mayors, Sheriffs, Militia, Members of Parliament, etc., and much genealogical information in the way of notes about the families. *The History and Topography of the County of Clare,* by James Frost, Dublin, 1893, is a mine of genealogical information extracted from original sources including Inquisitions, Forfeitures, Depositions, Convert Rolls, etc., and also a list of the Justices of the Peace of County Clare, extracted from *Liber Munerum Hiberniae,* 1661-1862 (pp. 615-622) ; a list of Members of Parliament, 1583-1886 (pp. 623-624) ; a list of the Grand Juries of County Clare, 1732, 1784, 1799, and 1805 (pp. 624-625) ; a list of High Sheriffs of County Clare, 1577-1892 (pp. 625-629). *The History of the County Down,* by Alexander Knox, Dublin, 1875, contains much family history and also a list of the Members of Parliament for the County of Down, from 1585-1874 (pp. 79-85) ; a list of High Sheriffs, a few before 1600, and the complete list from 1600 to 1874, with the years of office and in most cases the personal addresses (pp. 91-98). *The Ancient and Present*

State of the County and City of Waterford, by Charles Smith, Dublin, 1746, contains "A List of the Mayors, Baillifs, and Sheriffs of the City of Waterford, from the year 1377, to the present year 1745, inclusive" (pp. 159-166).

The above lists indicate that the offices, held by members of the various prominent county families, were to some degree through influence, passed down from father to son or from generation to generation within certain families.   Charles Smith's *The Ancient and Present State of the County and City of Waterford,* 1746, pp. 159-166, names some of the families in which the offices of Mayor, Bailiff, and Sheriff, were held from the 14th century until *c.* 1650.   Most of them were of Anglo-Norman or English origin as their names indicate: The Mayors were William Lumbard, 1377-1378; William Chapman, 1379; William Madan, 1380; Philip Spell, 1381; Robert Sweetman, 1382-1383; William Lumbard, 1384; William Forstall, 1385; Robert Bruce, 1386; William Lumbard, 1387; William Poer, 1388/89 (descended from Robert le Poer, Marshal to Henry II, in the Anglo-Norman invasion) ; Milo Poer, 1390; William Spence, 1391; William Chapman, 1392; John Rocket, 1393; Milo Poer, 1394; William Forstall, 1395; William Attaman, 1396; William Lincolne, 1397; Andrew Archer, 1398; John Eyenas, 1399; later mayors represent the above and other families of Brushbone, Walsh, Attaman, Power, Roberts, Rockett, Wickin, White, Holland, Russel, Dyer, Strong, Rice, Gough, Core, Mulgan, Rope, Corr, Commerford, Dobbin, May, Butler, Devereux, Sherlock, Morgan, Lincoln, etc.

The names in the above lists of Charles Smith are marked (M) for Mayor; (B) for Bailiff; (S) for Sheriff.   Among the Waterford families which appear to have held office in their control through generations are, for example, the following two families of Lincolne (Lincoln), and White: *Lincoln or Lincolne:* 1397, William Lincolne (M) ; 1417, William Lincolne (M) ; 1426, William Lincolne (M) ; 1428, Robert Lincolne (M) ; 1449, William Lincolne (M) ; 1478, William Lincolne (M) ; Up to 1521 there were no Bailiffs or Sheriffs; 1523, William Lincoln (B) ; 1526, William Lincoln (B) ; 1530, William Lincoln (B) ; 1535, William Lincoln (M) ; 1543, Wil-

liam Lincoln (M) ; 1571, James Lincolne (B) ; 1589, William
Lincoln (B) ; 1611, William Lincoln (S) ; 1627, Barthol. Lin-
colne (S) ; 1627, William Lincolne (S) ; 1635, William Lin-
coln (S) ; 1635, Garret Lincoln (S) ; 1645, Garret Lincoln
(M) ; 1645, John Lincoln (S) ; after this the name does not
appear. *White:* 1437, John White (M) ; 1450, William White
(M) ; 1455, William White (M) ; 1459, William White (M) ;
1525, James White (B) ; 1542, James White (M) ; 1591,
Thomas White (S) ; 1595, James White (M) ; 1598, Thomas
White (M) ; 1608-09, Nicholas White (S) ; 1615, Nicholas
White (M) ; 1631, Pat. White (S) ; 1637, James White (M) ;
1640, Henry White (S) ; 1642, Thomas White (M) ; 1643, And.
White (S) ; 1644, Lau. White (S) ; No Whites after this.

PUBLIC RECORD OFFICE OF IRELAND, DUBLIN: MSS. records
of Public Office:

1. Lodge's MSS., from which *Liber Munerum Publicorum
Hiberniae* was compiled as noted above. (Brief Calendar of
Lodge's MSS in 55th *Report,* pp. 116-122.)

2. Justices of the Peace: MS. Catalogue of Warrants for
Justices of the Peace, Co. Cork, 1663-1829. (55th *Report,* p.
138.)

3. High Sheriffs: List of, in Frazer MSS., Lot no. 208,
"High Sheriffs for various Irish Counties, 1302-1862," copy
of MS. in the Office of Arms. (55th *Report,* pp. 11-12, 142,
145.)

4. Grand Jury Books (Assizes): Assize Indictments. 2
vols. 1735-1775, 1777-1797. (See original in Armagh Public
Library; Catalogue of MSS. p. 6.) (56th *Report,* p. 411.)

5. Justices of the Peace: List of Magistrates, Co. Clare, appointed 1737-1863. (Original MS. in Royal Irish Academy.)
(56th *Report,* p. 411.)

6. The Commonwealth Council Books. A List of the Original MSS. with their places of deposit. (55th *Report,* pp. 134-
135.) These include among eleven collections, (5) The Civil
List of Ireland, 1654 (Betham Transcript) (Ad. MS. British
Museum, 19833) ; (6) List of the Established Ministers in the
several precincts throughout Ireland (Trinity College Library,

MS. 1040 (2)); (7) List of all the Schoolmasters within this nation (with their salaries) (Trinity College Library, MS. 1040 (3)); (10) Volume of payments, 19 Aug. 1651, to 22 July 1652, and 19 Oct. 1653 to 17 Nov. 1656 (in Office of Arms, Dublin Castle (Genealogical Office)).

DONEGAL COUNTY LIBRARY: The Donegal Grand Jurors, Books of Presentments, 1768-1783; 1815-1856. The National Library of Ireland has a microfilm of the records. (See VOLUME II., p. 271, herewith.)

PUBLIC RECORD OFFICE OF NORTHERN IRELAND, BELFAST: MSS. Records of Public Office:

1. Carrickfergus Papers, 1659-1822. Oaths of Mayors; Rolls of Burgesses and Freemen. (1925 *Report*, p. 7.) The Rolls of the Members of Parliament, Mayors, Sheriffs, and Freemen, are printed in *The History and Antiquities of the County of the Town of Carrickfergus*, by Samuel McSkimin. Belfast, 1909: A List of Members of Parliament (pp. 432-435); Mayors and Sheriffs (pp. 409-430); Freemen (pp. 276-284), with biographical and genealogical notes on the Chichester, Davys, Dalway, Ellis, Lyndon, Clotworthy, and Dobbs families (pp. 469-487); and biographical and genealogical sketches on past sheriffs: Adair, M'Cance, Legg, Wilson, Bruce, Burleigh, M'Garell, Kirk, Allen, Fenton, Greer, Stewart, Reid, Bell, MacMurray, Lepper, M'Ferran, Porter, Kelly, Craig, Pirrie, Wilson, Johnstone (pp. 502-507); "Biography, Eminent Persons"; M'Skimin, Jackson, Allen, Adrian, Reid, Riddell, Stannus, Campbell (pp. 525-528).

2. Justices of the Peace for Co. Fermanagh, 1663-1844, and a list of High Sheriffs, Co. Armagh, 1664-1681, 1687, 1704 (1930 *Report*, p. 10).

3. List of Sheriffs of Ireland (Co. Londonderry excepted), 1600-1891 (1931 *Report* p. 12).

4. Grand Jury Lists, Co. Londonderry, 1614-1819 (1951-53 *Report*, p. 18).

* * * * *

RECORDS OF FREEMEN AND FREEHOLDERS: A Freeman was one who was admitted to the freedom of an incorporated city, town or borough, according to its own customs and by-laws. A city or town corporation was a local administrative body formed for purposes of government by municipal officers. From medieval times city or town corporations were created by Patent held of the Crown. The rights and privileges of a freeman varied in detail but generally included the privilege of voting at a parliamentary election, and also allowed him freedom from all tolls and dues. Usually no person was admitted a freeman of a city or borough by gift or by purchase; the only qualifications being birth, apprenticeship or servitude, or marriage. A person of distinction was sometimes admitted as an honorary freeman. Members of the city guilds were freemen.

A Freeholder was the owner of a freehold. A freehold was a tenure of real property by which an estate of inheritance, in fee simple or fee tail, or for life was held, or the estate itself; also a similar tenure of an office or dignity, as a Freeman. Freeholders' lists give information such as the name of the freeholder, the name of the townland or portion thereof held by him, and the name of the landlord. The identification of the freeholder with his townland of residence makes it possible to trace the history of the tenure of the townland by means of the records in the Registry of Deeds which are indexed by townland in the Land Index.

The North Munster Antiquarian Journal, Vol. IV, 1944-1945, Appendix I, pp. 103-130, contains an article regarding "The Freemen of Limerick," and a list of the freemen, 1746-1836. Three sample records read: (1) Ivers, Anthony, Gentn., son-in-law to the late Thos. Dunn of Mungret, 29/6/1795. (2) Baylie, Edward, son of Sexton Baylee, Burgess, 12/9/1757. (3) Baker, George, son of the late Richard Baker, Ballydavid, Co. Tipperary, 6/8/1817. This article offers the following information:

Admission to the freedom of Limerick was by right or by grace. By right the candidate was (1) proved to be the first born of a freeman; over 21 years, and presently a resident of the city, or (2) married to the daughter of a freeman; over 21 years, and a resident of the city, or (3) one who had completed a seven years apprenticeship to a freeman who was a tradesman or merchant of the city.   In the case of an applicant who claimed the right to become a freeman by birth, he was required to prove legitimacy, primogeniture, and his father's record of freedom of the city.   If the applicant claimed the right by marriage, he must prove his lawful marriage and that his wife was the legitimate child of a freeman.   If the applicant claimed the right to become a freeman following a completed seven years of apprenticeship, he must prove his service and that his master was a freeman.   In early times the mayor had the privilege of naming two freemen by grace, and after the Restoration of Charles II, occasionally according to new rules, a tradesman of long standing might be made a freeman upon the payment of a fee of sufficient size.   The honor of freedom of the city was sometimes conferred upon a distinguished person of another locality for specified reasons, whereupon his certificate was usually enclosed in a gold snuff box, engraved with the arms of the city.   The fees for admission varied somewhat in different towns and cities.   In Limerick a man paid £1 for stamp duty when admitted by right; and £3 if admitted by grace as well as 10/6 to the Mayor for affixing the seal of the Corporation, the same fee to the town clerk and a fee of 2/6 to his deputy.   A freeman automatically became a member of the general body of the city council, with a vote in all matters excepting election of officers.   He was entitled to vote in Parliamentary elections and was made free of tolls excepting upon special occasions of raising money for specific purposes.

NATIONAL LIBRARY OF IRELAND, DUBLIN: Lists of Freeholders and Freemen.

1. A Handlist of the voters of Maryborough Corporation, 1760.   This is taken from a notebook which forms part of the Drogheda MSS. in the National Library.   This contains a list of the freemen and burgesses of the borough which was from 1 March 1738/9 to 29 Sept. 1754; a rough alphabetical list kept up to date by additions and corrections to 1759; an amended list to 1760 (MS. 1726, Ainsworth Report, Vol. 4,

p. 995). List printed in *Irish Historical Review,* Vol. IX, No. 33 (March 1954), pp. 67-85.

2. An alphabetical list of the freemen of the City of Dublin, commencing Jan. 1774, and ending 15 Jan. 1824. (I.H.S., Mar. '40, p. 19.)

3. A printed list for Co. Limerick, 1776.

4. *Report on Fictitious Votes,* 3 vols., 1837 (furnished to the Irish House of Commons), contains complete lists of the freemen of the corporate towns in all counties; the owners of rent-charges on estates in every county; also the returns of owners of houses in the towns of Armagh, Bandon, Coleraine, Dungannon, Galway, Lisburn, Londonderry, Newry, and Youghal. Rights of freemen of the various trade guilds are set out, especially in cases of Dublin citizens with many extracts of records showing the rights by descent from father to son, by marriage, etc.

5. Microfilms: Freeholders Book of Co. Armagh, 18th century; and Register of Freeholders, Co. Donegal, 1767-1768 (see VOLUME II, pp. 270-271, herewith).

6. Various lists of Freemen printed in historical and archaeological society journals, etc. Some examples are: (a) "Honorary Freemen of Cork since 1690," by M. V. Conlon, in *Journal of the Cork Historical and Archaeological Society,* Vol. 51, pp. 74-86. (b) "Studies in Waterford History, V." by S. Pender. Gives lists of freemen, Council members, masters and wardens of guilds of Waterford Corporation, 1656-1665; bonds of apprentices from 1664-1677, and a list of guild officers and freemen for 1664-1677. Information taken from Vol. II of the old Council Books of the Corporation of Waterford. Published in *Journal of the Cork Historical and Archaeological Society,* Vol. 53, No. 177 (Jan.-June, 1948), pp. 39-59. (c) "Alphabetical List of the Free Burgesses of New Ross, Co. Wexford, from 1658 to 30th Sept. 1839" (including genealogical notes), by Col. P. D. Vigors, *ed.,* published in the *Journal of the Royal Society of Antiquaries,* Vol. XXI, pp. 298-309.

7. Various County and Town histories contain lists of

freemen. *The Town Book of the Corporation of Belfast, 1613 1816,* by R. M. Young, ed., Belfast, 1892, contains the Roll of Freemen, 1635-1796 (pp. 246-300).

GENEALOGICAL OFFICE, DUBLIN CASTLE: Lists of Freeholders. This Office has copies of Freeholders Lists for the following counties: Armagh, 1753; Donegal, 1761-'75; Fermanagh, 1788; Limerick, 1776; Longford, 1830-'35; Meath, *c.* 1790; Queen's Co., 1758-'75; Tipperary, 1776; Westmeath, 1761. The list for Co. Fermanagh is contained in the Poll Book of 1788 which gives particulars of the abodes and freeholds of some 3,500 county electors (voters) who are grouped according to the initial letter of their surnames.

ROYAL IRISH ACADEMY, DUBLIN: This library has a printed list of freeholders for County Tipperary, 1776.

PUBLIC RECORD OFFICE OF IRELAND, DUBLIN: Lists of Freemen and Freeholders:

1. Transcript of Minute Book. Admission of Freemen, Guild of Weavers, Dublin, 1774-1807 (Abstracts, No. 1429, Gertrude Thrift Coll.) (56th *Report,* p. 54). See also abstracts and extracts of miscellaneous Guild Records, Freemen's Rolls in this same collection (56th *Report,* p. 55).

2. T. U. Sadleir MSS. containing List of Freeholders, Co. Meath, 1781, copied from MS. in Headfort collection (M1364) (58th *Report,* p. 25).

3. "The names of gentlemen and freeholders of the King's County hereafter named, sworn before the Lord Deputy the third of December, 1576 . . ." (58th *Report,* p. 27).

PUBLIC RECORD OFFICE OF NORTHERN IRELAND, BELFAST: Lists of Freemen and Freeholders:

1. Freeholders List of the Scottish in Ulster, *c.* 1613. Loaned to this Office for copying, by the Presbyterian Historical Society, Belfast (1929 *Report,* p. 11).

2. Freeholders Registers: Co. Down (principal names:— Agnew, Andrews, McCance, McCandless, Mahaffy, Morrow, Murray, Wallace, Waterson, Watson), 1746-1795. For Londonderry (principal names:—Andrew, Cairns, Fleming, Hil-

ton, Morrow, Murray, Torrens), 1761-1829 (1925 *Report,* p. 8).

3. Freeholders List (Drumcree Parish) 1747-1800, Co. Louth (1926 *Report,* p. 9).

4. Freemens Rolls and Burgess' Rolls, Carrickfergus, 1659-1822 (1925 *Report,* p. 7).

5. Marquis of Downshire, Hillsborough, Co. Down, Return of Freeholders in Barony of Lecale, 1790 (1928 *Report,* p. 10).

6. Freeholders List, District of Portadown, 1747-1802 (1931 *Report,* p. 13).

7. Roll of Burgesses and Freemen of Dungannon Corporation, Co. Tyrone, 1832 (1933 *Report,* p. 37).

8. Freeholders List, Co. Fermanagh, 1747-1768 (1946-47 *Report,* p. 12).

GUILD RECORDS: Some printed records of various guilds are listed in VOLUME II, pp. 249-252, herewith. Some other records are noted as follows: *The Ancient Guilds of Dublin,* by Edward Evans, is in the Public Record Office of Ireland, Dublin (55th *Report,* p. 14). The National Library of Ireland has the *Calendar of Ancient Records of Dublin in the possession of the Municipal Corporation of that City.* 19 vols. *Ed.* by John T. Gilbert, *et al.* Dublin, 1889-1944. These volumes include miscellaneous records of members of the various guilds. The Almanacks and Directories contain lists of officers of the guilds of Dublin, etc.

PUBLIC RECORD OFFICE OF IRELAND, DUBLIN:

1. Notes on the Guild of St. Loy (2 vols. and index), presented (55th *Report,* p. 137).

2. Copies of Charters and extracts from by-laws, registers, etc., of trade guilds, Dublin, 1296-1824 (W. Monck Mason) (Egerton MS. 1765, Cat. Add. MSS., British Museum) (55th *Report,* p. 137).

3. See also the Thrift Abstracts (55th *Report,* p. 137).

4. Two rolls of aldermen, sheriffs and guildsmen in Dublin Corporation, 1720, 1721. M1370, 1371. (58th *Report,* p. 47.)

PUBLIC RECORD OFFICE OF NORTHERN IRELAND, BELFAST: Indentures, Apprenticeship documents, Bonds, Leases, etc., 1694-1865, some 358 documents from the Downpatrick Estate Office (1933 *Report*, p. **10**).

UNIVERSITY LIBRARY, CORK: Deposited in the vault of the Library is a volume of MS. transcribed "Apprentice Indentures Enrolling Book," commencing 17 Jan. 1756, ending 4 Dec. 1801, transcribed by Richard Caulfield.

SCHOOL REGISTERS: Some printed Registers, etc., are listed in VOLUME II, pp. 231-232, herewith.   References to school records and lists of pupils in some cases are found in county and town histories. *The History of Belfast*, by D. J. Owen, Belfast, 1921, contains among its miscellaneous biographies, etc. (pp. 353-409), a few notes on the "Old School in Church Lane" (p. 379), with names of the early schoolmasters, Mr. Gordon in 1685, Robert Willis pre 1739, the Rev. Nicholas Garnet in 1752, and reference to an article by "Belfastiensis" (Isaac W. Ward) on the subject of "The Old Belfast Latin or Classical School and some of its Pupils," which appeared in the *Northern Whig* of 26 October 1905.

Articles of the older schools with lists of the masters are found in various Historical and Archaeological Society Journals.   "The City of Dublin Free School (*c.* 1477-1712)" by Michael Quane, is published in *The Journal of the Royal Society of Antiquaries*, Vol. XC, Part II (1960), pp. 161-189. This contains names, dates, and notes on various Masters of the school.

The King's Inns Admission Papers (1607-1867), edited by Thomas U. Sadleir, *c.* 1956, presents a collection of records relating to barristers, deposited in the King's Inns Library. During the 17th century the records of students lack particulars as to parentage.   However, up to 1880, all Irish law students were required to complete their education at one of the English Inns of Court in London; at the Inner Temple, the Middle Temple, Gray's Inn, or Lincoln's Inn.   Gray's Inn was attended by the majority and its Admission Registers *Gray's Inn, 1521-1889*, edited by Joseph Foster, 1889, provides the name, parentage, and residence of the students with date of entry. *Lincoln's Inn, 1420-1893,* 2 vols., 1896, contains names of many Irish law students. The Register of the *Inner Temple, 1547-1660, ed.* 1877, contains the same information regarding numerous Irish law students. The College of Arms, London, has complete transcripts of all the Inner and the Middle Temple Registers. From about 1720 the *King's Inns Admission Papers,* Dublin, usually show the parentage. During the 19th century further information is added such as the place of preparatory education, maiden name of mother.

Thom's Irish Almanac and Official Directory, 1844 onward, is full of lists of names of barristers with places of residence; lists of the officers and faculty of various colleges, schools (professional and otherwise), and miscellaneous information thereof.

PUBLIC RECORD OFFICE OF IRELAND, DUBLIN: This Office has among the Lodge MSS., his "An Alphabetical List of the Members of the Society of the King's Inns, Dublin, from ... 1607", containing various alphabetical lists of the members with date of admission, sometimes date of death and other particulars (1607-1771). (55th *Report,* p. 120). This Office has also a "Chronological list of Irish Students admitted to the Inner Temple, London, 1547-1657 (58th *Report,* p. 22). Among the Commonwealth Council Books is a "List of all the Schoolmasters within this nation (with their salaries)." (Ms. 1040 (3), Trinity College Library) (55th *Report,* p. 134).

PUBLIC RECORD OFFICE OF NORTHERN IRELAND, BELFAST: The 1926 Report of the Deputy Keeper of the Records (pp. 5-6), contains the following announcement concerning the deposit of School Registers: "The department [this office] was approached by the Ministry of Education with a view to the deposit in its custody of Registers of Public Elementary Schools. The reply was returned that, generally speaking, School Registers would not be acceptable as Public Records; but that, in view of the absence of any system of public registration of births in Ireland prior to 1864, the destruction of the Census Returns, which might have been used for proof of age for persons born before that date, and the frequent absence or incompleteness of Church Baptismal Registers, an exception might be made in the case of School Registers which were in use before 1880, since these would often show the ages of children born before the registration of births became compulsory. The Minister of Education accordingly addressed a circular to managers and principal teachers, informing them that it would sanction the disposal by deposit in this department of registers covering the period mentioned, and suggested that such deposit should be made. About forty-three registers have, so far, been received. Of these a detailed list is given in paragraph 12 below. There has been considerable resort to these registers, and there is reason to believe that age has been satisfactorily proved by this means when it could not otherwise have been determined." The information is further provided that there are some 2000 Primary Schools in Northern Ireland. From this date on, each *Report of the Deputy Keeper* contains, under "Receipts from the Ministry of Education," a list of the Primary Public School Registers received during the period covered by the *Report*. In the course of time, various private School Registers were also received. The lists are far too lengthy to print herein. A current list of the Registers in this Office is kept up to date. In addition, a Name Index of Students provides for each individual, the name of School, Town or County; Name of Register or Roll Book; sex of pupils; inclusive years of Register; age of pupil; religion; occupation of parents and place where living; date of entrance; number of days present; scholastic rating. The earliest Registers of Public Schools began c. 1829 but most are dated from c. 1860. The private school registers began earlier in many cases.

CHAPTER XX

NEWSPAPERS

The value of local newspapers to the historian and genealogist has long been recognized. The earliest 18th century newspapers were for the most part issued weekly. As time went on they were published semi-weekly or tri-weekly. Later several of the newspapers of the larger cities appeared daily. In addition, periodical magazines serving various purposes were published monthly or less frequently.

Newspapers portrayed the political, economic and ecclesiastical news of the day, usually highly flavored by the beliefs and viewpoints of the editors or owners. Thus several newspapers giving evidence of prejudice contrary to the interests of the Government were shortly discontinued. In some cases the editors were imprisoned or saw fit to leave the country.

Newspapers and various periodicals contain information regarding legal and court cases, military and other Government appointments to public office, social news regarding the more or less important families, as well as the birth, marriage and death notices, for the cities and towns or areas represented. They offer a wealth of miscellaneous news items ranging from criminal cases and reported accidents or unusual events, to biographies and family history. Many newspapers and periodical magazines ran an extended series of genealogical articles regarding county families. Those of seaport cities gave some place to lists of the people who departed from time to time by ship for America and other countries. A few examples of material and its use illustrate the value of these sources:

A History of the City of Dublin, by John T. Gilbert, Dublin, 1854 (3 vols.), contains a section at the rear of each volume, devoted to "Authorities" or references, for one chapter after another. Gilbert employed a wide range of printed authorities and MSS. materials from which he compiled his work which

sets forth the history of the residents of the city of Dublin,
street by street. His background of experience and knowledge
of Public Records made his choice of materials significant.
Among his "Authorities" were references to many newspapers
noted below in order as they appear in the first few chapters:
Sleater's *Dublin Chronicle* (1787, 1788); *Dublin Gazette*
(1706, 1707, 1710, 1729, 1732, 1738, 1754, 1755, 1756); *Dublin
Penny Journal* (1832); *Freeman's Journal* (1763-1776); *Dublin
Weekly Journal* (1725, 1726, 1728, 1730); Contemporary
Broadsides; Faulkner's *Dublin Journal* (1741, 1742, 1748,
1753, 1755, 1762, 1768); *Pocket Companion for Freemasons*
(1751); *Hibernian Magazine* (1771, 1775, 1778-1780, 1781-
1783, 1785, 1788, 1791); *Dublin News Letter* (1740); *Dublin
Intelligence* (1691-1692, 1695, 1709, 1729); *Pue's Occurrences* (1731); *Gentleman's Magazine* (1784, 1788); *London
Gazette* (1677, 1691, 1692, 1703); *Universal Advertiser*
(1754); *Dublin Mercury* (1706); *Volunteer Evening Post*
(1784); *Impartial News Letter* (1727); *Walsh's Dublin Post-
Boy* (1729); *Whalley's News Letter* (1714); *The Flying Post*
(1706).

Some 13,275 items are contained in *Irish Marriages, an Index to the Marriages in Walker's Hibernian Magazine, 1771
to 1812*, with Appendix from the Notes of Sir Arthur Vicars,
of the Births, Marriages, and Deaths in the *Anthologia
Hibernica*, 1793 and 1794. By Henry Farrar. Privately
printed for Subscribers, 1897, 2 vols.

The County of Londonderry in Three Centuries, with
Notices of the Ironmongers Estate. By J. W. Kernohan. Belfast, 1921. Reprint from *Coleraine Chronicle*.

The Story of St. Patrick's Church, Coleraine. Its History,
Heraldry, Sculptured Stones, Stained Glass, Old Families and
Alliances, Architecture and Traditions. By Sam Henry. Reprinted from the articles which appeared in the columns of
the *Coleraine Chronicle*.

*"Old Ballymena, a History of Ballymena during the 1798
Rebellion."* In the *Ballymena Observer*, 1857, under the title,
"Walks about Ballymena."

Lists of local emigrants printed in local newspapers

throughout Ireland from time to time, particularly in seaport towns. Examples: *Belfast News Letter:* Sailing notices in issues of 10 September 1754; 8 October 1754; 27 May 1755; 21 October 1755; 26 September 1755, all cover the sailings of Arthur Dobbs' colonists to North Carolina. The *Nation,* issue of 8 December 1850, has March 1850 Record of Sailings of Catholics from Ireland via Liverpool.

A short Bibliography of Sources of Newspapers and Periodicals is set forth in VOLUME II, pp. 247-248, herewith. To this should be added: *Poole's Index to Periodical Literature, to January 1887.* By William F. Poole and William I. Fletcher. 2 vols. Boston, 1882. London, 1888. (2nd Sup., 1st Jan. 1887, to 1st Jan. 1892, by W. I. Fletcher.) *A Handlist of Irish Newspapers,* by R. L. Munther, 1961 (Cambridge University Press, Cambridge, England, for the Cambridge Biographical Society).

*   *   *   *   *

The existing issues of certain important newspapers and periodicals and their places of deposit are listed below as follows:

BELFAST NEWSPAPERS AND PERIODICALS:

All of the following collections are deposited in the Linen Hall Library, Donegall Square, Belfast. (Library Catalogue 1917.)

1. *Belfast Commercial Chronicle,* Feb. 13, 1805 to Dec. 28, 1853, excepting issues for 1811, 1815, 1817-1832, 1835, 1837-1840, 1849.

2. *Belfast Co-operative Advocate.* Nos. 1-2. Belfast, 1830.

3. *Belfast Evening Post.* Nos. 300-315. June 12th to July 31st, 1786, excepting No. 303. See *Belfast Mercury.*

4. *Belfast Evening Post,* "Letters by a Farmer," originally published in 1787.

5. *Belfast Magazine and Literary Journal.* Belfast, 1825.

6. *Belfast Mercury or Freeman's Chronicle.* Began publication, June 1783. On June 12, 1786, the name was changed

to the *Belfast Evening Post,* issued on Monday and Thursday. It ran for 60 numbers.

7. *Belfast Mercury* (2nd Publication), 1851-1858.   Nine volumes.

8. *Belfast Monthly* Magazine. Belfast, 1808-1814.   13 vols. (wants vol. 12).

9. *Belfast Newsletter.* Collection begins with Vol. 2. No. 152, dated Feb. 16th, 1738-1915.   Wants 1737, 1740-1745, 1748, 1751, Mar.-Aug., 1755, Jan.-Sept., 1836.   The years 1738, 1746, 1752, 1753, are represented by only a few numbers.

10. *Belfast Penny Journal.* Vols. 1-2.   May, 1845, to July, 1846.

11. *Belfast Penny Punch.*   May, 1847 to July, 1848.

12. *Belfast Temperance Herald.*   June, 1846.

13. *The Bible Christian,* 1830-1835 (wants 1831, 1834). Second Series, Vols. 1-2.   1836-1837.   (Presbyterian.)

14. *Bolg an Tsolair; or, Gaelic Magazine.*   Belfast, No. 1, 1795.

15. *The Christian Freeman.* Vols. 1-3.   Belfast, 1832-1835. (Presbyterian.)

16. *The Covenanter.*   Vols.   1-3.   1830-1832.   (Presbyterian.)

17. *The Gleaner: or, Farmer's and Tradesman's Weekly Miscellany.*   No. 10.   Belfast, 1821.

18. *The Guardian and Constitutional Advocate.*   Belfast, 1829.

19. *The Irishman:* a weekly newspaper.   1819-1822.

20. *Irish Presbyterian.*   Vols. 1-6.   1853-1858.   (Presbyterian.)

21. *Literary Museum; or, Weekly Magazine.*   Vol. 1.   Nos. 2-5.   1793.

22. *The Magic Lanthorn.*   Vol. 1. Nos. 6-7.   Vol. 2. No. 12. 1815-1816.

23. *Microscope, The; or, Minute Observer.*   Vol. 2. 1800.

24. *Mirror, The: a weekly miscellany.*   Belfast, 1823.

25. *New Belfast Magazine.* Conducted by the Students of the Royal Academical Institution. Session 1833-1834.

26. *Northern Herald.* Sept. 28th and Oct. 12th, 1833.

27. *Northern Magazine.* March, 1852, to Feb., 1853.

28. *Northern Star.* Belfast 1792-1797. Established to advocate the cause of the United Irishmen. Suppressed in 1797.

29. *Northern Whig.* Belfast, 1824-1915. Wants 1851-1858; 1862-1871.

30. *Orthodox Presbyterian:* (a monthly magazine). Vols. 1-8. 1829-1837. New Series, Vols. 1-3. 1838-1840.

31. *Presbyterian Magazine.* Belfast, 1835.

32. *Quizzing Glass, The.* Sept. 1834 to Aug. 1835.

33. *Rushlight, The.* A weekly literary publication. Vol. I. Nos. 1-41. 1824-1825.

34. *Temperance Advocate.* Belfast, May, 1833.

35. *Ulster Magazine.* Jan. 1830. Vol. I, No. 1.

36. *Ulster Miscellany, The.* Belfast, 1873.

37. *Ulster Register:* a political and literary magazine, 1816-1818. Vols. 1-4. Belfast.

38. *Ulster Repository.* Vol. 1. n.d. [1785]

39. *Ulster Times.* 1841-1842. Belfast.

CORK NEWSPAPERS AND PERIODICALS:

The following are referred to in the *Journal of the Cork Historical and Archaeological Society* (Vol. 1 A, pp. 83-84, by C. G. Doran; Vol. 3 (1897), pp. 136-138, by James Buckley; Vol. 9, pp. 267-268, by E. R. McC. Dix; Vol. 11, pp. 93-95, by Richard Caulfield). Various issues have been collected by the Cork libraries, the British Museum, the National Library of Ireland, and Trinity College Library, Dublin.

1. *Irish Monthly Mercury*, No. 1, 1649. A London reprint of issue No. 1 (1649), is in the British Museum (Cat. E. 592 (5)).

2. *The Freeholder*, began publication in 1716. A small single quarto sheet.

3. *The Cork Newsletter*, began *c.* 1716; reached No. 828 in 1723 and appeared until 1725. Small folio. Double columns.

4. *The Medley*, began publication in 1738. Two sheets, small folio, about every eight days.

5. *The Serio-Jocular Medley*. Printed in 1738.

6. *Corke Journal* (George Swiney's), 1754.

7. *The Cork Evening Post*, 1754-1796. The National Library of Ireland has Nov. 1757 to Oct. 1758; 1773, Vol. XVIII, wants 9 Nos. (Jan. 4, 7, 18; June 4; Sept. 18; Dec. 17, 21, 25, 29). Trinity College Library has 1786-1799.

8. *The Corke Chronicle, or Universal Register.* 1764.

9. *The Hibernian Journal.* Trinity College Library has 1760 to 1771 (?).

10. *The Corke Chronicle or Free Intelligencer.* 1764-1768.

11. *The Corke Chronicle or True Intelligence.* Trinity College Library has 1772, Jan. 2nd (Vol. IX, No. 1).

12. *Hibernian Chronicle*, 1769-1802. The National Library of Ireland purchased all issues excepting 1771. The Baptisms, Marriages and Deaths recorded in this newspaper have been indexed. The Public Record Office of Northern Ireland has obtained a copy of the Index (1936 *Report*, p. 5; 1938-45 *Report*). Trinity College Library has issues for 1779-1787, and scattered numbers for the years 1790-1799.

13. *The Cork General Advertiser.* The National Library has the issue for Dec. 15, 1777 (Vol. II, No. 74).

14. *The Volunteer Journal or Weekly Advertiser.* Trinity College Library has issues for 1782-1784; and Jan. 2, 1786 (Vol. IV, No. 70).

15. *The Cork Gazette and General Advertiser, 1789-1797.* The National Library has issues, 13 Feb. to 11 Dec. 1793 (Vols. IV and V), and 9 Jan. to Dec. 1796 (Vol. VIII). Trinity College Library has issue, 11 April 1792 (No. 185).

16. *The New Cork Evening Post.* Trinity College Library has issue of Aug. 17, 1797 (No. 67, Vol. VII).

17. *The Cork Herald or Munster Advertiser.* The National Library has eight numbers, Nov. 3, 1798 to Dec. 5, 1798.

Trinity College Library has bi-weekly, Vol. 1, April, 1798 (No. 23), and Aug., 1798 (No. 58).

18. *The Cork Advertiser and Commercial Register.* The National Library has issues for 1799 (Jan. 29th, 31st; Feb. 2nd to July 18th). Trinity College Library has an issue for July, 1799 (No. 75).

DUBLIN NEWSPAPERS AND PERIODICALS:

Irish Bibliography. Tables Relating to some Dublin Newspapers of the 18th Century, by E. R. McC. Dix, Dublin, 1910, contains information regarding eight newspapers, as to extant issues and places of deposit. The repositories are the National Library of Ireland, the Chief Secretary's Library in Dublin Castle, the Royal Irish Academy, the Library of Trinity College, the Dublin Municipal Library, Marsh's Library, the Public Library on Lower Kevin Street, Dublin. Each of these libraries contains partial collections but between them there are fairly complete sets of each newspaper; *The Dublin Gazette,* 1706-1800; *The Dublin Journal (Faulkner's)* 1727/28-1800; *The Dublin Weekly Journal* (Carson), 1725-1737; *Pue's Occurrences,* 1717-1772/73; *Dublin News Letter* (Robert Reilly), 1737-1743; *Sleater's Public Gazetter,* 1758/59-1771/74; *The Public Register or Freeman's Journal,* 1763/64-1800; *Saunders' Dublin News Letter,* 1767-1800.

The Public Register; or, Freeman's Journal, 1763-1924, strongly pro-Government (*Irish Historical Studies,* Sept. 1938, p. 169), has been regarded by the National Library of Ireland as a valuable source for students of history and genealogy, and therefore a name and subject index has been in the course of work since about 1955. This is being filmed on micro-cards. The Royal Irish Academy has several numbers of the *Public Monitor* 1772-1773, bound with the first volume of its numbers of the *Freeman's Journal.* Both of these collections of newspapers contain a wealth of genealogical information including notices of births, marriages and deaths.

Various earlier Dublin newspapers in the libraries of Dublin to which John T. Gilbert had access and which he used as sources for some records in his *History of the City of Dublin,* 3 vols., have been mentioned above. An important periodical was the *Gentleman's Magazine*, 1731-1868. "Dr. Caulfield's Contributions to the Gentleman's Magazine," published in the *Journal of the Cork Historical and Archaeological Society* (Vol. IX, pp. 189-198; 268-274; Vol. X, pp. 48-56), calls attention to the work of great genealogists which appeared in this periodical and (*ibid.*, p. 189) makes the statement: "Down to the year 1868 the 'Gentleman's Magazine' was almost the only publication in the United Kingdom devoted to history, biography, genealogy, and antiquities, accessible to the general public, exclusive of the comparatively few 'Journals or Transactions' issued by such archaeological societies as were then in existence." This *Gentleman's Magazine* was indexed from 1731 to 1818, by John Nichols. *The Gentleman's Magazine Library* is a classified collection of the chief contents of the *Gentleman's Magazine* from 1731 to 1868, edited by G. L. Gomme (11 vols.). The Linen Hall Library, Belfast, has the above publication; a good collection of *Walker's Hibernian Magazine*, 1771-1812, and other scattered numbers of some Dublin newspapers, listed in its 1917 *Catalogue of the Books in the Irish Section*, pp. 75-76.

The British Museum, London, and the Dublin libraries have scattered collections of newspapers dating back to 1731, published in the larger cities and towns. Some of these are as follows:

KILKENNY:

The Kilkenny Journal, began 1791. It and the *Kilkenny Moderator* were listed in *Slater's Directory*, 1846, as active newspapers. *Finn's Leinster Journal*, published in Kilkenny, 1766 (?), is mentioned in *Irish Historical Studies*, September, 1938, p. 169.

LIMERICK:

Information regarding the Limerick newspapers is contained in *Limerick, its History and Antiquities*, by Maurice Lenihan, Dublin, 1866 (pp. 360, 414, 481, 487, 494, 752), as follows: *The Munster Journal* was said to be the oldest Journal in the Province of Munster. It was succeeded in about 1787 by the *Limerick Journal*. This was followed by the

Limerick Chronicle. After 1833, the *Limerick Evening Post* and the *Clare Sentinel* and later *The Star* were published in the same Mansion House in George Street. The *Limerick Herald* was being published in 1821. *The Limerick Star and Evening Post* began publication on 4th Feb. 1834. *The Limerick Reporter* began publication, July 12, 1839. *The Munster Telegraph,* started in 1819, continued for a short period. *The Munster Journal* began in 1832. *The Limerick Guardian* was published for a short time in 1833. Others were, *The Limerick Standard,* in 1840/41; *The Limerick and Clare Examiner* in 1845; *The Limerick Observer,* in 1856; *The Limerick Herald,* in 1853; *The Munster News,* established in 1852, and the *Limerick Southern Chronicle,* established in 1863.

LONDONDERRY:

A List of Books, Pamphlets, Newspapers, etc., printed in Londonderry, prior to 1801, by E. R. McC. Dix, is in the Linen Hall Library, Belfast.

Mr. T. MacCallum Walker, Librarian of Magee University College Library, Londonderry, in 1955 (presently Deputy Librarian, The University Library, Glasgow, Scotland), offered the following information regarding Londonderry newspapers:

1. Londonderry newspapers in Magee University College Library:

(a) *The London-Derry Journal.* Published from June 3, 1772 to the present time. After the first year, the run is broken. The Library is proposing to obtain microfilms of the missing issues from volumes in the British Museum and from other collections, wherever they can be found.

(b) *The Londonderry Sentinel.* Published from 1829 to the present time. At first the newspaper was a weekly; then issued three times a week.

(c) *The Londonderry Standard.* Published from 1836 to the present time.

2. Londonderry newspapers in the British Museum:

(a) *The London-Derry Journal.* Scattered numbers from various years. The run is broken.

(b) *The Londonderry Chronicle.* No. 1, etc., 18 Feb. to 7 Oct. 1829.

(c) *The Londonderry Guardian.* No. 1, etc., 30 Sept. 1857 to 28 Sept. 1871; then discontinued.

(d) *The Londonderry Journal.* No. 3814, etc., 15 Feb. 1825 to 19 March 1880. Continued as the *Derry Journal,* 19 March 1880, to date.

(e) *The Londonderry Sentinel.* No. 1, etc., 19 Sept. 1829, to date.

(f) *The Londonderry Standard.* No. 1, etc., 30 Nov. 1836 to 21 May 1888; continued as *The Derry Standard,* 23 May 1888, to date.

NEWRY:

The following newspapers of Newry, County Down, are in the Linen Hall Library, Belfast. (1) *The Newry Magazine: or, Literary and Political Register,* 1815-1818 (Vols. 1-4). Ends with July-Aug., 1818. (2) The *Newry Examiner and Louth Advertiser.* Vol. 1, March 17, 1830-July 2, 1831. This was continued through 1846 (see Slater's Directory).

TRALEE:

Newspapers for County Kerry were printed in Tralee, County Kerry. *County Kerry Past and Present* (A Handbook to the Local and Family History of the County), by Jeremiah King, Dublin, 1931, contains a list (p. 257) of the "Newspapers in the British Museum Library, printed in Tralee:-Chute's Western Herald 1812-35; Kerry Evening Post 1813-1917; Tralee Mercury 1829-39; Kerry Examiner 1840-56; Tralee Chronicle 1843-81; Raymond's Kerry Herald 1856; Kerry Star 1861-63; Weekly Chronicle 1873; Kerry Sentinel 1878-1917; Kerry Independent 1880-84; Kerry Weekly Reporter 1883-1925; Kerry News 1894-1917; Munster Life 1897; Killarney Echo 1899-1925." "Kerry People No. 1121 in 1925; The Post 1774; Journal 1782; Chronicle 1783; Mercury 1793; Herald 1793; Dispatch 1807, were printed in Tralee, but copies were not deposited in the British Museum before 1812; and that library has the best collection of Kerry newspapers.

Most of the local collections in Kerry have been destroyed by fire."

The Royal Irish Academy has nine volumes of clippings of a genealogical nature regarding County Kerry families, taken from the *Kerry Evening Post* (1774-1917). These genealogical articles appeared year after year from 1850 to 1917, and are of great value in tracing County Kerry families.

* * * * *

The *Ulster Journal of Archaeology* (2nd Series, Vols. VII, IX-XV) contains a bibliography of newspapers and periodicals published in Ulster towns of Armagh, Ballymena, Ballymoney, Carrickfergus, Coleraine, Downpatrick, Larne, Londonderry, Lurgan, Newry, Omagh, and Strabane.

The *Journal of the Waterford and South East of Ireland Archaeological Society,* 1906, contains a list of books, newspapers and periodicals published in Waterford, Carlow, Cashel, Clonmel and some other Munster towns.

The *Journal of the Cork Historical and Archaeological Society,* Vol. X, pp. 122-125, calls attention to the *Clare Journal* which was published in Ennis, Co. Clare, beginning in 1778. One issue, 15 Feb. 1779 (Vol. II, No. 13), is bound with other miscellaneous newspapers in the Newspaper Room of Trinity College Library, Dublin. Other Ennis, Co. Clare newspapers are the *Ennis Chronicle,* Vol. 11 (1794), containing 104 numbers now deposited in the National Library of Ireland, Dublin.

A *Catalogue of the Bradshaw Collection of Irish Books in the University Library Cambridge;* London, 1916 (3 vols.), contains an extensive indexed list of the periodicals and newspapers in the collection, under the cities and towns (Vol. III, pp. 1599-1602), referring to the annotated Bibliography in Vol. II, which contains the listings of periodicals and newspapers in the Bradshaw Collection, for Dublin and each of 92 provincial towns. Miscellaneous numbers of many newspapers regarding these towns are in this library.

I. *Slater's National Commercial Directory of Ireland,* London, 1846, contains a list of the newspapers published at that time in various cities and towns, with the names of the editors, the addresses, and the days of the week of each issue; the cities and towns being as follows: Belfast, Cork, Dublin, Kilkenny, Waterford, grouped as cities; and Armagh, Athlone, Ballina, Ballyshannon, Boyle, Carlow, Castlebar, Clones, Clonmel, Coleraine, Downpatrick, Drogheda, Dundalk, Ennis, Enniskillen, Galway, Limerick, Londonderry, Longford, Monaghan, Mullingar, Naas, Nenagh, Newry, Omagh, Parsonstown, Roscommon, Sligo, Tralee, Tuam, Waterford, Wexford.

CHAPTER XXI

IMMIGRATION, NATURALIZATION, EMIGRATION RECORDS

Unfortunately, there are no complete series of Immigration, Naturalization, or Emigration records in Ireland. Much has been written by historians, based upon State Papers, Court Records, Census Records and other sources to indicate the amount of immigration, naturalization, and emigration which occurred from time to time, and the particulars regarding many families.

The extensive series of records containing evidence of immigration; the arrival and settlement of the English in all parts of Ireland, the Scots in Ulster, the Huguenots in their various colonies, and the German Palatines in a few settlements, are set forth in previous chapters in PART THREE herein. CHAPTERS III-IX have described the source materials of the respective Church denominations. These contain many miscellaneous records relating to the arrival of individuals in Ireland. Court Records and State Papers described in CHAPTER XI include the Patent Rolls, Fiants, Inquisitions, Pipe Rolls and other Chancery and Exchequer Court Records which contribute evidence of the time and place of settlement of thousands of people who came to Ireland for permanent residence. These records are supplemented by the Plantation and Settlement Records discussed in CHAPTER XIII.

Naturalization records are found in the great collection of Lodge MSS. in the Public Record Office of Ireland, Dublin. These include Lodge's extracts from the Patent Rolls concerning "Denizations of the Irish, Scots and other Foreigners (Richard II - George I). Lists of persons to whom grants of English Livery [Liberty and protection by English Law] or Denization were made." At the end of the entries for the year 1607 is Lodge's note: "N.B.—From this time great numbers of the Scots Nation were naturalized and made free Denizons, many of whom were Mechanicks, Farmers, etc., but I have only mentioned such as were of some note." (55th *Report*, p. 119.) The Lodge MSS. in the Public Record Office also include "A List of Protestants who, in pursuance of an Act of Parliament 13 Charles II, for encouraging Protestant strangers and others to inhabit and plant ye kingdom of Ireland, took Oaths of Allegiance and Supremacy whereby they became liege, free and natural subjects of Ireland in every respect, condition and degree to all Intents, Constructions and Purposes as if born in Ireland and were free to exercise their calling in any City or Corporation of this Kingdom according to the tenor and effect of said Act." This list gives the occupation of the person, place of nativity, time of taking of the Oath (1662-1737/8) and reference in each case to inrolment (Patent Rolls, 14 Charles II - George II). (55th *Report*, p. 117.) Some published Naturalization Records (Ireland) are listed in VOLUME II, p. 235, herewith. A collection of Ulster Denization and Naturalization records was compiled by the Rev. David Stewart, D.D., and published in pamphlets by the Presbyterian Historical Society, Belfast. The nature of these records is described on pp. 557-558, herewith.

As a supplement to the meager Irish emigration records which will be discussed below, there are numerous original sources in the United States giving evidence of Irish immigration. These include the many series of Ships Manifests containing passenger lists of those landing at various ports of entry, also the Census, Naturalization, and Pension records. In addition there are the County Court records (Wills, Deeds, etc.) which furnish information concerning first generation immigrants in America, often with details or some clue as to their Irish origin. Some Irish emigration records are also noted. All are set forth in this VOLUME I, pp. 3-48, containing sources for "Preliminary Research in the United States." Published works are listed in "A Bibliography for Preliminary Research in the United States," contained in VOLUME II, pp. 289-346, herewith.

Evidence of early 17th century emigration from Ireland is contained in *Analecta Hibernica*, No. 4, Dublin, 1932, published by the Irish Manuscripts Commission, in an article entitled "Documents Relating to the Irish in the West Indies," collected and edited by the Rev. Aubrey Gwynn (pp. 139-286). This is a bibliography of the 17th and 18th century source materials, richly illustrated with samples of the records, relating largely to Roman Catholics who emigrated from Ireland to settlements on the Amazon, 1612-1623; Irish political prisoners transported to Virginia, 1620; Daniel Gookin's Irish settlement in Virginia, 1621-1623; other settlements in St. Christopher's, Montserrat, Barbados, etc., 1626-1712; the Blake family, Roman Catholics of Connaught (since 1306), transported from Co. Galway to Montserrat in 1656 (records in letters naming members of the family) ; and various indentures for service in Maryland and Virginia, 1677-1679. In addition (on pp. 285-286), there is a "Description of Barbados (1668)" preserved in the British Museum among the Sloane MSS. (3662), showing that Barbados population of 18,300 in the early 17th century, had dwindled in 1666 to 8,000 men after departures to Virginia, New England, and other places in the West Indies [at the end of periods of indentured servitude] (p. 251). *The Journal of the Commissioners for Trade and Plantations* (1750-1756), contains a description of the Roman Catholics of the various islands of the West Indies (pp. 282-286). Four-fifths of the inhabitants of Montserrat were Papists. Irish emigration during this period was increasingly directed towards the mainland rather than towards the Islands of the West Indies.

John P. Prendergast states in his *Cromwellian Settlement of Ireland*, Dublin, 1875 (pp. 88-93), "While the Government officials were thus employed in clearing the ground for Adventurers and soldiers, by making the nobility and gentry of Ireland withdraw to Connaught and the soldiery to Spain, 'where they could wish the whole nation,' they had agents actively employed through Ireland, seizing women, orphans, and the destitute, to be transported to the Barbadoes [Barbados] and the English Plantations in America. It was a measure beneficial they said to Ireland, which was thus relieved of a population that might trouble the Planters; it was a benefit to the people removed, who might thus be made English and Christians; and a great benefit to the West India sugar planters, who desired the men and boys for their bondsmen, and the women and Irish girls in a country where they had only Maroon women and Negresses to solace them. The thirteen years war, from 1641 to 1654, followed by the departure of 40,000 Irish soldiers, with the chief nobility and gentry, to Spain, had left behind a vast mass of widows and deserted wives with destitute families. There were plenty of other persons too, who, as their ancient properties had been confiscated, 'had no visible means of livlihood.' Just as the King of Spain sent over his agents to treat with the Government for the Irish swordmen, the merchants of Bristol had agents treating with it for men, women, and girls, to be sent to the sugar plantations in the West Indies. The Commissioners for Ireland gave them orders upon the governors of garrisons, to deliver to them prisoners of war; upon the keepers of gaols, for offenders in custody; upon masters of workhouses, for the destitute in their care 'who were of an age to labour, or if women were marriageable and not past breeding;' and gave directions to all in authority to seize those who had no visible means of livelihood, and deliver them to these agents of the Bristol sugar merchants, in execution of which latter direction Ireland must have exhibited scenes in every part like the slave hunts in Africa. How many girls of gentle birth must have been caught and hurried to the private prisons of these men-catchers none can tell."

Prendergast continues "Messrs. Sellick and Leader, Mr. Robert Yeomans, Mr. Joseph Lawrence, and others, all of Bristol, were active agents. As one instance out of many:- Captain John Vernon was employed by the Commissioners for Ireland into England, and contracted in their behalf with Mr. David Sellick and Mr. Leader under his hand, bearing date the 14th September, 1653, to supply them with two hundred and fifty women of the Irish nation above twelve years, and under the age of forty-five, also three hundred men above the age of twelve years, and under fifty, to be found in the country within twenty miles of Cork, Youghal, and Kinsale, Waterford, and Wexford, to transport them into New England. Messrs. Sellick and Leader appointed their shipping to repair to Kinsale; but Roger Boyle, Lord Broghill (afterwards Earl of Orrery), whose name, like that of Sir C. Coote, seems ever the prelude of woe to the Irish, suggested that the required number of men and women might be had from among the wanderers and persons who had no means of getting their livelihood in the county of Cork alone. Accordingly, on the 23rd of October, 1653, he was empowered to search for them and arrest them, and to deliver them to Messrs. Sellick and Leader, who were to be at all the charge of conducting them to the water side, and maintaining them from the time they received them; and no person being once apprehended, was to be released but by special order in writing under the hand of Lord Broghill."

"Again, in January 1654, the Governors of Carlow, Kilkenny, Clonmel, Wexford, Ross, and Waterford, had orders to arrest and deliver to Captain Thomas Morgan, Dudley North, and John Johnson, English merchants, all wanderers, men and women, and such other Irish within their precincts as should not prove they had such settled course of industry as yielded them a means of their own to maintain them, all such children as were in hospitals or workhouses, all prisoners, men and women, to be transported to the West Indies. The governors were to guard the prisoners to the ports of shipping; but the prisoners were to be provided for and maintained by the said contractors, and none to be discharged except by order under the hand and seal of the governor ordering the arrest. It is easy to imagine the deeds done under such a power! On the 22nd December of the same year, orders were issued prohibiting all the shipping in any harbour in Ireland bound for Barbadoes, and other English plantations, from weighing anchor until searched, in order that any persons found to have been seized without warrant should be delivered."

"All measures, however, were vain to prevent the most cruel captures as long as these English slave dealers had recourse to Ireland. In the course of four years they had seized and shipped about 6400 Irish men, women, boys and maidens, when on the 4th of March, 1655, all orders were revoked.

These men-catchers employed persons (so runs the order) 'to delude poor people by false pretences into by-places, and thence they forced them on board their ships. The persons employed had so much a piece for all they so deluded, and for the money sake they were found to have enticed and forced women from their children and husbands,- children from their parents, who maintained them at school; and they had not only dealt so with the Irish, but also with the English,'— which last was the true cause, probably, of the Commissioners for Ireland putting an end to these proceedings."

"Yet not quite an end."

"In 1655 Admiral Penn added Jamaica to the empire of England; and, colonists being wanted, the Lord Protector applied to the Lord Henry Cromwell, then Major-General of the forces in Ireland, to engage 1500 of the soldiers of the army in Ireland to go thither as planters, and to secure a thousand young Irish girls ("Irish wenches" is Secretary Thurloe's term), to be sent there also. Henry Cromwell answered that there would be no difficulty, only that force must be used in taking them; and he suggested the addition of from 1500 to 2000 boys of from twelve to fourteen years of age. 'We could well spare them,' he adds, 'and they might be of use to you; and who knows but it might be a means to make them Englishmen—I mean, Christians?' The numbers finally fixed were 1000 boys, and 1000 girls, to sail from Galway in October, 1655—the boys as bondsmen, probably, and the girls to be bound by other ties to these English soldiers in Jamaica."

All of the above quotation from Prendergast is well documented with his references to State Papers, etc., and other Commonwealth documents. His work contains illustrations of the capture of people for transportation to the West Indies. Quoting the State Papers (p. 338) he gives a typical occurrence in Laccagh, a district where stood the castle of Laccagh or Lackagh belonging to the family of the Fitzgeralds in the parish of Monasterevan, County Kildare. This family was founded by Sir Thomas Fitzgerald, second son of Thomas, seventh Earl of Kildare, and brother of Gerald, the eighth Earl. Sir Thomas, of Laccagh, was made by statute in a par-

liament held at Trim, A. D. 1484, Lord Chancellor of the Kingdom for life. Regarding this family after the victory of Cromwell's army in Ireland, Prendergast states: "All the Irish
of Lackagh of the Popish religion (except four who were
hanged for the benefit of the rest), to the number of thirty-
seven—being three priests, twenty-one women, and thirteen
men, were, on 27th November, 1655, delivered to Captain
Coleman, of the Wexford frigate, for transportation to the
Barbadoes. The names of the priests were James Tuite,
Robert Keegan, and John Foley. There was also the wife of
Blind Donogh, and the whole family of Mr. Henry Fitzgerald,
of Lackagh Castle. Mr. Fitzgerald's case was one of great
hardship. He and his wife, Mrs. Margery Fitzgerald (both
of the house of Kildare), were fourscore years and upwards,
and no one could charge them with being Tories or counten-
ancing them, and they could scarcely be deemed guilty of not
running after them with hue and cry. The Tories, too, had
frequently despoiled them. Yet they, with their son Maurice,
their daughters Margery and Bridget, Mary the widow of
their eldest son Henry, with their man servant and maid servant had to lie in prison till the ship could be got ready to
carry them with the rest of this miserable cargo. They were
assigned to the correspondents of Mr. Norton, a Bristol merchant and sugar planter, who was to be at the charge of trans-
porting them to the Indian Bridges, now called Barbadoes."

   Most of the English lords of the Pale, of families of English blood and name, settled there since the 13th century or
later, also the English planters of Queen Elizabeth's time,
had become Irish in their sympathies before the opening of
the Rebellion in 1641. These Anglo-Norman and English
lords of the Pale and those beyond the Pale were classed by
Cromwell's Parliament as Irish, together with the Gaelic-Irish
gentry. Their English and Anglo-Norman surnames were
carried to the West Indies and the English colonies on the
main land by the ruined, destitute, and convicted members of
the old English families after the Rebellion. These English
by blood but Irish by centuries or a few generations of residence in Ireland quickly lost their Irish identity in the new

world. It was to the interest of any one of English surname
to remember only his blood connection with England. For this
reason the origins of early colonial immigrants of English
surname should be sought in Ireland if there is no proof of a
direct emigration from England. The links of from one to
several generations between England and the new world may
lie in Ireland. For suggestions, see CHAPTERS IX, XI, and XIII.

Evidence of the continuation of the practice of kidnapping,
well into the 18th century, is brought out in the account of
the Annesley Peerage Case, contained in *Duffy's Hibernian
Magazine*, Vol. 1, October, 1860, pp. 176-185. Under the title
"The Vicissitudes of James Annesley," it appears from evidence given in the Courts at Dublin in the year 1743, that
James Annesley was the legitimate son of the late Lord Altham, by his wife, a daughter of the Duke of Buckingham.
When about thirteen years of age, after the death of his father,
Lord Altham in November 1727, James Annesley was seized
in Ormond market, Dublin, in the presence of his uncle, Richard Annesley, and was hurried off to the quay, placed in a
boat, and taken off to Ringsend, where he was put on board
a ship which was about to sail for America, in April 1728.
"The ship at once proceeded to the river Delaware in
North America, and there the heir to the house of Annesley
was sold as a slave. In that wretched position he remained
for thirteen years. At the end of that time he made his escape, and found his way to Jamaica. Here his story excited
the interest of Admiral Vernon, who sent him to England,
where he proceeded to take the necessary steps for asserting
his alleged rights."

Regardless of the outcome of the case, some interesting
facts regarding the procedure and practice of the times with
respect to shipping records is set forth as follows: After the
evidence of two witnesses who accomplished the above kidnapping: "We accompanied the boy and Lord Anglesey to
Ringsend, and saw the boy put on board ship," the story goes
on. Thus the fact of kidnapping was clearly proved; and it
certainly speaks very ill for the vigilance of the public authorities of Dublin at the time, that such an occurrence could take

place in sight of a multitude of people without any notice being taken of it. From further evidence given in the case it seems there was at that time a regular system of sending out servants to the colonies, or as they were called, "the plantations." Certain precautions were taken to ensure that those who were thus sent went of their own free will. They entered into indentures before the Lord Mayor at the Tholsel [City Hall], and a list was made of them, and retained in the archives of the Corporation. But how nugatory this protection was appeared from evidence in the case. The last thing that was done after all the servants had been got on board, and just before the ship sailed, was that an agent or clerk of the owner went on board, received from the captain a list of the servants, and called it over. This list so handed by the captain to the agent was taken as final, and from it there was no appeal; it was for it that the master was responsible to the owner. "Every person," said one of the witnesses, "found on board, when the list is taken of the servants' names, would be set down in the list as a servant, *even if he was to declare himself unwilling to go, or whether the clerk found him indented or not,* and the clerk would not on that account stop the ship." Of course, this left a wide door open to oppression, and it was very easy to avoid the ceremony of indenting a servant at the Tholsel, and to send a person off to the plantations whether he liked it or not. The present case was an example. The evidence of the two witnesses, Reilly and Byrne, shewed clearly that there could have been no time for indenting young Annesley, and at all events, though the captain's list, when produced at the trial, showed that he had a James Annesley on board, there was no record of that name in the Corporation's indenture-books, which were also produced. "The ship's destination, we may observe, was proved by the production of the Custom-house book of ship entries."

Some published Irish and Scotch-Irish emigration records are listed in VOLUME II, pp. 234-235, herewith. Miscellaneous records giving evidence of emigration appear in some county, town, diocesan, and regional histories and in newspapers, periodicals, and Church records. A few sources which illus-

trate the variety of published works containing evidence of
emigration are as follows:

BOLTON, CHARLES KNOWLES. Scotch Irish Pioneers in Ulster
and America. Boston, 1910. This is primarily a history of
the Scotch-Irish settlements in America. Information concerning those who attended the General Synod of Ulster in
the capacity of Minister, Ruling Elder, Commissioner, Witness or Petitioner, with regard to residence, Church activity,
emigration to America, has been extracted from the *Records
of the General Synod of Ulster, 1691 to 1820*. (3 vols.),
Belfast, 1890-1898, and other sources such as the *Journal
of the Association for the Preservation of the Memorials
of the Dead in Ireland*. Bolton has presented a list of about
1,100 names, the position of each in the Church, the year of
the record, and the home town.

CRIMMINS, JOHN D. Irish-American Historical Miscellany.
New York, 1905. This relates to New York City and vicinity, together with much interesting material regarding
immigrants who settled in other parts of the country. It
contains a large collection of records of the first generation
Irish in America, with notes as to the origins of many and
some later records.

HANNA, CHARLES A. The Scotch-Irish or the Scot in North
Britain, North Ireland, and North America. 2 vols. New
York and London, 1902. This is an important source, con-
taining much miscellaneous information regarding the
Scotch-Irish emigrants and their origins.

KERNOHAN, J. W. Londonderry in Three Centuries. Belfast,
1921. This contains a brief chapter on "Emigration,—
Trade and farming conditions,—Dobbs on the causes of
Emigration,—Pioneer Ulster Scots in America,—Character
of the emigrants,—Bann Valley exodus,—Persons of property and long settled in Ireland,—Wills and other records."

KIERNAN, T. J. The Irish Exiles in Australia. Dublin, 1954.
This concerns the settlement of Australia, principally after
1786, with many political prisoners, and others who went
voluntarily.

MARSHALL, W. F. Ulster Sails West. Belfast, 1943, 1944. In a little book of 78 pages, the Appendix II, pp. 60-67, contains the "Names of some Ministers, Licentiates, Students, or Emigrants who went from Ulster and served in the Ministry of the Presbyterian Churches in North America during the period 1680-1820, with the Presbytery of oversight, or district of origin where these have been ascertained, the date or approximate date of arrival, and the Provinces or States where they exercised their ministry." There are records of 191 men. Appendix III, pp. 67-70, contains "Names of some American-born ministers of the period 1730-1820, whose parents were from Ulster." Appendix IV, pp. 71-72, contains "Names of some American-born ministers of the period 1752-1820, of Ulster extraction, but not of parents from Ulster. Those marked with an asterisk had grand-parents from Ulster (24 in number), and some notes on place of residence of each.

MURRAY, THOMAS. The Story of the Irish in Argentina. New York, 1919.

MYERS, ALBERT COOK. Immigration of the Irish Quakers into Pennsylvania, 1682-1750. Swarthmore, 1902. This contains a collection of records concerning Irish Quaker certificates of removal from Ireland, received at the Monthly Meetings of Friends in Pennsylvania, 1682-1750; with genealogical notes from Friends' Records of Ireland and Pennsylvania, Genealogies, County Histories, and other books and manuscripts. The records give evidence of emigration and, in many cases, concern from two to several generations of a family, before and after emigration.

O'BRIEN, ERIS. The Foundation of Australia (1786-1800). With an introduction by Douglas Woodruff. London, 1937. This is a work of importance to those interested in the problems of Irish emigration, and in the history of the Irish in the Colonies. Many political prisoners were sent to Australia at this time.

O'HANLON, REV. J. Irish-American History of the United States. Dublin, 1902. The Very Rev. John Canon O'Hanlon has compiled a great work, carefully documented regarding sources and personal notes giving genealogical and historical information about Irish and Scotch-Irish emigrants who contributed in an important way to the affairs of the American Colonies or States.

SERLE, PERCIVAL. Australian Biography, Dictionary of. Sydney, 1949.

STEWART, REV. DAVID. The Fasti of the American Presbyterian Church. This is an Appendix to the *Fasti of the Irish Presbyterian Church*, 1613-1840. (For details, see p. 382, herein.) The American *Fasti* contains the records of 156 ministers who emigrated from Ulster to America. An Addenda (not included in all volumes), contains the records of eighteen other ministers who emigrated.

STEWART, REV. DAVID. The Seceders in Ireland with Annals of their Congregations. Belfast, 1950. (Unindexed.) It contains emigration records in a "List of Ministers who emigrated to America and Canada" (pp. 173-181). "Emigration of Ministers to Canada" (pp. 205-209). "Emigrants to the Carolinas" (p. 174). Miscellaneous information about Seceder ministers sent to America (p. 176).

WALLACE, W. S. Canadian Biography, Dictionary of. Toronto, 1926.

WITTKE, CARL. The Irish in America. Baton Rouge, 1956.

WOODBURN, JAMES BARKLEY. The Ulster Scot, His History and Religion. (2nd edition) London, 1915. This contains the important historical background of the Ulster Scots. A chapter is given on the "Emigration to America" (pp. 213-229).

*   *   *   *   *

PUBLIC RECORD OFFICE OF NORTHERN IRELAND, BELFAST

1. Emigration Lists presented by the New England Historic Genealogical Society: (1925 *Report*, p. 11).
   (a) List of Emigrants to America from Liverpool, 1697-1707.

(b) Emigrants from England, 1773-1776.

(c) Two Early Passenger Lists, 1635-1637.

2. Emigration of Protestants, 1718-1728. Typed copy in the Presbyterian Historical Society, Belfast, and also in the Public Record Office of Northern Ireland. Transcript made from documents (destroyed in 1922) formerly in the Public Record Office, Dublin (Rev. David Stewart).

3. Emigration from Ulster to North Carolina, etc., from papers of the late W. C. Houston, dated 1736-1737. Philadelphia, U. S. A. (1927 *Report*, p. 7.)

4. Chesney Diary. Mentions numerous County Antrim and County Down families who emigrated to South Carolina, North Carolina, Virginia, and Pennsylvania, 1755-1800. (1951-53 *Report*, p. 74.)

5. From Curator of the County Museum, Armagh, Lists of Passengers for New York, Philadelphia, etc., sailing from Newry and Warrensport, 1791-1792. (1936 *Report*, p. 9.)

6. Notes of Ulster Emigration to America, Archbishop King's Diary (Extracts). Drumgooland Vestry Book, 1789-1828. (1929 *Report*, p. 13.)

7. Emigration, Notes on, to America by R. J. Welch, Esq., Belfast. (1929 *Report*, p. 13.)

8. American Passenger Lists, 1804-1806, from British Museum (Add. MS. 35932). From June, 1804 to March, 1806, the lists cover 47 ships and 1,600 passengers. 11 sailed from Belfast, 11 from Dublin, 10 from Londonderry, 9 from Newry, 2 from Sligo, 1 from Ballyshannon, and 1 from Warrensport. Ports of arrival were for the 47 ships: New York, 30; Philadelphia, 8; Boston, 4; Baltimore, 2; Charleston, 2; New Bedford, 1. Passenger's names, addresses, and year of sailing are indexed in the 1929 *Report*. Thus on p. 33, are three Jameson entries: Jameson, Dav., Braid, Co. Antrim. *Pass. to Amer.* 1805. Jameson, Wm., Lisburn, Co. Ant. *Pass. to Amer.* 1805. Jameson, Wm., Loughbrickland, Co. Down. *Pass. to Amer.* 1806. (1929 *Report*, p. 15, and Index.)

9. Copies of Ordnance Survey Documents, deposited in the

Royal Irish Academy, Dublin, containing lists of persons who emigrated, 1833-1835, from various parishes in County Londonderry, Ireland, chiefly to the United States and Canada. These lists of names are arranged by parishes, and for each emigrant, his name, age, year of sailing, townland of residence, religion (R.C. or E. C., or P., for Roman Catholic, Established Church, or Presbyterian), and place of destination. The parishes are: Aghadowey, Aghanloo, Agivey, Arboe, Artrea, Ballyaghran, Ballynascreen, Ballyrashane, Ballyscullion, Ballywillin, Balteagh, Banagher, Bovevagh, Clondermot, Coleraine, Desertlyn, Desertmartin, Desertoghill, Drumachose, Dunbo, Dungiven, Enigal, Kilcronaghan, Kildollagh, Killowen, Kilrea, Magilligan, Tamlaght Finlagan. (*Reports* 1934, pp. 4, 5; 1935, p. 4; 1936, p. 4; 1937, p. 4; 1938-45, p. 6.) Copies of these lists were sent by this Office to The Libraries of the Canadian Archives, Ottawa, Ont., and The National Archives, Washington, D. C. The latter list has the Call No. (J V 6137 N 6 . . .). *Historical Gleanings from County Derry*, by Sam Martin, Dublin, 1955, contains the Emigration Lists of the Parishes of Aghanloo, 1833-1834; Aghadowey, 1833-1834; Balteagh, 1833-1834; Bovevagh, 1833-1834; Coleraine, 1833-1834; Drumachose, 1833-1834; Dunboe (Dunbo), 1833-1834; Magilligan, 1833-1834; Tamlaght Finlagan, 1833-1834.

10. Photostatic copies of a list of persons (including a number from Ulster) naturalized in New York, 1802-1814. (*Report,* 1948, p. 4.)

11. American Diary of James Stephens, 13 Oct. 1858 to 25 March 1860. (*Report,* 1938-45, pp. 31-34.)

12. Causes for Emigration to America. Transcripts of State Papers Relating to Ireland, 20 June 1727 to 31 Dec. 1729 (P.R.O., London): "The most notable topic is the commencement on a large scale of emigration from Ireland. This seems to have first attracted notice in the summer of 1728. On 27 July 1728, Thomas Whitney writing from Larne reported: 'Here are a vast number of people

shipping for Pennsylvania and Boston. There are three ships at Larne; five at Derry; two at Coleraine; three at Belfast; and four at Sligo. I am assured within these eight years there are gone about 40,000 people out of Ulster and the low part of Connaught, so if they go on those Colonies will be very strong. The landlords here have raised the rent . . . the tenants can not pay it.' " (*Report*, 1933, p. 22.)

* * * * *

PUBLIC RECORD OFFICE OF IRELAND, DUBLIN

1. Emigration: A series of letter books, 1827-1857, transferred from the Valuation Office, dealing with the management of Crown estates, etc., and emigration of destitute tenants from Crown estates. (58th *Report*, p. 18.)
2. Emigration of destitute tenants from Crown estates, with letter registers, 1850-1861. (58th *Report*, p. 18.)

* * * * *

The emigration records of the various parishes of County Londonderry, 1833-1835 (listed above under the Public Record Office of Northern Ireland), illustrate the tendency of members of one family or of the branches of a family, living in one or near parishes, to emigrate at the same time or to follow each other closely. These particular emigration records also show that in nine of the parishes of County Londonderry, the proportion of emigrant Roman Catholics to Protestants was a little less than one-fourth (201 to a total of 885), with some variation however, in the different parishes. Of the 201 Roman Catholics who emigrated from these nine parishes, 114 went to Quebec or St. Johns, Canada, while 87 went to New York or Philadelphia.

The records of emigrants in the McCloskey family (Roman Catholics) from the County Londonderry parishes illustrates the above emigration pattern as follows:

Parish	Name		Age	Year	Townland	Religion	Destination
Balteagh	John McCloskey		25	1834	Cloghan	R. C.	Quebec
"	Eliza	"	25	1834	"	"	"
Bovevagh	Patrick	"	18	1833	Dirnaflaw	"	"
"	Eleanor	"	22	1833	Ardanarn	"	"
"	Mary A.	"	20	1833	"	"	"
"	James	"	25	1833	Farkland	"	New York
"	Eliza	"	30	1833	"	"	"
"	Mgt.	"	14	1833	Drum	"	"
"	Grace	"	25	1833	Gortnahey Beg	"	Quebec
Drumachose	James	"	26	1833	Bolea	P.	Philadelphia
"	Jane	"	28	1833	"	P.	"
Tamlaght Finlagan							
"	" Owen	"	30	1834	Ballykelly	R. C.	Quebec
"	" Patrick	"	28	1834	"	"	"

CENSUS RETURNS (Ireland): 1851. Reports on Ages and Education. Tables of Deaths. General Report. (Alexander Thom & Son.) 4 vols. Dublin, 1855-56. The emigration statistics in Vol. I (pp. 148, 151, 152, 210, 212, 213, 215, 218, 219, 220, 223, 225, 227, 230, 232, 235, 243, 265, 278, 305, 314, 323, 330, 333, etc.), give the numbers of emigrants (Irish and Ulster Scots) who sailed from Irish ports and Liverpool or other English ports, from 1772/3 to 1851, and some figures on their countries of destination. "During the Emigrations chiefly in 1772 and 1773, many weavers and spinners with all their families went. They stopped when the war broke out. Protestants emigrated most. In the years 1771, 1772, and 1773, as many as 28,650 emigrants sailed from ports in the North of Ireland for America" (p. 148). "According to the Report of the Census Commissioners for 1841, the average annual emigration between 1831 and 1841 was 40,346, and from the 30th June in the later year to the end of 1845, it averaged 61,242, per annum. Such, however, was the effect of the potato blight . . . that the number rose to 105,955 in 1846, after which the emigration seemed to partake of the nature of an epidemic and, in 1847, the number who left the country more than doubled those who departed in the previous year" (p. 243). Further figures show that in 1848, only 178,159 emigrated; in 1849,

214,425 departed; in 1850, the emigration was 209,054; in 1851, 249,721 left Ireland (p. 243). "The total Colonial and foreign emigration from Ireland between 1831 and 1841 was 403,459, or an average of 40,346 per annum. Of these 214,047 embarked from Irish ports, 152,738 from Liverpool, and 10% was added for imperfect returns . . . From the ports of Ulster there went 76,905; from Munster, 70,046; from Leinster, 34,977, and from Connaught, only 32,119" (p. 227). "In 1844, the estimated emigration from Ireland . . . was 54,289, of which number 15,925 sailed from Irish ports and 38,364 from Great Britain" (p. 235).

CHAPTER XXII

BIRTH, MARRIAGE, AND DEATH RECORDS

The discovery of birth, marriage, and death records with evidence of family relationships is, no doubt, the primary objective of all genealogists. For the members of landed families, the proofs of birth, marriage, and death, have ever been matters of primary importance, relating to legal rights. This material, of the nature of public records, has been preserved to some extent, in one form or another, since medieval times.

The genealogist can expect to find scattered MSS. collections of birth or baptismal records, marriage records, and death or burial records, also printed transcripts or abstracts of many collections of original documents concerning birth, marriage and death. The primary sources are the Parish Registers and other Church records of the various denominations, tombstone inscriptions, Court records including Affidavits and Inquisitions Post Mortem, Petitions recorded in State Papers, Funeral Certificates, Marriage Settlements; also Wills, Trusts, Deeds, Leases, Assignments and other conveyances giving evidence of birth, marriage, or death; Census Records, Old Age Pension Records, newspaper notices and obituaries, School Registers, etc.

All previous chapters of this volume have contained some information regarding sources of vital records. Therefore, the object of this chapter is to present a summary of information and notes on certain collections of source material not yet described.

The registration of Protestant marriages began in Ireland on April 1, 1845. The registration of all births, marriages and deaths, became compulsory in Ireland on January 1, 1864. All registers of birth, marriage, and death prior to 1922 (and for the twenty-six counties of the Republic of Ireland, thereafter) are deposited in the Office of the Registrar General, Customs House, Dublin. The births, marriages, and deaths in the six counties of Northern Ireland, beginning in 1922, are registered at the Central Registry Office, Fermanagh House, Ormeau Ave., Belfast, Northern Ireland.

The National Library of Ireland has *Births Registered in Ireland: General Index.* Births Registered in Ireland in 1864-1866. Fol. H.M.S.O. Thom, 1873-76.

A brief history of the conditions in Ireland, affecting marriages in the seventeenth and eighteenth centuries is important as a guide in the search of marriage records and will explain why marriages of many Presbyterians, Methodists, and people of other denominations will be found recorded in the Parish Registers of the Established Church of Ireland. The Appendix to the 34th *Report of the Deputy Keeper of the Public Records of Ireland* (pp. 23, 25, 26), offers the following information:

"The state of the Civil Law as regards marriage in Ireland was as follows: Marriages between Roman Catholics and celebrated by Roman Catholic priests, have always been regarded as valid. Although Presbyterian marriages by Presbyterian ministers were admitted to be valid by the Civil Courts, yet Presbyterians who were married by their own ministers had often 'to confess themselves guilty of fornication, in their respective parish churches, or else pay a heavy penalty' (Latimer, *History of the Irish Presbyterians,* p. 130). In 1704, some Presbyterians residing at Lisburn were excommunicated by the Episcopal authority for the crime of being married by ministers of their own church (*id.* p. 136) . . . It was not until 1782 that the Irish Parliament passed a bill by which marriages of Dissenters celebrated by their ministers were legalized beyond a doubt . . . "

"But mixed marriages, or marriages celebrated between people of different religious persuasions, were on quite a different footing. By the Act 12 Geo. I, c. 3, marriages between two Protestants, or a Protestant and a Roman Catholic, by a priest or degraded clergyman, were declared null and void. This disability, as far as the Roman Catholics were concerned, was not removed till 1870 when, by the Act 33 and 34 Vic., c. 110, sec. 38, mixed marriages by a Roman Catholic priest were legalized. The position of the Dissenters may be seen from the following extract from a memorandum amongst Clogher Diocesan Papers (Causes of Office for Clandestine Marriages) :- 'Several of the Dissenting ministers of the Diocese solemnize marriage between members of the Established Church and those of their own sect, and claim it is their right to do so . . . in such cases (when it came to the knowledge of the Court) citations were issued against the parties so marrying, upon which they always came forward, obtained [a marriage] licence, and were married in [the Established] Church. The fact is, the Dissenting ministers would use every means in their power to break in upon the Bishop's jurisdiction and abridge his prerogative.' In 1840, the Armagh Consistorial Court declared that a marriage between a Presbyterian and an Episcopalian [Established Church of Ireland], performed by a Presbyterian minister, was illegal. Next year, a man convicted of bigamy carried the matter to a higher court, on the ground that his first marriage had been celebrated by a Presbyterian minister, although between a Presbyterian and an Episcopalian. In the Queen's Bench, three judges were for liberating the prisoner, and two for his condemnation. In the Lords, the Law Lords being divided, the decision of the inferior court was upheld and the marriage pronounced invalid. So great was the consternation on this decision that in 1844, the Government brought in and passed a Bill declaring valid not only any future, but any past mixed marriages celebrated by Presbyterian ministers."

"Mixed marriages by regularly ordained clergymen of the Established Church of Ireland, though without publication of banns or licence, were never void in Ireland, and only voidable in cases of minors and wards entitled to estates over certain limits, if an action were taken within a year (9 Geo. II, c. 11, s. 8), but both the clergyman and the parties rendered themselves liable to certain legal penalties, and the clergymen were often degraded by the ecclesiastical authorities. If such a clergyman, however, after being degraded by the ecclesiastical authorities, again ventured to celebrate a mixed marriage, he thereby committed a felony, and rendered himself liable to the provisions of the Act of 12 Geo. I, c. 3, the marriage also being null and void. By the Act of 32 Geo. III, c. 21 (1792) inter-marriage between Protestants and Roman Catholics was permitted, if duly celebrated by a clergyman of the Established Church."

"The custom of celebrating clandestine marriages, that is to say, marriages performed by clergymen, without the publication of banns or the granting of a licence, apparently dates back to an early period."

Considering the illegality of mixed marriages, and of those performed by Dissenting ministers before 1844, and the legal requirements before this date, of the publication of banns in the Established Church of the diocese in which the marriage was to be performed, or the issuing of a licence, preceding the marriage by a clergyman of the Established Church, it must be remembered that a great proportion of the marriages, regardless of the sect, were entered in the Parish Registers of the Established Church of Ireland.

Thus, except in the case of Roman Catholic marriages, the Parish Registers of the Established Church should be searched for possible records of marriages of Presbyterians and other Dissenters. The existing Registers are listed on pp. 280-308, herein.

In Ireland it was customary practice for the aristocracy to be married by licence of the Prerogative Court, under the jurisdiction of the Archbishop of Armagh, or by licence from the Consistorial Court of the diocese of Dublin. The papers of the former were called Prerogative Marriage Licence Grants. Those of the latter were Diocesan Marriage Licence Grants. In any search for marriage records, when the Parish Registers and Marriage Licence Grants are lacking, the next best evidence of marriage, which has been termed "primary presumptive evidence," is a Marriage Licence Bond. These Bonds are of value to the genealogist as their purpose was a guarantee that there was no impediment to the marriage. Before a bishop would grant his licence for a proposed marriage, he required this bond as a protection against action for damages in case any ecclesiastical or legal impediment existed to prevent the marriage. These bonds contained the names of the bridegroom and the bride, the date, their respective places of residence, and the names of the two sureties who signed.

Unfortunately, the original Marriage Licence Grants and Bonds were burned in the Public Record Office, Dublin, in 1922, but the Indexes were saved and these offer almost as much information as the original records. Also some of the original records had been transcribed and some Indexes had been printed. The Marriage records of this nature and other miscellaneous collections now in the Public Record Office of Ireland, Dublin; the Public Record Office of Northern Ireland, Belfast; and other sources, in addition to the Parish Registers, etc., mentioned above, are as follows:

THE PUBLIC RECORD OFFICE OF IRELAND, DUBLIN:

1. "Index to the Act or Grant Books and to the Original Wills of the Diocese of Dublin [*c.* 1638] to 1800." This is printed in the Appendix to the 26th *Report of the Deputy Keeper of the Public Records in Ireland*, Dublin, 1895 (pp. 1-1089). The Index contains about 59,895 entries which principally concern original Wills, Administrations, Marriage Licences, Marriage Licence Bonds, Grants of Office, etc. The Index is alphabetically arranged, by names of the principals in the instruments, with the year and nature of the document in each case, and often the residence in the diocese, particulars as to station, occupation, or condition (spinster, etc.).

2. "Index to the Act or Grant Books and to the Original Wills of the Diocese of Dublin, 1800-1858." This is printed in the Appendix to the 30th *Report of the Deputy Keeper of the Public Records in Ireland*, 1899 (pp. 1-1155). The Index contains about 63,500 entries, in continuation of the above Index, arranged in the same manner.

3. COURT AND REGISTER BOOK (Diocese of Killaloe): Court Book, Marriage Licence Grants, 1776-1845 (55th *Report*, p. 26).

4. GRANT BOOK, DIOCESE OF CASHEL, 1840-1845 (Probates, Administrations, and Marriage Licences). (55th *Report*, p. 10.)

5. MARRIAGE LICENCE BONDS AND AFFIDAVITS, INDEXES TO: These records are contained in large ledgers and constitute the *Index* to all of the Diocesan Marriage Licence Bonds which were burned in 1922. The Indexes are compiled by Diocese, each being arranged alphabetically, by name of the groom with the names of both the groom and the bride, and the year of the Marriage Licence Bond which was issued in the Consistorial Court by the Bishop of the Diocese. The Indexes now in the Public Search Room are for the following dioceses: (55th *Report*, p. 28).

(1)	Ardfert, see Killaloe.	
(2)	Armagh,	1727-1845
(3)	Cashel and Emly,	1664-1857
(4)	Clogher,	1711-1866
(5)	Clonfert, see Killaloe.	
(6)	Cloyne,	1630-1867
(7)	Cork and Ross,	1623-1845
(8)	Derry (five bonds), 1702, 1705, 1722, (See Diocesan and Testamentary Index).	
(9)	Down, Connor and Dromore,	1721-1845
(10)	Dublin (Marriage Licence Grant Books),	1672-1741
(11)	Dublin (Marriage Licence Bonds),	1718-1746
(12)	Elphin,	1733-1745
(13)	Kildare,	1790-1865
(14)	Killala and Achonry,	1787-1842
(15)	Killaloe, (and Clonfert, 1739, 1815-1844, and Limerick, 1827-1844, and Ardfert, 1820, 1835).	1719-1845
(16)	Kilmore and Ardagh,	1697-1844
(17)	Limerick, see Killaloe.	
(18)	Meath	1665, 1702-1845
(19)	Ossory, Ferns and Leighlin,	1691-1845

(20)   Raphoe,   1710-1755,   1817-1830
(21)   Tuam,   1769-1845
(22)   Waterford and Lismore,   1649-1845
(and the peculiar jurisdiction of Lismore, 1779-1802).

6. MARRIAGE LICENCE BONDS (DUBLIN).   Vol. A. 1749-1813
(and one Bond, Diocese of Leighlin, for "Dowse and Hope,"
1820), saved from the fire.   (55th *Report*, p. 29.)

7. *Original Marriage Licences and Marriage Licence
Bonds*, presented during the period from the destruction of the
Public Record Office in 1922 to the end of 1927.   These records
are dated from the 17th to the 19th centuries, giving the names
of the groom and the bride, the nature of the record, the
year of the document and the Court from which the Licence
or Bond was issued.   The documents are listed with other
presented Original Probates, etc., in Appendix II, of the 55th
Report, pp. 33-90.

8. CERTIFICATES OF ACKNOWLEDGEMENT OF DEEDS BY MAR-
RIED WOMEN, INDEXES TO.   1834-1852.   Contain the names of
wife and husband, the dates of certificate and deed, and the
Parish, Barony or Manor, etc., in which the lands affected by
the deed are situate.   (55th *Report*, p. 127.)

9. *Marriage Licence Bonds (Killaloe), 1680-1762, Transcript of* (Ad. Ms. British Museum, 31883).   (55th *Report*,
p. 139.)

10. *Marriage Settlements and Articles (Original, Copy, and
Memorials of)*.   Presented by Alexander Bell and Son, Solicitors (128 items), giving the names of the groom and bride,
the year and number of the document.   Also Marriage Settlements and Agreements, presented by E. J. French, Solicitor,
listed with the names of the groom and bride, the year, and
number of the document.   Both collections of presented documents are of the 18th and 19th centuries.   (56th *Report*, pp.
27-28, 29, 44-46.)

11. Marriage Licence Grants, Prerogative and Diocese of
Dublin (Transcripts), 1738-1818, collection presented.   (56th
Report, p. 54.)

12. Marriage Licence Grants and Marriage Licence Bonds,

transcripts and abstracts presented in 1928, listed alphabetically by name of the groom with that of the bride, dated 17th to 19th centuries. (56th *Report*, pp. 198-202.)

13. Dublin Marriage Licence Bonds, 1749-1813, Vol. A, and Marriage Licence Grants, 1776-1845, listed with Original Probates, etc., under names of the groom and bride (cross indexed), with town or parish, county, nature of the record, year of the instrument, Court or Registry, and Reference Number. (57th *Report*, Appendix I, pp. 62-324.)

14. Marriage Licence Bonds and Marriage Licence Grants of various dioceses, 17th-19th centuries, compiled among the Gertrude Thrift Abstracts, listed among Original Unproved Wills, etc., presented 1929-1930, giving the names of the groom and bride, the nature of the document, the year of the record, the Court or Registry (Diocesan or Prerogative), and the Thrift Abstract number or that of other "Original Document, Copy, or Abstract." (57th *Report*, pp. 325-420.)

15. BETHAM GENEALOGICAL ABSTRACTS: 241 Notebooks, among which are 16 volumes containing abstracts from Prerogative Marriage Licences, 1629-1801; 4 volumes (Nos. 57-60), containing abstracts from Prerogative Marriage Licences, 1629-1800; 54 volumes containing abstracts from Dublin Marriage Licences, 1660-1824; records collection purchased in 1935. In 1936, a Betham volume was purchased which is an addition to the above, being a volume of abstracts of Marriage Licence Bonds, Prerogative, 1629-1800 (G-Y). (58th *Report*, pp. 25-26.)

16. The Trustees of the Charlton Endowment Fund, 1932 & 1939, presented 4 bundles of certificates of marriages, *c.* 1795-1862, Cos. Longford & Meath, with a small number for Cos. Cavan, Louth, Offaly, Westmeath and Dublin City, and 8 bundles of applications for marriage portions & grants for advancement in life, etc. (58th *Report*, p. 31.) The miscellaneous collections of presented documents, listed in the 58th *Report*, contain very many marriage records dating mostly from the 17th or 18th century.

GENEALOGICAL OFFICE (OFFICE OF ARMS), DUBLIN CASTLE, DUBLIN: Marriage records:

1. Abstracts of the Prerogative Marriage Licence Grants, *c.* 1629-1800.

2. Dublin Marriage Licence Grants, 1638-1764; 1789-1800.

3. Abstracts of Dublin Marriage Licence Grants, *c.* 1660-1823.

4. A vast number of records of marriage are contained in the pedigrees and manuscript collections of this Office. Its library of printed reference materials contains the important sources.

PUBLIC RECORD OFFICE OF NORTHERN IRELAND, BELFAST:

1. Abstracts of Prerogative Marriage Licence Grants, *c.* 1629-1800 (copies of the records in the Genealogical Office, Dublin Castle).

2. Prerogative Marriage Licence Bonds, Extracts, 6 Books, *c.* 1629-1857.   (1938-1945 *Report*, p. 12.)

3. Pilson MSS., containing "Births, Marriages and Deaths, in the neighborhood of Downpatrick, 1693-1862," compiled by Aynsworth Pilson.   (1935 *Report*, p. 8.)

4. "Baptisms, Marriages and Deaths, 1769-1795, Alphabetical List of," recorded in the *Hibernian Chronicle*, checked and information added from other sources.   (1938-1945 *Report*, pp. 5, 12.)

5. "Diocese of Clogher Marriage Licence Bonds, 1698-1738," extracted from records in the Public Record Office, Dublin.

6. "Marriage Register of Rathfriland Presbyterian Congregation, 1782-1811."

7. Marriage records of individuals contained in MSS. collections acquired by this Office as gifts or by purchase, or transcripts, if dated prior to 1800, are usually listed in the Index of the *Report* in which the collection is noted.   Many thousands of Marriage Records are also entered in the Master Card Index in the Search Room.

PUBLISHED MARRIAGE RECORDS:

See VOLUME II, herewith, pp. 219-220, 228, 237.   See also

under Microfilms, p. 284. Printed Registers of the Established Church of Ireland are listed in PART THREE, CHAPTER III, herein; also see Huguenot and Presbyterian printed Registers listed in CHAPTERS VII, and VIII, respectively.

Published Death or Burial records, particularly contained in Parish Registers, and compiled transcripts of inscriptions copied from tombstones and memorial tablets, are listed in VOLUME II, 216, 227-228, and 237, herewith. Many other transcribed collections are included in county, town, and diocesan histories, and in Historical Society Journals. Microfilms of the Quaker Registers of Births, Marriages, and Deaths or Burials, are listed in VOLUME II, pp. 274-275, herewith.

Perhaps the greatest number of printed burial records, transcribed from tombstone inscriptions and memorial tablets, is contained in the *Journals of the Association for the Preservation of the Memorials of the Dead in Ireland;* later continued as the *Journals of the Irish Memorials Association* and, in 1937, incorporating the Dublin Parish Register Society. Vols. I-XIII, No. 2. 1892-1937.

This series of *Journals* contains many thousands of inscriptions copied from tombstones and memorial tablets in cemeteries and churches in all parts of Ireland, representing all denominations. Descriptions of any coats-of-arms on the tombstones or memorial tablets (or photographs, sketches or rubbings of them) are included. The material is amplified for numerous families by notes from Wills, Funeral Certificates and other sources, with the compiled records of well-known genealogists. This Journal was first published as the *Annual Report* of the "Fund for the Preservation of the Memorials of the Dead, in Ireland," founded in 1888, to compile a comprehensive tombstone encyclopedia for all of Ireland. The *Reports* of 1888-1891 were published as Volume I of the *Journal of the Association for the Preservation of the Memorials of the Dead in Ireland.* Dublin, 1892. Ten volumes were published under this title; Volume X covering the *Reports* for 1917-1920. Vols. XI-XIII, No. 2, bear the title *Journals of the Irish Memorials Association,* and include records of Parish Registers, being continuations of earlier published Registers, as listed in VOLUME II, pp. 216-217, herewith. A series of published indexes accompanies the work.

Vols. VII and VIII of the above Journals contain the Funeral Entries of the 17th and 18th centuries, contained in Funeral Certificates issued by the Ulster Office of Arms, Dublin Castle, and accompanied by any family coats-of-arms of the deceased. This series was copied from an original Ms. volume in the British Museum (Add. Ms. 4820), which was somehow detached from the other seventeen volumes preserved in the Office of Arms (now the Genealogical Office), and was deposited in the British Museum. The Funeral Certificates now in the Genealogical Office, Dublin Castle, are dated 1588-1698. An example of the number of generations included in the records of some of these Funeral Certificates is illustrated in PART TWO, CHAPTER IV, pp. 137-156, herein.

Some miscellaneous MSS. tombstone inscriptions of early date are contained in the Lodge MSS. in the Public Record Office, Dublin. *A Book of Inscriptions on Ancient Tombstones*, by Walter Harris, is deposited in the Armagh Public Library.

Prior to the "Burial Act" (31 & 32 Vic., Cap. 103), in July 1868, which relieved Dissenters and permitted their ministers to conduct burial services, the clergy of the Established Church held jurisdiction over funeral services for Protestants. The subject of burial regulations as late as 1865 is discussed in *A History of Wesleyan Methodism on the Armagh Circuit*, by Surgeon-Major Lynn, M.D., Belfast, 1887 (pp. 201-202). This author tells of a case of a Methodist preacher of this Circuit, the Rev. Edward Best, who in 1865 applied to the rector of the parish of Kilmore in which the town of Rich Hill is situated, for permission to conduct the funeral service of the late James Loney, in the parish graveyard, as the deceased was to be interred there in the family plot of ground. Permission was at once curtly refused. Whereupon the Methodist preacher, Mr. Best, performed the service on the public road opposite the graveyard. This breach of the Burial Act came before the Government which ordered an inquiry. At this late date the feeling was such that Parliament finally passed the above relief "Burial Act" of July 1868. Meanwhile, the inscriptions on the tombstones in the cemeteries or Protestant graveyards show that Dissenters as well as members of the Established Church were buried in the Parish burial grounds of the Churches under the jurisdiction of the Established Church. Thus the records of such burials were entered in the Parish Registers. Needless to say, dissenting ministers, particularly the Quakers, claimed the right to perform the services for their own members. Their burial records were well kept. The Presbyterian Registers do not contain burial records in the cases of most congregations. Examples of burial inscriptions of Dissenters in the graveyard and on memorial tablets in the Established Church, in the parish wherein the family of the deceased resided, are furnished as follows:

Enniskillen Parish and Town, by W. H. Dundas, 1913 (pp. 91-119), contains a chapter on "Memorial Tablets and Tombstone inscriptions, In the Church and In the Graveyard" (of the parish Church). Only tombstone inscriptions of Methodist preachers and Presbyterian ministers are given here as illustrations:

BAYLEY: "Sacred to the memory of Rev. Benjamin Bayley, Wesleyan Methodist minister who entered into eternal rest 10 Aug. 1879, in the 72nd year of his age and 47th of his ministry, and of his beloved wife Eliza. W. Bayley who fell asleep in Jesus 24th May 1874, in 68th year of her age. Prov. X. 7. Erected by their loving children (Headstone with railing)." (p. 99.)

BERKELEY: "Erected by the Presbyterian Congregation of Enniskillen in memory of their much beloved minister Rev. Thomas Berkeley who died 8 Dec. 1836, in the 9th month of his ministry at 23 years (Alter tomb)." (p. 100.)

NESBITT: "Underneath lies the body of the Rev. Thomas Nesbitt, Wesleyan minister who departed this life in the full triumph of a living faith, 13 June 1832, at 23 years. His favorite motto was "a sinner saved by grace." Also of his father Rev. John Nesbitt, Wesleyan minister who departed this life 18 Jan. 1858 at 82 years. And near this spot reposes the remains of his mother Margaret Nesbitt, who fell asleep in Jesus 9 May 1861 at 75 years. Prov. X. 7." (p. 112.)

STEVENSON: "Sacred to the memory of Margaret wife to Rev. E. S. Stevenson, Presbyterian minister of Enniskillen who departed this life 3 Mar. 1850 at 80 years. Also her husband Rev. E. Stevenson (Stephenson) who died 29 Apr. 1852 in the 87th year of his age and 48th year of his ministry." (p. 117.) *The History of Enniskillen*, by Trimble, Vol. III, p. 919, shows this was the Rev. Ephraim Stephenson who was ordained in the Presbyterian Church in 1802, and retired from the ministry of the Presbyterian Church, Enniskillen, in 1832.

WILSON: "Here lies the body of William Wilson, Methodist preacher who departed this life 22 Feb. 1808, at 53 years." There are six Wilson tombstones and two other inscriptions on tablets, the oldest being for William Wilson who died 25 Feb. 1703, aged 50 years (p. 119).

ARMSTRONG: "Here lies the body of Rev. Gustavus Armstrong who departed this life 25 March 1832 at 74 years. He was for more than 40 years a useful Preacher of the Gospel. Dan. XII. 3" (p. 98). There are numerous Armstrong inscriptions. This Gustavus Armstrong is identified in C. H. Crookshank's *History of Methodism in Ireland*, Belfast, 1885-1888 (Vol. I, pp. 251, 435, 436; Vol. II, pp. 180, 415, 421; Vol. III, pp. 159, 172): Gustavus Armstrong was converted (Methodist) at 12 years of age, living near Enniskillen, in 1771. He preached in Armagh, 1787; Dungannon, 1787; Bluestone, near Newry, 1800; Bandon, near Cork, 1816; superannuated, 1831; erected a chapel at Knockmanoul, 1832; death reported at annual Conference, 1832.

Occasionally, the parentage and origin of an emigrant is preserved by a tombstone inscription. The *Journals of the Association for the Preservation of the Memorials of the Dead in Ireland*, Vol. I (1888-1891), pp. 360, 361, contain the following:

Parish of Enniskillen, County Fermanagh, Ireland:

"Erected to the memory of James Cauthers of Waterinnerry, who departed this life, April 11, 1845, aged 60 years. Also Margaret his wife, who died December 27th, 1854, aged 70 years. 'Blessed are the dead who die in the Lord.' Erected by their son, James Cauthers, of New York, America."

Parish of Enniskillen, County Fermanagh, Ireland: "Erected to the memory of Henry Edmonson, of Enniskillen, who departed this life, Febry. 23rd, 1830, aged 58 years. Erected by his daughter, Letitia Cauthers, New York, America."

CHAPTER XXIII

WILLS AND PROBATE RECORDS

In Ireland, as in other countries, wills are one of the most fruitful sources of genealogical information. A will provides the approximate date of death of the testator. It may have been written, signed and witnessed some years before the time of death, but it was usually probated shortly after the death and this date was entered at the bottom of the will and on the Court copy. Wills were not only signed by the testator but if he was of an armorial family his armorial bearings, impressed on a wax seal, were attached to the original document. This offered an important clue to his family descent. A living wife was almost always mentioned by her given name and sometimes by her maiden surname. Some wills bequeathed property to all living children in order of their age; the bulk of the estate in most cases going to the eldest son according to the law of primogeniture. Usually all sons were named in age order, before the daughters were provided for accordingly with personal belongings and money. If a man had no son, the daughters customarily inherited the estate as co-heirs, rather than the male heir of a brother or other collateral line. When the dates of the signing and of probating a will were widely spaced, there is no certainty that all people named in the will were still living at the time of death of the testator, for men and women were careless about redrawing wills in the earlier days as they are now. Also a daughter, named as unmarried in her father's or mother's will, may have married shortly after the instrument was drawn. Thereafter she may have become a widow and married a second time. The signatures of witnesses must be carefully noted, for often relatives who were brothers, brothers-in-law, or sons-in-law performed this duty.

The destruction of records in the Public Record Office, Dublin, in 1922, at first seemed to present a hopeless situation with regard to the future study of Irish wills, but this has been overcome in several ways. The many thousands of certified copies of the original wills, administrations, transcripts or abstracts of the original documents, as well as the numerous original wills never probated, now form a great many scattered collections in various repositories. During more than a century these collections compiled by solicitors, legal agents, representatives of repositories, careful and well known genealogists, local historians and record searchers, have accumulated and are now contained in manuscript materials or in printed sources, representing replacements of the destroyed documents to an important extent.

Some printed sources of wills are listed in VOLUME II, pp. 259-261, herewith. Local histories and various periodicals often include abstracts of wills of the nobility and gentry, while family histories and genealogies commonly contain full transcripts or abstracts of the original wills of testators in one or more lines of the family.

Wills fall in three periods. The early or medieval wills are dated prior to the Reformation. Existing wills of this period are few and usually concern people of great estate. From the time of the Reformation in 1536 to 1858, the Ecclesiastical Courts of the Established Church of Ireland assumed jurisdiction over all probate matters. Wills and administrations within these dates were classed as Prerogative or Diocesan, according to the Court in which the estate was probated. In 1857, the jurisdiction of the Ecclesiastical Courts over probate matters was abolished, and from 1858 onward the proving of wills and administration of estates was transferred to the Civil Courts. The records will be discussed in order of these periods.

MEDIEVAL WILLS AND INVENTORIES

A very few early wills are deposited in the Royal Irish Academy and in Trinity College Library, Dublin. These are listed by collections in the catalogues and indexes of the repositories. In Trinity College Library are early Dublin Wills and Inventories. H. F. Berry has edited this collection of documents which has been published by the Royal Society of Antiquaries of Ireland, 1898, under the title of the *Register of*

Wills and Inventories of the Diocese of Dublin, 1457-1483. In addition to the Latin text, taken from MSS. 552 (E. 3. 32), an English translation is given. The Introduction presents information concerning early wills. Other sources are noted in the 55th *Report of the Deputy Keeper of the Public Records in Ireland* (pp. 132, 144), as follows: (1) The *Calendar of Christ Church Deeds* (containing some testamentary matter), edited by M. J. McEnery, and printed in the 20th, 23rd and 24th *Reports of the Deputy Keeper*. A manuscript continuation of the Calendar, 1605-1700, is in the Public Record Office, Dublin. (2) A *Calendar of Ancient Records of Dublin*, Vol. I (Gilbert). (3) *Chartularies of St. Mary's Abbey*, Vol. I (Gilbert). (4) Hardiman's edition of O'Flaherty's *H-Iar Connaught*. (5) The *Diocese of Limerick, Ancient and Medieval* (Begley). (6) The *Patent Rolls, Inquisitions*, etc. (see Vol. II, pp. 253-258, herewith). Inventories of lands held *in capite* and other possessions of the deceased were recorded in early and later Inquisitions Post Mortem.

PREROGATIVE AND DIOCESAN WILLS AND ADMINISTRATIONS, 1536-1858

As stated above, there were two classes of wills and administrations under the jurisdiction of the Ecclesiastical Courts between 1536 and 1858. These were Prerogative or Diocesan Wills and Administrations, according to the Court of probate.

The Archbishop of Armagh, Primate of all Ireland, or his representative, presided over the Prerogative Court which was the Supreme Court in all ecclesiastical matters. It extended jurisdiction over all of the minor Courts including the Consistorial Courts of the dioceses, particularly in cases pertaining to more than one diocese. Wills were proved in the Prerogative Court and intestate administrations were settled in this Court, if the deceased died possessed of property valued in excess of five pounds (sterling) in each of two or more dioceses.

The bishop of each diocese presided over its Consistorial Court, there being twenty-eight in number. This Court held ecclesiastical jurisdiction over matters of probate and other affairs pertaining to the one diocese. Thus if the deceased left property located in only one diocese, or property of less than five pounds (sterling) value in a second diocese, his will was proved or his estate, if intestate, was settled in the Consistorial Court of the diocese in which he had resided. As much the larger number of wills were Diocesan Wills, probated in a Consistorial Court, it is an important matter to determine in which diocese the family lived. The books of reference listed in PART ONE, CHAPTER II, herein, will help to identify the place of residence, as to the diocese in which it was located.

All original Prerogative Wills and Prerogative Will Books containing official copies of the wills, housed in the Public Record Office of Ireland, Dublin, before 1922, were destroyed in the fire, except for eleven original documents and the Will Books for the years 1664-1684; 1706-1708 (A-W) ; 1726-1729 (A-W) ; 1777 (A-L) ; 1813 (K-Z) ; and 1834 (A-E), which are still in this office.

The loss of Prerogative Wills of dates earlier than 1800 has been largely repaired for the genealogist, due to the fact that Sir William Betham had, between 1810 and 1830, made abstracts of all the Prerogative Wills proved between 1536 and 1800, numbering over 37,000, and about 5,000 Grants of Administration, 1595-1800. These abstracts contain all genealogical information in the wills and administrations, naming the testator or the intestate deceased, the heirs, executors, family relationships, dates, and residence, location or properties. The abstracts were entered by Betham in his series of 241 notebooks which are now in the Public Record Office of Ireland, Dublin (58th *Report*, p. 25), and will be described more fully. Sir William Betham, Ulster King of Arms, 1820-1853, used the information in his notebooks to prepare thirty-nine large volumes of "Will Pedigrees," drawn up as genealogical charts, which he called his "Genealogical Analysis" of his abstracts, showing all names, relationships and dates mentioned in the wills and administrations, but omitting any mention of property. Each of these genealogical charts contains the names in from two to many generations of a family, in some cases carried down in one line and in other cases showing the descent in various lines. Betham constructed the charts showing information in single wills and also in many cases he combined the information taken from a series of family wills in one generation after another, to make an extensive chart. The "Will Pedigrees" or genealogical charts of Betham are deposited in the Genealogical Office (Office of Arms), Dublin Castle.

In the course of time, Betham's successors in office added countless notes, mostly in the margins of the "Will Pedigrees," as they uncovered proven genealogical information regarding the families concerned in the Prerogative Wills and Administrations.

Sir Bernard Burke, Ulster King of Arms following Betham, had this entire series of "Will Pedigrees" copied for his own private use. The collection is contained in forty-two volumes, which were purchased in 1931 by the Public Record Office of Northern Ireland, Belfast. Each volume is of a size equalling the average deed book. The marginal annotations of the Betham collection are lacking in the Burke transcripts. While volumes one and two are arranged somewhat haphazardly, volumes three and four show a planned system, dealing with wills of dates earlier than 1700, arranged in alphabetical order. Each one, however, is not in perfect alphabetical sequence. The latter volumes, five through forty-two, contain the charts of the wills 1700-1800, being arranged in alphabetical order. Each volume is self indexed, both as to names of testators and alliances recorded in the wills. An additional volume index of names of persons whose property was subject to Prerogative Grants of Administration Intestate, has been compiled.

The *Index to the Prerogative Wills of Ireland, 1536-1810,* edited by Sir Arthur Vicars (Ulster King of Arms), Dublin, 1897, acts as an excellent guide to the existing abstracts dated from 1536 to 1800, in Sir William Betham's notebooks now in the Public Record Office of Ireland, Dublin. It also serves as an Index of the "Will Pedigrees" or genealogical charts in the Genealogical Office, and of the transcripts made by or for

Burke, now in the Public Record Office of Northern Ireland, Belfast. It should be noted that Vicars' Index includes the wills dated 1801-1810 which were not abstracted by Sir William Betham or included in his "Will Pedigree" charts. However, some omissions of wills in Vicars' Index, between 1536 and 1800 have been discovered and are shown in a typescript volume in the British Museum, entitled "Additions to and Corrections in Vicars' Index." It is estimated there are 38,654 wills listed in Vicars' Index, by name of the testator, his or her rank, occupation or condition (spinster, etc.); town, county, or other location in Ireland, and in some cases a residence in England, Scotland, or more rarely, America is given; and always the year in which the estate was probated.

Vicars' Index will be found in a number of the large genealogical libraries of the United States. Photostats of "Will Pedigree" charts of the testators listed in Vicars' Index, and any of Betham's Abstracts of Wills and Administrations in his notebooks may be obtained by contacting the respective repositories.

All original Diocesan Wills, and Diocesan Will and Grant Books containing the official copies of the original documents, were destroyed in the Public Record Office fire of 1922, except for one original Will and the Will and Grant Books for the Diocese of Connor, 1818-1820, 1853-1858; Diocese of Down, 1850-1858.

The heroic work of replacing the destroyed documents and locating transcripts, abstracts, manuscript collections of family records and published records which provide the information taken from the burned wills, has been extremely successful. As stated above, the copying of the records by qualified individuals has preserved the information in a good proportion of the Diocesan Wills and Administrations. Solicitors, family representatives and genealogists, and various repositories have presented copies of the records to the Public Record Office of Ireland, Dublin; the Public Record Office of Northern Ireland, Belfast; the National Library of Ireland, Dublin; or the Genealogical Office (Office of Arms), Dublin Castle; and in many cases these collections have been exchanged among the said repositories for making additional transcripts. In addition, some important genealogical collections of certified copies or plain copies of the records have been purchased or received by the repositories as gifts, while several thousands of original unproved Diocesan Wills have been acquired in one way or another. Thus it is important to know what documents once existed, before making a search for presently existing replacements.

Fortunately, the Indexes to the Diocesan Wills, Grants of Administration, and Administration Bonds were saved from the fire of 1922, as they were located in the Public Search Room of the Public Record Office, Dublin, which was not burned. These indexes and copies thereof (unpublished) are listed below under the repositories. Some published indexes are listed in VOLUME II, pp. 259-261, herewith. The indexes serve three purposes: (1) They provide the name of the deceased, his place of residence, and the year of probate which was most likely the year of his death. (2) They alert the genealogist to the possibility of locating a copy of a listed Will or Administration. (3) They indicate the time when, owing to death, the property of the deceased changed hands. A record of this is quite usually found in the Registry of Deeds, and often provides as much genealogical information as contained in the Will.

The Indexes and collections (original documents, transcripts and abstracts) of Wills, Grants of Administration, Administration Bonds, etc., are deposited in the repositories as follows:

THE PUBLIC RECORD OFFICE OF IRELAND, DUBLIN:

1. List of Testamentary Records, Indexes and Calendars saved, and of those presented or purchased from the time of the fire in 1922 to the end of 1927 (55th *Report of the Deputy Keeper*):

(1) Prerogative Grant Books (Grants of Administration), 1684-1688; 1748-1751; 1839 (p. 26). Prerogative Day Books, 1784-1788 (p. 26).

(2) Inventories (Prerogative Court), Index to, 1668-1858 (p. 28).

(3) Wills (Prerogative), Indexes to, 1536-1858 (p. 28).

(4) Wills (Unproved Prerogative), Indexes to, 1689-1858 (p. 29).

(5) Will Books, Prerogative, 1664-1684; 1706-1708 (A-W); 1726-1728 (A-W); 1728-1729 (A-W); 1777 (A-L); 1813 (K-Z); 1834 (A-E) (p. 31).

(6) Eleven original Prerogative Wills saved; names Clark, Clarke, Stevenson, Young, Younge, 18th and 19th centuries (p. 30).

(7) Diocesan Grant Books: Diocese of Cashel (Probates, Administrations, etc.), 1840-1845; Diocese of Derry and Raphoe (badly damaged), Administrations, 1812-1851; Diocese of Ossory, Administrations, and Administrations Will Annexed, 1848-1858 (pp. 26-27).

(8) Court and Register Book, Diocese of Killaloe (Administrations), 1845 (p. 26).

(9) Unpublished Indexes of Diocesan Wills as follows (pp. 28-29):

(a) Ardagh, 1695-1858. Includes parts of counties Cavan, Leitrim, Roscommon, Sligo, and Westmeath.

(b) Ardfert and Aghadoe, 1690-1858. Includes County Kerry and part of County Cork.

(c) Armagh, 1677-1858 (M-Y). (Also Drogheda District, 1691-1846, A-Y.) Includes parts of counties Armagh, Londonderry, Longford, Louth, Meath, and Tyrone.

(d) Cashel and Emly, 1618-1858. Includes parts of counties Limerick and Tipperary.

(e) Clogher, 1661-1858. Includes parts of counties Donegal, Fermanagh, Louth, Tyrone, and all of Monaghan.

(f) Clonfert, 1663-1857. Includes parts of counties Galway, King's and Roscommon.

(g) Cloyne, 1621-1858 (damaged). Includes part of County Cork.

(h) Connor, 1662-1858 (and one entry of 1859). Includes parts of counties Antrim, Down, and Londonderry.

(i) Cork and Ross, 1548-1858 (and two probates, 1454, 1479). Includes part of County Cork.

(j) Derry, 1612-1858. Includes parts of counties Antrim, Donegal, Londonderry, and Tyrone.

(k) Down, 1646-1858. Includes parts of counties Antrim and Down.

(1) Dromore, 1678-1858 (damaged). Includes parts of counties Antrim, Armagh, and Down.

(m) Dublin, 1536-1858 (fragments). (Printed in the Appendixes to the 26th and the 30th *Reports of the Deputy Keeper of the Records*). Includes parts of counties Kildare, Queen's, Wexford, Wicklow, and all of County Dublin.

(n) Elphin, 1650-1858. Includes parts of counties Galway, Roscommon, and Sligo (fragments).

(o) Ferns, 1601-1858. Includes parts of counties Wexford and Wicklow (fragments).

(p) Kildare, 1661-1857. Includes parts of counties Kildare, King's, Meath, and Queen's (fragments).

(q) Killala and Achonry, n.d. (fragments). Includes parts of counties Mayo and Sligo.

(r) Killaloe and Kilfenora, n.d. (fragments). Includes parts of counties Clare, Galway, King's, Limerick, and Tipperary.

(s) Kilmore, 1682-1857 (badly damaged). Includes parts of counties Cavan, Fermanagh, Leitrim, and Meath.

(t) Leighlin, 1682-1858 (fragments). Includes parts of counties Carlow, Kilkenny, Queen's, and Wicklow.

(u) Limerick, 1615-1858. Includes parts of counties Clare, and Limerick.

(v) Meath, 1572-1858 (fragments). Includes parts of counties Cavan, King's, Longford, Meath, and Westmeath.

(w) Newry and Mourne, 1727-1858 (fragments). Includes part of County Down.

(x) Ossory, 1536-1858 (very badly damaged). Includes parts of counties Kilkenny, King's, and Queen's.

(y) Raphoe, 1684-1858 (very badly damaged). Includes part of County Donegal.

(z) Tuam, 1648-1858 (very badly damaged). Includes parts of counties Galway, Mayo, and Roscommon.

(z-2) Waterford and Lismore, 1648-1858 (badly damaged). Includes parts of County Tipperary and all of Waterford.

Substitutes for most of the damaged indexes noted above are found among the printed Indexes to Diocesan Wills, listed in VOLUME II, pp. 260-261, herewith. These fill the gaps to the following extent: Cloyne, 1621-1800; Dromore, 1678-1858; Dublin, 1536-1858; Ferns, 1601-1800; Kildare, 1661-1800; Killaloe and Kilfenora, 1653-1800; Leighlin, 1652-1800; Newry and Mourne, 1727-1858; Ossory, 1536-1800; Raphoe, 1684-1858; Waterford and Lismore, 1645-1800.

(10) Unpublished Indexes to Diocesan Administration Bonds (p. 27);

(a) Ardagh, 1697-1850.

(b) Armagh, 1742-1857 (and Drogheda District, 1822-1846).

(c) Cashel and Emly, 1644-1858.

(d) Clogher, 1660-1858.

(e) Clonfert, Killala and Achonry, Limerick and Ardfert, 1738-1837.

(f) Cloyne, 1630-1857.

(g) Connor, 1636-1858.

(h) Cork and Ross, 1612-1858.

(i) Derry, 1698-1857.

(j) Down, 1635-1858.

(k) Dromore, 1742-1858, and Newry and Mourne, 1811-1845.

(l) Dublin, 1697-1800, 1801-1845, and Kildare, 1770-1848.

(m) Elphin, 1726-1857.

(n) Ferns, 1765-1833.

(o) Killaloe, 1704-1857.

(p) Kilmore, 1728-1857.

(q) Leighlin, 1694-1845.

(r) Meath, 1663-1857.

(s) Ossory, 1660-1857.

(t) Raphoe, 1684-1858.

(u) Tuam, 1692-1857.

(v) Waterford and Lismore, 1661-1857, and peculiar jurisdiction of Lismore, 1766-1846.

(11) Index Books: Dioceses of Cashel, Waterford, Lismore and Ferns. Grants of Probate and Administration, 1847-1858 (with list of Unproved Wills lodged in Cashel Diocesan Court, 1638-1856). Diocese of Waterford and Lismore: Grants of Probate and Administration, 1650-1788 (p. 29).

(12) A "List of Original Probates, Letters of Administration Will Annexed and Intestate, Marriage Licence Grants and Official Copies of Wills, Grants, etc., presented during the period from the destruction of the Record Office in 1922 to the end of 1927" (pp. 33-68). Records are indexed by name, with the year of the document, nature of the record, and Court or Registry (Prerogative, Consistorial (Diocesan), Principal or District Registry of the Probate Court).

(13) A "List of Original Unproved Wills (never lodged for Probate), Duplicates of Wills and Plain Copies of Wills, Grants, etc., presented 1922-1927" (pp. 69-90). Records are indexed and described as above. Thrift Abstracts are included.

(14) Inquisitions: Record Commissioners' Transcripts of Deeds and Wills in (Chancery), recited in Chancery Inquisitions. 30 volumes for counties Antrim, Armagh, Cavan, Carlow, Clare, Cork, (Cork City), Donegal, Down, Dublin, Fermanagh, Galway, Kerry, Kildare, Kilkenny, King's, Limerick, Londonderry, Longford, Louth, Mayo, Meath, Monaghan, Queen's, Roscommon, Sligo, Tipperary, Tyrone, Waterford, Westmeath, Wexford, Wicklow. These are dated mostly between the time of Henry VIII and William III (p. 115).

(15) Inquisitions: Record Commissioners' Transcripts of Deeds and Wills in (Exchequer), recited in Exchequer Inquisitions. 12 volumes for counties Carlow, Dublin City and County, Galway, Kildare, Kilkenny, Louth, Queen's, Meath, Westmeath. These are dated mostly between the time of Henry VIII and William III (p. 115).

(16) Deeds and Wills in Inquisitions, Index to (p. 125).

(17) The Officers and Directors of the Bank of Ireland in 1922, presented "Unclaimed Probates, Letters of Administration and Affidavits" (693 Documents) (pp. 6, 10).

2. Lists of Testamentary Records saved from the fire of 1922, and of documents presented in 1928 (56th *Report of the Deputy Keeper*) :

(1) Miscellaneous collections of Wills (Original Unproved) and Plain Copies of Wills and Probates; Administrations, Grants of (Official Copies) ; Probates and Letters of Administration Wills Annexed (Original), and other Administrations Intestate, are listed in this *Report* under the names of the donors (mostly solicitors), among presented collections, containing records of various classes (pp. 24-59).

(2) "List of Original Probates, etc., and Official copies of Wills, Grants, etc., presented, 1928; Wills in salved [saved] Prerogative Will Books, and Wills and Grants of Administration in the salved Down and Connor Will and Grant Books" (pp. 79-197). This list of records is presented alphabetically, by name of the principal, his residence, nature of the record, year, Court or Registry, and reference number. About 5,000 records are listed. It is estimated that 2,017 items are records of the Prerogative Court and most of the remainder are Diocesan records of Down and Connor. They are dated from 1664 to 1858, a few being of later dates.

(3) "Original Unproved Wills (never lodged for Probate), Duplicates of Wills and Plain Copies of Wills, Grants, &c., presented 1928, List of" (pp. 198-202). The records are listed alphabetically, by name of the principal, etc., as above. They are dated from the 17th to 19th centuries.

3. List of Testamentary Records saved from the fire of 1922, and of documents presented in 1929 and 1930 (57th *Report of the Deputy Keeper*) :

(1) Collections presented, acquired by purchase and loaned for copying, 1931-1936, are listed as received from solicitors and other individuals, with the classes of records, names of the principals, residences in some cases, dates of the records, etc. These collections contain a wealth of Wills (Copies) ; Wills (Abstracts and Extracts) ; Letters of Ad-

ministration; Letters of Administration Will Annexed, etc. (pp. 19-46).

(2) Appendix I contains Testamentary, Matrimonial and Ecclesiastical Documents: "A List of Original Probates, etc., and Official Copies of Wills, Grants, etc., presented, 1929, 1930; Grants in salved Prerogative Grant Books, 1748-1751, and 1839; salved Dublin Marriage Licence Bonds, "A" 1749-1813; salved Dublin Consistorial Cause Papers, . . .; Grants of Administration and Administration Will Attached in salved Ossory Grant Book, 1845-1858; Marriage Licence Grants . . ." (pp. 62-324). Records are listed alphabetically by name of the principal, with residence, nature of the document, year, Court or Registry, and source (with number) of the original Document, Copy, or Abstract.

(3) "A List of Original Unproved Wills (never lodged for Probate), Duplicates of Wills and Plain Copies of Wills, Grants, etc., presented 1929, 1930, and concluding part of the Testamentary, Matrimonial and Ecclesiastical portion of the "Thrift Abstracts" Collection (pp. 325-420). Records are listed alphabetically by name of the principal, his residence, nature of the document, year, Court or Registry, and source (Original Document, Copy, or Abstract), with number of the record.

4. Collections of Testamentary Records acquired by the Public Record Office of Ireland, Dublin, 1931-1950 (58th *Report of the Deputy Keeper*): Mr. Diarmid Coffey, Assistant Deputy Keeper of the Records, stated in this *Report*, p. 5, "Since the publication of the 57th *Report*, important collections of documents have been deposited, both by government departments and by private donors. I wish to return thanks to the many donors whose gifts have enriched the testamentary and other collections. As in former years, the list includes a large number of solicitors, whose presentations have done much toward building up an extensive collection of testamentary documents serving as substitutes for material destroyed in 1922."

Testamentary Records dated between 1536 and 1858, deposited in this Office from 1931 to 1950, are recorded under the headings of (1) Deposits by Government Offices; (2) Purchases of Record Collections; (3) Presentations of Record Collections.

"A Card Index is being maintained of testamentary documents received otherwise than from probate registries. It is hoped that this will supply the deficiency created from the fact that the lists of such material published in previous reports [the 55th, 56th, and 57th *Reports*] are not being continued. Since the publication of the Deputy Keeper's 57th *Report*, over 7,000 items have been added" (p. 8). This Card Index in the Public Search Room covers the purchased and presented collections of Wills which have mostly come to this Office among family papers, genealogical MSS., and from solicitors' offices. They are listed in the 58th *Report* by the name of the donor or the person from whom they were purchased, or the source from which they were loaned for copying. Under each collection are given the principal surnames of the testators, and in some cases the dates (by year) and location. The very large collections, such as that of Betham, are self indexed.

A few of the collections which are self indexed, are noted as follows:

(1) A copy of the Index to Armagh Wills, 1666-1837 (A-L), from Phillipps MS. No. 15294, in the Public Record Office, Belfast, in substitution for the original index, destroyed in 1922 (p. 8).

(2) A copy was made of the list of abstracts of wills in the Stewart-Kennedy Notebooks in the Library of Trinity College, Dublin (p. 8).

(3) The volumes of the Greene MSS. in the National Library entitled "Extracts from prerogative and diocesan wills," "Extracts from grant books and parish registers" and "Extracts from prerogative rule books, wills, diocesan and prerogative, and Castle Dermott parish registers," were transcribed and indexed (p. 8).

(4) Transcripts of the Diocese of Ossory Administrations, 1738-1804, contained in the T. U. Sadleir collection, and miscellaneous Deeds and Wills, etc., 1672-1868, contained in the same Sadleir collection (p. 25).

(5) Collection of 241 volumes known as the *Betham Genealogical Abstracts*, subdivided as follows:

80 vols. from Prerogative Wills, 1536-1800.

2 vols. from Kildare Wills, 1661-1826.

16 vols. from Prerogative Marriage Licences, 1629-1801.

60 vols. of which nos. 1-56 are from Prerogative Administrations, 1595-1800 and nos. 57-60 from Prerogative Marriage Licences, 1629-1800.

54 vols. from Dublin Marriage Licences, 1660-1824.

29 vols. of miscellaneous extracts from court records, pedigrees and memoranda (for details see indexed catalogue in P. R. O.).

(6) Eight volumes of papers of Sir William Betham (letters dealing with his genealogical researches and memoranda and extracts on genealogical subjects). M744-715. (p. 25).

(7) Betham MSS., viz.: (p. 26).

Volume of Abstracts of Grants of Administration, Prerogative, 1595-1802 (A-C). T7427.

Volume of Indexes to Clogher Wills, 1658-1849. T7429.

Volume of Indexes to Limerick Wills, 1631-1841. T7430.

Volume of Indexes to Meath Wills, 1635-1838. T7431.

Volume of Indexes to Prerogative Wills, 1641-1811; Waterford Wills, 1659-1838; Cloyne Wills, 1621-1838; Elphin Wills, 1669-1838; Kilmore Wills, 1682-1838. T7432.

(8) Dean Swanzy's Testamentary Notebook, giving genealogical abstracts of Wills, Administrations, & Marriage Licences for Prerogative Court, 1681-1846, Clogher Diocese, 1712-1750, & Kilmore Diocese, 1694-1770. T1746 (p. 41).

Mr. B. Mac Giolla Choille, Assistant Deputy Keeper of the Records, stated in 1955, "The Office of Charitable Donations and Bequests in Dublin, has abstracts of every Prerogative and Diocesan Will leaving any bequest of a charitable nature, from 1800 to the present time. Such bequests to a Church or other institution, were willed by common practice, regardless of wealth or circumstance. Thus this great collection of will abstracts of a portion of the Diocesan and Prerogative Wills (the originals and Court Copies of which were lost in the fire in 1922), bridges the period, 1800-1858. An Index of these abstracts is in the Public Record Office, with one gap, 1829-1839, because there are indexes to wills in this Office covering those years." The indexes and the accompanying records were sent by the Commissioners of Inland Revenue, London, and are listed in the 58th *Report*, p. 19, as follows: Irish will registers, 1829-1839; Irish Will indexes, 1828-1879; Irish administration registers, 1829-1839; Irish administration indexes, 1828-1879. The Irish Will Registers dated from the 4th quarter of 1828 to 1839 were taken to England by the British Inland Revenue Board, containing the abstracts of Prerogative and Diocesan Wills, showing the date of death of the testator, residence, date of will, the estate liable to duty (amount), the name of the executor and his or her residence, rank, occupation, or description (widow, etc.), where and when the will was proved. The Registers 1840-1879 are missing, but the Indexes for this period are an aid.

THE GENEALOGICAL OFFICE (OFFICE OF ARMS), DUBLIN CASTLE:

Material relating to Wills and Administrations is found in many sources in this Office but is largely contained in the following collections:

1. Sir William Betham's "Will Pedigrees," drawn up as genealogical charts, which he called his "Genealogical Analysis" of his abstracts of all the Prerogative Wills of Ireland, 1536-1800, and his genealogical charts made from his abstracts of the Prerogative Administrations Intestate, 1595-1800, have been described earlier in this chapter and also on pages 146-147, herein.

2. The "Index of Will Abstracts in the Genealogical Office, Dublin Castle, Dublin," compiled by Miss P. Beryl Eustace, and published by the Irish Manuscripts Commission, in its periodical, *Analecta Hibernica* No. 17, pp. 147-348, concerns

the abstracts of about 7,500 Wills in various manuscript collections. This is more fully described in this VOLUME I, p. 147.

THE NATIONAL LIBRARY OF IRELAND, DUBLIN:

Aside from the many published works containing material relating to Wills and Administrations, there are numerous manuscript collections containing family records including Wills and other testamentary documents, or transcripts or abstracts thereof. A typescript catalogue with descriptions of the contents of these manuscript collections, is in the Library. One such collection is the Greene MSS. of five volumes, containing original certified copies of Wills (Prerogative and Diocesan), Baptismal, Marriage and Burial Entries, extracts from 49 Officers' Rolls and Patent Rolls, and abstracts of Wills, Grants and other documents formerly in the Public Record Office, relating to various Greene families and other families connected with the Greenes by marriage. This manuscript collection also contains certified copies of Baptismal, Marriage, and Burial entries of members of allied families of Budd, Croker, Denis, or Dennis, Elliot, or Elliott, Greene, or Green, Hunt, Jones, Lewis, Mackesy, Newport, Poulter, Shearman, etc., in the parishes of Clonmore, Dunkitt, Fiddown, Kilbeacon, and Macully or Kilculliheen, Diocese of Ossory; parish of Innislonagh, Diocese of Lismore; St. Finnbarr's Parish, Diocese of Cork; and Shanagolden, Diocese of Limerick. This collection was borrowed by the Public Record Office of Ireland, Dublin, and was transcribed and indexed (57th *Report,* p. 56; 58th *Report,* p. 8).

TRINITY COLLEGE LIBRARY, DUBLIN:

One important collection of abstracts of Prerogative and Diocesan Wills is contained in the Stewart-Kennedy Notebooks, compiled from the records in the Public Record Office, Dublin, before 1922, by Mr. H. Stewart-Kennedy. Mr. Edward Phelps compiled a list of the Will abstracts which is in the Public Record Office, Dublin, at the present time (58th *Report,* p. 8). *Analecta Hibernica* No. 17, p. 148, notes this information and the fact that a copy is also in the Public Record Office of Northern Ireland, Belfast. The Deputy

Keeper's Report for this latter Office (1935 *Report*, p. 4) states that "A transcript was made of extracts from the wills of Ulster testators . . . some 500 in number, have been arranged in dictionary order of names, and bound in a single volume which has been deposited as a record. An index to the contents is embodied in Appendix B," of the 1935 *Report*.

THE REGISTRY OF DEEDS, DUBLIN:

Over 2,000 Wills were recorded in the Registry of Deeds, 1708-1800, primarily because they concerned real estate in Ireland. An index (MS.) of these wills was at first compiled by Miss P. Beryl Eustace, embodying the records 1708-1800. This was placed in the Genealogical Office (Office of Arms), Dublin Castle. Thereafter Miss Eustace compiled abstracts of the wills dated 1708-1745, and 1746-1785, totaling 1,464 in number, which have been published by the Irish Manuscripts Commission, under the title *Registry of Deeds, Dublin, Abstracts of Wills, 1708-1745; 1746-1785*, edited by P. Beryl Eustace, Dublin, 1954, 1956. Further details concerning these records are noted on pages 62-64, herein.

FRIENDS' MEETING HOUSE, 6 EUSTACE STREET, DUBLIN:

Among the hundreds of manuscript collections in the historical library, preserved by the Society of Friends, are six volumes containing Quaker Wills as follows:

1. Carlow Monthly Meeting, Book of Wills and Inventories, 1675-1740.

2. Edenderry Monthly Meeting, Book of Wills, 1628-1763.

3. Mountmellick Monthly Meeting, Book of Wills, 1755-1795.

4. County Wexford Monthly Meeting, Book of Wills, 1680-1760.

5. Dublin Monthly Meeting Books of Wills, 2 volumes, 1683-1772.

Quaker Records, Dublin, Abstracts of Wills, edited by P. Beryl Eustace and Olive C. Goodbody, and published by the Irish Manuscripts Commission, Dublin, 1957, contains abstracts of the 224 wills in the above Monthly Meeting, Books of Wills. Appendix I of the above volume contains a list of the only wills, 28 in number, which are preserved in the Records of Ulster Quarterly Meeting in the "Will Book of Ballyhagan Meeting." Abstracts of these were made by Lieut-Col. J.R.H. Greeves and published in *The Irish Genealogist*, Vol. 2, No. 8, October 1950. Appendix II of the above volume contains a list of some full copies of wills and some notes from wills which are deposited in the historical library at Friends House, Dublin. Further details about the published abstracts of wills are noted on p. 428, herein.

THE PUBLIC RECORD OFFICE OF NORTHERN IRELAND, BELFAST:

The "Chief Deposited Manuscript Collections," including "Solicitors' Collections," have been previously described herein (pp. 208-227). These and innumerable smaller collections of original, transcripts or abstracts of documents, have contributed many thousands of Prerogative and Diocesan Wills and Administrations, or the information extracted from the testamentary documents, of interest to genealogists. Furthermore, except for the very large manuscript collections, the names of the principals in each instrument are embodied (with their county or further description of residence, year of probate or date of Will, and nature of the record), in the Index contained in the *Report of the Deputy Keeper*, following the receipt of the record collection, in case the materials meet the principles of indexing stated on pp. 201-202, herein.

Undoubtedly, the most important of the "Chief Deposited Manuscript Collections," containing information taken from Prerogative Wills and Administrations, 1536-1800, is the Sir Bernard Burke collection of transcripts of Pedigree Charts made from Sir William Betham's "Will Pedigrees," constructed from Betham's abstracts of all the Prerogative Wills and Administrations of Ireland, 1536-1800. The Burke collection of transcripts is described earlier in this chapter, with Betham's records, and also on pp. 210-211, herein. One fact which might confuse the genealogist should be explained. While there are apparently some 16,000 pedigree charts in the Burke collection of transcripts of the work of Betham, these actually were constructed from the abstracts of over 37,000 Prerogative Wills, 1536-1800, and the abstracts of the Prerogative Administrations Intestate, 1695-1800. The Burke transcripts which accurately reproduce the pedigree charts of the Betham collection (with more legible handwriting and more space allowed for each name and dates, residence, etc.), show from two to many generations in each chart. In the longer charts the names, etc., from several wills of succeeding generations of a family have been combined in the one pedigree chart. All charts show at least the children or heirs named in the Prerogative Will or Administration Intestate of one person. Many charts show the children of each person in the second generation named in any of their wills, etc., and so on for succeeding generations. The lines of numerous families are continued for six or seven generations, and in some cases are further extended. Neither Betham nor Burke have indicated how many wills are represented in each chart. However, Sir Arthur Vicars' *Index to the Prerogative Wills of Ireland, 1536-1810,* serves as an Index to the testators named in any of these charts. This shows testators in three or more generations represented in a pedigree chart of six to eight generations. The Pedigree chart of the family of Nesbitt (Nesbit, Nesbet, Nesbett) illustrates this (Burke Collection, Vol. XIX, p. 154). There are fifty Nesbitt, etc., wills listed in Vicars' *Index,* three of which were used (and one Administration for Andrew Nesbitt, of Brenter, Co. Donegal, Esq., 15 Sept. 1692), to construct an eight generation chart.

PRINCIPAL AND DISTRICT REGISTRIES OF THE COURT OF PROBATE AFTER 1857

The average American genealogist may feel that the wills and administrations after 1857 are too late to be of interest. A brief review of Irish emigration statistics will serve to emphasize the fact that the period 1857 to 1875 or thereabouts is of great importance for the study of Irish Wills. It is shown that a large proportion of the Irish and Scotch-Irish who came to America and Canada or went to Australia or other parts of the British Empire after 1840, were under thirty years of age when they left home. Of these, the greater number were of ages between eighteen and twenty-five years. Most of the parents of these young people remained and died in Ireland. Relatively few emigrated when their children had become established and could send for them. The small number of emigrants aged forty or over, and the staggering figures of emigration during the great famine, 1846-1847, and for two decades thereafter, are sufficient evidence that in this period the parents of more young adult emigrants died in Ireland before or after their departure, than in any other like period of time. Statistics are taken from *The Census Returns (Ireland): 1851. Reports on Ages and Education. Tables of Deaths. General Report* (Alexander Thom & Son). 4 vols. Dublin, 1855-56. The emigration figures are quoted at the end of CHAPTER XXI, herein. Thus the genealogist may approach this period for the study of Wills and Administrations with great interest.

After 1857, the Established Church of Ireland no longer held ecclesiastical jurisdiction over probate matters, and testamentary jurisdiction was transferred from the Prerogative and the Consistorial (or Diocesan) Courts to the Civil Courts. "The Court of Probate and Letters of Administration Act (Ireland) 1857," (20 & 21 Vict. c. 77), created one Principal and eleven District Registries of the Court of Probate throughout Ireland. This means that Ireland was divided into twelve sections for matters of probate.

In the 3rd *Report of the Deputy Keeper of the Public Records in Ireland,* Appendix 11, next to P. 76, is a "Map of Ireland Shewing the Principal and District Registries of the Court of Probate, together with the County and Diocesan Divisions as existing at the time of the passing of The Probate and Letters of Administration Act (Ireland) 1857." The map (in various colors to set forth the respective Districts and Principal Registry) was printed by Forster & Co., Lith. to H. M. Stationery Office, Dublin. The scale is 27 miles to one inch. The map shows the District Number, the counties or area included in each District, and the Place of Registry in each District, as follows:

Dist. No.	Place of District Registry	Districts under Registry
1.	Londonderry	Cos. Donegal, Londonderry, and the Baronies of Strabane and Omagh in the Co. of Tyrone.
2.	Belfast	Cos. Antrim and Down.
3.	Armagh	Cos. Armagh, Louth, Monaghan, Fermanagh and Tyrone, except for the Baronies of Strabane and Omagh.
4.	Ballina	Cos. Mayo, Sligo, and Leitrim, except the Baronies of Mohill, Carrigallen, and Leitrim.
5.	Cavan	Cos. Cavan, Longford, and the Baronies of Leitrim, Mohill and Carrigallen, in the Co. of Leitrim.
6.	Tuam	Cos. Roscommon and Galway.
7.	Mullingar	King's Co. and Westmeath.
8.	Kilkenny	Cos. Carlow, Queen's Co., and Kilkenny.
9.	Waterford	Cos. Waterford, Wexford, and South Riding of Tipperary.
10.	Limerick	Cos. Limerick, Clare, North Riding of Tipperary, and Baronies of Clanmaurice and Irraghticonnor, in the Co. of Kerry.
11.	Cork	Cos. Cork and Kerry, except the Baronies of Clanmaurice and Irraghticonnor in the Co. of Kerry.

Principal Registry	Districts under the Registry
Dublin	Cos. Dublin, Kildare, Wicklow, Meath, and part of King's Co.

*   *   *   *   *

Mr. D. A. Chart, appointed Deputy Keeper of the Public Records of the new Public Record Office of Northern Ireland, Belfast, on 14 January 1924, gave the following information regarding the Northern Ireland Wills dated after 1857, and the general practice with regard to preserving the records in all Distict Registries:

"In view of the enormous destruction of records in Dublin in 1922, efforts were made to obtain copies of the destroyed documents from every possible source and, concurrently with the steps taken to obtain original documents, communications were addressed to Government Departments, solicitors, and private persons in whose hands such copies were likely to be found. Fortunately, it was possible to repair in part at once one of the worst losses—that of the original wills. Since the establishment of the Probate Registries a copy of each will proved had been preserved in the District Registry which issued the grant. These had been entered in large volumes known as Will Books. Belfast and Londonderry Probate Registries had each preserved Will Books containing copies of the wills proved in respective jurisdictions since 1858. The Will Books of the former Armagh District Registry for the same period had been transferred to, and were preserved in, the Principal Registry, Belfast. It was represented to the Lord Chief Justice that since the original wills which had been concentrated in Dublin were no longer available, a similar concentration of the copies for the convenience of searchers in Northern Ireland should be effected in this Office. Accordingly, with the Lord Chief Justice's consent, these Will Books, numbering 102 in all, and covering the period 1858-1900, were transferred here from both Northern Registries [including the Will Books of the former Armagh District Registry which were transferred first to the Belfast District Registry before it became the Principal Registry of Northern Ireland, at the time of the change in Government when Counties Cavan, Donegal, and Monaghan, joined the Irish Free State]. The loss, however, of the Grant Books and all other Testamentary Papers, particularly the "Schedules of Assets," will be severely felt." (1924 *Report of the Deputy Keeper*, p. 9.) The 102 Will Books, 1858-1900, are each indexed by names of the testators but there is no consolidated index for this series. The Calendars of Grants of Administration, now in the Principal Registry Office, Belfast, should be consulted for this period.

The principal and District Probate Registry records saved after the fire of 1922, and the replacements, now in the Public Record Office of Ireland, Dublin, are as follows:

The Grant Books containing Probates and Administrations for the various District Registries are as follows: Armagh, 1858-1861; Ballina, 1858-1875; Belfast (Probates only), 1867-

1869, 1871-1873, 1875-1877, 1883-1885; Cavan, 1858-1873; Cork, 1858-1869; Limerick, 1858-1868, 1873-1877; Londonderry (Probates only), 1862-1869; Mullinger, 1859-1869; Tuam, 1872-1886; Waterford, 1858-1865. The Grant Books also contain Administrations Will annexed for the following District Registries: Armagh, 1862-1873; Cork, 1885-1891, 1895-1901; Limerick, 1858-1865, 1895-1902; Mullinger, 1892-1903; Tuam, 1886-1903. (55th *Report*, pp. 26-27.)

The Grant Books of the Principal Registry, Dublin, are 1878 and 1883 (Special and unadministered and Probates); 1891 (Probates); 1893 (Administrations Will annexed). (*ibid.*, p. 26.)

Indexes are as follows: Wills (Unproved) Principal Registry, 1858-1899; Wills (Unproved) District Registries, 1858-1905; Armagh District Registry (Wills and Administrations), 1862-1877; Cork (Wills and Administrations), 1874-1879, 1898-1899; Limerick, 1900-1906; Waterford (General Index to Applications for Grants, Caveats, Unproved Wills, etc., 1889-1901. (*ibid.*, p. 29.)

Will Books for the Principal and District Registries, containing copies of Wills, transferred to this Office after 1922, are as follows: Ballina, after 1865; Cavan, 1858-1873; Cork, 1858-1876; Kilkenny, 1858-1874; Limerick, 1858-1875; Mullinger, 1859-1877; Tuam, 1858-1877; Waterford, 1858-1873. The Principal Registry, Dublin, Copies, 1869 (G-M); 1891 (M-P); 1901 (A-F). The Principal Registry Will Books, Dublin, are as follows: 1874 (G-M); 1878 (A-F); 1878 (G-M); 1878 (N-Z); 1891 (G-M); 1896 (A-F). (*ibid.*, p. 31.)

The 55th *Report of the Deputy Keeper*, Appendix II (B), pp. 33-68, contains a "List of Original Probates, Letters of Administration Will Annexed and Intestate, Marriage Licence Grants and Official Copies of Wills, Grants, etc., presented during the period from the destruction of the Record Office in 1922 to the end of 1927." Among the listed records are many from various District Probate Registries and from the Principal Registry in Dublin. The records are entered alphabetically, by name of the testator, with his title, or description (widow, etc.), the nature of the record and the Court or Registry. A further list is contained in the 56th *Report,* pp. 79-196, and pp. 198-202.

CHAPTER XXIV

GENEALOGISTS AND RECORD SEARCHERS
GENEALOGICAL BOOKSHOPS

Irish genealogists and record searchers do not advertise their services. Some of the compiled works of the most able and active genealogists are published in one form or another, i.e., family histories, genealogies, pedigrees, extracts from collections of wills, marriage records, tombstone records, school registers, etc., as the bibliography in the accompanying VOLUME II will show. The greater part of the work of genealogists remains in their manuscript collections. These are appraised by virtue of the proven ability of the compiler, and sought accordingly by the various historical societies, institutions, and official repositories of records in Ireland.

Qualified genealogists make a practice of contributing some part of their work to the historical society journals or other periodicals of note in their particular field and area of interest. VOLUME II, CHAPTER V (pp. 52-75) herewith, contains a "Family Index to Articles in Irish Periodicals: Relating to Family History, Genealogy, Pedigrees, and Biography (with a key to the periodicals)."

The reviews of recently published books of historical and genealogical interest appear in the semi-annual numbers of *Irish Historical Studies,* the *Journal of the Royal Society of Antiquaries of Ireland,* and some other periodicals. The outstanding articles in the more important magazines of a historical and genealogical nature are also noted, with the names of the contributors. The work of reviewing current material is entrusted to highly qualified critics.

A number of the large American libraries have subscribed to *Irish Historical Studies,* since its first number was issued in March 1938, or have lately acquired all numbers and now maintain an annual subscription. The same should be true of the *Journal of the Royal Society of Antiquaries of Ireland,* the *Ulster Journal of Archaeology*, and other periodicals listed in VOLUME II, pp. 43-53, herewith.

The volume of inquiries sent to the various repositories of records regarding genealogists is increasing so rapidly that some centralization of information seems necessary in Dublin and Belfast. In making inquiries many people mistakenly use the terms genealogist and record searcher synonymously. Thus more often one who asks for the name of a genealogist actually wants the service of a record searcher.

Before offering any suggestions regarding contacts with Irish genealogists and record searchers, a common ground of understanding must be reached as to the qualifications and work which establish one person as a genealogist and another person as a record searcher. It is true that all genealogical research is carried on by record searchers. But few record searchers engage in the character of work or attain the necessary qualifications of a genealogist. On the other hand many superior genealogists employ the services of record searchers to save themselves time and travel expense.

A competent genealogist has, in the course of his experience, acquired a wide knowledge of all classes of the pertinent records of each period. He knows their historical background, their extent, location, and the use which he can make of them. His ability is commensurate with a phenomenal memory for all manner of detail relating to or encountered in the records. He knows how and where to dip into one source after another for information. With the sixth sense of a detective, he will recognize any emerging clue and know how to follow it through one class of records after another while forming the next link in the chain of evidence. A genealogist must have a fund of imagination to help him determine what might have happened under given circumstances. He works by process of elimination. He is blessed with overwhelming curiosity. Once he becomes interested in a case he can never let it go. A genealogist of any note is exceedingly sensitive in his ability to recognize related evidence and to weigh cumulative presumptive evidence. In the course of his investigation he will strengthen his theory as to probabilities, based upon overwhelming circumstantial evidence, if no contrary fact can be discovered to disprove one weak link in the chain. But his suppositions are carefully qualified until substantiated with proof. He is of necessity his own severest critic, without pride, in his search for truth.

It is obvious that few purses are deep enough to pay for the knowledge and judgement of a genealogist of this order while he investigates all collections of all classes of records which could possibly pertain to a single case. The time given to research resulting in negative findings alone would shock an uninformed client and is hard to report. For this reason about half or more of a genealogist's time is usually donated during the course of any professional research. Thus he has reason to be selective in taking a case.

Record searchers in the full or part time employ of an institution or repository of records, may have begun working with the published or manuscript records in any capacity which gave them familiarity with the indexes and materials at hand. Experience has taught them what collections of records and indexes are available, where to find required information among the published or manuscript sources of various classes of records in one or more repositories of records. They are able to read original documents dating from the 16th century and to interpret and copy the text accurately. Some are specialists in Gaelic, Latin and early English calligraphy.

A professional record searcher employed in a library or other repository of genealogical records, or if working as a self employed person, fulfills his purpose when he follows directions to search for particular records among specified source materials and, if successful, to make transcripts, abstracts, or extracts, according to his orders. Having performed this duty his commission is completed. The use to which his copied records may be put is no concern of his.

A published list of names and addresses of genealogists and record searchers seems inadvisable. Time and circumstances cause continual changes in their activity and availability as new people come into the field and others drop away.

In the course of time the Genealogical Office (Office of

Arms), Dublin Castle, now operated as a department of the National Library, has become the center through which all inquiries relating to the work of genealogists and record searchers in Dublin are cleared. Inquiries may be addressed to Mr. Gerard Slevin, Chief Herald of the Genealogical Office, and Keeper of the Manuscripts of the National Library. Record searchers in the National Library work under the supervision of Mr. Alfred MacLochlainn, Assistant Keeper of the Manuscripts; Mr. Patrick Henchy, Keeper of the Printed Books; and Mr. Thomas P. O'Neill, Assistant Keeper of the Printed Books.

The practice of screening genealogists and record searchers has evolved as a matter of service and protection to those who could not come to personally examine the records in the various repositories in Dublin. The Genealogical Office has responded by assigning record searchers to fulfill each commission sent to this Office, for work in its own or other repositories, according to the requirements of the case. A report on the records concerning certain families, deposited in the Genealogical Office, is illustrated on pp. 148-154, herein. This will give an idea of what can be expected. It was the work of a qualified record searcher, performed under the supervision of Mr. Slevin. In this case no request was sent for the services of a genealogist or for research in any other repository.

The Ulster-Scot Historical Society, Law Courts Building, Chichester Street, Belfast, was organized to handle inquiries for genealogical research regarding Ulster families. It is operated as a department of the Public Record Office of Northern Ireland. Its director, Mr. Kenneth Darwin, is also Deputy Keeper of the Records in the latter Office. Record searchers in the employ of the Ulster-Scot Historical Society have access to all of the Card Indexes, Catalogues, MSS. collections, and the library of printed books in the Public Record Office of Northern Ireland. These record searchers will also work in other Belfast repositories.

Some private repositories such as Friends House Library, 6 Eustace Street, Dublin, and the Presbyterian Historical Society Library, 20 Church House, Fisherwick Place, Belfast, are equipped for members of their own staff to handle inquiries. Miss Helen D. Jones, Secretary of Friends House, and Miss Olive C. Goodbody, Keeper of the Manuscripts in Friends House Library, will supervise the work of examining the records of the Society of Friends and also some hundreds of family manuscripts deposited in the library. Miss Jeannie L. M. Stewart, Assistant Secretary of the Presbyterian Historical Society, will provide reports on the records and manuscript collections in this repository.

The names of genealogists and record searchers in the several counties may be obtained from the respective County Libraries, or from the Genealogical Office, Dublin Castle (for the counties in the Republic of Ireland), and the Ulster-Scot Historical Society (for the counties of Northern Ireland).

In 1955, this compiler while in Cork, inquired of Mr. P. J. Madden, Librarian of the County Cork Library, and of Mr. W. Cahill, Librarian of the University Library, Cork, for the names of any competent genealogists of the county. Three names were offered. Mr. Basil O'Connell of the National Library of Ireland, Dublin, was acclaimed as a scholar and genealogist of distinction, who knows more about the medieval and modern records of the families of the Province of Munster than any other living person. He has worked particularly on Irish Roman Catholic families of South Munster. Mr. John T. Collins, who may be contacted through the University Library, Cork, has the reputation of a fine genealogist who specializes in County Cork families, and their allied families from surrounding counties. He is a contributor to the *Journal of the Cork Historical and Archaeological Society*. Mr. J. Lankford, of Gortmuire, Assumption Road, Cork, also is a competent County Cork genealogist.

A County Cork genealogist has the advantage of knowing a great deal about the local families. He has two good libraries of published records for research. He also knows the locations of the churches. He can examine the existing Parish Registers and tombstone records. But the bulk of his research must, of necessity, be done in Dublin. Hence, if a County Cork genealogist takes a case pertaining to a local family, it will almost always involve some days of work in one or more Dublin repositories of records, or he must write for the services of record searchers to complete the research on the particular branch of the family under consideration.

As the preceding chapters have shown, most of the genealogical source materials concerning members of families of the counties in the Republic of Ireland are in Dublin repositories of records. Source materials in Dublin and in Belfast must be searched when tracing the members of an Ulster family.

Amateur genealogists, family historians and professional genealogists who can not personally work in the repositories of records in Dublin and Belfast or travel about Ireland, can do much to help themselves and reduce the expense of research. By carefully studying the source materials described and listed in this VOLUME I, and the accompanying VOLUME II, each person can plan his own program of research in relation to its particular requirements. He can make a choice of the collections of records to be searched, and select the items of which transcripts or photostats can be ordered directly from each repository.

Thus anyone can write directly to the Public Record Office of Northern Ireland, Belfast, or to the Ulster-Scot Historical Society, for transcripts or photostats of the following specific records:

1. Any family manuscript collection of records, listed in VOLUME II, pp. 111-166, herewith.

2. Any one of the hundred thousand or more items listed in the Indexes in the *Reports of the Deputy Keeper of the Public Records* (1924-1951/'53).

3. Any pedigree chart in the Burke collection of transcripts of the Betham pedigrees from Prerogative Wills, 1536-1800. Sir Arthur Vicars' *Index to the Prerogative Wills of Ireland, 1536-1810*, Dublin, 1897, contains the name, residence, and date of probate of all testators.

Transcripts or photostats of particular records in the Public Record Office of Ireland, Dublin, can also be ordered directly from this Office, by writing to Miss Margaret Griffith,

Deputy Keeper of the Records (recently appointed), for any of the following:

1. A copy of any collection of family records listed in VOL-UME II, pp. 169-196, herewith, excepting those marked with an asterisk. This sign indicates there are records for the family in this Office but they may be scattered among various collections, and must be located by a record searcher by means of indexes and catalogues in the Public Search Room.

2. The 55th to 58th *Reports of the Deputy Keeper of the Public Records in Ireland*, contain thousands of other listed records of families or individuals, copies of which can be ordered if the desired item is named with the number of the *Report*, and the page whereon it is listed.

3. Sir Arthur Vicars' *Index to the Prerogative Wills of Ireland, 1536-1810*, Dublin, 1897, serves as an index to the "Abstracts of Prerogative Wills of Ireland, 1536-1800," made by Sir William Betham and contained in his collection of 241 notebooks deposited in this Office.

Certified copies of memorials of Deeds, Leases, Wills, Marriage Settlements, etc., can be ordered directly from the Registry of Deeds, Henrietta Street, Dublin, if one has access to the microfilms of the Names and the Land Indexes to the records. These are described in this VOLUME I, PART TWO, CHAPTER I. The microfilms of the Indexes, 1708-1904, consisting of 122 reels of the *Names Index*, and 283 reels of the *Land Index*, are deposited in the Genealogical Society Library of the Church of Jesus Christ of Latter-Day Saints, Salt Lake City, Utah.

One morning in 1952, this compiler was working with the Old Deed Books in the Registry of Deeds, on the floor above the main office. A young woman working at another table was rapidly searching the records in one Deed Book after another and appeared to be thoroughly familiar with the records. At one point this compiler became puzzled over the obscure meaning of the peculiar wording of a paragraph, and finally approached the young woman to ask if she would read the deed and interpret the wording. She was cordial and helpful. In the course of a short conversation, upon request, she gave her name as Miss M. P. Read, 31 Raglan Road, Ballsbridge,

Dublin. She had recently been graduated from a Law School. After ten years she might be located at the same address, or contacted through Mr. J. W. Dobbs, Assistant Registrar, Registry of Deeds, Henrietta Street, Dublin. However, a search of the records of this repository can also be commissioned through the Genealogical Office, Dublin Castle.

A report or outline of the family records contained in any one of the published books of compiled family history and genealogy, listed in VOLUME II, pp. 4-33, and 34-37, herewith, or a search of any of the county, town, diocesan or parish histories, or any other printed works or microfilms in Ireland, listed in VOLUME II, herewith, will require the attention of a record searcher in the National Library of Ireland, Dublin, the Linen Hall Library, Belfast, etc. However, a photostat of any one of the short articles on the history or genealogy of a particular family, listed in VOLUME II, pp. 53-75, herewith, could be ordered directly from the National Library of Ireland, care of Mr. Patrick Henchy, Keeper of the Printed Books, Kildare Street, Dublin. The same service could be obtained by writing to the Genealogical Office, Dublin Castle, care of Mr. Gerard Slevin, Chief Herald and Keeper of the Manuscripts in the National Library.

Inquiries regarding genealogists and record searchers in the London area will be furnished by applying to Sir Anthony Wagner, Garter Principal King of Arms, College of Arms, London, E.C. 4. Important collections of Irish Genealogical source materials are deposited in London in the British Museum, the College of Arms, Friends House Library, Lambeth Palace Library, the Public Record Office, the Society of Genealogists Library, and Somerset House. The records include pedigrees, family histories, wills, and source materials relating to the English origins of many Anglo Norman and English settlers in Ireland. They went to Ireland between the 12th and the 18th century with the primary purpose of acquiring land. Their descendants who remained in Ireland eventually contributed to the flow of emigration to the American colonies, the United States, Canada and other British possessions. In many cases the Irish links between England and the colonies must be discovered before the English origin can be proved.

* * * * *

Any Irish bookshop which carries second hand books may have at least a small selection of the books listed in VOLUME II, herewith. Some large bookshops specialize in published historical and genealogical works of the 18th and 19th centuries, as well as the more recent printed source materials. If a particular book or series of volumes cannot be located it will pay to have a well-known bookshop advertise for any one or more desired items. A deposit for the service will probably be required.

This compiler was told in a Dublin bookshop that it would be almost impossible to find for purchase the entire series of the *Journal of the Cork Historical and Archaeological Society* owing to a fire in a warehouse where the undistributed issues were stored. When in Cork the compiler made an inquiry in the County Library for the name of anyone who owned the entire series and would sell it. A man was located who sold his set and other rare and desirable reference books in order to send a son to college.

Any one of the well-known bookshops may yield surprising "finds," as private libraries come on the market from time to time. In 1951, this compiler discovered a portion of the genealogical library of Col. James Grove White, at Fred Hanna, Ltd., Dublin, and acquired a number of basic reference books containing his bookplate or his autograph.

Books relating to Ulster records were found in Cork when they were seemingly unobtainable in Belfast, and books of Leinster and Munster interest had become dusty on the shelves of a Belfast bookshop. London bookshops often acquire very desirable Irish historical and genealogical reference books, family histories, etc. One can write to the county libraries listed on pp. 132-133, herein, for the names of any bookshops which carry second hand books and might have genealogical materials.

As books become more scarce and difficult to obtain by mail, due to the waiting lists for certain basic items, it seems best

for a person who is in the process of building an Irish genealogical library to write to any or all of the well-known bookshops and join the waiting lists for particular items. A charge
account can be opened in the larger bookshops if credit is
properly established. This compiler is impressed with the
safety and efficiency of the shipping services to the United
States which have been used by private sellers and bookshops.
All details are taken care of in Ireland. The following are
reliable bookshops which have supplied this compiler, except
for two names marked with an asterisk, which were supplied
by Mr. Alfred MacLochlainn, Assistant Keeper of the Manuscripts in the National Library of Ireland, when he recently
came to Chicago.

BELFAST:

The Cathedral Book Store. 18 Gresham Street, Belfast,
Northern Ireland. Mr. Hugh Greer, Director.

* The University Book Shop, Ltd. 50 University Road, Belfast 7, Northern Ireland.

CORK:

The Book Mart. 27 a, Washington Street W., Cork. Mr.
J. Kerrigan.

Lee Book Store. Lavitts Quay, near Patrick's Bridge, Cork.

The Mercier Bookshop. 4 Bridge Street, Cork. Directors:
Capt. J. M. Feehan and J. C. O'Connor.

DUBLIN:

Eason & Son, Ltd. 4041 Lower O'Connell Street, Dublin.
P. O. Box 42.

Green & Co. 16 & 18 Clare Street, Dublin, C 17. H. S.
Pembrey.

Fred Hanna, Ltd. 29 & 29 Nassau Street, Dublin, C 3. Directors: Arthur Hanna and Walter Hanna.

Hodges Figgis & Co. Ltd. 6 Dawson Street, Dublin. Directors: Frances T. Figgis and S. E. Allen Figgis.

* The Museum Book Shop. Kildare Street, Dublin. Mr. Day.
George Webb Book Shop. 5 & 6 Crampton Quay, Dublin.

LIMERICK:

O'Mahony & Co., Ltd. Limerick.

* * * * *

Northern Ireland Government publications, including *Reports of the Deputy Keeper of the Public Records of Northern Ireland*, etc., may be obtained at Her Majesty's Stationery Office, Chichester Street, Belfast.

Publications of the Government of the Republic of Ireland, including the *Reports of the Deputy Keeper of the Public Records in Ireland;* the Irish Manuscripts Commission Journal, *Analecta Hibernica*, and other works, etc., may be purchased at The Government Publications Sale Office, G.P.O. Arcade, Henry Street, Dublin.

FAMILY NAME INDEX

This Index contains the names of families and individuals mentioned within the text, when reference is made to a source of genealogical information, with the following exceptions:

(1) The 1847 List of Wesleyan Methodist Ministers on pp. 352-358.

(2) The principal families in Ireland, 11th to 17th century, pp. 450-461.

When there are references only to a few persons of one surname, page numbers for all are listed opposite the surname. When there are numerous references to a surname, first is given the surname (if reference is merely to the name); next the surname followed by the word "family" when reference is to the family as such, and then for individuals the surname is followed by the given name.

The General Index should be consulted for reference to thousands of self indexed collections (published, MSS., and microfilmed) concerning families and individuals.

S

Sackville	515
Sadleir, Col. Thomas	369, 370
Sadler, Henrie	557
St. Clair, *see* Sinclair	
St. Ferreol, de	333
St. John	359
St. Johnes, Sir Oliuer	557
St. Ledger (St. Leger, St. Legere)	328, 333, 359, 630
Salterson, Samuel	638
Sambrooke	515
Sampey, G.	376
Sample	620
Sandal	330
Sander, Col.	416
Sandes family	115
Sandham, Robert	416
Sandilands family	647
Sandos	329
Sands, William	638
Sandwith, William	415
Sapcotts, Jane	150
Sarsfield family	115, 170, 615, 619
Saunders	616
Saurin (De Saurin) family	325, 326, 329, 333
Sautelle, Capt.	328
Sautelle (Sautell), Major	165, 329
Sautelle (Sautell), Mary	165
Sauvage	334
Savage family	334, 610, 650
Savage, John	413
Saveroy	334
Savery (Savory) family	331, 334
Sawyer	623
Scardeville	334
Scharwell	334
Schomberg, Marshal	313
Scoffier	333
Scot (Scott)	238, 620, 649
Lieut.	346
Archibald	413
John	22
Scull family	169, 500, 624
Scullion, Ezechael	103
Seaver	611
Seeds	238
Segan (Segen)	331
Segrave	509, 600
Semerat (Simoe, Semirot)	331
Semple	620
John	384, 386
William	389
Seve	333
Severin	333

Seymour, Margaret (Dickson)	91, 93
Shadwell	620
Shaftesbury family	611
Shanaghan	166
Shannon, earl of	233
Shapcot, Rob.	638
Sharkey, Mary	21
Sharman C.	375, 376
Sharp, Anthony	414
Shaw	237, 238
Anthony; James	389
S.	376
William	416
Shearman family	166, 169, 500, 624, 734
Shee family	169, 170, 500, 614, 624, 630
Sheldon, W.	370
Shelley, T.	376
Shelmadine, John	328
Shepherd, Benjamin	425, 426
Sheppard, N.	376
Sheriff, Joseph	375
Sherlock family	623, 664
Sherlocke, James	507
Sherriff	237
Sheryveen, Mary	20
Shier	359
Shirley family	115, 600
Shoemaker	359
Shoppe	334
Shortal (Shortall)	630
Shoultare	359
Shunwire	359
Shutes, Michael	21
Shutter	236
Sicklemore, Capt. James	416
Sidney, Viscount	171, 644
Siggen, Thomas	507
Simpson, James	389
Simroe, *see* Semerat	331
Sinclair (St. Clair)	330
Skales	650
Slade, William	414
Slaret, Ta	425
Slater	650
Sleeper	359
Slowey	253, 255
Smith	236
	238, 333, 348, 600, 620, 649
Ann (Anne)	569
Jane	239
Jesse; Richard	557
John	638
Joseph	22
Katharine	416

GENERAL INDEX

This Index includes:

(1) All place names except (a) Parishes of Church of Ireland on pp. 281-296 and 301-308; (b) places designating Presbyterian Congregations on pp. 403-410; (c) places at which Methodist and Baptist ministers were located on pp. 352-358 and 375-376; and (d) towns listed on pp. 266-67.

(2) Names of all individuals not included in the Family Name Index, except some public persons such as sovereigns who are only mentioned incidentally.

(3) Records of the numerous estates, under the name of the estate or the family holding it.

(4) Each "collection" in the various repositories of records which is designated by a specific name.

(5) Subjects.

A

Abbeylara	510
Abbott, T. K.	128
Aberystwyth; National Library of Wales	136
Achonry, Diocese of (Roman Catholic)	464
Adair Narrative (1622-1670)	131, 401
Adair, H.	477
Adair, W.	362
Adams, J.	633
Adare estate	359
Administrations; see *Wills & Probate Records*	
Adventurers; see *Land Records*	
Aghadowey	131, 259, 401, 700
Aghagallon (Ahagallan)	252, 425
Aghalee	252
Aghaloo (Aghalow)	212, 513, 631, 638
Aghalurcher	253
Aghanloo	254, 700
Agivey	254, 700
Agnew, D. C.	318, 322, 330
Ahern, Mr.	123
Ahoghill	513
Ainsworth, John	135, 600, 661
Alexander, D.	268
Aliens; see *Naturalization, and Passenger Lists*	
Allen, Joseph	224
Almanacs	465, 471, 474, 527, 528
Aney	298

Annabeg	370
Annageliffe	252
Annagh	369
Annesley Collection	111, 506, 589, 594
Annesley Peerage Case	694
Antiquities, Notes on	525
Antrim, County and/or Town (see also *Plantations* and *Ulster, Province of*):	
Armorial tombstones, in	236
Census returns	173, 251, 257
Court records in P. R. O., Northern Ireland	224
Cromwellian settlement, in	565, 568
Crossle MSS.	213
Derry Cathedral Registers	266
Dissenters' petitions	216
Estate papers	604, 608, 610, 611, 612, 615
Huguenots, in	316
Land records	218
Office holders	637, 662
Plantation settlers, muster of	651
Poor Law Unions	529
Presbyterian Church Register	401
Public Record Office, Northern Ireland, in	205
Quaker records, in	131, 414, 421
Religious returns	512-13
Solicitors records for	223
Surveys	576, 593, 594

Antrim (continued)
  Tax records
      212, 214, 217, 633, 636
  Wills   725, 726, 728
Antrim MSS. (MacDonnells'
  estate)   209, 605
Antrim Parish   237
Antrim, Presbytery
  of   401, 402, 410
Appointments to Office, see
  Patent and Close Rolls
Apprentice records (see also
  Guild Records) 123, 223, 672
Aradh   369
Aran   614
Arboe   210, 254, 605, 700
Archdale family
  papers   209-10, 605
Archdall, Mervyn   167
Archibald, James E.   374
Archives, Dominion, Ottawa,
  Canada   525, 700
Archives Nationales, Paris 647
Archives, The National,
  Washingon, D. C.,
      14, 15, 17-28, 525, 700
Ardagh, Diocese
  of   167, 216, 725, 727
Ardagh and Clonmacnoise,
  Diocese of (Roman
  Catholic)   464
Ardbraccan   510
Ardee   510, 565
Ardfert and Aghadoe,
  Diocese of   709, 725
Ardlogh   350
Ardmayle   616
Ardmore   252
Ards   120
Ardstraw   513
Armagh, County and/or City
  (see also *Plantations*, and
  Ulster, Province of):
  Armagh County Museum,
    records in   118
  Census returns
        119, 215, 251, 258
  Church Registers   212, 266
  Cromwellian settlement,
    in   565
  Crossle MSS.   213
  Directory   478
  Estate
    papers 605-608, 611-613, 616
  Forfeitures and settle-
    ments   379, 542
  Freemen and free-
    holders 118, 142, 669, 670

Groves Collection   214
Huguenots, in   316
Inquisitions, in   214, 549
Land records   118 120,
    219-20, 512, 619, 620, 625
Libraries, in   118
Military records 119, 650, 653
Newspapers   686
Office holders 225, 637, 666
Plantation settlers, mus-
  ter of   651
Poor Law Unions   529, 534
Public Record Office,
  Northern Ireland, rec-
    ords in   205
Quaker records, in   413
Religious returns   510, 513
Solicitors records for   223
Surveys   576, 593, 594
Tax records   119, 217,
    257, 402, 632-636, 638
Wills   118, 725, 726, 728
Armagh County
  Museum   118, 609, 650
Armagh, Diocese of
  Diocesan Registry Office 119
  Escheated lands   120
  Inquisitions   555
  Manor court rolls   210
  Marriages   709
  Religious census 167, 216, 499
  Rent rolls   120, 258, 605
  Wills   211, 219, 725, 727
Armagh, Diocese of
  (Roman Catholic)   466
Armagh District Probate
  Registry   737-739
Armagh, Manor
  of   120, 210, 258, 605
Armagh Parish   513
Armagh, Presbytery of   402
Armagh Probate District 187, 198
Armagh Public
  Library 119, 512, 554, 584, 650
Armoy   237, 238
Arms, see *Heraldry*
Arms, Office of, see
  Genealogical Office
Army and Navy officers
  (see also *Directories* and
  Almanacs)   474
Arran and Athenry   254
Arthur, W.   335
Artnacrea   252
Artrea   210, 216, 513, 605, 700
Athboy   637
Athelstanford   387
Athenry Peerage Case   163

King, William 262, 390
King-Harmon papers 614
King's County (Offaly).
(See also *Leinster,*
Province of):
Antiquities of 525
Census returns 174, 254
Cromwellian settlement,
in 565, 568
Directories 474
English settlers, in 540
Estate papers 615, 616
Freeholders 670
Land rec-
ords 585, 621, 622, 623
Marriage records 711
Office holders 637
Poor Law Unions 533, 534
Religious returns 510
Surveys 576, 593
Wills 725, 726, 728
King's Inn,
Dublin 125, 168, 492, 510, 673
Kinsale
Catholics not trans-
planted 565
Directories 474
Estate papers 613
Forcible migration, from 690
Huguenots, in 316, 324
Office holders 637
Quaker records, in 416
Kirkcudbright (Scot-
land) 378, 387
Knights and Knights' Arms,
see *Genealogical Office* 140
Knight's fee, definition 626
Knockgraffan 416
Knocknabohilly 370
Knocknanarney 366
Knox, Alexander 663

L

Laccagh 692
Lacrom, Thomas Aiskew 577
Lacy 539
Laggan Presbytery 131, 401
Lamacraft, C. T. 143
Lambeg 237, 316, 324
Lambeth Palace Archiepisco-
pal Library 133, 198, 640
Lambstown 414
Lancashire and Yorkshire
families in Ireland 128
Land measurements in Ireland 90
Land Measures, Irish 90
Land Records (see also the

counties and provinces,
and the several reposi-
tories)
Catholics, lands of 439
Confiscations, forfeitures,
claims and grants 113-4,
119,-20, 127, 142, 144, 168,
171, 430-50, 500, 503, 512,
516, 539-41, 554, 558, 560-61,
578-9, 584-88
Court papers, in 494-7, 548-9
Cromwellian forfeitures
and settlements 364-65,
367, 431-2, 561, 565-6, 572
Deeds, miscellaneous 128, 618
Description of types of
ownership, leases and
occupancy 519-21
Estate papers 257, 597-617
Identification, as aid to 4
Index in Registry of
Deeds, Dublin 68
Inquisitions 541, 545-49, 555
Manor Courts, returns of 115
Patent and close rolls,
in 550-1
Plantation and settle-
ment records 169,
351, 492, 493, 535, 544-596
Poor Law Unions 526-534
Public Record Office,
Dublin, in 158, 169
181-82, 499, 547-8, 618-624
Published 625
Redistributions, 1660-
1685 579-586
Registry of Deeds,
Dublin 51-90
Rent rolls and lists of
owners 115, 120, 257-8, 621
Surveys, see *Surveys*
of Land and Occupants
Lane family collections 600
Lansdowne House, record in 577
Lankford, J. 747
Lanktree, Matthew 179, 336, 341
La Ponce MSS. collection,
de 126, 644
Larne 220, 224
236, 251, 258, 513, 605, 685
Lart, Charles E. 646
Lascelles, Rowley 660
La Touche, J. J.
Digges 173, 249, 319
Laughinshillen
(Loughinsholin) 512
Lavey 252, 510

Longford (continued)
Office holders 637
Poor Law Unions 532
Religious returns 510
Surveys 576, 593
Wills 725, 726, 728
Loughans 606
Loughguile 237
Loughinsholin (Loghen-
shollen) 95, 101, 254
Loughtee Upper 252
Louth, County and/or Town
(see also *Leinster,
Province of*):
Antiquities of 525
Census returns 174, 254
Cromwellian settlement,
in 565
Crossle MSS., in 213
Estate papers 605, 616
Forfeitures and
claims 217, 503
Freeholders 671
Genealogies 272
Huguenots, in 316
Inquisitions 490
Land records
210, 547-8, 619, 621, 622
Marriage records 711
Office holders 637
Poor Law Unions 532, 534
Religious returns 510
Survey and Distribution,
Books of 593
Wills 725, 728
Louth, Earls of 169, 600, 623
Lower Bann 399
Lowry, T. K. 603
Lumly, William 336
Lurg 215, 253, 634
Lurgan
Census returns 220, 251
Directory 478
Dissenters' petitions 513
Estate records 605
Huguenots, in 314, 316, 324
Land records 619, 685
Parish registers, ex-
tracts 212
Quaker records, in 222, 413,
414, 420, 421, 424, 425, 427
Schoolmasters, in 215
Lurganboy 227
Lygacory 422
Lynch estate papers 614
Lynn, J. M. 336

M

MacCormack, J. R. 571
MacDermott's Map, Philip 448
MacDonnell MSS. 218, 543
MacFirbis Collection, Duald 126
MacGiolla-Domhnaigh,
Padraig 247
MacLochlainn, Alfred 107, 746
MacLysaght, Dr. Edward 107,
137, 231, 241, 248, 509, 601
MacLysaght family col-
lections 600
MacMahon, Ross 542
MacNeill, Eoin 130
Macosquin 254
Macully 166
Madden, P. J. 123, 747
Madden MSS. 126
Magee University College
Library 131, 401
Magennis 543
Maghaberry 421
Maghera 220, 251
Magheradernan 602
Magherafelt 220, 251, 513
Magheragall 237
Magherastephana 253
Magheross 253
Magilligan 399, 700
Maguire, Myra 231
Mahaffy, Robert Pent-
land 568, 570
Mallow 416
Malone estate papers 614
Malpastown 510
Mansfield family papers 115, 600
Manuscripts, ancient and
medieval
Microfilms of 445
List of (in Gaelic) 461
Published 446-50
Manuscripts in private owner-
ship, survey of 509
Maps (see also *Land Records;
Surveys*)
42, 448, 524, 574-78, 738
Maquay 400
Markethill 215, 478
Markham, Capt. 364
Marriages and marriage rec-
ords (see also the various
denominations and reposi-
tories)
In general 704-705
Regulations re-
garding 264, 391, 705
Crown permissions 168, 493

Office of Arms, see *Genealogical Office*
Office holders (see also *State Papers*, and county) 145, 166, 491, 492, 637, 657, 660-666
O'Gallachair, P. 634
Oge, Garret; Thomas 538
O'Gorman family collections 600
O'Grady family collections 600
O'Grady, Standish Hayes 133
O'Hanlan, J. 697
Old Age Pensions, see *Census returns*, and *Pension records*
Oldcastle 421
Oldstone 385, 605
Omagh 209, 346, 351, 475, 513, 634, 685, 686
O'Mahony, C. 663
O'Malley, Sir Samuel 614
O'Neill Daunt family collections 600
O'Neill, Earl of Tyrone 539, 540, 542
O'Neill, Thomas P. 107, 746
Ordnance Survey Documents 27, 127, 525
Ormond 369
Ormond family papers 601
Ormonde, Earls of; Dukes of 169, 537, 580, 623
Ormonde **MSS.** 135, 516, 573, 583-585, 641
Orrery, Earl of Cork, and 601
Orrery estate papers, Armagh 611
Orrery estate papers, Cork and Limerick 601
Orrier 119
O'Shee-O'Shea family estate papers 614
O'Shee papers, Power 600
Ossory, Diocese of (Roman Catholic), Parish Registers of 464
Ossory, Diocese of Religious returns 167, 499
Wills 169, 186, 219, 726, 727, 731
O'Sullivan, Donald 604
O'Sullivan, William 559
Owen, D. J. 653, 672

P

Packolet (America) 226
Palatine settlers in Ireland 358, 359
Paisley 387

Pale, composition for 554
Pallas 359
Pardellstown 143, 234
Pardons (see also *Patent and close rolls*) 492-93
Parishes 38, 42, 281-296
Parish Registers, see the various denominations
Parkmount 212, 258
Parliament, members of (see also *Directories*, and *Almanacs* 115, 474
Parliamentary Records (see also *Public Record Office, Dublin; Public Record Office, Northern Ireland; National Library;* and *Genealogical Office, Dublin*) 185, 485-506, 578
Parliamentary Register 492
Parsonstown 686
Passenger Lists, see *Emigration*
Patent and close rolls (see also *State Papers* 491, 549, 583, 584
Patents, Northern Ireland, Index to 219
Paterson collection 219, 606
Paterson, T. G. F. 118, 219
Paul, F. J. 382
Pearson, A. I. 125
Pedigrees, Genealogical Office, in 138, 141
Pedigrees, Irish in France 646-647
Peerage and baronage (see also *Directories* and *Almanacs*) 168
Peers, lists of 138-141, 492
Penal Laws 436-8
Pender, Seamus 125, 126, 388, 433, 636, 669
Pennsylvania Historical Society 525
Pennsylvania, migration to 701
Pensioners, French 497, 657
Pension Act, Old Age 250
Pension Records 168, 184, 492, 656-659
Petitions (see also *Land Records*) 584
Petty, Sir William 573-578
Phelps, Edward 130, 734
Philipstown 510, 637
Phillips, Sir Thomas 558, 651
Phillips, Walter A. 340, 373
Pillow MSS. 220